ONE DROP OF BLOOD

ALSO BY SCOTT L. MALCOMSON

Tuturani: A Political Journey in the Pacific Islands

Empire's Edge: Travels in Southeastern Europe,
Turkey, and Central Asia

ONE DROP OF BLOOD

THE AMERICAN MISADVENTURE OF RACE

SCOTT L. MALCOMSON

FARRAR STRAUS GIROUX

NEW YORK

Farrar, Straus and Giroux
19 Union Square West, New York 10003

Distributed in Canada by Douglas & McIntyre Ltd.
Printed in the United States of America
Designed by Jonathan D. Lippincott
First edition, 2000

Library of Congress Cataloging-in-Publication Data
Malcomson, Scott L.
    One drop of blood : the American misadventure of race / Scott L. Malcomson.—1st ed.
        p. cm.
    Includes index.
    ISBN 0-374-24079-5 (alk. paper)
    1. United States—Race relations.   2. Racism—United States—History.   I. Title.

E184.A1 M265 2000
305.8'00973—dc21   00-024487

Grateful acknowledgment is made to *The New Yorker* and *The Village Voice,* in which some of the material in this book first appeared, in an altered form.

For Hannah and Benjamin
and in memory of Joe Wood

CONTENTS

III. WHITE FLIGHT   263

IV. A FAMILY IN TIME   395

ONE DROP OF BLOOD

THIS BUSINESS OF ANGELS

All the names, all those to-
gether burned
names. So much
ash to bless.
—Paul Celan, "Chemical"

The North Canadian River slips through Oklahoma City, which marches away from it, to the north and south, in an almost unbroken grid. Like many towns in the southern Great Plains, Oklahoma City grew up at a time when irregular curving rivers had given way to the more rigid lines of railroads (themselves soon replaced, on this level terrain, by straight highways). People came to Oklahoma because land was cheap; and evidently land remains cheap enough, for Oklahoma City is not built up. Even close to the center, people live in houses on evenly spaced lots. In a hot and moody climate the lawns and gardens stay green. During the dust-bowl years, Oklahoma land went from cheap to worthless, and tens of thousands of Okies, the poorest of the white Depression poor, left for yet another trek west; but when the bad weather had gone the state dammed the rivers, creating the lakes that provide the water that makes the lawns of Oklahoma City possible. On a rectangle of land you can make for yourself a garden, a lawn, a home. Oklahoma City is among the most man-made of

American towns; it is what we, leaving nature aside, create for ourselves. The proud city turns its back on the river, especially at night, when everyone has returned safely home and the river drifts quietly by like a winding secret.

In this orderly city a bomb brought down a government building one workday, killing 168 people, either immediately or after dehydration, suffocation, or dripping away enough blood to die. Every age and race of American was among the murdered; it was a democratic torturing death. More than a year later, the site of the building remained empty, surrounded by rickety Cyclone fencing. Twisted or stuffed into the fence were T-shirts with scrawled messages, business cards, flowers, toy animals, a child's pair of red sneakers. I visited the place on a sunny day in late autumn. A small but steady trickle of pilgrims passed slowly by this homemade shrine, reading certain messages out loud. Parents tried to explain matters to children. In a lot next to the fence stood an old tree, surprisingly unharmed, and an office chair; above them were two walls of buildings made useless by the explosion. On one, someone had painted a lengthy cry telling us that God demanded justice. On the other was the simple remark, "We Should Have Looted." From the bombing site itself rivulets of reddish-brown water flowed beneath the fence and into the gutter, where visitors stood deciphering the T-shirt messages. One read, "God Bless America and Help US ALL." We tiptoed and hopped about to avoid staining our shoes.

Many people had wedged sticks into the fence to form primitive crosses. There were dozens of them, and a few Christmas trees tightly bound to the wires. Were all of the victims Christian? There were many images and invocations of angels, and references to young victims who had become angels, and even some photographs of children now dead. I saw no pictures of adults, which was a surprise, because most of the bombing victims were not children. This business of angels came from the belief that children, upon death, unquestionably enter heaven. Adults, having no doubt sinned, cannot expect immediately to become angels. We are not assumed to be innocent. But it is worth recalling that children did not post these angel notices. In many cases their parents did. One family put together a holiday card with pictures of their two lost boys on one side and, on the reverse, a handwritten letter signed by those children from beyond the grave. The boys' letter said they were happy in the other world and asked all who read it to pray, not for them, but for their family—for the very adults who, in this world, had actually written the letter. When these adults speak of innocents they are talking to themselves, saying, *We are innocent.* This is one way to make sense of things.

Another strange detail of the popular shrine to the dead at Oklahoma City was that the pictures of victims, at the time of my visit, all portrayed white people, although many of the dead were not white. Perhaps nonwhite families had felt this was not a place for them to mourn, or that they were not members of this larger, stricken family. Certainly the national face of the tragedy had been a white face, that of a white child. Immediately after the bombing, a spontaneous assumption of many Americans was that the bomber must have been nonwhite and non-Christian—in the event, an Arab Muslim man. This was another way to make sense of things. Within forty-eight hours several attacks took place against people who were thought, however vaguely, to be Arab Muslims. Once a young white Christian, Timothy McVeigh, was arrested, those many Americans who looked as if they might be Arab Muslims could harness their particular fear, and presumably those Americans who had suspected them swallowed shame.

Many of us cast the Oklahoma City bombing as a story in which innocent, childlike white American Christians were victims, a story of Terror in the Heartland. The heartland was by definition Christian, white, and blameless. The shrine at Oklahoma City was a spontaneous expression of this idea—not a media spin or a planned commemoration, just America talking to itself. Even those who were not present there—blacks, for example—participated in that conversation by not talking. We heard much about unity, about coming together, after the bombing. Timothy McVeigh—if he is as he has been portrayed, a government-hating white Christian separatist "sending a message"—made the event a perfect paradox: he killed a representative sample of Americans to send his separatist message, and we, in our confusion and pain, reacted by separating ourselves, each to his or her heartland. Thereby we did what he, a madman, wanted.

McVeigh's madness lies in the belief that any of the American races can pursue a separate destiny and in that pursuit achieve a new life and freedom. Americans have believed this, in many different ways, for centuries. Our New World was indeed new, and full of possibilities for new forms of freedom—as well as limitless possibilities for chaos. The racial roles of Indian, black, and white were one leading aspect of American novelty. They formed channels through which social power might flow with some smoothness and social position might be understood. Since early-colonial times, none of these groups has ever been missing from the national equation. They came into being as part of the American experience, and their elaboration over the centuries is much of what makes America unique. Each is crucial to our collective imagination; without any one of them, we could not have a collective imagination. We could not have a nation.

Yet our American drive for newness has also led us into new forms of unfreedom. From the beginning, the people living out these racial roles of Indian, black, and white often felt them to be constricting. They wanted not to be reduced to instances of a race. So they sought to escape race by escaping—or controlling, separating off, eliminating, sometimes absorbing—that which alone made them racial, namely the existence of other races. One sought to go beyond race by escaping the reminders of one's own racialness, to "separate" in order to become fully oneself and free, to solve this problem of race by starting afresh. Such efforts never entirely succeeded. It was already too late. The history of the New World's three-part racial division stuck to Americans like a burr, pricking at their skin, even as they went west, always west, hoping to start over.

Oklahoma was the last place to start over, the last truly Western place: Indian Territory did not join Oklahoma Territory to form the present state until 1907. Oklahoma is an extreme example, one I will often return to in the pages that follow. The state has been a laboratory of separatism. Its first extensive settlement was by Indian tribes relocated there in part, or so many believed, as a way of preserving their racial identity. Both blacks and whites arrived at the same time, the blacks as slaves to Indians. Blacks and whites began moving in large numbers to western Oklahoma (Oklahoma Territory) and eastern Oklahoma (Indian Territory) in the last great westward migration following the Civil War. In the early years of the twentieth century blacks and whites outnumbered Indians in Indian Territory. And it is a very revealing feature of those years that the members of each of these three groups, within living memory of the Civil War, had precisely the same goal: a separate state dominated by their own race. An impossible desire animated their hearts. Each wanted to be free and unencumbered by the others; indeed, the idea of freedom, as they understood it, required racial separatism. Even apart from economic considerations, these Americans seem to have felt they needed their own racial place in order to escape the past, to remake themselves, to become new people—to become, at last, innocent, each to itself, after nearly three hundred years together.

Not quite a century after these unsuccessful efforts at separation Timothy McVeigh arrived in Oklahoma City to send his message. I couldn't help seeing his act, however hideous, and the commemorations that followed it as part of an American pattern. At the site of that vast killing, adults faced with the immensity of political terror and death were trying to recast themselves as children, who were not to blame, and in the process once again separating into people with races—which was the same separation that had led, in a way, to the terror and death. This suggested to me that the past was forming them, in spite of themselves. That past is the past of race in America—not the past of racism, but of race in itself, and of race in our selves. The racial roles we play as Americans have tended to be repeated over the course of American history; I should say, we have tended to repeat them. And we regret this, and tell ourselves that we will start fresh, the past will stop now, and will not hold us any more than it holds an innocent child. Then we repeat our race roles again.

I have done this, too. I think most Americans do. It cannot be undone, but perhaps it could be done differently. When I was growing up, in Oakland, California, I knew many different kinds of people. The city had a great mixture of peoples. I can remember, faintly, what it was like when, as children, we did not attach much significance to the colors of our skins. I can also remember, more clearly, what it was like when we fit into those skins and began to separate, friend from friend, into races—to think with our skins, so to speak, and to act in them—a painful and violent process. These were roles prepared by the American generations that had gone before; the past was forming us, and so we would carry that past into the future. I have never ceased regretting that process, because it diminished each of us.

We cannot successfully choose not to have a past. But we might find a common past that, if we can claim it in all its tragicomic fullness, with all its passionate murders and lasting intimacies, will enable us to do something more than repeat our racial roles, the divisions that steal among us to mock our humanity. Perhaps we can identify the past that haunts us—not to exorcise it but to live with it, and slow the pace of our repetitions, ease the sharpness of our separations, overcome the thoughtlessness of our racial roles.

The name Oklahoma was cobbled from two Choctaw words, for *red* and *people*. By coincidence, the dirt of western Oklahoma has a red cast, which is why the rivulets flowing from the bombing site appeared to come from a wound. In that flowing water I did see the color of blood, which is the same for all of us. In the popular commemorations I saw the color of skin, which is not the same for all of us; and I wanted to know why that separation had taken place, unbidden, probably unwanted, here at the site of this tremendous murder committed by my mad countryman.

PART ONE

AN INDIAN COUNTRY

■

The Cherokee nationalist David Cornsilk, dressed in shorts and a casual shirt, of medium height and build, was unremarkable in appearance save for his green eyes. He would often look away into some middle distance, whether when listening or speaking; he had that nervous and distracted quality common to political activists, an engaged loneliness born of a constant solitary effort to grasp allies and anticipate the enemy. At the moment, he was again fighting his tribe's government. The Cherokees' chief had got caught up in a battle with the tribal police force, which was investigating the chief for financial improprieties. Anxious for his power, the chief decided to fire the police force. The police responded in an unusual fashion: they chose not to recognize his authority. They appealed to the tribal court, which temporarily granted them a new home, right there in the courthouse. The officers took their patrol cars, computers, radios, and uniforms and simply moved.

So on a warm spring morning David Cornsilk and I met in the lobby of the courthouse in Tahlequah, Oklahoma, capital of the Cherokee Nation. From time to time a self-described policeman would wander by. The officers were behaving as if they had power, and, at least so far, some Cherokees were willing to agree, even though these "policemen" had, for example, no jail, and even though the tribe's chief had decided to hire a new force. It was a curious situation. These uniformed men made pots of coffee, logged in and out, smoked cigarettes on the back porch, and investigated crimes *as if* they were police officers, and as long as enough people agreed that they were policemen, weren't they? Various Cherokees had contributed thousands of dollars to pay their salaries. Cornsilk had come that morning to present them with the check, along with an eagle feather, sanctified by a medicine man, to give them strength. The policemen's predicament—their insistence, despite being technically unemployed, on their policeness—must have struck a number of chords with Cornsilk. He is perhaps the leading Cherokee nationalist today, a self-appointed spokesman for the tribe, respected and sometimes hated; a keen genealogist, he is also more than half white. He is spending his life trying to answer a nearly impossible question: What is an Indian?

"There was a lot of prejudice against us in my dad's family because we were half white. My grandmother, my dad's mother, always called us, you know, her half-breed grandkids." Cornsilk did not find being a half-breed grandkid easy. "Coming out of childhood into adulthood," he said in his thoughtful, deliberate way, "it was real hard to straighten out a lot of that. It was really very confusing for me." His father's mother made self-definition either simpler or more difficult, depending on how you look at it, because, while not herself genetically a full-blood Cherokee, she nevertheless believed herself to be a full-blood. "She would sit for hours combing her granddaughter's hair, which was straight and black. She just loved it, it was so beautiful. The whole while sitting there with her wavy hair. My grandmother had real wavy hair. But she considered herself a full-blood. She spoke the language and lived as a full-blood."

This was what David Cornsilk saw as a little boy, and it made an impression on him. He grew up in the countryside surrounded by full-blood Cherokees and feeling their particular prejudice against white people (and against blacks and half-breeds). His white mother, who was more or less rescued by his father from an abusive relationship with a white man, had decided to live as a Cherokee. "Her family are backwoods folks from Arkansas. We were not accepted into her family because we were half-breed Indians. So we were treated differently by them. I'm sure if we had been half-breed blacks they would have never even accepted that we existed. So my prejudices come from that side. It took me a long time to even—I'd never been around black people other than just the few who live up there and one or two other kids who'd come to my school." "Up there" refers to a hill overlooking Tahlequah, a place local whites and Cherokees call Nigger Hill. The black people who live up there today are still collectively known as "the freedmen" and are descendants of slaves brought west by their Cherokee owners from the tribal homelands in North Carolina, Georgia, northern Alabama, Tennessee, and parts of other states. Most of these ancestors came during the forced removal in the 1830s along what was called the Trail of Tears.

"So when I got into college and I started seeing more black people in school and stuff and—they're so *different* from us. I had this one friend and—I just cringe when I think of me doing this—I asked him if I could touch his hair. I would never do that to a white person. You know, that's awful. And he laughed, he thought it was really funny that someone'd want to touch his hair. Just because I'd never even been around someone like that. It took me a long time of associating with them and realizing that they're human beings and that's how you have to see them to even want to shake their hand. 'Cause I had all those prejudices that my mom's family had. You know, 'You guys are lucky that at least you're Indian and white, you sure wouldn't wanna be one of *them*.' I had a hard time even going to a restaurant and seeing a black person cooking, and thinking, 'Ecchh, I don't want to eat after that person has handled that food.' I think back on that person that I was and it just makes me sick." Cornsilk laughed a little in quiet amazement and shook his head.

Not that he got a much more positive view of blacks from his Cherokee family. But the picture there had some subtleties. There was, for example, the matter of lips. Cornsilk's are a big-lipped people. "So many of my family have really big lips, and that's a characteristic, I think, to a certain degree, of many American Indians. Many American Indians have full lips. But some of my family have *big* lips. Really big lips. I had one cousin, we used to call him 'Lips.' They were just *turned up*, I mean they were so big. But I tried to discern what that small amount of blood that runs through our family that is not Cherokee, on that side, really is. I found Irish, Scottish, English in that small strain. But no evidence that there's any African ancestry in there. Which wouldn't bother me at all."

The boy David Cornsilk, with his full lips, wavy hair, and restless green eyes, wandered about his rural Indian home in the late 1960s and considered his options. His neighbors treated him as something of a stranger; they did not welcome him into their tribe, especially when it came to group ceremonies. He knew that the essence of tribal identity—it is most important in religious matters—was membership in a clan, inherited through the mother's side. This matrilineal kinship system, based on seven clans, is older than recorded Cherokee history. Well into the colonial era, clan membership was the ground upon which Cherokee social relations were built, laws about property, marriage, and criminal justice. Cherokeeness, or a national identity, was a very baggy concept compared with clan identity. Having a white mother meant Cornsilk did not have a clan, and could never have a clan.

"I think I was probably about ten years old, and I was walking from my house to my grandmother's house, and I started thinking about how I had been treated at the ceremonial grounds. Because I don't have a clan. I'm not ashamed of being without a clan. My dad made the choice to marry a white woman and that's how I ended up being here. I've never really thought about being more than what I am. But when I'd made the decision that I was gonna get married— I think I made a lot of decisions when I was ten years old, I decided that I was gonna go to college, although no one in my family ever had—I decided that I was gonna marry me a woman with a clan." Cornsilk laughed when he said this because he'd adopted a hillbilly accent, the speech of his white family. Ah wuz gonna marry me a woman with a clan. Cornsilk wanted to "make sure that my kids had a clan. And that kind of evolved into—the way to find a woman with a clan was to marry a full-blood. That's what you looked for, because you knew that a full-blood, whether that person knew their clan or not, *had* a clan. There was a clan there somewhere. Fortunately, I married a woman who was both full-blood and knew her clan, so it worked out pretty well."

Many, perhaps most, Cherokees have no idea what their clan is. Cultural nationalists, such as David Cornsilk, want more people to "return" to their clans. "Over the last probably ten years there has been a kind of cultural awakening among Cherokees. So you have a lot of people *searching* for their clan. By the same token, you have these people that are clanless, like myself." The Ojibwas, he said, have solved this problem by creating a new clan. "They call it the Chicken clan. And anyone who's born without a clan is automatically the Chicken clan. Although I'm not sure that I'd wanna be from the *Chicken* clan. I'd wanna have a more interesting animal totem." He laughed, and I laughed. I could see it might be a little humiliating to be profoundly associated with a flightless barnyard bird. Cornsilk had thought about identity questions, attended to them in more detail, than most Americans ever would or could, but he also seemed to find them richly comic, which is probably not a bad idea. When we had finished laughing about the Chicken clan I suggested that perhaps the existing Cherokee clans had begun in a similar fashion: through force of circumstance, in an act of imagination.

"That's a possibility. The origin of those clans is so far back it's difficult to say. There's only a couple of them that really have origin stories. The Holly clan, sometimes called the Bear clan, they claim an origin with a child that was found underneath the holly tree, a girl child, and she fostered this clan of Cherokee people. That's the only one I can really think of that has an origin story. In order for us to move ahead, I think, as a people we're going to have to figure out some way for everybody to have an identifier, you know, something they can cling on to. And maybe clan is the answer. Because you get people in the tribe whose degrees of blood drop to one over four thousand and ninety-six. That's the lowest degree we've enrolled so far, and this person I think will find it difficult to figure out, How do I connect? How do I belong? Where do I belong? And if we have some automatic pocket for that person to fall into, it'll be easier for us not to lose that person. That's what I think is the key. You know, there's safety in numbers."

The concept of safety in numbers has specific resonance among Cherokees. It echoes an ancient idea of collectivity. Cherokees certainly had property, both movable goods and land; but these descended through the female line and were inextricably tied to the matrilineal clans. Land was understood to be collectively "owned." In daily life land belonged to whoever used it, and ceased to be theirs when they were through with it. Private accumulation of wealth beyond a basic level, whether in land or goods, was not an activity that made sense. The Cherokees accompanied this economic structure with concepts of group generosity and responsibility (including responsibility for crime and punishment).

Such were the core ideas, however attenuated, that reformers sought to eliminate in the nineteenth century. The Cherokee tribe today recognizes as citizens about 182,000 "Cherokees by Blood." The phrase is that used by the Dawes Commission, a turn-of-the-century federal outfit charged with deciding who was a real Indian. The United States, after about a hundred years of some-times serious effort, had succeeded in forcing the Cherokees and other tribes to accept land "in severalty," that is, to divide the land allowed to them by treaty into parcels that would be owned privately by individuals. The purpose of this was most clearly stated by Henry Dawes himself, a senator from Massachusetts, speaking, he believed, as a friend of the Indians to other well-meaning white friends of the Indians at a conference in 1885. He is reporting back after a trip to Indian Territory: "The head chief told us that there was not a family in the whole nation that had not a home of its own. There is not a pauper in that nation, and the nation does not owe a dollar. It built its own capitol, in which we had this examination, and built its schools and hospitals. Yet the defect of the system was apparent. They have got as far as they can go, because they hold their land in common. It is [the socialist writer] Henry George's system, and under that there is no enterprise to make your home any better than that of your neighbors. There is no selfishness, which is at the bottom of civilization. Till these people will consent to give up their lands, and divide them among their citizens so that each can own the land he cultivates, they will not make much progress." The latter nineteenth century was a time of brutal frankness—or of brutal confidence—among social theorists, and Dawes was no exception.

Before the Dawes Commission could accomplish its goal of instilling self-ishness in the hearts of Cherokees, it had to determine Cherokeeness, and this was done in the language of blood. (There were many impostors, mainly white, claiming Cherokee roots in order to get land allotments.) It required a shocking amount of paperwork. The commissioners interviewed thousands of Chero-kees, many of whom, after forced relocations, intermarriages, absconded parents, informal adoptions, and civil wars, had only the fuzziest ideas about where they were from. A significant number of Cherokees—usually members of or sympathizers with the traditionalist Keetoowah society, known as Nighthawks— refused to go along with the Dawes Commission's racial categorizing. These people were put on the Dawes lists thanks to genealogical assertions made by informants. Because the Nighthawks were known to follow traditional ways, and perhaps also because they were thought to dislike white people, they commonly were registered as full-bloods. (This was the case with Cornsilk's paternal grand-mother, she of the wavy hair, who was informed on by her neighbor Leonard and enrolled as a full-blood, although she wasn't one. When she found out, she went down the road and slapped Leonard in the face.) The Dawes Commission published neat lists, easily available today in public libraries and federal archives, with a column for blood quanta: $1/4$, $1/8$, $1/2$. F means "full." These lists are still the basis for determining Cherokeeness. The tribe today will not recog-nize anyone as Cherokee who does not have an ancestor on the Dawes rolls, though all it takes is one drop of blood.

As a Cherokee nationalist, David Cornsilk has spent much of his time expos-ing Indian artists he believes to be fraudulent. The market for original Indian art began to expand more than a decade ago; increased demand brought increased supply; and certain people not necessarily known before to be Indians started to make Indian art. As Cornsilk put it, anytime Indians have something worth money—land in 1890, oil paintings and casinos today—white folks will try to take it. So he and his friends hunted a few of these artists down, traced their genealogies by means of the Dawes rolls and other records, and exposed them as fair-weather pseudo Indians. They humiliated them. It is, by now, impossible to recognize many Cherokees as Indians because they have no phys-ical or speech characteristics that swiftly distinguish them from whites, blacks, Hispanics, or Asians. That is why Cornsilk had to do so much research, because many millions of people in the world could pass for Indian.

"You know, I got punched in the mouth in front of Wal-Mart by one of these people." The Cherokee capital has a Wal-Mart, as well as all the other chain stores and restaurants for which Wal-Mart has come to serve as the symbol. Tahlequah is, aesthetically, indistinguishable from numberless small American towns, except for the street signs in Cherokee. "He's a pretty vocal fella. He's a good artist. He does beautiful flowers and birds and things. He was taking our history and our mythology and our culture and twisting it to his own view of the world. And he may have painted a Cherokee man floating in a canoe through the Tennessee River . . . but that's how *he* saw it, that's not how I might have seen it, and that's not how the Cherokee people might have perceived that. And what right does he have to tell us how that event was? He doesn't have that right.

That would be like me going to Egypt and—you know, I have ancestors on one side who are Italian, and they came from Egypt to Italy. So I'm probably of Egyptian heritage. And I can go to Egypt and say, 'Hey, guys, I wanna come over here and do some sculptures and you guys accept it.' "

Evidently, Cornsilk had a distant ancestor named Alberti who went from Egypt to Italy in the early eighteenth century. "He was an architect for the Medici family in Tuscany. Then he killed somebody and fled to Poland. Then from Poland he was deported to Germany, then from Germany he came to America."

I asked, "Is that where the Alberty Cherokee name comes from?"

"That's where it comes from. We're all descended from this man."

"There's a number of Albertys."

"Yeah, there's a lot of them. My great-grandmother was an Alberty." The primordial American Alberty had three wives in succession and eight sons by his wives. "All eight of his sons married Cherokee women. This is like in the 1780s and '90s. So some of these Alberty families have married back in so much that they don't even know they have white ancestry." Those people would be full-bloods. "You'll ask them, 'Where does your name come from?' And they'll say, 'I don't know.' They don't have any clue. And then you have others that married back out of the tribe and they'll be as white as white." Those people would be what we call whites. "It's a fascinating family. We all trace back to Frederico Alberti, who came to America in the early 1700s."

Cornsilk and I rose from our chairs in the courthouse lobby and went back into the provisional police station to say goodbye and wish luck to the stubborn lawmen. Two of Cornsilk's friends, both fellow nationalists, joined us; we drove to a place on the highway called Goldie's and had cheeseburgers and iced tea. The two Cherokee men, one young and one middle-aged, were, like Cornsilk, educated and thoughtful, though more playful than their militant friend. They appeared just as white as he, and I supposed that, in their day-to-day life, they must enjoy the benefits that white men effortlessly get in most parts of American society: a basic unthinking respect, for example, and credibility; the precious privilege of not being seen as a special interest or an exception to the rule. I recalled that Cornsilk had told me he'd married a full-blood in part because he wanted to see in his own family "those little brown faces." He had also said that the tribe is steadily lightening in color, and that soon enough the Cherokees by blood will all "be white." Part of his work is to find a way that a white tribe can yet be Cherokee. Blood, as he sees it historically, is merely necessary, not sufficient.

How could someone having lunch at Goldie's that spring afternoon in Tahlequah have known that three of the men at our table were Cherokee Indians? Only by listening to the conversation. There was some talk about the arrogance of full-bloods, who apparently lord their language skills over mixed bloods. Cornsilk said that full-bloods often refuse to teach Cherokee even to their own children, much less to mixed bloods. He spoke of occasions when full-bloods had made fun of his efforts to master Cherokee; he called this "hurtful" several times, "hateful" once. He spoke as if the full-bloods were planning to take their knowledge—the knowledge he craved—with them to the grave in a suicidal, purist act of self-preservation, by keeping what they know pure in death.

Politics was a happier subject. The three friends gabbed cheerfully about other tribes, on whose affairs they were well informed. This was real politics, only it concerned Apaches and Navajos rather than Serbs and Mexicans. The younger man, a Web-site designer for a Memphis paper, talked about tribal Internet projects. I wondered whether his Memphis colleagues knew he was a Cherokee or if they thought of him as one. The three discussed the strengths and weaknesses of various medicine men and the relative vitalities of local ceremonial gathering places, or "stomp grounds."

Cornsilk spoke about Redbird Smith and the vagaries of traditionalist religion, which now goes loosely under the term *Keetoowah*. Redbird Smith, more than anyone else, was responsible for codifying and preserving modern Cherokee religion. Redbird's father, Pig Smith, had been a conservative in the Cherokee sense, in other words, a full-blood. (The name Smith came from his trade as a blacksmith; a pig is a unit of iron.) Redbird, born in 1850, grew up in an activist traditional Cherokee milieu. Cherokee society was at that time already well divided against itself, and its traditional forms of knowledge greatly lost. The Smith family's milieu was a mixture of Creeks, Cherokees, and, most importantly, Natchez. The French had destroyed the Natchez in the early eighteenth century, and a remnant was adopted into the Cherokee tribe. Some scholars assert that the Natchez were closest to the ancient Temple Mound cultures; the Natchez among the Cherokees in 1850 certainly had a store of traditional knowledge, a body of thought that overlapped extensively with that retained by their fellow southeastern Indians the Creeks and Cherokees. Within this world the Smiths and other families worked up a cultural blend, the essential elements of which continue today as the Keetoowah religion. By such adaptive methods the sacred Fire, in Cherokee terms, was kept burning.

It did not always burn brightly, and it was often divided. The Keetoowahs split several times, commonly because one group decided the main body had become impure. After Redbird's death his son Stoke Smith moved his father's Fire from its old place in the hills to Stoke's front yard. According to Cornsilk, Stoke went on to extinguish the Fires at other stomp grounds and take the medicine bottles beneath them to his own Fire. Not everyone went along, but the momentum was with Stoke, and many Fires gradually cooled. One stomp ground allowed drinking; its observances finally ended when dancing drunken men fell into their Fire.

Cornsilk said that Redbird's niece Katie, whose group still prospers, claimed that she had received a message from Redbird on his deathbed. He made two signs to her, one of which looked like the V for victory, and supposedly said the words "I was wrong." Educated in Christian schools, Katie took this to mean that Redbird had accepted Christianity. She created her own version of Cherokee spiritual tradition that incorporated Christian elements. Cornsilk said her stomp ground was south of Tahlequah, in the hills above Highway 82.

When we had exhausted the subject of medicine we paid the check and said our goodbyes in the parking lot. Cornsilk had mentioned that one of the Fires which Stoke Smith had extinguished still had its medicine bottles buried beneath. The table had gone somewhat quiet at the mention of this abandoned remnant. I thought of what might be in those bottles; of Cornsilk's efforts to purify Indian art, which he sees as representing Indian culture; and of another Medicine Bottle from another tribe. I have two pictures of him, by Joel Emmons Whitney (1822–1886), above my desk. The first, a stereograph, is captioned "Medicine Bottle, a Mdewakanton Dakota participant in the 'massacre' of 1862, as a prisoner at Fort Snelling, June 17, 1864, awaiting the gallows." His features are cut deep and are beautiful, he is a perfectly handsome man, with long dark hair. He has loosely wrapped about himself a blanket; his chin rests on his hands; his eyes are half open and look away. This was Indian art in the nineteenth century, for white viewers, an art of dying. In both visual arts and literature of the period the Indian commonly appears as someone not quite gone, a person expert in the endings of life. The other picture is captioned "Little Six and Medicine Bottle on the gallows, 1865." Through two ranks of soldiers you see in the middle distance a gallows and two men with sacks over their heads, hanging by their necks from ropes. The space between you as the viewer and the lifeless bodies must have been cleared for the photographer to get his shot. In front of the gallows are two open coffins. Before these in the clearing, looking away from the gibbet, stands a thin white dog, awkwardly turned, one paw extended forward, caught nervously pacing.

"ALL THINGS IN ABOUNDANCE"

COLONIAL AMERICA AS EDEN

■

Our country, at the beginning, was already a work of art. When the earliest European colonists arrived on the shores of North America, they were astonished by the beauty of their surroundings. Native tribes generally practiced both hunting and agriculture, and both of these required fire. One burned brush to remove the hiding places of game animals and to clear land for planting. The result of this was a man-made ecology that created great stretches of meadow and airy forests; together they resembled what we now call "English" parks. Fire-resistant trees grew tall, shading vast tracts free from undergrowth. You could, an English traveler noted, drive a coach through these woods. In such an environment valuable plants flourished, plants that provided food: persimmons and plums, wild grapes and strawberries and mulberries, black walnuts and hickories.

Colonial agricultural methods necessitated ending the fires; the great trees were felled for lumber; the brush returned, and choked away the persimmons and mulberries. Similarly, the meadows created by regular burning had attracted elk and bison from their pastures across the Appalachians, pastures that had themselves been extended and maintained by native burnings. Such large grazing animals, too, would disappear with time. But as long as native methods prevailed the land retained this parklike quality. Today we can only imagine its loveliness. In Cherokee-dominated northern Alabama it persisted into the nineteenth century; John Abbott, traveling with the famous colonel David Crockett, described the landscape there in 1813: "Upon the banks of a beautiful mountain stream there was a wide plateau, carpeted with the renowned blue grass, as verdant and soft as could be found in any gentleman's park. There was no underbrush. The trees were two or three yards apart, composing a luxuriant overhanging canopy of green leaves, more beautiful than art could possibly create. Beneath this charming grove, and illuminated by the moonshine, which, in golden tracery pierced the foliage, there were six or eight Indian lodges scattered about."

Some early travelers believed they had found paradise, though they had actually found something more significantly American—namely, that which comes just after paradise while keeping a paradisal memory. The distinctively American combination of aggression and nostalgia, of crude self-advancement permeated by wistful sentiment and loss, a culture obsessed with responsibility and its avoidance: this peculiar mind-set was born in the earliest days of our collective experience, and is with us still. Thoughtful colonizers of a biblical bent knew they were enacting the Fall and that the first step in creating their new society was to make, so to speak, its ruins.

Following Columbus's landing on the island of Hispaniola, now divided between Haiti and the Dominican Republic, in 1492, the Spanish and Portuguese set the tone for American life. Their model was essentially one of war followed by enslavement of the defeated natives—soon, also, of imported Africans. These slaves were expected to mine the earth, particularly to dig up gold and silver. There seems never to have been any doubt among the Iberians that their slaves, whether African or American, did not want to be slaves. They were dying in unimaginable numbers. The several million Arawaks on Hispaniola in 1492, for instance, were down to two hundred within fifty years. The Spaniards and Portuguese knew well what they were doing—they kept good records, and ruled their parts of America with efficient bureaucracies. The horrors of this time are mainly known to us now thanks to Iberian writers who, early on, were moved to set them down on paper.

The historian Robin Blackburn has written, "The most disturbing thing about the slaves from the slaveholder's point of view was not cultural difference but the basic similarity between himself and his property." This was true also between colonizers and Indians. People from European, African, and Indian tribes met one another in the bizarre New World and were puzzled by their similarities. Many tried to make sense of these similarities by emphasizing the differences—taking, for example, certain conceptions of race and using them to make a grid of social meaning. Consider the fate of Estevan, Morocco-born, the first African whose individual presence in America has been recorded. He left Spain with his master, Andrés Dorantes, in 1527, as part of an expedition to Florida and whatever might be beyond it. Once on land, the explorers marched briskly from misfortune to disaster. By 1529 their numbers had dropped from about four hundred to sixteen. After five years of enslavement by Gulf Coast Indians, only four travelers remained: Estevan, Dorantes, Alonso del Castillo Maldonado, and Álvar Núñez Cabeza de Vaca. They escaped together, found friendlier natives, and spent the next two years crossing the Southwest to Mexico.

In Mexico City, Dorantes sold Estevan to the Spanish governor, and the slave told many a story about cities of gold. In 1539 the governor dispatched an expedition to find these cities, with Estevan as guide. Estevan, according to the chronicler Pedro de Castañeda, broke away from the group and pushed north-ward in pursuit of "reputation and honor." Upon reaching an Indian town, Estevan submitted to questioning by the local leaders. "For three days," Cas-tañeda writes, "they made inquiries about him and held a council. The account which the negro gave them of two white men who were following him, sent by a great lord, who knew about the things in the sky, and how these [men] were coming to instruct them in divine matters, made them think he must be a spy or a guide from some nations who wished to come and conquer them." Why did they not believe Estevan? "Because it seemed to them unreasonable to say that the people were white in the country from which he came and that he was sent by them, he being black. Besides these other reasons, they thought it was hard of him to ask them for turquoises and women, and so they decided to kill him. They did this."

Such a clarifying political use of skin color was not the only choice. If skin color and behavior were consistently related, one might use the first as short-hand for the second. However, skin color by itself is an emptiness; one's actions matter, not one's color. For example, when Estevan and his three presumably lighter-skinned companions first reached New Spain, their identities, from the Indian point of view, derived not from their respective colorings but from the qualities of character they had exhibited in the course of their journey. Este-van's fellow traveler Cabeza de Vaca had admired many of the native people they met during their years of wandering, and some of the Indians evidently respected the sojourners, especially for their medical talents—so much so that when the wayward foursome and their Indian captor-companions finally encountered Spaniards, the Indians refused to give up their men. They refused because they could not believe that such good men as they knew could also be Spaniards. The Indians were willing to give their captives only to other Indians. "This sentiment roused our [Spanish] countrymen's jealousy," Cabeza de Vaca remembered. The Spaniards' leader "bade his interpreter tell the Indians that we were members of his race who had long been lost; that his group were the lords of the land who must be obeyed and served, while we were inconsequential." Why did the Indians not believe the Spaniards? Cabeza de Vaca writes: "Conferring among themselves, they replied that the Christians lied: We had come from the sunrise, they from the sunset; we healed the sick, they killed the sound; we came naked and barefoot, they clothed, horsed, and lanced; we coveted nothing but gave whatever we were given, while they robbed whomever they found and bestowed nothing on anyone. They spoke thus through the Spaniards' interpreter and, at the same time, to the Indians of other dialects through one of our interpreters." One has the sense that Cabeza de Vaca agreed with his captors that perhaps one could not be both Spanish and humanly decent. Cabeza de Vaca's newfound countrymen went so far as to propose to him and his companions that they enslave the Indians. This idea outraged the Spanish and African wanderers: "And to think," Cabeza de Vaca wrote, "we had given these Christians a supply of cowhides and other things that our retainers had carried long distances!" Cabeza de Vaca came very near to seeing his own countrymen as foreigners, at least in moral terms, and "to the last I could not convince the Indians that we were of the same people as the Christian slavers."

It was possible to imagine, even at the time, that these visually distinct peoples among whom one moved were of the same family as oneself and that the similarities were, finally, more significant than the differences. Such was the vision of Francisco López de Gómara, part of whose *Historia general de las Indias* of 1552 was translated into English in 1555, along with other Spanish reports, by the enticingly named Richard Eden.

López de Gómara wrote:

> One of the marvellous things that God useth in the composition of man is colour, which doubtless cannot be considered without great admiration in beholding one to be white, and another black, being colours utterly contrary. Some likewise to be yellow, which is between black and white, and others of other colours, as it were of diverse liveries. And as these colours are to be marvelled at, even so is it to be considered how they differ one from another as it were by degrees, forasmuch as some men are white after diverse sorts of whiteness, yellow after diverse manners of yellow, and black after diverse sorts of blackness . . . Therefore in like manner and with such diversity as men are commonly white in Europe and black in Africa, even with like variety are they tawny in these Indies, with diverse degrees diversely inclining more or less to black or white . . . By reason whereof it may seem that such variety of colours proceedeth of man, and not of the earth: which may well be although we be all born of Adam and Eve, and know not the cause why God hath so ordained it, otherwise than to con-

> sider that his divine majesty hath done this as infinite other [than]
> to declare his omnipotence and wisdom in such diversities of
> colours as appear not only in the nature of man, but the like also
> in beasts, birds, and flowers . . . All which may give further occa-
> sion to philosophers to search the secrets of nature and complex-
> ions of men with the novelties of the new world.

This idea of human diversity as a type of blessing, while unusual, cannot but
have occurred to many observers simply by virtue of its logic. The New World
had so many tribes of different colors, including various shades of European,
that it would have been odd not to entertain an idea of their basic unity, particularly given the powerful Christian belief that God "made of one blood all
nations," as Paul wrote. López de Gómara's rhapsody was, in Eden's translation,
among the most widely read American accounts in England and informed the
views of the first English adventurers. These men were the religious and political enemies of the Spanish, and in the New World their ambition, tempered by
circumstance, led them to attempt multiracial communities. Indeed, it was the
racial hierarchy of the Spanish that made a multiracial coalition seem an obvious choice to the English.

The earliest multiracial New World coalition to include white Englishmen
was led by Francis Drake. Once a slave trader himself, Drake presumably did
not act from moral considerations. Such considerations were, however, part of
the general mix. The English had a tradition of associating Spain with tyranny,
specifically, though not exclusively, Catholic tyranny and papal rule. This tradition was very much sharpened in the sixteenth century, not least because
Spain's New World wealth increased its desire and ability to threaten England,
and the reports of Spanish chroniclers and others as to the brutality of New
World life—the worst bits were quickly translated—transferred English hatred
of Spain into a new sphere. The slowly developing ideology of English freedom,
of the right of man to be free from monarchical despotism, found, when faced
with the despotic vision of Spanish rule in the Americas, a foreign-policy companion. Some among the English came to believe that their role, as both lovers
of freedom and lovers of power, was to undermine the Spanish by promoting
freedom in America.

Drake put this idea to practical effect in Panama. He wanted to seize the
Spanish gold shipment, up from Peru, at a town on the Atlantic coast where the
gold was loaded for its final transshipment to Spain, a place called Nombre de
Dios, or Name of God—a heist so big as to pass from theft into statecraft. At first
Drake attempted it on his own, but, not knowing the timing of the overland
pack-train delivery, he failed. Then he thought to enlist the aid of a sizable community living south of Nombre de Dios—the Cimarrons, escaped slaves some

three thousand strong. The Spaniards were terrified of the Cimarrons, who did not fear them and regularly raided Spanish settlements to free the slaves there. Probably a mix of Africans and Indians, though an English source described them as "valiant Negroes fled from their cruel masters the Spaniards," the Cimarrons endangered Spanish rule at a sensitive point. Drake, a masterful opportunist, approached the Cimarrons, who took him and his lieutenant, John Oxenham, to a peak from which the Englishmen first saw the Pacific Ocean. (They vowed to sail it one day, and did.) The Cimarrons infiltrated Panama City and discovered when the gold was to be moved. A combined English-Cimarron force—aided by French Huguenots, who had been working with Cimarrons for nearly a decade—succeeded in seizing the gold, and Drake left for England with a fortune. "This league between the English and the Negroes," a Panama official warned, "is very detrimental to this kingdom, because, being so thoroughly acquainted with the region and so expert in the bush, the Negroes will show them methods and means to accomplish any evil design they may wish to carry out."

Three years later, in 1575, Oxenham returned with fifty men and supplies for the Cimarrons. Oxenham's men took all the rigging from their ship, burned it to extract the hardware, then carried everything overland to the Pacific and built a new ship. The English-Cimarron crew proceeded to raid Spanish shipping and settlements and to free slaves, who then joined the Cimarrons. They also destroyed Catholic churches. The Spanish reported that the Cimarrons had all become "Lutherans," a Spanish catchall term for Protestants. The sources contain no evidence of racial friction in the black-English coalition; everyone seems to have marauded happily together. In the end, a substantial black-English threat to Spain was avoided by the capture and execution of Oxenham and his English comrades (and, presumably, many Cimarrons). The Spanish kept their peculiar racial system intact and choked back their fear that, if the English had been able to flee, "they would have returned in such strength that, aided by the negroes, they would have become masters of the Pacific, which God forbid, for this is the key to all Peru." And Peru was the key to Spanish power in the world.

Drake did not forget the value of the Cimarrons. In his trips along the South American coast he did his best to incite Indians to escape slavery and to become "Lutherans." One English sailor, stranded for fourteen years in Mexico, brought back tales of a northern Mexican tribe that, under the leadership of a Negro, was threatening Spanish control over its mines in that region. This story meshed promisingly with the successful multiracial Cimarron experience. Meanwhile, other Englishmen were thinking of colonizing North America, which they saw as their natural sphere of influence. The idea was to make the north a political counterweight to the Spanish south; to take the Protestant struggle against Catholicism to a new field; and to oppose Spanish racial hierarchies and slavery with English notions of equality and freedom. The ideal was muddled from the beginning. Armed opposition from Indians, for example, was not considered by the English an acceptable expression of political opinion. Nor did the English recognize the paradox of bringing freedom to peoples already free; instead, they seem to have believed that freedom, as they understood it, was an English concept and could only be spread under English leadership. From a practical European standpoint this may not have been far wrong. The Spanish and Portuguese conquests in America had been fantastically swift and thorough, and there was little reason to suppose that England's rivals would have more difficulty in North America than they had farther south.

A reconnaissance expedition in 1584 located Roanoke Island; the trip's chronicler, Arthur Barlowe, found the Indians friendly enough, and described the land in Edenic terms: "The earth bringeth foorth all things in aboundance, as in the first creation, without toile or labour." English planners, led by Sir Walter Raleigh, set about organizing a voyage to begin settlement. One of them laid down rules to ensure equal treatment of Indians, including a regulation that "no Indian be forced to labour unwillyngly." The colonists set off in five ships in April 1585.

A second, related expedition sailed in September of that year, led by Francis Drake. As always, Drake held cities to ransom and plundered as best he could. But he seems to have had another, more interesting project in mind. Over the space of a few months he raided Santo Domingo, Cartagena, and Saint Augustine, in each case freeing slaves and spreading a message of liberation. The Spanish were quick to grasp their English enemy's intention: to unite Indians and Africans under English leadership, and by bestowing freedom to create a multiracial rebellion. Drake sought to lure, as a Spanish source put it, "negro labourers who in his country are free." He had several hundred Africans and Indians—as well as, it was said, some Turks and Moors—with his fleet when he set sail for Roanoke.

Upon Drake's arrival there in June 1586, the colony was already foundering badly. Its leader, Ralph Lane, had not performed well. Many of the rank-and-file Roanoke colonists had probably been forced into going in the first place— England's hopes for America included using it as a vast workhouse for the home country's many unemployed and, at the far end, unemployable. Such men were the worst possible candidates for peopling a hardworking Protestant paradise. Likewise, the local Indians, though apparently civil on the whole, as yet showed no sign of wanting to give up their life of light, easily sustainable agriculture, controlled hunting, fishing, foraging, and honorable warfare for the English alternative of intense, sedentary farming and the production of agricultural exports for the London market; and one can't really think of any good reason why, in these earliest encounters, they should have. Lane and his colonists departed with Drake. Two later expeditions left colonists on the island, and both of these groups disappeared. In this way, the first great drama of Anglo-America entered history and our imaginations: the Lost Colony of Roanoke.

Much was lost at Roanoke between 1585 and 1587. The English had tried to start something new there, something that might have reversed the terrible pattern of American colonization begun in 1492: they had intended, apparently, and haltingly, to found a free society of Africans, Indians, and Europeans. The freedom of Roanoke would have been imperfect and born of circumstance, but that is true of all liberties. The alternative, exemplified by the Spanish, was so much worse. It was also well known to the English, because it was the American norm, and would soon enough take hold, with English variations, in North America. John Smith of Jamestown would advocate adopting the Spanish model. The seeds of an English version of Spanish racial empire were already there: the basic principle of European overlordship; a belief in the superiority of the colonizing civilization; and, somewhere deep in the European heart, a conviction that the lives of Indians and Africans were not as valuable or worthy of note as those of Europeans. The most profoundly tragic aspect of the Lost Colony of Roanoke lies in a textual silence, for while there are many records of the English expeditions, there is no mention of what happened to the Caribbean, South American, Floridian, and African voyagers presumably brought by Drake to freedom in Roanoke. Imagine them. Some would probably have been able to remember passing from freedom into a bizarre and pitiless servitude, only to set sail for yet another new life as free men and women in an unknown land. Why did the English forget them, while remembering themselves and the Spanish? We might say that with this sin of omission, this seemingly blithe constriction of the imagination when faced with human multiplicity, the English first became white.

The Roanoke story that has been recorded and remembered to this day is a white story, the first specifically white tale in English North America. It has been told to illustrate the gravity of the dangers faced by the first white people on these shores; to illustrate both the initial generosity and the lurking enmity of Indians. But the more likely story suggests just the opposite: that the people of Roanoke joined the people all around them; that they shed their separateness like a useless cloak; that they were not lost, but found.

———

Drake's effort at Roanoke was not the last attempt at a multiracial society of free men in the New World. The New England Puritans, too, for example, had to contend with an alternative vision, one rather more comic than the events of 1585–1590. The Pilgrims, or earliest New World Puritans, sometimes styled Separatists, had rebelled against what they saw as the mistaken course of the Protestant Reformation in England. The English church and state looked upon the Separatists poorly, and oppressed them. The tiny group removed to Holland for sanctuary, but after little more than a decade found the going too hard. As William Bradford, who led the first Pilgrims to New England aboard the *Mayflower* in 1620, later described it, the founding generation had been growing old in Holland, and feeble, "so as it was not only probably thought, but apparently seen, that within a few years they would be in danger to scatter, by necessities pressing them, or sinke under their burdens, or both." Meanwhile some among their children had begun to stray, even to many non-Separatists: They were being "drawne away by evill examples into extravagante and dangerous courses, getting ye raines off their necks, and departing from their parents . . . These, and some other like reasons, moved them [the Pilgrims] to undertake this resolution of their removall . . . The place they had thoughts on was some of those vast and unpeopled countries of America, which are fruitfull and fitt for habitation, being devoyd of all civill inhabitants, where there are only salvage and brutish men, which range up and downe, little otherwise than ye wild beasts of the same."

Ten years after the *Mayflower*, preaching to a shipload of Puritans prior to their debarkation in Boston, John Winthrop famously expressed their dream: "the Lord will be our God and delight to dwell among us, as his owne people and will commaund a blessing upon us in all our wayes, soe that wee shall see much more of his wisdome power goodnes and truthe then formerly wee have beene acquainted with, wee shall finde that the God of Israell is among us, when tenn of us shall be able to resist a thousand of our enemies, when hee shall make us a prayse and glory, that men shall say of succeeding plantacions: the lord make it like that of New England."

Bradford and Winthrop were obsessed with enemies. New World Puritanism was not an easy creed; it suppressed individual freedoms to a degree considered extreme, even perverse, at the time; and the desperate colonists believed themselves trailed by the Devil, who, as Bradford wrote, "may carrie a greater spite against the churches of Christ and ye gospell here, by how much ye more they endeavor to preserve holyness and puritie amongst them, and strictly punisheth the contrary." The seemingly inexhaustible cargo of fear that the Puritans carried across the ocean extended to the Indians, who haunted their imaginations—"ye salvage people," Bradford called them, "who are cruell, barbarous, and most trecherous, being more furious in their rage, and merciless where they overcome; not being contente only to kill, and take away life, but delight to tormente men in ye most bloodie manner." The Pilgrims, as Bradford knew, might not have survived without Indian assistance—he acknowledged the help of Squanto, particularly, in showing where to plant corn and how to fish—yet such knowledge somehow did not change the way he described the tribes he met.

Into this tense and unforgiving social situation ambled the louche figure of Thomas Morton, possibly an attorney and undeniably a bad poet, who arrived in 1622 to pursue the fur trade. The majority of seventeenth-century white New Englanders were not religiously motivated Puritans—just as most of the *Mayflower* passengers were not Pilgrims—and this may be doubly said of Morton. No less an opportunist than Francis Drake, he quickly sensed his chance to perform acts of liberation by means of, in this case, a biracial community. Morton had come over with a Captain Wollaston, who, like some others at the time, was a person of station in England with high hopes for American adventure. Wollaston settled just north of Plymouth with a few other gentleman companions and a horde of servants. His hopes were quickly dashed, and he left for Virginia with servants to sell. From Virginia, Wollaston wrote back to his partner Rasdall asking that more servants be sent. Rasdall agreed, then departed New England, leaving one Fitcher as his lieutenant.

Here Bradford picks up the story: "this Morton abovesaid, haveing more craft than honestie . . . in ye others absence, watches an opportunitie . . . and gott some strong drinck and other junkets, and made them a feast; and after they were merrie, he began to tell them, would give them good counsell. You see (saith he) that many of your fellows are carried to Virginia; and if you stay till this Rasdall return, you will also be carried away and sold for slaves with ye rest. Therefore I would advise you to thruste out this Lieutenant Fitcher; and I, having a parte in the plantation, will receive you as my partners and consociates; so may you be free from service, and we will converse, trade, plante, and live together as equalls, and supporte and protecte one another, or to like effecte. This counsell was easily received; so they tooke opportunity, and thrust Lieutenant Fitcher out a dores."

This was, in Bradford's view, not a happy development. Even within his own minuscule community there were doubters; and other white colonists presented many threats, secular and religious, to Puritan power. However, the simple existence of Morton's rough democracy might not have been a danger worth eliminating. While Puritans did participate in the trading of humans, it was not among their central concerns, and they would not have cared much if Morton wanted to interfere with Captain Wollaston's property rights in his servants. What seems to have touched the Separatists off were Morton's close relations with Indians; his strong belief, frequently stated, that Puritanism was ridiculous; his fondness for, indeed advocacy of, heavy drinking; and, related to these three, his erection, in 1628, of a maypole. Morton and his friends, according to Bradford, then devoted themselves to "drinking and dancing aboute it many days together, inviting the Indean women, for their consorts, dancing and frisking together, (like so many fairies, or furies rather,) and worse practises. As if they had anew revived and celebrated the feasts of ye Roman Goddess Flora, or ye beastly practices of ye madd Bacchanalians. Morton likewise (to shew his poetrie) composed sundry rimes and verses, some tending to lasciviousnes, and others to ye detraction and scandall of some persons, which he affixed to this idle or idoll May-polle. They changed allso the name of their place, and in stead of calling it Mounte Wollaston, they call it Merrie-mounte, as if this joylity would have lasted ever."

Thomas Morton enjoyed America. As he wrote later, in *The New English Canaan*, "The more I looked, the more I liked it." He brings an erotic richness to his descriptions of the landscape, with its "lusty trees," its "dainty fine round rising hillucks . . . and cleare running streams, that twine in fine meanders through the meads, making so sweet a murmering noise to heare, as would even lull the senses with delight a sleep, so pleasantly do they glide upon the pebble stones, jetting most jocundly where they do meet, and hand in hand runne downe to Neptunes Court." His sensibility was far from Puritan. But his humor and evident lubricity conceal a serious side, for he saw what was happening to the Indians, and he felt he knew what the Puritans, who "make a great show of religion but no humanity," were about. When Morton first came to New England he witnessed the aftermath of the epidemic of 1616–1619, itself probably caused by contact with Europeans. Some scholars estimate that 90 percent of coastal New England natives died in that short period. "For in a place where many inhabited," Morton wrote, "there hath been but one left a live, to tell what became of the rest, the livinge beinge (as it seems) not able to bury the dead, they were left for Crowes, Kites, and vermin to pray upon. And the bones and skulls upon the severall places of their habitations, made such a spectacle after my comming into those partes, that as I travailed in that Forrest, neare the Massachusets, it seemed to mee a new found Golgatha."

The Puritans were not much more gentle than the disease. In 1623 Captain Miles Standish of Plymouth heard a rumor of an Indian uprising. He set out with a small party and killed eight suspects, decapitating their leader and sticking his head on a post atop the Plymouth blockhouse as a "warning and terror." The Indians, according to Morton, then named the Puritans "Wotowequenage, which in their language signifieth stabbers or Cutthroates."

Morton fought the divine madness of Pilgrims, "those moles," with pagan lunacy, hungover poetry, and winking rage: dance music with a deep sad ache, a harmony with centuries ahead of it. "The setting up of this Maypole," he wrote, "was a lamentable spectacle to the precise seperatists that lived at New Plymouth. They termed it an idol; yea, they called it the Calfe of Horeb: and stood at defiance with the place . . . threatning to make it a woefull mount, and not a merry mount." The vehicle of this threat was Miles Standish, a short, stout man whom Morton consistently calls by his nickname Captain Shrimp. (Morton refers to himself, with no small conceitedness, as "mine host.") Standish arrested Morton and hauled him before a Pilgrim council. If ever a man deserved a stiff drink, that man was Thomas Morton. No one understood this better than he. "A conclusion was made, and sentence given," Morton wrote, "that mine Host should be sent to England a prisoner . . . So these Worthies set mine Host upon an island, without gunne, powther, or shot, or dogge, or so much as a knife to get anythinge to feede upon, or any other cloathes to shelter him with at winter than a thin suit which he had on at that time . . . He stayed a month at least, and was releeved by the Savages that took notice that mine Host was a Sachem [chief] of Passonagessit, and would bring bottles of strong liquor to him and unite themselves into a league of brother hood with mine host; so full of humanity are these infidels before these Christians."

At that time a fairly peaceful society of natives and immigrants together might have developed naturally—and in many parts of North America, for a century or more, it did. Leaving aside racial hatred and separatism for the moment, we can see how sensible Thomas Morton's somewhat unsteady vision was. For the natives, European arrival vastly expanded their markets, both locally—in agriculture, animal products, and fishing—and, of much more importance, internationally. European shipping technology produced, at a stroke, millions of new customers. Native Americans were positioned to take advantage of these opportunities, mainly in the region east of the Mississippi and south of the Great Lakes, an expanse comparable in extent to western Europe (excluding Scandinavia). In political terms, the area was reasonably stable, kept so through extensive diplomatic and trade networks. Boundaries between groups were widely recognized, though subject to dispute, and crossed by an infrastructure of roads and portages. This economic zone was well suited to provide what the Europeans initially wanted most: prepared animal skins.

Native Americans had a surplus of furs and skins. Western Europeans, by contrast, had, for commercial purposes, hunted out much of their territory, and in the sixteenth century a considerable portion of their furs came from Russia. The Dutch dominated the fur trade, while their Russian suppliers pushed ever farther into Siberia (and finally into North America) to find product for the

Amsterdam market. North America provided a new sphere of opportunity, and the Indians played the role of their Russian counterparts. English, French, and Dutch traders established their posts along the Atlantic coast and inland waterways at sites chosen for their proximity to the Indian supply lines, based on the existing infrastructure. The system lasted for nearly two hundred years, until the late eighteenth century. It was an industry huge in geographic extent and in complexity. The Indians knew how to find the product, extract it, transport it, and prepare it for export, none of which the Europeans were able to do so well. What the Europeans had were certain technologies—most importantly, firearms and steel tools—and access to the world market. Furs are not an especially important product now, but at the time demand was enormous, and within decades of the failure at Roanoke, North American natives were part of a global system of exchange. The scale increased steadily; in the period 1700–1715 shipments to England from South Carolina alone included 887,986 deerskins, the majority already dressed. Profits were high enough to compensate everyone for the labor involved. Dutch ships even took beaver furs from Atlantic ports to Russia for further refinement, then on to the Amsterdam market for sale to western European consumers.

None of this could have happened without the skills, hard work, and eager participation of American natives. They were willing to enter into the trade because the Europeans had things they wanted: firearms, powder, flints, and bullets; metal manufactures (hatchets and knives, kettles, hoe blades); and textiles. Guns made it easier to get meat. Hatchets and hoe blades made it easier to clear land and to farm it. The advantages of woolen and cotton clothing are less clear. Certainly, fashion provided a spur. A scarlet and blue cloth manufactured in the Stroud valley, Gloucestershire, enjoyed a real vogue among Indian consumers after 1690, greatly increasing the prosperity of Bristol, whence it was shipped to America.

Indian goods, then, and Indian purchases were critical in creating a place for North America within the seventeenth- and eighteenth-century world market. The trade was experienced as beneficial by both the Cherokee hunter and the English weaver (or at least the English mill owner). Many other goods improved life on both continents. The Europeans introduced sugar, the horse (and the drawn plow), pigs, sheep, and cattle, and the grasses necessary for intensive animal husbandry. From the New World, Europe received, among many new products, tobacco, potatoes, tomatoes, sweet potatoes, peppers, peanuts, several types of bean, and pumpkins and other squashes. Sometimes these products took roundabout journeys that illustrate the elaborate development of exchange circuits. Indian corn arrived on the slave coast of Africa much as breadfruit came from Tahiti to the West Indies: it improved agricultural yields in Guinea, enabling the land to provide more food and the human population to provide more slaves. The potato went from the New World to England and back; the Cherokees acquired it from the English, as well as peach and apple seeds from the Spanish. The watermelon, native to Africa, was part of the Cherokee diet by 1700.

Markets, like people, being imperfect, some products and customs were taken up slowly if at all. The widespread Indian habit of regular bathing puzzled the Europeans. Superior native obstetric methods were not adopted by non-Indian North American doctors until after World War II. The French explorer Jacques Cartier learned an Indian cure for scurvy, but the knowledge lay unused by Europeans for two centuries until a British physician read about it in Cartier's account of his travels. The natives were likewise slow, fatefully slow, at learning to repair guns.

In the seventeenth-century social economy the possibility of a fusion of populations cannot but have occurred to many. We may assume that Thomas Morton's Merry Mount produced some light-hued Indians or dark whites. The noted Powhatan Pocahontas famously married the Englishman John Rolfe in 1614. Many tribes allowed fur traders, all of them men, to marry into Indian society. Apparently such marriages were inoffensive and, at times, probably useful, in the way that intertribal family relations were useful in the pre-European period: they helped to strengthen the bonds between two peoples. Intermarriage was the rule in contemporary Spanish America and in the vast, though lightly held, French "possessions." It would soon prove to be otherwise in the English colonies, but it did not need to be. The fact that John Smith of Jamestown sold a white man—the surprised and disappointed young Henry Spelman—to a Powhatan chief does suggest a lack of what we would later call racial solidarity.

In political and military terms, the early Indian assumption appears to have been that the new players could be integrated into existing social arrangements, just as the precontact economic infrastructure was retooled to meet new market demands. The French, British, Dutch, Swedish, and Spanish might reasonably be viewed as tribes that would take their places within a familiar order of conflict and cooperation. This was, indeed, how they behaved. The European tribes fought and traded with each other in ways that must have been more or less recognizable to their native neighbors. Within a language group—English, for example—smaller units might break away, perhaps influenced by a charismatic leader, and find themselves in conflict with their former fellow tribesmen. (That is how Rhode Island began.) This, too, would have sparked recognition among Indian observers. Indian tribes and European tribes made and broke alliances in a pattern not wildly different from that of precontact America.

Yet in this evolving new world there were differences from the old, seemingly minor ones that rapidly grew in importance. Guns made hunting and warfare more efficient. Suddenly Indians could kill both animals and people on a scale unknown before. The desire for a more pleasant life—or greed, depending on how you look at it—led strong tribes to eliminate weaker competitors through force, in order to secure exclusive access to game resources. Soon, to get the furs they needed to exchange for the things they wanted, Indians had to kill Indians. Europeans were killing Europeans for just the same reason. Worse still, the whole process had a definite and foreseeable end. Game populations could not replenish themselves, given the high rate of resource depletion; eastern North America, and later the West, would be hunted out, just as western Europe had been. The early-colonial, or late-Indian, political economy in North America was simply not sustainable. And neither was a society in which Indian skills and labor commanded a premium. The eventual European acquisition, after about 150 years, of Indian intellectual capital, such that Europeans could locate, extract, and prepare the furs themselves and so dominate all aspects of production, came only as a final blow. At that point there were, in the European colonial mind, no strong reasons left for living together with other Americans in peace.

Before this point, roughly coinciding with the American Revolution, Indians on the whole do not appear to have considered themselves Indians—that is, as a significantly distinct people. No tradition existed for such a concept. No historical circumstance had ever required it. Although Native American polities had much in common, there were also a thousand differences of language and customs, religious beliefs, economies and resources, physical appearance, and, not least, memories of past injuries and injustices inflicted by one group upon another. Tribes guarded their lands zealously. They lived with each other roughly in war and delicately in peace. The arrival of European tribes gave them pause, but what is most remarkable in the early period is that, literally decimated (or worse) by disease, so many native tribes nevertheless maintained themselves and, in fact, eagerly assimilated many aspects of European life into their societies.

To a great extent, Europeans also thought of Indians as divided into distinct, stable political units. Europeans were themselves divided into groups on the basis of differences in language, customs, religion, economies, physical appearance; and historical circumstances, conditioned by the desire for wealth, forced them to recognize such differences among the native peoples. Militarily and economically, each European group—sometimes very small groups—had to recognize distinct tribal sovereignties in order to survive, then to prosper. There was no alternative.

There was, however, an alternative idea: that Indians were Indians. In 1585 the attorney Richard Hakluyt, an advocate of colonization, summarized his goals for Virginia: "The ends of this voyage are these: 1, to plant Christian religion; 2, To Trafficke; 3, To conquer; Or, to doe all three." As can be guessed from his language, the three were complementary. The process of converting heathens was a political one and nearly as old as Christianity. It took many centuries to convert the pagans of Europe; the distinctly rough-edged political consolidation of feudal Europe then enabled the area's warlords to turn their energies toward the Middle East, Muslim Spain, and Africa. The rise of the Ottoman Empire, culminating in the early fifteenth century, vastly raised the stakes of Crusader adventurism and tightened the bond, for Christians, between Church expansionism and their own survival. The Ottoman conquest of Constantinople and the swelling of the Muslims' Mediterranean fleet were followed within a generation by Columbus's landing at Hispaniola—and the discovery of an immense new world filled with non-Christians. An old principle suddenly had a new realm in which to work itself out. Hakluyt's second goal, "To Trafficke," or trade, stood in close relation to religion—Crusaders had sometimes formed a flying wedge for mercantile interests—and was, in the English case, much more important. (The early voyages were privately financed and for profit.) For Hakluyt's readers the third term, "To conquer," was nearly a redundancy, a nod to the goal of blocking Spain.

In Hakluyt's influential imagination the people in "Virginia"—a mental marker for a vaguely understood America—were generic heathens, not a political set of distinct sovereignties. When actual settlement got under way, this attitude necessarily changed, and distinctions were made, but the urge to see all Indians as the same was always there to be called upon. It was not in every case a question of hostility. Several prominent Englishmen in the infant Virginia colony wanted to construct a biracial society, but it would be *biracial*, a concept that must have made far more sense to Englishmen, who already suspected they were white, than to Powhatans, who had yet to learn they were Indian. In the event, according to one despairing white advocate of racial assimilation, most colonists opposed joint development: "There is scarce any man amongst us that doth so much as afforde them [the natives] a good thought in his hart and most men with their mouths give them nothing but maledictions and bitter execrations." Once the local natives had mounted a determined assault on the Virginia immigrants—in 1622—the latter leaped to a conclusion that some had nurtured from the beginning: Indians should be slaves. One argued that the Indians were "apter for worke than yet our English are"—no great compliment—while the colony's secretary wrote that the natives could "most justly be compelled to servitude and drudgery, and supply the roome of men that labour, whereby even the meanest of the Plantation may imploy themselves more entirely in their Arts and Occupations, which are more generous whilest Savages perform their inferiour workes of digging in mynes, and the like." The chronicler Samuel Purchas, commenting (after the 1622 fighting) on his friend Captain John Smith's history of Virginia, wrote, "Smiths Forge mends all, makes chaines for Savage Nation / Frees, feeds the rest."

This concept of slavery—enchaining one entire people as a means of freeing another—illustrates a difference between native and English thinking. Generally speaking, one native tribe did not enslave another. There is very little evidence of a permanent, ethnically marked class of slaves in a native society prior to regular Indian-European relations. Captives were enslaved (when not killed), but they were not compelled to marry other slaves and produce slave offspring. Rather, they and, more to the point, their offspring were often assimilated as tribal members. You might die a slave, but you were not born one. When whites were captured by one native tribe or another, they did not become the nucleus of a distinct racial slave caste; neither, in the early days, did Africans, whether escapees or captives. Indeed, small numbers of whites and, later, larger numbers of Africans escaped to the tribes. Some English captives, faced with rescue teams, even refused "repatriation," preferring to remain as adoptive Indians.

The English perspective on slavery was different. In 1639, just nine years after his arrival as founding governor of the Massachusetts Bay Colony, John Winthrop willed to his son Adam an island and "also my Indians thereon." Certainly Winthrop could distinguish among Narragansetts, Mohegans, Eastern and Western Niantics, and Pequots. He had been intimately involved in the Pequot War of 1635–1637, the first major conflict among allied English-native forces and the natives' unforgettable introduction to the Englishmen's military tactic of wholesale extermination (in this case, aimed at the Pequots). In war and trade, Winthrop never neglected the distinctions among tribes; knowledge of them formed the basis for much of Massachusetts's diplomacy. But in slavery, for Winthrop, a Niantic became simply an Indian. In all the English colonies Indian captives, often including women and children, were bought and sold. During the seventeenth century Indian slaves, like Africans, sometimes had limited terms of service; and, also like Africans, in the early eighteenth century Indians saw their prospective status, in the event of capture, change from servitude to lifelong slavery. In part because they escaped so easily when held near home, Indians were often traded away to the West Indies. This type of long-distance trading marked another radical departure from native practice. One did not often return from Barbados; nor was one "adopted" there into anything but lifelong slavery, a status that also applied to one's descendants, indefinitely. In 1693, during their first decade of regular contact with colonists, Cherokee chiefs traveled to Charleston to protest the sale of Cherokee captives by other tribes (Catawbas, Savannahs, and Congarees). Over the next several decades, with the encouragement of the Carolinians, Cherokees and neighboring tribes fought each other and sold the human proceeds. Charleston merchants then packed the captives off in lots to the Indies. Native protests continued during this period, apparently because they did not quite realize what was happening—that they had entered a system in which a captive became permanently a property. On at least one occasion Cherokee visitors to Charleston were assured that their departed tribal fellows would be returning from the sugar islands; but that was a lie.

By degrees, as seen most dramatically in the refinement of slavery, Indians were becoming Indians, a status that compounded cultural and "racial" qualities. More obviously cultural factors, as reflected in terms such as *heathen* and *savage*, gradually receded in importance as race grew. In a shadowy process that seems, from the few sources available, not to have been grasped by natives at the time, Indians were not only becoming Indians, they were entering the still more mystifying category of people of color—a group that, in a further move, was associated by colonists with permanent slavery. A Carolina slavery-regulation act of 1712, for example, used the legal formula "negroes, mulattoes, mestizoes and Indians." The distinct tribal self-conceptions of natives were being melted away by white power into something new and nearly unimaginable. As the century progressed, as colonial law and practice turned native tribal citizens into Indians, people of color, and sometimes Negroes—and as these unstable categories themselves acquired stability as synonyms for *slave*—natives slowly realized that a collective fate awaited them.

"A NEW KIND OF DISORDER"

A CHEROKEE UTOPIA AND THE RISE

OF RACIAL SEPARATISM 1730–1830

■

Among the Cherokees, the process of Indianization or colorization was brilliantly interrupted by an emissary bearing a very different concept of collective identity—universal brotherhood. A sober spiritual cousin of Thomas Morton, Christian Gottlieb Priber came to the Cherokees as an advocate of communism, and as an advocate of racial equality many years before that idea came into fashion.

Few solid records exist of how the Cherokees understood this strange, short fellow who, upon arrival in the leading native town of Tellico, immediately doffed his clothes and began to paint his skin in the local manner. It is impossible to guess at Cherokee expectations in that period. Certainly they had received odd, even grandiose, visitors before. In general, as a European, one would have had to have been a little bent, whether by greed or a less common force, to enter Cherokee territory at all. Sent by the English crown to solicit favor among the southeastern tribes in 1725, Colonel George Chicken wrote, in a typical entry (for September 8), "About Seven of the Clock in the Evening came in here a Young ffrench ffellow with a Chickesaw Woman who Stayed til the Dusk of the Evening about a Mile from the Town being very much afraid of these people knocking him on the head before he could come to the Sight of some White Person." Not only does this passage—the entire one for that day— show that for whites the identity marker of white already superseded, in some manner, national identities such as French or English. It also shows that young non-Indian men could be found blundering about the mountain woods in a state of anxiety over being knocked on the head. This dazed wandering was not, as we shall see, exceptional.

Christian Priber's predecessor in grandiosity among Cherokee visitors was the demented Sir Alexander Cuming. He had been sent, apparently, in a private capacity by King George II as an emissary to the Cherokees. The available evidence suggests that Cuming's wife had had a dream, of unknown content, that persuaded Cuming to seek his destiny on Cherokee land. Among his many schemes was a plan—it indicates the tenor of his thought—to settle three million Jews in the Cherokee hills, thus somehow retiring eighty million pounds of British debt. According to one source, "the government turned a deaf ear to all of his proposals," and rightly so, but not before Cuming had convinced a somewhat random assortment of Cherokees to visit England. He had indelicately urged the Cherokees as a whole to become subjects of the king; and, according to him, he succeeded, crowning Chief Moytoy as emperor in April 1730.

"This was a Day of Solemnity the greatest that ever was seen in the Country," Cuming wrote in his journal; "there was Singing, Dancing, Feasting, making of Speeches, the Creation of Moytoy Emperor, with the unanimous consent of all the headmen assembled from the different Towns in the Nation, a Declaration of their resigning their Crowns, Eagles, Tails, Scalps of their Enemies, as an Emblem of their all owning his Majesty King George's Sovereignty over them, at the Desire of Sir Alexander Cuming, in whom an absolute unlimited Power was placed." Cuming then packed off his seven volunteers to London— "we were only going to see England for our own pleasure," one of the Cherokees later recalled—where they were lodged in the basement apartments of a Covent Garden undertaker. They were popular dinner guests; they ate and drank freely and saw the touristic sights. When they met the king, they presented, along with eagle tails, "four Scalps of Indian Enemies," Cuming noted, "all of which His Majesty was pleased to accept of." English colonial authorities had long since adopted the practice of paying bounties, especially to whites, for enemy scalps.

The seven Cherokees signed a treaty forming a trade and military alliance with England. Upon meeting the lords commissioners, one of the Cherokees reportedly said, "We look upon the Great King George as the Sun, and as our father, and upon ourselves as his children. For though we are red, and you are white yet our heads and hearts are joined together." The Cherokees then returned to their own land without Sir Alexander, who remained in London to face fraud and embezzlement charges brought by South Carolinians.

The Cuming adventure was later interpreted as a general cession of power, and perhaps land, by the entire Cherokee Nation to the English. This was impossible, not least because the nation as a united political unit didn't exist.

The Carolinians had already tried, in 1721, to convince the Cherokees and themselves that Wrosetawasatow was "king," to little effect. The Cherokees' first serious efforts at governmental centralization didn't come until 1752. Their traditional social structure was loose, giving primacy to matrilineal clans, and they preferred it that way. This structure slowly broke down, as did the once-great authority of native doctors, whose medicine was useless, at best, against new infectious diseases, notably smallpox. The growing presence of whites and Africans, often as tribal citizens by marriage or adoption, further confused the situation. Into this fluid, somewhat crumbly society walked Christian Priber.

The best account of him is given by Antoine Bonnefoy, a *voyageur* who pushed off from New Orleans in August 1741 with a flotilla of small boats and large canoes for a trip up the Mississippi. Upon reaching the mouth of the Ohio River in mid-November, Bonnefoy's canoe and one other were ambushed by Cherokees. One canoe escaped. The rest of the French group reacted minimally from across the river—"the commander contented himself with hoisting his flag on his bateau"—as Bonnefoy and four others "were seized, each by one of the savages, who made him his slave." The eighty Cherokees spent a day dividing loot equally, then packing it. They fed their captives with the same food, in the same portions, as they had themselves. Bonnefoy noted this.

The expedition continued up the Ohio to the Tennessee River, at which point in his narrative Bonnefoy introduces his fellow captives: Joseph Rivard, Pierre Coussot, Guillaume Potier ("half-breed"), and "Legras's negro," who had been wounded severely. Bonnefoy alludes to slaves other than Legras's on the trip, but says nothing more about them. In early January he and his three fellow white slaves (including half-breed Potier) "were adopted by men of prominence in the party. I was adopted as brother by a savage who bought me of my master, which he did by promising him a quantity of merchandise, and giving me what at that time I needed, such as bed-coverings, shirts, and mittens, and from that time I had the same treatment as himself. My companions were adopted by other savages, either as nephews or as cousins, and treated in the same manner by their liberators and all their families." "My companions" evidently did not, in Bonnefoy's mind, include Legras's Negro, who was set free as his wounds worsened: "the head man of the party told him to return to the French, but not knowing where to go, he followed the canoes for two days. On the third . . . the savages, tired of seeing him, gave him over to the young people, who killed him and took his scalp."

Upon arrival at Tellico, Bonnefoy, Rivard, Coussot, and Potier were made to imitate the status of slave for about a day, a dramatic set piece stretching over two ceremonies during which they had to wear slave collars, each man carrying a white stick and a rattle, and sing songs ("which we did," on the first occasion, "for the space of more than three hours, at different times, singing both French and Indian songs"). These customs over, "the savages who had adopted us came and took away our collars. I followed my adopted brother who, on entering his cabin, washed me, then, after he had told me the way was free before me, I ate with him, and there I remained two months, dressed and treated like himself, without other occupation than to go hunting twice with him."

The observant Bonnefoy noticed at Tellico three English traders with two black servants; "a son of Andre Crespe and also Jean Arlois of Bordeaux"; "a negro and negress who formerly belonged to the widow Saussier"; fifteen Natchez refugees; and Christian Priber, "a German, who said in French that he was very sorry for the misfortune which had come upon us, but that it would perhaps prove to be to our happiness." One can see that this hint from a way-ward German might have seemed curious, not to say insane, to the semi-captive Frenchman, given the conditions in which it was uttered. Five days after arriv-ing in Tellico, Bonnefoy "had occasion to ask the German . . . who was lodging in the cabin of my adopted brother, what he wished me to understand. I prayed him to explain to me what was this alleged happiness which he promised us." The Bordelais Jean Arlois and the half-breed Potier were there as well, and these men gathered in the cabin, in mid-February 1742, to hear out the vision of Christian Priber: "He replied that it would take time to explain to us what he had to say to us, addressing himself to all three; that he thought we ought to join his society; that he would admit us to an establishment, in France, of a republic, for which he had been working for twenty years; that the form of the govern-ment should be that of a general society of those composing it, in which, beyond the fact that legality should be perfectly observed, as well as liberty, each would find what he needed."

The study group reconvened the next day. Bonnefoy wanted to know where Priber had learned French. The German replied that, "being of a good family, he had been instructed in all that a man ought to know; that after having com-pleted his studies, he had learned English and French." Priber said that he had been obliged to leave Germany because of hostility to his planned republic. He went to England, then to Charleston, South Carolina. (Coincidentally, Jean-Jacques Rousseau's beloved uncle, Gabriel Bernard, lived in Charleston at the same time. It would be some years before Rousseau, the eminent admirer of "noble savages," would expound his belief in the radical freedom of man in the "state of nature.") After Charleston, Priber passed some time in a frontier town-ship, as if to acclimate himself. In or around 1736 he proceeded to Tellico.

He told Bonnefoy he had been in Tellico four years, preparing to lay "the first foundations of his republic, under the name of the Kingdom of Paradise." What was the nature of this paradise? Priber told Bonnefoy "that in his republic there would be no superiority; that all should be equal there; that he would take the superintendence of it only for the honor of establishing it; that otherwise his condition would not be different from that of the others; that the lodging, furniture and clothing should be equal and uniform as well as the life; that all goods should be held in common, and that each should work according to his talents for the good of the republic; that the women should live there with the same freedom as the men; that there should be no marriage contract, and that they should be free to change husbands every day; that the children who should be born should belong to the republic, and be cared for and instructed in all things that their genius might be capable of acquiring; that the law of nature should be established for the sole law . . . The individual was to have as his only property a chest of books and paper and ink." Sources other than Bonnefoy add that Priber's republic would be a refuge for escaped debtors, criminals, and slaves. The trader Ludovic Grant, who married into a prominent Cherokee family and knew Priber, related that the utopian's republic would admit "Creeks and Catawbaws, French and English, all Colours and Complexions." Bonnefoy noted that Priber had instructed the Cherokees in the use of weights and measures — presumably to help them avoid being cheated by traders, as they often were — and in how to make steel.

The intrepid Bonnefoy escaped two months later and after a grim journey made it back to French America; so we must pick up Priber's story in other, English sources. The English feared Priber, supposedly because they believed he was an agent of France. The French did want to bring the southeastern tribes into alliance with them. Bonnefoy himself had taken time to tout the virtues of French cloth and guns. He admitted they were more expensive but said the quality was better. His apologetic tone reveals one reason why the French never prevailed: the English had more supplies, superior means to deliver them, and so lower prices. But French shortcomings were due to limited ambition. France wanted to trade for furs, not conquer and colonize. This modesty appealed to native tribes, and the English knew it. So did Priber, whose own ambitions were far greater than the English appreciated. According to one anonymous writer who claimed to have interviewed Priber, he intended "neither more nor less than to bring about a confederation amongst all the southern Indians to inspire them with industry, to instruct them in the arts necessary to the commodity of life, and in short, to engage them to throw off the yoke of their European allies, of all nations." Priber had a prediction: "Believe me, before this century is past, the Europeans will have a very small footing on this continent." He re-crowned Moytoy as emperor, this time of Paradise; titled himself prime minister or secretary of state; and laid plans for a new capital city southwest of Tellico.

Priber had to be stopped. When the South Carolina government began to receive letters signed by imperial secretary of state Priber, it determined to capture this "man of ill principles," as one Carolinian described him in a worried letter to the lords commissioners for trade and plantations in London. The Charleston government deputized a reluctant Ludovic Grant. "I found," Grant later reported, "that he was well apprized of my design and laughed at me[,] desiring me to try in so insolent a manner that I could hardly bear with it." Grant prudently withdrew.

A second attempt failed more slowly and comically. The trader and historian James Adair, who had a correspondence with Priber, recorded the effort of a Colonel Fox, whose strength, Adair noted, "was far greater in his arms than in his head." Fox tried force but found it "difficult to enter abruptly into a new emperor's court, and there seize his prime minister." Instead of a captive he received a speech from a warrior extolling the honesty of Christian Priber. The imperial secretary of state himself then expanded on this theme, emphasizing that he had come among the Cherokees "only to preserve their liberties." Priber mentioned that he was hoping to bring in experts who would instruct the Indians in how to make gunpowder. And he finished by noting that, as he "was not accused of having done any ill to the English, before he came to the Cheerake [Cherokee], his crime must consist in loving the Cheerake.—And as that was reckoned so heinous a transgression in the eye of the English, as to send one of their angry beloved men [a Cherokee political term] to enslave him, it confirmed all those honest speeches he had often spoken." A second Cherokee rose to speak along similar lines, telling Fox that the Cherokees wished to remain on friendly terms with the English as "freemen and equals." Priber tranquilly gave Fox an escort to return the colonel to Charleston in safety.

Adair was only half kidding in his sardonic remarks, written years later, about "the new red empire." Priber's republic posed more an ideological than a military danger; but his ideology was very threatening indeed. The English began to sense, as one put it, a new "intractability . . . in matters of trade," an attitude traced to Priber's natural-rights preaching. Finally, while traveling to Mobile, Priber was seized by traders and Creeks and sent to a prison in Frederica, Georgia. "The Creek Indians have at last brought Mr. Priber prisoner here," a correspondent wrote with relief in the South Carolina *Gazette* of August 15, 1743; "he is a little ugly man." Others had found him passably easy on the eyes, though no one said he was tall. "There was a book," the *Gazette* letter writer continued, "found upon him in his own writing ready for the press, which he owns and glories in." In this book, which, like Priber's alleged Cherokee dictionary, has been lost, he "lays down the rules of government which the town is to be governed by, to which he gives the title of *Paradise*. He enumerates many whimsical privileges and natural rights . . . it is a pity so much wit is applied to so bad a purpose."

An English traveler, writing under a pseudonym, took away a different impression of the utopian: "The philosophical ease, with which he bore his confinement, the communicative disposition he seemed possessed of, and his politeness, which dress, or imprisonment could not disguise, attracted the notice of every gentleman of Frederica, and gained him the favour of many visits and conversations . . . 'It is folly,' he would say, 'to repine at one's lot in life—my mind soars above misfortune—in this cell I can enjoy more real happiness, than it is possible to do in the busy scenes of life. Reflections upon past events, digesting former studies, keep me fully employed, whilst health and abundant spirits allow me no anxious, no uneasy moments;—I suffer,—though a friend to the natural rights of mankind,—though an enemy to tyranny, usurpation, and oppression . . . ' " And as such he died in a Georgia jail.

Christian Priber understood the Indians as possessing a full humanity. His interest in their Indianness seems to have been at once tactical, scholarly, and sincere, but not essential; he apparently planned to welcome English, French, and African converts into Paradise, as well as Catawbas and Creeks. He viewed all these peoples as having in common all the qualities that mattered. He did adapt one institution from his Cherokee teachers—the Town of Refuge, a sanctuary for lawbreakers that, in a limited form, existed before the utopian's arrival in Tellico. The rest of his vision came complete from his mind and the Europe that formed him. His example had little influence, outside Cherokee country, in his time, and none after his death.

Nonetheless, Priber was a precursor of the idealism that drove the American Revolution thirty-three years after his imprisonment. Leaving aside the question of family organization, two notions distinguish Priber's thought from that of the Revolutionary generation. These concern private property and race. The idea of private property contained a set of assumptions: that one could own land, objects, labor, and the money which measured their value; that these things were in some way transferable from one owner to another without changing their nature; that, in philosophical terms, property was "naturally" private; and that the simple taking of property, notably by the state, was a crime. As a principle, private property was basic to the Revolution and to modernity. It was not an uncontroversial idea at the time, which is why Massachusetts's 1780 Declaration of Rights included "the right . . . of acquiring, possessing, and protecting property." Ownership of property and the pursuit of property had to be demanded as natural rights, that is, rights that adhered to each individual in society. Without these rights modern society might be a scene of constant struggle, of theft and murder, rather than a state of justice and peace. Priber, however, would likely have argued that the private pursuit of property was itself a cause of strife, and so conclude that the ideal society—his Paradise—could only be happy if private property were abolished, which was what he proposed.

The Revolutionary generation also held views opposite to Priber's on race. In general, the revolutionaries believed humanity to be divided into identifiable races, each with its own characteristics. The Declaration of Independence characterized Native Americans as "merciless Indian savages, whose known rule of warfare is an undistinguished destruction of all ages, sexes, and conditions." Not everyone, not even all the declaration's signers, quite agreed with this description, but the fundamental consensus remained that Indians were Indians, a distinct race not part of we, the people. Africans, including their free descendants, were likewise thought to be meaningfully distinct as a group and so not part of the people. Priber, of course, believed all humans were humans; taking this belief to its logical conclusion, he appears not to have recognized the importance of race at all.

Revolutionary thought differed from Priber's on the questions of private property and race partly because of slavery. The institution of chattel slavery brought together private property and race, because slaves were human property and were of a race—in essence, a "slave race." Identification of this "race" presented sizable difficulties. One relatively stable term, *African*, existed alongside a host of less precise terms, such as *Negro, black, Indian, mulatto, colored,* and *mestizo.* The less-exact terms were more common, because slaves were a motley group. At bottom their identification hinged on their being not-white, as can be seen in the language of a Virginia act from 1691: "whatsoever English or other white man or woman being free shall intermarry with a negroe, mulatto, or Indian man or woman, bond or free, shall within three months of such marriage be banished and removed from this dominion for ever." Importantly, this act aimed at regulating *whites*, because regulating whiteness, protecting its status, was critical to the evolving racial system. Being white meant not being the property of others. It meant being free, and fully human. Given the historical circumstances, it also meant creating the not-white, however imprecise that category might be.

It was only historical circumstance that led to the bizarre overlapping of private property and race. There had been light-skinned slaves throughout Europe, around the Mediterranean rim, and into subcontinental Asia as late as the thirteenth century. Even in 1614 the Portuguese traveler Fernão Mendes Pinto was able to relate tales of being enslaved here and there, without respect to his presumably light coloring. For Europeans, as you would expect, the most important question about slavery was whether one could oneself be made a slave. This was the subject of very lively debate among Europeans in the years coinciding with New World colonization; however, it was not a racial debate but a more generally human one. It had to do with full and free possession of oneself—and, ultimately, self-possession as a form of private property.

Modern notions of private property grew from earlier debates over personal freedom, debates that were at once religious and political. The rise of Protestantism after Martin Luther's revolt of 1517 fueled the conviction that one's relationship to God was private in nature, or nearly so. One would then measure one's personal freedom in terms of the absence of constraints on belief. People being social animals, Protestants quickly came to rebel against constraints on expression, assembly, political representation, and, in the end, property. In England the long, slow, bloody, and inconclusive Puritan revolution may be dated from William Tyndale's translation of the Bible into English, beginning in the 1520s, to the Act of Toleration of 1689, the same period in which Englishmen established themselves in North America. For American purposes, several features of English Protestant revolutionary thought would prove critical: the extreme emphasis on personal and group liberty; the belief that one could remake oneself or be reborn; a root-and-branch rejection of "custom" as a guide to social life and of inheritance as a license for power; popular resistance to any intermediaries between oneself and power, or God; belief in the nation (in this case, England) as having a special covenant with God; and the rhetoric of opposing "slavery" to a natural freedom. As the revolutionary Puritan poet John Milton wrote in 1649, basing himself on Martin Luther, "the right of birth or succession can be no privilege in nature to let a tyrant sit irremovable over a nation free born, without transforming that nation from the nature and condition of men born free into natural, hereditary, and successive slaves."

English Protestant or Puritan thinking, which provided the substance of American Puritanism, was based on a distinct mix of the Bible, nature, reason, national history, Greek and Roman classical writings, and the revolutionary literature of personal freedom that was such a marked feature of the Protestant argument with Catholicism. (When the Puritan preacher Alexander Whitaker wrote back home in 1613 with his Good Newes from Virginia, for example, he urged the shared humanity of the English and the Indians by citing "the law of Nature," the "grounds of reason," and common descent from Adam.) From such a soup, anything might be justified, except, perhaps, for slavery. References to slavery abound in English Protestant writing; defenses of slavery do not, nor do they feature in anti-Protestant writing. A literature of personal freedom could not easily accommodate slavery as anything but a negation of free will. Slavery was, at best, a "custom."

In English America, however, slavery of Indians and Africans was rapidly becoming a social fact with which thoughtful minds had to wrestle. Certain aspects of English Protestantism could be useful in that effort, such as one nation's or group's special covenant relationship with God and the exclusion from it of heathens. Still, depriving certain people of free will forever on the grounds of a hereditary accident, such as being born Indian or African, was not a simple trick, even for the adept. We can see this in the work of John Locke, whose almost religious use of the concept of private property would be so influential for our modern world.

In America, Locke has been recognized as a great philosopher of liberty. His bold conceptions of the social contract, limited government, and natural rights retain their power today. Yet he was an enthusiastic participant in the slave trade. In the 1670s he helped write a constitution for Carolina which held that "Every freeman of Carolina shall have absolute power and authority over his Negro slaves, of what opinion or religion whatsoever." Locke was a shareholder in the Royal African Company, which from 1672 held the monopoly on English slave trading, building forts along the African coast and outfitting slave ships. In 1673 and 1674 he was secretary to the Council of Trade and Plantations. From 1696 to 1700 he was among the half-dozen active members of the Board of Trade and Plantations, attending, in all, 372 meetings. Locke could hardly have been much more familiar with the nature of American racial slavery; he was among its architects.

Locke's political philosophy gave a crucial role to individual private property. In essence, Locke saw man as owning himself. His natural right to security of person, even to selfhood, was, so to speak, a property right; and from this basic property right flowed his right to own what we more commonly think of as property. ("Lives, liberties and estates . . . I call by the general name property.") Locke had a vision: his propertied man would go forth in search of unimproved property; he would, with his labor, improve it, enlarging both his own and the general wealth. This process would be infinite in extent. The moral power of private property lay in the broader progress achieved through countless acts of self-aggrandizement.

Where did slaves fit in this scheme? Locke gives some hints. He seems to have believed that people who did not work much, or failed to improve the property available to them—in other words, people who did not guide their lives fully toward the individual pursuit of property, thus slipping the moorings of the social contract—were not fully human. By giving up their ownership of themselves, in part or in whole, they gave up some portion of their natural rights. For example, as a member of the Board of Trade and Plantations, Locke addressed the problem of healthy English beggars. He proposed incarcerating them and requiring three years of forced labor. If one of them forged a pass to escape such bondage, he should lose his ears; the second offense should be punished by transportation to the colonies.

If a person did not work, he should be forced to work. And if property lay unused, it should be taken and put to use. The best example of such "waste" property he found in nonwhite America, where "a king of a large fruitful territory feeds, lodges, and is clad worse than a day-labourer in England." Such a king clearly lacked "Reason to guide him," and the correct policy, when faced with this primitive pauper-king, was "not allowing him the privilege of his nature, to be free." A natural right then became a privilege that could be taken away.

It was people such as Locke, defined by their grasp of private property, who could do the taking. This belief does not seem to have sat entirely well even in the mind of John Locke. He strove to find a reason why the slave should be a slave, referring conventionally to master-slave relationships as "the state of war continued, between a lawful conqueror, and a captive." This tired and forced interpretation of the old practice of enslaving war captives could not have held much power for Locke. His concern was with rational expansion of property rights, not military codes—with the spread of liberty, not the law of nations. And the facts of New World racial slavery as he knew them could not conform to the limits of military jurisprudence. There simply was no unending "war" that could justify the endless use of martial law.

Locke needed some deeper formulation to encompass the slave. He already believed that each individual's relation to itself was that of a property owner and that giving up that property was a type of suicide. Reasoning backward, he determined that the slave must have, "by his fault, forfeited his own life, by some act that deserves death." The great rationalist was edging himself toward the irrational. What act could a helpless captive, or an infant born into slavery, possibly have committed? But Locke was onto something profound and horrible: in the slave system Locke had helped create, by his own logic, the slave really was subhuman and so a living corpse. He did not own himself. Having lost that ownership, he could not even commit suicide, because to do so would be merely to destroy his owner's property, not gain control of himself—suicide would bring the slave no closer to freedom. And *freedom* was, finally, Locke's passion, as it was the passion of Englishmen throughout his century. In a closed system where people are property, the slave could only regain his free humanity by somehow making the master give up his own, by making the master forfeit his own life, that is, his property—by making the master kill that part of himself that was his slave. And so, "Whenever he finds the hardship of his slavery outweighs the value of his life, 'tis in his power, by resisting the will of his master, to draw on himself the death he desires." Locke had logically and systematically trapped himself within the psychology of slavery. In one of the more bizarre passages of modern Western philosophy, he recognized that modern slavery contained, far within, a suicidal murder.

This terrible psychic tangle of human property and human progress, of freedom and death, was reality in Locke's lifetime and in Priber's. The link between race and slavery—or between inherited racial slavery and private property—was, even for Locke, irrational and maddening, a historical accident that could overwhelm the most powerful of minds. Confronting the social system he made and that made him, Locke philosophized his way toward death. Priber tried to outflank the system and died in prison. The Cherokees, not wanting a life so awash in death, and finding Priber's alternative impracticable, had to find some other way of being and surviving. They had to brush their destiny against the American grain of private property and race, and see what they could see.

After Paradise came tremendous fear. The old means of holding Cherokees together had faltered. The spiritual doctors whose medicine and worldview had stabilized the tribe in the face of nature were clearly weakened. A smallpox epidemic in 1738–1739 had carried off as much as half of the tribe; a smaller epidemic in 1759–1760 reemphasized the medicine men's feebleness. Without hope for a cure, some smallpox victims killed themselves. The trader James Adair, Priber's ironic correspondent, wrote that "many threw themselves with sullen madness into the fire, and there slowly expired, as if they had been utterly divested of the native power of feeling pain." By the 1750s the Cherokees had invented a dance. "In it the dancers wore elaborate false faces," the historian William McLoughlin writes, "portraying horrifying spirit figures; they shouted and frightened the children. Some say it was designed to scare the young into obedience, but others believe it grew out of the pervasive fears of death and destruction wrought by white invaders. It seemed to teach that there was a new kind of disorder loose in their world."

In this condition the Cherokees entered the Seven Years' War. The conflict was partly over colonial territory (in America and India) and partly over European supremacy, ranging France, Austria, Russia, Saxony, Sweden, and Spain against Britain, Prussia, and Hanover. In its American form, the French and Indian War, it pitted Britain against France, with both sides fielding native allies. The French were stronger among the natives; the English were simply stronger. The Cherokees allied with Britain, taking action against the French and Shawnees. Yet the alliance was inevitably fragile, because the Cherokees knew the greatest long-term threat came from British colonists. As a Scotsman wrote of British colonial society in the 1760s, "No nation was ever infested with such a set of villains and horse thieves." The British frontier colonists were, on the whole, desperate, unscrupulous, and, to the Cherokees' dismay, infinitely replenishable. Worse still, the British colonial social structure was wildly unstable, such that the British chiefs could hardly control their frontier subjects; treaty promises meant little to frontiersmen. Cherokee chiefs were likewise losing their authority, particularly over young warriors who increasingly saw treaties as hopeless compromise and war as the only solution. A minor incident between starving, wandering fighters and remote settlers in Virginia ended the British-Cherokee alliance. In 1760–1761 British troops entered Cherokee territory and, in several actions, burned more than half of the towns, destroyed at least fourteen hundred acres of crops, and drove Cherokee families into the hills. "It was," a Cherokee chief wrote of that time, "an Ishmaelitish period when tribe was against tribe and nation against nation, when cunning met cunning, cruelty retaliated cruelty, and perfidy circumvented perfidy and deeds of desperate heroism defied the sword, the scalping knife, the fagot and torture." After one successful engagement, a Carolina militiaman wrote, regarding his Indian enemies, "we have now the pleasure, sir, to fatten our dogs with their carcasses, and to display their scalps, neatly ornamented, on the top of our bastions."

Cherokee culture became a culture of war. The Cherokees fought and retreated, ceded land here or there as if tossing meat to a predator. The predation never ceased, and the defeat of France in 1763 left all the frontier tribes without a counterweight to England. Yet the problem was not precisely with England. The Cherokees, like most eastern tribes, had decided between 1740 and the Revolution that their enemy was white people as a whole. A new idea — racial hatred — had been hammered into their minds, along with a new understanding of themselves as a race, "red" or "Indian." And this idea, which probably surfaced among Cherokees as early as the 1720s, brought a corollary: racial separatism.

In July 1777 Cherokee chiefs met with commissioners from North Carolina and Virginia to negotiate the cession of lands in western North Carolina and southwestern Virginia (today a part of Tennessee). Over the preceding five years the tribe had sold or otherwise relinquished 41,068 square miles of land; now they were to sell another 6,174. After long negotiation a tract had been decided upon, but the American commissioners — "American" in the newest sense, for their revolution was only a year old — wanted still more. The chiefs elected Corn Tassel (Onitositah) to speak for them. Described as a "stout, mild and decided man, rather more comely than otherwise," Corn Tassel delivered one of the more penetrating speeches in our history:

> It is a little surprising that when we entered into treaties with our brothers, the whites, their whole cry is *more land!* Indeed, formerly it seemed to be a matter of formality with them to demand what they knew we durst not refuse. But on the principles of fairness, of which we have received assurances during the conduct-

ing of the present treaty, and in the name of free will and equality, I must reject your demand.

Suppose . . . I were to ask one of you, my brother warriors,
under what kind of authority, by what law, or on what pretense he
makes this exorbitant demand of nearly all the lands we hold
between your settlements and our towns, as the cement and consideration of our peace. Would he tell me that it is by right of conquest? No! If he did, I should retort on him that *we* had last
marched over his territory; even up to this very place which he
has *fortified* so far within his former limits; nay, that some of our
young warriors . . . are still in the woods, and continue to keep his
people in fear . . .

If, therefore, a bare march, or reconnoitering a country is sufficient reason to ground a claim to it, we shall insist upon trans-
posing the demand, and your relinquishing your settlements on
the western waters and removing one hundred miles back
towards the east, whither some of our warriors advanced against
you in the course of last year's campaign.

One would like to know the commissioners' reaction to this proposal of sending
their people back to Jamestown. However, Corn Tassel well understood that he
was scoring a debater's point only. The fact of white power had, by this time,
been brought home: "Let us examine the facts of your present eruption into our
country . . . What did you do? You marched into our territories with a superior
force; our vigilance gave us no timely notice of your manoeuvres; your numbers
far exceeded us, and we fled to the stronghold of our extensive woods, there to
secure our women and children. Thus, you marched into our towns; they were
left to your mercy; you killed a few scattered and defenseless individuals, spread
fire and desolation wherever you pleased, and returned again to your own habitations." Corn Tassel, in his warrior's pride, wished to chide his opponents for
failing to fortify their forward positions. He nonetheless knew that they didn't
really have to, because their fire could return at any time, and his taunt could
not conceal the anxiety from which it sprang. The whites had the power, and
believed they had the right. Concentrating on the latter point, Corn Tassel
raised his oratory to a higher level and drew the logical conclusion:

You talk of the law of nature and the law of nations, and they are
both against you. Indeed, much has been advanced on the want
of what you term civilization among the Indians; and many proposals have been made to us to adopt your laws, your religion,

your manners and your customs. But, we confess that we do not yet see the propriety, or practicability, of such a reformation, and should be better pleased with beholding the good effect of these doctrines in your own practices than with hearing you talk about them, or reading your papers to us on such subjects.

You say: Why do not the Indians till the ground and live as we do? May we not, with equal propriety, ask, Why the white people do not hunt and live as we do? . . . The great God of Nature has placed us in different situations. It is true that he has endowed you with many superior advantages; but he has not created us to be your slaves. *We are a separate people!*

The language, the way of describing the world, that Corn Tassel used would last to our own day. Whites were whites, Indians were Indians. Somehow they were radically different and should remain so. This would require considerable overhauling of Corn Tassel's own society. As early as 1745, Chief Skiagunsta had complained, "My people cannot live independent of the English . . . The clothes we wear we cannot make ourselves. They are made for us. We use their ammunition with which to kill deer. We cannot make our own guns. Every necessary of life we must have from the white people." Strictly speaking, the Cherokees did not need these things, and in bad times, such as the 1760–1761 war, they had returned to deerskin clothing, and to bone arrowheads in place of brass. But, strictly speaking, the English didn't *need* sugar, tobacco, or furs, either. John Locke had premised his moralism of conquest on conditions of scarcity; scarcity, however, is in the eye of the beholder. The modern drive for growth has never been securely based on need. It has been based on desires in surplus of need, and most often beyond the reach of both honor and religion; and this has lent modern expansions their moral particularity.

The morality of modern expansionism, as Corn Tassel explained, often came wrapped in a civilizing mission associated with a culture—in this case, what the chief described as "white" culture, an association he could only have learned from whites themselves. It had a spiritual element, as shown by his reference to the "great God of Nature." For an American this mental complex— with Indians and whites as distinct civilizations or races, charged by God with distinct missions—dates from the latter half of the eighteenth century, coming into its own only after the defeat of France in 1763.

It had been incubating for some time. According to the historian Gregory Evans Dowd, the earliest recorded manifestation of what would become a Pan-Indian separatist movement occurred along the upper Susquehanna around

1737. The Susquehanna had become home to native refugees from farther east—a station, as it turned out, in the piecemeal flight of uprooted people west to the Allegheny, then west and south into the country of the upper Ohio. These people often had little in common other than a general Indianness and, increasingly, a shared enemy that thought of them only as Indians. In 1737 a seer among the exiles reported that the supreme deity, the Master of Life, had said Indians were doomed unless they ceased trading skins for liquor. Alcohol was denounced again along the Susquehanna in 1744, among dispossessed Shawnees and Delawares. A white missionary described there "a devout and zealous reformer, or rather restorer of what he supposed was the ancient religion of the Indians."

The Master of Life appeared again to the Delawares in 1751. They informed missionaries that "God first made three men and three women, viz: the indians, the negro, and the white man," in that order. Because the Indians had come first, whites "ought not to think themselves better." "The notion of the separate creation gave legitimacy to the Indians' way of life," writes Dowd. "It explicitly challenged not only those Indians who had converted to Christianity but also those few who had grown too close to the Anglo-Americans . . . Claiming that only Indian ways could lead Indians to salvation, the theology of separation implicitly attacked Indian clients of the Anglo-Americans. The notion had radical implications for Indian identity. Attachments to the older, local, linguistic, and lineage-oriented conceptions of one's people now competed with a decidedly innovative pan-Indianism."

This "theology of separation" first appeared among mixed refugees and so was polyglot—a mixed answer to a problem of mixture. It included, roughly, a self-cleansing rejection of alcohol; a command to wean oneself from foreign manufactures; polemics against greed or "covetousness," which was construed as culturally non-Indian; a highly problematic "return" to ancient ways, with emphasis on precontact religion; and a strong sense that God was punishing his chosen people for moral laxness, promiscuity, mixture with whites, and squandering of their patrimony (notably game animals). God's punishments included smallpox.

Indian separatist theology needed, by its nature, to be cobbled together. Some elements had a noticeable Christian flavor. Along the Susquehanna, around 1752, a Munsee prophet first employed a chart—a quick way to avoid linguistic obstacles—that showed heaven and hell, with the latter distinguished by the presence of Europeans and rum. The Munsee prophet also promoted rituals, at least one of which was probably new: a twenty-four-hour ceremony that climaxed in collective weeping. The chart approach was taken up by the greatest of the early prophets, the Delaware Neolin, who by 1761 had a large following. His chart showed heaven and hell, with the path to heaven blocked by a symbol representing white people and a set of strokes indicating "ye vices which ye Indians have learned from ye White people." By 1763 some Delawares had adopted a southeastern native practice, set to a new purpose. They drank an herbal tea that made them vomit, purifying them of "White people's ways and Nature." Ritualized vomiting spread among the displaced tribes. One center of radicalism became known to whites as "vomit town."

The political aspect of Pan-Indian separatism was something like holy war. The Delaware Neolin spoke openly of a coming conflict; it arrived in 1763, led by the Ottawa Pontiac. Taking into account the numbers of tribes and individuals involved and the geographic extent of operations, Pontiac's War was the largest united effort in Indian history. By its end, two years later, the war had cost the British nine of thirteen posts besieged along the frontier and had inspired Britain to prohibit settlement west of the Appalachians—a proclamation London was powerless to enforce.

Pan-Indian militancy surfaced again, briefly, in Lord Dunmore's War of 1774, then with vehemence throughout the Revolution, ending only in 1794—twenty years of almost constant conflict. In May 1776, as the Continental Congress in Philadelphia debated how to declare independence from Britain, a delegation of Mohawks, Ottawas, and Shawnees arrived in Cherokee country. According to a British witness, a Shawnee unrolled a war belt and told his potential allies that "red people who were once masters of the whole country hardly possessed ground enough to stand on." The Shawnee believed it "better to die like men than to dwindle away by inches." Militant Cherokees picked up the belt, to the displeasure of their cautious leaders. Not for the first time, Pan-Indianism had created division. It had always been directed toward individual Indians, in the sense that it sought to spring them from tribal loyalty to Indian loyalty and to substitute a racial concept for a tribal one. But each tribe had its elite, and part of what those elites did was negotiate with whites—for their own tribes. These negotiations gave the tribal elites power: money, goods, trading privileges. For local chiefs, Pan-Indian war songs posed many dangers. They wished to preserve what they had, including their tribe's land, or what remained of it. It was not by chance that much of the militant Pan-Indian leadership came from tribes that had little or nothing left to lose.

By 1776 it had become clear to many that wars with whites were wars one lost. The Cherokees, hard-pressed by large settler populations and too far from British supply lines, had a more precarious position than their neighbors to the north or southwest. For the northern militants (and their many Cherokee and, soon, Creek allies), this was slightly beside the point. As the Shawnee ambassador had said, the choice was already, to some degree, between a quick death and a slow one. In the event, most Cherokees opted for war with the new Americans and allied with Britain.

Their choice immediately proved disastrous. In less than four months Revolutionary border militias had led four expeditions against the Cherokees—an extraordinary concentration of firepower—and managed to destroy nearly all of the tribe's towns, homes, and crops. The elder chiefs sued for peace, while sizable militant forces withdrew west or abandoned Cherokee country altogether, a nearly unprecedented step. They joined the Northerners and fought, at last, not as Cherokees but as Indians. Some were still fighting in 1794, at the Battle of Fallen Timbers, the decisive defeat that ended the largest organized racial uprising in American history, before or since. They had kept fighting for thirteen years after the British surrendered at Yorktown.

After the Battle of Fallen Timbers the Indians' holy war briefly subsided until, again, a seer arose among the beset Shawnees: Lalawethika, brother of the warrior Tecumseh. Born just before the Revolution, Lalawethika lost his right eye as a child, and by his adolescence was on his way to being a drunkard. He continued down that path, earning a reputation only as a chattering braggart; his name meant Rattle or Noisemaker. He trailed his elder brother as Tecumseh, who had fought bravely at Fallen Timbers and refused to sign the treaty that followed it, led their band from hunting ground to hunting ground in Indiana. Lalawethika was a figure of ridicule. He could not hunt, and depended on others to feed him and his family. He associated himself with a medicine man who eventually taught him about herbs and healing, but Lalawethika also failed at this. In April 1805 he collapsed, and his wife prepared his funeral.

Then he revived. He had indeed died, he said, and been taken to heaven, where he saw happy Indians, plentiful game, and fields of corn. He also learned of the torments of hell, where drunkards were forced to swill molten lead. The Master of Life sent him back to earth to guide his people. Lalawethika told his listeners that he would never touch whiskey again, and that he had a new name, Tenskwatawa, The Open Door.

The Shawnee prophet soon gathered followers—Senecas, Wyandots, Ottawas, as well as Shawnees. He had further visions of the Master of Life, from whom he received teachings. Tenskwatawa, also known simply as the Prophet, taught that Indians should respect their elders and traditional ways, cease quarreling, swear off alcohol, and give food and shelter to widows, orphans, and the helpless. They should not practice polygamy and should honor their spouses. Indian women living with white men should leave them and return to their people; mixed-blood children should be barred from tribal life. Individuals should not accumulate private property, because selfishness was evil. Indians should eat only traditional foods. Domesticated animals and bread were forbidden. Indians should dress in traditional clothes, and set aside metal for wood, fired clay, bone, and stone. The Americans, the Prophet taught, were not children of God but agents of the Great Serpent. The Master of Life wanted his true children gradually to abandon all ties with the children of evil. When they had completed this work, he would "overturn the land, so that all white people will be covered and you alone shall inhabit the land."

The Prophet directed his message against whites, against Indians who adopted white ways—and against traditional shamans who didn't recognize the new dispensation. He advised followers to throw away their old medicine bundles, extinguish their old fires and light new ones, cease old ceremonies and practice those he offered in their stead. The Prophet provided followers with conversion ceremonies, which they took to other villages as they spread the faith. Converts were to confess their sins and shake hands with the Prophet. New disciples received a rosary of beans, which symbolized "the flesh of the Prophet." Those who resisted the message were warned of consequences. Some of the Prophet's followers identified witches, and killed them.

During this period white Americans were signing treaties with a succession of enfeebled, and not infrequently drunk, chiefs, picking off the lands of Delawares, Miamis, Wyandots, Sauks, and Ottawas. Young warriors from these tribes and others drifted toward the Prophet. By the middle of 1806 William Henry Harrison, then governor of Indiana Territory (and later president), had grown worried. He challenged the Prophet to demonstrate his spiritual power. "Ask him to cause the sun to stand still," Harrison said, "—the moon to alter its course—or the dead to rise from their graves. If he does these things, you may then believe that he has been sent by God." In one of the odder twists of our history, the Prophet knew that an eclipse was due. He announced that he would take Harrison's challenge and make the sun disappear, which it did. Word of the Prophet's act rushed among the villages of defeated tribes, and men left their homes to join Tenskwatawa and his strong elder brother.

Tecumseh believed in his younger brother, once so lost. And he had a political vision to match his brother's spiritual power. In late 1807 he began to speak out. Tall, handsome, powerfully built, and relentlessly articulate, Tecumseh urged all Indians to unite and to move no farther west. He traveled without cease along the American frontier, among the dispossessed and desperate, spreading the word. In 1810 he addressed an increasingly nervous Governor Harrison: "I am a Shawnee. My forefathers were warriors. Their son is a warrior. From them I take only my existence. From my tribe I take nothing. I have made myself what I am. And I would that I could make the red people as great as the conceptions of my mind . . . The way, the only way to stop this evil [of white expansion] is for all the red men to unite in claiming a common and equal right in the land, as it was at first, and should be now—for it never was divided, but belongs to all. No tribe has a right to sell, even to each other, much less to strangers, who demand all, and will take no less." This was what the United States feared most—a mirror of itself, a racial republic, the united Indian states. As early as 1805 the secretary of war had sent out a circular instructing his agents to prevent an assertion, by the southern tribes, of common, intertribal land title.

Tecumseh had taken the theology of separatism to its final stage. Tribes meant nothing; only the race mattered. In 1811 he carried his message south, to the Cherokees, Chickasaws, Choctaws, and Creeks. He asked them, "Where today are the Pequot? Where the Narraganset, the Mohican, the Pokanoket and many other once powerful tribes of our people? They have vanished before the avarice and oppression of the white man, as snow before a summer sun . . . Will we let ourselves be destroyed in our turn without making an effort worthy of our race?" The Creeks had a prophet of their own, Hillis Hadjo, and some from Hadjo's tribe went north with Tecumseh to aid him there; some crossed the Mississippi as ambassadors to western tribes, while other Creek diplomatists visited Florida to rally the Seminoles. The practical Cherokees, too, had their prophets. A messenger in the sky above a Georgia mountain in 1811 told a man and two women, "You yourselves can see that the white people are entirely different beings from us; we are made from red clay; they, out of white sand." The messenger was not unreasonable; he ordered that houses be built for white people "who can be useful to the Nation with writing." Useless white people, however, had to go. And land must be returned. A second messenger, following Tecumseh's embassy, explained that "God is not pleased that the Indians have sold so much land to the white people." In 1812 further heavenly messengers took a harder line. Cherokees were commanded to "put aside everything that is similar to the white people and that which they had learned from them." Cherokees who declined would be taken away by divine force, as if they were white, for the whites would be taken away, too.

Tecumseh turned to war in that same year. The British had been encouraging dissatisfaction among the northern tribes for some time, a constant irritation to the insecure Americans. This, combined with quarrels over shipping rights and British impressment of American sailors, caused the two white nations to stumble their way toward battle. Tecumseh saw his chance. He took whatever men he could find to Canada. They gathered at Fort Malden, on the Canadian side of the Detroit River: Kickapoos, Shawnees, Potawatomis, Delawares, and Wyandots, Sauk and Fox, Chippewas, Sioux and Winnebagos. Britain gave Tecumseh command of the Indian force, which proceeded with the British to take Fort Detroit.

The War of 1812 did not go well for Britain. In September 1813 American ships destroyed the British fleet on Lake Erie, cutting supply lines to Tecumseh and his British allies. The British prepared to retreat, enraging Tecumseh. William Henry Harrison moved west with a large force, compelling Tecumseh and his British counterpart, Henry Procter, to drop back a hundred miles to the Thames River. There Tecumseh made his stand against his nemesis, Harrison, on October 5, 1813. In the mid-afternoon Harrison's cavalry charged Procter's line, which collapsed in minutes with Procter fleeing on horseback. Tecumseh and his men remained. As the Prophet watched from a nearby hillside, Harrison's men advanced on his brother. After thirty minutes Tecumseh was dead, and his soldiers retreated into the forest.

The War of 1812 shattered Tecumseh's racial dream. The southeastern tribes split over it: many Creeks sided with Britain and were mercilessly defeated by Andrew Jackson with the help of Cherokees and Choctaws—and pro-American Creeks. Even if all the tribes had been united, in 1812 Americans between the Appalachians and the Mississippi outnumbered Indians seven to one. The upper Ohio region had already been lost after the Battle of Fallen Timbers. The lower Ohio, with Kentucky on its southern bank and the new territories of Indiana and Illinois to the north, now formed an impenetrable white barrier between the Great Lakes tribes and the Cherokees, Creeks, and other southeastern tribes. Whites in Louisiana and the Missouri Territory likewise pressed in from the West. Resistance continued only on a local, and more tribal, basis—among the Seminoles in Florida, who fought intermittently until 1842; or among the Sauk and Fox, who, influenced by a Winnebago prophet, tried to reclaim their land in 1831, only to be crushed in the pathetic, harrying massacre known as the Black Hawk War.

Tecumseh himself became, curiously, a somewhat heroic figure to white Americans. Men such as Harrison sought to take their measure in him; they saw him as an opponent worthy of themselves, the westward-striking leaders of an expanding nation. Perhaps Tecumseh's racial goals felt familiar to the whites. He was, in that important respect, like them. White historians would pay him a significant compliment by saying he was lighter-skinned than his followers (although he wasn't). White artists would take away his nose ring and realign his features. An 1856 sculpture has him in glistening white marble, eyes closed, about to expire, another Indian caught in the art of dying.

This business of Indian dying was a complicated one. The United States in 1813, so young in some ways, was yet already a haunted country, a setting for ghost stories. White Americans knew quite well that they had taken their coun-

try with sword and gun from its inhabitants called Indians, and public murders have a way of remaining in the public consciousness. The nation named
itself with Indian words: Connecticut, Massachusetts, Adirondack, Allegheny,
Appalachian, Kentucky, Tennessee, Mississippi, Missouri, Ohio, Illinois, Alabama. Linguistic borrowing of Indian words eerily tracks the success of white
military force: after a sharp rise in the first decades of contact, it plummets from
1622, when Virginia Indians struck at Jamestown, to a nadir at King Philip's
War (1675–1676). After that New England conflict, word borrowing picks up
speed and soars after the Revolution, dips again for the Civil War, then reaches
its peak around 1900, with Indian lands finally divided into private property and
Indian population at its historic low.

Months after the death of Tecumseh, Washington Irving wrote, "notwithstanding the obloquy with which the early historians of the colonies have over
shadowed the character of the ignorant and unfortunate natives, some bright
gleams will occasionally break through, that throw a melancholy lustre on their
memories. Facts are occasionally to be met with in their rude annals, which,
though recorded with all the colouring of prejudice and bigotry, yet speak for
themselves, and will be dwelt upon with applause and sympathy when prejudice shall have passed away." Or they might not; the natives could simply disappear, they might "vanish like a vapour from the face of the earth," Irving
continues, "their very history will be lost in forgetfulness, and 'the places that
now know them will know them no more for ever.' " This intense sense of past
crimes and crudities, of a general "prejudice," and of melancholy loss was widespread, in literary circles, from the first decades of the new republic. It is unsur-
prising that Irving built much of his reputation on haunting, supernatural tales;
he lived in a country haunted by Indians.

White Americans would not have been haunted by Indians if they had not
seen in Indians something of themselves. And they would not have been so
morbidly preoccupied with the Indians' art of dying if they had not sensed in it
something of their own deaths. Indians had represented many horrible things to
white Americans, but they had also represented freedom, dignity, honor, mobility, the unimportance of wage work, nonacquisitiveness, and intimacy with
nature. In a way, they even represented stability: Indians were timeless, they
knew themselves, whereas whites were pursued by time and want, nomads
always pushing west, gripped by a need for accumulation and possession, fencing and plowing and controlling. They did not know themselves at all. White
American society had begun as a nomadic society. From the moment of first
landing most white Americans never hesitated to move on, to pack up their car-
avans and head west. The peculiarity of the white-Indian encounter was, in
some sense, the reverse of its customary expression: white nomads were over-

running settled societies. But these new nomads, unlike most previous nomadic cultures known to history, had remarkably little in common. In contrast to the Indians they encountered, they often had no shared language, no collective past, little religion, weak social hierarchy, few if any institutions, and only the sketchiest idea of where they were.

The tribal identification that these nomads developed, of course, was that they were white. The American "is either an European or the descendant of an European," the Frenchman Crèvecoeur wrote in 1782, "hence that strange mixture of blood, which you will find in no other country." The "American" could not be Indian, however, and this was tremendously important in part because Americans, in Crèvecoeur's sense, had such a fragile hold on themselves; being individualist nomads, they could hardly keep their society together. They were haunted, in many ways, by the possibility of merging with the Indians. As early as 1612 white men were executed—variously burned, hanged, broken on the wheel, or shot—after being caught at what might not seem to be a crime: living with Indians in preference to whites. The tendency of whites to "become Indians" was noted with alarm through the Revolutionary period. As Crèvecoeur wrote, "Thus our bad people are those who are half cultivators and half hunters; and the worst of them are those who have degenerated altogether into the hunting state . . . as Europeans and new made Indians, they contract the vices of both." This type of "reversion" was exceedingly common along the shifting frontier from earliest colonial times well into the nineteenth century. More often than not, settled agricultural natives encountered white nomads who survived by hunting, foraging, and occasional pillaging. The nomads would be followed by others who practiced an agriculture more sedentary and intensive than that of the natives; but these would not come until they had been preceded by members of their own tribe who inaugurated the white presence by acting more like Indians than did the Indians themselves.

This muddling at the margins was mirrored, as white America coalesced into a distinct national tribe, by the idea that whites and Indians would merge. The notion had already occurred to William Byrd (1674–1744), who felt that an opportunity for a thoroughly mixed race had been missed in early-colonial times. He wrote that there was only one "way of converting these poor infidels and reclaiming them from barbarity, and that is charitably to intermarry with them." By "them" he meant Indian women, not men. The offspring would be, if not white, white enough: "Even their copper colored complexion would admit of blanching, if not in the first, at the farthest in the second generation. I may safely venture to say that the Indian women would have made altogether as honest wives for the first planters as the damsels they used to purchase from aboard the ships." This idea still held at the other end of the eighteenth century, to different degrees, for Byrd's fellow Virginians George Washington and Thomas Jefferson. Washington's policy as president was to recognize tribal sovereignties while aiming at the education, material uplift, and eventual assimilation of Indians as citizens. Typically, Jefferson added to this a belief in racial absorption. "In truth," he wrote in 1803, the year he completed the purchase of Louisiana from Napoleon, doubling U.S. territory, "the ultimate point of rest and happiness for them is to let our settlements and theirs meet and blend together, to intermix, and become one people." In this way Indians and whites would "finally consolidate our whole country to one nation only." That same year, however, Jefferson also wrote that if a tribe should "take up the hatchet" it ought to be driven across the Mississippi as "a furtherance of our final consolidation." As president, Jefferson addressed an Indian delegation in 1808, emphasizing the importance of individual landownership—private property—then adding, "you will mix with us by marriage, your blood will run in our veins, and will spread with us over this great continent."

Ultimately, what Byrd and Jefferson sought was for Indians to become white—to join the tribe that had won. The idea was not unreasonable. It was not even strange within many tribes' understanding of how war worked. "They would," Jefferson wrote in 1813, "have mixed their blood with ours, and been amalgamated and identified with us within no distant period of time." But the moment had passed. The Indians' own thinking had advanced too far down a certain American road to look well on amalgamation and identification with whites.

Yet the sense among white Americans that part of them was Indian did not go away after the War of 1812 and the death of Tecumseh. Rather, it was transformed into a sense of melancholy, tragedy, and romance. In finally becoming a unified white nation, and in making the transition from nomadic, uprooted struggle to a rough stability, this portion of the American people had to begin the process of losing a part of itself—the part that was free and mobile and an aspect of nature rather than its subjugator. It had both to honor this part of itself and to kill it. For this nascent racial and national collective, radical individual freedom and mobility had to be tamed and made past. The imaginative figure for this historical act was the Indian.

A changing idea among white people about themselves created a new Indian, wild, free, glorious, unalterably separate in racial terms, and doomed to extinction. To this end, the drama of miscegenation had to be played out, in the popular imagination, both to integrate and to reject the foreign, Indian element. In Lydia Maria Child's 1824 novel *Hobomok*, for example, the white female protagonist marries an Indian, and they have a son. The novelist proceeds to show how the marriage cannot last; the Indian husband withdraws west in a dignified fashion, with his son staying east to become white. But the son becomes white in a distinctively American way, because he retains enough Indi-anness to distinguish him from an Englishman. The Indianness of the Ameri-can offspring is both erased and retained, as if the drop of native blood makes the boy truly white, rather than European—in other words, a true American.

More influential and popular than Child's book were James Fenimore Cooper's Leatherstocking novels, the earliest of which, *The Pioneers*, appeared in 1823. Cooper has been considered the first major American novelist, and *The Pioneers* introduced the basic elements of what would become the literary genre of Westerns. The story turns on two types of racial mixing. The first con-cerns the novel's hero, who is thought to be part white and part Indian. He shows an implacable anger toward the local white property magnate, a judge, and argues the prior claim of Indians to the judge's land. At the novel's end, however, it is revealed that the hero is Indian only by adoption (or choice), not by blood, and his claim against the judge is that of one white man against another. This reconciles him with the judge, whose daughter the hero marries. The Indian land claim, having been debated, can now be forgotten, and the part-Indian hero becomes fully white—but only after having been, in the white imagination, Indian.

The second type of racial mixing in *The Pioneers* is that of Leatherstocking himself—also known as Natty Bumppo, Hawkeye, and Deerslayer—with his Indian partner, Chingachgook. "The Leatherstocking . . . had imbibed, uncon-sciously, many of the Indian qualities," Cooper writes, "though he always thought of himself as a civilized being." Leatherstocking and Chingachgook prefer the "savage ways" of the forest, Leatherstocking by disposition, Chin-gachgook by "nature." Cooper in many ways codified these savage, putatively Indian ways, basing his knowledge on white sources. Cooper's savage ways became those of his Indians and of generations of white writers who succeeded him. His savage was a man, physically powerful, eloquently direct, and bound by honor. Not cruel, he still had a loving command of the means of violence, the hatchet, rifle, and knife. In the forest he knew the meaning of every snapped twig and whispering feather: nature spoke to him as one of her own. He was individualistic, alone and lonely because his time had passed. The native tribes were dying, the land being enclosed, game disappearing.

Cooper created Leatherstocking and Chingachgook to embody this idea of life and to embody its death. For Chingachgook death comes in *The Pioneers* as suicide, when he allows a forest fire to burn him. Meditating at Chingachgook's grave, the not-really-Indian hero of the novel judges, with exquisite brutality, that the Mohican's "faults were those of an Indian, and his virtues those of man." This is where Leatherstocking himself comes in: his own virtues are those of an Indian and of man. He doesn't actually have any faults at all, except that he loves a life that cannot last. Completely white, he is, then, the greatest of

Indians, because he has all their virtues and none of their faults. And the reason he doesn't have the Indians' faults is that he has no Indian blood. From the white point of view, as Cooper expresses it, the Indians are racially doomed but Indianness lives on in whites—it is a crucial part of what makes those whites American. The demise of Indians then becomes a white American tragedy, and a part of white Americans' self-understanding, somehow a necessary stage in "the march of the nation across the continent," the novel's last words.

The unbridgeable racial gulf between whites and Indians entered, during this period, into jurisprudence. The question was whether Indians had a right to their land—which was one way of phrasing the question, Did the United States have the right to take Indian land? In considering this issue, judges emphasized that whites and Indians were so distinct that they could not mix, and that the right of conquest gave the former a claim on the property of the latter. Such were the beliefs of Supreme Court justice John Marshall, a Virginian who served on the Court from 1801 to 1835. In a decision published in the same year as *The Pioneers*, he recognized that most often, when one people conquers another, "The new and old members of the society mingle with each other; the distinction between them is gradually lost, and they make one people." This could not happen in North America, however, because "the tribes of Indians inhabiting this country were fierce savages, whose occupation was war, and whose subsistence was drawn chiefly from the forest. To leave them in possession of their country was to leave the country a wilderness; to govern them as a distinct people was impossible, because they were as brave and high spirited as they were fierce . . . What was the inevitable consequence of this state of things? The Europeans were under the necessity either of abandoning the country, and relinquishing their pompous claims to it, or of enforcing those claims by the sword, and by the adoption of principles adapted to the condition of a people with whom it was impossible to mix . . . or of remaining in their neighborhood and exposing themselves and their families to the perpetual hazard of being massacred."

Put simply, it was the Indians' own racial distinctiveness that forced the Europeans (identified elsewhere in Marshall's opinion as "whites") either to withdraw altogether or to conquer and expel. Marshall places the cultural responsibility for their death and displacement on the Indians themselves and their incapacity for change. It is indicative of the times that Marshall also admires them as "brave and high spirited" and even allows for the "pompous" nature of European claims. These qualities of admiration and self-criticism would be greatly amplified by the other great jurist of those early decades, Joseph Story of Massachusetts, who served on the Supreme Court from 1811 to 1845. Story, writing in 1828, saw in the conquest of North America no motive besides "ambition and lust of dominion" and believed that European talk of civilizing influence and Christianization was simply a lying justification for greed. Nonetheless, Story wrote, the Indians had to die. "By a law of their nature, they seem destined to a slow, but sure extinction. Everywhere, at the approach of the white man, they fade away. We hear the rustling of their footsteps, like that of the withered leaves of autumn, and they are gone forever . . . They have perished. They are consumed. The wasting pestilence has not alone done the mighty work. No,—nor famine, nor war. There has been a mightier power, a moral canker, which hath eaten into their heart-cores—a plague, which the touch of the white man communicated—a poison which betrayed them into a lingering ruin."

Joseph Story was the leading legal scholar of the first half of the nineteenth century—even Marshall, the browbeating chief justice and architect of the early republican Court, deferred to his friend's learning—and he had no trouble expressing himself clearly. Yet what is one to make of this "moral canker" in the "heart-cores" of Indians, or of "the touch of the white man" that communicates it? Story's remarks read like something near madness; they have a mystical quality. A simple touch: as if the white man were the god of death. And it is to death that Story turned when he wrote that, in death, the gulf between white and Indian will be crossed.

Before death, it cannot be crossed. "Reason as we may," Story wrote, "it is impossible not to read in such a fate much, that we know not how to interpret; much of provocation to cruel deeds and deep resentments; much of apology for wrong and perfidy; much of pity, mingling with indignation; much of doubt and misgiving as to the past; much of painful recollections; much of dark forebodings." But it must be so, because "the red men are incapable of . . . assimilation . . . They can neither be tamed, nor overawed." The Indians, because of their racial character, must be removed from among white people, whose own racial nature included the touch of death. "Humanity," concluded Story, like the hero at Chingachgook's grave, "must continue to sigh at the constant sacrifices of this bold, but wasting race."

Story did not mention his concurrence in Marshall's 1823 decision that encouraged the "inevitable" removal of the remaining eastern Indians. Neither did he speak of the enormous efforts on the part of Indians to succeed on white terms—to adopt white institutions and to abandon every aspect of their own cultures except their land. Story, Cooper, perhaps even John Marshall, and certainly Washington Irving, four men who, together, were the leading creators of American law and literature for the post-Revolutionary generation, were haunted by Indians. And it seems that, however painful this may have been, their white generation preferred living with these accusing ghosts to sharing their new country with living Indians.

"WELCOME, NEGRO, WELCOME"

THE INDIAN AS SLAVE AND SLAVEHOLDER

■

This was the world that greeted the Cherokee Elias Boudinot, born around 1804, a man who had many ambitions but did not want to be a ghost. His parents, David Oo-watie and Susannah Reese, were among those Cherokees who had moved away from small towns, the traditional basic unit of Cherokee society, and onto family farms. They left the old town of Hiwassee, in southeastern Tennessee, and started farms strung along Oothcaloga Creek, in northwestern Georgia. Oo-watie's brother, The Ridge (later called Major Ridge), also came with his family. These families abandoned their matrilineal clan ties and much of communal life. The children of Oo-watie and The Ridge took their fathers' names, ratifying the new patrilineal system. The families lived apart from each other, working for themselves. Without a town there would be no council house and stomp ground, no traditional ball plays for the boys to learn warriors' skills. The men would be farmers, not warriors and hunters. The women would stay in the home, not plant crops; they would card, spin, weave, and sew, prepare meals, and raise children. The U.S. government provided materials and instruction—the do-it-yourself kit for a way of life.

David and Susannah's first son, who would become Elias Boudinot, was named Buck; their second, Stand. The boys grew up with their cousins, the Ridges. Buck became fast friends with the Ridges' son John, who was slightly older and lighter skinned. Both boys were about one-sixteenth white. In 1811 Buck joined John Ridge at the Moravian mission school at Spring Place, twenty or so miles up the Oostanaula River, among the Blue Ridge Mountains. They had only six classmates, some of them white.

The Cherokees were transforming themselves at a fantastic pace. In hardly more than a decade they had abandoned most of their old towns and moved onto farms. They were trying hard to live like whites. By 1809 the nation had over 19,000 head of cattle, 3 sawmills, 13 gristmills, more than 6,500 horses, and 583 slaves. Three hundred forty-one whites lived in the nation, more than a hundred of them being white men married to Cherokees. Many of the white men worked as tenant farmers for Cherokee landlords. (The federal survey did not tabulate white women or Cherokees with African ancestry.) The total population stood at 13,319, a substantial increase over the approximately 10,000 in 1794.

This prosperity, and the way of life it required, created divisions. A portion of the tribe, perhaps a tenth, was doing well, and a few Cherokees lived the dream of large plantations worked by slaves. Many of these had white relations, either from among the missionaries and settlers or, further back, from among the Tories, mostly of Scottish heritage, who had fought alongside Cherokee allies against the Revolution. Such families, which included the Ridges and Waties, were already being referred to as the mixed bloods. The term is somewhat misleading, because it does not include mixtures among tribes or mixtures with Africans; more importantly, it refers to behavior as well as genes. A mixed blood who lived as a full-blood was essentially a full-blood, the reverse also being true. An element of choice was thereby introduced. The man who would become leader of the full-bloods, John Ross, had little Cherokee blood and spoke Cherokee with difficulty. The men who would dominate mixed-blood politics, such as Buck and Stand Watie and John Ridge, were almost entirely Cherokee. White relatives had importance in that they could make white people seem less foreign, and in some cases helped children to learn English. But beyond that, one's race was determined by one's actions.

Nonetheless, the language of blood was used to make sense of behavior. Whites also used it, for the roots of this language lay in the white view of the world. Return Meigs, who acted as the U.S. agent among the Cherokees from 1801 to 1823, advocated intermarriage because he believed that "the adult real Indian will alter his habits but in a partial degree," whereas "by their intermarriages with the half Blood and with the whites" the "real Indian will disappear." This was war by other means: "the shades of complexion will be obliterated and not a drop of human blood be lost." Many Cherokees believed or feared this, too—that, in Meigs's words from 1805, "where the blood is mixed with the whites . . . there is an apparent leaning toward civilization, and this disposition is in proportion to its distance from the original stock." In one sense, the Cherokee Nation, regardless of birth, had become assimilated, because Cherokee imaginations now labored in the language of race.

The federal government sought to use the division between mixed bloods and full-bloods to achieve the goal of removing Cherokees from their lands. Return Meigs had decided by 1808 that the entire tribe should remove across the Mississippi to "preserve their national existence." He felt that only a few hundred of the tribe, the successful mixed bloods, had the wherewithal to succeed in an increasingly white world; the rest would be cheated and destroyed. The shift away from George Washington's policy of material uplift and integration was under way. Evidently, the Cherokees were not becoming white quickly enough. Or it may be that they were becoming white all too well, becoming fully human in the Lockean sense, that is, owners of property. As such, they would be entitled to the respect of government and hard to displace. (A Georgia congressman would explicitly link U.S. policy of "civilizing the Indians" with "rendering them permanent upon their lands"—lands that Georgia wanted.) And so the U.S. government, which had tried so hard to make Indians behave like whites, now wanted them to be Indians again. That is why Meigs, addressing a Cherokee council in 1808, tried to instill race pride in his Indian charges: "You have your choice," he said, "to stay here and become industrious, like white people . . . or go over the Mississippi." The latter option would mean they could remain Cherokees, which Meigs urged them to do, though in a very peculiar way. "Brothers," he said, "it is well known everywhere that the Cherokees stand on the highest ground of reputation as a Nation of Red men. The Cherokees have more knowledge as farmers, as manufacturers, and have more knowledge of literature than any nation of Red men in America, I may safely say, than all the Red men in America put together . . . You have more money, more cattle, more horses, more and better cloathing than any other nation of Red men . . . I wish to excite in yourselves a just pride, that is, to have you value yourselves as *Cherokees*; the word 'Cherokee' or 'Cherokees' should always convey an Idea of Respectability to your people."

Here was a true stew of identity. The U.S. government wanted Cherokees to take pride in themselves generally as the best of their red race, while the specific sources of that pride were all the activities that made them "like white people." Further, the only way to guard this bewildering racial identity was to leave the ancestral lands and live in complete isolation from white people. Meigs was exhorting the Cherokees to become assimilationist racial separatists.

Many chiefs took his advice. The Cherokees divided in two, each side sending a delegation to Thomas Jefferson, nearing the end of eight years as president, in Washington. One group, dominated by mixed bloods, emphasized tribal progress "in agriculture & domestic manufactures much beyond their own expectations or the expectations of their white Brethren of the United

States & that by the schools many of their children have made great advancement in the useful facts of english education, such as reading, writing, and arithmetic." They asked Jefferson to continue in encouraging such advances among a people "between whom & the white people the great Spirit has made no difference, except in the tint of their skins." The delegation said that "the great Spirit loves his red children as well as his white children" and "their final destination is the same," by which the delegation meant death. A second group, representing older chiefs, the less well-off, and the less white, gave Jefferson a different message. These Cherokees were, they said, "deturmed to move over the missippa if they like the Cuntry when they exploar it, pervided there father [Jefferson] will assist them in their persute." They requested boats and guns.

Then the pendulum swung back. The two groups returned home and, within nine months, reunited the Cherokees. They informed a disappointed Meigs that his government would now face a national council, one unwilling to leave the old lands. Meigs tried again his arguments about national pride, but his audience drew its own conclusion—namely, that the Cherokees should keep their national pride intact on their national territory.

Yet the divisions were there, and they were deep. Those who lived in white ways continued to do so, with pride. And those who lived, as they saw it, as Cherokees refined further their belief in racial separatism. They developed myths, widely believed, holding that white, black, and red were the primordial divisions of humankind. Many of these stories resembled that of Cain and Abel or of Noah and his sons: Once all men had been brothers, but the brothers fought. They committed the basic crime that led to the basic punishments for humans: that they would be dispersed to different lands and have different colors, and when they came together again there would be conflict and ruin. In these circumstances the divine messenger told the Cherokees in 1811: "the white people are entirely different beings from us; we are made from red clay; they, out of white sand."

That vision came in the year that Buck Watie, age about six, joined John Ridge at the Moravian school in Spring Place. The Moravians had a finely honed sense of their civilizing mission. They not only taught reading, writing, and arithmetic; they also tried to convert their charges to Christianity—a slow process—and to impart the skills of hoeing, plowing, and spinning cotton. They kept their students apart from other Indians, anxious that they not revert to heathenism. School vacations, for that reason, were kept short. There would be no ball plays or all-night dances for the flower of Cherokee youth.

Buck and John did well at school; John, in particular, had a charismatic hold over his peers. In 1817 an emissary arrived in Cherokee territory from the interdenominational American Board of Commissioners for Foreign Missions. The board was looking for "foreign" students to place at its new school in Cornwall, Connecticut—that is, in the fabled North, which, among Cherokees, was already associated with racial liberalism and civilized friendliness in contrast to a grasping, white-supremacist South. The emissary said that he represented "great and good men at the North who loved them and wished to do them good." The following June, Buck, two other Indian scholars, the American Board emissary, and a pastor traveled on horseback to New England. (John would soon follow.) On the long journey to Cornwall, Buck and his party stopped in Monticello to visit Thomas Jefferson, now retired from the presidency; they called on James Madison, himself just retired from eight years as president; and they met in Washington, D.C., with President Monroe.

Proceeding north, the group of riders spent an evening in New Jersey with Elias Boudinot, a tall, handsome, elegant white man well into his seventies. Buck Watie appears to have taken Boudinot's name as his own earlier that year. A number of Cherokee students had adopted the names of American Board luminaries; Boudinot was a member of the board as well as founding president of the American Bible Society. Son of an Antiguan woman and a Princeton postmaster whose paternal American ancestry stretched back to the 1680s, Boudinot had been a somewhat reluctant but effective revolutionary, a fast friend and admirer of Washington. He livened his retirement by writing Christian tracts, notably his curious final work, of 1816, *A Star in the West; or, A Humble Attempt to Discover the Long Lost Ten Tribes of Israel, Preparatory to Their Return to Their Beloved City, Jerusalem*. In that book the white Boudinot approvingly quoted, at length, Washington Irving's 1814 article on Indians, whom Irving called that "race of beings, whose very existence has been pronounced detrimental to public security" and whose "rights . . . have seldom been deeply appreciated by the white man." Boudinot wrote, "For more than two centuries . . . the aborigines of America engaged the avarice and contempt of those who are commonly called the enlightened nations of the old world. These natives of this wilderness have always been considered by them as savages and barbarians, and therefore have given them little concern, further than to defraud them of their lands, drive them from the fertile countries on the sea shores, engage them in their wars, and indeed destroy them by thousands with ardent spirits [liquor] and fatal disorders." Not surprisingly, the Indians "were disgusted and soured with the general character and conduct of white men." Against the white view of Indians, Boudinot held out the "possibility, that these unhappy children of misfortune, may yet be proved to be the descendants of Jacob and the lost tribes of Israel."

No record exists of how Buck and his companions reacted to these views of the aging revolutionary—a tribal theory of biblical circumstance that was nearly as old as the first European landings in the New World, but had fallen from fashion by 1816. Certainly no one in Cherokee country pined for Jerusalem. Buck Watie doesn't seem to have believed the lost-tribes argument, but he did, apparently, feel an affection for Boudinot, and Boudinot liked him. The white man offered him a stipend to help pay for his studies.

So Buck Watie entered the American Board school as Elias Boudinot. The school had opened only the previous year but was eagerly gathering students. In 1821 it would have a Tahitian and a Maori, two men from Maui and two from Hawaii, a Malay, an Oneida, and a Tuscarora, two Choctaws, two Mohawks, three Mohegans, and the Cherokees. The school preferred its students to keep their native names—it made an exception for Boudinot—and showed a fascination with native peculiarities, encouraging students to give presentations on their home cultures. Yet the school was also dedicated to giving the young scholars a thoroughly European and aggressively Protestant education, with the idea that they would return home to lead their people in acculturation to the norms of Cornwall, Connecticut, and speed the deaths of the diverse cultures they represented.

Elias Boudinot excelled at school, studying history, geography, surveying, rhetoric, philosophy, trigonometry. He read Virgil; one wonders what he made of the *Aeneid*, which can be understood as the story of a tribe broken by war and forced to travel west in search of a new home. ("For years / They wandered as their destiny drove them on / From one sea to the next.") Cornwall students worked every day in the garden, learned such mechanical arts as ironmongering, and did manual labor. The school immersed its students in Christian instruction—prayer every morning at six and again every evening—and by 1820 Boudinot had converted.

Cornwall's citizens were invited each year to a presentation by the students. A visitor in 1821 reported for the Presbyterian *Religious Remembrancer*, of Philadelphia, on the anniversary exercise, which featured prayer, a sermon, the display of a Hawaiian idol (made of wood and silver), and talks by the Cherokees, "among whom the appearance and performance of Elias Boudinot, John Ridge, and David Brown . . . would have done credit to the best white young men of their age. Elias Boudinot, in a declamation, confuted the idea more completely by his appearance than his arguments, that savages are not capable of being civilized and polished." Even as a teenage student, Boudinot had style. He liked wearing fine clothes, and sometimes carried a parasol for protection against the sun.

In 1822 Boudinot and John Ridge headed back to Cherokee country. Both had health problems, but John had another reason for leaving. He had fallen in love with a local white woman, Sarah Northrup, and she with him. Her family opposed their engagement. They asked the couple to wait for two years, hoping to interest Sarah in white suitors. Boudinot and John Ridge traveled to Charleston, South Carolina, where John addressed a church audience on the theme of Cherokee advancement. He attacked the view that separate races should remain separate—that they were better off that way. He cited "the degraded Hottentot" in Africa, "the wild Arab," and "the Hindoo," as well as the Native American. Who of them would prefer to remain in his native state when he could have the "well regulated pleasures of a Herschel or a Newton, who surveys the regions of the universe . . . and who demonstrates, with mathematical exactness, the rapid flights of the comet, and its future visits to our solar system!" "Will anyone believe," John asked, "that an Indian with his bow and quiver . . . actually possesses undisturbed contentment superior to a learned gentleman of this commercial city, who has every possible comfort at home?" No, salvation lay, as John C. Calhoun had told a Cherokee audience three years before, in "becoming like the white people."

Elias Boudinot spent 1823 in Cherokee country, looking after his ailing mother, who had converted to Christianity and changed her name to Susannah Charity. It was probably in this same year that Boudinot wrote the first published fiction by an Indian author, a short story called "Poor Sarah; or, Religion Exemplified in the Life and Death of an Indian Woman." Boudinot places Sarah as a destitute elderly woman of no particular tribe in eastern Connecticut. There she encounters, around 1815, a financially comfortable white woman identified as Misse, who narrates the story. In the course of the encounter Misse learns about herself—that her own piety is small and her life easy, compared with those of Sarah. "Oh, what a lesson, thought I, for my repining heart!" Misse exclaims as Sarah describes her abjectness: "I no steal, no eat stolen food, though I be hungry ever so long. Then God gives me a small look of himself, his Son, and his glory. And I think in my heart, they all be mine soon; then I no suffer hunger any more, my Father's house have many mansions." Sarah has no community. She can't even tell friends of her troubles. "So I be quiet," she says to Misse, "tell nobody, only cry day and night for one good friend."

Sarah decides that she has to become new, to be born again. Jesus will be her friend. "Then I kneel down, and tell Jesus take my bad heart—can't bear my bad heart, pray give me the Holy Spirit, make my heart soft, make it all new." When Sarah's abusive and unbelieving husband dies, she is able to tell Jesus, "I be all his; serve him all my life; beg the Holy Spirit to come and fill all my heart, make it all clean and white like Jesus." Sarah lives on, nourished by God and crusts of bread, until her final triumph of dying: " 'Then I be quiet like a child, don't want to go till he call me.' Much more she said upon this interesting subject, which indicated a soul ripe for heavenly glories . . . In the course of three weeks from this time, I heard that Sarah was removed to a better world."

"Poor Sarah" is an act of tortuous ventriloquism: an Indian man not yet twenty years of age posing a dialogue between two Connecticut women, one white, one Indian, in which the former's cozy piety and philanthropic ease are undermined by the latter's pure degradation. Boudinot was already dabbling in the art of Indian dying. He apparently never wrote another fiction, though "Poor Sarah" was well received. It was first published in English in 1823 and later, in Boudinot's translation, in Cherokee. A Philadelphia printer paired it with a longer piece on the conversion of William, a slave, who tells the narrator, "though me be chief of sinners, Jesus will save me, though me be only poor black negro . . . Me love all men, black men and white men too; for God made them all." A white congregation receives William, adding some verses to a standard hymn:

> Welcome, negro, welcome here,
> Banish doubt, and banish fear:
> You, who Christ's salvation prove,
> Praise and bless redeeming love.

Boudinot would probably have winced at the implication of the Philadelphia edition that a black conversion and an Indian one were two instances of a single action: the conversion of a nonwhite. He would have recognized it, though, as well as the fact that both stories narrate this action as a moment in the psychic life of white people and the workings of their Savior. He might even have noticed that, in such white Protestant American stories, God functions as a safe repository for interracial love.

At the end of 1823 John Ridge traveled to Cornwall to marry Sarah Northrup. Her family had tried to keep the engagement secret but failed, and condemnation hit them from the newspapers and the pulpit. The editor of the local *American Eagle* wrote that the "subject of INTERMARRIAGES with the Indians and blacks of the missionary school" was "not a subject for irony." Certainly he did not waste himself on irony. He felt he had to "shrink from recording the name of the female thus throwing herself into the arms of an Indian," noting that "the public at large . . . feel indignant at the transaction" and some among them had said "that the girl ought to be publicly whipped, the Indian hung, and the mother drown'd." This girl, he wrote, "has thus made herself a *squaw*, and connected her race to a race of Indians." John Ridge and Sarah Northrup were married at the end of January 1824. They left Cornwall hastily, facing angry crowds at each stop of their coach as they hurried from New England.

Not everyone in Connecticut hated John and Sarah. Poems were written celebrating the interracial marriage, such as these lines from Silas McAlpine:

O, come with me, my white girl fair,
Come, seek with me the southern clime,
And dwell with me securely there,
For there my arm shall round thee twine;
The olive is thy favorite hue,
But sweet to me thy lily face;
O, sweet to both, when both shall view
These colors mingled in our race.

There were less favorable poems. Emily Fox of Cornwall recorded that John had taken Sarah, "snatch'd her from the mother's breast / And his tawny arms did her embrace."

Come all young maids I pray take care
How Indians draw you into a snare,
For if they do I fear it will be
As it is with our fair Sarah.
And what a dreadful, doleful sound
Is often heard from town to town,
Reflecting words from every friend,
How our ladies marry Indian men.

The *Eagle*'s editor continued his campaign against the school, writing that "the young men of the town, poor white boys, were often cast into the shade by their colored and tawny rivals." Some white bachelors of the Cornwall valley rallied themselves and pluckily released a set of resolutions, the second of which was that "though we feel no spirit of boasting . . . still we spurn at the intimation that we have been cast into the shade, by our rivals, white or tawny." Colonel Benjamin Gold, a pillar of Cornwall and friend of the school, joined seven others in a letter to the *Eagle* calling its charges "base fabrications."

This soon put Colonel Gold in an awkward position, because Elias Boudinot, too, was in love with a white woman of Cornwall, the colonel's daughter Harriet. And Harriet, as she told her parents in the autumn of that same year, wished to marry Boudinot. Benjamin Gold refused to give permission. Harriet soon became ill, and remained ill until her father relented. They attempted to keep the prospective wedding secret and succeeded through the winter. But the mission school itself found out.

It took the news badly. Following the Ridge-Northrup marriage, the school had announced that no further such joinings would occur. Some school backers and administrators told Harriet that either she give up Boudinot or they would announce the engagement. Harriet refused to abandon her fiancé, so the school functionaries published the news, adding "that after the unequivocal disapprobation of such connexions, expressed by the [school's] Agents, and by the christian public universally; we regard those who have engaged in or accessory to this transaction, as criminal; as offering insult to the known feelings of the christian community: and as sporting with the interests of this charitable institution."

Colonel Gold feared for his daughter's safety, and hid her. Through the window of her hiding place she could see the village green. She later described what she saw there: "In the evening our respectable young people Ladies and Gentlemen convened on the plain to witness and approve the scene and express their indignation. A painting had before been prepared representing a beautiful young Lady and an Indian . . . The church bell began to toll one would certainly conclude, speaking the departure of a soul. Mr. John C. Lewis and Mr. Rufus Payne carried the corpse and Brother Stephen set fire to the barrel of tar—or rather funeral pile. The flames rose high, and the smoke ascended— some said it reminded them of the smoke of their torment which they feared would ascend forever." Stephen was Harriet's elder brother. Harriet wrote to relatives, with that precise irony she shared with her intended, "Even the most unprincipled say, they never heard of anything so bad even among the heathen as that of burning a sister in effigy."

Boudinot read newspaper accounts of the burning. He received death threats from Cornwall and as far afield as Boston. He also had supporters, such as a writer in the *Niles' Weekly Register* of July 9, 1825: "Why so much *sensibility* about an event of this sort? A gentleman who was thought fit, by many thousands of people, for the office of president, openly and frankly recommended an incorporation of the Indian race with the citizens of the United States, by intermarriages . . . It is a strange world." Boudinot left Cherokee country to marry Harriet. Before entering Cornwall, he adopted a disguise. One wonders what kind of disguise it was—he already dressed as a white man. Harriet and Elias married on March 28, 1826, then rapidly left. The American Board, unable to appease white Cornwall opinion, soon closed the school, nine years after it had opened.

The reactions of the citizens of Cornwall to two of their daughters' marrying Indians had a bracing effect on the Cherokees. To them, John Ridge and Elias Boudinot were the best, in a sense, that the nation could offer: enormously gifted, carefully prepared, self-possessed men in their mid-twenties who were to lead their tribe into a future of equality with whites. Ridge and Boudinot had done everything white society had urged Indians to do—everything toward which American policy, at considerable expense, had been dedicated since the

Revolution—and yet, even in the North, they had been rejected, and in Boudinot's case symbolically murdered, for having crossed racial lines in the name of love. Such crossings had been fairly common in Cherokee life for a century; for that matter, they had been fairly common in white society, under certain historical conditions, even in the state that took the Indian name of Connecticut.

But racial distinctions throughout North America were steadily hardening, and each of the three great racial groups was coming to understand itself in a new way. Among the Cherokees material prosperity was soaring: their number of plows increased nearly sixfold between 1809 and 1824, the stocks of swine and sheep more than doubled, there were three times as many schools and enrolled students, almost five times as many wagons. Meanwhile, the number of whites in Cherokee society had decreased by 29 percent—and the number of Negro slaves had grown by 119 percent, from 583 in 1809 to 1,277 in 1824. The tribe had begun to pass laws regulating intermarriage. It would eventually adopt many features of the more thorough Southern slave codes.

At the same time, the tribe's white Southern neighbors had made it clear that an Indian among them would be considered a "free person of color," as the governor of Tennessee put it—not white, and therefore not a full citizen. The governor of Georgia explained that Indians would be "in a middle station between the negro and the white man" and that, "without the possibility of attaining the elevation of the latter, they would gradually sink to the condition of the former." Cherokees would be "integrated," if it came to that, as Negroes. This was not a prediction unique to Georgia and Tennessee. Eighteenth-century statutes identifying Indians with blacks as "people of color" were returning in new, refined forms. It was a general trend; within fifteen years Indians throughout the South would find themselves redefined by statute, judicial decision, and census practice as people of color, facing the same severe restrictions as free blacks—even including, by the 1850s, the possibility of being sold into slavery.

Elias Boudinot knew that his people continually threatened to split, as they briefly had before Jefferson in 1808, between those who considered themselves progressive, civilizing, and in some way white and those who were reviving traditional observances and practices with the aim of remaining, or becoming, in some way Cherokee. He also knew that integration into U.S. society was impracticable, not least because whites, for racial reasons, would not allow it. And he knew integration would be disastrous for Cherokeeness. If each family owned its own property, then that property could be sold. Whites were not scrupulous in real-estate matters. They would buy up the lands of the weakest Indians, those attracted by a temporary windfall. These Indians, the majority of the tribe, without education or advanced skills, unable to speak English, in a hostile white environment—they would become destitute wandering laborers, at best. A people would be reduced to individuals, or individualism. It was already happening among those who, illegally, sold their land. The Cherokees would dissolve from view like grains of salt in water.

Boudinot did not want that to happen, and the only way he could think to prevent it was to reinvigorate the civilizing program begun under Washington—but directed now by Cherokees themselves. In 1826, at the request of the tribal council, he traveled east on a speaking tour to raise funds for a printing press and type. The idea was to purchase one set of type in English and one in the new Cherokee alphabet invented by Sequoyah around 1821—the first American tribal alphabet. (Sequoyah knew no English; he simply saw the need for a written language, and made one up.) The Cherokees could then publish a newspaper, the first Indian newspaper, edited by Elias Boudinot.

Boudinot visited the major Eastern cities, speaking at churches and town halls. He had a set speech, which he published in Philadelphia under the straightforward title "An Address to the Whites." Boudinot was a new sight to many in his audiences, an impeccably dressed gentleman, better educated and better spoken than some of his white listeners, but still, he emphasized to them, "You here behold an *Indian*, my kindred are *Indians*." He reiterated the Christian belief that "of one blood God created all the nations." He urged his white listeners to forget the bitter warfare of "ancient times," just as he said the Indians would forget the cruelties of Cortés and all those who came after him, for we were entered upon a new era, in which Indians, among whom Cherokees made the vanguard, would break "the fetters of ignorance" and leave behind "the vices of heathenism." He detailed the advances of the Cherokees: their material growth, their new system of government modeled on that of the United States (but without private real estate, and without freedom of speech), their alphabet and the translation into it of the New Testament. "The shrill sound of the Savage yell," he said, "shall die away as the roaring of far distant thunder; and the Heaven wrought music will gladden the affrighted wilderness." His tribe had ceased to practice polygamy, and clan blood revenge, and the executing of witches.

For his audience Boudinot divided people into two types, good and bad. Good whites were the leaders of human development, the summit of civilization. Bad whites were, for example, those who tended to live near Indians and "differ from them chiefly in name." Boudinot had a low opinion of what presidents and secretaries of war had begun calling "real Indians." The good Indians were people like Boudinot. The bad ones he consigned to the older generation, men and women who were probably doomed, he said, to "grovel on in ignorance and die in ignorance," lost in "deep darkness."

He asked the good white people of Boston, New York, and Philadelphia to save the Indian race. If the Cherokees, and then the other remaining Indians, could complete their work of civilization, then we could make "this world of the West, one continuous abode of enlightened, free and happy people. But if the Cherokee Nation fails in her struggle, if she die away, then all hopes are blasted, and falls the fabric of Indian civilization." He knew which was more likely. "We have seen every where the poor aborigines melt away before the white population," Boudinot concluded. "We have seen, I say, one family after another, one tribe after another, nation after nation, pass away; until only a few solitary creatures are left to tell the sad story of extinction. Shall this precedent be followed? I ask you, shall red men live, or shall they be swept from the earth? . . . They hang upon your mercy as to a garment. Will you push them from you, or will you save them?"

Boudinot's trip raised about fifteen hundred dollars. Type was struck, a press purchased; after many delays Boudinot proudly announced in February 1828 the first issue of the *Cherokee Phoenix*, later changed to the *Cherokee Phoenix and Indians' Advocate*—"the first paper," he wrote, "ever published in an Indian country." Now the great work could begin. No more savagery and ignorance, no more "deep rooted prejudices" among Indians, no return to the days "when it was thought a disgrace, for a Cherokee to appear in the costume of a white man." The Indians, all Indians, would improve themselves, and, he emphasized, *"in their present locations."*

Less than a month later Boudinot ran straight into trouble. The U.S. government, it seemed, had decided that Indians could not improve—it was not in their Indian nature. Therefore, they should leave. Or so said the House Committee on Indian Affairs. "It appears that the advocates of this new system of civilizing the Indians," Boudinot wrote, referring in his sarcasm to the revivified federal plan for removal, "are very strenuous in maintaining the novel opinion, that it is impossible to enlighten the Indians, surrounded as they are by the white population, and that they assuredly will become extinct, unless they are removed." Boudinot was not one to use irony lightly: "Where have we an example in the whole history of man, of a Nation or tribe, removing in a body, from a land of civil and religious means, to a perfect wilderness, *in order to be civilized?*"

Boudinot continued trying to civilize the Cherokees where they were, where he lived. He and Harriet had begun a family, as anticipated in the poem about John and Sarah Ridge, "when both shall view / These colors mingled in our race." Harriet's parents, Colonel Benjamin and Eleanor Gold, visited in 1829. The colonel wrote home saying that his daughter and son-in-law's town, New Echota, was "truly an interesting and pleasant place; the ground is as level and smooth as a house floor." He noted, with some surprise, the prosperity of the Cherokee capital, comparing it favorably with Cornwall: "The stores in the nation are as large as the best in our town in Litchfield County; their large wagons of six horses go to Augusta and bring a great load, and you will see a number of them together. There is much travel through this place. I have seen eleven of these large wagons pass by Mr. Boudinot's house in company." As to his son-in-law, "Mr. Boudinot has much good company and is respected all over the United States, and is known in Europe." Colonel Gold was also pleased with the Boudinots' "two beautiful and interesting children (Elinor and Mary) who would pass in company for full-blooded Yankees."

Colonel Gold wrote his letter on December 8, 1829, the same day that Andrew Jackson first addressed Congress as president. Jackson said that he advocated removal of the Cherokees to the West. This came as no surprise. Jackson and his Democratic Party had achieved power partly due to the votes of white Western men and those many white men in the Eastern and Southern states who planned or dreamed of Western fortunes. The Western states, notably Ohio in 1803, had led in expanding voter suffrage. In these Western states the old Eastern rules—property and taxpayer qualifications for voting—could not apply. The expansion of the white male electorate spread back east, in part because the Eastern voting elites wanted to hold on to their populations. In this way, the total number of voters had expanded dramatically by the 1828 election, as had voter participation. In 1824 fewer than 27 percent of adult white males voted; four years later 58 percent went to the polls. The Jacksonian Democracy allied these new voters with a decisive portion of the Southern plantation oligarchy. In terms of social class this was an odd and volatile partnership. But it worked, for a while, and one of the reasons it worked was that it pioneered a broad national consensus that promised to eliminate class differences through indefinite physical expansion of an explicitly white America. Jackson's ally Senator Thomas Hart Benton had warned his constituents earlier in 1829 that the Democrats' opposition, "in every question between the white people and the negroes or Indians, regularly, officially, impertinently and wickedly takes part with the Indians and negroes against their white fellow citizens and fellow Christians."

This held obvious implications for Indians, and particularly Cherokees. The racialization of Indians and the taking of their land had become critical issues for the white people who were Jackson's professed constituency and who were in the majority. (Federal sales of ceded Indian land were also an important source of government revenue.) For a variety of reasons, white people in this period felt an acute need to affirm their whiteness, and a correspondingly acute need to affirm the blackness of blacks and the Indianness of Indians. They were also going through their first economic depression. The time-tested means for

white Americans to improve their prospects was to move west. All that stood in
their way were Indians.

Jackson singled out the Cherokees because they had imitated the United
States too well. Not only had they created a political body based on race, and
enacted laws to keep that race pure, they had also made for themselves a constitution and representative government mirroring that of the United States. In
other words, they had erected a nation within a nation—an *imperium in imperio*,
as the phrase went. The bulk of the land and population of this Cherokee state
was within the limits of Alabama and, particularly, Georgia. The Georgians
wanted that land. Jackson devoted much attention in his first address to this
problem. He said that most Indians "have retained their savage habits," while "a
portion . . . having mingled much with the whites . . . have lately attempted to
erect an independent government within the limits of Georgia and Alabama."
This was unacceptable. "Would the people of Maine," Jackson asked, "permit
the Penobscot tribe to erect an independent government within their State? . . .
Could the Indians establish a separate republic on each of their reservations in
Ohio?" He raised these questions to indicate their ridiculousness. The federal
government, he argued, would not defend the Indian claims, as it could hardly
"aid in destroying the States which it was established to protect."

Jackson paused to review the history of whites and Indians. "Our conduct
toward these people," he told Congress, "is deeply interesting to our national
character." He described the steady dispossession of native tribes "by persuasion
and force." Jackson considered this a sad story, but one for which the current
generation of white people ought not to shoulder the blame. In any case, all the
Indians should go west, where they might combine into a single state free from
white people, and "raise up an interesting commonwealth, destined to perpetuate the [Indian] race and to attest the humanity and justice of this [white] Government." Within weeks Georgia had passed legislation to extend its laws and
governance over the Cherokees within its borders.

Washington hammered away at just how Indian Indians were; and Elias
Boudinot's editorials became harsher. He pointedly ran news items on uncivilized happenings in civilized countries. He lampooned the old language of deference, when Indians would present themselves as "children" to their "father"
in Washington. Boudinot had become a racial nationalist, a separatist. "While
he possesses a national character," he wrote in 1829, "there is hope for the
Indian." Yet what would that character be? Boudinot wrote "historical" editorials—it was part of his mandate—about Cherokee traditions. They were not well
informed and had not a single positive aspect; he wrote about Cherokee traditions in order to bury them. The only distinctive Cherokee phenomenon he
praised was the keeping of land in common, and even this he never praised as

Cherokee. He just asserted it as that without which there could be no Chero-kees. Why Cherokees should be Cherokees he never did say, or what made them different from whites or anyone else. They simply should; they simply were.

Boudinot's assertions of Indian success at adopting white ways grew more and more hysterical. He ranted because he had been betrayed. He had made himself into something that white power had encouraged, even praised, but somehow could not allow to exist, certainly not under Andrew Jackson: an Indian who was also white but still an Indian. Boudinot wrote of "what *we* call *oppression, systematic oppression.*" And the House Committee on Indian Affairs released a new report, arguing "that the maxim, so well established in other places, 'that an Indian cannot work,' has lost none of its universality in the prac-tice of the Indians of the South . . . that the condition of the common Indian is perceptibly declining . . . [that] the mass of the population of the Southern Indian tribes are a less respectable order of human beings now, than they were ten years ago." Boudinot replied, in April 1830, "We know of many Indians who not only *work,* but work *hard . . . the common Indian among the Cherokees is not declining, but rising.*"

The next month the neighboring Choctaws buckled under to Jackson and his Democrats. They agreed to go west. Jackson ordered his agent to withhold the Cherokees' annuity—payments for previously ceded land—from the tribal treasury, which paid both for the *Phoenix* and for lawyers to fight removal. In December, Jackson gave another long talk to Congress about Indians, in which he outlined his theory of history and proposed a new and fascinating compari-son between whites and Indians—one that made them nearly the same. "To fol-low to the tomb the last of his race," Jackson said of the representative Indian, "and to tread on the graves of extinct nations excite melancholy reflections. But true philanthropy reconciles the mind to these vicissitudes as it does to the extinction of one generation to make room for another . . . Nor is there any-thing in this which, upon a comprehensive view of the general interests of the human race, is to be regretted. Philanthropy could not wish to see this conti-nent restored to the condition in which it was found by our forefathers . . . The tribes which occupied the countries now constituting the Eastern States were annihilated or have melted away to make room for the whites. The waves of population and civilization are rolling to the westward, and we now propose to acquire the countries occupied by the red men of the South and West . . . Doubtless it will be painful to leave the graves of their fathers; but what do they more than our ancestors did or our children are now doing?"

This was an extraordinary admission, the heart of a set of baffling contradic-tions. Some Indians were becoming too much like whites, thereby threatening the coherence of the white United States—and so all Indians should go west, where they could continue being something they really weren't any longer, that is, real Indians, and could even create a racially separatist state—except that, if they actually wanted, out west, to "retard the progress of decay," they would need to "cast off their savage habits"—except that, as the whites were themselves steadily going westward, it would again in the future be too late for the Indians. It would always be too late. The story of the Indians would always be like a suicide note written for them by whites. Now, in 1830, Jackson was taking this maze of argument to a new level. He was saying that, in the end, whites and Indians were actually alike, all nomads pushing westward, starting over again and again.

Who, really, was treading on whose graves? Andrew Jackson was born in the Carolina backcountry in March 1767. His father died that year—an Irishman who had only just arrived on these shores. Jackson joined the Revolution at the age of fourteen, a farm boy with a gun. He was captured, and wounded by a British officer to whom he would not defer. In that same year his mother and two brothers died, all apparently as a result of the war. An orphan, Jackson drifted among employments; he gambled and brawled. Andrew Jackson was, in short, an American by merest chance, whose childhood was characterized by abandonment, bloodshed, and rootless wandering. In 1788 he naturally went west; he also made his first recorded purchase of a human being, Nancy, "Eighteen or Twenty Years of Age," about the same as Jackson. He would make his name and fortune as a lawyer and land speculator, then a politician, a judge, above all a warrior. He fought the Creeks (whom he defeated thanks to Cherokee aid), and later the Seminoles and their black allies. And he fought the hated British, most famously in the slaughter of the Battle of New Orleans. That conflict left seven hundred British dead. Jackson lost eight men. Only afterward did news arrive that the War of 1812 had ended several weeks beforehand.

This was the world Jackson knew: white orphans fighting and grasping and pushing on west past the graves of their ancestors. He was just twenty-five when he wrote to a colleague of his dread of Indians and the pointlessness of making treaties with "a Savage Tribe." He later wrote that "fear is better than love with an indian"—but whose fear, whose love? After all, it was Andrew Jackson, not Elias Boudinot, who wrote home to put some spine into an overseer, saying he must not be reluctant with the whip. Jackson's slave Betty, he wrote, "is capable of being a good and valluable servant, but to have her so, she must be ruled with the cowhide." What savagery was this?

So it is interesting that Jackson, in speaking to Congress in 1830, should argue that whites are like Indians, and vice versa, and that the happiness of both should be found in the same activity: always going west, separately yet oddly together. Doubtless, the president said, it would be painful to leave one's father's grave. Yet: "To better their condition in an unknown land our forefathers left all that was dear in earthly objects. Our children by thousands yearly leave the land of their birth to seek new homes in distant regions. Does Humanity weep at these painful separations from everything, animate and inanimate, with which the young heart has become entwined? Far from it. It is rather a source of joy that our country affords scope where our young population may range unconstrained in body or in mind, developing the power and faculties of man in their highest perfection." The Indians, Jackson told Congress, were lucky to have government help in relocating. "How many thousands of our own people," he exclaimed, "would gladly embrace the opportunity of removing to the West on such conditions! If the offers made to the Indians were extended to them, they would be hailed with gratitude and joy. And is it supposed that the wandering savage has a stronger attachment to his home than the settled, civilized Christian? Is it more afflicting to him to leave the graves of his fathers than it is to our brothers and children?"

Jackson was talking about himself. By extension, he spoke for the white men who had elected him, men who carried within a perfectly contradictory idea of themselves as settled and civilized yet also unconstrained and indifferent to rootedness. And always in the president's language lay a sharp awareness of death, of graves left behind, and the terrible ecstasy of this weeping rush westward toward one's "highest perfection." It is as if leaving home were the primordial act of the American, with each generation inheriting the duty of departure, a crystalline act both betraying the past and honoring the impulse that created the only past Americans had. White Americans, specifically, were a tribe condemned to wander; no, free to wander; free and insatiable and so not free. In this view, whites were like their image of Indians, only better, because whites had no attachments at all, just the elusive goal of self-made glory. The only collective tie or root whites had was racial. And the only tie or root Jacksonian whites honored in Indians was likewise that of race.

The Cherokee elite at once rejected this racial identity and swallowed it whole. Elias Boudinot traveled east in the fall of 1831 to raise funds for the *Phoenix* and to help John Ridge rally support. Ridge told a friendly meeting of whites: "You asked us to throw off the hunter and warrior state: We did so—you asked us to form a republican government: We did so—adopting your own as a model. You asked us to cultivate the earth, and learn the mechanic arts: We did so. You asked us to learn to read: We did so. You asked us to cast away our idols, and worship your God: We did so." Just a few years after Elias Boudinot had been burned in effigy by the citizens of Cornwall for courting a white woman, the Cherokee leaders had done everything they could to become just like the citizens of Cornwall, except to divide land privately and to hate Indians.

For a moment Ridge and Boudinot entertained hope: the Supreme Court, in *Worcester v. Georgia*, had decided that Georgia could not extend its sovereignty over Cherokee lands in violation of treaties between the Cherokees and the U.S. government. But Jackson soon made it clear that he would not enforce the Court's decision. He had already stated, regarding a previous decision, that a president was not obliged to follow Court decisions unless he adequately respected "the force of their reasoning." And Jackson greatly feared the larger implication of *Worcester v. Georgia* that federal laws held sway over state laws — the implication of secession, which had haunted the American republic almost since its founding. South Carolinians were already threatening, vigorously, to secede over federal tariffs that favored the North, meanwhile refining the theory of nullification, which held that states could accept or reject federal laws as they chose. At the same time, Alabama and Mississippi had passed laws similar to Georgia's regarding Indian lands. There was a general anxiety that, if the Court's decision were enforced and Georgia prevented from getting Cherokee lands, then Georgia, Alabama, and Mississippi would join South Carolina in nullification and even secession. This was exactly the type of division that Jackson's Democratic coalition had been made to prevent; it was the major fault line of white national consensus.

John Ridge knew that Jackson and Georgia, working in concert, would render the Court's decision unenforceable. He wrote that "the Chicken Snake General Jackson has time to crawl and hide in the luxuriant grass of his nefarious hypocracy." Yet soon Ridge met with Jackson, and the president came away believing that Ridge was in "despair" and convinced "that it is better for them to treat and move." Jackson was right about Ridge. The debate in Washington had been bitter. Cherokee allies from Northern states had argued vehemently against removal. Six thousand citizens had petitioned Congress not to proceed with Indian removal. Even in Georgia, the *Milledgeville Recorder* printed an article that asked, "Is it honest then to seize on, and take by force, a piece of property that pleases our fance, but does not exactly belong to us?" The writer suggested that Georgians would be like the Spaniards, who had pursued a policy similar to that of Georgia, and so become a "miserable race" as "a punishment from Heaven for the injustice and cruelty practised on the Indians." But Georgia hadn't the slightest intention of backing down; beating Indians was what elected governors in Georgia. Jackson would not back down, either. Uniting the white populace and gaining new land for it were central to his administration and vision. So Ridge and Boudinot, after consulting their influential white friends, backed down.

When Boudinot returned to Cherokee country, he made it known that he now favored negotiating a treaty for removal. The principal chief, John Ross, and the national council decided, therefore, that he should no longer edit the *Phoenix*. Boudinot submitted his letter of resignation on August 1, 1832. "I do conscientiously believe it to be the duty of every citizen," he wrote, "to reflect upon the dangers with which we are surrounded . . . I could not consent to be the conductor of the paper without having the right and privilege of discussing these important matters—and from what I have seen and heard, were I to assume that privilege, my usefulness would be paralyzed by my being considered, as I have already been, an enemy to the interests of my country and people. I love my country and I love my people, as my own heart bears me witness, and for that very reason I should deem it my duty to tell them the whole truth, or what I believe to be the truth. I cannot tell them that we will be reinstated in our rights, when I have no such hope, and after our leading, active, and true friends in Congress, and elsewhere, have signified to us that they can do us no good."

Chief John Ross replied that "toleration of diversified views to the columns of such a paper would not fail to create fermentation and confusion among our citizens, and in the end prove injurious to the welfare of the nation. The love of our country and people demands unity of sentiment and action for the good of all." Ross was about thirteen years older than Boudinot, raised more as a Scot than a Cherokee. He knew white people very well and was successful both as a businessman and as a politician. By the time of Boudinot's resignation, Ross had become the acknowledged leader of the illiterate mass of the Cherokee population, while Boudinot, John Ridge, Major Ridge, and their friends had become identified as leaders of a small minority that consciously distanced itself from what might be called actual Cherokee life. Boudinot's argument was essentially that he knew best and that Ross wanted to keep the tribe from the truth by silencing Boudinot's group, soon known as the Treaty Party. Boudinot knew white people, too. He knew the people of Cornwall, and he knew the whites who came in increasing numbers to Cherokee land, staking claims to whatever they wanted at the point of a gun. The danger, he wrote three days after resigning, was "immediate and appalling": "And think, for a moment, my countrymen, the danger to be apprehended from an overwhelming white population—a population not unfrequently overcharged with high notions of color, dignity, and greatness—at once overbearing and impudent to those whom, in their sovereign pleasure, they consider as their inferiors. They should have, our sons and daughters, be slaves indeed." Georgia had, as part of its strategy, enacted racial legislation to bring Indians nearer the status of blacks. And by 1833 President Jackson was reaching for new language in telling Congress why the Indians must go: "Established in the midst of another and a superior race, and without appreciating the causes of their inferiority or seeking to control them, they must necessarily yield . . ."

The minority Treaty Party faction was pushed, and pushed itself, ever further from the tribal government led by Ross. Boudinot and John Ridge were openly portrayed as traitors. It is important to note that the tiny Cherokee elite, Ross included, did not disagree on the essentials of Cherokeeness. They wanted gradually to exchange them for those of "civilized man," as Ross and two others had said in a letter to John Quincy Adams. "The Cherokees," their letter stated, "if permitted to remain peaceably and quietly in the enjoyment of their rights, the day would arrive, when a distinction between their race and the American family, would be imperceptible; of such a change, the nation can have no objection. Complexion is a subject, not worthy consideration, in the effectuation of the great object—for the sake of civilization and preservation of existence, we would willingly see the habits and customs of the aboriginal man extinguished, the sooner this takes place, the great stumbling block, *prejudice*, will be removed." The elite debate was not one of assimilation versus separatism. Cherokee leaders wanted to assimilate on their own terms, separately; their debate was about how to be separate, for how long, and where, and under whose leadership. And so, faced with the inevitability of removal, the Cherokee elite split into factions. Within the space of a month in early 1835, Ross negotiated with the United States a proposal for removal west at a price of five million dollars—and opened talks with Mexico to establish a colony there for the Cherokees and, he hoped, other tribes. "I am confident," he wrote to the Mexican chargé d'affaires, "that the Creeks Chickasaws & Choctaws would also follow as well as every tribe which have been removed under the present policy of this Govt. from their Native lands not from choice, but from necessity." Neither negotiation went anywhere: Ross himself killed the first one, Mexico killed the second. And the Cherokee elite had begun killing each other. One man was already dead. The chiefs now sometimes traveled through Cherokee country with guards.

Boudinot and the Treaty Party had their own plan, which Jackson endorsed, sending them back to Cherokee land with a letter. "You are now," the president wrote to the tribe, "placed in the midst of a white population. Your peculiar, customs which, regulated your intercourse with one another, have been abrogated by the great political community among which you live." The man who had done so much to construct a white idea of nationhood, and who saw whiteness as a positive quality synonymous with civilization, nonetheless urged the inferior Indians to flee from "the effects of a white population. Where you now are, you are encompassed by evils, moral and physical, and these are fearfully encreasing." One hesitates in interpreting such a passage. It seems to suggest that Andrew Jackson believed that whiteness contained within itself a quality of moral evil. It also suggests he knew that white frontiersmen, in their push west, were not really realizing their "highest perfection."

In late December 1835 Boudinot and seventy-four other Cherokees, as a self-appointed council, approved a treaty for removal west, the direction associated in Cherokee belief with death. Boudinot signed because he felt the tribe had no choice; but he knew that the great majority opposed removal. Chief Ross fought hard against the treaty, even proposing that Cherokees become citizens where they were rather than move. Jackson's opponents and moralist Northerners renewed their attacks. The Senate approved the treaty in May 1836, by a margin of one vote. In his last annual address as president, later that same year, Jackson said, "The national policy [toward Indians], founded alike in interest and in humanity . . . may be said to have been consummated by the conclusion of the late treaty with the Cherokees."

The tribal split deepened. Ross continued to battle the treaty and convinced the majority of Cherokees not to emigrate. Most Cherokees continued to plant and harvest, ignoring the May 1838 deadline for voluntary removal. An English traveler in 1837 had been impressed by Cherokee prosperity and surprised by the notion of Cherokee inferiority: "An observer could not but sympathize deeply with them; they were not to be confounded with the wild savages of the West, being decently dressed after the manner of white people, with shirts, trousers, shoes and stockings, whilst the half-breeds and their descendants conformed in every thing to the customs of the whites, spoke as good English as them, and differed from them only in a browner complexion, and in being less vicious and more sober." Yet Elias Boudinot had given up on the political good effects of this whitening. He believed that if the Cherokees remained on their land, as John Ross still hoped would happen, "The final destiny of our race . . . is too revolting to think of. Its course *must* be downward, until it finally becomes extinct or is merged in another race, more ignoble and more detested." This other race was the black race, which Boudinot saw as a social grave. Boudinot and John Ridge left with their families for Indian Territory in what would become Oklahoma.

Few Cherokees left voluntarily after the 1835 treaty. Most waited for Chief Ross to save them, which he failed to do. After the 1838 deadline passed, the United States sent in troops to round up the Cherokees. Soldiers called at each house and brought the Indians to stockades. The process was degrading to everyone. The commanding officer, General Winfield Scott, hated the job. Soon the horrors of taking roughly fifteen thousand unwilling people from their homes became too much for the government, which gave in to John Ross's request that he manage the removal himself together with his brother and business partner, Lewis. The brothers divided the tribe into thirteen convoys, which departed between late August and early December. At least several thousand died along the Trail of Tears.

Political disagreement did not diminish in the new land. The following spring a council was held that failed to unite the competing groups. After the council a small committee met, which itself formed a still smaller committee of assassins. One of those present later recalled that "numbers were placed in a hat for each person present; twelve of these numbers had an X mark after the number which indicated the Executioners. All present were asked to draw." One group found John Ridge at home at daybreak. They pulled him from his house; some held him while others stabbed; then each man walked over his dying body. All this Sarah saw from the house. Meanwhile, John's father, Major Ridge, was riding out in the company of a slave when assassins killed him with five bullets. And Elias Boudinot was walking along about nine that morning when four men approached and asked him to get some medicine—he had charge of the dispensary. Boudinot set out on foot with two of the men. One soon fell behind and stabbed Boudinot. The other killed him with seven blows of a hatchet to his head.

The assassins were carrying out tribal law, which regarded the selling of tribal land as treason.

The Cherokee tribe fell further apart, for a while. A friend wrote to Boudinot's brother, Stand Watie, who was away lobbying in Washington, D.C.: "Several persons have been *killed* since you left. Don't Know Them, except old 'Corn Tasel' who lived in Flint he was killed at home and a negro boy taken off. Some persons Stole Two Negro boys from Wes. Creek, and Two *Mules*, got away with them." A similar letter arrived later that year from Watie's brother-in-law: "I think there is now to be no end to bloodshed, Since the Starr boys & the Ridges have commenced revenging the death of their relatives. A dozen or so are implicated and I am afraid that some of them will be more desperate than the first ones. Murders in the country have been so frequent until the people care as little about hearing these things as they would hear of the death of a common dog."

It took six years for the bloodletting to end and the tribal factions to sign a treaty of unity. After the 1846 unification Cherokees settled into a period of consolidation and growth along the then-prevalent Southern model. "The traveler, passing through the Cherokee nation," wrote a white trader, "is struck with the contrast between an occasional stately dwelling, with an extensive farm attached, and the miserable hovels of the indigent, sometimes not ten feet square, with a little patch of corn . . . Most of the labor among the wealthier classes of Cherokees, Choctaws, Chickasaws, Creeks, and Seminoles, is done by negro slaves; for they have all adopted substantially the Southern system of slavery." Collective landownership made a plantation system both tremendously profitable for those who could buy slaves and wildly divisive in class terms. The use of land went to the person who could till it. Those who could afford to hire labor—to buy laborers—would be able to till vast tracts. Those who had only their own labor . . . had only their own labor. Capital was spent on slaves, not land, because you couldn't buy land. So collective landownership made slavery even more central than it was in a private-ownership system. The population of slaves relative to that of Cherokees increased slowly but steadily from 1824 to 1860. John Ross's enterprising brother, Lewis, understood immediately how important slaves would be to developing new lands. Even as he was organizing the removal of the tribe (with its slaves) to Indian Territory, Lewis sent boats down the Mississippi to buy more slaves, five hundred in all, whom he sold to the newcomers once they arrived in the West. Five hundred enslaved people was a lot by anyone's reckoning; the demand for labor was that intense.

Labor became so valuable after the Trail of Tears that Cherokees and whites alike took to stealing slaves the way they had once, back in Georgia, Alabama, and Tennessee, stolen horses. Quick and lawless markets were easily found. The kidnappers had a particular interest in taking children, often directly from their parent or parents, because children were more easily managed as captives. A market also existed for free blacks. Apparently, whatever protests they might have made to buyers that they were actually free could be expected to have no effect. One wonders if they even made them. Skin color had become a definitive marker of slave status. It was difficult to prove that you were free if you were dark-skinned. In a way, freedom, more than ever, was a social position granted by the nonblack majority at its pleasure.

Cherokee society in the new territory, as envisioned by the white advocates of removal, became more "racialized." The Cherokees did not become more Cherokee, nor did they become more white, exactly—after all, they had just been humiliated by whites acting, in their own words and minds, as whites. The Cherokees simply became more nonblack, a pure negative self-definition, as if to say: I do not know what I am, but I know I am not *this*. The national council worked hard at defining what *this* was; most importantly, they worked at dissolving the social distinction between freedom and slavery, replacing it with a pure concept of race. Such was the reaction of this American tribe to the most desperate moment in its history.

So removal both weakened Cherokeeness and strengthened the Cherokee desire to control blacks—indeed, to create them. Prior to removal there had been some sympathy for blacks. African blood did not necessarily make a Cherokee an outsider. The movement against the international slave trade had been backed by many in the (slaveholding) elite. Elias Boudinot appears to have been subtly antislavery, and his *Phoenix* had published information sympathetic to abolitionism, which was then gathering momentum in American society. Boudinot's *Phoenix* also failed to approve the new "scientific" and other theories coursing through the Southern press in response to abolitionism. Before removal, slaves often could attend schools and churches. Many masters thought education of slaves made them more valuable. (Slaves sometimes acted as interpreters for their owners.) The Cherokee laws of the 1820s proscribing, for example, black-Cherokee marriages and black entrepreneurship showed a hardening line; but there was still room for maneuver.

The Cherokee council's first law after removal west was titled "An Act to Prevent Amalgamation with Colored Persons." It replaced an earlier act; its major innovation was to outlaw marriages not just between "free" citizens and slaves but between citizens and any "person of color." A language of skin tone or race replaced one of social status. An act the following year made it illegal for "any free negro or mulatto, not of Cherokee blood, to hold or own any improvement within the limits of this Nation." The law did not specify what degree of Cherokee blood transformed someone from Negro to Indian. Another act provided for patrols—a Southern institution—to roam the countryside and detain any "negro or negroes" found going about without a pass from their masters. "They was always a bunch of patrollers around to watch everything we done," a former slave recalled decades later. "Dey would come up in a bunch of about nine men on horses and look at all our passes, and if a negro didn't have no pass dey wore him out good and made him go home. Dey didn't let us have much enjoyment." The year 1841 also brought a law prohibiting anyone from teaching free blacks or slaves how to read or write. Laws the following year frustrated owners from freeing their slaves and further limited the lives of free blacks.

Some of these laws were in reaction to fear of slave escapes and uprisings. The first mass revolt occurred in 1842, when thirty-five slaves armed themselves and fled into the adjoining Creek territory. The tribal council authorized and paid for a squad of one hundred Cherokees to chase them. The impromptu Indian army captured the runaways and returned them to their owners. The tribe's new paper, the *Advocate*, meaningfully published news of slave uprisings and conspiracies elsewhere in the world. And it published runaway-slave notices, because in fact slaves were escaping in greater numbers. They had witnessed the Indian master class losing control of itself as well as being forced on a thousand-mile march by whites. Besides, they now might escape to Kansas or the open West. Before they would have escaped into white Alabama or Georgia or Tennessee, which was no escape at all. The old *Phoenix* never once had an escaped-slave notice from a Cherokee owner; its Western successor, the *Advocate*, had plenty.

Interestingly, before their own removal west some in the tribe had advocated removal of Negroes to Africa. There, it was thought, Negroes would be able to be themselves. (There was at least one active branch, with a black membership, of an African colonization society in Cherokee country.) Apparently Cherokee supporters of African colonization failed to consider that they were suggesting for blacks precisely the fate they fiercely resisted for themselves, even though the language and concepts used were almost identical. But the connection may have been present subconsciously, for once the Cherokees had been forcibly colonized in the West, plans to colonize "their" blacks in Africa ended. Instead the tribe made them blacker and blacker, right where they were. In 1860 black slaves—not counting free blacks—made up more than 11 percent of the Cherokee Nation.

The question of black slavery—or of the racial character of the nation—was, of course, already dividing the United States by the 1840s. The *Advocate* exulted when California's white leaders, many of whom had resided on the West Coast for but a few years, succeeded in having California admitted as a non-slave state in 1850; its editor hailed the Compromise of 1850 "between the North and South, upon the slavery question," and hoped "that the Union will finally be saved." But the admission of California and other Western lands as states or territories—white states and territories—also appeared as a draining hourglass for Indians. The new white Californians vigorously set about killing coastal Indians. The Kansas-Nebraska Act of 1854 created two territories whose leaders worked hard to force Indians out. Similar policies would soon prevail in Minnesota and the Dakotas. Within twenty years of Cherokee removal it had become clear that the limitless and unwanted West had limits and was wanted, indeed coveted, by white people, most of whom either opposed slavery or opposed having black people in their midst. They also wanted to get rid of Indians.

In 1860 William Seward, then a senator from New York, gave an important speech in Chicago titled "The National Idea: Its Perils and Triumphs." The speech contained much on the westering destiny of free white men and their families. Republican Party thought, of which Seward and Abraham Lincoln were leading exponents, promised indefinite expansion of white people across the continent free from competition by black slave labor. Seward spoke in Jacksonian terms of civilization's advance. And he told his Chicago listeners that "Indian territory, also, south of Kansas must be vacated by the Indians."

Seward gave his speech in October; by December, Lincoln had been elected president—Seward would be his secretary of state—and South Carolina had seceded. The Confederate states moved quickly to bring Indians onto their side. By the spring of 1861 the Choctaws, Chickasaws, Seminoles, and most of the Creeks—four of the five large slaveholding tribes in Indian Territory—had joined the Confederacy. The Cherokees held out, for a while. The tribal split between a slaveholding upper class and a slaveless majority had become reflected in a political division between a secessionist faction, led by Elias Boudinot's brother Stand Watie and Boudinot's son Elias Cornelius, on one side, and the abolitionist Keetoowah Society on the other, with the aging chief John Ross attempting to hold a middle ground. The Keetoowah Society was a typically complex, even contradictory, Cherokee institution. Founded under the tutelage of two white Baptist missionaries, Evan Jones and his son John, the Keetoowahs wanted to restore the structures and honor of traditional Cherokee society. How exactly this fit with Baptist soul saving is hard to imagine, but it did fit. The Joneses were part of the Northern Baptist Church, as distinguished from the Southern Baptists. (The Baptist Church split in 1845 over slavery.) Evan and John were strong abolitionists; by 1853 they had expelled, or allowed to leave, all their slaveholding parishioners.

Against these divisive forces John Ross tried to hold the tribe together. In his annual message of October 1860 he attacked abolitionism: "Slavery has existed among the Cherokees for many years, is recognised by them as legal," Ross had told his tribe, "and they have no wish or purpose to disturb it, or agitate it—others have no excuse for doing so, coming from whatever quarter they may. It is not an open question among us, but a settled one . . . Our locality and institutions ally us to the South, while to the North we are indebted for a defence of our rights in the past, and that enlarged benevolence to which we owe chiefly our progress in civilization. Our political relations are with the Government of the United States." Ross, who himself owned fifty black people in 1860, wanted to keep the tribe neutral. The Confederacy, not surprisingly, felt neutrality to be impossible. Southern diplomats sped among the tribes crammed into Indian Territory, and one by one those tribes joined the cause. Union troops were abandoning their forts in Indian country, while Southern forces enjoyed a string of victories. And Stand Watie was threatening to set up his own, pro-Southern government, without Ross. Ross held out until August 1861, forcing the Confederate government to grant terms superior to those given by the United States. In his annual address of October 1861 Ross spoke of the "unanimity of sentiment" among Cherokees for a Southern alliance. He felt the South would win—"The unanimity and devotion of the people of the Confederate States must sooner or later secure their success"—adding, "Our Geographical position and domestic institutions allied us with the South."

Ross also seems to have sensed the parallel between Confederate states' rights doctrine and tribal sovereignty. "Our rights of self Government," he noted, "will be more fully recognized" in the Confederate States of America. Similarities between the secessionist cause and tribal autonomy are not hard to find. The Southern states seceded partly because their self-defined leading race—their white citizens—wished to preserve their rights of self-government, in particular their racial rights. This was exactly what the Indian tribes wanted to do in their respective territories.

The war went horribly for the Cherokees. The Keetoowahs, or at least the radical abolitionist offshoot called Pins, gave themselves up to raiding, murder, and pillage—or enrolled in the Union army. Stand Watie practiced a higher form of terrorism, battling the Keetoowahs with their own methods while also leading regular Confederate troops in Indian Territory. Watie appears to have hated black people. In at least one engagement, against a mixed white-black Union force, his troops simply shot the black soldiers dead wherever they could find them. They were not allowed to surrender.

With so many men going to war, Indian Territory had been emptied out by 1862. Some slave owners moved their property down to the Red River and Confederate Texas. Not every family could arrange such a journey, as can be seen in the young diarist Susan Foreman's entries from the middle of that year:

> Tues. 15th What a day this has been! The Pins came and took our blacks and our horses and have threatened Pa's life. They say they are bound to have it tonight! . . .
>
> Weds. 16th They did not come last night though, I sat up all night expecting them every minute. It was a fearfully long night. Today Charity and Mary talk of going. We poor children will be left all alone . . . The niggers are riding about today looking so saucy. They came and inquired of the blacks, where Pa and John are and when Pa will come in. It is terrible to be in such suspens and misery I endure. I am afraid of the niggers too. Nan's going to stay all night with me.
>
> Thurs. 17th Everything seems to be quiet this morning. Have seen only one nigger pass. I do not feel in quite as much distress today.

On August 5 a rumor of battle passed through, and the remaining blacks left. ("Yesterday the niggers all cut out.") Susan Foreman went with her father and brother as a refugee into Texas, where she died while the war continued.

The girl Susan Foreman may or may not have known how slight the difference could be, in white eyes, between Indians and blacks. The similarities among nonwhites received important confirmation, from President Lincoln, in a series of events that began soon after the Foremans' slaves fled the place of their bondage. Abraham Lincoln had been hopeful about colonization of African Americans since the 1850s. In his first annual message to Congress as president he had suggested colonizing rebel slaves and whatever free blacks might also want to leave. The emancipation by Congress of Washington, D.C., slaves in the spring of 1862 provided the right opportunity for Lincoln's colonization experiment. In two bills Congress appropriated $600,000 toward colonizing the ex-slaves of the capital city, that is, the black people living all around the Union's representatives, senators, and president. Lincoln located a spot in the Isthmus of Panama. To captain this project he appointed Kansas senator Samuel Pomeroy—whose previous relevant experience had been in removing Indians from their Kansas lands. The Panama scheme failed, and Pomeroy turned his energies to the Indian variant, urging the Indian Office toward "the *removal* and *consolidation* of the small tribes into one distinctive Indian country." The next year Pomeroy again worked for Lincoln on a plan to colonize blacks, in Haiti; this, too, failed.

Lincoln felt that, ideally, America should be white. He explained to a black delegation in 1862 that the white and black races could not coexist in the nation, adding that the presence of blacks in America was currently causing white people to fight each other. The next year, in March, Lincoln met with Indian leaders. He had not known many Indians. He began by explaining that the world is round. ("We pale-faced people think that this world is a great, round ball.") He then considered the "great difference between this pale-faced people and their red brethren both as to numbers and the way in which they live." Indians, he said, live by hunting, whereas white people farm, and "I can only say that I can see no way in which your race is to become as numerous and prosperous as the white race except by living as they do." Lincoln also told his Indian listeners of another difference between the two races: "Although we are now engaged in a great war between one another, we are not, as a race, so much disposed to fight and kill one another as our red brethren."

One might have thought that the carnage of a civil war between white people, widely understood as such at the time, would have undermined the belief in white civilization as superior, not to mention more peaceful—perhaps even have undermined the belief in whiteness itself. White people were killing each other all around Lincoln; he was himself directing much of the killing; and so his seemingly mad assertion of the white race's comparative amiability must have answered a deep need to take an observable, unattractive feature of white behavior and attribute it to another race. If that race were removed from the nation, then would not the unwanted behavior cease as well? In which case the white American race could advance to prosperity and reach that destiny uniquely its own.

The Civil War, however, was a truly American conflict; all three races fought on both sides. A majority of Indians fought for the Confederacy, even after John Ross was captured by Northern troops and declared his tribe's loyalty to the Union. Yet Indians in the Northern ambit, and some without, fought for Lincoln. (While Elias Boudinot's son Elias Cornelius distinguished himself for the Confederacy, another son, Frank, died fighting for the Union in Virginia.) Everyone's racial fate was in the balance during the Civil War, and all three races came together in the Battle of the Crater. It was an atypical battle in many ways; but in some sense, it may have been the most typically American battle in America's most horrifying war.

The Battle of the Crater took place before the city of Petersburg, Virginia. The Confederates' defensive line stretched for thirty-five miles, beginning west of Petersburg, guarding the Bermuda Hundred peninsula, and continuing across the James River to a point northeast of Richmond. If the Union could breach this line and take Petersburg, the way would be open to Richmond, the Confederate capital, where Elias Cornelius Boudinot had his seat in the Confederate Congress. Among the troops defending Petersburg were Catawba Indians in the Seventeenth South Carolina. The Confederates settled in for a long defense in the early summer of 1864. The siege would last for over nine months.

On the Northern side the U.S. Colored Troops set about digging trenches to parallel the Confederate defenses. Killing technology had advanced rapidly during the war; by 1864 rifles (with the new minié ball) had improved enough to necessitate long-term trench warfare, as greater accuracy over distances had made it deadly to raise one's head within less than two hundred yards of the enemy. Most Indians during the Civil War fought as Indians in Indian regiments (usually with white commanders), but some fought as white people, and a few fought as Negroes. With the Thirty-first U.S. Colored Infantry at Petersburg was one Austin George, a Mashantucket Pequot from Stonington, Connecticut. Like all the colored troops, he was paid roughly half what a white soldier of the same rank earned. With his colored comrades, the Pequot George labored at arranging felled trees and digging trenches in a sweltering Virginia June.

Among the white Union troops was Colonel Henry Pleasants of the Forty-eighth Pennsylvania Infantry. He had many coal miners in his unit, and proposed building a tunnel at a narrow point in the no-man's-land — 150 yards.

Pleasants suggested a five-hundred-foot tunnel; his men would pack the far end with four tons of gunpowder. After the explosion Union soldiers would push through on either side of the resulting crater and take Petersburg.

Pleasants's superiors rejected the idea, but the Forty-eighth started digging anyway late that June. General Burnside of the Ninth Corps recommended that his colored troops, including Austin George's Thirty-first, lead the attack. Colored troops trained while the Forty-eighth dug. After the intense heat came heavy rains in July, turning the Union trenches into sewers. But the work continued, and at the end of July the tunnel was complete and the colored soldiers ready for battle.

Presented with an accomplished fact, and having lost many men in fruitless charges against the Confederate lines, the top Union generals decided to go ahead with Pleasants's idea. There was to be only one change: General Meade wanted white soldiers, whom he thought more capable, to make the charge. The decision came down only hours before the fuse was to be lit. Among the "white" soldiers were Indian sharpshooters from Michigan, Senecas with the Fourteenth Heavy Artillery, and other Indians with the Thirty-seventh Wisconsin Volunteer Infantry. They were to be led by General Ledlie, a man famed among his officers for drunkenness.

The first fuse didn't stay lit. Pleasants and two men returned to the tunnel, relit the fuse, and ran back to the entrance. The explosion came at 4:44 a.m. It opened a crater 170 feet long, 60 wide, and 30 deep. The killing was vast: 278 men from Virginia and South Carolina died in the explosion, including soldiers with the Seventeenth South Carolina—which included the Catawbas.

The "white" troops, battle weary, untrained, and generaled by Ledlie, were confused by the smoke, the terrible noise, the fire. They hesitated, then poured into the crater. The Confederates regrouped and trained their guns into the burning hole. It was a hot morning, the Southern guns blazed away. Soon no sounds came from the crater. It was filling with dead and dying white men and Indians. "Blood," an officer recalled, "was streaming down the sides of the crater to the bottom, where it gathered in pools for a time before being absorbed by the hard red clay."

More blood: after two hours the "colored" troops were sent in. Their white general abandoned them. The Pequot Austin George went in with the Thirty-first Colored, as did Clinton Mountpleasants, a Tuscarora Indian. The Confederates began their counterattack at 7:30 a.m. One Union officer remembered, "The men of the 31st . . . were being mowed down like grass." Mountpleasants lost his life in battle. George was nearly killed by a bullet in the shoulder—it missed his spine by three inches—and the wound would plague him for the rest of his life.

All three races met each other in the sink of blood at the bottom of the crater. Indians died there as blacks, as whites, and as Indians. At the end of the battle the Union had taken almost 3,800 casualties, the Confederacy 1,500. The Thirty-first Colored left 136 dead. And upon these black and Indian corpses a few last racial distinctions were to be made. Those behind Confederate lines were left by the Southerners to rot, and colored prisoners were killed by bayonet or bullet. The day after the Battle of the Crater, a Union general noted: "The wounded seem to be mostly colored men that are writhing with their wounds in this insufferable scene and I think the neglect of them must be intentional." Two days after the battle, under a truce, Union soldiers were able to cross the lines and retrieve their putrid dead.

"GRAND AND GREAT—
THE FUTURE STATE"

SOME TWENTIETH-CENTURY SOLUTIONS

TO THE INDIAN PROBLEM

■

The experience of the Civil War did nothing to diminish racial separatism among Indians. One of the more surprising racial issues they had immediately to face after Confederate defeat was the U.S. government's insistence that former slaves become members of their former owners' tribes. The slaves' pressing problem upon being freed was that they had nowhere to go. When Works Progress Administration (WPA) researchers interviewed former slaves in Oklahoma in the 1930s, Patsy Perryman recalled for them what happened when the war ended. She, her family, and their Cherokee owner, Judy Taylor, had earlier fled to Texas. After the armistice, Judy Taylor "started back to the old home place, but wasn't going to take us with her until mammy cried so hard she couldn't stand it and told us to get ready. We drove through in an ox wagon and sometimes had to wait along the way because the streams were flooded and we couldn't ford. We found the old house burned to the ground when we got back and the whole place was a ruin. There was no stock and no way for any of us to live. The mistress told us we were free anyway and to go wherever we wanted to."

Despite decades of tribal legislation, the line between blackness and Indianness remained somewhat indistinct. Out-of-wedlock mixed-race children were not uncommon. Some Cherokees did have African ancestry, and many of their slaves had Indian ancestors; the same held for the other slaveholding tribes, who together made up the great majority of Indian Territory's nonwhite peoples. Further, many of the black slaves of Indians identified with Indian culture.

They often spoke the tribal language. They prepared Indian dishes and participated, however peripherally, in Indian festivities such as the Cherokees' Green
Corn celebration. Patsy Perryman's story of her brother, Lewis, illustrates at least
one of the psychological byways possible for a former slave of Indians: "My
brother Lewis married a full-blood Indian woman and they got lots of Indian
children on their farm in the old Cherokee country around Caney Creek. He's
just like an Indian, been with them so much, talks the Cherokee language and
don't notice us Negroes any more. The last time I saw him was thirty years ago
[about 1908] when he come to see mammy at the agency. We started out walking and pretty soon he dropped behind, leaving me to walk in front. I looked
back and there he was standing in the middle of [the road] with his eyes shut.

" 'What's the matter, brother Lewis?' I wanted to know. 'Sister wants you to
come on,' I told him.

" 'I darn tired looking at Negrees!' he said, keeping his eyes shut tight, and I
knew just how he felt. That's what I used to tell Mistress Taylor when I leave my
own mammy and run to the mistress, crying to stay with her, even after the
peace come that set us free. 'Honey,' Mistress Judy say kindly, 'stay with your
mammy, she cries for you.' "

Some slaves of Indians ran away during the war, and some of these fought
for the Union—including under Indian officers. Many returned to Indian Territory after the war ended, hoping to reunite with family members or simply to
see again the only homes they knew. Enough came back for Indians to perceive
them as a danger. Occasionally Indians became night riders—a post-slavery
equivalent of the old slave patrols, only there were no masters to whom the riders could return their prey. So sometimes Negroes still had to run. And it seems
likely that some Indians rode with the Klan, which was active in Indian Territory as it was throughout former slaveholding lands. Yet Indians eventually had
no choice but to accept their ex-slaves as tribal citizens, with a right to tribal
lands and a voice in tribal politics. In this way, black people became more like
Indians, and Indians, to their general dismay, became more like blacks. However, Indians fought the integration of blacks into their society by various
means, and black Cherokees had to struggle, through countless appeals to
freedmen commissions, to secure their rights as tribal members. In fact, that
struggle hasn't ended even today.

As part of Reconstruction, the United States decided to create in Indian Territory a single political unit whose membership would be determined largely by
race. All of the tribes resident there were expected to merge into a government
of Indians generally—though one that incorporated former slaves of Indians as

citizens—and to accept among them such Indians as the United States in future succeeded in displacing from other states and territories. The United States also proposed that no "white person . . . will be permitted to reside in the territory, unless formally incorporated with some tribe, according to the usages of the land." The federal government intended to keep a tight administrative grip on Indian Territory. The land of racial self-determination would then become a racial ghetto or internal homeland of a type more familiar in the next century.

The Indians knew that this final melding into a race implied a final dissolution of tribes. Paradoxically, the loss of tribal sovereignty meant a loss of Indianness, because the content of one's Indian identity, the collective memories, practices, and traditions, existed almost entirely at the tribal level. There was precious little of Indian tradition in 1866. *Indian* was a political term within a racial society; Indian culture as such was a political one expressed by a racial name. It gained its meaning chiefly in relation to the other political-racial names prevalent at the time, *white* and *black*. In any event, tribal leaders negotiating with the victorious Union in 1866 had little leverage to preserve tribal power. Their people were sick and broken; the Cherokees alone lost perhaps four thousand in the war years, roughly a fifth of the tribe. (A vicious cholera would sweep through in 1867.) Most of the Indian Territory negotiators came to the table representing defeated powers. They no longer had divisions to exploit among the white Americans; the white nation was at last firmly united. Nor did the Indians have anywhere left to flee to and start over. A U.S.-Cherokee treaty of 1828 had contained an intriguing, perhaps unique geographic curiosity: the Cherokee Outlet. This was a strip of land, fifty-five miles wide, which the Cherokees did not inhabit. It stretched west from the settled district to the Mexican border and was called the Cherokee Outlet because its essential nature was that of an escape route. Although a piece of land, it really represented a state of mind. It was drawn so as not to cross white territory. The Outlet stood as a reassurance for the Western Cherokees that they would always be able to get away from white people and into the great liberating nothingness of yet another West.

Thirty-eight years later there was no West. New Mexico had been ceded to the United States in 1848 (though the Apaches there would continue fighting until 1886). The tribes had no place to escape to. In this situation the Cherokees' new chief, William Ross, spoke to his tribe, assembled together for the first time in five years. He addressed them in terms that could be considered minimalist, at best: "I most devoutly thank the Great Ruler of the Universe that it is my privilege to address you as one people. I thank Him that amidst the carnage, the horror and the desolation of those long, dark years of conflict, we have not been swept entirely off the face of the earth." Their chief told the Cherokees, "If you firmly resolve to become one people, you will become one people," and that was all.

While the treaty of 1866 between the United States and the larger tribes of Indian Territory raised racial Indianness to a new institutional level, it also contained the seeds of a different sort of amalgamation: permanent second-class racial status. The United States wanted and got concessions on railroad through rights. It sought to erect U.S. courts on Indian land and the right to build military outposts—in short, to assume judicial and police authority over Indians. The United States created a general council of all the tribes, with some powers of governance. But the Indians immediately saw the council as a forum for resisting what it called the "adventurous spirit of the white man." The council did comply with one aspect of its new racial role—attempting to conciliate the rebellious Plains Indians, with whom most of the Territory Indians had little in common—but it soon bridled, demanding an independent elected bicameral government, an elected executive, and its own judiciary. Neither President Ulysses Grant nor Congress would accept this. They intended to keep a veto power and to determine all major appointments.

Congress continued to press for ever more control over Indian affairs. The Indians wanted to control themselves. In 1872 their delegates memorialized Congress to the effect that Indian Territory should be a self-governing unit within the United States. The delegates argued that their territory was far more advanced than most of the white territories. "It has a smaller area than any other and a larger population than any except Utah and New Mexico," they pointed out to Congress. "It has more acres under cultivation than Washington Territory, over one-third more than Utah, and more than twice as many as Colorado or Montana." In other words, Indians were, to borrow Lincoln's expressions, more "numerous and prosperous" than comparable whites even without quite "living as they do." This demonstration of achievement worked no better in 1872 than it had in Georgia in 1830, when Elias Boudinot wrote of "Indians who not only *work*, but work *hard*." In 1873 Chief William Ross was predicting the "gradual blending of the Indians under the same form of government . . . the allotment of their lands in severally, the gradual extinction of all civil distinction between them and citizens of the United States, and their ultimate absorption as a portion of their [the United States'] population." Two years later the all-Indian national council was dissolved.

Congress, greatly encouraged by the railroad companies, continued looking for ways to dismantle what remained of Indian autonomy and to make as much of Indian land as possible available to non-Indian (primarily white) settlers. The first land run on formerly Indian Territory occurred in 1889; a year later the Oklahoma Panhandle was added to the resettled counties to form Oklahoma Territory. This divided the old territory into two: Oklahoma Territory in the West, and a reduced Indian Territory in the East. Smaller tribes—the Sauk and Fox, the Iowa, the Potawatomi—ceded their small reservations along the western edge of Indian Territory. The most spectacular land run of all came on September 16, 1893, when the Cherokee Outlet was made available. The thermometer registered one hundred degrees that day at noon, when the Outlet officially opened. A hundred thousand people, by horse or wagon or on foot, entered the Outlet, many of them coming south from Kansas, fleeing a drought that had scorched the Great Plains. Some men killed others to get their 160 acres of baking land. One white group frightened off a black claimant with threats of lynching, which their white neighbors in that open stretch of territory echoed, crying, "That's right; we don't want any niggers in this country!" Another man arrived in the Outlet already lost; he "appeared demented, wandering around in a circle and asking helplessly, 'Where can I stake a claim? I want to get a home.'"

The congressional act that opened (or closed) the Cherokee Outlet in 1893 also created a commission to negotiate separately with the major Oklahoma tribes, with a view to dividing their lands into individual, private parcels and eventually eliminating tribal governments. Cherokee opposition to division of lands was led by the Keetoowahs. This group represented "full-blood" conservatism, even though its 1859 revival had been led by the white Baptist missionaries Evan and John Jones, of Welsh ancestry. A reorganization in 1874 was likewise carried out by a Baptist preacher. Redbird Smith and Zeke Proctor, two prominent Keetoowahs, had a German grandfather and a white father, respectively, and the Keetoowah Bob Ross had numerous white relations. Keetoowah cultural revivalism itself mixed Baptist Christianity with Cherokee, Creek, and Natchez elements. Nonetheless, the Keetoowahs were synonymous with full-bloods and traditionalism. They had opposed slavery and "progressive" plantation society in the Civil War, after which they aided in the murder of perhaps dozens of U.S. marshals attempting to bring U.S. police power into Indian Territory. The Keetoowahs split in 1889 into a warlike faction dedicated to the Red Path of vengeful justice and a second group hewing more to the White Path of peace and spirituality.

Despite Keetoowah efforts, traditional religious observances had all but disappeared by the 1890s. Cherokees no longer met for stomp dances, or the Friends Made, Green Corn, and New Moon ceremonies. The imminence of tribal dissolution, propelled by the U.S. Congress's belief in the universal excellence of private-property relations, seems to have inspired a reconstruction of traditional practices and a rebirth of interest in medicine men. The first stomp dance of this nativist revival occurred in 1896, at the home of a Creek widow. Some Creeks had kept alive traditional knowledge, and the first sacred Fire of the revival was a Creek fire. Soon the Keetoowahs had recovered the seven-beaded wampum belts of the Cherokees. They studied the symbols woven in the belts in an attempt to divine the tribe's future. Medicine men again took their patients at night beside streams, lit fires, and conjured. At one of the new stomp dances an old man strapped turtle-shell rattles to his ankles and taught women how to do shell shaking. It was a women's dance, but none of the women knew how to do it.

The Keetoowahs, of course, refused to recognize Congress's power to recognize Indians. When Dawes Commission agents showed up to count Indians, the Keetoowahs hid until the agents were gone. But by degrees a majority of the tribe was brought around to accept a final extinguishing of Indian land title. After nine years of resistance the tribe ratified an enrollment agreement in 1902. Thousands of whites tried to pass as Cherokees in hopes of acquiring land, and weeding them out took time; probably no large American racial group has been so extensively interviewed about its genealogy as the Cherokees. The thousands of interviews constituted the Indians' last chance to agree with the United States as to what an Indian was.

The five leading tribes of Indian Territory—Cherokee, Choctaw, Creek, Seminole, and Chickasaw—mounted one final attempt to create an Indian state. According to treaties, the United States could not place any tribe's land into a state or territory without the tribe's consent. The first bill to make Indian Territory a U.S. territory, thus eliminating tribal power and violating treaties, appeared in Congress in 1870. It would be followed by many others. None had the support of the tribes, and none took effect. Yet a distinct momentum existed in Washington, one complemented by a series of judicial decisions culminating in the Supreme Court's judgment, in 1903, that Congress could break treaties whenever it liked: "Plenary authority over the tribal relations of the Indians has been exercised by Congress from the beginning, and the power has always been deemed a political one . . . When, therefore, treaties were entered into between the United States and a tribe of Indians, it was never doubted that the power to abrogate existed in Congress, and that in a contingency, such power might be availed of from considerations of governmental policy, particularly if consistent with perfect good faith towards the Indians." Therefore treaties did not matter.

The movement toward integration of Indian Territory into the United States was strengthened, at the turn of the century, by the dramatic increase in white and black populations in the territory and the wish of the neighboring Oklahoma Territory to absorb Indian land and make a single state. Indians in Indian Territory were already outnumbered nearly four to one in 1890; ten years later there were at least six non-Indians for every Indian. None of these non-Indians had political rights, and they were not supposed to own land, but that did not make them leave. It did make them agitate for integration into the United States.

As pressure for single Oklahoma statehood increased, the five tribes responded by calling for their own state in the union. The *Cherokee Advocate* editorialized in 1904: "A great deal is being said at this time about statehood, both by the single and double staters, but not one has ever said—let's put the matter to a vote of the Indians. They are the original settlers and owners of the Indian Territory, and they should at least be asked to express their wishes in the matter . . . For the past forty years our people have looked forward to the time when we would have an Indian state. Are we to be disappointed?" That year, James Norman, a mixed-blood Cherokee, proposed calling the state Sequoyah.

On August 21, 1905, the Sequoyah Constitutional Convention began in Muskogee. Three hundred five delegates had been elected to the convention— Indians and whites and all the possible mixtures, as well as five men identified as black. (Two of the black men also served on committees.) There were no female delegates, though women attended the convention in large numbers and extensive, if ultimately futile, arguments were made for women's suffrage. After a "hot discussion" of what the state should be named—suggestions included Indianola and Tecumseh—the convention agreed to Sequoyah. The immediate inspiration for this was allegedly an 1898 poem by J. S. Holden, who wrote of the Cherokee alphabet's inventor:

> *Untutored, yet so great;*
> *Grand and alone his fame—*
> *Yes, grand and great—the future state*
> *Should bear Sequoyah's name.*
> *In ages yet to come,*
> *When his Nation has a place,*
> *His name shall live in history's page,*
> *The grandest of his race.*

A vocalist at the convention somehow sang this to the tune of "Dixie."

A final draft of the Sequoyah Constitution was ready on September 5. On that day the chairman of the convention and principal chief of the Creeks, Pleasant Porter, issued a proclamation, which concluded, "our present governments shall not be annihilated but transformed into material for a nobly builded state. 'Thus shall we have life not death.'" Death seems to have been much on the delegates' minds. When Pleasant Porter called the convention to full session on September 6, another poem was read, by a Delaware, one Mrs. Duckworth. Her meandering, almost incomprehensible verse reads more like a dirge than a hymn of nationalist hope. It may well have reflected the mood of many at the convention. The poem begins, "Sweet the solemn intonation, sad the chimes so faint so low, / Marking the time for dying nations, once supreme, now fading so," and ends, "All glory to the dying nations to heaven and nature's own refrain."

Pleasant Porter's remarks made it clear that Sequoyah was not something the Indians expected to gain U.S. approval. They simply saw an Indian state as their right. "From time immemorial," Porter said at the convention, "the Indians as a heritage of the original inhabitants have been promised a state, an empire of their own. Driven west by successive invasions the Indians were forced to settle in this territory . . . They have taken on the dress, the customs, and the religion of the white man and they welcome him as a brother. The national government must grant us separate statehood or make a confession."

The Indian statehood campaign soon got under way with the support of most tribal leaders. The majority of Indian Territory newspapers—there were 105 of them, serving a population of less than 400,000—opposed separate statehood and attacked it in the bludgeoning style of that period's journalism. But a great deal of support existed, even among whites, most of whom were Southerners and did not like their white neighbors in Oklahoma Territory, who tended to come, if not from the North, at least from Kansas. When, on November 18, 1905, the final vote tabulation arrived, 59,279 people had supported ratification of the Sequoyah Constitution, and 9,073 had opposed it.

The Indian state of Sequoyah never really had a chance. President Theodore Roosevelt, House Speaker Joseph Cannon, and the powerful senator Albert Beveridge had all declared their opposition to it. The Indians had substantially accomplished what Jefferson, Monroe, Jackson, and so many others had urged on them: to build a separate racial state that was identifiably Indian yet conformed to white norms. But from a white perspective, this was a historical footnote. The fate of the Indians as Indians had already been determined by whites to be a poetic rather than a political one. At this point the Indians' considerable value to whites was symbolic, a complex of thoughts that white Americans had about themselves. One of these thoughts, from Washington Irving and James Fenimore Cooper to Theodore Roosevelt, had to do with the pastness of Indians. In January 1906 Senator McCumber of North Dakota futilely introduced a bill for the admission of Sequoyah as a state. On June 16 Roosevelt signed a bill making Oklahoma Territory and Indian Territory a single state.

Indian symbolism took an interesting turn with Oklahoma statehood. The Oklahoma Constitution adopted almost every aspect of the Sequoyah Constitution. The state seal of Sequoyah was transformed into that of Oklahoma. Indian symbols pervaded the new state, down to its Choctaw name. The musical *Oklahoma!* would be based on a novel by Lynn Riggs, who was a Cherokee, as was Will Rogers, soon to be the state's favorite son. Some of the white and Indian Sequoyah activists would go on to dominate Oklahoma politics. At the official statehood celebration in 1907, after a reading of Roosevelt's declaration that Oklahoma had become a state, the organizers staged a mock wedding between Miss Indian Territory and Mr. Oklahoma Territory. It took place on the grounds of the Carnegie Library in Guthrie. In real life the bride was already married— Mrs. Leo Bennett, of Cherokee descent. She wore a satin gown and gloves and carried a mauve chrysanthemum. Mr. C. G. Jones, her symbolic intended, was a white man in black morning coat and striped trousers. Thomas Jefferson's belief in intermarriage had at last found this fulfillment.

There was to be one other fulfillment of Jefferson's racial vision for America. The new state set out to be, as the *Daily Oklahoman*'s editor put it in 1915, "a white man's state . . . and must forever be a white man's state." The legislature in its first session segregated Oklahoma. The Indians, of course, had long since segregated their territory; when land was allotted, "freedmen" and their descendants got less than Indians, and the Cherokees grouped black tribal members together in internal homelands. (They had also created separate black schools.) And in Oklahoma, at least, when the white leadership segregated their state, they recognized Indians as not being black. For many decades Indians would drink at the white fountain, sit in the white seats at the cinema, attend white schools, have lunch at the white counter, and vote as full-fledged white people.

With Oklahoma statehood in 1907 and the end of independent tribal government, Indianness either went underground or disappeared, depending on your perspective. One of the many miracles of racial identity is that it can change. One can "rediscover" oneself as a racial being more or less indefinitely, on terms that vary with the times. Americans with a few ancestral generations on American soil—that is, the majority—probably can find in their families two if not three racial heritages, white, black, and Indian. Those who cannot may easily partake, in an imaginative act, of the triracial national tradition, the only national American tradition that makes any historical sense. There is, of course, a second tradition that operates in tragic, comic, undeniably productive and destructive counterpoint—the American tradition that the three races are and probably should be separate. Whether the first tradition can function without the second remains to be seen.

In the case of the Cherokees, many after 1907 integrated themselves as quasi-white people into what was then imagined as mainstream American life—a segregated society taking whiteness as the national norm. They believed they were doing the right and sensible thing. The durability of this conviction may be measured in the final passage of Grace Steele Woodward's 1963 *The Cherokees*, still one of the best general histories of the tribe. "After statehood," Woodward writes, "full-blood Keetoowahs retreated to the flinty hillsides and valleys in eastern Oklahoma, where they sought to keep alive ancient traditions and by this method shut out reality. Eastern Oklahoma Cherokees have yet a long road to travel, if they are to overtake the more progressive members of their proud race. But they may yet throw aside their present lethargic habits, abandon their listless contemplation of the future, and, like Sequoyah, explore the unknown. For, given the proper incentive, no mountain, it seems, is too high to climb, no current too swift to swim, if one is a Cherokee."

As Woodward noted, the Keetoowahs, standing in for the concept of true Cherokees generally, continued to resist assimilation. In 1910 Redbird Smith, leader of the Nighthawk Keetoowahs, told their council, "Our pride in our ancestral heritage is our great incentive for handing something worthwhile to our posterity. It is this pride in ancestry that makes men strong and loyal for their principle in life. It is this same pride that makes men give up all for their government." Redbird and his son John traveled to Mexico with hopes of finding a new land, just as Chief John Ross had sought a Mexican dispensation decades before. Sequoyah himself had journeyed toward this last West, looking for a Cherokee fragment said to be living there; Sequoyah curled up and died alone in the wilderness before reaching the old Spanish lands. Redbird and John Smith had in their hands a deerskin treaty from about 1820 that gave a portion of Mexico to some Cherokees. In Mexico City father and son met with the American ambassador and a Mexican lawyer. The attorney told them the deerskin treaty gave them no claim on Mexico's government. The Smiths left Mexico City disappointed; soon the Mexican Revolution began, further weakening whatever hold a ninety-year-old treaty might have had.

In 1914 Redbird and John Smith went to Washington, D.C., to argue the Keetoowah case. They hoped the government would help create a homeland for full-blood conservatives of the five large Oklahoma tribes. The U.S. commissioner of Indian affairs wrote to President Wilson, whose policies abroad turned so significantly on the value of national self-determination, that "this matter but again presents the call of the Red Man for a return to ancient customs and tribal forms of government, which they realize is fading away from them by enforcing civilization and citizenship. For this I do not find it in my heart to condemn them." Redbird Smith appeared before a joint congressional commission and was politely received, but left Washington with nothing. Upon

Redbird's return to Indian country, the Nighthawk Keetoowahs met and decided to become a primarily religious organization. They also declared that clan memberships should be made public. Although, or because, clan membership was the key to cultural Cherokeeness, clan ties had been kept secret for decades—in part from fear of conjuring, because an ill-intentioned conjurer became more effective when his target's clan was known. The result was that ever fewer people knew to which clan they belonged. In the circumstances of 1915 the Keetoowahs apparently felt that the seven clans would need to be publicly acknowledged if they were to survive at all. So some Cherokees again consulted elderly men and women in order to discover the truths of their own existences.

The Keetoowahs' move was basically a withdrawal, not only from white and black society but from the Cherokee majority. It occurred in the context of what looked like nearly inevitable tribal disappearance. Taking American Indians as a whole, the various allotment policies and the inability of many Indians to preserve individual land title resulted in Indian lands shrinking, between 1887 and 1934, from 138 million acres to 52 million. In Oklahoma about 30 million acres were allotted under various programs; fewer than 3 million remained in Indian hands in 1951. Off the reservations the poorest Indians, who were more likely to be full-bloods, lost their lands first, just as Boudinot had foreseen. The better-off Indians, who were more likely to be mixed bloods, often had the education and white connections necessary to hold or increase their properties. But they were also intermarrying with whites at a growing rate, such that within decades their Indianness might become a distant and anachronistic part of their self-understandings. The Choctaw historian Muriel Wright, in her 1951 *Guide to the Indian Tribes of Oklahoma*, wrote, "the Indian population has been so thoroughly absorbed into the general population of the state that many 'Indians' themselves, if asked to answer the question of 'race,' would very likely reply 'white.'" In this situation, the Keetoowahs segregated themselves, only as Indians rather than, as the majority did under Jim Crow, Indian whites. In 1950 one dissident group took the ultimate step, forming a separate tribal band recognized by the U.S. government: the United Keetoowah Band of Cherokee Indians.

The elimination of tribal communal landholding and sovereignty left the Cherokees and other tribes unable to support themselves as tribes. They therefore became dependent on the state. The United States did not want dependents; it wanted people to integrate themselves, one way or another, as individuals. The government tried various forms of forced assimilation. One was boarding schools: if Indian children were to get a basic education, they would have to leave home. Visits home were often restricted, and children severely punished for speaking their native language, even when they knew no other way to speak. In many areas tribal dances and other religious observances were effectively outlawed. This harshest period of assimilation eased in the 1920s, in part because Indians fought (in white units, this time) in World War I, despite not being citizens. (Indians received U.S. citizenship in 1924, with the proviso that the Bill of Rights not cover them. Indians could not vote in all states until 1948; the Bill of Rights was extended to them in 1968.) From the 1920s through the 1950s U.S. policy continued to press assimilation, just somewhat more gently. The government spent large sums on education, health care, and programs (such as credit unions) to ease Indians into a cash economy. The government also pursued aggressive policies of termination (ending the legal existence of tribes) and relocation (luring rural Indian families to distant cities with great promises, rarely fulfilled, of jobs and prosperity). The relocation program was designed by Dillon Myer, President Truman's appointee as head of the Bureau of Indian Affairs. Myer had previously directed the internment of Japanese Americans during World War II.

The U.S. government sought to improve Indian lives by destroying Indian cultures, using both carrots and sticks. To a degree these measures succeeded, particularly among tribes, such as most of those in Oklahoma, that had received individual allotments rather than reservations. Without a tribal property base day-to-day life for most Indians necessarily involved individual advancement— the "selfishness" that Senator Dawes had considered the basis of civilization. To prosper materially, particularly in Jim Crow days, Indians had to get white. One manifestation of this was the steady decrease in full-blood Indians as a proportion of the tribal whole. Yet reformers such as Dawes had not anticipated the tenacity of some Indians' attachment to collective life. They had mistakenly thought that Indians' primary attachment as Indians was to land; if the land became private, thus losing its tribalness, then tribal members would lose their tribalness as well. But tribal members' primary attachment was not to their land, it was to each other. Very few American Indians live on the land their ancestors occupied prior to European arrival. The tribal bond can survive transplantation; it can even survive on next to no land at all.

The idea that a tribe exists when its members think it exists is, of course, rather self-fulfilling. But it could hardly be otherwise. Any group must, at some level, will its own existence. In the case of many Indian tribes, this will has been extremely resilient. It can also be elastic. What is an Indian? What is a Cherokee? Beginning sometime in the middle of the twentieth century, an extraordinary development occurred: more people became Indians. This trend continues to the present day, as we can see by looking at census returns. From 1910 through 1950, broadly speaking, census enumerators counted as Indians those people who looked to them like Indians. This must have been an interesting operation on the ground, and full of subtleties. The enumerators' instructions varied somewhat from census to census. In 1910, for example, the Census Bureau said, "all persons of mixed white and Indian blood who have an appreciable amount of Indian blood are counted as Indians, even though the proportion of white blood may exceed that of Indian blood." This sounds more scientific than it was, because obviously the enumerators were not looking at blood at all. They were looking at people's faces, and perhaps asking around as to whether Jack's neighbors believed Jack was Indian.

The enumerators' marching orders for 1930 included the following: they "were instructed to return as Indians, not only those of full Indian blood, but also those of mixed white and Indian blood, 'except where the percentage of Indian blood is very small,' or where the individual was 'regarded as a white person in the community where he lives' . . . 'A person of mixed Indian and Negro blood should be returned as a Negro unless the Indian blood predominates and the status as an Indian is generally accepted in the community.' " What does this mean, exactly? We must keep in mind, first, that the term *blood* had little to do with the red fluid universally recognized as blood. It had to do with facial features and skin tone; dress, perhaps; language, maybe; family name (surely someone called Whitekiller is an Indian?); and the general tenor of a community. We should also bear in mind that the enumerators were overwhelmingly white. The enumerators' perception of community acceptance is especially interesting to ponder. Given that the enumerators could hardly be expected to know when a person's "percentage of Indian blood is very small"—how could you tell?—the weight of judgment must have fallen on whether that person was "regarded as a white person." But regarded by whom? Similarly, the status of a black Indian must have been determined largely by whether that person was "generally accepted in the community" as Indian. The fascinating thing is that the enumerators were not ordered to find out whether a black Indian was "accepted" as black or a white Indian "regarded" as Indian. The Census Bureau evidently accepted an implicit racial hierarchy of community choice. It wanted to look at the faces of light-skinned Indians and ask around as to who was passing for white; lower on the racial scale, it would look at dark-skinned Indians and ask around as to who was passing for Indian. Presumably it was whites who did the "regarding" in the first instance and Indians who did the "accepting" in the second. A dark person's being accepted as black was of no interest or consequence, nor was a light person's being accepted as Indian.

That would soon change. The 1960 census was the first to leave it up to respondents to judge what race they were. Instead of using enumerators, the

Census Bureau sent forms through the mail. The number of Indians in America then jumped by 46.5 percent, from 357,499 to 523,591. This spectacular increase cannot be explained by an excess of births over deaths or by greater efficiency of counting methods. It simply indicates that many more people—more than 100,000—believed themselves to be Indians than the enumerators had believed to be Indians. The Choctaw Muriel Wright's assurance in 1951 that most Indians would consider themselves white had evidently broken down.

It happened again in 1970: the American Indian population increased by 51.5 percent, to 792,730. The demographer Russell Thornton writes, "The events of the 1960s, especially the political turmoil arising from the civil rights movement and subsequent 'ethnic pride' movements, probably had a large, albeit unmeasurable, impact on the growth of the American Indian population . . . during this time it became acceptable, if not actually popular, to claim a distinctive ethnic heritage—American Indian or otherwise. This was a marked departure from earlier times in the history of the United States . . ." Among Indians ethnic pride had never been entirely lost, even among the elite. In 1948 tribal leaders met to form the National Congress of American Indians, which would serve as a model for subsequent racial organizations. In 1961 the National Indian Youth Conference was able to proclaim, "We are products of the poverty, despair, and discrimination pushed on our people from outside. We are the products of chaos . . . We are also products of a rich and ancient culture which supersedes and makes bearable any oppressions we are forced to bear. We believe that one's basic identity should be with his tribe. We believe in tribalism, we believe that tribalism is what has caused us to endure."

Seven years later President Lyndon Johnson put the seal on assimilationist policies, saying to Congress that government must recognize "the rights of the first Americans to remain Indians while exercising their rights as Americans." The American Indian Movement was founded that same year. Then, in November 1969, came Alcatraz. The unoccupied prison island in San Francisco Bay seemed an excellent spot for Indian militance. California Indian rebels had done time there in the 1890s. Bay Area political culture in 1969 was sympathetic, at the very least, to radical gestures, and a sizable Indian activist community had grown up around the American Indian Center in San Francisco. Five Sioux militants had made a first pass at Alcatraz in 1964, one year after Attorney General Robert Kennedy closed the prison. The Sioux landed in full tribal garb and claimed Alcatraz under the 1868 Treaty of Fort Laramie, which allowed any adult male of a tribe party to that treaty to file a homestead claim on unused federal property. The hopeful Sioux were quickly escorted from the island by federal marshals. On November 9, 1969, fourteen activists from various tribes tried the same tactic, setting out from Sausalito in the afternoon intending to buy Alcatraz. They had with them twenty-four dollars' worth of glass beads and red cloth, which is said to have been the price paid by the Dutch for Manhattan. Their offer was not accepted, and the occupation lasted just nineteen hours. Then, on November 20, a larger group of Indian men, women, and children sailed for the Rock. This occupation would last nineteen months.

The Indian occupiers of Alcatraz had water, food, camping equipment, and a heightened sense of humor. "We will give to the inhabitants of this island," they proclaimed, although there were no inhabitants, "a portion of the land for their own to be held in trust by the American Indian Affairs and by the Bureau of Caucasian Affairs to hold in perpetuity—for as long as the sun shall rise and the rivers go down to the sea. We will further guide the inhabitants in the proper way of living. We will offer them our religion, our education, our life-ways, in order to help them achieve our level of civilization and thus raise them and all their white brothers from their savage and unhappy state." This was arguably the largest-scale parody yet made by Indians of white people.

Although Alcatraz never did become Indian land—it would be fixed up as a tourist attraction instead—the occupation received much media attention and fueled the fashionability of Indianness. Jonathan Winters, Anthony Quinn, Jane Fonda, and Candice Bergen visited occupied Alcatraz, as did Merv Griffin. A certain Indian aesthetic would briefly excite Hollywood, in such films as *Billy Jack, Little Big Man,* and *A Man Called Horse.* Many of these films involve a white man whom circumstance has led to behave in Indian ways; the Indianness of the films is dramatized by a central white character, or at least a white performer, acting like an Indian. Thus the Indian drama became a white drama. A major feature film written, directed, and produced by Indians, with Indian actors, would not appear until nearly three decades after the 1969 landing at Alcatraz.

The Indianness revival did not escape the attention of popular musicians. The group Creedence Clearwater Revival provided a boat for ferrying Indians and sympathizers between San Francisco and Alcatraz. Cher recorded "War Paint and Indian Feathers" and "Half Breed." Elton John, who is white and British, released "Indian Sunset" in 1971, the year the Alcatraz occupation ended. He sings the first-person narration of an Indian warrior sometime in the late nineteenth century. The song is an imaginative cocktail of Indian-related items and acts: "a painted tepee," "war lance," "tomahawk," "Great Father of the Iroquois," "ride a painted pony," "run the gauntlet of the Sioux," "my squaw." John's character leaves his cowardly Iroquois chief and heads west, "where the red sun sinks in the hills of gold," to fight an abundantly doomed rearguard action against the white man. His pony leaves hoof tracks across the plains. He hears of Geronimo's death—"he was laying down his weapons when they filled him full of lead"—then soon meets his own. "Peace to this young warrior," John sings, "comes with a bullet hole." In real life Geronimo died at Fort Sill, Oklahoma, in 1909, after twenty-three years of confinement. But dramatic Indian death is critical to the song, making John a 1970s heir to James Fenimore Cooper, who had pioneered this art of Indian dying in white popular culture some 140 years before.

Just how much of a role films and songs played in altering white, black, and Indian ideas about the races' respective Indian qualities is impossible to say. More serious work also flowered during this period: Vine Deloria, Jr.'s books *Custer Died for Your Sins* (1969) and *God Is Red* (1973), Dee Brown's *Bury My Heart at Wounded Knee* (1970), a popular 1972 reissue of *Black Elk Speaks*, with an introduction by Deloria. Indian history as history (rather than anthropology) also became a legitimate subject for research at the nation's universities. Indian power, when faced with federal and state governments, grew rapidly—tribal autonomy became federal policy, and in 1971 the Cherokees elected their own chief for the first time since Oklahoma statehood. Indian militance grew as well. American Indian Movement (AIM) members marched to Washington in 1972 along the "Trail of Broken Treaties" and occupied the Bureau of Indian Affairs; the next year AIM took over Wounded Knee, South Dakota, and stood off federal agents there for sixty-nine days.

The 1980 census brought startling news. The American Indian population had grown by 72.4 percent in ten years, reaching nearly 1.4 million (excluding Eskimos and Aleuts). Of these, 232,344 were Cherokees, making the tribe by far the largest in the country. (The Navajo were second, at 158,633.) Cherokee population growth was highest in California, having gone, according to census figures, from 258 in 1930 to 51,394.

The Census Bureau continued to use self-declaration as its basic method, but it had added a new question, item 14, which sought to determine ancestry. Respondents were asked to "print the ancestry group with which the person *identifies*." Multiple ancestry was allowed, though in most cases the bureau only tabulated the first two ancestries given. The result was that 6,754,800 Americans said they had Indian ancestry. (The North American Indian population at European contact is generally estimated at six million.) Of these 6,754,800 Americans who believed themselves to have Indian blood, the great majority (5,173,500, or 76.6 percent) listed their race as non-Hispanic white. Blacks, Hispanics, Asians, and others accounted for just 5.4 percent of ancestral Indians; the rest were simply Indians. This disproportional representation of whites among those claiming Indian ancestry at least suggests that whites also make up a high proportion of those who, between 1970 and 1980, changed their race to Indian. The trend continued in 1990. Although the increase in Americans of

Indian, Eskimo, or Aleut race slowed to 38 percent—still far exceeding the excess of births over deaths—the number of people listing Indian ancestry leaped to 8,708,220. That means that just short of two million Americans found Indian ancestors in ten years.

Where did these tens of thousands of formerly white Indians come from? And why did they switch? This was not supposed to happen. Indians were meant to disappear. Yet not only did they not disappear, they were increasing in number; some mixed-blood whites were choosing to become mixed-blood Indians, thereby changing their race overnight; and yet another population, though one cannot say how large it is, was declaring itself Indian or part Indian without any Indian blood at all. It is as if white American culture, or some part of it, no longer needed Indians to die. On the contrary, it seems to have wanted them to live, such that tens of thousands of whites could decide that their Indianness was, at some level, more precious than their whiteness.

HOMELANDS

∎

Indian militants of the 1970s had a racial as well as a tribal vision. Intertribal powwows remain frequent and popular, particularly in the West. (The word *powwow* is Narragansett for "conjurer" or "meeting"; it entered English after 1605 and is now a general Indian term for get-together.) But the basic unit of identity is still one's tribe. One has a tribe first; then one becomes an Indian. Even after all these centuries the racial concept has failed to displace the tribe.

Indians are understandably ambivalent about the numbers of new Indians and self-imagined Indians. Who can join the tribe? The sharpest distinction in Indian country seems to be between those tribes that have something, such as a reservation, and those that do not. Propertied tribes have tended to be more exclusive, in part from fear of losing federal recognition and thus losing tribal property (as well as federal aid). Less propertied, and larger, tribes have tended to be more inclusive. Yet even here the distinctions break down, mainly because so many Indians marry non-Indians. More than a third of Indians in the 1970 census had married non-Indians; ten years later more than half had. In such a situation an exclusive tribal-blood policy would almost certainly lead to tribal disappearance. This is especially true given that marrying someone of another tribe is not, from one's strictly tribal point of view, any different from marrying a Chinese or black person. There is probably no tribe today that can limit itself to full-bloods; that would constitute a collective suicide, as well as a repudiation of love.

Increased federal recognition of tribal sovereignty has also had the effect of increasing tribal wealth. This has been true in the obvious sense that you can't have tribal wealth until you have a tribe. Beyond that, in a tribe, as in any corporation, the pooling of wealth leads to the possibility of investment and the creation of more wealth (as well as the creation of skills). Finally, sovereignty has enabled tribes to provide products and services unavailable under neighboring sovereignties—mainly, states.

One of the services is gambling. The Indian Gaming Regulatory Act of 1988 had its genesis in an effort to ease state-tribal conflict over bingo games. The statute additionally mentioned "promoting tribal economic development, self-sufficiency and strong tribal governments." Many states and localities prefer not to have gambling, or, more commonly, like to keep the business and its revenues under state control (as in lotteries). Yet more people want to gamble than states and localities are able to satisfy. Therefore, many tribes have seen a market opportunity and seized it. Most tribes building casinos get their start-up capital, expertise, labor, and customers from non-Indian populations, but they generally are careful to keep as much revenue as possible for the tribe and to negotiate contracts that will eventually lead to exclusive tribal ownership. In this way, some tribes—especially those near populous cities—have become rich.

Indian tribes tend to distribute resources evenly among tribal members, in accord with the tradition of collective ownership. For some tribes this makes being an Indian financially attractive to a degree not seen since the final big land allotments at the turn of the century. The most famous examples today of materially desirable Indianness are in Connecticut: the Mashantucket Pequots (with their Foxwoods casino) and the Mohegans (with the Mohegan Sun). The history of Indian self-definition since European arrival is rich in ironies, but the pure concentration of historical ironies in the pretty, forested hills upriver from New London, Connecticut, probably exceeds that in any other part of our country. The first English war of extermination against Indians had been against the Pequots, most notably in 1637 with the massacre of a fortified village in Mystic. "[T]here were about four hundred souls in this fort," an English captain at the scene reported, "and not above five of them escaped out of our hands." Those who did try to escape, he wrote, "our soldiers received and entertained with the point of the sword. Down fell men, women, and children." Among the English allies in this action and the skirmishes that followed were the Mohegans, led by Uncas. The name would be used nearly two centuries later by James Fenimore Cooper for his own Uncas, the doomed hero, "the last warrior of the wise race of the Mohicans."

Uncas was not quite the last Mohegan. After the Pequot War the tribe continued to be powerful until the English no longer needed it. The surviving Mohegans dispersed. In the late twentieth century Mohegan territory consisted of a tiny church on half an acre atop a hill outside Montville, Connecticut. There a handful of Mohegans met and worshipped and kept alive some fragments of tribal tradition. In the 1970s they began seeking federal recognition. The government does not make it easy to be recognized as a tribe. The process requires not only lawyers and lobbyists but anthropologists, who must prove continuous tribal existence—specifically, an unbroken bloodline. The Mohegans' effort puttered along until a group of businessmen approached the tribe, offering to fund its recognition effort in exchange for the contracts to build and operate a casino. The Mohegans agreed, and ten million dollars later, in 1994, became a federally recognized tribe.

At this point the Mohegans needed money and expertise, and both arrived in the form of Sol Kerzner, a South African hotelier turned casino developer. A short, blunt man—he is a former boxer—Kerzner turned a small fortune from hotels into a huge fortune from casinos on the strength of one brilliant idea. White South Africans wanted to gamble, but a certain Calvinistic turn of mind kept them from allowing gambling on white territory. Meanwhile, as part of the rigid racial separatism called apartheid, the South African government had created internal homelands. Whites forced black South Africans to live in these homelands in order to keep the races separate.

Kerzner realized the homelands were perfect for casinos. They had semi-independent "governments" that would be easier to work with, so to speak, than the white national government. Casinos would bring money to the desperately poor homelands. And white gamblers would come because this black space would be ideal for doing things they didn't think they ought to be doing in their own, white homeland, such as gambling and having interracial sex. Kerzner built Sun City in Bophuthatswanaland and made a mint. He also pioneered a fascinating form of architecture: a meticulous reconstruction of a place that barely existed. The main attraction of Sun City today is the Lost City, which "revives" an ancient African civilization. Surrounded by a man-made jungle, it is like a temple commemorating an imagined, magnificent death. One goes to play in the vast spaces of this memorial. Its features include a fake volcano that erupts and a man-made lake with simulated waves for surfing. From here Kerzner went on to build the lost city of Atlantis in the Bahamas, with a simulated marine environment. Then he came to Connecticut.

The Mohegans' contractors built a casino that is "Mohegan-themed," which means that its four main entrances are named after the four seasons and Indian motifs abound. It has a fiberglass forest and fake pony-hide banquettes and turtle-shell sconces and an artificial cliff representing a real one from which Uncas is said to have leaped across a river. The main drinking spot is called the Wolf Room because Mohegans are the Wolf People.

In a distant and relatively underdecorated part of the casino, I met one day with Roland Harris, a mild-mannered land surveyor and chairman of the Mohegan tribal council. He wore khakis and a light-blue blazer in a tight herringbone. He said that there had been some on the tribal council who argued against having a casino. "On the other hand," he said, "there were those who realized money is power."

Harris, who traces his ancestry back thirteen generations to Uncas, believed that the "traits" of Uncas have carried on today: "We have the ability to understand"—Harris paused—"the white-Indian balance. Bitterness doesn't work." The Pequots, he said, are uncommunicative, while the Mohegans like to communicate. The Pequots separate themselves, while the Mohegans trade. The Pequots, Harris added, are still not talking to the Mohegans.

I asked whether Sol Kerzner's South African experience had been useful in his Mohegan work. Harris mentioned the Transkei, a black homeland where Kerzner had done some business with the native government. "It's really," Harris said, "what an Indian tribe is."

Ten miles of good highway take you from the Mohegan Sun to the Pequots' Foxwoods. It is not as strongly Indian-themed as the Sun, but it does have a small museum below an artificial waterfall. (A larger museum is planned.) The flowing water makes the air in the museum refreshing. "For the past three centuries," a display reads, "the Mashantucket Pequots have struggled to regain their land and bring their people home." The museum displays narrate the various events of Pequot history. The only video is devoted to the Mystic massacre. It has sounds of gunfire and screaming and an English captain saying, "We must burn them!" This is the critical moment in Pequot history, when the tribe realized its world contained only enemies. The video makes sure to mention Mohegan involvement on the English side.

By the 1950s there were two Pequots on Pequot land, Elizabeth George and Martha Langevin. Both died in the early 1970s, at which point several Pequots in the surrounding area reorganized the tribe. They tried to come up with development projects—principally, making maple syrup and firewood. In 1983 the Pequots received federal recognition and 214 acres for a reservation. Then came the Indian Gaming Regulatory Act in 1988, some fresh thinking about the Pequots' old bingo hall, some non-Indian money and political helpers—and, just over a decade after federal recognition of the Pequots, the largest casino in the world.

Gambling chips at Foxwoods are called wampum, and the cocktail waitresses wear short skirts like those of Disney's Pocahontas. Some wear feathers in their hair. The waitresses are not, on the whole, as far as they know, Indians. The Indians gather instead at Pequot headquarters in a valley beneath the casino. One approaches it along a winding road that follows a creek bed; flanking the road are large new houses set tastefully back in the forest. I went to the tribal offices knowing that the Pequots' chief would not speak to me—he doesn't like interviews—but I thought seeking an interview would be a good way to see the place. The lobby receptionist worked at a large desk near the center of a two-story cavern. People wandered in from time to time, and the receptionist would politely inquire, Are you a member of the tribe? If the answer was yes, they could then go about their business. It was odd to see these Pequot faces. Some were black, some were brown, some seemed Asian, while others seemed Indian and others white. After a while the whole idea tended to break down. Following the Pequot War some Pequots were sold into slavery. In later years many worked as sailors, traveling the world, notably on whaling ships. Many were employed in the shipyards in New London, which attracted workers of every imaginable ethnicity. In short, this tiny massacred tribe's survivors had opportunities to intermarry with every known type of person. When word got out that being a Pequot was worth a great deal of money, ancestral memories were rekindled. An ingathering of the tribe followed. Now, when you see the Pequots wandering in and out of the lobby, or gaze at the displays of photos from tribal baseball games and picnics, you see all the world in the faces of Pequot Indians. It remains a minuscule tribe, with a blood-quantum requirement set at one-sixteenth and expected to go lower for survival's sake, yet as a collective, it looks just like America.

If a tribe looks just like the society surrounding it, is it still a tribe? Historically, the answer has been that it is not. The further twist, in America, has been that becoming not-a-tribe involves becoming part of the larger culture that is itself somewhat tribal—the white tribe. This tribe, however, has had a self-definition elastic enough that its members can be white and not-white ("just an American") at the same time. This can make white separatism a somewhat cloudy affair. In any case, logically, if not always practically, there is no reason why other tribes could not offer roughly the same elasticity of being. Indeed, the startling increase in the population of American Indians suggests that the white example of changeability is being followed today among Indians. It was how many tribes operated with regard to tribal membership before European arrival and, frequently, up to the early nineteenth century.

The official enrolled population of the Cherokee tribe in eastern Oklahoma—as distinct from the Eastern Cherokee band, in the Smoky Mountain area, and the United Keetoowah band—has gone from about 12,000 in 1975, to 63,400 in 1981, to somewhere near 180,000 today. That makes 168,000 new Cherokees in twenty years. Each of them had to identify an ancestor on the

Dawes rolls. The Cherokee nationalist David Cornsilk, not surprisingly, sees this growth as a good thing. But he does so within the framework of a very American idea: citizenship only dimly tied to race. Yes, the Dawes rolls are based on blood, however doubtful some of the results; but they also include many blacks. And whites, depending on your definitions. "Cherokee blood doesn't make you special," Cornsilk insisted that afternoon back in Tahlequah, the Cherokee capital. "If I believed that Cherokee blood made us special, then I would be a racist. And I don't *want* to be a racist. What makes us special, what makes us unique in this system that has been imposed on us, is that we are citizens of an indigenous nation that was here before any of you all were." He should perhaps have emphasized *in this system,* but he didn't.

Cornsilk's insistence on citizenship, as distinct from race, has led him into some trouble with his tribe. In 1983, he said, the tribal council decided that only Cherokees "by blood" could vote. (Supposedly the incumbent chief's opponent had been courting the "freedman" vote.) This disfranchised black Indians. "I think there was a racial motivation behind it," Cornsilk said as we sat in the Cherokee courthouse. "Because these people *are* black. They're up there on top of a hill and everybody here in town calls it, you know, that hill, I don't even want to use the word."

"They call it Nigger Hill."

"Exactly. These are wonderful people who live in abject poverty. You go up to their houses, and their houses are collapsing around them and, you know, a dozen little dogs in the yard. If you didn't have a black person standing in that front yard you could swear that was probably where some of these Cherokees lived." Cornsilk laughed nervously, although he was by no means a nervous man. His laughter may have been nervous because many full-bloods, as he told me, feel a self-doubt, based only on blood, "that maybe our Indian blood makes us incapable." It is a kind of terror one has of oneself. "These people [on Nigger Hill] live like Cherokee," Cornsilk continued. "They communitize themselves. Many of them even speak Cherokee. There's a lot of them who, their grandparents spoke the Cherokee language, and they even have passed it down." They might be more Cherokee than most Cherokees.

"Throughout the history of our tribe, we have always made people who came into our tribe and established a true connection to us—either through marriage or adoption—we made them one of us. And then suddenly to have an entire branch of our family, the freedmen branch of our family, to be cut off, to be simply severed and told, 'Now you're no longer one of us,' for political reasons, for racial reasons, is more than I can tolerate." Cornsilk said that the Cherokees who might be considered, or who consider themselves, closest to the black Cherokees—the full-bloods—hate them with a special passion. "You should hear some of the remarks made. In fact, my wife, because she's full-blood and I think has a lot of the prejudices of full-bloods—they have their own set of prejudices against mixed bloods, against white people, against black people—and she said, 'I can't imagine why people want those colored people in our tribe.' That's not the word she used. She said, 'We're Indians.' She said, 'We're supposed to be Indians.' She accused me of thinking like a white person." I said that it sounded like the opposite of the way a white person would think—wanting to include blacks in the tribe—but his wife may have had another idea in mind: that whites think Indians are colored people. Historically, she had a point.

Nevertheless, her husband was pressing ahead with his insistence that "you can be a Cherokee and not be an Indian." "If the freedmen's descendants were all allowed to enroll," he said, "and they all enrolled, we would probably grow by a hundred thousand people. That they all would enroll is probably not the case. I spoke to a very intelligent, articulate young man in Washington, D.C., who's an attorney, and I tried to get him to take this case. And his response was, 'I am an African American. Why would I want to be a Cherokee?' And I understand that. His sense of identity is strictly with the African American community. I tried to explain to him that you can be an African American and be a citizen of the Cherokee Nation. Are you not an African American and a citizen of the United States? Isn't that possible?"

Cornsilk had the gift of being completely logical about something that is illogical. He was also implacable. He had gone looking for a plaintiff to bring a case in tribal court demanding the right to vote without being on the Dawes roll as a Cherokee by blood. He found Bernice Riggs, up on Nigger Hill. "She lives up here on the hill," he told me in an excited voice. "Very sweet lady, she's seventy-seven years old. And I intentionally selected her as the plaintiff in this case, because—for two reasons. One, she's an elder, and respected in this community. Even though there's so much racial prejudice in this community, she is well known and respected by most of the people here. And my second reason is that she actually possesses Cherokee blood through her father, and through his father, and through his father. Which is why her family was placed on the roll as freedmen, rather than as Cherokees by blood. Because in order to get on the by-blood section of the roll, your Cherokee blood, if you were part black, had to come through your mother." This matrilineal rule "didn't apply to people if they were part white or part Chinese or whatever, but it applied to people that were black. If your mother was black, you were black. They claimed it was the Cherokees' matrilineal descent, you know, that historically we've always traced through the mother. But they didn't apply it across the board. They resurrected it to apply to the blacks." This meant that, because the Cherokee blood in a black family was likely to come from a Cherokee man with a black woman, most black Cherokees would be defined as black rather than Cherokee.

"As a people," Cornsilk said, "I think we have a moral responsibility to them. Certainly, we are placed in the middle of a larger nation, and it wouldn't be detrimental to them in the long term if they didn't have citizenship in our nation. They enjoy citizenship in the United States. But I feel like we have to act *as if* we are the only ones here. And in that circumstance, what would be the status of these people? Where would they be, *if we were the only ones here*, and we had done that to them? They would be second-class citizens, and then we would have an apartheid situation where we would probably even have separate drinking fountains. I look at it as if we are the only ones here, and what would we do in that situation. The answer has to be that there has to be justice for everybody here, regardless of race, color, creed. And looking at citizenship in the nation, it has to be based on what the constitution says.

"I've been called nigger lover, you know, 'You're lettin' niggers into the tribe.' That word just drives me nuts. But you know, I don't like the word *red-skin*, either."

PART TWO

THE REPUBLIC OF NEW AFRICA

■

Velma Ashley's father was an uncompromising man. "You were supposed to be independent," she told me. "You weren't supposed to bow to anybody. He moved out here so he wouldn't have to bow to white people." In 1907 Ashley's father, Mr. Dolphin, moved from Beatrice, Alabama—at the border of the old, pre-removal Choctaw lands—here to Boley, one of twenty-nine all-black towns in what would become Oklahoma. (When he moved, it was still two territories.) The black leader Booker T. Washington visited Boley and wrote that it represented "a wholesome desire to do something to make the race respected; something which shall demonstrate the right of the negro, not merely as an individual, but as a race, to have a worthy and permanent place in the civilization that the American people are creating." This may have been what Dolphin had in mind—Washington's ideas would animate his daughter's life. Then again, Dolphin's feelings might be more accurately inferred from a newspaper article designed to attract blacks to Boley. It began with a simple question: "Have you ever experienced complete freedom?" The article went on to explain the nature of Boley as a town "of superior culture . . . where your supreme thoughts can be put into action without any fear of hesitancy." The all-black towns may have provided a place designed for racial uplift, or for individualist achievement; or perhaps the people who have lived in them wanted something of both.

Velma Ashley's comfortable, well-kept house stood catty-corner from Boley's public school. Ashley was eighty-five years old. Sitting on the piano bench in her living room, hands in her lap, back straight, legs properly folded, she did not look as if she had bent once in her life, unlike her father, who had lived in Alabama as the slave of his father. Dolphin never did tell Ashley her grandfather's name. "Whenever I would ask him about it," she said in her formal, deliberate voice, "something would always come up, so that he couldn't go into it. But I also sensed that he didn't want to go into it." Born around 1855, he was freed at age eight or nine. Until his death Dolphin would refer to his father, when the subject arose, as the Master or "my Master."

Dolphin's mother married a Mr. Stallworth, whom Dolphin did not like. When he needed to take a family name, Ashley's father "was working for somebody and they sent him down to Mobile to get something, on the train, and he looked out, you know, across the tracks, and he saw a big sign on a boxcar . . . He saw the word *dolphin*. And he took it, because he didn't want to be a Stallworth. And when he got back to Beatrice, he got on his horse and went to Monroeville, which was the county seat, and established his name." Dolphin began to raise a family in Beatrice, but by the turn of the century he had started to worry about the fate of his children. Lynchings were common. Dolphin had done well enough that his sons owned horses to ride just for fun. "Whites," Ashley said, "felt 'niggers' weren't supposed to ride horses of their own for pleasure." When Dolphin heard about Boley, he came.

What did Dolphin find in Boley? An opportunity to work hard. He and his wife managed to get a large family through the Depression without anyone going hungry, an immense accomplishment. He died in 1943. There is a population of Dolphins in the old Boley cemetery, now overgrown with grasses and brambles, a patch of ground across Highway 62 from the town.

Ashley had spent nearly all her life in Boley, separate from the white world, devoted to uplifting her race in the way she thought proper. The town was at its height in her youth, before cotton went into its long decline as a cash crop, before urbanization drew ever more people away, before the interstate turned Highway 62 into a relic. She taught for decades at the town's school, mainly English, though she spent one year teaching history, and was even superintendent for a while. In an all-black town "you grow up with a better appreciation of yourself," she says. "We were never told to sit in the back of the room, or to stand behind white people."

Now, however, Ashley thought Boley could use some white people. They had a "background" black people did not have, a self-esteem, and a social discipline. "Somewhere along the line we have, to use an expression of yesteryear, we have missed the boat." Children grew up without fathers; students didn't apply themselves to studying the sorts of things Ashley had taught, like *Beowulf* and Lincoln's Gettysburg Address and the Constitution. (Ashley tended not to teach black literature or black history. She said there was hardly enough time to teach the "mainstream" subjects.) Black people used to have rules, she said, rules her parents taught her—for example, that "every girl should have one good white dress and one good black one." But today "the basic things are not being taught. And I'm hoping that they still do it in the white communities."

"Maybe they do," I said. "I don't know. There are millions and millions of white people."

"I mean," she said, in a practiced scold, "just generally speaking."

Years ago Boley's town poet, Uncle Willie Jesse, sang,

> *Oh, 'tis a pretty country*
> *And the Negroes own it, too*
> *With not a single white man here*
> *To tell us what to do—in Boley.*

This laconic humor took on a harder edge with time, to judge by the title of an oral-history video made by the head of Boley's chamber of commerce, Charles "Chip" Coleman: *I'm Not Dead*. Boley once had a population of over five thousand. Now it was down near five hundred, or less, not counting inmates of the nearby prison or the state-financed "boardinghouses" for people who couldn't take care of themselves—about the only white folk one saw in Boley. The prison and boardinghouses were leading employers, along with Smokaroma, a small manufacturer of barbecue and hamburger cookers owned by Maurice Lee, Jr., who came from an old Boley family. Lee, a trim, businesslike man, told me that Boley was working to attract retirees and expand tourism. He was keenly aware that his town had seen better days and that its young people tended to leave— sardonically, he quoted an old proverb, "The white man's ice is colder." But, he pointed out, Boley was still doing better than Castle, a white town six miles east. Nearly empty, unpaved, white Castle was almost a ghost town.

One afternoon I was driven around Boley by Theodore Roosevelt McCormick, an athletic octogenarian and lifelong entrepreneur who owned the local motel, which might be described as open on request; the newer of Boley's two cemeteries (the well-maintained one); and various other interests. He put up many of Boley's postwar buildings and graded many of its roads. To enter Boley, from Highway 62 you crossed a stream and drove uphill onto Main Street, passing, on the left, the tiny city hall/police station/firehouse McCormick built. As you neared the crest, on the right was a corner where the Masonic lodge once stood, a three-story building with marble stairs, the pride of Boley and a site for conventions bringing together blacks from all over Oklahoma. On the left you passed what was the first black bank in Oklahoma, the Farmers and Merchants State Bank. The bank was closed, as were the other two that had financed Boley in better times.

As we inched along in his car, McCormick would say, "Houses all along in here," gesturing at plots taken over by new-growth forest. It requires, he said, about twenty to thirty years for forest to reclaim emptied land. Some of the former homes, with vines creeping over them and trees in what were once sitting rooms, had clearly been grand. "All through here was houses," McCormick would say. When we nosed back onto Main Street and headed down toward the highway, McCormick said that the street had once been full of commercial buildings, with not one empty lot. Now, if you hit Main Street at the right time of day, you might not see a soul.

McCormick was a relative of Abigail Barnett McCormick, a Creek freed-woman on whose land allotment Boley was founded just after the turn of the century. The town came to be named Boley—as Ashley and other Boleyites told the story—because of a disagreement between two white employees of the Fort Smith and Western Railroad, a Mr. Moore and a Mr. Boley. The railroad needed towns every six to ten miles along its line to ensure an adequate water supply. However, the land between the white towns of Paden and Castle was populated by the families of former Creek slaves. Moore believed blacks couldn't run a town responsibly and opposed recognizing a black town, whereas Boley believed they could, or deserved a chance to prove themselves. So the town was named Boley. As Ashley said, the railroad figured that whites "were close enough, in Paden and Castle, if things go wrong."

When large numbers of blacks (and whites) began arriving in Oklahoma Territory and Indian Territory during and after the great stampede of 1889, black leaders organized to put blacks in each of the territories' districts in hopes that, when the time came to join the Union, Oklahoma would be admitted as a majority-black state. That is why the territory had so many all-black towns so quickly—it was the last chance for a black state. Oklahoma's whites and Indians, however, were set against the idea, and blacks were already being expelled from some areas in 1891. When Oklahoma achieved statehood in 1907, just months after Mr. and Mrs. Dolphin arrived from the South, the new legislature's first act was, of course, to segregate it. The Creeks, like the Cherokees, already had a segregated society, which made the transition fairly simple. Creeks just became juridically white. Blacks remained black. The resurgence of the Ku Klux Klan in the 1920s, then, had relatively little effect on all-black towns (though it tore up Tulsa, where blacks and whites lived near each other). "We have never been bothered by Klansmen," Ashley said, perched on the piano bench. Why? "Because they *wanted* all the Negroes to get together. Wanted to give one of the states to them." Black separatism fit right into the Klan's plan.

Ashley said that her father could pass for white but always told his children not to think they were special as a result. He refused, she emphasized, to enter whites-only places. "They wouldn't know he wasn't white," she said, "but he wouldn't do it. He wouldn't go in because I couldn't go with him." His children came in many shades, although "he didn't have a single child who could pass for white." In segregated Oklahoma, Ashley knew how much, and perhaps how little, it meant not to be able to pass for white. She recalled needing a drink of water one day at Montgomery Ward in the city. There were two fountains, one brown and one white, at the end of a long, wide aisle. "They were wide in those days," she recalled, though she was just a little girl at the time, and doesn't everything look huge to a child, or in the memories of an adult? Were the fountains given colors to help people who couldn't read? They had signs above them for the literate. Ashley went to drink at the brown fountain. A white girl was drinking at the white fountain. The white girl said, "I wonder if the water you're drinking tastes any different from mine." Ashley said, "You can come over and taste it." The white girl replied, "I can't taste yours, but you can taste mine." Which Ashley did, and she said it tasted the same.

Dolphin's children were teased because their father looked white, in a town where, as Booker T. Washington wrote, "no white man has ever let the sun go down upon him." Ashley brought out a photo of her father for me to see. I looked hard at Dolphin, an old man in farming clothes—he farmed all his life—standing a bit restlessly, or so it seemed, on a porch. Even at this age he appeared physically powerful, his shoulders and chest thick. Did he look black, or white? The picture was a bit fuzzy. I leaned forward over the coffee table better to see his stern face. I looked at his nose, to see if it was broader . . . but I couldn't do this, and sat back up and looked away from Dolphin.

Booker T. Washington believed that white and black were separate fingers of a single hand. He thought that blacks would best develop toward civilization if they were apart from whites. He also believed that most of human civilization was the creation of white people. This belief Ashley shared, but, having lived most of her life apart from whites, she no longer believed separatism was viable. And so Boley needed white people: "I think that would help more than anything I see right now." Being around only blacks could be a "handicap." White children would introduce more competition into the school. White people knew about history and politics and medicine. She said that she could clear a room of her colleagues by bringing up such subjects. "The only person who would stand around and talk to me about it was the history teacher." White people listened to classical music, not the "ugly music" she heard in Boley. (She particularly disliked the pianist at the Baptist church she attended, one of Boley's seven churches. Music should be played "as it's written," but the pianist was always "jazzing it up": "I don't know whether to pop my finger and look around for someone to dance with, or whether I should sit down and take my place. The woman plays all over the keyboard.") Above all, perhaps, white people were well-spoken. She told about a meeting with some white people who came to town during which one Boley man—Theodore McCormick, in fact— said "we is." That, she said, was "humiliating. It's a big barrier to overcome, to get into the mainstream of speaking correctly."

White people, however, had nothing to learn from black people. "I can understand why there are white people who don't want to be bothered with black people. I can understand that. Because I know what we have to offer, and if you're going to have to stop and teach me along the way, you won't want to be bothered.

"The greatest thing we have going for us is that we are loyal. We are loyal to a fault. Every white man I know who's worth, say, a million dollars has a black man that he would trust with anything. Limousine to drive, a family. The only thing he wouldn't let that black man do is to marry his daughter. That's the only part of it I don't understand." Ashley, who often spoke in parables, told the story of a cousin who had spent her life working for a white man. She still lived down South. "I went down there with the intention of getting her to come home with me and spend some time. She said, 'Velma, I can't go right now because Doctor is away on vacation and I have to take care of his house.' This girl is living in what might have been a house, what might have been twenty-four by twenty-four. The windows look like somebody took a saw and cut a square out of the wood and then placed leather hinges on it.

"Now, that was her window. In the summertime she would take a frame that she had with a screen on it and stick it in the window. Now, that's the way she was living, in this man's back yard. Not asking why, nothing; she's just blind loyal. She helped to rear him. She's—oh, I guess she would be well into her nineties now. She might not even be working now. If she had to have medical attention, or she dies, she'll get whatever she actually needed. She didn't live in the House. And she wouldn't even consider coming out here for two weeks.

"I mean, getting back to this now, I would say that one of the greatest things we have going for us is that we are loyal to people who put their trust in us. I'm sorry I can't say we are loyal to each other in the same way, because we're not." When Ashley said "people," she meant "white people."

A last parable: "Maybe I told you about the black boy who was reared by white people down at Okemah? Mr. and Mrs. Berry had a servant—I mean, the woman came in on a regular basis. If the weather was bad, she stayed there. They treated her more like a member of the family than they did as somebody working, but she knew where her place was and stayed there. This woman became suddenly ill, and died, but before she died she asked Mrs. Berry if she would take care of her son. She told her, 'Yes, he won't suffer for anything. And I'll teach him.' "

"Mrs. Berry raised him from a little baby," Ashley continued. "If he were in this room now with you and four or five other white men, and I were in that dining room listening, I wouldn't be able to tell who was a black man. He sounded just like you. When he was eighteen, he spoke just as well as you do now. Do you see what I mean?

"I'm not one of these persons that's black and, regardless of what's the situation, I like my situation. No, I don't. I've always wanted better for us than what we were getting. That's why I fought so hard to get the school to where children would be proud to say, 'I am from Boley.' "

"THE GRAND HAM"

RACIAL IMAGINATION IN THE OLD WORLD

■

Who was the first black separatist? The question implies a prior one: Who was the first black? The scientific consensus today is that humans like us originated in Africa some hundred thousand years ago. What skin color they had is hard to say. To the extent that skin color, from an evolutionary point of view, correlates with anything, it correlates with climate. Africa was once cooler than it is now, but within the evolutionary life of Homo sapiens it has always been on the warm side. So presumably our distant ancestors were darker than many of us are today. Migrations took some of them to new climes, where they experienced a very gradual lightening. The geneticist Luigi Luca Cavalli-Sforza believes that Europeans, who would become the white people known to modernity, were a mixture of Asian and African—65 percent and 35 percent, respectively, give or take 8 percent—and that the migrations that created this mixture were relatively late, about thirty thousand years ago.

Color variations are visible in the art of Egypt beginning in the third millennium B.C., and it would appear that, in northeast Africa and the eastern Mediterranean, they had some significance. What that significance was it is difficult to know. Perhaps it was simply the sort of thing one noticed in passing. Skin color as an identifier of people is conspicuously missing from the Pentateuch, the first five books of the Bible, which narrates events throughout northeast Africa, the Middle East, and the Arabian Peninsula. Its stories concern some peoples who were indisputably dark-skinned, such as the Ethiopians or Cushites, yet these peoples are not identified as black; nor are others called white. (In Numbers 12:10, God does punish Miriam by making her the color of "snow," but this is a skin disease, not a racial curse.) The "black and beautiful" in Song of Solomon 1:5 refers poetically to sunburn from too much time in the vineyard. The first biblical reference to skin color as an inherited marker appears in Jeremiah, whose author lived several centuries after the historical events of the Pentateuch and the death of Moses. "Can Ethiopians change their skin," Jeremiah asks, "or leopards their spots? Then also you can do good who are accustomed to evil." This is a wispy thread from which to hang any conclusion about racial thinking among eastern Mediterranean peoples in the early sixth century B.C. (Besides, Jeremiah was rescued from imprisonment in a cistern by an Ethiopian.) Skin color is most noticeable in the Hebrew Bible by its absence—despite the fact that the various books cover an area that had both light and dark peoples, and despite the authors' obsession with genealogies and tribal purity.

The Greek historian Herodotus, writing a century and a half after Jeremiah, notes skin color from time to time, specifically black skin, which he evidently saw as exceptional. It was the color of peoples in Ethiopia, in the unknown lands south of the Sahara, and in India. While this color is, to Herodotus, unusual, it has no negative connotations or indeed connotations of any kind other than suggesting a nearness to the sun. Herodotus refers to Ethiopians (Greek for "burned-faced ones") as reputedly the tallest, longest-lived, and "most beautiful men in the world." Their king, facing down the empire-building Persian Cambyses in the 520s B.C., may have been not only good-looking but unusually sensible. Addressing Cambyses' spies, the Ethiopian king, according to Herodotus, said that the Persian was unjust in his expansionism. "Were he just," the king says of Cambyses, "he would not have coveted other land besides his own, nor would he have led into slavery men who have never done him any harm. Here, now, give him this bow, and do you speak to him these words: 'The king of the Ethiopians counsels the king of the Persians that when you Persians can draw so easily, as I do now, bows as big as this one, then come against the long-lived Ethiopians—and come in overwhelming force. Till then, be grateful to the gods who have not put it into the heads of the sons of the Ethiopians to win land additional to their own.' "

As far as written history is concerned, the best opportunities in the ancient world for dark-skinned and light-skinned people to meet each other—and, therefore, to have the possibility of giving their respective skin colors some meaning—were in Egypt and on either side of the Red Sea and the Gulf of Aden, though Herodotus locates an Ethiopian community on Cyprus. It is interesting in this respect that some biblical confusion exists about two places closely associated with Africa: Cush and Sheba, or Seba. The latter was apparently in what is now Yemen, at the southern tip of the Arabian Peninsula, but biblical geographers also located it in Ethiopia. Similarly, biblical Cush is generally considered to have been in what is now upper Egypt and Sudan, but there was another Cush in Arabia. The two most famous "black" women in the Bible, neither of whom is identified there as black, are Moses' wife, Zipporah (of Cush), and the Queen of Sheba. But which Cush, and which Sheba? Were these women black, or not? The Bible answers neither question definitively. One might guess that the biblical authors did not think the answers were important. It would be up to later writers to turn the Red Sea from a highway into a racially significant barrier between black "Africa" and not-so-black "Arabia."

Later writers would find all manner of phenomena in the Bible that aren't there. One of the things they discovered was that all black people descended from Ham, the son of Noah, and that Noah said the sons of Ham should be slaves. It took about ten centuries to develop this theory, which is based on Genesis 9:18–27:

> The sons of Noah who went out of the ark were Shem, Ham, and Japheth. Ham was the father of Canaan. These three were the sons of Noah; and from these the whole earth was peopled. Noah, a man of the soil, was the first to plant a vineyard. He drank some of the wine and became drunk, and he lay uncovered in his tent. And Ham, the father of Canaan, saw the nakedness of his father, and told his two brothers outside. Then Shem and Japheth took a garment, laid it on both their shoulders, and walked backward and covered the nakedness of their father; their faces were turned away, and they did not see their father's nakedness. When Noah awoke from his wine and knew what his youngest son had done to him, he said, "Cursed be Canaan; lowest of slaves shall he be to his brothers."
>
> He also said, "Blessed by the Lord my God be Shem; and let Canaan be his slave. May God make space for Japheth, and let him live in the tents of Shem; and let Canaan be his slave."

According to Genesis, the sons of Ham went on to settle much of northeast Africa and considerable portions of Palestine and the eastern Mediterranean coast, much of the Arabian Peninsula, Syria, and Mesopotamia. If this was the case, then many indeed are the sons of Ham; and we should note that in Genesis the specifically cursed sons of Canaan are placed not in Africa but in Palestine and some Phoenician cities. The curse against Ham's progeny—rather, against Canaan's sons—does not come up again, despite many opportunities.

Indeed, the Ham story may well have been related to the Israelites' need to find a scriptural basis for their rule over the Canaanites, who preceded them in Palestine.

Nevertheless, the words were there, waiting for opportunistic interpretation. And there was at least some significance attached to skin tone in the ancient world by the fifth century B.C. (Sadly, the Greek epic poem *Aethiopis* has not survived. It was among a cycle of lost poems, the "Epic Cycle," narrating world history from the beginning to the late heroic age, and probably written in the sixth or seventh century B.C.) Homer had described the Ethiopians as the most distant of peoples, and this, along with the dark coloring, flat noses, "woolly" hair, and climatological speculations one gleans from Xenophanes and Herodotus, provided a rudimentary template that would develop over some two millennia. At one end of the earth, to the north, live very white people (Thracians in Xenophanes, later Scythians, Turks, Slavs). At the other end live black people (Cushites, Ethiopians, Nubians, Zanj, Moors, Garamantes, Beja). Their distinctiveness results from climate; whites get little sun, blacks get a lot. The norm is Mediterranean—the land of our ancient authors. To them their own skin tone was unremarkable, indeed colorless.

It is hardly surprising that this basic structure would acquire some ethical weightings. The possibility occurs as early as Aristotle (fourth century B.C.), who wrote in his *Politics*: "Those who live in a cold climate and in Europe are full of spirit, but wanting in intelligence and skill; and therefore they retain comparative freedom, but have no political organization, and are incapable of ruling over others. Whereas the natives of Asia are intelligent and inventive, but they are wanting in spirit, and therefore they are always in a state of subjection and slavery. But the Hellenic race, which is situated between them, is likewise intermediate in character, being high-spirited and also intelligent. Hence it continues free, and is the best-governed of any nation, and, if it could be formed into one state, would be able to rule the world." Aristotle does not speak here of Ethiopia (or of skin color), but the basic principle—of a superior "temperate" people sandwiched between two intemperate ones and having the virtues but not the vices of both—could and would be applied along a north-south, white-black axis.

There seems to have been a weak classical consensus that, as for Menander (342–?292 B.C.), the varieties of skin color simply indicated the diversity of humankind. The turning point, as far as moralizing about color goes, was probably in the influential writings of Origen (A.D. ?185–?254), who lived in Alexandria, Egypt, and was the first great scholar among the Greek Christian Fathers. Origen argued for equality before God, picking up the classical rhetorical device of using Ethiopians to represent that which is furthest from the norm. Origen insisted that the mission of the Church could extend even to the

Ethiopians. The essential concept is in the word *even*: the distant Ethiopians, so different in appearance, illustrated by their acceptance of God the universality of the Church. This would be a double-edged sword for Ethiopians and the "blackness" they represented.

Black as a color already had associations with death and evil. As early as A.D. 100 the Devil had been nicknamed the Black One. Origen played with these color associations in discussing the Ethiopians. Contrasting outer blackness (being Ethiopian and burned by the sun) with inner blackness (sin), Origen discussed the "black and beautiful" woman in Song of Solomon: "We ask in what way is she black and in what way fair without whiteness. She has repented of her sins; conversion has bestowed beauty upon her and she is sung as 'beautiful' . . . if you repent, your soul will be 'black' because of your former sins, but because of your penitence your soul will have something of what I may call an Ethiopian beauty." It is revealing that Origen felt he had to ask how someone could be fair without looking white. His notion of Ethiopian beauty suggests an answer: he had to argue that one could be black but still be beautiful by converting. Apparently, he need not say that one could be white and beautiful, because that was assumed.

The black Ethiopians thus came to symbolize both the unimportance of color and its importance. The Christian Gregory of Nyssa (?335–?394) may have been the first to fuse the real and the spiritual in the concept of becoming white. He wrote that in the city of God "Gentiles become dwellers of the city; Babylonians, Jerusalemites; the prostitute, a virgin; Ethiopians, radiantly white." The Ethiopian's color and the prostitute's condition were in some way seen as similarly distant from God. This schema was picked up by Gregory's contemporary Saint Jerome and by Saint Augustine (354–430). Himself a North African, Augustine wrote of Ethiopians: "Those are called to the faith who were black, just they, so that it may be said to them, 'Ye were sometimes darkness but now are ye light in the Lord.' They are indeed called black but let them not remain black, for out of these is made the church to whom it is said: 'Who is she that cometh up having been made white?' " The language is clearly symbolic, but it must be said that all language that attributes meaning to skin color, apart from some speculations about climatic effects, is symbolic. And the language of blackness used here obviously accords it a low status—with the understanding that it was part of the early Christian genius, and especially of Augustine's writing, to make the low high. Augustine argued that before God we are all Ethiopians, and all slaves. Yet in life he did not blacken his skin, sell himself into slavery, or move to Ethiopia to make himself more divinely abject and so nearer to God. Unfortunately, there don't appear to be any sources telling us what black Christians in this period thought about being made white.

There are, however, Muslim sources on the subject, from a slightly later period. The circle around the prophet Muhammad included people of Ethiopian descent, among them Bilal, the first muezzin, who gives the call to prayer. Ethiopian Christian forces had been active on the Arabian Peninsula since the early sixth century. In 615 eighty Muslims, including Muhammad's daughter Rukayya, received refuge in Ethiopia. A close relationship developed between Christian Ethiopia and the persecuted Muslims, and when the king of Ethiopia died, Muhammad said the Muslim funerary prayer for him. In short, there was regular contact between black Ethiopia and not-precisely-black Arabia, across the Red Sea, in the sixth and seventh centuries.

The Arabs' attitudes toward people whose skin looked different appear to have changed dramatically after the first Muslim conquests in the seventh and eighth centuries. The Muslims were imposing a religiously inspired government, based, in principle, on the universal Koran, but in practice carrying a great deal of cultural arrogance and miscellaneous tribal baggage. Muslim warriors lost sight of the famous Koranic verse "Men, We have created you from a male and a female, and made you into nations and tribes, that you might get to know one another. The noblest of you in God's sight is he who is most righteous." Soon enough, the black poet Suhaym (d. 660), born a slave, could write these sad lines: "Though I am a slave my soul is nobly free / Though I am black of color my character is white," and "If my color were pink, women would love me / But the Lord has marred me with blackness."

The equation of slavery and blackness was not unique to Suhaym and would quickly grow common. This requires some explanation, because it was destined to become an article of faith among Christians, Muslims, and Jews alike—part of the content of blackness. Dark-skinned slaves had existed in the Mediterranean world for some time. They had been present in Egypt (as had dark-skinned conquerors) for many centuries. Outside Egypt at least some of the black people represented in classical art were slaves. A trader's handbook from the first century A.D. records exporting slave markets in the Horn of Africa ports at Malao and Opone. The Roman Empire needed vast numbers of slaves, acquiring them through war and trade and as tribute. One estimate puts the empire's slave intake between 50 B.C. and A.D. 150 at half a million per year. Such a number is staggering to contemplate; the majority of these slaves would not have been sub-Saharan African, but some portion was. Christian expansion in the early centuries after Christ—like the preceding Jewish expansion, which reached the African Atlantic coast—would at least have increased the exposure of Christians to black slaves. The Arab Muslim conquests in Africa enabled a commerce that dwarfed any Christian, not to mention vestigial Jewish, trade in black slaves; an unprecedented number of dark Africans could soon be found in Mediterranean cities. The sadness of Suhaym can be appreciated in this context.

Yet we should remember that white slaves, too, were numerous north of the Sahara. Mediterranean and Levantine peoples not only enslaved each other, they purchased huge numbers of people from the north; the word *slave* itself comes from *Slav*. The classical paradigm of a temperate, superior people between extremes of white and black served later generations as an explanation of why whites and blacks were more appropriate as slaves. One writer at the turn of the tenth century expounded the merits of the temperate Iraqis, "who are done to a turn in the womb. They do not come out with something between blonde, buff, blanched, and leprous coloring, such as the infants dropped from the wombs of the women of the Slavs and others of similar light complexion; nor are they overdone until they are burned, so that the child comes out something between black, murky, malodorous, stinking, and crinkly-haired, with uneven limbs, deficient minds, and depraved passions, such as the Zanj, the Ethiopians, and other blacks who resemble them. The Iraqis are neither half-baked dough nor burned crust, but between the two." The temperate zone could even be extended, with sublime self-interest, as far north as Germany, where Albertus Magnus picked it up in the thirteenth century. The hot south, he wrote, produced black people naturally "quick-witted in invention and outstanding in philosophy and magic"; the cold north produced whites, vigorous but "dull-witted and untutored"; while in temperate climes people "live easily among themselves, practice justice, keep their word, respect peace and the society of men."

You might think Europeans to the north, in their paleness, would have had firmer ideas on the curse of Ham and black slavery, but the opposite was the case. While European Christians did take Scripture as their main guide in understanding the world, almost none of them had any sound idea of what was actually in the Bible. Before the advent of printing in the fifteenth century, and Martin Luther's emphasis on Bible reading in the succeeding century, very few people had much access to the Bible. Similarly, the vast majority of people would never see a map in their lives. The very notion of Asia, Africa, and Europe as continents was extremely fuzzy; these names, when used at all, represented the eastern, southern, and northern coasts of the Mediterranean, respectively, with indefinite hinterlands beyond them. One early-fourteenth-century map called Europe Africa, and vice versa, though this was a fairly clear mistake even then.

So we may not be surprised that the geographic placement of Noah's sons Japheth, Shem, and Ham varied considerably over time. The cleanest textual tradition with influence over Christian writers extends from the Jewish writer Flavius Josephus, in the first century A.D., who had Japheth's descendants in

Europe and Asia, Ham's in Africa and Asia, and Shem's in the Middle East. Presumably the priority for Josephus, as for any Jewish commentator, was to locate Shem's progeny, because Genesis clearly gives Shem as the ancestor of the Israelites. However, Christians also sometimes laid claim to ancestry through Shem, in accord with their own wish to see themselves as the chosen people. In any case, Ham and Japheth were all over the map. An early medieval Jewish source has Japheth in Ethiopia, rather than Ham or his son Cush—an identification repeated in several fifteenth-century Christian sources.

The immensely influential *Travels* of the pseudonymous Sir John Mandeville—a collection of tales from books rather than the real thing, and by an unknown author—had Shem taking Africa, Japheth getting Europe (some editions change this to Ethiopia), and Ham in Asia. Mandeville writes, in the 1371 edition, "Ham was the mightiest and the most powerful and from him came more descendants than any of the others. From one of his sons [Cush, in Genesis], Nimrod the giant was born, who was the first king in the world and who started to build the tower of Babel." This identification of Ham with royal power—Mandeville once considered the Khan of the Mongols to be the Grand Ham—may be what led the house of Luxembourg and, later, the Habsburg Maximilian I to be portrayed as sons of Ham. The *Nürnberg Chronicle*, as late as 1500, has Ham's descendants (with one exception) as white. The black descendant is white in some editions, black in others and on one occasion migrates to a different chart and becomes a descendant of Shem.

The noble "white" and Asian Hams somehow coexisted, in late-medieval writings, with their opposite, the servile Ham. This Ham was also white, or nearly so. He served to make sense of the existence in Europe of serfs, the majority of the population; Ham helped justify the persistence of servility in a changing European culture. In non-Mediterranean Europe, by the fourteenth century, most people were Christian; the last pagan holdouts, the Lithuanians, had been forcibly converted by 1386. And most people were no longer slaves. Slavery disappeared very gradually among what later generations would consider white people, and for a host of reasons. A full-blown slaveholding economy was the rule throughout Europe until the eighth century A.D. at the earliest. It waned, thereafter, very unevenly; perhaps a tenth of England's population was still in slavery by the tenth century.

Among the many reasons for slavery's decline in non-Mediterranean Europe were the solidification of Christianity and the inefficiency, in new political conditions, of making people work by making them slaves. Christians had happily been enslaving Christians for centuries, but by the eighth century, the Church, as a sociopolitical structure, had a good reason for changing its policies and disapproving slavery: Christians were in fierce competition with Muslims, who did not, as a rule, enslave other Muslims. This was one aspect of Islam's appeal in its spread westward, with Muslim invaders inciting Christian slaves against their masters. Christianity could hardly prosper if it appeared to be the gospel of relative unfreedom.

Meanwhile, the main sources of new slaves for Christians—the pagan peoples of Britain, the Slavic lands, and other northern and eastern territories—were drying up as those peoples accepted the faith. So there weren't enough pagans left at home, and enslaving, or continuing the enslavement of, one's Christian neighbors had become politically unwise. At the same time, the fragmented and competitive structure of northern medieval society forced rulers to evolve a system in which their laborers had a greater share in social power than that of a slave. Expansionary European feudal lords from the tenth century onward had to lure peasants into loyalty. Slavery would not count as a lure. By 1226 Toulouse was a "free city"—residence there of a year and a day conferred freedom—and other cities such as Korčula and Bologna offered a similar appeal.

Central to this process was a new sense of shared citizenship-like culture that could not accommodate slave status. One shared with others a religion and a place and even a common language; loyalty to a lord or city took these as a premise and extended them in people's minds. Many of those minds could remember slavery, which had been the norm in an older order—and which grew into a powerful symbol of what one was not.

Yet the differences between slavery and serfdom, while great, were not always considered great enough by serfs. Peasant revolts had been a serious concern of feudal elites since the eleventh century, and especially after the English rising of 1381. Rebel serfs often cited the Christian belief in human equality as grounds for revolt. However little peasants might know of the Bible, it took no effort to understand, for example, that the last shall be first, and the first last. Medieval thinkers responded to this problem in several ways. An early, and increasingly useless, strategy was to claim that servile populations descended from those who had chosen the wrong side in wars against Muslims or pagans, and so had inherited servile status. A related, more lasting Christian variant of this argument held that all people were slaves in that all partook of Adam's original sin—though this belief never adequately explained why some people (the majority) were more slave-like than others. Here is where the curse of Ham came in: it made it possible to say that one human portion was naturally servile. That is how white serfs, in the opinion of some late-medieval writers, became sons of Ham.

———

In the Mediterranean, slavery continued in force and had a color scheme on which to draw. The importance of color should not be overstated even there. There are many ways of identifying people, color being one, and color certainly was important in labeling chattel. Barcelona records from the late thirteenth century show how ethnic (or tribal), religious, and color labels were all used to distinguish one slave from another: Moor of intermediate color (*loro*, or neither white nor black, also expressed as "olive colored"), black Saracen (*Saracen* meaning Muslim), white Saracen, *loro* Saracen, white Tatar, Bosnian, Greek. In color terms, for Barcelona in the latter half of the thirteenth century, according to one sample, the slave population was about 52 percent white, 20 percent Saracen, 18 percent *loro*, and 10 percent black. Obviously the many terms could overlap; someone identified as Saracen might have been white, black, brown, olive. And we should always remember that these many-hued slaves were to some degree assimilated, their descendants eventually becoming free. One scholar has tentatively estimated that, in the period 700–1500, over four million sub-Saharan Africans, that is, "black Africans," were transported across the desert to Mediterranean markets. They could not all have died without having children. Given the scale of the trade, we can safely say that a large, if unmeasurable, number of Mediterranean and European people have ancestors who were African or, if you like, "black."

In the Mediterranean, unlike farther north, it made sense to have a word meaning "intermediate" to designate people between the understood extremes of white and black. It was a practical term, as it corresponded to the long-standing notion of Mediterranean oliveness, or whatever it was, as a norm. A rough equating of white and black, northern and southern, as naturally inferior populations continued, within the Mediterranean, well into the fourteenth century, as seen in the writings of two of the greatest thinkers of the late-medieval period, the Jewish philosopher and theologian Moses Maimonides and the Muslim historian Ibn Khaldun. Maimonides, born in Córdoba, Spain, in 1135, composed his *Guide for the Perplexed* toward the end of the twelfth century while working as a physician in Egypt. In a concluding passage concerning nearness to God, he offers the simile of a king whose subjects are partly in the country and partly abroad. Those in the country are trying by various means to approach the king. Those abroad are uninterested. The king represents God. But who are these uninterested people, symbolically represented as foreigners? "The people who are abroad," Maimonides writes, "are all those that have no religion, neither one based on speculation nor one received by tradition. Such are the extreme Turks who wander about in the north, the Kushites who live in the south, and those in our country who are like these. I consider these as irrational beings, and not as human beings; they are below mankind, but above monkeys, since they have the shape and form of man, and a mental faculty above that of the monkey." These irrational beings provided a disproportionate share of the slave population.

Maimonides does not mention skin color, though by this point it is likely that north and south, Turk and Cushite, sufficiently conveyed notions of color. The Tunisian Muslim Ibn Khaldun, in *An Introduction to History* (written between 1374 and 1377 in a fortified Algerian village), stated that the qualities of peoples in the far north and south come primarily from climate. That is why blacks are black and their qualities "close to those of dumb animals . . . The same applies to the Slavs. The reason for this is that their remoteness from being temperate produces in them a disposition and character similar to those of the dumb animals, and they become correspondingly remote from humanity."

Ibn Khaldun tends not to describe the Northerners as white, preferring ethnic terms. He does, however, rather brilliantly remark, "The inhabitants of the north are not called by their color, because the people who established the conventional meanings of words were themselves white. Thus, whiteness was something usual and common to them, and they did not see anything sufficiently remarkable in it to cause them to use it as a specific term." But who precisely were these people establishing "the conventional meanings of words"? They certainly were not Slavs or Celts, Jutes, Germans, Finns, Scythians, or Turks. Nor were they black; one presumes blacks found blackness as unexceptional as whites found whiteness. The establishers of meaning were people like Ibn Khaldun and Maimonides—or Herodotus and Xenophanes—Mediterranean, temperate people. And such people seem in general, at least since classical times, to have considered themselves more white than not. Herodotus did not note whiteness in the way he noted blackness; as far as physical markers went, Mediterranean authors of the classical period and later were more fascinated by Northerners' hair than by their light skin. Mediterranean terms for dark people tended to incorporate a color element, while their terms for light people usually did not. In medieval Arabic the same word was used for black slave and black person, while the word for a white slave never came to mean "a white." From classical times, then, despite the appealingly geometric north-south, black-white division, there appears to have been a Mediterranean bias toward thinking of oneself as closer to "white" than to "black." And, for all of us in the Western Hemisphere, it is Mediterranean people who have recorded most of our early history. That an antiwhite sentiment existed is undeniable; the antiblack sentiment was stronger.

Who knows why? Perhaps the fact that outdoor work makes people darker, and that such peasant labor was associated with low social status, had a decisive effect on color symbolism. Perhaps the repeated military incursions, often suc-

/

cessful, of white or whitish tribes from the steppes and the German lands, even from the northern Atlantic coasts—maybe these focused Mediterranean minds on the tribal distinctions to be made among whites, or at least troubled any easy contempt. The history of skin color might have been different if the boastful king of Ethiopia had taken his big bow and long-lived men against Cambyses in Persia. But dark-skinned expansionism northward was nearly nonexistent if you except the centuries of North African domination in Spain. Mediterranean peoples experienced black Africans, especially after the Muslim conquests, mainly as slaves. White people they knew in a wider variety of roles and, indeed, a wider variety of colors; Arab writers sometimes describe them as pink, red (a color term also applied to Persians), and even, at an imaginative extreme, blue. Finally, the competition between olive Mediterraneans and white Northerners was, from the seventh century onward, primarily religious—Muslims versus Christians—and so faith, rather than skin color, was the leading means of identification for both sides. Africans, by contrast, presented no political or doctrinal unity that might have superseded physical appearance as a collective identification. When dark Africans did come north in groups, they did so as Muslims. When they arrived in the north as individuals, they did so, to an apparently decisive extent, as "blacks."

Not long after Ibn Khaldun published his thoughts on white people as dumb animals, some of those same people would sail their ships down the Atlantic coast of Africa and take the story of blackness to a new level. Paradoxically, perhaps, it would be these somewhat despised white people—so like blacks, when viewed from the Mediterranean—who would give the legend of Ham its modern form.

European expansion into Africa began in earnest in the thirteenth century, along the North African coast. There seems to have been little anxious preoccupation with skin color in this period, and it isn't hard to see why. The North African population in the thirteenth century must have been exceedingly mixed in appearance, whatever Ibn Khaldun's thoughts on the matter. Muslim slave traders had been posted in West Africa since the ninth century. From that time forward the black slave trade was key to political developments both in the savanna and trading belt of sub-Saharan Africa—from Senegal clear across to the Red Sea and Ethiopia—and in North Africa. One important political factor was blacks enslaved as soldiers. The first substantial Muslim government in North Africa west of Egypt, the ninth-century Aghlabid dynasty of Tunisia, used black slave forces; so did the mid-century Abbasid governor of Egypt, with black slaves from the upper Nile and lighter ones from Greece and the Black Sea ports. The tenth-century Fatimid dynasty, based at the new capital city of Cairo and active from Morocco to Palestine, also had a substantial black element. The economic historian Ralph A. Austen conservatively estimates the number of slaves shipped north across the Sahara, between the years 900 and 1100, at 1,740,000—working as miners, agricultural laborers, and domestic servants as well as soldiers. Austen has another 1,650,000 slaves across the Sahara in the period 1100–1400. It is safe to say, then, that dark faces were not a novelty anywhere along the southern Mediterranean coast in the thirteenth century, when northern Mediterranean merchants began to seek greater access to the trans-Sahara trade.

The thirteenth-century Europeans along the African coast mainly came from Spain (Aragon, Castile), Portugal, France, and Italy. Some were mercenaries—Portuguese served the rulers of Marrakesh around 1220, while a Catalan company soldiered for Tunis. Some were missionaries, most successfully the Dominicans, who opened an Arabic-study department in Tunis in 1250. More common were merchants; Sicilian traders had negotiated agreements with North African rulers since the eleventh century, followed by Pisans and Genoese. In the train of merchants came ambitious knights. Iberian kings had a strong interest in Africa, reviving an old Gothic dream. They had succeeded, bit by bit over centuries, in extending their power over Muslim Spain and the Balearic Islands. In 1291 the kings of Aragon and Castile actually met to divide up Africa into an east (Aragon) and a west (Castile). This foreshadowing of European imperialism went nowhere—neither kingdom had the strength or will to unseat the North African powers—but it indicates Iberian intentions. To the northern kings, invading Africa appeared a fairly natural extension of the "Reconquest" of Spain.

Looking south, Europeans on the Mediterranean African coast saw many things: strong local powers, followed by a great deal of sand, and beyond that a little-known but plentiful source of slaves, agricultural products, salt, and, above all, gold. Sub-Saharan Africa had a lot of gold—about two-thirds of the world supply in 1350. If anyone had doubted this, their skepticism would have been overcome by the famous pilgrimage of Musa, the ruler of Mali, to Mecca in 1324. Stopping in Egypt for three months with his entourage, he threw around enough gold to cause a serious inflation. So the Europeans, seeing that their chances in the desert were small, began to finance voyages westward, with faint hopes of outflanking the Sahara trade and getting gold from the source.

The way ahead was not obvious. In the same year, 1291, that Aragon and Castile wishfully carved up Africa, the luckless Vivaldi brothers sailed west from Genoa, "for the regions of India by way of the Ocean," and were never heard from again. But more ships went, and by the 1330s Europeans had gained a pretty sound understanding of the Canary Islands, off the Atlantic coast of Africa. The king of Portugal said he had "turned the eyes of our mind" toward the Canaries in 1345. The king of Castile that same year staked a claim to not only the Canaries but the larger goal of Africa, which he imaginatively asserted had belonged to his putative Visigothic ancestors, saying, "the kingdoms of Africa are of our conquest." By 1351 two missionaries from Majorca had established a diocese on Grand Canary. More ships sailed, often with investment from the ubiquitous Genoese; and pirates raided the Canaries, too, taking slaves. In 1393 France got involved. The scramble for Africa—and the scramble for the Americas—would be rehearsed in the Canary Islands.

The conquest of the Canaries became a serious affair in 1402 with the arrival of Jean de Béthencourt, an unscrupulous freebooter at the head of a patchwork crew. Or, as his loyal scribes, the monk Pierre Bontier and the priest Jean Le Verrier, begin their account, "It was the custom in old times to record in writing the deeds of chivalry and marvellous feats of the valiant conquerors of former days . . . We here propose to speak of the enterprise undertaken by the Sieur de Béthencourt, chevalier and baron, born in the Kingdom of France in Normandy, who set out from his house in Grainville . . ." The conquest of the Canaries was recorded within the mind-set of a romance novel. A nobleman sets out from his house one day and conquers the world. The romance is of a very particular kind, as when one Berthin attempts to placate a troop of Spaniards with wine, food, and women: "he even took away by force, and against their will, some women who had come from France, and delivered them up to the Spaniards, who dragged them down to the beach, and violated them in spite of their loud cries and shrieks of distress."

What were these people thinking, and where did they think they were? They did not think much, and they had little notion where they were. They grasped at religion and greed and romance as their unsteady guides; they blundered. They had no idea they were making our future. The Canaries, as they found them, were populated by a people about whom relatively little is known. Bontier and Le Verrier discuss them, on the whole, in positive terms: "in all the world you will nowhere meet with a finer or better formed people [gens], both male and female, than the people of these islands. They are very intelligent, and require only instruction." The inhabitants of one island are described as "of strong intelligence, and very firm in their law [loy], and have a church where they make their sacrifices." The Canarians had few manufactures or substantial buildings, and were underdressed by European standards. Our French authors describe the people of each island in respectful language, dwelling on warlike qualities (considered good), diet (barley, hogs, sheep, delicious goat's meat, and, as one would expect exiled Frenchmen to note, excellent cheeses), political structure, and physical appearance.

The women were uniformly beautiful. At no point do the Frenchmen mention skin tone, nor do they speculate as to whether the natives were from anywhere except the Canaries. Bontier and Le Verrier do not wonder, for example, whether the Canarians came "from Africa," even though they had Africa very much on their minds. Much of the thrust of their narrative consists in recommending that de Béthencourt be funded to conquer and convert the mainland, which our authors understood as inhabited by "Saracen" Muslims immediately to the east, and farther to the east and south by various peoples including one group, isolated on an island, called "black people." The authors believed that as one proceeded down the western coast of Africa, "the country of the Moors" gave way to "a great kingdom called Guinoye," or Guinea (derived from the Arabic sources' "Ganah," as in modern Ghana). In short, the two Frenchmen in 1406 knew perfectly well where Africa was and that it contained some distinctly black people, but they did not attempt to corral the Canarians into categories of black or white. Nor did they describe the Canarians as "natives," "tribes," or "primitives" in any sense; they naturally referred to them as "peoples" (*peuples* or *gens*).

Postwar twentieth-century historians have considered the Canarians the first Indians or native Americans, slated for imperialist extermination; relatedly, they have emphasized that the Canarians were not black, that they were part of a new third group between white and black with which the European imagination had to grapple. But these two curious and observant Frenchmen, at least, did no grappling at all. However compelling the black-Indian-white triad would later be, it seems to have had no purchase on the minds of Bontier and Le Verrier. Primarily, the monk and the priest saw the Canarians as pagans to be brought to Christ; secondarily, they were people to be conquered for France; finally, they were a potential obstacle between the conquerors and Canary resources. These three considerations the Frenchmen bound together, for example in their discussion of archil, a dye plant: "if only this island be once conquered and brought into the Christian faith, this plant will prove of great value to the lord of the country."

From a modern perspective the most remarkable aspect of the Frenchmen's narrative is how unremarkable they found the Canarians to be, and how quickly their conversion and conquest, and the exploitation of their lands, could be integrated into Bontier's and Le Verrier's existing concepts. But is this really so strange? Christian powers from Jerusalem to Gibraltar, Scotland to Riga, had been conquering local pagans, converting them, and then exploiting their resources from late Roman times. They had done it with savage Britons and wild Lithuanians, shaggy Goths, godless Germans. This was the story of Christianity's advance, and it would not have been ancient history to a conquering churchman in 1406. Its methods were the political norm. Invaders terrorize the populace until they can scare up some turncoats in the local leadership; the target elite splits; sooner or later a new leadership is installed by force, persuasion, and intermarriage; and history has a new Christian people. Ethnographic particularities, whether of the Finns or the Canarians, could certainly be of interest along the churchly way, but they were not central to the project. Ethnic, religious, and, at the limit, "racial" (that is, skin-color) concepts had overlapped since classical times, at least. Modern peoples have tended to fold ethnicities into nations, nations into races; we have tended to fold religions into the more secular idea of civilizations. Each of these concepts may then be read backward into history, more or less indefinitely. Musa's splendid spending habits in 1324 can be construed as an index of black or African civilizational achievement; the Normans' displaying of a decapitated Canarian man's head on a pike may be seen as a revealing episode in European or white imperialism. But if the concepts involved did not exist, or barely existed, at the time, can they honestly be used?

The myth of Ham, that lodestar of racial thinking, does make an appearance in Bontier and Le Verrier's narrative. The clerics devote several chapters to some highlights of the Pentateuch, intending them as a little catechism for "those of the island." In a typically late-medieval mix of biblical exegesis and scientific niggling, they write that God told Noah "to build an ark of wood squared and polished, and to smear it within and without with bitumen. Bitumen is a glue so strong and tenacious that when two pieces are brought together and joined with it, they cannot be separated by any means except by the natural blood of women's flowers." The churchly chroniclers go on to demonstrate their lack of access to Genesis by explaining that Nimrod, rather than Noah, presided over the earth's division into three parts: Shem got Asia, and Ham took Africa. Presumably Nimrod kept Europe for himself. The most striking thing about this catechistic chapter is that the clerics raise the Ham-Africa connection in the midst of their fund-raising appeal for the conquest of Africa, then drop it entirely. They do not argue that Ham is black, or Nimrod white. They draw no conclusions or even implications from this garbled story of the origins of humankind. Evidently, they were far more interested in the possibilities for using menstrual blood as a glue solvent than in dividing humanity into three. Yet they did want to conquer Africa, one might say regardless of what color the people there might be.

To that end, Bontier and Le Verrier introduce a description of sub-Saharan Africa. In the tradition of chivalric romance, this appears as the paraphrasing of an alleged book written by an alleged Spanish friar who had traveled across the continent, from Guinea to Ethiopia, through the realms of the Christians, "the Pagans, and the Sarracens." The friar's tale has him passing south along the coast from Morocco to "Guinea," then east "through many countries" to Nubia. He then proceeds down the Nile, sails back to Morocco, and down the coast once more, around Cape Bojador, to Guinea's River of Gold, where large ants bring up the precious metal as a by-product of their subterranean home building. Now, it's known that gold is not mined by giant ants, whether in Guinea or elsewhere (a similar story appears in Herodotus, with an Indian locale). Someone here is not telling the truth. However, the general picture of African rivers south of Cape Bojador, up which there are rich gold mines, was accurate; proceeding upriver and then eastward, one would indeed have passed many countries and eventually have reached Nubia. This was the sub-Saharan belt of states, with urban centers presiding over brief empires. The story as related mentions black people once, living on "an island named Paloye," but otherwise does not identify people by skin color or any other marker. This is the Africa the two Frenchmen in the Canaries expected to find if they and de Béthencourt could just get enough money. They expected to find lively states, one of them incidentally black, and there to conquer, convert, and exploit resources. Much of this did happen, though without Bontier and Le Verrier.

In the mid-fifteenth century, when Portuguese captains finally learned how to round Cape Bojador and navigate the African coast as it arced eastward, south of the Senegal River, to the Niger River delta, they encountered peoples with many centuries of experience at trading slaves and gold. Inland states from Lake Chad westward traded by camel caravan to the east and north, and by boat and portage to the west, downstream from the headwaters of the Senegal, Gambia, and Niger Rivers to the coast. An active trade existed as well along the Atlantic shore, though it was undertaken in smaller, shallow-draft boats rather than oceangoing vessels. European captains, privately funded and expected to make a profit, only gradually made their way into these trading zones. It took almost a century from the earliest settlement of the Canaries to the rounding of Cape Bojador, two hundred miles to the south. Regular trade as far as Benin did not begin until 1485. Over this period of a century and a half, such small European voyages made their money by bringing back to Europe gold, slaves, and a pepper called malaguetta.

This trade gradually caused a shift from the nearly colorless worldview of Bontier and Le Verrier to a heightened perception of "white" and "black." However many millions of black Africans had been integrated into Mediterranean society, including the European coastal regions, over the preceding centuries, the taking of large numbers of black people by Europeans was something new. Presumably black captives transported previously across the Sahara or up the East African coast became Muslims (and Christians)—their descendants certainly did—and in European eyes the descriptive category of black, as we have seen, overlapped considerably with more religious terms for Muslims, such as *Saracen* and *Moor*. These new black captives, by contrast, were generally pagan, and henceforth Europeans would learn to distinguish between Moors as Muslims and blacks (*nigri*, etc.) as pagans, with *black Moor* and *blackamoor* as bridging terms. A few northern Mediterranean dreamers had hoped to find a Christian kingdom south of Morocco; they wishfully extended the black Christian states of Ethiopia and Nubia westward in their minds, with the thought of an African (incidentally black) alliance creating a Christian belt that might then be tightened against North African Islam. An Ethiopian embassy had come to Spain in 1306 to propose a joint Christian effort against the Muslims; more than a century later, in 1428, the royal houses of Aragon and Ethiopia came close to concluding an alliance by marriage. Whatever ill opinions Iberians may have had concerning dark skin, they evidently did not preclude political alliance by the intimate means of marriage and reproduction. This was indeed what occurred between some prominent native Canarian converts and their erstwhile European conquerors, and it would happen soon in sub-Saharan black Africa.

Nonetheless, the combining of black skin and pagan faith in the bodies of significant numbers of enslaved captives brought about a turning point: it was the beginning of what one might call modern blackness, and thus of modern whiteness. This was a complex psychological process, first perceptible, with any clarity, in the narrative of the Portuguese royal chronicler Gomes Eanes de Zurara, writing in about 1453–1454 of African events in 1444. He describes the capture of a group of "Moors" near the mouth of the Senegal River. The Europeans,

> shouting out "St. James," "St. George," "Portugal," at once attacked them, killing and taking all they could. Then might you see mothers forsaking their children, and husbands their wives, each striving to escape as best he could. Some drowned themselves in the water; others thought to escape by hiding under their huts; others stowed their children among the seaweed, where our men found them afterwards, hoping they would thus escape notice. And at last our Lord God, who giveth a reward for every good deed, willed that for the toil they had undergone in his service, they should obtain victory over their enemies . . .

Zurara's language, so heartbreaking in its specificity, suggests that the Christians' military work could not easily be integrated into the chivalric conventions that had served Bontier and Le Verrier in the Canaries fifty years earlier. These hysterically terrified families were hardly enemies in any chivalric sense. Helpless, they appear not to have put up any resistance.

Zurara relates that the captives were taken to Portugal and displayed to Prince Henrique. The Portuguese group's leader addresses the prince, urging him to take his "royal fifth" of the merchandise, these people who have such "great sorrow . . . at seeing themselves away from the land of their birth, and placed in captivity, without having any understanding of what their end is to be." The next day the captives are assembled in a field near the town of Lagos, "a marvellous sight; for amongst them were some white enough, fair to look upon, and well proportioned; others were less white like mulattoes; others again were as black as Ethiops, and so ugly, both in features and in body, as almost to appear (to those who saw them) the images of a lower hemisphere. But what heart could be so hard as not to be pierced with piteous feelings to see that company? For some kept their heads low and their faces bathed in tears, looking one upon another; others stood groaning very dolorously, looking up to the height of heaven, fixing their eyes upon it, crying out loudly, as if asking help of the Father of Nature; others struck their faces with the palms of their hands, throwing themselves at full length upon the ground; others made their lamentations in the manner of a dirge, after the custom of their country."

Then these people were divided into fifths for distribution, "and then it was needful to part fathers from sons, husbands from wives, brothers from brothers. No respect was shewn to either friends or relations, but each fell where his lot took him. O powerful fortune, that with thy wheel doest and undoest, compassing the matters of this world as pleaseth thee, do thou at least put before the eyes of that miserable race some understanding of matters to come; that they may receive some consolation in the midst of their great sorrow. And you who are so busy in making that division of the captives, look with pity upon so much misery; and see how they cling one to the other, so that you can hardly separate." Portuguese from the surrounding region had left off work to see the Africans. As they watched them, in the chaotic scene of their division, some helped to separate the people, while others wept.

Zurara first justified the capture and distribution of Africans as slaves in religious terms. They would be brought to the Lord by these means, and Zurara speaks of generations of their descendants in Portugal as "good and true Christians." One of these early captives Zurara later knew as a Franciscan friar. He relates at some length how popular these slaves were in Portugal, so much so that they often lived as "free servants" did, while others were "set free and married to women who were natives of the land." Zurara does not dwell on the skin color of these new Christians, though elsewhere, discussing another slavery episode, he writes: "And here you must note that these blacks were Moors like the others, though their slaves, in accordance with ancient custom, which I believe to have been because of the curse which, after the Deluge, Noah laid upon his son Cain, cursing him in this way:—that his race should be subject to all the other races of the world. And from his race these blacks are descended . . ." Zurara also writes that at least some Africans "had no knowledge of bread or wine, and they were without the covering of clothes, or the lodgment of houses; and worse than all, through the great ignorance that was in them, in that they had no understanding of good."

In Zurara's account the Portuguese clearly wondered about their own understanding of good. Some separate the people, but others weep, while Zurara seems to have done both. The possibility of redemption, for the slavers and the enslaved, comes through religious conversion of the latter. This is not the traditional matter of converting Muslims. Though he has trouble locating the difference, Zurara struggles to separate Muslim Moors from pagan blacks. It is important to do so because, in this moment, a new type of person is being created (the black) and a new social idea: inherited racial slavery, rather than, say, slavery as a result of religious war or simply sale. The black slave trade was and would be propelled first by economic desire, but Zurara needed something more than this, something more, even, than the furtherance of the Church, to make sense of what he saw. And he reached for blackness. The materials were there for the grasping: the rough reality of skin color, the itinerant fragments of the Ham story, a certain distaste among some European and Mediterranean peoples for dark skin, a feeling that the heavily dressed in stone houses have a deserved edge over those with light clothing and houses of wood and straw. But only now, nineteen hundred years after Herodotus wrote of the woolly hair and black skin of his beautiful Ethiopians, did these materials come together and form the black race. Faced with an extreme situation, Zurara reached an extreme resolution. All around him his people engaged in the new process of enslaving blacks as blacks; dark people became the black race as a result of this process. Such were the means of understanding available to a Portuguese royal chronicler in 1453.

If the slavery business had continued as mere slave raiding, one wonders how it would have worked out. The numbers involved would have stayed relatively small. And we see in Zurara these Portuguese villagers, peasants leaving their fields for the day, weeping at the sight of black Africans being enslaved. Evidently the peasants could identify with them. Most Portuguese in Zurara's time would have had their own ideas about the slave life. Would a peculiar institution based on kidnapping and murder have long withstood such sympathy? Besides, Zurara writes of black Africans converting and becoming Portuguese, just as some millions over the centuries had already become Arab, Berber, Catalan—and Portuguese.

But the Atlantic slave trade would not be based on raiding. Very quickly the Europeans discovered that sub-Saharan western and central Africa was ruled by substantial states with substantial armies. These had no intention of allowing their subjects to be carted off at will for use abroad. No, they preferred to sell them and make a profit doing so. They had been selling their neighbors and subjects north for time out of mind. Now a new market had appeared providentially at river's end. European raiding did continue, but it brought gains too short-term even by European standards, and naturally tended to spoil the market. From the 1470s peaceful diplomatic relations would become the rule all along the African coast, and the slave trade a cooperative one. Rulers of the African states along the coast and upriver reckoned their social capital more in terms of people, including slaves, than of land. If the price of a person sold to slavers exceeded the value of that person as a laborer at home, then that person would likely be sold. Additionally, less organized African peoples served as a slave population to the degree that they could be captured in "war," as would the people of more powerful but defeated states. European merchants found in much of sub-Saharan Atlantic Africa a populous land that evidently, from its elites' perspective, could afford to sell, as it happened, millions of people. The slave trade would lead to an overall net loss to the slaving parts of West Africa and an economically disastrous depopulation. But that was in the future, and a profitable trade rarely waits for long-term consequences. From the late fifteenth century well into the eighteenth, slavery seemed a good business to most African sellers.

From a non-slave African point of view, the trade was mainly in luxuries. Africans imported textiles, raw iron and finished metal products, jewelry, currency, liquor, and such war matériel as firearms and horses. With the exception of some military goods—usually a contraband trade, in the case of firearms— none of these products was new to African purchasers, nor were any of them especially necessary. Textiles were purchased as a prestige good and often for reasons of fashion; European sellers devoted much attention to consumer whims so as not to be stuck with unwanted merchandise in African ports. British merchants brought cotton and linen from India and Holland because British woolens were, understandably, not as popular as lighter fabrics. All of this trade existed atop a large internal market. Africans already had excellent iron and steel—superior African smelting methods, taught by Africans, would be used in Brazil until 1800. Africans already had textiles, jewelry, liquor, and so forth, and purchases from Europeans were a small part of the overall economy. African buyers did not "need" what Europeans had to sell. Soon enough, they would take up tobacco smoking, yet another contribution of New World slave labor to Old World leisure. African consumers simply wanted the products and paid the lowest price they could to get them. They paid in gold, though this trade diminished after 1550. They paid in malaguetta pepper, in textiles such as Allada cloth and the Senegambian mats so popular in Europe. They paid in carved ivory. Above all, they paid in people.

Initially, the Atlantic slave trade operated within a fairly narrow compass, from the southern Iberian ports (mainly Seville and Lisbon) through the near Atlantic islands (first the Canaries, then São Tomé, Príncipe, Cape Verde, Madeira, and the Azores) then into the rich deltas of the African coastline. European ships had reached the Congo River, in west-central Africa, by 1483. This was a world of what would later be called racial mixing. Portuguese, principally, as individuals and in groups, established themselves in the islands—all previously uninhabited except for the Canaries—and along the coast. The Canaries were, in many ways, a special case, being inhabited and, after decades of warfare, conquerable. Free Canarians married into the new ruling society and became, in some sense, "European." Enslaved Canarians remained, for a few generations, Canarians. Along the African coast, by contrast, the people were not conquerable at all, and so Portuguese married into local society and became, in some sense, "African."

In the freshly settled islands affairs were more complicated. Investment came primarily from Europe but also from Africa. Labor, free and slave, came from Europe, the Canaries, and Africa. At the northern ends of this circuit, in Seville and Lisbon, the identifiably black population swelled, soon reaching between 5 and 10 percent of the urban totals, that is, somewhat lower than the official black population of the United States today.

For purposes of understanding later American developments, the Atlantic islands are especially important. The colonists there needed to make money. After some experimentation they fastened on three products: wine (especially on Madeira), sugar, and cotton. The latter two were produced in a rough plantation system, the model for America, and worked mainly, though not exclusively, by slave labor, most often from the Canaries and Africa.

Christopher Columbus of Genoa knew this world well. He lived in the minority-black cities of Lisbon and Seville. He sailed through the Atlantic islands—his father-in-law from his first marriage possessed an island off Madeira—and along the African coast. He knew about black slaves and black slavers; Canarian slaves and Canarian slavers; and about sugar plantations. According to his son Ferdinand, Columbus's African voyages got him thinking: "one thing leading to another and starting a train of thought, the Admiral while in Portugal began to speculate that if the Portuguese could sail so far south, it should be possible to sail as far westward, and that it was logical to expect to find land in that direction."

Columbus's idea was not new. Educated people had long understood that the earth was round and that, in theory, one could sail in one direction and return from the other. Columbus was simply the first to go so far, to sail from Gomera, the westernmost of the Canaries with a deepwater port and still uneasily occupied, and, after a difficult month, reach a new island. Ferdinand, basing his account on Christopher's papers, describes this first American encounter:

> At daybreak they saw an island about fifteen leagues in length, very level, full of green trees and abounding in springs, with a large lagoon in the middle, and inhabited by a multitude of people who hastened to the shore, astounded and marveling at the sight of the ships, which they took for animals. These people could hardly wait to see what sort of things the ships were. The Christians were no less eager to know what manner of people they had to do with . . . Being a people of primitive simplicity, they all went about as naked as their mothers bore them; and a woman who was there wore no more clothes than the men. They were all young, not above thirty years of age, and of good stature. Their hair was straight, thick, very black, and short—that is, cut above the ears—though some let it grow down to their shoulders and tied it about their heads with a stout cord so that it looked like a woman's tress. They had handsome features, spoiled somewhat by their unpleasantly broad foreheads. They were of middle stature, well formed and sturdy, with olive-colored skins that gave them the appearance of Canary Islanders or sunburned peasants. Some were painted black, others white, and still others red.

It is striking that the Columbuses saw the "Indians" as both of an intermediate or olive tone, like Canarians or serfs, and given to changing their skin color. The New World was indeed where all our colors changed into their modern shades. In terms of white and black, as we have seen, Mediterranean people (such as the ancestors of Columbus and his crew) had long been neither. They had been intermediate, temperate, olive-colored. The impact of widespread black slavery, and direct contact with black populations, had by the 1450s brought the idea of blackness into regular circulation in Seville and Lisbon— though with the possibility of assimilation, including color assimilation. Now, after 1492, the northern Mediterranean peoples suddenly confronted a huge pagan population much like that of sub-Saharan Africa but not, despite being at the equator, nearly as dark. Moreover, these people, the "Indians," were from Christopher Columbus's own account of his first voyage intended to be servile. One result of this was that the olive Mediterraneans such as Columbus rapidly became white.

The transition appears in the tortured writings of Bartolomé de Las Casas. In his *History of the Indies,* written in the 1540s, Las Casas described the same moment of contact related above by Ferdinand Columbus: "The Indians . . . were astonished when they saw the Christians, frightened by their beards, their whiteness, and their clothes; they went up to the bearded men, especially the Admiral since, by the eminence and authority of his person, and also because he was dressed in scarlet, they assumed him to be the leader, and ran their hands over the beards, marvelling at them, because they had none, and carefully inspecting the whiteness of the hands and faces." These Indians, of course, could not communicate except by gesture, and it is very difficult to imagine how Las Casas (or Columbus) could have known that what astonished the Indians was whiteness. Indeed, the Indians have already been described elsewhere as resembling Canarians or sunburned peasants, that is, as looking more or less just like Columbus and his crew. What this otherwise inexplicable passage must reveal is Las Casas marveling at his own whiteness, and Columbus's, because they had only recently become white. In the Iberian mind Iberians had become white, blacks had become black, and Indians had become Indian all in about seventy years—say, in the time between the separation of the captured black slaves on a Portuguese field in 1444 and Las Casas's recommendation, in 1516, that black Africans be imported to the Caribbean in preference to using Indians as slaves.

Las Casas was born in 1484 in Seville. He went to Columbus's town of Santo Domingo, on Hispaniola, in 1502, still a teenager, and established himself there, acquiring Indian slaves and starting a business. By 1510 he had become a priest—he never did explain why—and saw himself as more compassionate toward his slaves than were other men. But Las Casas the famous "Defender of the Indians" remained unborn until the following year. This new man was conceived at the end of 1511, when a Dominican friar delivered the first notable blow against American slavery. Antonio Montesinos spoke in the church of Santo Domingo about Saint John in the desert. Montesinos told his audience of Spanish colonists that they had made the paradise of Hispaniola into a human desert. "With what right and with what justice do you keep these poor Indians in such cruel and horrible servitude?" he asked. "By what authority have you made such detestable wars against these people who lived peacefully and gently on their lands? Are these not men? Do they not have rational souls? Are you not obliged to love them as yourselves?"

The little colony demanded that Montesinos recant and spare it any further sermons by returning at once to Spain. Less than two decades had passed since Columbus found Hispaniola, yet a terrible fever had gripped the Spaniards following him. Within ten years of his first voyage Columbus was complaining: "They all made fun of my plan then; now even tailors wish to discover." More than discover, they wished to make money. To do so, they wanted slaves, both as merchandise and for labor. From the earliest days the Americas were seen as part of the Iberia-Africa-Atlantic-islands circuit. Columbus himself understood what he was doing in this way. He enslaved Americans almost immediately on arrival and soon would propose resale in Iberia and the Atlantic islands ("I believe those from Guinea are not now enough"). Several thousand Americans were sold in Europe between 1493 and 1501, this was one means of financing voyages. Many thousands more were enslaved to work the new American plantations; they lasted a year, perhaps two, in bondage, then died. Much had happened by the time Montesinos asked, "Are these not men?"

Las Casas remained a slaveholder for three more years until, he says, he "began to consider" a passage from Ecclesiastes: "He that taketh away his neighbor's living slayeth him, and he that defraudeth the laborer of his hire is a blood-letter." After further consideration of "the misery and slavery that these people suffered," he decided that "everything which had been done to the Indians in the Indies was unjust and tyrannical." He gave up his slaves and devoted the rest of his long life (he died in 1576) to defending the Indians.

Yet his solution in 1516 to the "misery and slavery" of Indians was to replace it with the misery and slavery of Africans, who were already being imported to the Indies in large numbers in 1510. Were they not being defrauded of their labor? What was the difference between these two peoples? Both were pagans, recently contacted, in warm climates, with their own states. Both were, if one used a little imagination, dark-skinned. Both were enslaved and traded as property from the earliest days of contact with Europeans. In Columbus's mind, and not only his, the people of Guinea and of Hispaniola were nearly indistinguishable, part of the same useful population of slaves.

Nevertheless, Indians soon found advocates for their rights, and Africans did not. Indians visibly troubled the European conscience, while open concern for Africans remained many years away. Queens and kings, scholars, clergymen, and jurists debated the nature of Indians and of European power over them, including the power of enslaving; they did not do so for Africans. Pope Paul III, in 1537, blamed the Devil himself and his minions for spreading the idea "that the Indians of the West and the South, and other people of whom we have recent

knowledge, should be treated as dumb brutes . . . the Indians are truly men."
But were not black slaves also men?

A number of factors may account for these divergences. There was a tradition of African slavery, and, probably more importantly, African slaves were sold as merchandise by Africans. By and large, Europeans bought black people already enslaved; logically, the responsibility for enslavement would be somewhat more diffuse in the European slaver's mind than was the case in the Americas. Control over the bodies of black slaves was already established; it just passed from African hands into European hands. Similarly, Europeans had little access to Africa beyond the coastal marketplaces, and almost no control over black African land, culture, or anything else. There was no conquest and so no need to debate the nature of the conquered or of the conquering. Given the broad acceptance of slavery as such, there was little spur to European reflection. (It is suggestive, in considering white people of a later period, that moral abolitionism would insist that black slaves had been captured by whites rather than sold by blacks. It was, apparently, necessary for whites to place themselves at the heart of the racial-slavery drama before being able to see the moral importance of ending it.) Indians were legally royal subjects, and their fate was critical for Europeans in that it was critical for Europeans' own divisions of power—most importantly, for the endless struggles between central, monarchical power back home and slave masters on the ground in America. Black Africans, by contrast, were in independent states, and black slaves were legally nothing more or less than slaves. European powers in Africa competed for market share. In America they competed for countries.

In Africa, Europeans saw products. In America they saw something of themselves. As Richard Eden would later write, after perusing the Spanish sources, the Indians "may well bee lykened to a smoothe and bare table unpainted, or a white paper unwritten, upon." This was a situation unlike that in Africa. The American experience provoked Europeans to consider themselves in new and strange ways. They did so negatively, by dwelling on the differentness of Indians. But they also sought resemblances. Even Columbus gave hints of finding Hispaniola very much like home. And Las Casas describes some Indians as being "as white as us and better hair." On one hand, Las Casas has Indians marveling at Spanish whiteness; on the other hand, he sees some Indians as already white. We can watch him stretching about this fairly new concept of whiteness. Las Casas wanted to include Indians in the human family, but the sheer scale of apparent human difference seems to have overwhelmed his ability to do this within the traditional structure of Christian equality before God. The less than amazing reality of the rustic Canarians was one thing; the Americans were quite another. Christian egalitarianism simply lacked the power to assimilate the humanity of these battered and tortured people. Perhaps it was the battery and torture itself, committed by self-identified Christians, that rebounded to undermine the conquerors' Christianness and Christianity's strength of conviction. What could have been Christianity's triumphant period of conversion threatened to become its greatest debacle. The spreaders of Christianity in America had, after all, to be restrained by their own pope. All this was happening as Las Casas sat at home writing his enraged *History*. In it he reached for something to help make sense of this bloody world, and that something was race. He could use it to judge the nearness of his beloved Indians, some "as white as us." Perhaps he reached for race because of its neutrality; Christians betrayed Christian principles, but whites couldn't betray white principles because a skin color doesn't have principles. Yet this neutrality was deceptive. He reached out with whiteness to include but also to exclude, and within the white idea lived its opposite, blackness, the very feature that distinguished the people whom Las Casas recommended as replacements to save the Indians. The modern triad of black-white-Indian was now in place. It is almost as if whites needed Indians to become fully white, and to make blacks fully black.

Las Casas himself realized this drift when it was too late. In his long old age he bitterly regretted having urged the export of black people as slaves to America. He wondered whether his involvement in slavery might prove to be the act that would keep him from being accepted at his death into heaven.

"COAL BLACK IS BETTER

THAN ANOTHER HUE"

LOVE AND RACE IN SHAKESPEARE'S ENGLAND

■

By the time the English began seriously exploring the New World, racial ideas about blacks, Indians, and to a lesser extent whites had taken on lives of their own. Christian methods for understanding pagans and human equality now could be supplemented, or even replaced, by a division of humanity into races with moral as well as physical characteristics. An account of the first English voyage to equatorial Africa, in 1553, says little about African appearances, concentrating instead on shipboard feuding and the tough bargaining tactics of the local black king. But Robert Gainsh's narrative of the second trip, in 1554, referred to those who were "in olde tyme called *Ethiopes* and *Nigrite,* which we now call Moores, Moorens, or Negros," as "a people of beastly lyvyng, without a God, law, religion, or common wealth, and so scorched and vexed with the heate of the sun, that in many places they curse it when it ryseth." These accounts were published in 1555 by Richard Eden as part of his anthology, to which he appended his own similarly unflattering remarks on Africans.

Eden devoted little space to Africa, and much to the New World narratives of Peter Martyr, Oviedo, and López de Gómara. The New World held more political, economic, and ethnographic interest for Eden and, presumably, his readers. By means of these stories the English, like the Spanish and Portuguese before them, could triangulate themselves as white. Discussing Columbus, Martyr writes of the admiral in the Indies "considering with himself the corporature of this people." Columbus wanted to know why the Indians were not black, given that they lived at the same latitude as the Ethiopians. If the

Ethiopians were black because of closeness to the sun, why were the Indians, just as near the sun, not as black? "For the Ethiopians," Martyr writes, "are all black, having their hair curled more like wool than hair. But these people of the island of Puta (being as I have said under the clime of Ethiopia) are white, with long hair, and of yellow color." The language of black, white, and Indian, then, was available to English readers in their earliest source of firsthand information. So was the rejection of a strictly climatological explanation for blackness; and so were negative images of black Africans as being something like beasts. Only four years after Eden, one William Cunningham could confidently state that sub-Saharan Africans were "blacke, Savage, Monstrous, & rude." In 1577 George Best demonstrated the results of discovering that blackness was not simply an effect of closeness to the sun. He offered two complementary alternatives: that "blacknesse proceedeth of some naturall infection of the first inhabitants of that Countrey [Africa], and so all the whole progenie of them descended, are still poluted with the same blot of infection," and that this infection was due to Africa's first inhabitants being descended from Ham.

The first black captives of Englishmen had arrived in London in 1555. Many more followed. They quickly became fashionable as musicians and servants, such that Queen Elizabeth, who herself had an African entertainer and an African page, decreed in 1596 that "negars and Blackamoores" be expelled from England. She feared they were taking English jobs. A second decree followed, then a commission to a foreign merchant, in 1601, to deport all blacks. Elizabeth's decrees failed; too many people wanted blacks in their homes. This suggests that English people did not think blacks were quite beasts. Rather, they were fascinated by blacks and by the spectacle of humans appearing so different yet still being humans. While the bulk of sixteenth- and early-seventeenth-century English references to black Africans were uncomplimentary, two of the most important works, one by William Shakespeare, the other by Ben Jonson, present a more complex image. The premise was first expressed by the mysterious John Mandeville, whose *Travels* found many readers in English translation in Elizabeth's time. Mandeville wrote that the Numidians thought darkness of skin "a great beauty, and aye the blacker they are the fairer they think them." Mandeville's Numidians even blacked up those cursed with light skin. This relativistic idea appears again in *Titus Andronicus*, Shakespeare's first and uneven attempt at writing tragedy, a new form in Elizabethan theater. The play's most fascinating character is Aaron, a "Moor" and a man who boasts of his evil nature, which Shakespeare equates with his blackness. Aaron is unstoppably bitter, cruel, and godless, second in these qualities only perhaps to the white queen Tamora, whose vengefulness drives the play.

Queen Tamora loves Aaron, "my sweet Moor, sweeter to me than life!" Those around her are appalled by this, but not only because it is adultery against the king—they also despise Aaron because he is black. As one character (soon dead) says, upon finding the white queen and the black man together, "Believe me, Queen, your swart Cimmerian / Doth make your honor of his body's hue, / Spotted, detested, and abominable." Presumably Shakespeare was playing on a loathing of blackness already current among his London audiences. By this time—1594—they would have seen many black people in the city's streets, most often as slaves or servants. Yet the undeniably white Tamora does love this black man, and Shakespeare has her express this love in adoring, beautiful language without any hint of hesitation or apology. She does not love him because of or despite his dark skin; she simply loves a man. And Shakespeare shows no strain in imagining or expressing such a love.

Later in the play Tamora bears a child, Aaron's son. The English had already learned from practical experience that, as Aaron puts it, "where the bull and cow are both milk-white, / they never do beget a coal-black calf." A nurse brings the baby before Aaron and two of Tamora's lighter sons. "A joyless, dismal, black, and sorrowful issue!" the nurse cries. "Here is the babe, as loathsome as a toad / Amongst the fair-fac'd breeders of our clime."

"Is black so base a hue?" Aaron replies.

The nurse says that Tamora wishes the baby be killed. The queen's elder sons move to kill him, but Aaron snatches the boy from the nurse and draws his sword. "Stay, murtherous villains," Aaron says, "will you kill your brother?" Aaron tells his son's half brothers that no one, not they nor any greater man, not even "the god of war, / shall seize this prey out of his father's hands."

> *What, what, ye sanguine, shallow-hearted boys!*
> *Ye white-lim'd walls! Ye alehouse painted signs!*
> *Coal black is better than another hue,*
> *In that it scorns to bear another hue;*
> *For all the water in the ocean*
> *Can never turn the swan's black legs to white.*

What are we to make of this expression of black-skin-color pride by Shakespeare, and of the dramatization of a literal kinship between black and white? It seems that modern racial consciousness, with its extremes, intimacies, and ambivalences, already existed. There is plenty of racial hatred in the play—and there is the closeness of a common parent, as when Aaron tells Tamora's elder sons that the dark baby

> *. . . is your brother, lords, sensibly fed*
> *Of that self blood that first gave life to you,*

> *And from your womb where you imprisoned were.*
> *He is enfranchised and come to light.*

We can hardly know what Shakespeare thought privately about race, but in this play he conveys an aching sympathy for Aaron—more exactly, for Aaron's predicament of being black. Shakespeare makes it quite clear that skin color alone identifies the baby as illegitimate (a white baby is quickly substituted to cover Tamora's adultery). Aaron rages at the injustice that darkness should keep his son from becoming royalty.

And, importantly, he refers to his child, while rushing him to safety, as a "slave." The play does not require this. Aaron is himself hardly a slave, and his son's being one really makes no sense, except in that, for late Elizabethan Londoners, blacks were seen as slaves by virtue of their color. More precisely, Aaron's son is born not into slavery to anyone in particular, but as a slave to his skin color itself—to the social perception of what his appearance means. Slavery evidently could be understood as the condition into which a baby was born if that baby had dark skin. Yet the play makes it equally apparent that this is an absurdity imposed on Aaron's son by the white people surrounding him. Thus one paradox of modern racial thinking—that blacks are and are not naturally inferior to whites, that they are kin and not kin—is already present just forty years after the first English voyage to sub-Saharan Africa. And Shakespeare, at least, considered it significant enough, and important enough to the English, to make it central to his first tragedy.

The paradox of whiteness and blackness also drives the first fully developed modern English masque, a dramatic form with various antecedents that reached its artistic maturity in Ben Jonson's *Masque of Blackness*. Jonson was a friend and competitor of Shakespeare; they used to square off in wit contests in taverns. Sometime around 1604 Queen Anne—Elizabeth having died in 1603 and been succeeded by Anne's husband, James—asked Jonson to write a masque in which she and her ladies would be black. Why the queen wanted temporarily to be black, we do not know. Jonson worked up a musical playlet featuring the river Niger personified, "in form and colour of an Ethiop," according to Jonson's description, "his hair and rare beard curled . . . his front, neck, and wrists adorned with pearl." A song introduces him:

> *Fair Niger, son to great Oceanus,*
> *Now honour'd, thus,*
> *With all his beauteous race:*
> *Who, though but black in face,*
> *Yet are they bright,*

And full of life and light.
To prove that beauty best,
Which, not the colour, but the feature,
Assures unto the creature.

Niger has arrived with his daughters at England's shore, where he falls into discussion with Oceanus, who wonders why the African has come so far from home. Niger blames his daughters. Being very black, he says, they are beautiful, for the sun, "in their firm hews, draws / Signs of his fervent'st love; and thereby shews / That in their black, the perfect beauty grows." He also praises their superior curly hair and mentions that they are descended from the earliest of peoples. (Jonson adds a scholarly footnote to the effect that those "which dwell under the south, were the first begotten of the earth.") Even "death herself (her self being pale and blue) / Can never alter their most faithful hue."

However, their perfect black life, Niger reveals, was disturbed by the intrusion of foreign poetry, which praised the beauty of light-skinned women. Niger's daughters took this to heart and despaired; they even believed a tale that all people had once been white. Then one night they were gazing miserably into a pool and saw there a message saying they should go to a land whose name ends in Tania, where they would become beautiful. So Niger and his daughters set out, first reaching "Black Mauritania," then "Swarth Lusitania" and "Rich Aquitania," none of which was the right spot. Now they have reached Albion, as Oceanus explains—a blessed land whose name is derived from the Latin for "white." But Albion does not end in Tania, an obvious difficulty until the sudden appearance of the moon, "Her garments white and silver . . . The heaven about her was vaulted with blue silk, and set with stars of silver, which had in them their several lights burning." The set and designs for this masque were by Inigo Jones, concoctions of wood and fabric, metals, jewels, all lit by cunningly placed candles—a spectacle that might have made us worry about fire but in 1605 was the height of technological ingenuity, with the most powerful persons of the time swanning across the creaking boards acting out their little drama for themselves. The moon is called Ethiopia—for that, Jonson believed, was how Ethiopians addressed the moon—and she says, "Niger, be glad." For he and his daughters have reached Britannia, ruled by a sun "whose beams shine day and night, and are of force / To blanch an Ethiop." This British sun "can salve the rude defects of ev'ry creature. / Call forth thy honour'd daughters then . . . / Their beauties shall be scorch'd no more." Queen Anne and her ladies then become white and no doubt remained happily so while their dancing and singing continued far into the night, as would be the custom at Jacobean courtly masques.

Jonson packed a great deal into his brief play about blackness. The world he showed was that of an emerging imperial Britain actively conquering the world. Such is the significance of the transformation of Albion into Britannia. Ethiopia, the moon, explains:

> *This blessed isle doth with that Tania end,*
> *Which there they [Niger's daughters] saw inscrib'd, and shall extend*
> *Wish'd satisfaction to their best desires.*
> *Britannia, which the triple world admires,*
> *This isle hath now recover'd for her name; . . .*
> *With that great name Britannia, this blest isle*
> *Hath won her ancient dignity, and style,*
> *"A world divided from the world": and try'd*
> *The abstract of it, in his general pride.*
> *For were the world, with all his wealth, a ring,*
> *Britannia, (whose new name makes all tongues sing)*
> *Might be a diamant worthy to inchase it,*
> *Rul'd by a sun . . . of force*
> *To blanch an Ethiop.*

With these compact lines Jonson has summarized a new English view of English destiny. England is now Britain, perfect in itself and so perfect in its extension across the world, even unto the Ethiopians. This process was well advanced by 1605. Under Elizabeth, England had pushed herself to the conquest of Ireland, in many ways the English counterpart to the Canaries, and foraged into sub-Saharan Africa and the Americas. Under her successor, James, the crowns of Scotland and England were at last united, creating Britain, and James further pursued expansion in America. However bloody this expansion was in reality, in Jonson's *Masque of Blackness* the conversion of the non-British to Britishness appears as the fulfillment of "their best desires." Symbolically and literally, Jonson expressed this desire of the most distant foreigners to become British as the desire of blacks to become white. He handily pilfered the ancient Mediterranean climatic understanding of human diversity by making Britain's sun "temperate"—surely a stretch even for Britons—yet also of such mysterious force as to make people white rather than darken them. And nowhere does he mention that other ancient, semi-European understanding of human diversity, that faith which led the Spaniards to denounce themselves at such an early date: the Christian doctrine of equality before God. In *Masque of Blackness* all humans are equal in that all are, or at least aspire to be, white.

White Englishmen, then, in 1605, had at least the capacity to think of the world in secular terms of black and white, and to do so with loving optimism, believing that the world might become white and British in essence if not in appearance. This marks a crucial difference between the British approach to Africa and America and that of the Iberians. Yet alternatives do exist within Jonson and Shakespeare, as they existed for Las Casas, Montesinos, López de Gómara, even Zurara. Shakespeare and Jonson both wrote effortlessly of black-skin-color pride, and Jonson had stated emphatically that character, not skin color, was what mattered in judging humans. Unfortunately, that view could not be reconciled with the demands of his audience. In *Masque of Beauty*, a sequel to *Masque of Blackness*, a group of whiteness-seeking black women once more tosses about in the sea, this time on a floating island. (Again, Queen Anne is playing.) When they reach their goal at last, Jonson has a song in which the harmonizing of human difference into whiteness is expressed in terms of secular love:

> *When Love at first, did move*
> *From out of Chaos, brightned*
> *So was the world, and lightned,*
> *As now. (Echo: As now! Echo: As now!)*
> *Yield night, then to the light,*
> *As blackness hath to beauty:*
> *Which is but the same duty.*
> *It was for beauty that the world was made,*
> *And where she reigns, love's lights admit no shade.*
>   (Echo: *Love's lights admit no shade.* Echo: *Admit no shade.*)

To these words of his Jonson can only respond in a footnote: "For what country is it thinks not her own beauty fairest, yet?"

Yes, what country doesn't? But a country is not a race. However similarly their envies, bitternesses, and prides may be expressed, a country cannot extend itself with the same assimilating or excluding force as can a race. A country cannot be enslaved, transported, and identified for generation after generation in the way a race can. A country can have a harmless pride, idly in its territory. Races don't exist in such isolation, nor do their exclusive prides, which will always act to diminish someone.

A secular British understanding of blackness, as exemplified by Jonson, did not entirely dominate the field. Britain was riven by religious conflict through the sixteenth and seventeenth centuries. Britons took their religion, or religions, very seriously. And while religious division could separate them into almost microscopic, angry groupings (such as the Pilgrims), a generality of Christian faith remained the powerful norm. Within that faith was an idea of human unity, one increasingly at odds with British practice as more men and women went abroad. The resulting tension can be seen in the work of Reverend Samuel Purchas, the preeminent compiler of travel chronicles after his predecessor Hakluyt. His first book, *Purchas His Pilgrimage*, was published in 1613. He included in his discourse on blacks a consideration of "the cause of that their black colour." He admitted, "I cannot well answere this question." He dismissed various current arguments, such as closeness to the equator (disproved by the varieties of people found at a similar latitude), heat, dry air, and soil conditions (all similarly disproved). He rejected the black-semen theory, then alluded to some speculators who searched the stars for an answer.

> And there will I leave them; yea, I will send them further to him that hath reserved many secrets of nature to himselfe, and hath willed us to content our selves with things revealed . . . His incomprehensible *unite*, which the Angells with covered faces in their *Holy, holy, holy* hymnes resound and *Laude* in *Trinitie*, hath pleased in this varietie to diversifie his works, all serving one humane nature, infinitely multiplyed in person, exceedingly varied in accidents, that wee also might serve that *one-most* God; the tawney Moore, black Negro, duskie Libyan, Ash-coloured Indian, olive-coloured American, should with the whiter Europaean become *one sheepe-fold*, under one great shepheard, till *this mortalite being swallowed up of life*, wee may all *be one, as he and the father are one.*

Purchas continues in this vein, with an escalating detonation of italic type and capital letters. The third edition added a concluding "Amen."

This was close to López de Gómara's paean to the "diverse liveries" demonstrating God's inscrutable omnipotence, written more than half a century before and available in English since 1555. But Purchas's cry is in every sense a prayer: forceful, anxious, intended to overcome grave doubt and to pass human power away into the hands of God. Purchas published his enormous book to celebrate and encourage the exploration by England of the bigger world's mysteries—an exploration that had a strong whiff of impiety in seventeenth-century England, as it had had in imperial Greece and Rome. Exploration implied a dissatisfaction with what God had given you. Purchas celebrated exploration but seems to have stopped short of believing humans could or should "know" everything, specifically that they should ever know why their many appearances were so different. Purchas saw that such "knowledge" might irreparably damage the doctrine of human equality. As a clergyman, he would have known how critical that doctrine was to sustaining the faith's appeal among unprivileged Britons, the great majority; indeed, the argument for a direct relation between each man and God might be seen as the mainspring of Protestantism, not to mention British parish politics in relation to royal power.

And yet the truth remained that the celebrated explorers were building societies based on enslavement and not infrequently murder of black Negroes and olive-colored Americans. They commonly saw these people as inferior to "the whiter Europaean." The disjuncture between such a reality and spiritual doctrine must have been nearly intolerable to a sensitive mind. As we have seen, the common reaction was to place race in a mental sphere separate from religion. Another tactic, as in Jonson, was to accommodate race within a Neoplatonic, harmonizing scheme that, with the right lighting and costumes, might at least overwhelm the pitiless contradiction at its heart. Purchas could do neither of these, but he could reach for the one quasi-biblical device that might mitigate the terrible power of human equality: the curse of Ham. He had dismissed it in 1613. Perhaps the pressure had become too much by 1625, for in that year and the following he published *Hakluytus Posthumus, or Purchas His Pilgrims,* in which he deleted the long yearning prayer, substituting, under the running headline "Chams Curse continuing still. Black colour, whence," a new passage on black slaves: "They are descended of Chus, the Sonne of cursed Cham; as are all of that complexion, Not so by reason of their Seed [semen], nor heat of the Climate; nor of the Soyle . . . but rather from the Curse of Noe upon Cham." One might observe that, in context, this is not the fortuitous discovery of a biblical basis for racial hierarchy. Rather, it is the forced, straining rescue of religious faith from impotence when faced with racial domination. One might also wonder how soothing it really was to white (or "whiter") Christian minds.

The passage Purchas quoted concerning the biblical and natural slavery of dark-skinned people came from the account by George Sandys of his Middle Eastern travels. In one of history's coincidences, Sandys—a poet and acclaimed translator of classical Latin verse—would play an important role in the early Virginia colony. He arrived there as treasurer and director of industry and agriculture in 1621, two years after the first recorded arrival of blacks in Virginia. Whether he brought the curse of Ham with him is unrecorded, though it was not the sort of idea an educated man in his position was likely to leave behind.

Virginia's main problem in 1621 was labor. First, it tended rapidly to die.

Virginia was a death trap for workers. Second, labor was, after Jamestown's first ghastly ten years or so, capable of producing excellent profits (from tobacco) only if it was carefully controlled. There were two possible solutions to this situation. The attractive solution was provided by George's brother Edwin, friend of liberty and foe of royal absolutism. (Their father was archbishop of York.) Edwin Sandys had joined the Virginia Company as a modest investor in 1607, the year Jamestown was founded. He became a keen reformer and upon gaining the treasurer's position in 1619 initiated an ambitious program. His and his allies' first move was to place some of the company's land in individual hands as a spur to initiative. Likewise, they instituted a representative government and granted land to the government's officers with the idea that officers' tenants would provide the necessary governmental revenue, eliminating the need for taxation. Edwin also launched somewhat far-fetched or bookish schemes to start an iron industry (without a decent source of iron), silk raising (with cocoons courtesy of King James), biracial educational enterprises to encourage a melding of the British and Indian populations, and so on. The idea was to have a diversely based economy—eliminating, Edwin and his king hoped, the unhealthful business of tobacco—peacefully worked by an enfranchised population of whites and Indians. Edwin Sandys immediately began sending hundreds of people over to Virginia, most of them pulled from destitution.

And most of them soon died in Virginia. They died, somewhat indirectly, because of people like Edwin's brother George. These men chose the second, less attractive solution to the labor problem. George Sandys and the other leading officers of Virginia became rich by ignoring almost every one of Edwin Sandys's programs, except those that provided them with land, men to work it, and political power to force that work. They took the company tenants due them as officers and employed them privately, adding as many other servants (and possibly slaves) as they could. The few well-placed men in Virginia grew wealthy by making their laborers grow tobacco for export, rather than food for nourishment. As their workers keeled over from malnutrition, exhaustion, or alcohol poisoning—ships visiting in summer were floating gin mills—the officers and successful planters demanded more. They enforced obedience by torture and execution. Upwards of three thousand workers perished during Edwin Sandys's tenure, which ended in 1624. Brother George lived in Virginia from 1621 to 1625. His own long life ended in 1664; his travel writings influenced Francis Bacon and John Milton, while his Latin translations earned the praise of John Dryden and Alexander Pope, who called him "one of the chief refiners of our language."

The men and some women dying in this period were overwhelmingly white in appearance and Christian. One assumes they were not victims of racial and religious prejudice. The problem for early Virginian masters was how to compel labor—how to keep workers in a useful form of bondage. "He maketh us serve him," one of George Sandys's men wrote of his master, "whether wee will or noe and how to helpe yt we doe not knowe for hee beareth all the sway." That "sway" was mainly political, economic, and legal (in the form of indentures and other binding labor contracts). As long as all or most non-elite white men and women were bound by contracts, they could reasonably be compelled to work. That many in the early period died before their contracts expired was convenient for those who owned their labor, as long as that labor did not disappear too quickly and could be replaced; the servant was effectively a lifetime slave. He was bought and sold as chattel. For a time Britain provided a nearly adequate supply of such people. One did not require a racial theory to keep them in subjection, though descriptions of the seventeenth-century poor as savage, uncivilized, rude, dirty, and so on used a language that could later be laid upon "races" without amendment. Some Englishmen did propose forms of enslavement for the British poor (even on a quasi-racial basis for some Irish and Scots). More generally, the elite view of the European poor as a separate people already had a long tradition to sustain it.

Nonetheless, the seeds of a modern racial conception of the American laboring class were present in the 1620s. They had no particular connection to the poet Sandys's interpretation of blackness in Genesis, nor to the "20 and odd Negroes" of 1619 noted by John Rolfe in a letter to Edwin Sandys. For white Virginians the first American race was Indian. In 1622 the local Indians revolted, killing 347, including the hopeful administrator, George Thorpe, charged with erecting Edwin Sandys's biracial designs. The massacre eliminated whatever misgivings the dwindling Jamestown population had about killing and enslaving Indians. Thorpe had already noticed that the bulk of Jamestown's whites—the castaways of English poor-relief rolls and those slightly better-off—despised Indians. Within a few growing seasons of the 1622 massacre the white dead had been avenged several times over. The cycle of white Virginian life became one of tobacco and staple planting punctuated by murderous raids into the native hinterland. The idea of enslaving Indians for life fastened upon the minds of white Virginians, particularly those who could not afford to buy or intimidate labor in the manner of their social superiors. An Indian slave would likely be more troublesome than a bought white servant; but he or she was free for the capturing, as long as one was willing to lower oneself to what may be considered the basest humanity. For many poor white men in and around Jamestown this would have seemed a tiny step. Their degradation was already pretty complete.

Such men could take the degrading language of deserved servitude applied to them by their superiors and transfer it to Indians, with the added twist of a racial label that, by going to the nature of a person rather than merely to his or her temporary social condition, could apply for life and to the slave's progeny. This Indian-race concept had many holes in it, not least the belief that Indians were in fact white. Yet circumstances were such that an Indian racial identity could be asserted by whites with some broad credibility. Applying this notion to blacks might seem natural and would have many advantages: blacks came already captured and enslaved, lived as property outside any category of royal "subject," were easily identified, did not know the terrain, and had no chance of escaping homeward. Yet the black-slave-race idea took some time to develop, primarily because few Africans of any shade lived in Virginia. Compared with British term servants, they cost too much. English Barbados would switch from white servants to black slaves in the 1640s, but transport costs from Africa to Barbados were significantly lower than to Virginia, making black-slave-labor prices relatively lower on the island. Potential British laborers knew that sugar raising, Barbados's economic foundation, was hopelessly grim work, and that the possibilities of setting oneself up (after serving one's term) on a little island were small compared with those on the American mainland. Beginning in mid-century, the rise in British wages at home also made British indentured labor dearer abroad.

In Virginia, however, after the killing years of the 1620s, white society slowly stabilized and extended itself. White Virginians organized themselves to enclose pastures, increasing their stores of cattle and swine; representative government advanced under capable administrators; and the surviving local Indians, after a second, bloody uprising in 1644, were reduced to tributaries. This was a comparatively sunny period for the few blacks in Virginia. Though most probably came to the New World as slaves, they worked alongside whites as near equals and sometimes bought or received freedom. Some actually forced their shift from slave to indentured servant through the simple expedient of working so slowly that their masters had to negotiate limited terms of service if they wanted any work at all. (A Puritan source from 1638 conveys the essence: "Negros" were "more easily kept as perpetuall servants." Blacks shipped from Africa had no contracts, and so were necessarily lifetime servants; but the language used implies that both black and white servants, with or without limiting contracts, often sought a practical "renegotiation" on the ground. The language also implies that masters tried their best to force servants of all colors to work as long as possible, even despite contracts, which was in fact the case.) Other Africans came to Virginia under terms of indenture. They worked off their contracts and bought their own indentured servants to work their lands. However few in number, black masters did live in Virginia in the 1650s.

Yet as early as 1639 the Virginia legislature passed an act specifically discriminating against "Negroes"—they were not to be provided with arms or ammunition by the colony. (The first black slave uprising against Englishmen had occurred the year before in a Puritan West Indian colony.) Blacks were a nearly insignificant proportion of the Virginia population in 1639, but the legislature was evidently confident that they were distinct from everyone else, recognizable as a separate population, and not to be trusted by the majority. This distrust probably arose not from blackness as such but from slaveness: slaves could not be trusted with arms, and while not all blacks were slaves, many slaves were black (recognizing that the term *Negro* sometimes included Indians). Antiblack legislation and court decisions tended to spring, in the early decades, from a social need to control slaves (rather than to control blacks)—a social need to control the distribution of liberty. Ownership of black slaves for life is clearly recorded in Virginia from the 1650s; however, slavery rather than skin color truly determined one's status. After all, one of the earlier human-chattel cases, from 1654, arose when a black master (Anthony Johnson) successfully imposed lifelong bondage on a black servant (John Casor) who had believed himself to be only indentured. Racial lawmaking and enforcement were born from the coincidence of skin color and slavery and were directed at controlling labor more than race relations.

Controlling labor remained the great preoccupation of wealthier Virginians. By the 1650s the higher price of indentured labor of whatever color had powerfully combined with a growing colonial population of free but landless, or nearly landless, men. The servants were getting restive; the landless ex-servants, mostly white, were already restive. Their masters' reaction was to extend terms of service, restrict land sales, limit voting to the propertied, raise the penalties for running away, and impose sundry other burdens. The first servile revolt occurred in 1661, and a fashion developed among the lower classes for rebellion. This trend climaxed with Bacon's Rebellion in 1676, which mobilized landless men, white but also black, in an explicit race war against Indians. Nathaniel Bacon and the other leaders were reasonably well off men who realized that the discontent of disfranchised whites (and some blacks, including slaves) could be concentrated by appealing to fear and hatred of Indians. (Years later, in 1746, the earliest surviving poem by an African slave would concern a massacre by "the awful creatures," Indians.) While Bacon's premature death kept him from having a lasting influence, the rebellion did succeed in inspiring the restoration of the vote to landless freemen. It also brought legislation (later renewed) to the effect that anyone who captured an Indian from 1676 forward could enslave him or her. Such enslavements had occurred since the 1620s; the difference now was that a legislature representing a non-Indian population had

decided that Indians—that is, a racial group defined by people outside it—
could be enslaved for life.

One is reminded of the Cherokees' and other Indians' efforts to insist on
their own nonblackness. Blacks might likewise have sworn up and down that
they were not Indian, and for nearly identical reasons. Those blacks who fought
alongside Bacon—one of the last bands to surrender had eighty blacks and
twenty English servants—were, like the Cherokees who began enslaving blacks
not long afterward, living in an emerging triracial world over which they had little control, but within which they were determined to press whatever advantage
they could. Each calculated as any person would calculate, as Anthony Johnson
had calculated in taking to himself the life of John Casor. It was not for them to
change the world. Only whites had the power to do that. Whites had made this
world.

The political hardening of white racial attitudes toward Indians in Virginia
coincided exactly with the hardening of white racial attitudes toward blacks.
Morgan Godwyn identified the essence of this hardening in 1680 by noting that
the terms "*Negro* and *Slave*" had "grown Homogeneous and Convertible" and
that the meaning of blackness for whites was simply an instance of accepting
"for *Truth* [that] which shall make for Interest," which is to say, for profit. The
1660s, 1670s, and 1680s saw the more or less clear definition of races in legislation. The important remnant of religious misgiving—that Christians could not
be slaves, which had done so much to eliminate white slavery in previous centuries—was legislated out of existence. The principal categories of white, black,
and Indian now lived in the law books, while the critical non-category category
of mulatto (and similar terms) continued a vagrant legal existence. Slavery was
explicitly and implicitly associated with dark skin: blacks, Negroes, mulattoes,
Indians. The regulation of labor had been transformed, partially but decisively,
into the regulation of race.

At the same time, two basic paradoxes had been established. Under relentless pressure from the lower classes, a broad social liberty had been born, but at
the cost of a complete denial of liberty to a portion of society. This was, in the
words of the twentieth-century historian Edmund Morgan, "the American paradox, the marriage of slavery and freedom." The legal and social institutionalization of American blackness came principally as a result of decades of negotiation
between whites over the nature of their bondage to each other. The American's
distinctive liberty evolved with and through the concept of being white and not
a slave; the black's (not the black American's) distinctive unfreedom evolved
with and through the concept of being black and a slave.

The second paradox is more general. To the extent that Europe, Africa, and
the New World together made what we think of as the global condition of

"modernity," that condition had as an essential component the inheritance of social status. Modernity is often considered hostile to inherited social status, given that modern societies tended to undermine genealogical aristocratic privilege (soon to be widely considered irrational). But modernity also created and fixed a global notion of inherited slave status and "savage" status, and of an inherited racial identity for whites, blacks, and Indians. Whether modernity can exist as such without these blood notions remains an open question. But we can be certain that, for most of its life, it has not.

By the eighteenth century in North America blacks had been saddled with all the major characteristics of modern blackness, which is to say that, among other things, they could not be Indian and they could not be white. The racial codes in this era were mainly devoted not to explaining blackness but to establishing whiteness by negative example. They aimed at preventing mixing of "white blood," that is, at protecting the normal population of free people from the abnormal population of the unfree. It is striking how much legislative ink was spilled in trying to prevent blacks and whites from having children together. Because legislatures in those days did not make laws simply to pass the time, we can guess that interracial lovemaking was not altogether exceptional. Of particular concern to white male lawmakers and justices were white women (in short supply) having children with black men, in or out of marriage—though one George Ivy, probably white, did petition for the repeal of Virginia's law against intermarriage. As for Shakespeare a century earlier, for white Virginians a belief in black inferiority lived against an obvious backdrop of intimacy. One assumes that not all whites found their black lovers unworthy. The reverse would also have been true.

Perhaps the most important aspect of American writing on black identity in the late seventeenth century is its rarity. However deep the roots of black inferiority may have been in the white mind, whites did not congratulate each other in the streets of Jamestown or anywhere else for having solved, at last, the black problem. They did not dwell on their wisdom in understanding that blacks really were meant to be slaves. They even failed to praise racial slavery as the key that unlocked the door to collective white freedom. (To the extent that early whites celebrated racial victories, these were victories against Indians.) Rather, whites do not seem to have had anything good to say about racial slavery. It solved a labor problem. It did not solve a black-white racial problem because there had not been much of one to solve.

It did, however, create a racial problem, one that received, not surprisingly, racial solutions. Slave or free, blacks in 1700 did not make up a large proportion of the colonial population. But once racial slavery had been codified, imports of blacks soared. The need for labor remained high, while the cost of indentured whites rose—as did wages back in Britain. By 1770 the black colonial population would reach its peak, more than 20 percent of the total. This massive importation of black people quickly led to a thorough set of white associations—the stereotypical content of early American blackness. South Carolina's turn-of-the-century racial code noted first that black slavery was essential to the colony's development, then immediately added that a separate set of laws to govern blacks was essential because of their "barbarous, wild, savage natures" and "the disorders, rapines, and inhumanity, to which they are naturally prone and inclined." A justifiable fear of black revolt—the first serious uprising came in 1712, in New York City—motivated the development of powerful stereotypes. Governor Alexander Spotswood of Virginia, having recently seen a conspiracy put down, told the assembly in 1710 that, of all threats to their colony, blacks, "by their dayly encrease seem to be the most dangerous; and the tryals of last Aprill court may shew that we are not to depend on either their stupidity, or that Babel of languages among 'em; freedom wears a cap which can without a tongue, call together all those who long to shake of[f] the fetters of slavery and as such an insurrection would surely be attended with most dreadfull consequences so I think we cannot be too early in providing against it, both by putting our selves in a better posture of defence and by making a law to prevent the consultations of those negros."

The differences in language between the Carolina code and Spotswood's speech are worth noticing. The Carolinians, influenced by Barbadians, saw blackness as a natural savagery. Spotswood at most thought blacks were stupid, but he respected their overcoming linguistic confusion to unite in revolt, and he saw them as *naturally* inclining to revolt because they were humans and no human would want to be a slave. Early in the eighteenth century some white men had already grasped that creating a racial slave caste was not a very good way of solving a human labor problem. The attribution of negative qualities to blacks as blacks grew in response to a white need to ignore the qualities of blacks as humans—mainly because humans, everyone knew, would not accept a life of slavery. They could be expected to fight for their freedom.

So early American whites had got themselves in a real predicament with amazing speed. On one hand, racial slavery had enabled many of the colonies— including Georgia, after it abandoned its antislavery policy in the late 1740s— to prosper, and had led to a perceptible easing of tensions between the white classes. Georgia, at its founding in 1733, had pioneered a system of collective landownership and no blacks, slave or free. By 1738, some Georgia settlers were arguing vehemently for introducing private property and allowance of racial slavery, "which if granted, would occasion great Numbers of white People to come here, and also render us capable to subsist ourselves." In the eyes of these men the difference between bare survival and prosperity was precisely the difference between the cost of free labor and slave labor. They knew that Georgia's premise was, in part, moral—the colony would be an example of (white) human equality. Equality, however, they prized less than liberty, specifically the liberty to amass wealth, which was the reason most white people came to America in the first place. Without that liberty, they felt like slaves; to acquire that liberty, they needed others to be enslaved. In a remarkably sarcastic way, this point was made in an appeal to Georgia's ruler: "You have afforded us the Opportunity of arriving at the Integrity of the *Primitive Times*, by intailing a more than *Primitive Poverty* on us: The Toil that is necessary to our bare Subsistence, must effectually defend us from the Anxieties of any further Ambition . . . The valuable Virtue of Humility is secured to us, by your Care to prevent our procuring, or so much as seeing, any *Negroes*, (the only human Creatures proper to improve our Soil) lest our Simplicity might mistake the poor *Africans* for greater slaves than ourselves." A few years later, with immigration to Georgia at a standstill, slavery was introduced. Soon "great Numbers of white People" arrived, as did black slaves, and Georgia prospered, just like its vigorous neighbor South Carolina, which by this time had a black majority.

On the other hand, racial slavery meant introducing into society a large internal enemy. What to do? Most colonies opted to tighten racial codes. Blacks would not be allowed to vote, as they had in Virginia until 1723. They could not learn to read and write; they could not worship freely; they could not gather together, earn money, learn trades, move about. They would be made racially separate.

Some mid-century minds saw two large difficulties with this: it was a wretched way for white people to live, and it greatly complicated the emerging vision of a distinct American people. A middle-aged Benjamin Franklin faced these difficulties head-on. His approach is characteristically practical in the American sense: it attempts to think rationally within the irrational context of race. Writing in 1751, he begins with economics: " 'Tis an ill-grounded opinion that by the labour of slaves, *America* may possibly vie in cheapness of manufactures with *Britain*. The labour of slaves can never be so cheap as the labour of working men is in *Britain*." Slaves were too expensive, didn't work hard enough, required the employment of drivers, and stole, "almost every slave being *by Nature* a thief . . . Why then will *Americans* purchase slaves? Because slaves may be kept as long as a man pleases, or has occasion for their labour; while hired men are continually leaving their master (often in the midst of his business), and setting up for themselves."

Having expressed the central problem—free white labor is unreliable, while black slave labor, however imperfect, is not—Franklin fails to resolve it. Instead, he goes on to note some negative effects of racial slavery. Looking at the English Sugar Islands, he sees excess and degeneracy: "The negroes . . . have greatly diminished the whites there; the [white] poor are by this means depriv'd of employment, while a few families acquire vast Estates, which they spend on foreign luxuries . . . The Whites who have slaves, not labouring, are enfeebled . . . Slaves also pejorate [degrade] the Families that use them; the white children become proud, disgusted with labour, and being educated in idleness, are rendered unfit to get a Living by industry." Franklin also remarks that slaves are ill treated and therefore tend to die early, "so that a continual supply is needed from *Africa*."

Black slaves, Franklin reports, have already "blacken'd half *America*." This must stop. Why? Because America should be white and English. Franklin concludes:

> Why should *Pennsylvania*, founded by the *English*, become a colony of *Aliens*, who will shortly be so numerous as to Germanize us instead of our Anglifying them, and will never adopt our language or customs, any more than they can acquire our complexion? Which leads me to add one remark: That the number of purely white people in the world is proportionably very small. All *Africa* is black or tawny. *Asia* chiefly tawny. *America* (exclusive of the new comers) wholly so. And in *Europe*, the *Spaniards*, *Italians*, *French*, *Russians* and *Swedes* are generally of what we call a swarthy complexion; as are the *Germans* also, the *Saxons* only excepted, who with the *English* make the principal body of white people on the face of the earth. I could wish their numbers were increased. And while we are, as I may call it, *scouring* our planet, by clearing *America* of woods, and so making this side of our globe reflect a brighter light to the eyes of inhabitants in *Mars* or *Venus*, why should we in the sight of superior beings, darken its people? Why increase the sons of *Africa*, by planting them in *America*, where we have so fair an opportunity, by excluding all blacks and tawneys, of increasing the lovely white and red? But perhaps I am partial to the complexion of my Country, for such kind of partiality is natural to Mankind.

This may be said to summarize white common sense in the middle of the eighteenth century. America was meant to be a white, English-speaking country.

Never mind why, or to what end. Franklin doesn't speak of a white destiny or mission in the world. Rather, whiteness is a type of natural reality. Blacks live in this white country by virtue of the fact that they can be enslaved and, when enslaved, provide an arguably more efficient labor than do free people. However, ideally there would not be any black people in America.

Efforts to abolish slavery must be understood in this context. Moral abolitionism had existed among a small minority of white colonists since at least 1688, when the Mennonites of Germantown, Pennsylvania, asked, "have these Negroes not as much right to fight for their freedom as you have to keep them slaves?" Quakers continued to argue against slavery on moral grounds from the 1690s onward. But most Americans were not Quakers and did not listen to Quaker preaching; besides, many Quakers owned slaves. More common was a perception that Africans were, after all, human beings, and human beings, as Governor Spotswood noted anxiously in 1710, are unlikely to accept enslavement with any grace. This minimal (and fearful) recognition of a common humanity combined with a general sense, as set out above by Franklin, that black slavery was bad for white people. It made them haughty and lazy. Owning black slaves also tended, as the Quaker abolitionist John Woolman put it in 1762, to "deprave the Mind."

A fear of blacks, then, and a fear of the effects of black slavery on white characters were the main motivations behind abolitionist sentiment in the mid–eighteenth century. What was missing was a strong sense among whites of identification with blacks—a sense that one might as easily have been born black as white and that the merest coincidence made one free rather than a slave. However, the reasons white people had for wanting to abolish slavery were secondary in importance to abolition itself. And abolitionism made enormous strides between 1760 and 1800. As revolutionary notions of liberty and equality gained momentum, numerous white writers saw the contradiction between advocating human freedom and holding slaves. One of the earliest strong defenses of colonial rights against British power, by James Otis in 1764, showed where the emerging secular revolutionary doctrine of human equality might lead: "The Colonists are by the law of nature free born, as indeed all men are, white or black . . . Does it follow that tis right to enslave a man because he is black? . . . Can any logical inference in favour of slavery, be drawn from a flat nose . . . ?" A Massachusetts writer in 1774 assailed slaveholding American patriots for "making a vain parade of being advocates for the liberties of mankind . . . thus making a mockery of your profession by trampling on the sacred rights of Africans." In that same year George Washington made the explicit connection: "we must assert our rights, or submit to every imposition, that can be heaped upon us, till custom and use shall make us tame and abject slaves, as the blacks we rule over with such arbitrary sway."

In this particular way the white Revolutionary generation saw its commonality with black slaves. Slavery and freedom were incompatible. Between 1777 and 1804 slavery was abolished, by one means or another, from Pennsylvania on north. Emancipation was at least seriously debated in the upper South, beginning in Virginia in 1777. The freeing by masters of their own slaves was greatly eased during this period, and increased, notably in Virginia. Abolition societies sprang up after the Revolution everywhere but the Carolinas and Georgia. At the turn of the century, if not before, most of the great revolutionaries— Franklin, John Adams, Washington, Jefferson, Patrick Henry, Madison, Thomas Paine—were antislavery, even as some of them continued, rather shamefacedly, owning slaves because it was economically expedient.

Being antislavery did not mean being pro-black. For one thing, neither an ideology of equal natural rights nor Christian egalitarianism was relativistic. Both maintained that blacks were in no important way different; therefore, "blackness" should not exist. In such systems of thought, being pro-black would make no sense. Further, the enemies of slavery had fought hard against the prevailing ideas of blackness, all of which either were negative or (in the case of fitness for labor) had negative results. Abolitionists argued strenuously that the characteristics of blackness were the result of being a slave, correctable by education and freedom. Blackness was the other side's idea.

Rather than being pro-black, those whites who disapproved of slavery were more likely to be not antiblack—that is, they were against "prejudice," a term that had been increasingly applied to racial ill feeling since the 1760s. Writing in 1788, James Madison said that integration of freed slaves would be "rendered impossible by the prejudices of the whites." The prejudice argument held that whites' low opinion of blacks came either from some innate color aversion or from miseducation. If black slaves were petulant, illiterate shirkers, this was due to their being slaves, not to their blackness. Blackness as such, from the anti-prejudice point of view, had no content at all, positive or negative. Blacks were or could be just like whites, only darker.

The inherent difficulty with this was that, while blacks might be just like whites, they could not be white—a distinction Madison, for one, seemed to find at once insignificant and decisive. As long as whiteness had some importance, a black person could at best be almost white. One can easily see how unattractive this would have been: to have endured a thousand miseries at the hands of people whose power came from their color, only to be told by one's white friends that one was just as good and human as they were, must have seemed a backhanded compliment. Taking such a compliment sincerely would have meant forgetting the realities of white domination and accepting the power of white people to reinvent themselves as innocent and unaffected by their racial past. Why would one want to help any white person, much less the white collective, in this self-cleansing, self-absorbed act? One might well wish to forget the terrible black past for oneself, but was there any good reason to forget it on behalf of whites? How could one agree that racial slavery had just been, so to speak, an honest mistake?

Unfortunately, there are no sources to indicate what blacks thought about this anti-prejudice trend in white American thinking. Certainly, it held potential benefits. But it also held the pitfall of making one's freedom dependent upon the elimination of blackness. Because negative blackness or "prejudice" was widely thought to be entrenched in white minds—and because dark skin color as such could not be removed—many whites who were sympathetic to blacks concluded that the solution to the problem of race was the separation of blacks from white society. So it is perhaps not too surprising that white abolitionists, actively or passively, tended to be racial separatists. This was even more true of the milder opponents of slavery. Former slaves, after all, were not expected to bring anything of value to the republic. The value of slaves to American society lay in their cheapness relative to free labor. That and their ready availability were the keys to the growth of slavery in America. With this critical factor removed, it was very difficult for white Americans to imagine blacks as anything but a burden—or, in the slaveholding states, a threat. In the North white people who concerned themselves with racial issues usually ignored the question of what should happen with free blacks. Educational efforts—the obvious solution, and very much on white minds with respect to whites—were few and ineffectual. Northern voices were resoundingly silent as to the means for black integration. Relatedly, Northern abolitionism all but disappeared after the Revolution, despite the fact that the great majority of blacks remained in bondage. Perhaps, because Northern abolitionists had focused so intently on their own sinfulness, they did not, with their local guilt removed, think racial slavery was any longer very interesting. They had cleansed themselves, and that was what mattered.

The white Southern view necessarily differed. If black slaves were to be free, they would be free right next door. They would compete with white people for jobs, land, love, and everything else. A white society only recently grown accustomed to a rough equality within itself would have to face equality with that other population whose oppression had made white equality functional. And so the rather passive (for the moment) separatism of Northerners turned more active in the South, among those many whites who seriously considered emancipation. The earliest proposal for colonizing blacks had appeared in a Philadelphia paper, from the pen of an abolitionist, in 1768. But the real center of colonization sentiment was in Virginia, the cradle of both slavery and freedom, birthplace of our first presidents, and home to 40 percent of the black population. In 1777 a proposed emancipation bill suggested that freed blacks be sent to some other locales where they might become truly free and independent, and that the same number of white people be imported to take their place. One of the three authors of this bill was Thomas Jefferson, whose opinions on the matter would soon carry great weight.

Jefferson refers to the colonization plan in his *Notes on the State of Virginia*, which he wrote in 1781 while recovering from a bad fall and revised in the winter of 1783–1784; he published these notes after arriving in Paris as a diplomat in 1784, and they quickly became influential. He expected the colonization scheme to be revived once the Revolution ended. Having described colonization, he immediately raises an obvious issue:

> It will probably be asked, Why not retain and incorporate the blacks into the State, and thus save the expense of supplying by importation of white settlers, the vacancies they will leave? Deeprooted prejudices entertained by the whites; ten thousand recollections, by the blacks, of the injuries they have sustained; new provocations; the real distinctions which nature has made; and many other circumstances, will divide us into parties, and produce convulsions, which will probably never end but in the extermination of the one or the other race.
>
> To these objections, which are political, may be added others, which are physical and moral. The first difference which strikes us is that of color . . . And is this difference of no importance? Is it not the foundation of a greater or lesser share of beauty in the two races? Are not the fine mixtures of red and white, the expressions of every passion by greater or lesser suffusions of color in the one, preferable to that eternal monotony, which reigns in the countenances, that immovable veil of black which covers the emotions of the other race? Add to these, flowing hair, a more elegant symmetry of form, their own judgment in favor of the whites, declared by their preference of them, as uniformly as is the preference of the Oran-utan [ape] for the black woman over those of his own species . . . Besides those of color, figure, and hair, there are other physical distinctions proving a difference of race. They have less hair on the face and body. They secrete less by the kidneys, and more by the glands of the skin, which gives them a very strong and disagreeable odor . . . They seem to require less sleep. A black after hard labor through the day, will be induced by the slightest amusements to sit up till midnight, or later . . . They are

at least as brave, and more adventuresome. But this may proceed from a want of forethought . . . They are more ardent after their female; but love seems with them to be more an eager desire, than a tender delicate mixture of sentiment and sensation . . . In general, their existence appears to participate more of sensation than of reflection. To this must be ascribed their disposition to sleep . . . [Blacks are] in reason much inferior . . . in imagination they are dull, tasteless, and anomalous.

Jefferson was not one to give unmixed compliments. He had a mathematical mind, even a talent for arithmetic, and he mathematically undermines his kind remarks about blacks with qualifications. He also finds them at once needing little sleep, yet sleepy. In any case, these are not the sort of people he would want in the country he was helping to create.

It is important to remember that, elsewhere in the *Notes*, Jefferson argued at length that he did not want more foreigners, either, in the prospective United States. Like Franklin thirty years earlier, he wanted the new land to be peopled through a natural increase of "the lovely white and red" already propagating so well. "It is for the happiness of those united in society to harmonize as much as possible in matters which they must of necessity transact together . . . Every species of government has its specific principles. Ours perhaps are more peculiar than those of any other in the universe. It is a composition of the freest principles of the English constitution, with others derived from natural right and natural reason. To these nothing can be more opposed than the maxims of absolute monarchies. Yet from such we are to expect the greatest numbers of emigrants. They will bring with them the principles of the governments they leave . . . These principles, with their language, they will transmit to their children. In proportion to their numbers, they will share with us in legislation. They will infuse into it their spirit, warp and bias its directions, and render it a heterogeneous, incoherent, distracted mass."

Jefferson makes an exception for talented "artificers," then goes on to mention that the Virginia assembly had at least tried to ban the importation of slaves, which might have helped "stop the increase of this great political and moral evil." This at first seems a non sequitur. Of all his many reasons for despising blacks, Jefferson at no point criticizes them for importing the "maxims of absolute monarchies." But Jefferson is attempting to define the United States and what makes it a nation. One characteristic of the nation is the best of Englishness. Another is Americans' miraculous combining, alone in the universe, of this Englishness with natural right and reason. A third is whiteness, but therein lies a difficulty: not all whites are American. Further, white Americans such as Jefferson did not want to think that their skin color was part of what made them deserve their own distinct nation. That would have been both ridiculous and humiliating. So, when considering European immigrants, those immigrants were not white. Only their despotic inheritance mattered. But when considering blacks, the prospective replacements for slaves are identified as white, and only as white. In a real sense, the Europeans become white in America.

Yet we can imagine that, if all blacks were "removed beyond the reach of mixture," as Jefferson put it, white Americans might cease to be white. America could then become its higher self, the one for which men had so recently fought and died. The discussions of African removal, and of manumission, suggest that something like an urge not to be white motivated many thoughtful white men in the immediate post-Revolution period. First, economic desire — that commanding master which had caused the slaveholder Patrick Henry to whisper with reluctance, "I am drawn along by ye general Inconvenience of living without [slaves]; I will not, I cannot justify it"—had lost some of its force. Virginia was already exporting slaves to the deeper South; it needed them less. In a related vein, the presumed sanctity of property rights, which would be so important in later slavery struggles, appears to have waned in importance. While Virginians were debating colonization of blacks, they were also tightening restrictions on private manumission. Restricting a master's ability to free his slave property was an explicit violation of the master's property right. And, on the whole, the colonization proposals, made by slave owners, did not speak of compensating slave owners for their property loss. So the economic and property factors in racial slavery appear not to have played a large role in the minds of those slave owners hoping to expel blacks from the new nation.

Second, the colonization debates and proposals did focus, intensely, on white prejudice. This is the first extensive discussion in our literature of the nature of white people. It was carried on by whites, slaveholding whites. And they could not find a single good thing to say about white people. The major problem with freeing blacks, they said, was that white people were prejudiced against them, and this prejudice was generally viewed as a shortcoming. Discussing integration of freedmen, St. George Tucker wrote in 1796, "Who is there so free from prejudices among us, as candidly to declare that he has none against such a measure?" Tucker advocated colonization, as did Ferdinando Fairfax, who had actually come up with a plan in 1790. Integration would be impossible, Fairfax believed, because "prejudices, sentiments, or whatever they may be called would be found to operate so powerfully as to be insurmountable."

It is a little odd to hear white slave owners in the 1790s criticizing themselves, or at least whites in general, for being racially prejudiced. But at the time there was little content to whiteness apart from prejudice against blacks and a certain fondness for one's own appearance. These men knew perfectly well that racial slavery was evil, not to mention against their principles. They knew they probably didn't even need it to prosper, at least in Virginia. This was the rack upon which they tortured themselves. The problem, in the end, was not slavery, which they were ready to do without. The problem was a white way of thinking, from which they felt unable to extricate themselves or their country. They desperately wanted to start over, on fresh principles. Wasn't that a goal of the Revolution? But they could not imagine starting over with a population of free blacks. Perhaps this is because the presence of blacks was, in fact, the reminder that societies don't really get to start over.

Plans to colonize free blacks in the 1790s never went anywhere. The expense would have been staggering, the necessary political will immense. The Northern states were uninterested; they had already solved their problem by abolishing slavery and, not just coincidentally, having relatively few blacks in the first place. A moderate, day-by-day racial separatism would suit them fine. Apart from Pennsylvania, the states most likely to receive freed slaves—Ohio, Maryland, Delaware, and Kentucky—had in short order passed laws prohibiting the in-migration of free blacks. South Carolina and Georgia, utterly dependent on slave labor for their prosperity, had never been interested in colonization, while North Carolina was more interested in fighting Indians. The colonization idea was, in any case, a nearly insane one. But its madness sprang from the heart of the new country, which is why it would reappear, like racial separatism, again and again.

"WE CAN BE AS SEPARATE

AS THE FINGERS"

SEGREGATION FROM THE AMERICAN REVOLUTION

TO THE GILDED AGE

■

It was, to be sure, a shared sort of madness. The earliest record of blacks in America wanting to separate themselves along racial lines appeared in 1773, when four slaves in Boston petitioned the legislature for help in returning to Africa. "We are willing," they wrote, "to submit to such regulations and laws, as may be made relative to us, until we leave the province, which we determine to do, as soon as we can, from our joynt labours, procure money to transport ourselves to some part of the Coast of Africa, where we propose a settlement." This was desperation. "Some part of the Coast of Africa" suggests that the men felt they belonged among black people—that their skin color held an importance beyond that of a state, tribe, or lineage. This was not the opinion of people who actually lived on the coast of Africa, unless they were entirely caught up in the slave trade. And the Boston men did not want to go to Africa in order to be caught up, again, in the slave business.

The basic idea of getting away from white people, however, had deep roots. There had been two black escapee states in Brazil in the early and middle seventeenth century. The Cimarrons on the Central American isthmus had also set a powerful example. Following the success of Francis Drake and others at forming black-white alliances, Spain made a treaty with one important Cimarron group, recognizing its sovereignty (and ending its cooperation with the English). Escapees, most famously in Jamaica, had formed durable, if economically marginal, communities.

The fundamental desire seems to have been for freedom, not for any type of racial mission. Because blackness was so much a creation of white power, an escape into blackness might well have been nonsensical. Rather, one would have wanted to escape into a full humanity. In America the Revolutionary environment raised hopes enormously, as whites were quick to realize, and the abolitionist surge after 1776 would have encouraged confidence in a new, multiracial (or nonracial), free America. However, it was evident by 1787, with slavery becoming fixed in the Constitution, that blacks would not be accorded full humanity among white people. In that pivotal year eight black men met in Philadelphia to found the Free African Society, the first significant independent black racial organization. Within months some of the eight joined with others in the first recorded nonviolent action against unequal segregation. At St. George's Methodist Episcopal Church in Philadelphia, a group of blacks arrived one Sunday morning and, at the moment a prayer began, took their seats as usual, then knelt to pray. As they prayed, white men came to them and said they should move to the rear. The worshippers asked to be left alone at least until the prayer had ended. The agitated whites insisted. It must have been such a distracted and chaotic prayer. When it was done, the black worshippers quietly stood and walked out. This act began the process of establishing a separate black church denomination in America. The first black school was founded in that year, in New York City, and by this time some free blacks had already begun separate Masonic lodges and mutual-aid organizations.

Also in 1787, the year of our Constitution, Britain established Sierra Leone as an African home for returning slaves—and Prince Hall led the first large-scale call by American blacks for a return to Africa. Hall, who had organized the first black Masonic lodge in Boston in 1775 and, like thousands of blacks, fought for the Revolution, spoke for seventy-three "African blacks" in telling the Massachusetts General Court of the "disagreeable and disadvantageous circumstances" characteristic of free black life in New England. These "and other considerations which we need not here particularly mention induce us to return to Africa, our native country, which warm climate is more natural and agreeable to us; and for which the God of nature has formed us; and where we shall live among our equals and be more comfortable and happy, than we can be in our present situation." Prince Hall also demanded equal educational opportunity for blacks in Boston. The coincidence of these two ideas—racial equality in America and a return to Africa—implies that as a free black person one felt oneself to be not only a partial American but a provisional one, dependent on future developments. This is a bizarre social status on its face, but, of course, many whites had exactly the same conception of how blacks fit, or didn't fit, into the new society whites considered their own.

As it happened, the early peaceful efforts at racial self-determination coincided with violent ones: the revolt of Haiti's blacks (slave and free) against France and the planter class, and Gabriel Prosser's uprising in Virginia. The Haitian revolution had several stages, beginning in the 1780s and culminating in full independence in 1804. Prosser's revolt, in 1800, was briefer and unsuccessful. Prosser had amassed a core group of a few dozen, whose plan was to take Richmond and go on to make Virginia an independent black state with a white minority. Apparently, several thousand slaves were ready to rise up, but when the attackers assembled, two slaves informed on them. A huge thunderstorm followed, washing out a key bridge. Prosser postponed the invasion, but it was too late to go unnoticed back to the plantations, for the rebels had already been betrayed. Prosser and more than thirty of his men were hanged.

At their trial one of the rebels said, "I have nothing more to offer than what General Washington would have had to offer, had he been taken by the British and put to trial by them. I have adventured my life in endeavouring to obtain the liberty of my countrymen." The rhetoric of American liberation had returned to hit its white beneficiaries with a vengeance. A contributor to a Virginia newspaper commented, following Prosser's revolt: "Liberty and equality have brought the evil upon us. A doctrine which, however intelligible, and admissible, in a land of freemen, is not only unintelligible and inadmissible, but dangerous and extremely wicked in this country, where every white man is a master, and every black man is a slave. This doctrine, in this country, and in every country like this (as the horrors of St. Domingo [Haiti] have already proved), cannot fail of producing either a general insurrection, or a general emancipation." The writer pointed out that whites habitually spoke of liberty and equality even when their slaves could hear, as, for example, at dinnertime when they were serving. "What else then could we expect than what has happened?"

The uprisings in Haiti and Virginia, a surge in private manumissions, and Northern abolition combined to focus in white minds the notion that blacks were united as blacks. As a race, blacks were widely thought to spend much of their mental time imagining a day when they could kill whites and take over the country. Whites attributed to blacks a racial mission. They reacted to it, on one hand, by tightening slave codes and, on the other, by restricting the movement of free blacks. It also became standard white opinion around this time that blacks of whatever condition should not be educated, as a little knowledge would probably take them a long way toward demanding equality. Antiblack laws were extremely common throughout the young republic, not only in the South and the states bordering it but in, for example, the antislavery state of Massachusetts. Within one roughly twenty-four hour period Massachusetts had both proscribed the slave trade and restricted free blacks. The two could be, and often were, part of the same impulse. One could easily be antislavery and antiblack.

White separatism created black separatism, and the solidifying of both coincided with the creation of our nation. Neither race, at this point, appears to have assigned much positive meaning to its racial identity. As we have seen, whites did not desire to be white as such. Their principal wish as whites was not to be black. Similarly, free blacks in the immediate post-Revolutionary period probably did not want to be black. They did not write on the particular excellence of blackness. Blackness was a condition forced upon them. But having noticed, particularly in the Northern states recently freed of slavery, that whites in the new republic were determined to maintain their superiority, black leaders decided to make the best of blackness by organizing themselves along racial lines.

Around 1810 a free black-Indian sea captain in Massachusetts, Paul Cuffe, began thinking of ways to start a trade in black immigrants to Africa. (Prince Hall had died in 1807, his back-to-Africa dreams unrealized.) In 1811 Cuffe visited Sierra Leone and met in England with its backers, the African Institution. Upon return home, he helped organize tiny African Institutions among free blacks in Baltimore, Philadelphia, and New York, as sources for the trade. The work was meant to help Africa itself: Cuffe believed American blacks would, with their Christian faith, uplift the presumably non-Christian Africans they met.

Cuffe had bad luck with his timing. Britain and America were at war by 1812, and Sierra Leone was British. Cuffe petitioned Congress for permission to trade with the enemy. The bill was widely debated; it passed the Senate and went to the House, where one white Cuffe ally argued that immigration of free blacks to Africa would help remove "a part of our population which we could well spare." But the voting went seventy-two to sixty-five against. In early 1816, with the war over, Cuffe did land thirty-eight blacks in Sierra Leone. The British took the colonists but refused, under the terms of the recent peace treaty, to trade with Cuffe. In all, the captain lost about four thousand dollars.

Nevertheless, Cuffe's initiative stirred interest in colonization—at least, among whites, for example, Reverend Robert Finley, who had corresponded with Cuffe. The times were rife with benevolence. A reinvigorated Protestantism had spawned countless societies aimed at the improvement of just about everything. This was the field of action for any ambitious clergyman, and Robert Finley had ambition. He had married well—to the foster daughter of New Jersey's Elias Boudinot, the same Boudinot who took such an interest in Cherokees. The Boudinot connection gave Finley access to men of wealth and distinction. In 1816, casting about for a benevolent cause, Finley hit on African colonization. It would benefit America by helping the country "be cleared of" free blacks and those freed slaves who were no longer needed or wanted. Colonization would benefit Africa by giving that continent some "partially civilized and Christianized" newcomers, who might there achieve an equality not possible for them in America.

Finley first took his idea to the synods of New York and New Jersey, then to a small group of interested people in Princeton. New Jersey whites had watched the state's free black population nearly quadruple in thirty years; this was one source of the Princetonians' interest. Finley argued that having free blacks in the neighborhood was "unfavorable to our industry and morals" and might lead to "intermixture." His proposed colonization society would be directed from Washington, under congressional auspices, and would be national in scope, because racial slavery, "the great violation of the laws of nature," was a national crime requiring a national "atoning sacrifice" for the "injuries done to humanity by our ancestors." Africa's bosom had begun "to warm with hope and her heart to beat with expectation and desire," as she was "panting for the return of her absent sons and daughters."

Finley went to Washington and immediately enlisted the aid of Elias Boudinot Caldwell, his wife's brother, who had taken on the name of his foster father. Caldwell was chief clerk of the Supreme Court—the Court met in his home after the British burned the Capitol in 1814. He knew all the justices, of course, as well as Daniel Webster, Henry Clay, John C. Calhoun, Lafayette, and other notables. Caldwell brought in his good friend Francis Scott Key, an able attorney as well as author of "The Star-Spangled Banner." Finley, Caldwell, and Key knew everyone in Washington and formed the activist core of the nascent American Colonization Society.

Henry Clay, the Speaker of the House, presided over their first hopeful meeting. "Can there be a nobler cause," he asked, "than that which, whilst it proposed to rid our country of a useless and pernicious, if not dangerous part of its population, contemplates the spreading of the arts of civilized life, and the possible redemption from ignorance and barbarism of a benighted quarter of the globe!" Evidently, blacks, who were useless and dangerous in the United States, would become propagators of civilization once they crossed the Atlantic.

Elias Boudinot Caldwell emphasized that, because of prejudice, blacks could never be equal in America, so they should leave. Educating them was a fool's errand: "the more you cultivate their minds, the more miserable you make them." Caldwell, like Clay and like John Randolph of Roanoke, who spoke later, urged that the slavery question be avoided. On that basis, the American Society for Colonizing the Free People of Color in the United States came

into being. It united many of the most distinguished men of the nation; the secretary of the treasury quickly joined, as did the future president Andrew Jackson.

The colonizationist movement would gain support in nearly every corner of
white American society between 1817 and 1835. Some saw it as a step to aboli-
tion, others did not. But all agreed that being rid of free blacks was an excellent
notion. Of the Revolutionary generation, Jefferson, Madison, Monroe, and
Samuel Adams had approved the idea; so would Supreme Court justice John
Marshall and former justice Bushrod Washington, the presidents of Yale,
Columbia, Princeton, and Harvard, politicians such as Clay, Webster, Stephen
Douglas, Millard Fillmore, and the future abolitionist leaders Gerrit Smith and
William Lloyd Garrison. Dozens of auxiliary societies sprang up across the
country. Fourteen state legislatures would eventually give their official endorsement to black removal. Clergymen of various faiths preached colonization as a
social reform; the voluntary removal of free blacks to Africa became a special
subject of Fourth of July sermons, when collections for it were taken. White
American opinion could hardly have been more unanimous. Everywhere, the
free black population was increasing, perceived to increase, or expected to
increase. Everywhere, whites did not want free blacks near them. And everywhere that the subject was discussed, whites agreed that blacks could never be
equal because white prejudice would not allow them to be. Virginia's position
in the 1790s had become the national position.

White Americans widely perceived colonization of blacks, by this time
numbering several million, to be moderate and rational, a practical compromise. It could bring about a gradual emancipation of slaves by their masters
without needlessly upsetting the latter. It would separate two antagonistic populations, enabling both to pursue self-determination alone. Colonization sought
a middle course between abolitionism and continued slavery. The first would
simply split the Union; the second would gradually destroy the soul. Colonizationists also expected racial slavery to wither away as free labor, in line with population increase, became cheaper. Given this trend, thoughtful men believed
black removal to be a timely measure for easing the black race and slave labor
out of the picture.

That such an absurd scheme as colonizing three million or so people would
appear as the sensible solution to America's racial problems indicates just how
much race had unhinged the American mind by about 1820. Many white
Americans felt themselves to be under increasing psychological torment
because slavery reflected so poorly on them. Some found relief in an argument
favored by Thomas Jefferson: that slavery and the presence of blacks in America
were not their fault. These had been the fault of Britain, or of one's unwise
ancestors, or of a colonialist greed since eliminated by the self-improving men

of the nineteenth century. The present white generation, including slave owners, was blameless. Once the physical reminder of the guilty past—black people—had been removed, so too would that past itself, and America would start fresh, much as it would have in 1787 except for the persistence of slavery. Additional solace could be found in the emerging belief that blacks really were different by nature, a scientifically distinct set of people, probably inferior but in any case best kept separate. This belief, of course, needed its companion, that whiteness was a category of nature, an important one, with positive qualities. Each of these three beliefs grew in power from the 1820s onward.

Free blacks, too, were tormented. In some ways, they lived in the same psychological trap as whites did. Most of them, or their ancestors, had been slaves, which gave them an inheritance mainly of pain, shame, and self-doubt. However temporarily hopeful they may have been about their prospects in an independent United States, they began to perceive whites as radically and permanently different, a separate race incapable of changing itself. This perception had its twin: that blacks were a race, created more by circumstance than by nature but separate nonetheless, and perhaps with qualities all its own.

Blacks reacted to the American Colonization Society with ambivalence. Reverend Finley met some free blacks in Philadelphia, and Paul Cuffe's black emigrationist friend James Forten, a prosperous sailmaker, wrote to him of the reaction in January 1817: "Indeed, the people of color here was very much frightened. At first they were afraid that all the free people would be compelled to go, particularly in the southern states. We had a large meeting of males at the Rev. R. Allen's church the other evening. Three thousand at least attended, and there was not one soul that was in favor of going to Africa. They think that the slaveholders wants to get rid of them so as to make their property more secure. However, it appears to me that if the Father of all Mercies is in this interesting subject (for it appeared that they all think that something must and ought to be done, but do not know where nor how to begin), the way will be made straight and clear . . . My opinion is that they will never become a people until they come out from amongst the white people." The meeting passed resolutions decrying "the unmerited stigma . . . cast upon the reputation of the free people of color." They did not want to visit "the savage wilds of Africa." America was their home, and their racial fate as free men and women could not be unlinked from that of slaves: "We will never separate ourselves voluntarily from the slave population of this country."

The last sentiment is especially important. Free blacks as blacks were expressing a racial solidarity with slaves, a gesture of profound generosity. It represented a historical depth—a refusal to abandon the past—that must have been nearly incomprehensible to many white minds. Why find in yourself a part that is enslaved? Why dwell upon such suffering? Why not forget as best you can this regrettable slavery business and start over?

The Philadelphia resolutions also rejected Africa, seeing the black part of that continent as backward and inferior. The blackness of these Philadelphia men was not African but a racial condition shared by freeman and slave in the United States (although free-black societies habitually titled themselves African). A group of Richmond free blacks was more receptive to the society's propositions but did not want to go to Africa. They preferred a colony out West, along the Missouri River, or in some other North American location. After meeting with Philadelphia blacks, Reverend Finley reported: "The more enlightened they were, the more decisively they expressed themselves on the desirability of becoming a separate people." The white preacher was among the more thoroughgoing of early black separatists.

Forten had neatly summarized the situation. One had to do something, but what? The whites would use colonization to force people from their homes to a strange and unknown land where people just happened to be black. Emigration, by removing free blacks and the example of freedom they set, and by providing a safe depository for the troublesome, would simply improve the slaveholders' hold on their slaves. And yet it seemed impossible to Forten that blacks could ever realize their desire (or his desire for them) to become "a people" while living with whites—a people just as whites were a people.

Black colonization involved deep paradoxes. One was that it essentially proposed to blacks that they go to a black place so that they could cease being black—so that they could be human like anyone else. This alludes to a more profound paradox of racial separatism, at least in 1817: it represented an urge to be in a race and yet not to be in a race, to be "race-free." In future days we would learn that racial separatism can be small as well as large, that you can "separate" in myriad tiny ways from a banished thought to a smile, in your choice of casual language, in what you don't say to someone of another race, in the way you wear your hat. But in the period from 1817 to 1835 racial separatism was a large affair, at the core both of one's self and of national life.

The paradox of wanting to be in the black race and not wanting to be in it or any race steadily worked away at black society. Some thousands of blacks, already free and newly freed, would go to Liberia under the American Colonization Society plan. They did not go because they thought themselves "useless and pernicious." Some developed a positive view of Africanness and blackness, the beginnings of a cultural nationalism. The sources for this are difficult to locate with precision. In 1787 Count Volney, who was white, published, in French and English editions, *Travels through Syria and Egypt*. After gazing at the flat-nosed Sphinx and consulting Herodotus, Volney concluded that "the ancient Egyptians were real negroes" and went on to say: "How are we astonished . . . when we reflect that to the race of negroes, at present our slaves, and the objects of our extreme contempt, we owe our arts, sciences, and even the very use of speech; and when we recollect that, in the midst of those nations who call themselves the friends of liberty and humanity, the most barbarous of slaveries is justified; and that it is even a problem whether the understanding of negroes be of the same species with that of white men!" Volney returned to the theme in his contemplative 1791 masterpiece, *The Ruins,* in which a wise phantom informs the narrator, "A race of men now rejected from society for their *sable skin and frizzled hair,* founded on the study of the laws of nature, those civil and religious systems which still govern the universe." Volney supported this with a lengthy footnote citing classical sources: "we have the strongest reason to believe that the country neighboring to the tropic was the cradle of the sciences, and of consequence that the first learned nation was a nation of Blacks." *The Ruins* had as its theme the rise and fall of empires and the degeneracy of man. Volney argued that the source of evil in society lay with the decision of some, through the perversion of self-love, to hold themselves over others, and to make those others labor while their oppressors luxuriated in self-congratulation. Such societies, however, could never be sustained indefinitely. The ultimate example was blacks, once first in greatness, now first in debasement.

Volney's argument for African glory well served his bitterly ironic philosophy of history. Volney was known among Americans; *The Ruins* received its best English translation with the help of the American poet Joel Barlow, a friend of Thomas Jefferson. Barlow published the work in Paris in 1802. As a student, Volney had attended the same salon as Benjamin Franklin. He traveled through the United States in 1795–1798 and found a welcome in prominent circles. Perhaps he converted one or two people to his vision of Africa? He certainly influenced Henri Grégoire, another Frenchman with many American friends, including Thomas Paine (and Joel Barlow). Grégoire labored all his life against slavery, and as part of that work wrote *On the Cultural Achievements of Negroes* (1808). He wanted to respond to Jefferson's influential remarks in *Notes on the State of Virginia* concerning black inferiority. To that end, he cited Volney, and supporting classical writers, to argue that civilization as his generation understood it originated in Africa, among black people. He also provided a gallery of distinguished black people through the ages—the first instance of a black race-pride tradition that continues today. "The natives of Africa and America," Grégoire wrote, "would long ago have risen to the highest level of civilization if this good purpose would have been supported by a hundredth part of the efforts, the money, and the time that all have been given over to tormenting and butchering many millions of these unfortunate people, whose blood calls for vengeance against Europe." Grégoire sent a copy of his book to Jefferson, who was unimpressed, as he explained in a private letter to the ubiquitous Joel Barlow.

Whether Grégoire or Volney had much direct influence on black American thinking is hard to say, but the arguments they pioneered do appear as early as 1827 in a black source—*Freedom's Journal*, the first black newspaper in the country. Following their premier issue the editors published "Mutability of Human Affairs," which meditated on how empires rise and fall, including that of ancient, black Egypt: "Mankind generally allow that all nations are indebted to the Egyptians for the introduction of the arts and sciences; but they are not willing to acknowledge that the Egyptians bore any resemblance to the present race of Africans; though Herodotus, 'the father of history,' expressly declares that the 'Egyptians had black skins and frizzled hair.' All we know of Ethiopia, strengthens us in the belief, that it was early inhabited by a people, whose manners and customs nearly resembled those of the Egyptians."

Like white Americans and Indians in the same period, blacks were composing a story of racial destiny. Generally it mixed classical learning with archaeological evidence and biblical passages. These were laid out in a progressive scheme: ancient glory, followed by decline, followed by a slow but certain rising of the race. The scheme was common to each of the three major races in America. Blacks and whites, however, in contrast to Indians, tended to locate their origins in more or less the same place—or at least neighboring places, Greece and Egypt/Ethiopia. They could be seen almost as history's twins, separate and inseparable. (Robert Alexander Young's extraordinary *Ethiopian Manifesto* of 1829 prophesied a black savior who would appear to be white.) Certainly, in the 1820s and long afterward, black nationalists saw black culture in much the way that whites saw white culture, with nearly the same sources and the same goals of liberty, equality, and middle-class Protestant gentility.

From a distance it seems strange that the two races should have so greatly resembled each other, given that they were in the process of discovering themselves as polar opposites, and given that one race was tyrannically powerful and the other, on the whole, subjugated. But in many ways their experiences were the same. They were both uprooted, New World peoples. They had fought and worked together for generations. They had learned to want the same things. Indeed, this fundamental sameness, tuned to a certain key, is what made the racial division in America so unbearable. Having embarked down this path, both races soon perceived the same destination: a war of racial extermination. By the 1830s apocalyptic logic seems to have dominated moderate white opinion. Alexis de Tocqueville wrote, "When I contemplate the condition of the South, I can only discover two alternatives which may be adopted by the white inhabitants of those States; viz., either to emancipate the negroes, and to inter-mingle with them; or, remaining isolated from them, to keep them in a state of slavery as long as possible. All intermediate measures seem to me likely to ter-minate, and that shortly, in the most horrible of civil wars, and perhaps in the extirpation of one or other of the two races." His opinion was shared by the moderate colonizationist W. M. Atkinson of Virginia, who believed that eman-cipation without black removal would "end in the extermination of the one race or the other—and if so, I do not doubt it would be the African." Henry Clay, whose political skill it was to express consensus, said in 1839: "In the slave States the alternative is, that the white man must govern the black, or the black govern the white . . . An immediate abolition of slavery . . . would be followed by a des-perate struggle for immediate ascendancy of the black race over the white race, or rather it would be followed by instantaneous collisions between the two races, which would break out into a civil war that would end in the extermina-tion or subjugation of the one race or the other."

That some of the most powerful white men in a country ruled by white men could have seen enslaved black men as their equals in terms of basic drives, lust for domination, and racial unity tells us much about white Americans of the period. David Walker, whose Appeal in Four Articles of 1829 reached a wide audience and received a terrified white response, shows how similar tensions could play themselves out in the mind of a thoughtful free black man. He com-pared whites to "devils," calling slaveholders the "natural enemies" of black people. Whites are characterized by their poor qualities:

> I know that the blacks, take them half enlightened and ignorant, are more humane and merciful than the most enlightened and refined European that can be found in all the earth. Let no one say that I assert this because I am prejudiced on the side of my colour, and against the whites or Europeans. For what I write, I do it candidly, for my God and the good of both parties: Natural observations have taught me these things; there is a solemn awe in the hearts of the blacks, as it respects *murdering* men: whereas the whites (though they are great cowards), where they have the advantage, or think there are any prospects of getting it, they mur-der all before them, in order to subject men to wretchedness and degradation under them. This is the natural result of pride and avarice.

The aversion of blacks to murdering, Walker adds, explains why whites can take advantage of them. But " 'Every dog must have its day,' the American's is coming to an end." Unless "you speedily alter your course," Walker tells white Americans, "*you* and your *Country are gone!!!!!!*"

The characteristic pridefulness and will to power of whites extends, Walker believes, even to white women who would marry black men: "I would not give a *pinch of snuff* to be married to any white person I ever saw in all the days of my life. And I do say it, that the black man, or man of colour, who will leave his own colour . . . and marry a white woman, to be a double slave to her, just because she is *white*, ought to be treated by her as he surely will be, viz.: as a NIGER!!!!"

Concerning blackness, Walker alluded, as would many writers after him, to a passage in Psalms: "Princes shall come out of Egypt; Ethiopia shall soon stretch out her hands unto God." He mentions the accomplishments of "the sons of Africa or of Ham, among whom learning originated, and was carried thence into Greece, where it was improved upon and refined." He also speaks of Hannibal, "that mighty son of Africa . . . who defeated and cut off so many thousands of the white Romans or murderers." Hannibal would have taken Rome if Carthaginians had been united, "but they were dis-united, as the coloured people are now, in the United States of America, the reason our natural enemies are enabled to keep their feet on our throats." As well as being more humane than whites, blacks are better warriors.

Walker describes an America in which, "Even here in Boston, pride and prejudice have got to such a pitch, that in the very houses erected to the Lord, they have built little places for the reception of coloured people." Meanwhile, too many blacks release themselves into sloth, ignorance, racial shame, and racial betrayal. Some even reach for colonization, "a plan got up, by a gang of slave-holders," for deliverance. But blacks are here to stay. They enriched the land with their labor, and will stay. Whites must change: "I speak Americans for your good. We must and shall be free I say, in spite of you . . . And wo, wo, will be to you if we have to obtain our freedom by fighting. Throw away your fears and prejudices then, and enlighten us and treat us like men, and we will like you more than we do now hate you, and tell us now no more about colonization, for America is as much our country, as it is yours. — Treat us like men, and there is no danger but we will all live in peace and happiness together. For we are not like you, hard hearted, unmerciful, and unforgiving . . . Treat us then like men, and we will be your friends. And there is not a doubt in my mind, but that the whole of the past will be sunk into oblivion . . . ."

Like Henri Grégoire, Walker took as his main polemical opponent Thomas Jefferson, whose *Notes on the State of Virginia* Walker called "as great a barrier to our emancipation as any thing that has ever been advanced against us." But Walker came from a later generation than Jefferson, one that had lived through the Protestant Second Great Awakening and had an increased attachment to worldly progress as a divine activity. The general idea was that one walked backward into the future, sweeping away the detritus of an unwise past as one advanced—yet one also walked confidently face forward, accumulating sensible wealth and happiness as one steadily approached fulfillment of the orderly, divine plan. This middle-class way of thinking had enormous power, as it provided many men and women with a reason to believe that their hard work would always be rewarded. It also banished a more tragic cast of mind to the upper and lower reaches of society—those who knew that little work could bring huge rewards, and those who saw their own vast labors bringing no rewards at all. Finally, this modern way of thinking had an explosive quality. It raised expectations, which could take on apocalyptic forms, such as the prophecy of End Times that, after its failure, became known as the Great Disappointment.

Being wholly responsible for oneself could liberate, but it also fed a particularly American terror, an overpowering fear of failure, of losing. The revolutionaries had been an elite that identified its political vision as a truth recovered from the past and systematized by present wisdom. American democracy after about 1820 had nothing to do with the past, almost no systematization, and often an indifference to wisdom. It honored the fight for money. This is the period when Andrew Jackson wrote—approvingly, anxiously—of trampling the forefathers' graves in the rush to self-advancement, when a European visitor wrote that in America "the children glide away from their parents . . . brothers and sisters stream off to the right and left, mutually forgetting one another, and being forgotten by their families." As Tocqueville said, "no one cares for what occurred before his time." Such a society could cohere only in constant motion. The new white Americans feared any kind of social control, and they equally feared losing self-control. It was an era of fantastic, selfish violence— and of self-help, in temperance societies, home medicine, and church groups. The future would bring everything, if you had enough desire and enough self-possession. Perhaps more importantly, the future would excuse everything. Forgiving and forgetting became nearly synonymous. Both were considered virtuous. In the headlong rush toward self-advancement, it could probably not have been otherwise.

The principal way in which this individualist culture acted collectively was to wage semi-declared war on Indians and blacks. By 1838 most states had made it illegal for free black men to vote. In the 1830s violence against free blacks in the Northern states was commonplace. This was whites' response to David Walker's urging them to change: they changed for the worse. And blacks responded by becoming more black. They solidified their separate church denominations, they held colored-peoples conventions, they read black papers, formed yet more black societies, wrote numberless petitions. They told themselves that empires rise and fall, that they were descended from the first civilized people on earth, the Ethiopians/Egyptians, that they would rise again as prophesied in the Bible.

They talked then of colonization, as they talked of war. Whites, of course, spoke of these too. But then, as the black nationalist Martin R. Delany wrote, blacks had "merged in the habits and customs of our oppressors." The same obvious, ludicrous "solutions" to the race problem—separation, extermination—occurred to both races at the same time. The faint possibility of assimilating free blacks while preserving slavery had been brusquely closed off by the Fugitive Slave Act of 1850, which in effect made every free black person a potential slave. The act legislatively united black America, capping the trend toward black separatism that began in the 1780s. Many, probably most, free blacks would still have followed the timeserving advice of the Colored National Convention of 1848: "although it may seem to conflict with our views of human brotherhood, we shall undoubtedly for many years be compelled to have institutions of a complexional character, in order to attain this very idea of universal brotherhood. We would, however, advise our brethren to occupy memberships and stations among white persons, and in white institutions, just so fast as our rights are secured to us . . . By so acting, we shall find many opportunities for removing prejudices and establishing the rights of all men." However, this provisional, meliorative separatism, as well as the mundane business of converting whites to their own ideals, had more fiery complements. Henry Highland Garnet had already addressed the National Negro Convention in 1843 on the subject of war. Just one vote prevented the convention's adopting his speech as reflecting the consensus. Garnet had directed his remarks at slaves: "You had better all die—*die immediately*, than live slaves and entail your wretchedness upon your posterity. If you would be free in this generation, here is your only hope. However much you and all of us may desire it, there is not much hope of redemption without the shedding of blood. If you must bleed, let it all come at once . . ." Even the 1848 convention, while referring to "the great law of progress," also recommended that freemen school themselves in "military tactics."

So by the 1840s a population of dark people had become, as James Forten had put it, a people. They were coming out from among the white people. Given slavery, the gradual exclusion of blacks from any equality in the Northern states, and their preemptive exclusion from the new Western states, the final alternatives did seem to be either Garnet's mass suicide or emigration. Garnet advocated colonization, as did Delany and, at one bleak moment, Frederick Douglass. This removal idea, so congenial to whites across the nation from the 1820s onward, reached its antebellum culmination among blacks with the National Emigration Convention of 1854 and the founding of the African Civilization Society in 1858, with Garnet as president. Still, very few blacks actually emigrated, and opposition to the white American Colonization Society remained, on the whole, vehement. Emigration was more an activity of the mind, an interior relocation mirroring the external separation. It was no more practical when advocated by blacks than when urged by whites.

Racial emigration was a very American act, in every sense. Many black colonizationists did not want to go to Africa. From 1830 onward there was much talk of Canada, which had small but growing black communities just over the border—the final destination of escaped slaves, particularly once the Fugitive Slave Act rendered all of the United States enemy territory. Many looked to South and Central America, others to Haiti, where Columbus had founded his first town and where Toussaint-Louverture had forced the first black republic into being. (A few blacks actually did relocate to Haiti.) A good number of free blacks, particularly before the passage of restrictive laws and of the 1850 act, thought their race should be given some land in the limitless West, just like Indians or just like whites, depending on how you view it. Some slave owners did resettle their chattel as free men and women on Western lands; and some of these blacks were later expelled, or at least cordoned and immiserated, by Western whites.

Most free blacks felt that America, not Africa, really was their motherland. If they had to lead racially separate lives, they would prefer to do so in America. Africa was far away and little understood. And black Americans knew perfectly well, despite abolitionist rhetoric about kidnapping and man stealing, that their African ancestors, by and large, had been sold by other Africans. As Frederick Douglass said in 1859, "the savage chiefs on the western coast of Africa, who for ages have been accustomed to selling their captives into bondage, and pocketing the ready cash for them, will not more readily see and accept our moral and economical ideas, than the slave-traders of Maryland and Virginia." Douglass was referring to the fact that black colonizationists in Africa, or thinking of Africa, intended to Americanize that corner of the Old World. They believed themselves superior to the natives, whom they would Christianize and teach to grow cotton plantation-style. (One of the more intriguing economic arguments for colonization held that transplanted ex-slaves would raise enough cotton in West Africa, as freemen, to undercut the Southern cotton system and so remove the profit motive from American slavery.) They would build neat American towns with American names, walk the African streets dressed like Americans, sing American hymns in American churches. They believed that American manners and customs were the best in the world, indeed the standard of truest humanity, a standard they took with them and expected others to admire and, when reason had prevailed, to emulate. What could be more American than that?

They did not want to return to Africanness. Their American idea was to eliminate the past, not embrace it. The belief in ancient African glory appears to have been psychic rather than practical. It extended even to Frederick Douglass, whose hatred of black-removal policies knew few bounds: "No one idea has given rise to more oppression and persecution toward the colored people of this country, than that which makes Africa, not America, their home." The same Douglass had gone on for pages, in 1854—they were published as a pamphlet—about how "the ancient Egyptians were not white people; but were, undoubtedly, just about as dark in complexion as many in this country who are considered genuine Negroes." However, Douglass finished by saying it did not matter, ultimately, whether black slaves descended from the builders of pyramids. A man is a man; a black man dreamed the same American dream as his white counterpart. "The poor bondman," Douglass wrote, "lifts a smiling face above the surface of a sea of agonies, *hoping on, hoping ever*. His tawny brother, the Indian, dies, under the flashing glance of the Anglo-Saxon. *Not* so the Negro; civilization cannot kill him. He accepts it—becomes a part of it."

That was the main point: blacks had become part of Anglo-Saxon civilization. This was the Protestant, democratic, middle-class-uplift view not only of an ardent assimilationist such as Douglass but of colonizationist, back-to-Africa black leaders as well. The Reverend Alexander Crummell, who lived in Liberia from 1853 to 1872, had a set speech with him when he toured the United States in 1861. It began with several passages from the French historian and politician François Guizot, among them this: "Is it not apparent that civilization is the main fact, the general and definite fact, in which all others terminate, and are included? . . . This is so true that, with respect to facts which are from their nature detestable . . . as despotism and anarchy, for example, if they have contributed in some degree to civilization, if they have given it a considerable impetus, up to a certain point we excuse and pardon their injuries and their evil nature; insomuch, that wherever we discover civilization, and the facts which have tended to enrich it, we are tempted to forget the price it has cost." For blacks like Crummell, there was much to pardon and forget. But his point was that, morally, one should forget, because that was the price exacted by the moral advance of Christian civilization, the fact in which all other facts terminate.

West Africans, in Crummell's view, the people from whom black Americans descended, had no past worth speaking of, just "vista upon vista of the deepest darkness . . . So far as *Western* Africa is concerned, there is no history. The long, long centuries of human existence, there, give us no intelligent disclosures. 'Darkness covered the land, and gross darkness the people.' " This was owing to

West Africa's complete isolation from "civilization": "Thrown thus back upon herself, unvisited by either the mission of letters, or of grace, poor Africa, all the ages through, has been generating, and then reproducing, the whole brood and progeny of superstitions, idolatries, and paganisms, through all her quarters. And hence the most pitiful, the most abject of all human conditions! And hence the most sorrowful of all histories! The most miserable, even now, of spectacles!"

Yet hope endured, and arrived in the form of Christianity, the English language, and "Anglo-Saxon life and civilization." It was a "most singular providence" that those "who have most largely participated in the slave-trade," that is, "the Anglo-Saxon race," should bear responsibility for saving Africa. Still more singular was that their agents should be blacks, former slaves but also an "advanced and superior people": "Not for death, as the Indian, not for destruction, as the Sandwich islander [Hawaiian], has the Negro been placed in juxtaposition with the Caucasian; but rather that he might seize upon civilization; that he might obtain hardiment of soul . . . and thus, himself, be enabled to go forth, the creator of new civilizations . . ."

Crummell's lecture may be the clearest example of what could happen to a person fully caught up in the American way, circa 1861, of racial thinking. An American ideal—men and women blazing their middle-class trails without a whisper of history to distract them—collided with this mysterious matter of color. In Crummell's case, the result was a rejection of Africanness as a cultural nullity, a vindication of the Anglo-Saxon race, and a characterization of racial slavery as simply a tough preparatory school for future black achievement. It is as if Americans, wanting not to have a past, yet at the same time having their collective past written in the colors of their skins, an indelible reminder that they were not the universal human prototype after all but a people bound by history—it is as if Americans faced a stark choice between self-hatred and the acceptance of white superiority. In that blacks and Indians were also Americans, the second option was itself, from the national point of view, a form of self-hatred and, when enforced, a form of self-destruction. The Civil War embodied both choices at once. It showed our ancestors incomprehensibly massacring one another, their mysterious colors burning together.

The war could be, and was, blamed on the existence of races. One of the beliefs contained in racial separatism—that whites could never accept nonwhites as equals—easily migrated into the view that the Civil War resulted from the presence of blacks in the United States. In his first meeting as president with a delegation of black men, in 1862, Abraham Lincoln said: "I need not recount to you the effects upon white men, growing out of the institution of Slavery. I believe in its general evil effects on the white race. See our present condition—the country engaged in war!—our white men cutting each other's throats, none knowing how far it will extend; and then consider what we know to be the truth. But for your race among us[,] there could not be war, although many men engaged on either side do not care for you one way or the other. Nevertheless, I repeat, without the institution of Slavery and the colored race as a basis, the war could not have an existence. It is better for us both, therefore, to be separated."

In this manner, President Lincoln indicated that white people—not Southern whites, but all white Americans—had created in their minds an unmovable belief in black inferiority, which was synonymous with blackness itself. Why white people had done this he could not say. Personally, he seemed to regret it. ("There is an unwillingness on the part of our people, harsh as it may be, for you free colored people to remain with us.") But the practical fact remained that whites would not tolerate blacks as equals. The problem lay not with slavery, Lincoln said, but with racial thinking itself; and an end to slavery would not end whites' belief in their own superiority. This would imply that the responsibility for the Civil War resided in white prejudices. However, that was not quite the conclusion Lincoln drew. Presumably, it would have been intolerable, even for him, to believe that the United States was premised on a mistaken notion of white specialness—to put it another way, that the nation he was fighting to preserve, at the cost of terrible slaughter, had in its basic national conception an error. Perhaps this is why he told the five black men he had brought to Washington that the presence of "the colored race" in America was itself the basis for the war. Blacks as such were the cause of dissension among whites; remove the cause, and the dissension ceases.

Lincoln was not unintelligent, irrational, or incapable of expressing his thoughts. Yet in these remarks to the five assembled black men, Lincoln's phrasings are clotted, and one struggles to extract their significance. Why should whites and blacks be separated? "You and we are different races," he explained. "We have between us a broader difference than exists between almost any other two races. Whether it is right or wrong I need not discuss, but this physical difference is a great disadvantage to us both, as I think your race suffer very greatly, many of them by living among us, while ours suffer from your presence. In a word we suffer on each side. If this is admitted, it affords a reason at least why we should be separated."

In attempting to answer this great racial question, Lincoln speaks nonsensically. How could a "physical difference" ever be "right or wrong"? What is the president talking about? He does at least hint at how whites "suffer from your presence"—that black presence has caused whites to be at each other's throats.

And toward the end of his address Lincoln also implies that the differences between whites and blacks are not only physical; his "right or wrong" may have been referring, in a way probably unclear even to Lincoln, not to physical but to mental differences, specifically to black mental inferiority. He had called this meeting to urge the free black population generally to leave North America. He sought a few men, as few as twenty-five, to lead the exodus. He told his visitors: "It is exceedingly important that we have men at the beginning capable of thinking as white men . . ."

What can we make of this statement? Lincoln has just finished explaining that white men as a group have the signal quality, however inexplicable, of not liking black people. Yet the deliverance of those black people will come about by their being able to think like whites. Could it be that blacks might enter into a full humanity only by learning to despise themselves—and to do so for no good reason—in other words, only by learning to become white? One has to wonder whether, somewhere in the white mind circa 1862, there wasn't a deep reservoir of self-contempt, a sense perhaps of incompleteness, treachery, or delusion. How else could one say, as Lincoln suggested, that white people were characterized, in their whiteness, by an unreasoning prejudice and excessive self-love, and yet insist that the nonwhite's great hope lay in incorporating white qualities into himself? It was whiteness, its interior operations, that troubled Lincoln. He was no fool, and any fool in that year knew that white people were murdering each other by the tens of thousands, that whites had killed and expelled the Indians from their midst, that they yet kept some four million black people in chains. This might have been a moment for a collective abandonment of racial pride. Certainly, even the most militant black nationalists, in their way, sought such an abandonment. Yet think what this would have meant for whites: an acceptance of their ancestors' miserable cruelty and of their own dependence on that cruelty for their present opportunities. It would have meant an end to newness, fresh starts, and innocence; it would have meant an exchange of bright optimism for an enduring sense of tragedy. It would have required whites, in some respects, to turn black, to grasp their country's past in its fullness and thereby reach a fuller humanity for themselves.

Perhaps it would have required an altogether different country. As it happened, whites took the opposite course. They had been steadily whitening since 1787, and at a particularly strong pace since the 1820s. They had been doing so legally, politically, and culturally. Far from shedding whiteness, they had clung to it more tightly, so much so that Abraham Lincoln in 1862 could believe that the mere presence of four or five million dark bodies on the North American continent had caused white people—his race, as he said—to go berserk and kill each other. In such a situation, wanting to preserve white innocence, a moderate, practical mind such as Lincoln's needed to travel a certain road: the end of whiteness, if it was to have any meaning at all within the concept of a common humanity, had to be that all people would become white, at which point whiteness would cease to exist and white people would at last be free from the torment of being defined by their skin color. Within this way of thinking, the only practical solution was to separate the races, particularly the black and white races, until such time as visually nonwhite people were capable, with white help, of thinking as white people. At that point, as François Guizot or Alexander Crummell might have put it, all could be forgiven, and forgotten.

When Lincoln met with the black delegation, he was already preparing a proclamation of partial emancipation. The way had been prepared by the House Select Committee on Emancipation and Colonization, which submitted its report in July. The committee found that, "apart from the antipathy which nature has ordained, the presence of a race among us who cannot, and ought not, be admitted to our social and political privileges, will be a perpetual source of injury and inquietude to both. This is a question of color, and is unaffected by the relation of master and slave. The introduction of the negro, whether bond or free, into the same field of labor with the white man, is the opprobrium of the latter . . . The committee conclude that the highest interests of the white race, whether Anglo-Saxon, Celt, or Scandinavian, require that the whole country should be held and occupied by those races alone." Typically for moderate white men of the time, the committee members deferred any discussion of racial essence, rather emphasizing that white prejudice was an unalterable fact: "It is useless, now, to enter upon any philosophical inquiry whether nature has or has not made the negro inferior to the Caucasian. The belief is indelibly fixed upon the public mind that such inequality does exist. There are irreconcilable differences between the two races which separate them, as with a wall of fire."

Lincoln's own commissioner of emigration, Reverend James Mitchell, had already sent the president in late May a lengthy letter, separately published, which stated again and again that the existence of black people had brought on the Civil War and that a happy democracy required a population of people who looked more or less like each other: "Our republican institutions are not adapted to mixed races and classified people. Our institutions require a homogeneous population to rest on as a basis." Mitchell recommended sending all blacks to Mexico, which he saw as already a mixed-race country.

It was Mitchell who had found and brought the black men to their meeting with Lincoln. Mitchell did not know that the president, beginning in early July, had gone daily to a quiet room in the Military Telegraph Office to work on a document freeing slaves in the rebel states. Lincoln met with the five black men in August; in September he issued a preliminary proclamation, to be put into effect on January 1, 1863, freeing the slaves of states still in rebellion at that date. The document dwelled on the prospects for colonization of freed blacks outside the continent. In his annual address to Congress on December 1, Lincoln offered a constitutional amendment in three articles. The first proposed that any state that would abolish slavery prior to January 1900 would be compensated for each slave; if it later reintroduced slavery, it would have to pay the money back. The second article said that any slave who gained freedom "by the chances of the war" should remain free, though loyal slaveholders would be compensated for runaways. The third article provided for voluntary colonization of free blacks. "I cannot make it better known than it already is," Lincoln told Congress, "that I strongly favor colonization." While he recognized that many blacks at present resisted the idea, he perceived that "opinion among them, in this respect, is improving" and did not doubt that freed slaves "will gladly give their labor for the wages, till new homes can be found for them, in congenial climes, and with people of their own blood and race."

The Civil War colonization proposals bore little fruit. (One Lincoln cabinet member later wondered whether the president would have gone ahead with the Emancipation Proclamation if he had known that colonization would fail.) About twelve thousand men and women, many of them slaves freed for the purpose, had immigrated to Liberia thanks to the American Colonization Society and its affiliates; several hundred more had gone to Haiti, led there by a white journalist, James Redpath, who also made his offer to Indians. Given an acknowledged black population of over four million, these numbers were small. The principle of racial separation they symbolized, however, remained strong in white and black minds. Lincoln had been intent on permitting individual states to keep blacks from voting, a policy nurtured by his successor, Andrew Johnson. This would have made blacks a separate and debased racial caste—an adaptation, in essence, of Northern and Western racial politics to the conditions of the post-slavery South, for the non-slaveholding states and territories had been carefully eliminating black civil rights since the Revolution.

This likely trend had been clear since 1863, the year of the Emancipation Proclamation. It extended from the fact that, in the course of the war, white opinion outside the South had slowly warmed to the notion that the division of the nation resulted not from slavery but from the fact of black skin coloring. This can be seen, obversely, in the way that Northerners addressed Southerners as their brothers: they accepted that the North benefited from slavery just as the South did. As Lincoln had put it in his 1862 address to Congress, "It is no less true for having been often said, that the people of the south are not more responsible for the original introduction of this property [slaves], than are the people of the north; and when it is remembered how unhesitatingly we all use cotton and sugar, and share the profits of dealing in them, it may not be quite safe to say, that the south has been more responsible than the north for its continuance." This reasonable, welcoming admission of collective white responsibility for slavery, rather than, for example, easing the acceptance of blacks into non-Southern white society, seems to have hardened the conviction that slavery had not, after all, been the premier racial issue—that, in the words of the House Select Committee on Emancipation and Colonization, "This is a question of color, and is unaffected by the relation of master and slave." A minority of thinkers on the subject, most eloquently Frederick Douglass, had argued for decades that whatever poor qualities had been exhibited over the years by blacks, individually or as a class, resulted primarily from their having been daily degraded, shunned by mainstream society, beaten with impunity, and for the great majority, through two centuries, bought and sold, separated from kin, whipped, tortured, shackled, raped, prevented by law from learning to read, add, subtract, multiply, or divide, kept from unsupervised worship, and told in myriad ways that they were by nature contemptible and always would be. To which an emerging white consensus replied that slavery did not define nor shape the black person. Color defined the black person, and eliminating slavery could not eliminate color.

Douglass had attacked this conception of color in 1862 with his habitual angry satire:

> This is the trouble, and the fact is another proof of man's perverse proclivity to create the causes of his own misery.—When there are so many real causes to vex and disturb the human mind and heart, is it not strange that men will contrive artificial ones for their own special torment? A man who should make himself miserable because the sky over him is blue, not white, because the stars are only visible at night, because water instead of ascending like smoke, descends like water, or because all the horses, cattle, and dogs, fish and fowl are not of the same color, however much we might pity him, would nevertheless be only a most unnatural fool, having only himself to thank for his vexation. Now we do not thus characterize those who are so greatly troubled about the hopeless blackness of the Negro, but we think they might, upon reflecting, learn to be content with the known laws of diversity which pervade the universe.

Douglass had thought to laugh the idea out of school. He had hoped that the color idea, once revealed in its absurdity, would recede from the minds of reasonable people, eventually to disappear. With it would disappear the temporary necessity of a separate black society. By 1865 he had decided that such hopes had been premature. Douglass traveled to Baltimore, the city in which he had been a slave, to give an address at the inauguration of the Douglass Institute, a black institution dedicated to black uplift. It must have been a bewildering occasion for him. Douglass had never been a racial separatist or nationalist. He saw blacks as slight in their achievements when compared with whites. He attributed this to their having been enslaved and to the prejudices of whites. He did not believe in blackness, as he did not believe in whiteness. He had memorably satirized, in a friendly way, the idea of African self-love, as when he described a visit by the black nationalist Martin Delany to Rochester: "he has gone about the same length in favor of black, as the whites have in favor of the doctrine of white superiority. He stands up so straight that he leans back a little . . . He is the intensest embodiment of black Nationality to be met with outside the valley of the Niger." Douglass favored assimilation, not to white norms as such but to a model of Protestant middle-class striving. He frequently looked to physical amalgamation through intermarriage as a way to take the American population as a whole beyond black and white. He appears to have believed that the end of slavery would bring the beginning of an end to race.

Yet here he was faced with a promising institution, named for him, which aimed to be a black institution. "The establishment of this Institution may be thought by some a thing of doubtful expediency," Douglass told his audience. "There was a time when I should have thought it so myself. In my enthusiasm, perhaps it was my simplicity . . . I once flattered myself that the day had happily gone by when it could be necessary for colored people in this country to combine and act together as a separate class, and in any representative character whatever . . . It seemed to me that colored conventions, colored exhibitions, colored associations and institutions of all kinds and descriptions had answered the end of their existence, and might properly be abandoned; that, in short, they were hindrances rather than helps in achieving a higher and better estimation in the public mind for ourselves as a race." However, "the latent contempt and prejudice towards our race . . . the persistent determination of the present Executive of the nation, and also the apparent determination of a portion of the people to hold and treat us in a degraded relation, not only justify for the present such associate effort on our part, but make it eminently necessary."

Black racial unity would remain needed just as long as white power took the forms that it did. Blackness was a temporary political and cultural tool. It soon became obvious that the tool needed sharpening. Four months after the Balti-

more address Douglass and other black leaders met with President Andrew
Johnson to urge him to allow blacks to vote. Johnson refused because, he said,
such a policy "will end in a contest between the races, which if persisted in will
result in the extermination of one or the other." Johnson based his analysis on
the resentful prejudices of poor Southern whites, which were in turn a product
of the condescension of slaves toward their non-slaveholding white neighbors.
He directed his argument particularly toward Douglass, whom he asked:

> "Have you ever lived upon a plantation?"
> Mr. Douglass: "I have, your excellency."
> The President: "When you would look over and see a man
> who had a large family, struggling hard upon a poor piece of
> land, you thought a great deal less of him than you did of your
> own master's Negro, didn't you?"
> Mr. Douglass: "Not I!"
> The President: "Well, I know such was the case with a large
> number of you in those sections."

Johnson had himself once been in the servile white class, as a tailor's apprentice. He believed that putting the black and white poor on an equal footing
would enrage the latter, just as it enraged him. For this he blamed blacks, whom
he saw as representing, in a sense, the white rich. Blacks were the rich man's
laboring tool for keeping poor whites down. And rage being something one tends
to direct, in practical terms, at the near rather than the far and the defenseless
rather than the protected, Johnson the former apprentice directed a share of his
at blacks. The obvious alternative to poor whites' hatred of blacks was an alliance
of the two groups against their common class enemy, the rich. This was just what
Douglass proposed to Johnson, a channeling of Southern class conflict into
democratic, nonracial politics. To this Johnson, an insecure, self-educated ex-
apprentice faced with an imposing, self-educated ex-slave, responded, "You touch
right upon the point there. There is this conflict, and hence I suggest emigration."

Emigration had already got under way by 1865, but it was an internal emigration. Many in the slaveholding states were preparing for a postwar world by
thinking of ways of ensuring white supremacy without slavery. Their efforts
reached clear expression in the Black Codes of 1865 and 1866, passed by state
legislatures throughout the South, which sought to create a form of racial slavery while accepting that people could not be traded as property. The states
hoped to shape blacks into a disfranchised serf class and to preserve the large-

plantation system of gang labor. Blacks, on the whole, refused to go along with this. Former slaves withdrew to poor, hilly land, where they could be away from whites. They abandoned white churches, where they had worshipped under the eyes of their masters, and formed black churches. They founded colored societies, held colored conventions, began colored unions (the National Negro Labor Union started in 1869). In alliance with the federal Freedmen's Bureau and sympathetic whites, they organized separate schools—nearly four thousand of them within seven years of emancipation. Blacks, with white help, had founded half a dozen black colleges by the end of 1866. The racial separation Douglass had hoped would pass away asserted itself with astounding speed.

For a time it appeared that some Northern whites, particularly the radical Reconstructionists, would, in league with blacks, north and south, be able to force through a legal structure that would guarantee the basic civil rights of black people—most importantly, the right of all men to vote. Blacks did indeed gain citizenship rights, against great resistance (and not only in the South). They did not get much more, and in the course of the 1870s even the right to vote was steadily whittled away. Blacks were killed in large numbers after the war and would continue to be killed well into the twentieth century because of their skin color. Into the 1870s whites fought blacks in countless small battles, particularly at election time, and the consolidation of white power was advanced by little murders. The South, at last, finally had its race war, so long anticipated.

It became clear that the price of peace for the nation was an acceptance that blacks could not be equal to whites. Such was the essence of the Compromise of 1877, which let blacks know that Northern whites and the federal government would no longer protect or advance them. The Supreme Court had already begun drifting in this direction by 1873. The power of whites in individual states to determine the racial nature of their societies was becoming policy.

The alternative was not at all beyond imagining. It had been famously expressed in the Capitol by the black congressman Robert Elliott. The House, in 1874, was debating a civil-rights bill. Former Confederate vice president Alexander Stephens had attacked the bill. Elliott responded: "The last vestiture only is needed—civil rights. Having gained this, we may, with hearts overflowing with gratitude, and thankful that our prayer has been granted, repeat the prayer of Ruth: 'Entreat me not to leave thee, or to return from following after thee; for whither thou goest, I will go; and where thou lodgest, I will lodge; thy people shall be my people, and thy God my God; where thou diest, will I die, and there will I be buried; the Lord do so to me, and more also, if aught but death part thee and me.' (Great applause.)" The radical Elliott had a House packed with some of the most powerful white people in the nation cheering the loving discourse of a black man. What did they hear in this expression of Ruth's longing to remain with her mother-in-law, Naomi? Did they hear self-effacement and servility? Did they hear desire? Did they hear kindness? Elliott was proposing the intimate unity of a national family, a single "people." His audience must have heard that, at least; and in the moment they wanted it.

But to achieve it required, paradoxically, a recognition of race. It required helpful policies aimed at blacks as blacks. Perhaps more importantly, it required the white majority to consider its own whiteness—the historical facts of it, and the unearned privileges—and somehow to convince the many thousands of their white brethren engaged in murder and intimidation to cease those activities and accept their equality with blacks. It would have required former masters to join with former slaves, and slaves with masters. And this huge work being completed, the business of racelessness might commence.

One part of this journey was indeed being made: the reconciliation of whites, north and south. Racial separatism was one aspect of that reconciliation. The assimilationist or integrationist side of racial politics, symbolized among black leaders by Douglass, slowly receded in the face of white reconciliation and black retrenchment. Douglass's old white friend and ally Wendell Phillips had declared after the war, "Slavery is dead. We have not only abolished slavery, we have abolished the Negro. We have actually washed color out of the Constitution." This idea of abolishing the Negro had deep roots in abolitionism, most spectacularly among colonizationists and those many abolitionists in the North who advocated Northern secession, which would have eliminated slavery within a purer, smaller nation by abandoning the black majority. At some level, this indicated a common white desire to eliminate slavery as it affected whites— as it reflected upon their historical character. This would in turn entail abolishing the Negro, who in his or her appearance marked the indelibility of American history, white and black. The Negro, then, had somehow to leave, or at a minimum to be safely contained.

Postwar black separatism evolved in this context, in parallel with white developments. It evolved, to a degree, in response to white developments, but only to a degree. The vast majority of blacks after the war were ex-slaves. As black slaves, they had developed a culture of their own—an American culture, certainly, and as such in part a white and an Indian culture, but it was also African, and in its relation to power and the history of slavery it was none of these but uniquely itself. It was a blues culture, with blues humor and blues pain, with a life of its own. Blues culture provided a usable past, yet one not premised on falsehood. If not separatist, it was inescapably separate, and exclusive of whites.

Blues culture was, in part, a culture of waiting, and this did not recommend it to strivers. Ambitious, educated (including self-educated) blacks in the postwar years desired inclusion in the American mainstream at a time when the mainstream was making itself increasingly white. Black leaders, at great risk to themselves, fought their way into power, and did all the things powerful people customarily do to keep it. But power resided in whitening institutions, especially after the Compromise of 1877 and the Supreme Court's undermining, in 1883, of the 1875 Civil Rights Act and the Fourteenth Amendment. The latter was a particularly harsh blow: eight out of nine justices of the party of Lincoln had agreed that private institutions such as hotels could legally bar people, on a racial basis, from walking through the door. Justice Harlan alone dissented, as he dissented from a similar decision in 1896 on *Plessy v. Ferguson*, though we should remember what he wrote regarding the later case: "The white race deems itself to be the dominant race in this country. And so it is in prestige, in achievements, in education, in wealth, and in power. So, I doubt not that it will continue to be for all time, if it remains true to its great heritage and holds fast to the principles of constitutional liberty."

The prospects for a raceless integration—for becoming fully human without becoming white—seemed to dim, then disappear. And so black leaders began to think more concretely of a separate destiny. One example had already been given in the Exoduster movement of 1879. This movement was not an elite effort. In fact, it excluded the elite, whom many poorer blacks saw as self-interested and too close to white power. The exodus first took form in 1870 with the founding of a clandestine group called the Committee, which, according to one member, sought to "look into affairs and see the true conditions of our race, to see whether it was possible we could stay under a people who had held us under bondage or not." A consensus emerged that blacks had to come out from among white people. An 1875 convention in New Orleans resolved on immigration to the North, the West, or Liberia; the following year, the Committee became the National Colored Colonization Council. The council began to gain adherents, mainly in Louisiana—perhaps a hundred thousand by 1879. In the meantime, the Liberian Exodus Joint-Stock Steamship Company in South Carolina, the Edgefield Real Estate Association in Tennessee, and similar groups elsewhere had been organizing. Immigration by black families to new lands, particularly Kansas, had begun on a significant scale as early as 1870; in 1879 and 1880, the peak years, perhaps sixty thousand black people left the South for Kansas and Indiana, some with the mistaken idea that Kansas would be a black state. It was not a well-organized movement. It was desperate, the zero degree of self-determination. The exodus met armed opposition from white Southern employers, who did not want to lose their powerless laborers. Yet tens of thousands managed to escape the white blockades and make it to new lands.

Frederick Douglass opposed the exodus as a concession to an idea he had given his life to fighting: "the idea that colored people and white people cannot live together in peace and prosperity." It was indeed such a concession, and not a surprising one. It was the most dramatic demonstration of passive racial resistance in American history to that time, a reluctant separatism, a quest only for, as one Committee man said, "somewhere where we could live in peace and quiet." The exodus enraged Douglass. It stirred in him the unquiet spirit of assimilation, the strange elixir of racial emulation that ran in the American vein: "Suffering and hardships made the Saxon strong," Douglass said, urging the Exodusters to stay and fight at home, "and suffering and hardships will make the Anglo-African strong." Such language had never come from Douglass before, and would not come again. The emergence of a rigid color politics independent of slavery had derailed him, tossed him into the wilderness of racial mission—the belief that races had destinies. For a person of education, possibilities, and self-regard, this could and would lead to an interior dialectic of contempt and desire, distancing and imitation. One could see glimmerings of such an attitude in David Walker's 1829 *Appeal*: that black and white sprang from nearly the same sources and traveled together forward in time, secret sharers of a dream of omnipotence. For the black majority caution prescribed a less grand, almost silent removal, the creation of black spaces in the South, in the mind, and, for some, a new racial beginning in the West not unlike that sought by whites. They went throughout the West, particularly to Kansas, Oklahoma, and Texas, settling lands but recently taken from Indians. They started black towns as far afield as California. In many cases they worked to keep white people out of those towns—though they also fought segregation.

If black elites perceived this popular black secession as the tail wagging the dog, the tail wagged well. Black church denominations continued to grow. The National Negro Labor Union continued to organize state and local unions on the basis of color. In 1888 the Colored Farmers' National Alliance and Cooperative Union began in Texas. The National Afro-American League started in Chicago in 1890. The Colored Women's League was founded in 1892, the National Federation of Afro-American Women in 1895, the American Negro Academy in 1897, the National Afro-American Council in 1898. Blacks organized in fraternal lodges, the Knights of Pythias, the Masons, True Reformers, and Odd Fellows. The contacts made there, together with the educations earned in black colleges, enabled the gradual accumulation of black capital and the formation of black banks and insurance companies. Segregated by whites, blacks created a separate society.

If black leaders wanted to lead blacks—they did not have the option of leading anyone else—a separate society was the only one they had to lead. White leaders did the same, but they had white voters and real political power. By 1901 the black vote, which had once put Ulysses Grant into the presidency and seventeen black men in Congress, had dwindled nearly to insignificance. Various Southern tactics had disfranchised millions of blacks. The last black congressman of the era, George White, told his colleagues at his departure in 1901 that it was "perhaps the Negro's temporary farewell to the American Congress." Two years later he founded a black town in New Jersey, called Whitesboro.

Black leaders and intellectuals guided a people who had little power, and so they had little power themselves. It is in the nature of leaders sometimes to question their constituencies. For white leaders, however, any kind of race betrayal was all but impossible. Whites constituted a majority of the population. White superiority was grounded in the law and the sciences. It bore the weight of custom. Aspiring to power, one assured the white public that one did not intend to alter the reality of white domination. It was hardly necessary to go on and on about the subject. At the time, simple inaction could suffice. One had only to talk about Americans, their greatness and future prospects, and everyone of every color knew that one meant white Americans. This method of making the visible unseen was, indeed, the wisest course, because the incongruities of a racially divided country could still unsettle the white mind, particularly as they reminded whites of their past. A branch of the Colored National League once addressed President William McKinley, in 1899, on the question of silence. The petitioners wondered why, given the wrongs they were suffering—lynchings of blacks, for example, were then running at over one hundred per year, sometimes with advance advertisement in newspapers—why had he never said a word? Why was it that "you have at no time and on no occasion opened your lips in our behalf. Why? we ask. Is it because we are black and weak and despised? Are you silent because without any fault of our own we were enslaved and held for more than two centuries in cruel bondage by your forefathers? Is it because we bear the mark of those sad generations of Anglo-Saxon brutality and wickedness, that you do not speak?"

A black leader, by contrast, could hardly be silent about his or her race. In slave days, yes, perhaps even under Reconstruction, but not in the Gilded Age. For a black leader in that era the black race was at once the only source of power and the symbol of powerlessness. The one leader who openly synthesized these qualities into a political whole was Booker T. Washington, who rocketed to power in the same year Douglass died, 1895. Washington's separatism was a perfect creature of his time. He told a mainly white audience in Atlanta that blacks were "the most patient, faithful, law-abiding, and unresentful people that the world has seen." Himself born into slavery, Washington said: "In all things that are purely social, we can be as separate as the fingers, yet [he made a fist] one as the hand in all things essential to human progress." When the applause at last waned, Washington concluded his talk: "The wisest among my race understand that the agitation of questions of social equality is the extremest folly, and that progress in the enjoyment of all the privileges that will come to us must be the result of severe and constant struggle rather than of artificial forcing."

Washington, at age thirty-nine, had come up with a uniquely workable American racial separatism. He showed a genius at balancing social forces. He legitimized the laboring lives of the black majority and never ceased feeding their resentment of educated blacks who, in their eyes, possibly did not want to be black. He championed the black yeoman farmer and small tradesman in much the way white politicians, particularly of earlier generations, had championed their white counterparts: as honest, hardworking people on the rise who should not, however, rise so far as to lose the simplicity that made them great. Washington capitalized on the immemorial American prejudice against politics and against intellectualism. He combined this with a shrewd understanding of white sentiment: most whites wanted blacks to be or at least feel inferior, and they wanted blacks to be happy.

The progress of Jim Crow segregation only quickened after Washington's speech. His implication of (temporary) inferiority, that blacks as a race were not ready for equality, must have been solace to many whites. Powerful white men adopted Washington as their black representative. He used his power as racial gatekeeper with skill and cunning; he enjoyed it. His enemies knew this and struggled against him accordingly. The novelist Charles Chesnutt said, after Washington's Atlanta address, "It is not a pleasing spectacle to see the robbed applaud the robber." Yet Washington's black opponents were not so unlike him as they might have been. The turn-of-the-century black elite—people such as Washington, W. E. B. Du Bois, the long-lived Reverend Alexander Crummell, even the bravest of them all, Ida B. Wells—concurred in viewing the black masses as something like an apprentice population still unprepared for equality. Washington wanted the black majority apprenticed to him and to whites. Washington's opponents wanted their race apprenticed to themselves, the college educated, the Talented Tenth of the population, those who had plumbed the abstractions and skills of European civilization. Black leaders differed in their relationship to white power, particularly in regard to political and legal forms such as citizenship rights and segregation laws. They differed on lynching, which most fought to end (through appeals to white power) but which Washington sought to outflank through accommodation and a steady rising of the race, which would make blacks indispensable to those whites who had the power to protect them. But the black elites generally agreed that the greatest problem over which they had any control was the poor quality of their racial constituency. Therein lay the racial mission. "Be the requirement just or unjust," Sutton Griggs has a black-activist character say in the 1902 novel *Unfettered*, "the polished Negro is told to return and bring his people with him, before coming into possession of that to which his attainments would seem to entitle him." Mass racial mobilization, then, could only come by grace of the necessarily deferred self-fulfillment of fortunate individuals. Polished people prescribed racial solidarity and self-help, a combination similar to that which had swept white society in the 1820s, a universe of temperance societies, literary and debate clubs, and regular church attendance, all with people who looked like oneself. The difference was that black separatism should be provisional— indefinitely so for Washington, more briefly so for his opponents—whereas for whites, at least since Jackson's presidency, racial separation could be imagined as somehow permanent. Black separatism was, by its nature, changeable, adap tive, and therefore creative. White separatism aimed at permanence and the silencing of the past, resisted change, could not absorb or adapt, and was therefore less creative than dead.

Nonetheless, white Americans held all the power and claimed the European inheritance as their own, as well as any other good thing that might cross the national mind. This was the text, so to speak, that any ambitious black person read. So it cannot be accidental that much black literature of the period focused on the mulatto. This writing literally embodied a search for sameness within a world of difference by dwelling on the differences between people who looked the same. The dance of racial ambivalence had characterized black literature from its earliest publications. In William Wells Brown's 1853 novel *Clotel*, the titular character is the mixed-race daughter of a president (based on Thomas Jefferson) and his servant. Frank Webb's *The Garies and Their Friends*, of 1857, tells of two Southern families, one black and one mixed. The black family survives the peculiar strains of Northern white cruelty, while the mixed family does not. Harriet E. Wilson's *Our Nig* (1859) likewise treats racial mixing and the hypocrisy of Northern whites, "professed abolitionists, who didn't want slaves at the South, nor niggers in their own houses, North." These prewar works, in their focus on mulattoes and thus on the intimacy, however fraught, of the black-white bond, at least glimpsed a type of integration; at the same time, in focusing on Northern white racial aggression they foreshadowed the postwar national settlement of racial separation without slavery. Given black prewar novelists' recognition of such a possibility, the massive self-segregation of Southern blacks immediately after the war appears less remarkable.

Black Americans published little fiction after the war until the mid-1880s, when a quasi-permanent separation of black and white in North and South alike came clearly into view, and the gentle visions of a Robert Elliott would have seemed antiquated. Mulattoes become both more and less important in the late-century literature, as do white people. Martin Delany had anticipated this in his novel *Blake* (1859), which first presented the attractiveness of a black-separatist uprising and urged upon mulattoes allegiance to the black race. Frances Harper's *Iola Leroy* (1892) picked up the second theme, emphasizing the moral necessity of light-skinned Iola Leroy's choosing blackness. Leroy believes that "the best blood in my veins is African"; the novel then argues that black racial loyalty is also loyalty to humanity, because allowing blackness to degenerate (in this case, into whiteness) would be to remove something valuable from the general human cultural stock.

Mulattoness and black separatism dominated the work of Sutton Griggs, beginning with his 1899 novel, *Imperium in Imperio*. The story's main characters are two men, one black (Belton) and one mulatto (Bernard). Both seek racial deliverance through black separatism and conspire with others to that end. They differ as to the pace and methods of change. The black man, patient and courageous, feeling a loyalty to his country, recommends that "we spend four years in endeavors to impress the Anglo-Saxon that he has a New Negro on his hands and must surrender what belongs to him. In case we fail by these means to secure our rights and privileges we shall all, at once, abandon our several homes in the various other states and emigrate in a body to the State of Texas," where they will "secure possession of the State Government." The mulatto, however, has no time for four years of persuasion. He wants to enlist foreign allies, infiltrate the navy, and commence insurrection. Perhaps his inner white person pushes him to such ferocity; Griggs does suggest that Anglo-Saxon blood instills a certain brutality. If we take blood as metaphorical, this equation makes a haunting sense. For the black separatism toward which Griggs hurtles his characters did indeed take its tenor from white thinking, and so it is not paradoxical that the most militant black separatism should come from a man part white. The torn mulatto is not a representation of "racial confusion." He is an example of American unity.

The black man, in his patriotism, is executed. The mulatto goes insane. Like James Fenimore Cooper's white Indian in *The Pioneers*, Bernard has a graveside speech: "Float on, proud flag, while yet you may. Rejoice, oh ye Anglo-Saxons, yet a little while. Make my father ashamed to own me, his lawful son; call me a bastard child; look upon my pure mother as a harlot; laugh at Viola in the grave of a self-murderer; exhume Belton's body, if you like, and tear your flag from around him to keep him from polluting it! Yes, stuff your vile stomachs full of all these horrors. You shall be richer food for the buzzards to whom I have solemnly vowed to give your flesh." In Griggs's book the drama of racial separation takes on the quality of suicide. It evokes, in a different setting, the mystical reflections of Joseph Story in mid-century, when the great jurist wondered at the extinction of Indians, victims of "a plague, which the touch of the white man communicated—a poison which betrayed them into a lingering ruin." In the case of American Indians, it was whiteness as killing agent; for Griggs, in the case of blacks at the turn of the century, it was a whiteness inside, as well as outside, that had the touch of death. It shows the depths of Griggs's empathy, his very American empathy, that he could see whiteness as self-destructive. In a breathtaking passage he has the part-white Bernard argue that violence alone can make blacks equal to whites. But using such means—racial murder—toward self-realization will bring a particular kind of equality and a particular kind of whiteness: "if we die on the mountain side, we shall be shrouded in sheets of whitest snow, and all generations of men yet to come upon the earth will have to gaze upward in order to see our whitened forms."

The equation of whiteness and self-destruction could, of course, be turned outward, such that the white idea, by constant expansion, might defer its implosion. Always starting over, in new territory, with new people, it could renew itself by destroying others in lieu of understanding how it destroyed its own, that is, white people. This is essentially what whites did from the 1880s through World War I, extending whiteness across the globe in a mad racial mission. And as Griggs saw a deathly whiteness in black separatism, some black thinkers of the early part of the century found in themselves a white imperialism that could, because it was within them, be colored black and provide a racial mission.

Black imperial dreams built on the older beliefs that the human race began in Africa and that civilization had originated among dark people in Egypt and the upper Nile kingdoms. Among black writers this black civilization was more a state of mind than a set of ideas, values, or practices. It represented the fact of historical achievement and power—a reality of racial power that beckoned to a present-day desire for the same. It had little African content as such; rather, emphasis was placed on its nearness to its successor, Hellenic Greece, which was the preferred civilizational fetish of white people. Similarly, black imperial thought was overwhelmingly Christian, the biblical pivot being, as it had been for a century, the promising Psalm "Princes shall come out of Egypt; Ethiopia shall soon stretch out her hands unto God." This Psalm and the few other biblical references that could be linked to black Africa constituted a defensive breastwork against whites taking Christianity for themselves. Here again the racial contest was over ideological or psychological materials that were remarkably similar and in many ways identical. White power in this imperial period was extending itself through the world with, in its hands, the somewhat vague but powerful ideas of civilization and Christianity. In many cases black power, such as it was, clutched the same ideas and claimed them for itself. The primal drama was one of theft by one brother from another, by white from black. It was in the end a family affair. What relation this all bore to ancient Greece and Africa, the House of David and the reign of Pharaoh, was, in a sense, purely coincidental. The relation it bore to turn-of-the-century America, however, was central and organic.

The notion that blacks and whites were similar peoples using similar ideologies to reach similar goals transferred "separate but equal" onto a cosmic plane. W. E. B. Du Bois, for example, longed for a Talented Tenth of all the world's darker peoples to lead the global nonwhite majority. (One hears in this an echo of Benjamin Franklin's perception that white people were, worldwide, a minority.) Such a transcendent scheme carried a heavy freight of mulattoness, the mulatto being the figure in whom racial sameness and difference concentrated. The global-racial-contest concept was itself, in its way, a mulatto concept, in that it had as its root a common humanity, though one subject to endless struggle—again, a basically fraternal mode of thinking, one closely related to the old American anticipation of inevitable race war, the idea that the races were identical in their desires for mastery. Such is a paradox of racial conflict. In the logic of deathly struggle it posits a sameness.

However, for some blacks, at least, death had a distinctly white color—just as social power, the power to control others' lives, to dominate others, had a whiteness to it. This was Griggs's insight, and it takes an interesting form in Pauline Hopkins's 1903 novel *Of One Blood*. Hopkins's hero, Reuel Briggs, is an outstanding black physician who appears to be white. On an expedition to Africa, for which Briggs serves as doctor, a group of explorers finds an isolated Ethiopian civilization far in advance of Europe or America. The Africans recognize Briggs as their long-lost king. Briggs takes power, converts his people to Christianity, and recognizes himself as black. The route to imperial blackness, then, might appear to lead through a period of whiteness; or, more precisely, the black American's experience of whiteness (and Christianity) fit him—it was always a man—to lead the black race, indeed to define blackness. This had been Alexander Crummell's argument decades before, and it had not changed much. Indeed some black activists, such as Edward Blyden, supported European expansion in black Africa itself as a civilizing influence.

Hopkins belonged to a black-nationalist circle that included Du Bois, Crummell, Anna Julia Cooper, Alain Locke, and William Ferris. Ferris took the notion of inner whiteness to an extreme in his one book, *The African Abroad*, which he began writing in 1902. "God has given the Anglo-Saxon the dominion of the earth," Ferris argued, "only because he has obeyed His moral laws." Ferris coined a race name to overcome the apparently negative connotations of *Negro*. He suggested "Negrosaxon." Ferris wrote, "after the Negrosaxon has been made over into the likeness of the white man he can hope to be made into the image of God."

There was a real logic to this, however mad it may seem. White thinking, sophisticated or rude, did include a white racial mission premised on the race's superiority. Generally speaking, white thought on the matter did not dwell on first causes, that is, attempt to explain why exactly whites were special. While occasional reference might be made to the whiteness of Aristotle, Jesus, Plato, or Pharaoh, these were specialists' arguments of small importance compared with the day-to-day, rocklike implacability of white self-importance. That assurance held racial power; and one way to racial power for someone not white was somehow to take that assurance for himself or herself. Given the times, the white example of overwhelming racial power could not be ignored, as it was the only example around. Ferris's internalization of whiteness on the road to a better blackness was one possibility. As metaphor, his Negrosaxonism, as we have seen, was not at all uncommon. The other, related, possibility was to argue that the black race was in fact superior to the white, or destined to be in time, a thought Ferris sometimes expressed but that was put most clearly by his contemporary J. Max Barber, who wrote that "the future belongs, not to the degenerating, morally putrid and cruelly avaricious white man, but to the virile, puissant races in whose hearts there is mercy and justice." David Walker had sounded the same note eighty years before, arguing that the differences between whites and blacks amounted to an excess of cruelty and greed among the former, and the qualities of mercy and forgiveness among the latter. It is a small, but intriguing, literary tradition.

THE NEW NEGRO

THE BEAUTIFUL DESPAIR

OF THE HARLEM RENAISSANCE

■

The high point of black racial separatism in our history arrived at precisely the time when racial mixing became national in scope. Between 1910 and 1930 the black share of the populations in Chicago, New York, and Detroit trebled. Roughly 200,000 black Southerners had come north between 1890 and 1910; in the succeeding decade somewhere between 300,000 and a million migrated, most to the cities. They came north against the forcefully expressed wishes of white Southerners and against the advice of much of the older black leadership, which preferred a stable population and did not want trouble. Cities were associated with trouble—specifically, in the black case, with "urban pathology," cardsharps, pimps and prostitutes, jazz, and small savings frittered away on cigarettes and drink. Black and white leaders alike feared the newly urbanized black masses would simply exchange rural peonage for slum-dwelling criminality.

Marcus Garvey, however, saw in the black city an opportunity. In 1914 he had begun his Universal Negro Improvement Association (UNIA), in Jamaica, the country of his birth. Among its goals: "To promote the spirit of race pride and love . . . To assist in civilizing the backward tribes of Africa. To strengthen the imperialism of independent African states . . . To promote a conscientious Christian worship among the native tribes of Africa." Garvey was not tall, but he was big; in ambition, he was enormous. He had the gift for embodying contradictions that marks nature's demagogues. He celebrated the ordinary man— and he said that most blacks in Jamaica were "really unfit for good society." He railed ceaselessly against black elites, hammering at their pretensions and con-temptuousness and accusing them of wanting to be white. He also asserted, time and again, that only a cultured elite could possibly lead a race he saw as generally backward.

Perhaps the only opinion Garvey held without contradiction was that races should be separate. He rarely hesitated to seek white help. That whites rarely did help must have been a disappointment to him, for he saw himself as engaged in a black version of white work. "The black and white races are now facing the crucial time of their existence," he once explained. "The whites are rightly and properly crying out for a pure white race, and the proud and self-respecting blacks are crying out for a morally pure and healthy Negro race." The alternatives to their peaceful separation, Garvey believed, were, first, even-tual starvation of blacks by a growing white race that would have no use for them. This had been, minus the starvation, a favored solution among white writers since Benjamin Franklin. Whether through European immigration or natural increase, white leaders looked to a future of overwhelming white num-bers; Lincoln had lectured Congress at length, in 1862, on the sunny prospect of a burgeoning white population. Scientific opinion contributed theories of racial degeneracy (the inevitable dwindling of nonwhite races) and the sterility of mulattoes. Many whites looked to the decennial censuses, which showed a tiny but steady decline of black population share, as harbingers of the wished-for black disappearance. The second alternative Garvey saw to racial purity and separation was race war. The third was the absorption, through racial mixing, of the black race in the white, also a pet theory of some white social scientists and anthropologists. Such racial mixing, Garvey argued, would be race betrayal and would harm humanity by removing one of its great constituent elements.

By 1919 Garvey had based himself in Harlem, taking over a former Baptist church on 138th Street for his Liberty Hall. The UNIA as yet had few followers, but Garvey could stir crowds and soon established himself as a player in the small and politically weak milieu of black leaders. William Ferris, for one, soon decided Garvey might be the long-awaited racial redeemer. The race, not to say the nation, certainly could have used a redeemer in 1919. Black soldiers had fought with distinction in World War I, in segregated units. Veterans expected something in return, such as racial equality. What they got instead were torture and murder. The annual number of reported lynchings had been in decline since the turn of the century, from the low hundreds to the low fifties. But a race riot in East St. Louis, over two days in July 1917, left at least 39 blacks dead, and the number of lynchings had leaped to seventy-six by 1919. In that year there were twenty-six race riots across the country, the worst of them in Chicago (23 blacks dead), taking about 120 lives in scarcely more than three months. The

Ku Klux Klan, revitalized in 1914, was experiencing phenomenal growth—its membership would soon reach into the millions—while the National Association for the Advancement of Colored People (NAACP) more than quadrupled its rolls between 1917 and 1919. The NAACP grew in large part by taking its politics to the left and adopting a rhetoric of racial consciousness. The leftward shift was very much of its times: perhaps one in five American workers struck during 1919. According to Leon Trotsky, the Soviets that year expected world revolution to topple the capitalist powers in a matter of months. At times white and black workers made common cause, as in Bogalusa, Louisiana, where the price paid (at the hands of the Great Southern Lumber Company) was death. More commonly, unions and cooperatives organized along racial lines, with a markedly increased racial militancy on both sides. Whites were, of course, more effective at this game than were blacks. The most emotional and destructive appeals to white solidarity were made on behalf of returning white soldiers, who saw black industrial workers as a particularly dangerous, and humiliating, threat.

This was the year of Garvey's opportunity. In March a disaffected Garveyite had labeled the leader "impractical, utopian, and Jackassical." In May, Garvey launched the Black Star Line, playing on the name of the white-owned White Star Line, which had once launched the *Titanic*. (The American Irish had a Green Star Line.) The Africa trade was booming, and ships had a magic appeal in an imperial era. More significantly, Americans had recently grown accustomed to buying stocks and bonds. People with unremarkable incomes liked the idea that their small savings might do for them what their daily work could not. Most had had their first speculative experience in buying Liberty Bonds, a fund-raising tool for the war effort. Garvey took the powerful experience of interest-bearing patriotism and transformed it into interest-bearing racial loyalty, while promising more than the government's humble 4 percent. The idea was not original, but no one could promote it quite as Garvey did.

The UNIA showed off its first ship, the thirty-year-old *Yarmouth*, at the end of 1919. The *Yarmouth* leaked water often and money always, but for a time it at least neared William Ferris's prediction that a Black Star Line boat "will send a thrill to the Negroes of two hemispheres and will lift the standing of the Negro race throughout the civilized world." The UNIA was soon bringing in tens of thousands of dollars through stock sales and membership drives. Garvey responded to his many critics by buying more boats: the elderly steamer *Shadyside* on April 10, 1920, and the decrepit yacht *Kanawha* two weeks later. Garveyites across the country sold five-dollar shares in this world-straddling enterprise of racial uplift, giving people of average means a positive sense of participation and giving their hopes of racial greatness a small anchor in reality.

Garvey gave birth to mass black politics. He talked of Africa, the actual Africa as well as the Africa of the mind. He emphasized that the UNIA was all black, not an adopted child of white philanthropy. He spoke of black military strength, dressed himself in a martial medley of fraternal-lodge styles, and appeared in uniform with his top men. In August 1920 the UNIA held its first convention, in New York City. Twenty-five thousand people came to Madison Square Garden to hear Garvey. The convention adopted a lengthy declaration combining denunciation of antiblack prejudice, lynching, segregation, and white imperialism with positive race goals: "by the principle of Europe for the Europeans and Asia for the Asiatics," the convention announced, "we also demand Africa for the Africans at home and abroad . . . We demand complete control of our social institutions without interference by any alien race or races." Garvey was elected provisional president of Africa, a place he had never seen.

The Justice Department had already decided that Garvey was "the foremost pro-negro agitator in New York," and for a time that was true not only in his eyes but in those of the black masses. Even Du Bois, whom Garvey often and brutally attacked as a white toady and race mixer, wrote with admiration, late in 1920, of Garvey's business plan to "redeem Africa as a fit and free home for black men." The Black Star Line, however, had been a doubtful prospect from the start. It was managed by people who knew very little about the shipping business. The ships cost far more, especially for repairs, than they made, and the line soon faced enormous debts. The *Yarmouth* made three limping voyages south from New York. It never did reach Africa. Financing came from stock sales, later from loans and race-patriot contributions. In 1922 a resident of Boley, Oklahoma, was querying the NAACP, "I am writing you in the defence of my race now we have men goin around repersenting marcos garvin and getting 5 dollars from each pupil and they say they will make you become a member of the African government and a stockholder of the black star line and I want you to rite me a letter and tell me is that so or a lye."

Later that year an embattled Garvey, having failed at wooing the Liberian elite, made a hopelessly logical move. He went to the American South. He traveled in the warmth of June. In New Orleans he said, "This is a white man's country. He found it, he conquered it and we can't blame him because he wants to keep it. I'm not vexed with the white man of the South for Jim Crowing me because I'm black. I never built any street cars or railroads . . . And if I don't want to ride when he's willing to let me then I'd better walk." Within days Garvey was sitting down for a two-hour meeting in Atlanta with Edward Clarke, the number-two man in the revived Klan. Clarke was a publicist. He had sold the Salvation Army, the Red Cross, and the YMCA. Now he was selling the Ku

Klux Klan, and doing very well at it. No record exists of what the race leaders discussed. Perhaps Clarke liked the image of two men walking together into a future where they would no longer have to see each other: an amicable separation. Garvey was desperate, but he had always been desperate.

He had met his secret sharer. "I was speaking to a man who was brutally a white man," he would later say, "and I was speaking to him as a man who was brutally a Negro." Garvey prized the straight talk of the Klan, which he felt, "through an honest expression of the whiteman's attitude toward the Negro, prepares him [the Negro] to help himself." This was the slavery-as-racial-training argument scored for the history-less twentieth century. "Between the Ku Klux Klan and the . . . National Association for the Advancement of 'Colored' People group," Garvey said, "give me the Klan for their honesty of purpose towards the Negro. They are better friends to my race, for telling us what they are, and what they mean, thereby giving us a chance to stir for ourselves, than all the hypocrites put together . . . away with the farce, hypocrisy and lie. It smells, it stinks to high heaven. I regard the Klan, the Anglo-Saxon Clubs and White America societies, as far as the Negro is concerned, as better friends of the race than all other hypocritical groups of whites put together. I like honesty and fair play. You may call me a Klansman if you will, but, potentially, every whiteman is a Klansman, as far as the Negro in competition with whites socially, economically and politically is concerned, and there is no use lying about it."

Grammatically, that last sentence suggests that Garvey believed he was a white man, which can't have been what he intended but does have truth in it. We should also note how a group of black leaders chose to portray Garvey when, after the Klan adventure, they rounded on him in force. They wrote to the U.S. attorney general, urging that Garvey and his lieutenants were chiefly motivated by "intense hatred against the white race."

At the higher levels, then, those preoccupied with racial destinies walked about in a forest of mirrors. Yet all around them was a black culture that had little use for mirrors, and none at all for white people as such. The separate black churches, bars, restaurants, barbershops—for that matter, one black family at home—created a space in which a separate black culture could develop and thrive. At the turn of the century some in the black elite began to show an interest in folktales, and a national black urban market created the possibility for black music and theater, in particular, to reach into the written record. Obviously, the elements of these did not suddenly begin their existence at the turn of the century. The generations born between the end of the Civil War and 1901 did indeed produce an outsize number of innovative musical geniuses, from Scott Joplin (born in 1868) through W. C. Handy, Buddy Bolden, King Oliver, Jelly Roll Morton, Bessie Smith, Fletcher Henderson, Duke Ellington, and Louis Armstrong (born in 1901). Nothing in the far larger white culture could approach their achievements. But these people, like Florence Mills and Bert Williams in the theater, innovated within a tradition whose own innovators we don't know by name. We don't know who dreamed up the songs any black Baptist churchgoer would have known by heart in 1870, the songs Joplin or Handy would have heard; much less can we know who first sang the songs that were forgotten by that year. Who could have first sung this folk refrain recorded in Missouri?

> *This world is not my home*
> *This world is not my home*
> *This world's a howling wilderness*
> *This world is not my home*

One presumes the author was not white, but who knows? One former slave, Sina Banks, whose master's plantation had been in Missouri, recalled for the Works Progress Administration a song:

> *I'm going home, I'm going home*
> *I'm going home to die no more.*
> *To die no more, to die no more*
> *I'm going home to die no more.*

She had learned the song "when I was just a little child going along with my brothers to white folks church." There were songs from slavery days that white folks probably would not have sung, in or out of church, such as:

> *Ha! Ha! White folks going for to see,*
> *Ha! Ha! White folks going for to see,*
> *Going for to tell you this, that and 'tother*
> *Fell in love with a great waterfall*
>
> *Fell in love with Dinah Crow,*
> *Teeth was shining like banks of snow,*
> *Eyes as bright as rings of the moon*
> *Teeth as sharp as a 'possum or coon.*
>
> *(Dat nigger's teeth was plenty sharp—*
> *Great consolation between us niggers.)*

One of the most widespread and popular slavery songs was "Run Nigger Run," or "The Patteroll Song," which refers to the patterollers, or slave patrols, posses of white men:

> *Run Nigger, run,*
> *De Patteroll git ye!*
> *Run Nigger, run,*
> *He's almost here!*
>
> *Please Mr. Patteroll,*
> *Don't ketch me!*
> *Jest take dat nigger*
> *What's behind dat tree.*

These latter songs could be seen as coming from black culture in that they make no sense without a distinct, collective black life. They also make no sense without the white culture that created patterollers, and so cannot be understood as independent of whiteness. This is the paradox of biracial (at minimum) slave culture, which was the culture so many Americans shared, to varying degrees, from earliest times to 1865.

It is true that a distinct blues culture evolved among blacks that had little or no reference to whites. Was this a "racial culture"? Many elements came from Africa. Many elements came from Europe. To argue that the former were inherent to black people — a natural inheritance — while the latter were borrowings or even imitations would be to underestimate the originality of black artists and storytellers as they worked with African, European, Indian, and other materials. W. C. Handy and King Oliver did not come from Africa; on a strict racial theory, what they did with call and response or the twelve-bar three-line stanza, both more African than not, could be seen as an assimilationist corruption of pure African form. If black cultural pioneers of the nineteenth century had been interested in racial identity, presumably they would have struggled to emphasize the African or the black and to weed out the white. They would have revived African religion and abandoned Christianity, taken African names, substituted African words for English ones, sung of Africa.

That such classic nineteenth-century nationalist strategies were at most partial, and often nonexistent, among black Americans suggests that the racial-identity impulse in blues culture was weak. The racially black person as such appears in slave songs and tales most often as the nigger, implying an ambivalence toward personal blackness that is not, in context, very mysterious. Blues culture, like blackness itself, came out of slavery and flowered under segregation, both of which were primarily creations of white power. As LeRoi Jones wrote decades later in *Blues People*, "The Negro could not ever become white and that was his strength; at some point, always, he could not participate in the dominant tenor of the white man's culture. It was at this juncture that he had to make use of other resources, whether African, subcultural, or hermetic. And it was this boundary, this no man's land, that provided the logic and beauty of his music." To some degree, being black was what white people wanted of black people. In this perspective, it is less surprising that blues culture did not attempt to purify its African qualities. Rather, it took what it liked with a freedom uniquely its own, improvising right up to the limits of structure, prizing quickness of transformation, bending notes, securing its profundities in fugitive beauty. It was not so much racially separate as independent of race, even antiracial, in that accepting the logic of racial thinking, as in Garvey's case, ultimately meant accepting the necessity of the white race. That was the assimilation blues people could not enact. Whiteness had to be kept contingent, alterable, part of history rather than of nature; blues blackness, then, defended these qualities. Among other things, it kept alive in our shared culture a spirit of nonracial humanity. That spirit might not have survived otherwise, for any of us. It was an American spirit.

And it was an American spirit of escape—from America, and from race. The spirituals dwelled lovingly on escape. The slave's possibilities for escape were few. One might escape in the transformative instant: the pulsing transcendence of the ring shout, the spiritual mergings as the deacon lined out a song and the chorus raised and lowered it, or the breath-catching offbeat of a work song, all higher rhythms with their origins in Africa and their hardest realities in the slave South. One might, just might, escape north, though after the war this seemed less like a true break and more like a change of venue. One might, in theory, escape to Africa, a possibility encoded in such forms as the "fly away home" motif, a spirit-life concept that has been traced to West Africa.

We might wonder why the African home had to be *encoded*. The people in slavery lived under a power that worked hard to eliminate the means by which one held the past: family and linguistic ties, religious continuities, social structure, open communication, literacy, access to books and periodicals. The American system bound slaves in an endless present, a static existence ideally without a past and therefore—this was the masters' goal—without a future. So Africa may have appeared in code because Africa as a past was both very real (in the African practices that survived the crossing) and utterly unreal in that one's connection to it quickly became symbolic, that is to say, timeless. We should also recall that most Africans were enslaved, in Africa, by other Africans, and this must have made one's relationship to Africa as a whole—as a real place—highly problematic. In so many cases the original race betrayal took place in the racial homeland. It seems logical to assume that one did not experience this betrayal in the moment as racial, any more than one understood one's homeland in Africa as a racial homeland. We can imagine that both concepts settled in with the death-like nature of racial slave life in the New World. Finally, a belief in return to a literal Africa must have implied, emotionally, a certain abandonment of what one had built here, in America, be it only a house of memories, and what one's friends and ancestors had built. With these factors in mind, it seems sensible that Africa should have been encoded, not so much because it had to be hidden but because its nature was that of a hiding place—something a real Africa couldn't be, an imaginary homeland where one's longings could go in life and one's spirit in death. This was a very specific kind of escape. The coded references to Africa in slave spirituals overlap with references to the world one would find in death—the freedom waiting there. This earthly world was not home. Slavery was, in an abstract sense, a living death, so it is not surprising that slaves would emphasize the free life in death. That was the one escape every person could be certain of making.

The appreciation of blues culture among elite blacks—the collecting of folktales, the enjoyment of blues and jazz and spirituals, black theater, and black storytelling—had been a long time coming. Pride in being descended from freemen rather than slaves, so important to elite thinking after the Civil War, had receded with the generations. The related pride in light skin—essentially, a pride in being closer to the human norm, understood as white, and therefore removed, however partially, from race, understood as blackness or nonwhiteness—also dwindled after the turn of the century. Whites at the time were indulging as national myth the idea of a peaceful plantation past in which blacks had been pleased at their natural subordination and Klan violence was justified, a trend that culminated with D. W. Griffith's film The Birth of a Nation (1915). White Southerners were proposing public recognitions of black loyalty during the Civil War. These developments seemed to portend the ultimate reconciliation of North and South, and they cut deep at the black elite. A film such as The Birth of a Nation equated black loyalty, even patriotism, with black slavery, precisely the equation that the elite, through careful accommodation, had sought to avoid. Melting-pot assimilationism, so important in the face of high European (and high non-Protestant) immigration, likewise had a disappointing aspect. A theory of American newness, it honored the power of American culture to assimilate foreigners. These foreigners, however, were light-skinned, as was the America assimilating them. In a note to the 1913 edition of his popular play *The Melting Pot*, Israel Zangwill wrote, "Melanophobia, or fear of the black, may be pragmatically as valuable a racial defence for the white as the counter-instinct of philoeucosis, or love of the white, is a force of racial uplifting of the black." In short, white opinion in the period appeared to be consolidating its exclusion of blacks.

By 1920 much of the bloom had gone off the white rose. The spectacle of whites slaughtering each other in a world war for no very good reason under-mined the connection between whiteness and civilization. The term *civiliza-tion* itself had become a target of black intellectual scorn. More than forty years after the end of Reconstruction, elite blacks could not fail to notice that all the black literary societies in creation were unable to effect a dramatic change in white opinion. Meanwhile, the growth of a national, black, urban market made possible a black life not wholly wrapped in poverty. The straight-backed solitude of the upwardly mobile black American might perhaps be eased. Finally, some in the elite had seen, for example in the Atlanta riot of 1906, that it was the repudiated black lower class, rather than the Talented Tenth, that actually opposed white power with black power, feeble as the latter was. In the most har-rowing circumstances one might rather have a street tough than a well-read dea-con at one's side.

Black intellectuals, who were nearly all from the middle class, soon hit upon a concept related to Israel Zangwill's new American, itself an echo of Crève-coeur's "new man" of 1782. Now into the world came the New Negro, inaugu-rating the most elaborate black cultural-separatist movement in our history. Alain Locke, in his famous introductory essay to the collection *The New Negro*, summed up the hopes and contradictions of this new man. Locke wrote in 1925 that the black elite had been preoccupied with the Old Negro of slavery, while black life had gone in a different direction. "Recall how suddenly the Negro spirituals revealed themselves," Locke wrote; "suppressed for generations under the stereotypes of Wesleyan hymn harmony, secretive, half-ashamed, until the courage of being natural brought them out—and behold, there was folk-music. Similarly the mind of the Negro seems suddenly to have slipped from under the tyranny of social intimidation and to be shaking off the psychology of imitation and implied inferiority. By shedding the old chrysalis of the Negro problem we are achieving something like a spiritual emancipation."

Locke pointed out that the Negro as a historical character had, with the first great migration north, shed the sectional identity of Southernness and become national, "a deliberate flight not only from countryside to city, but from medieval America to modern." Locke identified two contradictory trends. On one hand, he resisted the idea of a common blackness, especially given increased class differentiation within the black world: "if it ever was warrantable to regard and treat the Negro *en masse* it is becoming with every day less possible, more unjust and more ridiculous." On the other hand, he celebrated the coming idea of a common blackness, born of segregation but poised to transcend it. He took Harlem as his example: "So what began in terms of segregation becomes more and more, as its elements mix and react, the laboratory of a great race-welding. Hitherto, it must be admitted that American Negroes have been a race more in name than in fact, or to be exact, more in sentiment than in experience. The chief bond between them has been that of a common condition rather than a common consciousness; a problem in common rather than a life in common. In Harlem, Negro life is seizing upon its first chances for group expression and self-determination. It is—or promises at least to be—a race capital."

Locke, then, expressed, without resolving, the tension between individualism and collective racial identity that informed the Harlem Renaissance, for which his essay served as manifesto. That tension predated Locke and survived him. It is a tension common among intellectuals in a racial milieu, though hardly unique to them. The black race, simply by numbers, was overwhelmingly working-class, tenant-farming, or servile (as domestics, porters, and so on). To leave that class was to leave, in some way, the race. And as one rose higher, one's world grew whiter. Moreover, the means of rising in a segregated society normally involved, first, capturing a black market—say, by opening a funeral parlor, a shop, or a real-estate business. So one needed one's race in group form before one could leave it—transcend it, in money terms—as an individual. Class and race thus overlapped, as did the betrayal of both, in a way nearly unique to black America (the nearest comparison would be to American Indians). Certainly, as an Italian, Pole, Jew, or German, one might, with prosperity, feel that one had betrayed one's ethnicity or religious group, perhaps lost one's truer identity. But one was not betraying one's race, and in America that made a difference. Under pressure, whiteness could make room for many shades of white, even Irish Catholic, Jewish, Turkish, or Egyptian white. It could not, on the whole, accommodate black white. Under such conditions a truly black destiny had to be separate and nonindividual if it were to remain black—at the least, if it were to remain nonwhite. This helps to explain the millennial, all-or-nothing quality of black prosperity in nationalist schemes; an abiding sense that worldly power sprang from deception; a deep ambivalence toward race leaders; and the magical nature of some militant racial-uplift solutions, such as a return to Africa or the idea that five dollars could buy a position in that continent's government. An impossible racial situation encouraged an impossible politics.

The New Negro as artist took this tension between the racial individual and the racial collective, and the achiever's dilemma of solidarity and abandonment, into cultural work. The paradoxes surface clearly in Langston Hughes's

1926 essay "The Negro Artist and the Racial Mountain." "One of the most promising of young Negro poets," Hughes began, "said to me once, 'I want to be a poet—not a Negro poet,' meaning, I believe, 'I want to write like a white poet'; meaning subconsciously, 'I would like to be a white poet'; meaning behind that, 'I would like to be white.' And I was sorry the young man said that, for no great poet has ever been afraid of being himself . . . But this is the mountain standing in the way of any true Negro art in America—this urge within the race toward whiteness, the desire to pour racial individuality into the mold of American standardization, and to be as little Negro and as much American as possible." In a few lines Hughes had set up a number of assumptions: America was white; the black person's true self was black, not white (or American); and the black artist's greatest problem was failing to recognize these two points, accept them, and work within them. He does not state that a white poet should revel in his or her whiteness. Hughes found nothing good among white Americans or their culture—nothing *racially* good. He found little good within the black middle class, which he saw as wanting to be white.

He did find some redeeming qualities in the black working-class majority, despite the real possibility he raises that it would ignore the Negro artist. He liked "the low-down folks . . . Their joy runs, bang! into ecstasy. Their religion soars to a shout. O, let's dance! These common people are not afraid of spirituals, as for a long time their more intellectual brethren were, and jazz is their child." These folks would, Hughes believed, provide the materials for a true racial art. He allied himself with Bessie Smith and Paul Robeson, the writers Rudolph Fisher and Jean Toomer, the artist Aaron Douglas. "We young Negro artists who create now intend to express our individual dark-skinned selves without fear or shame. If white people are pleased we are glad. If they are not, it doesn't matter. We know we are beautiful. And ugly too. The tom-tom cries and the tom-tom laughs. If colored people are pleased we are glad. If they are not, their displeasure doesn't matter either. We build our temples for tomorrow . . ."

In Hughes's view the New Negro artist would at once represent the race and ignore it. The artist, like the merchant, needed the race to be a group. Unlike the merchant, the artist did not, in principle, think about money or this-worldly success, and so he need not worry over turning white or betraying blacks. The race artist would operate independently of day-to-day race matters because the race existed primarily in his imagination. The tension between the individual and the collective might be resolved, then, by merging the collective into the individual. The artist might withstand the apathy, misunderstanding, or active dislike of race individuals with the faith that he encompassed in himself their true collective nature, in spite of them. He could be a race of one, building his temple in a tomorrow he was unlikely to see.

Hughes loved the blues. The racial self he described did have a blues quality in its association of individual and collective freedom—the undivided self—with a dim, unknown place or state of being. That place could harbor an inconceivable moment of release; it could be Africa, or freedomland, or death, all temples of tomorrow. This was the place to which slave spirituals led. As we have seen, blues culture was not a racial culture but a human one and in an important sense anti-racial. It was also not progressive but transcendent. However, the New Negro of the Harlem Renaissance wanted a past, in contrast to the new (white) man of Zangwill's melting pot. And much of the usable black past resided in blues culture. Blackness needed to take content from the past in a way that whiteness did not, probably could not. White people of the time liked to say that blacks had no past and no culture—they were comic or frightening imitators of the white norm, no more—and that they were best off in servitude, the natural condition of a people without history. Such was one reason for the New Negro's needing a past.

Yet the New Negro also wanted to be new, and so one had to determine what of the old Negro should be kept, what discarded, and what imagined. The Harlem Renaissance, then, had a fraught relation with the black past. Locke, Hughes, and others clearly rejected the shuffling, loyal, humble Negro, a figure they could abandon at the white doorstep as being in essence a white creation and so not truly Negro. Similarly, the black middle and upper classes, the blue-vein societies and Old Philly and the D.C. aristocrats could be understood as wanting to be white and therefore, from a black (though not white) point of view, actually white, peripheral at best to the New Negro mission. This was a harsh judgment, but one with deep roots.

Some blacks of this generation tried to point out black contributions to the arts and sciences, but this business of contributions had its limits. The contributions somehow seemed always to enlarge the receivers rather than the givers. As Du Bois once explained, "Just as soon as true art emerges; just as soon as the black artist appears, someone touches the race on the shoulder and says, 'He did that because he was an American, not because he was a Negro; he was born here; he was trained here; he is not a Negro—what is a Negro anyhow? He is just human . . .'" Hughes's radical gesture, and that of the Harlem Renaissance after him, was to say there would be no more contributions. Henceforth, race would matter in a new way. Blackness would be preserved not by whiteness's slippery logic of American invisibility but by black rules of presence and visibility—above all, to blacks themselves.

The major terrain for this activity was cultural and necessarily threw black intellectuals onto the past. What they found there were a slave culture and Africa. The latter was at once more easily grasped and less useful. The old, common black stereotypes of Africa as a backward, pagan, bloody place to be redeemed by African Americans gave way to stereotypes of Africa as a harmonious, communal, pleasingly barbaric place close to nature and the distinctive race pulse. "There are mountains in Africa too," Arna Bontemps wrote in a 1926 poem,

> *Treasure is buried there:*
> *Gold and precious stones*
> *And moulded glory.*
> *Lush grass is growing there*
> *Sinking before the wind.*
> *Black men are bowing*
> *Naked in that grass*
> *Digging with their fingers.*
> *I am one of them:*
> *Those mountains should be ours.*

Garveyism had formed a kind of burning bridge from the old view of Africa to the new. Neither led to the material Africa, but the new view did give a valuable richness to the African harbor of the mind. African visual arts, in particular—from German, French, and British collections—finally gave companionship to the shells and ceramic shards that, inexplicable to white eyes, had for centuries decorated the graves of Africans and descendants of Africans who had died in the New World.

The slave past proved more resistant than a mythic Africa to assimilation into the New Negro vision. The principal difficulty was that the most abject, miserable period of black life in America also seemed the most authentically black. One had the sense that racial vitality had actually declined since the end of slavery. There could be no escape from this dilemma, for blackness had indeed been hammered into being in captivity. The tales, songs, and spirituals were slave-culture materials. They had, it appeared, a depth of blackness inaccessible to later generations. "Dese spirituals," an anonymous Kentucky woman was reported (in an 1899 magazine article) to have said, "am de best moanin' music in de world, case dey is de whole Bible sung out and out. Notes is good enough for you people, but us likes a mixtery. Dese young heads ain't wuth killin', fur dey don't keer bout de Bible nor de ole hymns. Dey's completely spiled wid too much white blood in 'em, and de big organ and de eddication has done took all de Holy Spirit out en 'em, till dey ain't no better wid der dances and cuttin' up dan de white folks." The woman's lacerating analysis provided a later generation with the hopeless choice between becoming more like whites or becoming more like slaves. Small wonder that so many of the poems of the Harlem Renaissance, which seemingly ought to have been full of bright mornings, lingered on the theme of death.

But the wish to wring racially positive content from slavery days was inherently contradictory. If black racial identity had been forged in slavery, then any return to blackness implied a return, in some way, to slavery. One could readily find an inconsolable nostalgia for slave days in Toomer's *Cane* (1923), the greatest work of the early Renaissance. Toomer considered it a "song of the end." "The folk-spirit," he believed, "was walking in to die on the modern desert." In *Cane*, Toomer appears as the son, dipping south to rescue somehow what is left of the race:

> *Now just before an epoch's sun declines*
> *Thy son, in time, I have returned to thee,*
> *Thy son, I have in time returned to thee.*

> *In time, for though the sun is setting on*
> *A song-lit race of slaves, it has not set;*
> *Though late, O soil, it is not too late yet*
> *To catch thy plaintive soul, leaving, soon gone,*
> *Leaving, to catch thy plaintive soul soon gone.*

> *O Negro slaves, dark purple ripened plums,*
> *Squeezed, and bursting in the pine-wood air,*
> *Passing, before they stripped the old tree bare*
> *One plum was saved for me, one seed becomes*

> *An everlasting song, a singing tree,*
> *Caroling softly souls of slavery,*
> *What they were, and what they are to me,*
> *Caroling softly souls of slavery.*

What a word to choose, *caroling*. Within a few years Toomer announced that he was not a Negro, going on to argue that no one was. The race had had its moment, then become impossible. Toomer did not say he had become white, he said he was an American, but we can imagine that in practical terms, at least, the difference was slight.

Blues culture did provide a way out of this dilemma—choosing between whiteness and slavery or, in a sense, between whiteness and blackness—yet in its distinct rejection of racial thinking blues culture made an awkward fit with the racial separatism of the later, radical Renaissance inaugurated by Hughes's essay. Sterling Brown, probably the bluest of the Renaissance poets, worked the old themes of grand futility and permanent homelessness. He sounded the American blue notes of pointless departure, doomed beginnings, and social mystery:

> *I is got to see some people*
> *I ain't never seen,*
> *Gotta highball thu some country*
> *Whah I never been.*

This was blues indeed, unromantic and nonracial (if lacking in humor), and it was of scant utility for the New Negro. The blues had to be pro-black in order to be useful to the New Negro; it had to be racially progressive. Neither Brown's blues nor Toomer's aching dusk could really fulfill these functions. Paul Laurence Dunbar, in 1902, had already created the first blues character in the black novel, and that character's name was Sadness. The more progressive Renaissance figures had only a measured amount of time for sadness. They needed action.

This led to an often raging emphasis on the "low-down folks," suggesting that true blackness resided among the poor and uneducated and, at the limit, criminal—as it had once resided with the slave. The Talented Tenth concept had been inverted to a point where race pride could look like willful simple-mindedness, as in Helene Johnson's lines:

> *Gee, brown boy, I loves you all over.*
> *I'm glad I'm a jig. I'm glad I can*
> *understand your dancin' and your*
> *Singin', and feel all the happiness*
> *And joy and don't-care in you,*
> *Gee, boy, when you sing, I can close my ears*
> *And hear tomtoms just as plain.*
> *Listen to me, will you, what do I know*
> *About tomtoms? But I like the word, sort of,*
> *Don't you? It belongs to us.*

Not the smallest problem with this approach was how appealing it could be to whites, some of whom were more than content to imagine blacks as a passionate underclass utterly separate from white society. By far the oddest Harlem Renaissance twinning was that of Carl Van Vechten and Claude McKay.

Although Van Vechten, who was white, lost interest in Harlem after the repeal of Prohibition, he did for several years act as ringmaster of a crowd of whites interested in blackness. A white person nosing around the Harlem clubs was "van vechtening." Van Vechten wrote to H. L. Mencken in the early 1920s, "Jazz, the blues, Negro spirituals, all stimulate me enormously for the moment. Doubtless, I shall discard them too in time." Two years later he was wondering whether black authors would "write about this exotic material while it is still fresh, or will they continue to make a free gift of it to white authors who will exploit it until not a drop of vitality remains." Within months he had answered his question with the novel *Nigger Heaven*. His heroine was a middle-class black woman yearning to return to true blackness. "Savages! Savages at heart! And she had lost or forfeited her birthright, this primitive birthright which was so valuable and important an asset, a birthright that all the civilized races were struggling to get back to—this fact explained the art of a Picasso or a Stravinsky. To be sure, she, too, felt this African beat—it completely aroused her emotion-ally—but she was conscious of feeling it. This love of drums, of exciting rhythms, this naive delight in glowing colour . . . this warm, sexual emotion, all these were hers only through a mental understanding." In short, Van Vechten linked middle-class blacks to whites and saw both as bereft of authentic bar-barism. He dwelled lovingly on sex, liquor, jazz, hate, and tom-toms.

The book was a best-seller. Harlem reaction seems to have been mainly negative. Van Vechten was made unwelcome at some clubs. There was talk of burning him in effigy. Du Bois characterized *Nigger Heaven* as "one damned orgy after another." But many New Negro luminaries praised the novel, includ-ing Langston Hughes, Nella Larsen, Wallace Thurman, and James Weldon Johnson. Two years later they would also praise Claude McKay's *Home to Harlem*, which resembled *Nigger Heaven* in many ways except that it was by a black writer, drew its characters more deeply, and ignored the middle class. It had plenty of prostitutes, pimps, and gamblers. The *New York Times Book Review*'s critic said it had "the real stuff, the lowdown on Harlem." Hughes wrote to McKay, "it is the finest thing 'we've' done yet." One reviewer felt that McKay had "out-niggered Mr. Van Vechten," while another characterized McKay's novel as "*Nigger Heaven* in a larger and more violent dose." *Home to Harlem* became the first novel by a black author to reach the best-seller list.

This was separatism of a sort, one capable of appealing to white audiences and even being performed by a white writer. It did not lead far. Jim Crow remained unmoved, white tastes changed, and the Depression sent Harlem unemployment to 50 percent. For every white baby that died in infancy, two black babies died. In 1930 Hughes published a novel, *Not without Laughter*. His hero loves blues, dancing, and survivor's humor, but he also sees these aspects of black life as products of racial oppression and hopes to leave them behind. He takes as his heroes W. E. B. Du Bois, Frederick Douglass, and Booker T. Washington. It may be wondered how much Hughes had meant what he said in "The Negro Artist and the Racial Mountain." The extreme disunity he had advocated in the name of unity—the race individual building temples for an imaginary race—had a corrosive effect Hughes tried to remedy in his novel and, soon, by turning to socialism. For the essay, in arguing against wanting to be white, he had yoked black pride to the life of the black poor. This not only had the effect of putting racial poverty in a positive light—something Washington had done, too—it also conceded a great deal to whites, including prosperity and its heedless power. And it made race rage blind, a thing to itself; left to itself, it fed there, ultimately giving blackness the quality of suicide. Certainly the New Negro band of sisters and brothers had a gift for collective self-destruction. The thirty or so people who made the movement jump could divide into about as many factions. After all, Hughes's manifesto had been written in response to an antiseparatist broadside by the black writer George Schuyler, "The Negro-Art Hokum," which claimed that "the Aframerican is merely a lampblacked Anglo-Saxon . . . Aside from his color . . . your American Negro is just plain American." And Hughes had begun the essay with an attack on a fellow black poet, Countee Cullen, one of exactly two whose work could bear comparison to that of Hughes.

One way out of this auto-da-fé was to conceive of racial separatism as a temporary stage. This tendency stretches far into the past; indeed, it touches the heart of separatism's impossibility. The various returns to Africa from Revolutionary days onward had been seen as a chance for the race to become normal and so cease to be a race. Black institutions before and after the Civil War had been understood as expedients preparatory to assimilation, perhaps assimilation as quasi whites but far more commonly as human beings among whom race would be unimportant. Garveyism had envisioned a black race triumphantly indistinguishable from the white race, taking for itself whites' full humanity and inhumanity. One can even see this tendency at work in Hughes's essay, which implies in its trajectory not wanting to be black but wanting to make blackness something one would want to be, in other words, to become black by creatively eliminating much of black reality. What, then, was the goal? To embrace blackness or to flee it—to absorb and transform the past, or to walk away from it? In Not without Laughter, Hughes wrote that blacks were "laughing all the time because they must forget." But perhaps they laughed because they could not or should not forget the great, tragic joke of race. Hughes wanted the race to remember, then forget, one might even say to remember in order to be able to forget. The hero's path in Not without Laughter consists in his immersing himself in the black folk, selecting what he wants, then moving on to wanting all that anyone might want regardless of race, such as a home, prosperity, independence, social distinction. Black cultural nationalism in this scheme is a stage one goes through on the road to becoming normal and individualist.

Seen in such a way, blackness remains static, just as the lives of the characters in late Renaissance novels (including Van Vechten's) exhibited a motionless frenzy that, when it went anywhere, went downward. It is very difficult to see this as unrelated to the intense concentration on race in itself. Few people want to be poor for long; few artists want to be race artists all their lives; few, if any, races want simply to be races. Each exercise involves an unavoidable diminishment of the self. The notion of making oneself racial, or one's race a race, as a temporary measure accommodates this emotional, political, and aesthetic problem. Yet it also contains an ambivalent violence: I will fight to become this thing so that I can no longer be it. It is a form of starting over that heralds its own end.

The brief militant period of the Harlem Renaissance began with Schuyler's satire and ended with several others, including one by Schuyler. Rudolph Fisher's 1928 *The Walls of Jericho* was kind: it finishes with Harlem's Talented Tenth and the lower class united against drugs and crime. Schuyler's *Black No More* (1931) was hilarious and so evenly mean-spirited as to seem sweet. The story features an apparatus that turns black people white. Few could resist the machine's lure. Schuyler's raffish, blanched hero joins up with a white-supremacist Atlantan to work the skin game in a comic version of Marcus Garvey's Southern coalition building. At the end, the whiteness machine's inventor announces that "in practically every instance the new Caucasians were from two to three shades lighter than the old Caucasians," which leads to crowded beaches and a land-office business in complexion darkeners: "Everybody that was anybody had a stained skin." Yet *Black No More* is not entirely lighthearted. Just prior to the mulatto denouement, Schuyler broke tone to describe the castration, torture, and burning of two white supremacists mistakenly thought to be (invisibly) black. He then titled his conclusion "And So On and So On." One senses a weary blues paying a visit, and a laughter that couldn't forget.

The last satire of the Harlem Renaissance came from Wallace Thurman in 1932, *Infants of the Spring*. Thurman had been the brilliant party master for the younger crowd in their delirious frolics at the house called Niggerati Manor. His satire ends not in reconciliation or a mordant free-for-all of color madness but in suicide and the victory of whiteness. Thurman's hero, Raymond, has wanted to "break the chains which held him to a racial rack and carry a blazing beacon to the top of Mount Olympus so that those possessed of Alpine stocks could follow in his wake"—that is, to escape race in order to exceed the accomplishments of whites. He has wanted to "free himself from racial conscious-ness." He feels that he has failed; he feels his generation has failed. Thurman dramatized this, in the final pages of *Infants of the Spring*, with matching por-tions of comedy and tragedy. A Renaissance writer—"Paul the debonair, Paul the poseur, Paul the irresponsible romanticist"—has killed himself in a vivid way. In bright eccentric clothes he has cut his wrists in the bathtub. He has strewn his posthumous masterpiece across the floor with an eye toward public-ity. But he left the water on: "Ironically enough, only the title page and the ded-ication were completely legible." Beneath the dedication "he had drawn a distorted, inky black skyscraper, modeled after Niggerati Manor, and on which were focused an array of blindingly white beams of light. The foundation of this building was composed of crumbling stone. At first glance it could be ascer-tained that the skyscraper would soon crumple and fall, leaving the dominating white lights in full possession of the sky."

Less than two years later Thurman's doctor warned him that his tuberculosis was worsening. Thurman drank steadily for a month, collapsed, and by the end of 1934 had died. Rudolph Fisher followed him four days later.

"THIS SPECIAL WAY OF LIFE"

■

Black separatism went into a lengthy slumber after the demise of Garveyism and the Harlem Renaissance. Increasing militance among workers, and the pitiless lessons of the Depression, transferred some of the social energy that might have gone into race politics to unionism, socialism, and communism. Since 1928 the Communist International had advocated that the Black Belt of the South be controlled by black farmers rather than white landowners. The American party urged that a separate black state be made of those regions, with its own government and laws. There seems to have been some presumption that the state would be communist in organization. The other major proposal for a separate black state came from the Nation of Islam.

A mysterious man named Wallace Fard appeared in Detroit midway through 1930, selling silks door-to-door and offering a vague religious message. Fard could have passed for white, an odd echo of the *Ethiopian Manifesto* of 1829, which had foreseen a racial deliverer who looked white. Fard's early follower Elijah Poole, later known as Elijah Muhammad and the Nation's architect, recalled that Fard's father had married a white woman "so he could get a son to live more like this civilization of the whites so as to be able to get among them and they will not be able to distinguish him." When Poole first met Fard, the young man suggested that Fard was Jesus. Fard apparently agreed and soon took up Christ's identity. Among Fard's ideas was human sacrifice—the murder of four white "devils" gave one "free transportation to Mecca," as Elijah recalled—

and apparently one follower did kill his white boarder. A concept such as human sacrifice naturally attracted police attention. In May 1933 Fard was thrown out of Detroit, and quickly disappeared.

Fard believed, according to Elijah Muhammad, that all people had once been black and lived in peace along the Nile as God's chosen. Then, sixty-six hundred years before Fard, Yakub was born, and he wanted power. Exiled, he and his scientists spent six hundred years on an island turning blacks into whites. Lightening bred the decency out of them; it made them evil. They tried to subdue black people, and for this they were banished to Europe. Their numbers and evil grew. They crushed blacks across the world. This would end as prophesied in Revelation. God would send the Mother of Planes, "the largest mechanical man-made object in the sky," to eliminate whites. In the meantime, American blacks should have their own state, with seed funding from "our former slave masters," to advance toward self-realization. What that self would be it is hard to say. Muhammad or Fard saw nothing good in black life as it was lived. That life was a product of slavery and the reign of Yakub. Muhammad urged his followers to "observe the operations of the white man. He is successful." In practice, they would live a communal Victorianism with its component of female submission greatly enhanced, and with a prohibition on pork. It was, in important ways, a rather white life.

The communists had more influence, for a while. Their proposed racial separatism was not their strongest suit, it being impractical and an awkward fit with proletarian solidarity. The communist self was a worker's self, not a racial identity. But communism did have a worldview that felt familiar. It did not seek to imitate the ruling class. It saw property as theft, a concept of which slavery had been the thorough enactment. And it saw the masses as embodying history in its purest, most profound form. This bottom-up, redemptive vision, in which the last shall be first, struck many chords within black America. The novelist Richard Wright played each of them in his 1937 "Blueprint for Negro Writing." He emphasized the black church and folklore, connecting both to slavery. The black church, he believed, had been "revolutionary" under slavery but "archaic" and quietist without it. Folklore, however, retained its power. "It was . . . in a folklore moulded out of rigorous and inhuman conditions of life that the Negro achieved his most indigenous and complete expression. Blues, spirituals, and folk tales recounted from mouth to mouth . . . work songs sung under blazing suns—all these formed the channels through which the racial wisdom flowed." Wright somewhat unfairly criticized post–Civil War black writers for neglecting these traditions: "Two separate cultures sprang up: one for the Negro masses, unwritten and unrecognized; and the other for the sons and daughters of a rising Negro bourgeoisie, parasitic and mannered."

Wright, allied with communists at the time, saw black nationalism as a necessary, desirable stage. He understood it as critical to (nonwhite) self-understanding and (non-bourgeois) collective mobilization: "at the moment when a people begin to realize a *meaning* in their suffering, the civilization that engenders that suffering is doomed." Yet the meaning came specifically from suffering. It took form in invidious racial circumstances, creating "a Negro way of life in America. The Negro people did not ask for this, and deep down, though they express themselves through their institutions and adhere to this special way of life, they do not want it now. This special existence was forced upon them from without by lynch rope, bayonet and mob rule."

The black writer had to work with what he, as a black person representing the racial collective, had available, deepening the blues—that culture formed by blacks in "the whole special way of life which has been rammed down their throats." Black writers must "feel the meaning of the history of their race as though they in one life time had lived it themselves throughout all the long centuries." Once they and black people generally had done this, they could transcend racial nationalism. Wright had encapsulated the eschatology of racial nationalism or separatism, its philosophy of End Times—the race must deepen itself in order to escape that self. He did not dwell on the paradoxically suicidal nature of such an enterprise, its Christian roots, or the oddness of mobilizing people on the basis of principles that ought to be, at a later date, discarded. He did believe that black slave culture bore gifts to the twentieth-century black wage slave. Psychologically, the crucial aspect of this cross-generational solidarity was that it did not issue into American whiteness or the economic violence of an achiever's individualism.

That meant a lot in 1937 and later. The trend of the 1930s had been toward greater racial militance, most importantly in the North. Black politicians were learning to harness the race vote, a practice white politicians could readily comprehend. Roosevelt and the New Deal finally lured black voters from the party of Lincoln to the Democrats, making black voting power nationally significant for the first time since Reconstruction. This was the traditional separatism of colored conventions—a provisional strategy whose goal remained integration. The Buying Power movement, for example, boycotted and picketed white businesses in order to force them to hire black workers. The NAACP directed its lawyers toward desegregating graduate schools, a perfect marriage of Talented Tenth interests and activism. Then, in 1941, the unstoppable organizer (and former Garveyite) Asa Philip Randolph threatened a black march on Washington to force integration in war industries and the armed forces. Randolph met with an upset Roosevelt. Seven days later the president banned discrimination in war industries. It was the first executive order on behalf of blacks since Lincoln. The march never took place.

World War II amplified the lessons of the previous world war. Blacks contin-ued leaving the South for industrial jobs in the North and, increasingly, in the West. They fought for the Allies across the globe; and they fought against two peoples in particular, the Germans and the Japanese, whose ideologies of war had a pronounced component of racial superiority. To some degree, black American soldiers were fighting a species of white Southerner. The leading black national paper, the *Pittsburgh Courier*, launched a Double V program—victory at home and victory abroad—while government war propaganda emphasized the multiracial character of America as a tool for mobilization. (Ed Sullivan pitched in with *Harlem Cavalcade*.) White America needed blacks in those years, and blacks knew it. Even white unions began taking in large num-bers of black members, who in turn brought civil-rights advocacy into the labor mainstream. Court decisions were chipping away at segregation. The first restaurant sit-in, at Stoner's in Chicago, occurred in 1942. Refusing to give up one's "white" seat on a segregated bus or streetcar appears to have become a political pastime during the war, at least in Alabama.

Black Americans did not want a reprise of the Great War and 1919, though to an extent they got one. There were violent incidents and race riots through-out the war—1943 being an especially bad year—and after victory a number of black returnees were murdered by whites. But this was mild compared with 1919 or the earlier days, still within living memory, when more than a hundred blacks could be lynched in a single year. There would be no return to that sta-tus quo. On one hand, black Americans had become too enmeshed in white institutions as equals. They were voting and getting college degrees and buying property, working in formerly white factories, joining formerly white unions, excelling in formerly white sports. Black novelists began to write books with white central characters, a trend that continued well into the 1950s. On the other hand, black social advances, in terms of fighting segregation, tended to come from blacks organizing as blacks. Their claims on white society, aimed at eliminating racial distinctions, were based on racial distinctiveness. In a sense, as Wright had foreseen, black nationalism conspired toward its own demise.

This created a tension in what became known as the civil-rights movement: a tension between blackness and humanness; also, a tension between wanting what whites had and not wanting to be white. The institutional culture that could sustain these tensions was the black church. One might even say that these tensions defined the black church. It is startling to think that the social institution most responsible for desegregating the United States was also its most persistently, and voluntarily, segregated one. (The black historian E. Franklin Frazier, writing in 1964, called the black church "the most important institu-tional barrier to integration and the assimilation of Negroes.") Yet the specific blackness of the black church made it an ideal place for a movement that sought not only to destroy the structures of white oppression but to transcend racial thinking in a way that, as with the blues, was at once black and not black.

The historically based transcendence of history was, after all, the particular activity of the black church. To a degree, this is true of most churches: religion provides a culturally specific tradition of leaving the world. What distinguished the black church from its white counterpart was that it incorporated the American racial past more fully and openly. The white church tended to understand itself as being ideally nonhistorical and certainly not racial. By contrast, and despite the many congregations that sought to suppress all evidence of blackness, the black church as a whole was distinctively black, in two respects: it took, formed, and reformed African and blues modes in an irrefutably black American way; and it stretched at transcending (not ignoring) race. The white church had always thought it was universal and fully human and so could not perceive its daily failure to be either. It could not transcend what it couldn't see. The black church, in its segregation, could perceive the social weight of race rather well and so had daily experience of what it actually meant to try to transcend race. The black church was racially conservative, which allowed it to work at changing racial roles without cutting off the past. In church one could loosen the ties of blackness without worrying that all might be lost.

Anxiety about a loss of blackness was not small in the 1950s, particularly after the Supreme Court's *Brown v. Board of Education* decision in 1954, which found racially "separate but equal" schools to be inherently unequal and illegal. The whole world of black businesses with black customers, of black newspapers and insurance companies, of black Wall Streets, threatened to disappear, and many people (including Langston Hughes) feared that something precious about blackness would disappear with it. Besides, the trend toward integration had been greatly motivated by factors unrelated to black life as it was lived. The white elite worried about its image overseas, notably among nonwhite peoples, whose loyalty was one subject of the contest between America and the Soviet Union. The white elite worried about its own cohesion, particularly after white Southern Democrats rebelled against their party in reaction to Democratic civil-rights legislation. Finally, the United States had fought a war against the racial-supremacist governments of Japan and, especially, Germany, which put domestic Jim Crow in a new light. All these were fine reasons to dismantle segregation, but they were not black, or even pro-black, reasons.

If anything, they foretold the elimination of a distinctly black life. Much of the legal thinking against segregation, for example, based itself on the emerging sociological concept of black pathology. The concept had significant antecedents, such as the "slave mentality" once thought to make freedmen unfit as citizens or beliefs in low black self-regard, all of which predated the Civil War and had been retailed ever since by whites and, more importantly, by blacks. These various conceptions of (temporary) black inferiority formed the negative content—the blackness that had to be transcended—of nineteenth-century assimilation. The Harlem Renaissance, when it prized what Du Bois called the "debauched tenth," operated as a pivot: blackness rose from the "darky" slave mentality, twirled about in the nationalist honky-tonk, then arced downward into black pathology. To the extent that pathology doctrine had an origin, it lay with Dr. Robert Park, who left his work as a ghostwriter for Booker T. Washington to become the founder of the Chicago school of sociology. The general Chicago idea was that racial discrimination had created a black underclass with pathological habits. Du Bois, Douglass, and many others had explored a similar conception, but they fished in deep waters. Park waded in the shallows, as would Gunnar Myrdal in *An American Dilemma* (1944). The liberal recognition of black misery easily drifted into a belief in black pathology; one more small step brought one to the impression that blackness and some socio-moral sickness were indistinguishable. Integration could then be viewed, and often was, as an uplifting not only from destitution but from blackness itself.

If, then, integration had a certain antiblack quality, and tended to the destruction of independent black life (particularly black business), it becomes less startling that the determinedly segregated black church led the struggle against segregation. As long as one had the church, one could not be assimilated as white, nor could one be pathological, even to oneself. Only the black church had the historical, institutional, and psychological wherewithal to hold the goals of wanting to be fully human and not wanting to be white in a creative tension.

It is telling that the church movement did not emphasize racial equality, a concept that moved in self-contradiction. Equality implied sameness. Racial equality implied not only that black and white were equal quantities but that they had equal qualities—race without content, so to speak. (The term *racism*, which became popular at mid-century, had a similar effect in transforming a historical process or drama into something like a medical condition that either had to be purged, somehow, or, in the defeatist view, would always remain, like an inherited blood disease.) The rush from content implied by racial equality meant that race had no past and no future, only an eternal inexplicable present. That was, in essence, a white view of race, against which the black church (with exceptions) and blues culture had quietly, peacefully struggled for an exceedingly long time. The black church movement did not emphasize equality, it emphasized freedom—above all, freedom from race, a freedom that could only come with understanding, in Toomer's words, "what they were, and what they are to me, / Caroling softly souls of slavery." That understanding would have required whites and blacks to come to terms with what they shared—and what they shared with Indians, Indians with them—an American historical understanding composed primarily of these three overlapping sets, an understanding of race that could not, in the end, be exclusively racial if it was ever to be a beginning, that is, if it was to be free.

An understanding that, of course, could not ever be white. In his moment of greatest doubt and resolve, in a Birmingham, Alabama, jail cell in 1963, Martin Luther King, Jr., thirty-four years of age, confronted this problem alone, scribbling frenetically in the margins of a newspaper. The civil-rights movement had been collapsing around him. The Kennedy administration, needing the support of white Southern Democrats, had perfected the arts of delay and denial; the white civil-rights agitators on Capitol Hill were often Republicans. The Mississippi voter-registration drive, undertaken by the Student Nonviolent Coordinating Committee (SNCC), had recently demonstrated that local white powers would contest the vote of every single black person, one at a time, with seemingly inexhaustible patience, just as night riders would shoot SNCC workers one at a time. Many a black activist, upon approaching a sharecropper's door, found it closed to him or her; as a Georgia activist put it, "When you ask a man to join you, you are asking for a confession that his life up until now has been lived upside down"—not an easy confession to make, particularly when the reward for acting on it could be death. Black businessmen were more than weary of agitations. A few days before entering the Birmingham jail, King had spoken of "traitors to the race," a phrase that did not come quickly to him. Many of his advisers had not wanted him to offer himself up for imprisonment. His father had asked him to wait for a better time. The sympathetic Northern media had begun to anticipate the movement's demise. Like the white and black moderates of Birmingham, Northern editorialists found King too irritating. *The New York Times* felt he demanded too much; *Time* wrote that King's protests and boycott in Birmingham "inflamed tensions at a time when the city seemed to be making some progress, however small, in race relations."

This missed the point, because King's goal was not an improvement in race relations but an improvement in human relations. He scribbled in the margins of a newspaper because he was in solitary, for disobeying an injunction against demonstrations; the newspaper had been smuggled to him; and in it he read about some moderate white pastors who felt he was inciting hatred and violence and urged an end to these "untimely" demonstrations. Of all the reports brought to King by his lawyer, this was the one that enraged him. Moderates and liberals, reasonable people, were both closest to him and furthest away. The white segregationist was an open enemy with a clear public policy. The segregationist was, in a way, close to the black person because he or she had a race;

and one could see, sometimes, the white segregationist raging around in his skin, trapped in it, in a fashion that, however distant, had a familiar quality. From a religious point of view, the segregationist had a sin or addiction that operated the way other sins or addictions operated, attracting and repelling its host, emptily laughing, an elusive companion destroying with solitude. The moderate and reasonable person was altogether different and vexing. The moderate was difficult to locate. That which the moderate opposed seemed always to have been done by someone else. The moderate appeared to be without sin, at least to himself, which made him fundamentally a mystery to religion. Without sin, no salvation. (Two years later Malcolm X would write, "the one people whom Jesus could not help were the Pharisees; they didn't feel they needed help.") The moderate did not wrestle with the Lord. Disengaged from sin, was he not also, in the end, inaccessible to righteousness? In context, the moderate, unlike the segregationist, did not think of himself as white and so could not imagine being black.

King struggled with his words. He was not a natural writer. The Southern preacher's technique of abruptly changing registers—from anger to thoughtfulness, absurdist pastiche, or comfort—worked through the linkages of physical voice and expressive body, but on the page it could look like narrative insecurity, even coyness. King scribbled from tone to tone, from self-important to scholarly to truth telling. Then he hit his stride when faced with the command to be reasonable and patient. "I guess it is easy," King wrote, "for those who have not felt the stinging darts of segregation to say, 'Wait.' " And he unleashed one of the longer sentences in our literature:

> But when you have seen vicious mobs lynch your mothers and fathers at will and drown your brothers and sisters at whim; . . . when you suddenly find your tongue twisted and your speech stammering as you seek to explain to your six-year-old daughter why she can't go to the amusement park that has just been advertised on television, and see tears welling up in her little eyes when she is told that Funtown is closed to colored children, and see the depressing clouds of inferiority begin to form in her little mental sky, and see her begin to distort her little personality by unconsciously developing a bitterness toward white people; when you have to concoct an answer for a five-year-old son asking in agonizing pathos: "Daddy, why do white people treat colored people so mean?"; . . . when you are harried by day and haunted by night by the fact that you are a Negro, living constantly at tiptoe stance never quite knowing what to expect next, and plagued with inner

fears and resentments; when you are forever fighting a degenerating sense of "nobodiness"; then you will understand why we find
it difficult to wait.

King in his cell was telling white moderates what it meant to him to be
black. He took them to the primordial scene of race recognition, when the child
looks at himself or herself in the mirror in a new way, through white eyes, when
one's skin acquires a color that will never go away. He wrote of being harried
and haunted by "the fact that you are a Negro." This was the transformation he
demanded of white moderates, a transformation he had once believed ought
not to be so difficult for them: that they were black; that being black had a quality of nobodiness, a sense of incompletion; that they were nobody, too. When
you are forever fighting a degenerating sense of nobodiness, then you will
understand. Such was King's gift for love that he sought to draw to the white
moderates' attention their own lack of human fullness, which found its earthly
expression in their inability to imagine being black.

Such was his anger that he wrote, "I have almost reached the regrettable
conclusion that the Negro's great stumbling block in the stride toward freedom
is not the White Citizen's Counciler or the Ku Klux Klanner, but the white
moderate who is more devoted to 'order' than to justice." The Klansman actually could imagine what it was to be black. The segregationist's fear was precisely a fear of being black. It was all too imaginable. This imagination
apparently exceeded the capacities of white moderates.

King had his letter sent to the men featured in the newspaper story. Their
leader, Bishop C. C. Jones Carpenter, read it, then remarked to a colleague,
"This is what you get when you try to do something. You get it from both sides."
King left jail and returned to a movement not much altered from when he had
last been free. Reasonableness and fear seemed to be gaining much ground.
Logically, then, the task of saving the movement fell to a lunatic (who could not
be reasonable) and to children, who have a more creative relationship with fear
than adults do. The lunatic was a white mailman named William Moore, a former marine, raised in Mississippi. He started off alone from Chattanooga, walking the highways and wearing two signboards: they read END SEGREGATION IN
AMERICA and EQUAL RIGHTS FOR ALL MEN. He had spent some time in a mental
hospital in the mid-1950s, after which he wrote a book describing how he found
himself at an angle to the world, "and where the world was not like the ideal, I
believed the world was wrong and so did not adjust my behavior to reality." In
1963, days after King left jail, Moore pushed his cart out of Tennessee, through
a bit of Georgia, and into Alabama. His goal was Mississippi, where he planned
to call on the governor and urge him to "be gracious and give more than is

immediately demanded of you." Only a Southerner would think to use *gracious* in such a way. A radio reporter caught up with Moore along Highway 11. Moore told the reporter he was unafraid of violence because he knew Southerners and was one himself. A mile farther on he was found dead, lying faceup, with his placards, and with two bullets in his head.

The sacrifice of the holy fool was followed by that of the children. King found the black adults of Birmingham tired of protest. They would volunteer for jail after a sermon but stay home at call-up time. It just didn't seem worth it; the movement asked too much. Thanks to the efforts of King's colleagues James Bevel and Diane Nash Bevel, however, schoolchildren were growing eager for jail. Many of them had but recently experienced the moment of recognition King described in his letter. Bevel and Nash went after the best students and sports stars, and the other kids followed. As children, they already knew much about artful battles against arbitrary authority. They signed up by the hundreds and marched by the hundreds into the teeth of police dogs and the jets of water cannon. The adults, including the children's parents, watched them walk into paddy wagons and fill the jail. After they filled the jail, they filled the jail yard. The black children of Birmingham set an American record for arrests in a nonviolent protest. Even some adults joined them. One of the pillars of Birmingham's black establishment at last dropped his opposition to the demonstrations after watching, from his window, a little girl being tumbled down the street by the force of a water cannon's stream. Eventually, an unelected group of leading white citizens agreed to revisions of Birmingham's segregation practices.

To the extent that the civil-rights movement in 1963, after Birmingham, had leaders, those leaders were adults. But to an incredible extent the movement was propelled by children, who took to the streets in cities and towns across the country. In the ten weeks after Birmingham there were 758 demonstrations in 186 places, with nearly fifteen thousand arrests. This was not about water fountains. It was not about race, in any narrow sense, or accumulated grievances and pent-up resentments. What historical grievance does a ten-year-old girl have? Perhaps this one: that that moment of race recognition, seeing oneself through white eyes as somehow destined for submission, fear, and bitterness, should not have happened.

The early civil-rights movement, however complex its workings, yet had that childlike simplicity. But racial thinking had a grip on adults, who were reluctant to yield their privileges and their protections against each other, however strangely conceived those privileges and protections may have been. The movement placed an unbearable pressure on American identity because it suggested that race really was an arbitrary matter of skin tone and that the nation really had been living upside down. The adult mind sped to register this notion, so unthreatening to a young person recently embarked on life, or to a holy fool, but deeply disturbing to a grown-up for whom the past was meant to be something other than an accumulation of shame and error. Adults tend to understand social relations in terms of justified power. In the fight against the power category of race, King had imagined that power came only from God, who has no race—therefore race had no power. To understand this would be like suddenly awakening after the sleep of one's life, to be like a child again.

Conceptually, the major difficulty King faced was the implication that the past did not exist, that Americans actually were children and their nation potentially brand-new, in 1963. King was playing on the centuries-old theme of newness, itself related to the collective longing for innocence. These were powerful, volatile materials. King sought to drain them from their traditional vessels of racial separatism into the greater vessel of American identity—he was forever invoking the principles of 1776, the noble bequests of Jefferson and Lincoln, and the American dream—but the wine was not so easily mixed. White innocence had special qualities for those who believed in it. For example, what moved many whites about Birmingham was not King in his cell, or for that matter any number of black adults trooping off to jail, or the murder of black civil-rights workers here and there in the South. The general attitude of white America seemed to be a hope that all this regrettable strangeness would go away. Most whites remained unmoved, too, by the unprecedented spectacle of teenagers and children down to the age of six parading by the hundreds straight to prison—six hundred jailed in a day. Rather, what finally moved white America was the violence of white policemen against innocent children. It was that little girl tumbling down the asphalt and thin, fifteen-year-old Walter Gadsden offering his abdomen to the teeth of a police dog. And it is hard not to think—because so much had gone before, unnoticed—that what whites saw here was their own innocence under attack. This wounded them. Broad white American support for black civil rights can be dated from that innocence-threatening afternoon in Birmingham on May 3, 1963, between the hours of noon and three.

However, white support often had as its premise the need to restore white innocence, a racial rather than human goal. This was the kernel of white racial separatism, which was itself the motor of our other separatisms. Needing white support, the civil-rights movement began then to drift into separatism, at just the time when it became an interracial struggle. SNCC, for instance, began debating a plan to bring hundreds of recruits into Mississippi for what would become Freedom Summer. SNCC's Mississippi project had been small, with forty-one workers in 1963. It paid single young people subsistence wages to register black voters, spread information about civil rights, and generally try to organize local blacks in small towns and rural areas to a point where they might feel something slightly more positive than fear. For this, SNCC workers and their sympathizers had, since the first mission to Mississippi in 1961, been killed and beaten, their houses and meeting places burned. After nearly three years they had little to show for their efforts. An infusion of recruits might put new energy into the Mississippi fight. Those new recruits, however, would mostly be white Northern college students. SNCC had been avowedly interracial; as its most revered organizer, Robert Moses, said late in 1963, keeping whites out would have made SNCC a "racist movement . . . the one thing we can do for the country that no one else can do is to be above the race issue." The great majority of SNCC workers up to that point, however, had been black. And the decision to bring in white volunteers was based in part on the perception that white America—to which SNCC reasonably felt it had now to appeal if the Mississippi project was to move forward—would react more strongly to the idea of a dead white activist than it had to news of dead black ones. White Americans might more readily see a dead white person as an innocent victim.

This was opposing racial thinking with racial thinking. It had an immediate effect. When two white SNCC workers and one black SNCC worker disappeared early in Freedom Summer, the government and Northern press reacted as if something had at last happened to innocent human beings rather than Negroes. The parents of the missing white men met with President Johnson. An enormous federal investigation got under way and eventually found the bodies and the killers. Seven were convicted. White bodies really were worth more than black bodies.

In appealing successfully to white America through the spectacle of white death—in appealing to the basest and most contemptible of white thoughts, that white people are simply more valuable than others—SNCC had strangled something in itself. It lost track of human unity; it lost contact with any higher power; it had played the white game by white rules, and sold its soul. At a February 1965 meeting Robert Moses announced he was leaving SNCC and changing his last name and "will no longer speak to white people." And yet the idea of opposing race with race, whiteness with blackness, took hold in 1964 and would have a long future. It was, fundamentally, a desperate response to Northern or national white thinking—including that of white sympathizers—rather than Southern white peculiarities. Southern segregation was, after all, crumbling. President Johnson's signing of the Civil Rights Act in July 1964 led immediately to peaceful desegregation across the South; the Voting Rights Act the next year eliminated the formal hurdles to black voting. What had seemed utopian in 1963 had become reality. Yet these triumphs brought only passing joy. Indeed, they acted to reveal the limitations of formal equality, which prompted the horrified realization that Jim Crow had simply been the visible face of an enemy who now carried on unseen. White innocence had been restored in its characteristic Northern form, color blindness, which condemned racial discrimination but failed to recognize that white people tended to be blind to color mainly, if not exclusively, when the color was white. Against this undisturbed norm of whiteness, blackness and black separatism reemerged.

Black separatism after 1964 took three main forms. The first consisted of race-based destruction. When in 1965 the black neighborhood of Watts in Los Angeles rioted, black people looted white stores and attacked white people on a remarkably straightforward racial basis. This was inhumanity in vivid action and brought no significant gains to anybody. The second form often had a religious element. King himself wrestled with it, saying, "It is absolutely necessary for the Negro to have power, but the term Black Power is unfortunate because it tends to give the impression of black nationalism." It gave that impression for good reason. Gaining racial power required some kind of nationalist thinking, if only a small Africa of the mind that might provide space for reflection and shoring up of the self. That was the direction King began leaning toward, but he stubbornly kept his focus on economic problems after the Selma voter-registration campaign of 1965. It was abundantly clear, once Jim Crow went into decline, that formal racial rights were worth relatively little when one was brutally poor because, at least in part, of one's skin color. However, the genius of Northern whiteness was to portray black poverty as an economic, not racial, phenomenon—or, if it was racial, the source of it was a black pathology. Black leaders responded to the black-pathology argument with positive blackness, to "colorblind" economic realities with Black Power.

The more churchly leaders faced an exquisite bind. They had long held among themselves the most successful form of racial power, and so Black Power, once the initial defiant thrill had (quickly) worn off, seemed less than exotic to them. At the same time, they knew that the power of the black church came not merely from racial separatism but through a highly mediated blackness that reached away from race toward God—a profoundly religious faith that power, in whatever form, ultimately came from a source that had nothing to do with race.

In July 1966 the newly organized National Committee of Black Churchmen, led by the race-and-religion commissioner of the interracial National Council of Churches, published its Black Power manifesto. "The fundamental distortion facing us in the controversy about 'black power,' " the churchmen wrote, "is rooted in a gross imbalance of power and conscience between Negroes and white Americans." The Negroes had conscience without power, which led them into "a distorted form of love [for whites], which, in the absence of power, becomes chaotic self-surrender." Whites, by contrast, had power without conscience, which led them to destroy blacks and would lead to national self-destruction. While deploring the violence of riots, the churchmen pointed to their causes, which lay "in the silent and covert violence which white middle-class America inflicts upon the victims of the inner city. The hidden, smooth, and often smiling decisions of American leaders which tie a white noose of suburbia around the necks and which pin the backs of the masses of Negroes against the steaming ghetto walls—without jobs in a booming economy; with dilapidated and segregated educational systems in the full view of unenforced laws against it; in short: the failure of American leaders to use American power to create equal opportunity in life as well as in law—this is the real problem and not the anguished cry for 'black power.' "

Theologically, the churchmen resolved the problem of earthly versus godly power by arguing that whites had set themselves as a race to rival God—taking his power—which, evidently, made it permissible for blacks to do the same, using their own race as a proxy warrior for God with the ultimate aim of returning to God the power usurped by whites. This would mean that Black Power was a temporary expedient for redressing an imbalance of power. How temporary would this expedient be? For individuals, judging from the manifesto, it might not be temporary at all. Blacks needed to "find a way to a new self-image in which we can feel a normal sense of pride in self, including our variety of skin color and the manifold textures of our hair. As long as we are filled with hate for ourselves we will be unable to respect others." The churchmen did not explain—who could?—what a normal sense of pride in one's racial self might be, apart from a lack of racial shame. Much rested on the word *normal*. How could one discover a normal sense of racial pride? What was the norm? Rather than dig into this quandary, the churchmen hurried to the conclusion that all groups should have race or ethnic pride and the power that comes from it—including "the need for . . . white Anglo-Saxon Protestants . . . to have and to wield group power." But white power, the churchmen felt, needed to have an element of shame. Implicitly, this meant that blacks, on their road to normal blackness, should eliminate their shame (as crippling), while whites, on their road to a democratic, normal, healthy whiteness, should develop a sense of shame and keep it indefinitely as the spur to conscience. Put differently, black self-hatred, as a result of powerlessness before whites, would be transformed into white self-hatred, as a result of whites' recognition of their own abuses of power. The clergymen avoided the deep questions of why any group would give up power; how much power was the right amount, or "normal"; and, ultimately, the surpassing reality that whites did not think of their power as racial.

One can imagine that this new self-hating white power, had it occurred, would have led to an unstable and moody cast of mind. It would also have transferred white innocence to blacks, which would give blacks—to combat self-hatred, to guard against white abuse of white power—the responsibility for instructing whites as to when whites' shame was not enough. In a subtle way, this would have both inverted the existing structure (in which whites controlled the apportionment of racial self-images) and preserved it, in that blacks' position as the national or white conscience was exactly the thankless social role the clergymen were struggling to shed. But the only alternative, by this logic, was for whites to develop a racial consciousness and a racial conscience on their own. And if they failed, as would seem likely, what then?

The price of failure might be national destruction, a possibility which the clergymen raised and which seemed imminent as the death tolls in Newark and Detroit mounted; after King was assassinated, in April 1968, blacks rebelled in 126 cities, and forty-six persons lost their lives, the cruelest eulogy for a peaceful man. The price of white failure might also be eternal black racial dissatisfaction, a sense that whites were deaf to the caroling of their own "souls of slavery" and so likely, for some time, to hide themselves in those suburban rings that the pastors had likened to a noose. The committee's black churchmen came mainly from Northern white denominations and so knew the Northern white mentality in a way that King and his comrades in the Southern Christian Leadership Conference did not.

The churchmen wanted to avoid these alternatives. What they hoped for was a two-stage historical advance, with Black Power as its instigating force. In the first stage, the nation's various ethnic and racial groups would come to a self-consciousness, each perfect unto itself, creating a multiple separatism of normal and healthy groups based on unknown standards of normality and health. In the second stage, each of these groups would renounce, partially or wholly, its separateness in favor of a common humanity and the national good of what the clergymen sincerely called "our beloved country." Ultimate power would be returned to God.

A final, more secular form of black separatism emerged from SNCC in the work of Stokely Carmichael, James Forman, and H. Rap Brown. The phrase "Black Power" itself had reached popular consciousness in the course of the June 1966 Memphis-to-Jackson march. Secular Black Power grew, in part, from the SNCC experience of organizing small black Southern communities. The main institutional settings for this, apart from loose-limbed SNCC itself, were black churches and, to a lesser extent, schools. The blackness of the black church, so to speak, and perhaps the sheer blackness of black life in segregated Mississippi may help explain why early SNCC workers did not spend much time worrying about the nature of blackness in black community organizing.

Besides, SNCC people were hardworking, innovative, and young, and thought they could win, in a relatively short time, against the white hatred that surrounded them. Yet some recognized what that hatred might imply for a black community and for SNCC in the event of not winning. As Robert Moses explained to an interviewer in early 1964, "the problem is whether . . . you can move Negro people from the place where they are now the victims of this kind of hatred, to a place where they don't in turn perpetuate this hatred." The church had long fulfilled that function, but by 1966, at the latest, many movement activists had lost patience with Christian churchly ways, seeing them as leading toward unacceptable compromise if not degradation. The meaning of winning changed; and the soul killing of Freedom Summer had changed SNCC.

Secular Black Power sought to avoid hatred by avoiding the makers and shapers of racial hatred, namely white people, and avoiding white ways of think ing. By 1967 Chicago SNCC had published a pamphlet that called for "learning to think Black and removing white things from our minds." It spoke of filling ourselves "with Hatred for All White Things"—with hatred, significantly, not of white people but of the inner white person who fought one's blackness. As the activist Julius Lester wrote in 1966, "the white man" was "simply to be ignored . . . For so long the black man lived his life in reaction to whites. Now he will live it only within the framework of his blackness."

What was this blackness, particularly without the black church? Where did it lead? It seems invariably to have led somewhere else—to a folding of blackness into something larger than itself. The anxiety of defining blackness in isolation was unbearable, and so often took the form of deciding what wasn't black, or black enough. There was much talk of Uncle Toms, of the black bourgeoisie feeding off the people, of people who married white, of the preferred or acceptable or token blacks: of race traitors big and small.

The rush to a racial identity soon produced a crisis with little hope for resolution in the terms it set itself—determining true racial identity could too easily be a process of elimination. Black Power activists quickly turned to broader fields than blackness. For many the broader field was Marxism and Third World (especially African) solidarity, which retained skin color, class politics, and the American history of racial oppression while making all three more generally meaningful. For others the broader field was religion—not the Nation of Islam, which was widely viewed as black-capitalist and curiously imitative of whites, not least in its rejection of the black American heritage, but the Christian, Muslim, and even, at a stretch, Jewish religions. One could also combine these fields. The "Black Manifesto" of 1969, chiefly authored by SNCC's James Forman, was a revolutionary Marxist, Black Power document addressed to, of all things, "the white Christian churches and the synagogues in the United States of America and to all other racist institutions."

After some purist denunciation of black capitalists, "black power pimps and fraudulent leaders," Forman wrote of solidarity with Africa, "our Motherland." (Africa needed dark Americans, "the most advanced technological group of black people in the world.") He predicted that "the day will come when we can return to our homeland as brothers and sisters. But we should not think of going back to Africa today, for we are located in a strategic position. We live inside the United States, which is the most barbaric country in the world, and we have a chance to help bring this government down." Forman looked to "long years of sustained guerrilla warfare inside this country," with the goal of total black control of the nation. This was not meant to be inhumane. On the contrary, blacks "are the most humane people within the United States." That was why blacks should rule, specifically "revolutionary blacks who are concerned about the total humanity of the world." Manifesto demands included reparations at "fifteen dollars per nigger," millions of dollars for a Southern black land bank, black media institutions, a black strike fund, a black university, and an International Black Appeal to capitalize cooperatives in the United States and Africa. The initial attacks were to be on white churches and synagogues, because missionaries had aided colonialism and, more importantly, because "active confrontation inside white churches is possible." The manifesto noted in conclusion, "We see this focus on the Christian church as an effort around which all black people can unite."

Like other racial separatist movements, Black Power wanted to get beyond racial separatism. It held within it, toward that end, an ideal of common humanity, of which Forman (and King, in his fashion) believed blacks had more than their share. This was indeed a world turned upside down, but not, for that, entirely different. Many radicals at the time spoke of black Americans as a colonized people tied by blood to the colonized in Africa, a notion familiar to the pro-colonizationist white generations of Abraham Lincoln, Andrew Jackson, and John C. Calhoun. The National Committee of Black Churchmen wrote in 1969 of reparations and human identity in a way that would have made sense to the slave-trade commissioner John Locke: "We [Americans] are a people who have always related the value of the person to the possession of property, or the lack of it. Hence, the sharing or the restoration of wealth is a significant gesture toward the restoration of personhood." It was an extraordinary admission for Christians to make. But so many black radical phenomena of those years seemed like tangled, hopeless echoes of white ideas that had been similarly flawed in their own eras. Tangled, because black and white were permanently tangled; hopeless, because the white majority would always win a racial contest fought with its own weapons. As it turned out, the black church, having struggled so hard for integration, remained separate from the white church and kept its power. It was the main holder of black racial power before the movement, during it, and afterward. And the church continued to take its power both from race and from a world well beyond race, which must be the key to its endurance.

Indeed, many secular Black Power leaders turned to religion. Some, like Stokely Carmichael, opted for the racial deliverance of Pan-Africanism; he moved to Africa, and hoped for the rest of his life for a following. Rap Brown became a Muslim minister. Ron Karenga simply invented a racial-religious holiday, Kwanza. There just had to be a power, and a form of human contact, greater than American race for racial life to be bearable. This, in turn, meant that one's racial worldview aimed at the transcendence of race. That was where Malcolm X had arrived early, in 1965, at the age of thirty-nine. His distinct Nation of Islam, sting-like-a-bee sense of humor ("Plymouth Rock landed on us") had lost its heart. And Elijah Muhammad, the anointed of God, now looked too much like a crazy man. Malcolm traveled to Mecca. After the hadj he wrote a letter describing it: "There were tens of thousands of pilgrims, from all over the world. They were of all colors, from blue-eyed blonds to black-skinned Africans . . . We were *truly* all the same (brothers)—because their belief in one God had removed the 'white' from their *minds*, the 'white' from their *behavior*, and the 'white' from their *attitude*. I could see from this, that perhaps if white Americans could accept the Oneness of God, then perhaps, too, they could accept *in reality* the Oneness of Man—and cease to measure, and hinder, and harm others in terms of their 'differences' in color."

Malcolm was saying that one could not free oneself from race without freeing oneself toward something beyond race, in this case God. Malcolm got his sense of humor back. According to Eldridge Cleaver, when Malcolm was asked "if he could accept whites as members of his Organization of Afro-American Unity, Malcolm said he would accept John Brown if he were around today—which certainly is setting the standard high." The white man John Brown, a friend of Frederick Douglass, had led a band of rebels, black and white, in 1859. They raided a federal arsenal, hoping to spark an insurrection (mainly black) that would lead to the bloody end of slavery. Brown believed he was an instrument of God. He was executed on December 2; just over a year later South Carolina seceded from the Union. Many at the time considered Brown the only great white man in our history, as have many since.

The old advertisement for the all-black town of Boley had asked, "Have you ever experienced complete freedom?" I wonder if anyone has ever been able to answer, "Yes." I wonder how you could possibly know when you are free. When I returned to Boley, Velma Ashley suggested I meet her on Sunday for church. It was a featureless morning. That part of Oklahoma, down along Highway 62 — which had taken so many hungry Arkansans west to California in the Depression — has a flattened, dusty quality. The dry wind mocks the traveler; you have to adjust your vision to notice the differences between one mile and the next. I drove to Ashley's Baptist church and laughed when I saw all the cars. The town is so small, but folks still wanted to drive. Ashley herself drove about four blocks.

It was an old church, and little. We all sat around before the service, in no apparent order, and from time to time, for no apparent reason, an old man (usually) or a woman would line out a song. Then we would respond. No one read from a hymnal. We did not look at one another. The songs came in through a window, visited, left a light coat of prayer dust. A deacon made announcements, then we broke up into study groups: men's, women's, children's. There were a dozen women and half as many men, about the usual gender balance for a traditional Southern black church. We men gathered in a corner, taking as our text Matthew 18:23 — Jesus' parable of the king and the servant. One day the king decided to make an accounting of all that his servants owed to him. One of his servants owed ten thousand talents, which he could not pay. The king ordered that he and his family be sold as payment.

> The servant therefore fell down, and worshipped him, saying, Lord, have patience with me, and I will pay thee all. Then the lord of that servant was moved with compassion, and loosed him, and forgave him the debt.
>
> But the same servant went out, and found one of his fellowservants, which owed him an hundred pence: and he laid hands on him, and took *him* by the throat, saying, Pay me that thou owest. And his fellowservant fell down at his feet, and besought him, saying, Have patience with me, and I will pay thee all. And he would not: but went and cast him into prison, till he should pay the debt.
>
> So when his fellowservants saw what was done, they were very sorry, and came and told unto their lord all that was done. Then his lord, after that he had called him, said unto him, O thou wicked servant, I forgave thee all that debt, because thou desiredest me: Shouldest not thou also have had compassion on thy fellowservant, even as I had pity on thee? And his lord was wroth, and delivered him to the tormentors, till he should pay all that was due unto him.

> So likewise shall my heavenly father do also unto you, if ye
> from your hearts forgive not every one his brother their trespasses.

No sociological or historical parallels were drawn from this parable. We simply discussed the poor character of the servant, who had not understood the importance of forgiveness—knowing that each of us, sometimes, behaved like that servant. We talked about the necessity of forgiving your enemies. Associate Pastor Shannon joined us, a young man with the unseasoned, forceful humility of a junior pastor. He was pleased with the chosen text and vigorously argued that forgiveness was the essence of the Christian way. We held hands, closed our eyes, and prayed that God forgive us for being slow ourselves to forgive.

I sat with Ashley during the service. The pastor gave a fine, if unremarkable, sermon. (He had to serve several churches. Few, if any, of the old, rural black churches in those parts could support a full-time minister.) There were perhaps forty of us in all. We sang, and the pianist did indeed jazz it up a bit, as Ashley had warned me—though her frown reminded me that my ears were not so finely tuned to impropriety as her own.

Ashley invited me to her home for Sunday supper. I asked her about the white people in the service: a shy man with a plaintive tenor voice who had sat in back, and a little girl who sat near the front. The man lived in one of the state-supervised boarding homes for "people who can handle themselves all right, they can get up and down and all, but they don't have any connections." Ashley said, "He's the only white person I've known who has lived here and come to church here." Except for the girl, whose name was Ebony. Ashley thought she had been named Ebony because of her hair. "That's all about her that's black," except for her adoptive parents. Ebony came to Boley as an orphan, and a local couple grew attached to her. She did seem a bright and lively girl. She gets teased at school for being white and has had some scrapes, but she just "replies that her father is her daddy, and her mother is her mama."

We had an excellent meal: ribs, black-eyed peas. Ashley recalled that her mother had been a gifted cook. She couldn't read, so had to cook from memory. She had a set of spoons and measured by them. She was careful about those spoons. She wouldn't let anyone else use them.

Ashley returned time and again to the high expectations she has for others, an appropriate topic for a retired schoolteacher. She had high expectations for her race and was frequently disappointed. "We don't have enough pride," she said, "in the person that we are."

I asked, "Do you think white people have more pride in who they are?"

"Yes I do. Because they have never had to overcome a racial stigma." She mentioned a white salesclerk who once miscounted the change: "My thought then was, 'Well, miss white lady, you been free all your life but my ancestors were slaves. You ought to know how to handle arithmetic a little better than that.' " Ashley's high expectations did include a historical element.

I couldn't help thinking of little white Ebony, who actually did have to overcome a racial stigma. I also found myself preoccupied with Ashley's views on white people. She saw their advantages as coming from historical circumstance and their pride as coming, not from their race status, but from a lack of racial stigma. It seemed a small leap to conclude that whites' pride came not from race but from a lack of it. I wondered about Ebony's pride. And I wondered about that of Ashley and her black town. There was so little black about Boley. It had reproduced every institution present in every white town of the same size. The differences lay in the histories people brought to those institutions—not the aspirations, not even the institutional forms, but the histories. So there was much that was black about the proud town of Boley. Yet certain questions remained unanswered. Could you have a pride without a racial past, as whites apparently did? Was there an American pride that was not simply a sophisticated form of forgetting? In my room at Theodore McCormick's sometime motel, on the nightstand by the kerosene heater, a previous guest had left the program for a revival held in Boley. He or she had transcribed there the day's text from Deuteronomy ("thou shalt remember all the way which the Lord thy God ledd thee these forty years in the wilderness"), then scrawled, "Someting to Painful to Remember and to Danger to forget," "To Painful Remember and To Danger to Forget," "To painful to *Remember and Danger to forget*," and finally, "Moses—Call *Israel*." What forgiveness, then, what forgetting?

Ashley mentioned a friend of hers who had "an aversion to white people"— "She just hates them"—so I went to visit Millie Coleman. She sat in a chair next to an elevated sickbed, wearing a white T-shirt with two packs of cigarettes in the breast pocket. "She white!" Coleman said of Ashley. They had passed quite a bit of time over the years debating the assimilation issue, not least when Ashley wouldn't allow students to have Afros. "She what we black folks call *white*. And we were reared that way. My generation and her generation"— they're nearly the same age—"that's the way we were reared as black folks. To imitate you—all right? We were reared that way. And it wasn't until James Brown come along and say, 'I'm Black and I'm Proud,' had all that hair and— and I felt like I was *somebody*. Miss Ashley didn't ever learn. But she is somebody special."

Ashley educated Coleman's children. "That school was like a beacon light in this community. Miss Ashley was superintendent. She was a tough old bird, I tell you. She ran that place like a soldier." The school had been on the skids recently because white people had joined the staff. "Some of your folks in there, messing us up."

Coleman's dapper son Malcolm, fifty-three, entered, and she asked him why black history wasn't taught at Boley's school. He talked about the lack, until recently, of good research into black history and the Eurocentrism that dominates school curricula in America. And, he added, "If you've been taught that everything that is white is pretty and everything that is black is evil and ugly, then you start having self-hate."

"Do you really think," his mother asked, "Miss Ashley had that in her mind?"

"I'm trying to figure out how she could not have it."

After a pause Malcolm said: "What these communities do is, they offer a haven so that hopefully by the time — if you stay there long enough, by the time you have to deal with the problems, your psyche's at least strong enough to know that you have some skills. The outside world will teach black children they have nothing." By "outside world," he meant "the white world."

Malcolm left, and Coleman talked about how "living in Boley has been a blessing for me." She had raised five children here. "They didn't have to be exposed to what I was exposed to in Mississippi. 'Cause the Ku Klux Klan came to my door at night to get a little boy six years old 'cause he told a white girl she was pretty."

We discussed Ashley, and I slowly gathered that these two women, who disagreed on the most fundamental questions of black life, were best friends. "I tell you, I respect that old lady," she said, "and when she taught my kids, she was some teacher." Of Malcolm she said, "You can't ask that boy nothing he don't know something about. And he's from Boley." Coleman believed Ashley should have taught the children more about black history and literature, should have raised their racial pride. Instead, she made the kids memorize *Beowulf.*

"Hey, you can't hardly read *Beowulf*! How you gonna memorize it?" Coleman's voice dropped to a whisper. *"They had to memorize* Beowulf." Ashley kept one of the Coleman boys after school to work on memorizing *Beowulf.* "He had to say it at church one night. 'Cause she'd take the kids and have a program at church. And I had gone over it with him. And he got up there and forgot it and made up a *Beowulf.* He was so creative. Didn't nobody know in the audience but me and Miss Ashley."

Ashley was furious. But Coleman told her, " 'Everybody else thought he was cute.' I said, 'Everybody else thought he did good. So you better just join in the club.' She said, 'I'm gonna flunk him! I'm gonna flunk him!' And I said, 'Well, he tried.' *Beowulf*!"

Coleman did have some misgivings about hating white people. "There was a lady in Boley who told me, 'Girl, if you don't watch it disliking white people gonna keep you out of heaven. 'Cause you got to love everybody.' " And historical circumstance had recently played a trick on Coleman which, as Ashley had told me, "just drives the whey out of her": "The predicament I'm in now: I can't walk, and I belong to something called Americare. And they come in and get me out of the bed, bathe me, come back three times a day." She dropped into a lovely mocking whisper. *"They all white, most of 'em!* And let me tell you something, brother, if I'm not getting a revelation in this world. It's just amazing what life can deal you. There're some good white folks! Them white guys coming here bathing me every day! Can you imagine that they doin' this, help bathe a black woman? I told Miss Ashley, I said, 'Honey, you would not believe the life I'm living these days.' "

PART THREE

WHITE FLIGHT

■

▐ first saw the accused terrorists Reverend Willie Ray Lampley, Cecilia Lampley, and J. D. Baird in a Muskogee, Oklahoma, courtroom during a hearing. They entered in chains. Ray was bent over, his face pale and blotchy, the sleeve of a long undershirt dangling, ripped, from beneath his dark-green prison jumpsuit. Baird was no more formidable. When he briefly took the stand and was asked to recall a number, he reached out his hands and did the sums with his fingers. Cecilia was the youngest (at forty-seven) and healthiest of the three, her nicely coiffed brown hair just beginning to gray; she seemed almost girlish, following the proceedings with care, chatting animatedly with Ray and their attorneys at the defense table.

In the months after the Oklahoma City bombing, thefts of explosives and other materials used by the bombers rose dramatically. A train in Arizona was derailed and credit claimed by a right-wing group; two military boys, admirers of the Ku Klux Klan, murdered a black couple; in Arkansas a bomb went off with, near it, a note alluding to the federal government's "conspiracy" against its people. The Klanwatch Project of the Southern Poverty Law Center announced that there were at least 858 extremist groups active in the United States in 1996, of which 380 considered themselves armed militias. This was a 6 percent rise over the year of the bombing.

Among those groups was Reverend Lampley's Universal Church of God (Yahweh), which occupied a decaying, one-story white wood-framed house in

rural Vernon, Oklahoma, with a washer and dryer on the screened front porch.
The church was set up like a home office, with printing devices, desks, wall cal-
endars with scrawled deadlines, stacks of pamphlets, and, next to the front door,
a framed photograph of the Branch Davidian compound in Waco, Texas, burning. Apart from this photograph, there were no devotional items in Reverend
Lampley's church, no altars, no chalices or crosses. Along with his church,
Lampley had a tiny militia. Here are some excerpts from a transcript of an FBI
surveillance tape recorded in and around the church seven months after the
Oklahoma City bombing. The speakers are Ray Lampley and Richard Schrum,
the FBI informer, wired for sound. "C four" is an explosive made from cooking
down ammonium-nitrate fertilizer, the same explosive used in Oklahoma City.
The transcriber tries to reproduce speech; "thank," for example, usually means
"think."

LAMPLEY: And, now, we fill that to about like that with black powder, so that
   this is directly in contact with it and it'll flame.
SCHRUM: Uh, huh.
LAMPLEY: We'll fill the rest of that, with this. Crimp it good, and then put
   these wires out like, well we n . . . we'll need to put the wires out this way. So
   what we'll do is we'll wrap this with a (*buzzing noise*) 'lectrical tape and then
   wrap those wires back this way so that all the shock goes directly into the C
   four. (*Squeak*)

(*They discuss grinding explosive powder in a kitchen blender.*)
SCHRUM: You thank that'll do it, I mean I don't know that much about a
   blender.
LAMPLEY: We make flour, with our blender.
SCHRUM: Oh you do? . . .
LAMPLEY: Yeah. Corn and make meal out of it.
SCHRUM: Oh you do?
LAMPLEY: Yeah.
SCHRUM: I'll be doggone.
LAMPLEY: We're survivors.

The next day federal agents entered the church and several trailer homes
around it and seized, among other items, guns, a toaster (allegedly used to provide a detonator), a blender from Sears, six bags of C-4, and *The Anarchist's
Cookbook*. Reverend Lampley was arrested in a McDonald's parking lot on the
turnpike.
   I next saw Reverend Lampley in prison. We sat in separate rooms and spoke

by telephone. We could see each other through a small window. We had to lean forward and squint, for the glass was murky. Reverend Lampley believed that the United Nations, "the Beast of Revelations 13," was set to invade the United States. Why the United States? Because "the American people are from the tribe of Ephraim, from the House of Joseph, we're Israelites." The Antichrist was coming to punish the Israelites because they had been in rebellion against God's law. Through his church, Reverend Lampley had tried for seven years "to warn the [American] people either to get in harmony with God's law or the whole system is coming down . . . It's still the matter that, it either gets in harmony with God—well, it's too late now . . ."

Reverend Lampley believed he was one of the two "witnesses" mentioned in Revelation 11. The witnesses call down plagues after the people fail to heed their warnings. "What we have done is we have filed lawsuits in eleven states, in federal district courts, letting them know that this conspiracy to overthrow the government of God and the government . . . uh, they have made a determination to overthrow God in the land, and this is nothing but a conspiracy and this is about to come to an end. So basically what I'm saying is, we have filed lawsuits throughout the land to *warn* everyone in political office that you either change, or you are going to die. And that's what it amounts to. That doesn't mean that *we're* going to kill them, it simply means that, uh, that they are going to be *killed*. I mean, all of these officials are going to die because they refuse to obey God."

Among Lampley's few friends at this time was Reverend Robert Millar, who had come to the arraignment to offer support. According to the FBI transcript, Lampley and his followers had thought to test their bomb at Elohim City, Millar's isolated hamlet—six and a half miles up a rough dirt road from a lonely highway. J. D. Baird had misgivings because, as he said, "the Feds were all over that place . . . tryin' to spook 'em into doin' somethin' so they can jump on their shit."

Reverend Millar was just finishing lunch when I knocked on his trailer door at Elohim City. He helped his ailing wife back to the darkened living room and onto the couch; wordless, she nearly disappeared into it. She must have been quite strong once. She had raised five children and spent two and a half decades with her husband building Elohim City out of the Ozark forest. A girl arrived to look after Mrs. Millar, known to all as Grandma just as the reverend was Grandpa. Before we sat down to chat, Reverend Millar cleared the dishes, adding them to the pile in the sink. The compound's water system was blocked; some of the men were out trying to fix it. His wife's health was failing, but Millar himself, at seventy, looked in fine shape. With a belly for ballast, a white beard, and emphatic eyebrows, he appeared somewhere between Santa Claus and Joseph Smith, like an Old Testament prophet only smaller and livelier: Isaiah as sprite.

At the kitchen table Millar gestured toward a letter from a Posse Comitatus group, one more of the far-right outfits that popped up in the 1990s. Such groups, Millar said, look to him for spiritual guidance, and he, in turn, looked to them for a way to expand his ministry. In 1959, still just in his mid-thirties, Millar suffered a heart attack. This left him with time to think and browse ("I've always been a browser"), especially in the Bible, where he noticed that the original texts had a number of names for *man*. "Pursuing that, I came to the conclusion that all erect bipeds are not the offspring of Adam, according to the Scripture . . . That led me into a conviction that all flesh are not the same flesh."

Browsing further, Millar concluded that God "has especially chosen some people, that is, some race of people." This conclusion itself, of course, was not new. What made the interpretation fresh, to Millar, was his belief that these chosen people need "to be clearly differentiated from the, what are today called, or in the Bible are called, Jews." He maintained that northern Europeans, "these people which together compromise [*sic*] less than 9 percent of the world population, that these people, together, are the inheritors of the promise made to Abraham, Isaac, and Jacob, and that they are the lineal descendants." Millar and his eighty or so followers, gathered here on an eastern Oklahoma mountainside within view of the Arkansas border, believed they, in turn, were the vanguard of the true Israelites and first among the inheritors of the promise made to Abraham. As part of their responsibility, they armed themselves to face the Tribulation and the Last Days, following which they who survived would lead in building the New Jerusalem, of which Elohim City was a model.

Millar pursued a determined multiculturalism. Cultures are in part "a result of the DNA code" and not to be trifled with: "I think the destruction of any ethnic group is really a violation of respect for fellow man and of respect for God's creation." A Canadian by birth, Millar gave native Inuits as an example: modern technology had led them away from their traditions. "To impose our changes unilaterally on other cultures can be very disruptive, and also no doubt a result of a profound arrogance on our part."

Wouldn't this, I asked, mean that he and I, both primarily, or at least patrilineally, of Scottish origin, ought to be wearing kilts, tossing cabers, cutting peat? The answer was no, because modern technology is a white achievement and therefore part of our racial tradition—even when it's brand-new. "All of life is progressive and changing, and this is especially true of Caucasian man. He tends toward change and progress." Caucasians have been inclined, "since the 1400s," toward "technological development." A spiritually successful society needs to divide tasks according to the particular geniuses of its constituent cultures. Each culture must know itself. "I think Alex Haley," Millar said, "I think he did an awful lot for white people with his book called *Roots*." Haley helped point the way toward a well-informed separatism.

"I think often lack of psychological balance, nervous problems, are the result of intermarriage," Millar continued. "Intermarriage—I'm not talking about Germans with French, English with Welsh. I'm talking about Caucasians with non-Caucasians, or Asiatics with Negroes." Such mixing was carefully avoided in Elohim City. "We teach our young people to consider very seriously their genetic inheritance and the genetic inheritance of any intended spouse." Elohim City children received a complete education at the compound, in accord with Oklahoma's home-schooling guidelines. The teaching of history included knowledge of the special role and destiny of Caucasians. Millar himself taught the children ancient Hebrew, to put them in touch with their roots.

Racial mixing formed part of the combination of social forces leading to apocalypse. "I think we're going to have bloodshed here in America," he said. "I think we're gonna have race wars. I think we're gonna have international intervention, that is, foreign nations on our soil. And I anticipate it more shortly than in the distant future." The signs were everywhere; everything was a sign. "I think that we are scheduled for a housecleaning. That's already going on." He slowly listed the banes being visited upon the world as retribution against white people for having betrayed their covenant with God. "Earthquakes, floods, famines, pestilence, plagues. Because we've had so much, and been such terrible stewards. But I do believe that a remnant of this group is destined to be a light, an example, to the other civilizations. Following the cleansing."

During our conversation Reverend Millar shifted seats almost constantly and the girl looking after Grandma wandered into the kitchen, stared at the dirty dishes, then wandered back to the dark living room. Millar suggested we go for a walk through the compound. He was restless, and worried that our conversation might be keeping his wife up.

We walked along a path in the chill mountain air, and Reverend Millar jumped onto a low railing, balanced himself along its length, hopped off. He didn't break his conversation. He said he had never been more content than with his present ministry. "I have this concept that the prayer, 'Thy kingdom come, thy will be done, on earth as it is in heaven,' now that is not only a possible fulfillment, it actually will be fulfilled, His kingdom will come on earth. And then the question arises, Why should we not move in that direction?"

The theology called Christian Identity, which the reverends Lampley and Millar shared, is one of many religious imports from Britain. It has its roots in the early and middle nineteenth century, when "Anglo-Israel" thought got off the ground with its leading idea that the English were among the chosen—that they could be "identified" as Israelites. Researchers traced the royal family back to the Old Testament. Some among the better classes of New England liked this notion and broadcast it on our shores. Christian Identity wandered in various circles only to be taken up between the wars by some formidable anti-Semites, including the alcoholic newsman William Cameron—an adviser to Henry Ford during the industrialist's openly anti-Semitic period—and Gerald L. K. Smith, an influential polemicist and advocate of Christian Nationalism who believed that Jews were "sons of Satan." Coincidentally, the leading architect of segregation in Oklahoma, William H. Murray, promoted Christian Identity beliefs. He ran the Constitutional Convention prior to statehood in 1907 and later served as governor (as did his son). Murray was one of those politicians characterized as "colorful." Thus his nicknames, Alfalfa Bill and the Sage of Tishomingo. He had been just another tobacco roader up from Texas until he married a Chickasaw Indian from good family—he believed the Chickasaws were also Israelites—and entered politics. Murray, though white, had been a key player in the Indian effort to make Indian Territory the Indian state of Sequoyah. He took that experience with him when he designed the white state of Oklahoma. He remains the most famous of the state's politicians and is remembered affectionately in its conventional histories. These histories do not normally quote from his Identity-influenced 1951 book, *Adam and Cain* ("Communism can never be checked till press and Gentiles attack the Jews as a people"), which includes a short version of *The Protocols of the Elders of Zion*, nor from his 1948 volume, *The Negro's Place in the Call of Race*.

After World War II, Christian Identity thought lay somewhat fallow, only to be adopted enthusiastically by the extreme right in the 1980s, influencing such celebrated religio-terrorist groups as the Order and Aryan Nations. These organizations committed sundry murders and bank robberies until the federal government closed many of them down. The surviving leaders then decided, in a typically semi-organized way, to promote "militias." Reverend Millar told me he would be willing to serve as the "spiritual leader" of the "militia movement." He saw this as part of his calling, and the militias as leading players in the coming battles of End Times.

Millar had made some progress in establishing himself as a spiritual leader. On the day of the Oklahoma City bombing (and the anniversary of the Waco fire), Reverend Millar, in his clerical capacity, visited Richard Wayne Snell on death row. Snell was awaiting execution for murdering a black Arkansas state trooper in 1984. He had previously murdered a Texarkana pawnbroker; supposedly he had believed, wrongly, that the pawnbroker was Jewish. By the time Millar arrived, Snell had already watched the Oklahoma City explosion on television. Millar had visited Snell weekly during his ten years in prison and had seen much progress in the convicted man's spiritual outlook. According to press accounts, Snell said before dying, "Hell has victory," and some took this as a reference to the bombing. Reverend Millar maintained Snell's words were, in fact, "Hail His victory"—the press version was "a definite misquote." Millar took Snell's body back to Elohim City for burial.

Snell's old comrade James Ellison, after serving a ten-year sentence (for racketeering), moved to Elohim City and married Reverend Millar's granddaughter Angie. Ellison had once had his own compound—Zarephath-Horeb, in Arkansas, about a hundred miles east of Oklahoma—and his own movement, the Covenant, the Sword, and the Arm of the Lord, or CSA. The compound's most famous feature, Silhouette City, was a mock American inner city, used as a practice ground for urban warfare. Ellison's followers helped pay the mortgage by robbing stores ("plundering the Egyptians"). Ellison, in the Christian Identity tradition, gradually came to understand that he was descended from King David. Reverend Millar recognized the value of his ministry by anointing him "James of the Ozarks." Federal agents surrounded Zarephath-Horeb in 1985, and Millar was brought in to convince Ellison to surrender, which he did.

Later, defense attorneys for Timothy McVeigh had tried to identify a conspiracy behind the Oklahoma City bombing. Their investigations kept leading to two men resident at Elohim City prior to the bombing, and to Reverend Millar. The FBI was particularly interested in Elohim City because records showed two calls having been made to the compound from McVeigh's phone, one only minutes after he rented a Ryder truck. "I think he probably met some of our young lads at some gun show," Millar told me, "and got our name by that means. You know, there's a certain camaraderie some people have at gun shows."

In Elohim City I stayed with Richard Snell's daughter Mary Ruth and her husband, Ed, in a trailer across from Elohim City's church. (About half the houses there were trailers.) I never asked Mary Ruth about her father because that would have been ungracious. Once, though, she and I were discussing religion, and she recalled that her father often preached and that he was a good preacher, too.

One cool morning Ed took me to see Snell's grave. The cemetery lay on a muddy track just beyond the burned ground of Elohim City's fire circle, where revivals were held in summer. Three community members had been buried there so far, so there were three simple crosses on the hillside overlooking the fire circle. Taking care of the cemetery was one among Ed's many jobs. He showed me a rectangular depression at the head of Snell's grave. Ed had plans to pour concrete markers for the three dead.

From the cemetery one could look back over Elohim City, the houses and trailers scattered in no apparent order among deciduous trees and some pines. In the distance, on the left, was a pasture for the community's sheep; above and slightly rightward, the community's sawmill; and above that, the mountaintop, highest point for miles around in this stretch of the Ozarks. Everywhere the smell of wood smoke, the gray or blue or black smoke from the dozen hearths of a dozen white families in hiding. Ed and Mary Ruth came here, he said, to get away from "the niggers" in the city, whom they feared in part because of Mary Ruth's parentage. We stood for a while on the road, and Ed told me about his conversion. He had not been living right. He did this and that as a laborer, he partied hard, he passed some time in prison. Then one day his body began to rebel. He lost his will. He was overcome with terror. He became feverish and stayed in a fever for many hours. He was being visited by an awesome power he was helpless to describe. Mary Ruth asked him if he needed a doctor; but he wanted nothing save to remain in that fever until it ended of itself.

Now, he said, people ask him, Where is the old Ed? And he replies, I don't know. I haven't seen him. He was here, but now he's gone, and no one knows where he went nor how to find him.

One night at Ed and Mary Ruth's trailer I sat on the porch for a while with Pete, Ed's friend. He was doing his best to look like a woodsman. He had grown a beard, kept his clothes sloppy, and carried a gun. Looking at Pete, you would never guess that he was born in Nairobi, Kenya, the son of missionaries, and grew up in Africa and California.

He asked, "How do you think the world's gonna end?"

"I don't know," I said. "I think it'll happen after I'm dead, anyway."

"No," he said, shaking his head, one cheek filled with tobacco. "It's gonna happen while I'm alive. There's gonna be a race war, against niggers, spics, and the Jewish people. And I'm gonna be ready."

We went inside. Pete sat in a comfortable chair, chewing tobacco, his rifle close to hand. Ed and Mary Ruth were on the sofa. Mary Ruth had had a bad fall, which led to partial paralysis, and, as part of her therapy, she was building a little ideal American town from bits of plastic and yarn that you buy through the mail. She had half a dozen buildings up already, on a shelf next to the television set. Now she was working on a flower shop. Ed said that when she gets it finished, he wanted to mount the whole town on a board covered with AstroTurf and contribute it to the church for display there.

Ed was in charge of the television remote. We were waiting for his favorite show, starring Chuck Norris, in which Norris plays a Texas lawman. But first, a TV movie concerning a miracle and its misuse by an unscrupulous preacher. One of the main characters, a black woman (the organist), warned, "Anything that comes from God can be dangerous in the wrong hands." Next to my chair, on a table, was a slip of paper with a swastika. I watched it, out of the corner of my eye, for some time, then finally reached over and picked it up. "Fight crime . . . ," it read. "Deport Niggers." Beneath it was a copy of *The Turner Diaries*, a best-selling novel about a militant cadre of white Americans who lynch Jews, kill blacks, and blow up buildings.

Eventually Chuck Norris came on. The plot concerned a lunatic whom Chuck had put in prison—and who had escaped, determined to wreak terrible vengeance on everyone who had wronged him (a long list) and, in the end, on Chuck himself. A jowly, sweaty man, the killer was also an explosives expert. Over the course of the program he would incinerate a number of people; each time, as his eyes widened and his finger neared the fatal button, he quoted Scripture. His final act was to blow up the entire neighborhood where he had been a boy, a typical affluent suburban street with nice houses on quarter acre lots. He blew the houses up one by one, an immense conflagration, and the whole neighborhood burned.

On Sunday morning Ed, Mary Ruth, and I put on our church clothes, crossed the muddy pathway, and entered a building shaped like an igloo—the church. The service began with singing and dancing. Then each family took its turn standing before the congregation, singing a song, after which each member, beginning with the youngest and ending with the father, would step forward and give thanks to Yahweh. They would give thanks for the community, for the feeling of God's love, for a new dress. Often a speaker would weep, with embarrassment, pride, and sometimes, it seemed to me, out of gratitude for being able to weep.

Many gave thanks that a young man who had been hit in the face by a swinging log had not been hurt more badly, for God had protected him. And when it came to be his turn, this thin, laconic boy with the swollen face and the scabs could hardly express his thanks to everyone around him, many with tears in their eyes. His jaw still painful, he could hardly stammer out his thanks to God. He wore a T-shirt with the Confederate flag on it, which has two stripes in an X. The T-shirt also bore a slogan: YOU HAVE YOUR X, I HAVE MINE. This was a reference to Malcolm X. Malcolm took X as his last name because he considered his family name a "slave name," that is, the name of a white person who had owned one of his paternal ancestors.

Many also gave thanks that another young man had decided to marry and return to stay in Elohim City. The community's greatest fear was that teenagers would move outside, where there were jobs and new faces—that they would choose to live in what they called "the world" and so relinquish in some sense their covenant.

Following the family testimonies a young man posted himself by the main entrance with an assault rifle while someone from each family marched forward to receive the family's flag. These representatives joined in a rigid circle. James Ellison was there for the family of Ellison, in his fatigues and blue scarf, wearing knives and, just for this ceremony, a straight flat sword in a red scabbard. The ceremony affirmed each tribe and recognized everyone's roots in the Torah and their special role in prophecy.

After more music the children were gathered together on benches. People at Elohim City spoke far more of family than of Yahweh. Every resource was directed at serving the children, who made up half or more of the population and gave their little home the air of a playground or summer camp. In practice, every adult was a parent to every child. The children always had someone older whom they could talk to about their problems, someone who would gladly listen. Ed told me the children understood the theology of the community even more rapidly than did the adults.

The children, by squeals and general acclamation, brought burly James Ellison up from his chair. In folksy tones Ellison sidled into what I slowly realized was the parable of the loaves and the fishes. He told it well. He emphasized that it had been a young boy who gave Jesus the loaves and fishes (John 6:8; in Matthew and Mark it was the disciples). Ellison concluded: "If you do whatever you do to help your mama and daddy or your brothers and sisters or your friends, all these might seem like little things but they're not. They're what it's all about. So remember that even if you're little, you can give a lot, and you can bless other people."

After the children left, I rose to preach. Reverend Millar had asked me to. I had not expected this. I had never composed a sermon in my life, but Reverend Millar, knowing that I am the son and grandson of Baptist ministers, asked me to address his flock. This was how the reverend and I got along with and understood each other—as members (me rather by proxy) of the fraternity of those who deliver the Word. To have refused would have been impolite; also, I felt an obligation not to be silent. But what could I say to a congregation, however small, of lightly armed white-separatist Christian fundamentalists waiting in serene, perhaps hungry anticipation of global travail and horror in a remote mountaintop commune in Oklahoma? What could I say that would neither encourage nor offend? And wasn't it strange to think that, just here, of all places, I was accepted as part of some larger historical purpose because of the color of my skin? I considered these questions as three teenagers made their way through a tinkling tune called "Fighting the Beast." I couldn't preach from Scripture. I didn't know Scripture well enough. The only parable I could recall without effort was that of the prodigal son, my father's favorite. I did not want to preach on the parable of the prodigal son in part because that story concerns God's forgiveness and I preferred not to preach, in this setting, about forgiveness. I should perhaps have preached as King often had, about a love beyond forgiveness. Or maybe I should have preached on John Brown. But these ideas did not come to me at the time.

In my weakness, fear, and lack of imagination, I fashioned a sermon from real stories. I took them from my last book. They were three parables about identity and nationalism—from Bulgaria, Turkey, and Uzbekistan. Each case had its own set of variables, concerning conflicts among different ethnic groups or races. The participants usually failed to resolve these conflicts. The result was terror, pain, and bloodshed. I ended with the parable of the Uzbeks, in which an ethnic majority is ruled by an allegedly universalist ethnic minority (the Soviet Russians) for decades. The majority, that is, the Uzbeks, separates itself into truculent localisms to preserve autonomy, only to find, upon independence, that each locality distrusts the others and the nation refuses to build itself. According to the Uzbeks, I preached, "the problem is that, if anything bad happens, crime or whatever excuse people might want, then the neighborhoods are going to go against the neighborhoods, and there won't be any way to stop that. And that's the fear they live with now. And that's my third and last parable."

When I had finished my sermon, the congregation at Elohim City stood and applauded. I begged them to sit down. I was out of breath and tried to hide next to Ed, who smiled in support. Reverend Millar nodded his head thoughtfully, gravely, then made some appreciative remarks about the different histories of people and how fascinating these are, about "footprints in the sands of time," which led, willy-nilly, to his recalling (in German and English) something Adolf Hitler once said about "Blood and Land." My sermon had brought the phrase to mind.

Reverend Millar climbed to his pulpit, a huge carved platform that put him near the ceiling, a window behind him to let in a simulation of the light from heaven. He no longer looked short. Holding himself at an angle to his congregation, he roared: "There was a flood over certain parts of the earth. As it affected Caucasian man, the purpose of the flood was to wipe out the mixture that had been produced . . . He sent the flood and, out of that, saved a *people*. Which is a prime example of divine eugenics. God was interested in the DNA code long before Adolf Hitler got any kind of ideas about things like that. And He did something about it, that's the purpose of the Flood. The Bible says specifically, Thou Noah, perfect in his genealogy, his bloodline inheritance."

Western civilization, Reverend Millar preached, had been advancing for nineteen hundred years. But every age has an end. His text was 1 Corinthians 15:51–52. Paul is speaking: "Listen, I tell you a mystery: We will not all sleep, but we will all be changed—in a flash, in the twinkling of an eye, at the last trumpet."

His voice grew and grew, until I could hardly believe such a small body could bring forth such a sound. "There's a windup of this age. And at the windup of this age, there's a *last trumpet* to be blown! And in the blowing of that last trumpet, *God help us* to move in the blowing of the last trumpet, to *participate* in it, to *be* that last trumpet!"

This was where a good preacher pauses, tells some story or other, appears to be an average person, leaving your exaltation in abeyance until some part of you wonders if it will return. And when it returns, it does so slowly, cunningly ("And let me tell you something . . ."), edging around the corner (". . . the great Flood . . .") then picking up speed (". . . before it occurred . . .") until you begin to realize (". . . was preceded . . .") with fear and joy that it is running straight at you—"by a man blowing a trumpet! Giving a message! The Flood didn't just *come*, apart from human instrumentality! God anointed a man that blew the trumpet! And it brought *destruction!*"

Then a good preacher slows it way down, he rescues you from your fear. And so, so softly: *"But He saved eight souls."* And after the last trumpet, Reverend Millar knew, quoting the famous lines from Isaiah, "Death is swallowed up in victory."

"THE ESSENCE OF WHITENESS"

SPAIN, ENGLAND, AND THE COLORS OF EMPIRE

■

Trying to locate the origins of a specifically white sense of specialness is a vexed business. As we have seen, within the premodern written records of, globally speaking, light-skinned people, references to white people as white people, as a race, are remarkably scarce. Certainly, references abound to white as a color of purity, chasteness, virtue, beauty; white, for lighter-skinned people, has also been the color of fear and apprehension, aging, death, bones, cold, emptiness, and ghosts. Yet there is no evidence that light people thought of themselves as inherently ghostlike. When a light person is truly white, he is dead. Likewise, when he is quite brown, he is dirty. Some have drawn racial conclusions from the latter fact (not the former), the idea being that light people cannot help equating dark skin with uncleanness. However, blond hair, for example, is yellow. Urine is yellow. Yet no tradition exists of an association between blond people and human wastes. Similarly, black and brown hair have, one supposes, long been common among European peoples. Yet there is no tradition of the light-skinned shunning such people as having dirt on their heads. In short, it is silly to conclude from the association of white with, say, purity that light people have something like an ingrained sense of their own superiority that travels along untroubled by historical circumstance. That they, like all peoples, often have liked themselves best is a separate matter.

The identification of light people as "white" appears most frequently as a result of comparison to the less pale—for example, in the thirteenth-century labeling of some slaves as "white" to distinguish them from black and olive-colored slaves. Even here, Mediterranean people could view themselves as more white in comparison to dark Africans but less white when faced with northern Europeans (and coming out on top either way). The thread seems to be not skin color in itself but the perception of difference from oneself. As Ibn Khaldun explained, white people did not identify themselves as white because they thought they were normal, their color unexceptional. And in this, one must admit, they were entirely correct. When they became white, they became abnormal. Being white represented a departure from being fully human.

The evolution of light-skinned people into white people has to be understood partly in terms of their reluctance to become white. There have been light people, of African and Asian ancestry, walking the earth for something less than thirty thousand years. The fact that they spent roughly twenty-nine thousand of those years—including many centuries when black Africans lived in the Mediterranean world, with a few making it as far north as Britain—not thinking they were significantly white wasn't due to a mental slowness on their part. And when they began to become white, it did not sit altogether well. Whiteness, beginning in the fifteenth century, was a puzzlement. Light Europeans, going ever farther from home to expand their wealth and power, confronted people apparently different from themselves—darker. This caused some Europeans, as seen in the writing of Las Casas, to marvel not only at the diversity of human life but at their own whiteness.

And it was a marvel. Imagine going all your life being light-skinned and not giving it a thought. Then, suddenly, you see yourself through others' eyes and realize that you are different. One reaction would be to deny the significance of the difference—to think that you were not actually white, but human, and that the dark person before you was likewise not dark, but human. We will never know how many light-skinned people held this view. Not noticing race, or not giving it significance, is inherently something that would never appear in the record. The writer does not jot down that which he considers insignificant; this is why Bontier and Le Verrier, writing about the conquest of the Canaries, did not mention skin color. It was not until social power took racial form—when the West African seagoing slave trade began in the middle of the fifteenth century—that white skin became socially valuable as a token of group membership.

A second reaction would be to see skin color as interesting but unimportant. Writers such as López de Gómara and Samuel Purchas occasionally held to this opinion. It foundered, however, on the reality that whites alone were expanding their territory. Others were being conquered and enslaved. Yet even given this reality, a strong sense of whiteness did not immediately develop. Light-skinned people were divided among themselves. Their self-understandings came from political loyalty, language group, home culture, religion—not from whiteness. No one planted the flag of whiteness on a Caribbean beach. White racial solidarity was almost nonexistent in early imperial days. Whites fought each other constantly. Nor does there appear to have been much higher consciousness of a shared white bond. Sir Walter Raleigh wrote A *History of the World*, not A *White History of the World*. No one in the pioneering imperial period seems to have had a very developed white consciousness.

A third reaction to the moment of race recognition—to the realization that you might be white—would be to say, Yes, I am white in appearance, but fully human, whereas you are not white in appearance, and not fully human. This was probably the dominant opinion among light-skinned people in the early days of European expansion, judging from what Europeans said and didn't say, what they did and failed to do. Whites in the New World did not massacre each other. They massacred Indians (when they could, and felt they needed to). Whites did not usually enslave one another (though early indentures were not far from that). They did keep black Africans and Indians as slaves for life, and often, with Indians, enslaved them by force. That whites did not do these things as whites—in the name of white rights, white power, white destiny—suggests that whites had a weak sense of racial identity. When among themselves, their solidarity extended only to the recognition of certain minimal norms, such as no enslavement and no massacring. When whites faced nonwhites, these norms, on the whole, no longer held. It seems evident that it was the norms themselves, rather than whiteness, that mattered to whites. They did not think of them as white norms.

Why not? The norms that whites shared in the New World (and Africa) had developed in the cultures from which these people came—Catholic, Protestant, English, French, Dutch, Spanish. These norms had no connection to race, except in that one spoke of "the English race." They were of immense importance to colonizers, even as men and women found them difficult to maintain, so far from home. They were also distant from the norms of native Americans, and differently so from those of African slaves (whose overriding norm, from their masters' perspective, was that of being a slave). Finally, the various Europeans had towering rivalries to divide them. When we put these factors together, it makes sense that whites considered themselves white only in limited circumstances. Further, to have been white would have been to place oneself in a position relative to blacks and Indians—to have invited comparison as equals—which would have had the effect of reducing one's powerful norms to racial peculiarities, as well as jettisoning most of what one thought was important. It might even have made what one was doing—killing, enslaving, taking other people's land—seem strangely unjustifiable, inhuman or beastly.

When "white" people protested evil acts against Indians, for example, they did not ask, Are these not white men? They asked, Are these not men?

The historical conditions of the New World, then, were conducive to a highly limited sense of whiteness while, in large part, they operated against just such a sense. In the early years race—being reduced to a color—was something whites attributed to other people, not to themselves. Like all people, whites wanted to think of themselves as normal, or a little more. Somehow, reinventing themselves as "white people" would have deprived them of their normality. Nevertheless, the nonwhite peoples in the New World did come, and fairly quickly, to think of whites as whites. It was blindingly obvious that whites generally behaved better toward each other than they did toward oneself, despite all their divisions. Becoming a Christian and submitting to their power, even imitating them in every way, did not, in a decisive number of cases, make them accept you as an equal, as one of them. This naturally led one to wonder what united these people in their distance from oneself. How were they to be understood? What characterized them, what was their essence? The only name that fit that essence was white.

In this way the attitude of whites toward nonwhites, and nothing else, made them white. For whites, that often meant that nonwhites made them white. This went against the grain of how whites saw themselves. Moreover, the content of this particular whiteness was almost entirely negative—arrogance, wanton destruction, ill-tempered power. So we can hardly be surprised that whites did not embrace it. European colonizers knew perfectly well what they were doing in their struggle for wealth and distinction or at least a bare living and some religious freedom. They knew they were committing terrible acts. Voices within their own communities had been raised against them from the beginning, whether Thomas Morton and Roger Williams, or Las Casas, Montesinos, Zurara, Pope Paul III, and George Thorpe. Colonizers did not, however, want to be reminded of their bloody acts. The horrors they had committed, which gave whiteness its content, were precisely the acts colonizers wanted to forget. Nonwhite people functioned as a reminder of the terrible white past. To forget that past, one sought to forget the existence of nonwhites—to remove them from one's memory as well as, physically, from one's daily life. Success in this effort would enable one to regain one's full humanity, rather than settling for the crabbed, diminished status of whiteness.

Whiteness in America, then, developed in a psychologically covert fashion. While use of the term *white* as a collective description predated the American colonies—and even, among olive-colored Mediterranean writers describing northern Europeans, the Atlantic slave trade itself—it was hardly the preferred term among light-skinned colonizers in the seventeenth century. Overwhelmingly, the preferred markers were national (English, Scots, Dutch), religious (Christian), and social (free, servant). Beyond these, people other than blacks and Indians were identified by personal name or as a man or a woman, that is, as human beings without a race. The idea that white people were white obviously existed, and had for centuries; the important point is to see how slowly and reluctantly whites accepted their skin color as their distinguishing characteristic. When they did so, it was not, on the whole, in reaction to Indians, whom many colonizers, particularly in North America, believed to be white or quasi white, and quite possibly a degenerate form of an earlier white American people. Whiteness, despite such events as Bacon's Rebellion, developed primarily as a response to blackness, particularly as blackness and slavery were made, by nonblacks, synonymous. We can see this if we consider the pre-*white* terms mentioned above. Each has a positive content. This is what we would expect, granting that humans rarely choose to understand themselves in negative terms. However, as the seventeenth century progressed, there grew up in the colonies a population described by the powerful in almost entirely negative terms, namely blacks. The solidifying of this negative race gave birth to its positive antonym, namely white people.

Perhaps *positive* is not quite the correct word. It was more in the way of a double negative—not nonwhite—a collective description forced into the imagination by the existence of its maligned opposite and resisted all along the way. The seventeenth-century laws and judicial acts concerning race in North America tended to hedge *white*, when it was used at all, with positive terms, most importantly *free*. The use of *white* without positive qualification appears most pointedly in early writings against black slavery. In 1652 a somewhat reduced (by secession) Rhode Island legislature, noting that "English men" had been buying "negers," resolved "that no blacke mankind or white" should serve more than ten years. This reference to white mankind was exceptional at the time. Light-skinned Americans generally continued referring to race as something other people had until 1691, when Virginia legislators introduced the legal terms "white man or woman." Obviously, the Virginians did not conjure these terms from nothing. Maryland, seeking in particular to prevent the coupling of free women with slave men, had gone from "freeborn *English* women" in 1664 to "free-born *English*, or white women" in 1681. (The earlier law bound such a woman to her Negro husband's master for the husband's life and made their children perpetual slaves. Apparently, some women thought this a reasonable bargain, suggesting how close their servant condition was to slavery, and masters were willing, perhaps eager, to have the resultant mulatto slaves. The 1681 law sought to curb the creation of white slaves by making the women and any children in such unions free.) When the Mennonites of Pennsylvania, in 1688, published the first extended protest against enslavement of blacks, they wrote, "though they are black, we cannot conceive there is more liberty to have them slaves as it is to have other white ones." But, again, it was the perception and codification of blackness—especially, in the American case, the equation of blackness with slavery—that led over time to the codification, seemingly so obvious, of whiteness.

The codification of whiteness still did not elicit any great enthusiasm among the people who could be called white. When we consider that being white brought nothing but power and privileges, we must be struck by the fact that white people were so reluctant to become white. They were, certainly, eager not to be black—to distance themselves from blackness. But they did not mount arguments in favor of whiteness, except by exclusion; that is, whites, unlike all others, did not gain their racial character from their race. Their character was a human character. Other peoples' characters were racial characters. This is important to keep in mind when examining the history of white separatism. After 1690, when white separatism might be said to begin in earnest, it had the nature of a racial separatism aimed at the exclusion of others rather than the consolidation of itself. Only under great pressure did whites think of their urge to separatism as explicitly white. What they wanted was to be normal and free; that was the thrust of their pronouncements and stated dreams for themselves. This required the exclusion from their society of the abnormal and the unfree, two social categories that by 1690 had become closely associated with having a race. White Americans generally, at this point, did not expound on the superiority of the white race. They certainly thought of themselves as superior, but they did not think of themselves as superior because they were white.

By 1700 a slightly stronger notion of whiteness had begun to settle in. It furthered the argument that whites were fully human while nonwhites were not. Advanced European thinkers had already prepared the ground for this belief. François Bernier, in 1684, divided human races into four: Europeans, Hindus, and (probably) American Indians; Chinese and Japanese; black Africans; and "vile" Laplanders. Significantly, Bernier did not describe what distinguished the first race, his own, except to say that Hindus' dark hue was "only accidental," whereas the darkness of Africans was "essential." In other words, what distinguished the race soon to be known as white was that it had no distinguishing characteristics. In comparison, other races were exceptional. To believe otherwise would raise the specter of relativism, which would in turn threaten to remove the standard by which one could proudly measure oneself against others—exactly the predicament many enlightened thinkers sought to escape.

Yet once one began to think racially, it was very difficult to escape that predicament. If anyone in Europe could have avoided the equation of light skin with full humanity, it should have been John Locke, whose central argument held that the human was a creature of experience, not essence. Logically this would mean that whiteness, if it had any significance at all, was a physical characteristic akin to hairiness. However, that is not quite the drift of his examples. When he published *An Essay concerning Human Understanding*, in 1690, he already had many years' experience of the slave trade and its uses in America. Discussing how an English child would frame "the idea of a man," Locke thought such a child would include several ideas, "whereof white or flesh-colour in England being one, the child can demonstrate to you that *a negro is not a man*, because white colour was one of the constant simple *ideas* of the complex *idea* he calls *man*." Locke does not show that a black boy could equally demonstrate that a white person is not a man, that John Locke is not a man, or that John Locke's whiteness is of no importance to his humanity. Rather, Locke finds whiteness to be essential in a white man, not relative. "When I consider him as a man I have nothing in my mind but the complex idea of the species man. So likewise when I say 'Caius is a white man,' I have nothing in mind but the bare consideration of a man who hath this white colour. But when I give Caius the name 'husband,' I intimate some other person." Locke still equates whiteness with the insignificance of physical appearance, but the quiet association of white with humanity seems to be playing with the philosopher. Later, he writes: "how certain soever it is, that man is an animal, or rational, or white, yet every one, at first hearing, perceives the falsehood of these propositions; *Humanity* is *animality*, or *rationality*, or *whiteness*: and this is as evident, as any of the most allow'd maxims. All our affirmations then are only in concrete, which is the affirming, not one abstract idea to be another, but one abstract idea to be join'd to another . . . *v.g.*, A man is white, signifies, that the thing that has the essence of a man has also in it the essence of whiteness, which is nothing but a power to produce the idea of whiteness in one, whose eyes can discover ordinary objects." Locke does not explain what compelled him to place whiteness, of all things, alongside rationality and animality when considering the nature of humanity. Of course, to say simply that true humans are always white would have necessitated some genuinely strange reflections on what it meant to be human and what role reason should play in being human. Perhaps we should return to Locke's English child, here in the nursery, first seeing the world, a child human and white who "certainly knows, that the nurse that feeds it, is neither the cat it plays with, nor the Blackmoor it is afraid of."

Such scientific and philosophical thoughts on race may not have had much influence on early-eighteenth-century Americans. They were practical and religious people, and often both, not much given to science. The question of race was for them largely a practical and religious one, mixed with what would later be called prejudice. When Samuel Sewall of Boston wrote against slavery, in 1700, he did so on the biblical ground that all men are equal. He made the argument, so important to a later generation, that liberty was an absolute that could not be reckoned in money or otherwise traded away. Sewall further argued against slavery on practical grounds, specifically that blacks made poor slaves because they didn't want to be slaves and that whites did not want them around in any case: "all things considered, it would conduce more to the welfare of the province to have white servants for a term of years than to have [black] slaves for life. Few can endure to hear of a Negro's being made free, and indeed they can seldom use their freedom well; yet their continual aspiring after their forbidden liberty renders them unwilling servants. And there is such a disparity in their conditions, color, and hair that they can never embody with us and grow up into orderly families, to the peopling of the land, but still remain in our body politic as a kind of extravasat [sic] blood."

Sewall's position on assimilation became common among whites in the course of the century. Racial slavery certainly had its defenders, and among them were some who attributed poor qualities to blacks as a race. More common were people who saw blacks—however inferior, whether by nature or circumstance—as human beings. Blacks were normal in a way that mattered greatly to Americans of all shades: they wanted to be free. At the same time, more and more white Americans saw themselves as a "body politic" that was also literally a body. It was a white body, but that whiteness had no substance to it. When Sewall tried to define the white body politic, all he could do was point to its exclusion of black bodies. The idea that America should be a country of white bodies seems to have taken hold surreptitiously. Whiteness had stolen upon white people like a ghost, a result of their thoughts and actions toward nonwhite people. There was little in this whiteness to embrace. The best that might be said of whiteness was that, in Benjamin Franklin's words from 1751, "perhaps I am partial to the [white] complexion of my Country, for such kind of partiality is natural to Mankind." This was whiteness as innocent self-love. What Franklin lost sight of was that white self-love in a society of racial slavery could not be innocent. Three years later John Woolman, writing against racial slavery, made the point with precision: "When *Self-love* presides in our Minds, our Opinions are bias'd in our own Favour; in this Condition, being concerned with a People so situated [in slavery], that they have no Voice to pleade their own Cause, there's danger of using ourselves to an undisturbed Partiallity, till, by long Custom, the Mind becomes reconciled with it, and the Judgment itself infected."

White Americans, faced with what they were doing to nonwhites and wanting to love themselves, did indeed raise themselves in their own minds to an "undisturbed Partiallity." Keeping that partiality undisturbed was much, perhaps all, of the work of whiteness. The best means for keeping one's partiality undisturbed, as Woolman knew, was to convince oneself that it was not partiality but human nature—or that, as Franklin so quickly asserted, "such kind of partiality is natural to Mankind."

North American whites in the latter half of the eighteenth century, the Revolutionary generation, pursued both these strategies at the same time. On one hand, they told the world and themselves that they, white Americans, were not white at all but universal humans. They were, in fact, the culmination of universal human development to that date, the perfect combination of secular and religious, of Greece, Rome, and Europe. "In the formation of our constitution," Noah Webster (he of the dictionary) wrote in 1787, "the wisdom of all ages is collected—the legislators of antiquity are consulted—as well as the opinions and interests of the millions, who are concerned. In short, it is an *empire of reason*." The revolutionaries would build a model of human society for all the world to emulate, as James Wilson of Pennsylvania said: "By adopting this system, we shall probably lay a foundation for erecting temples of liberty, in every part of the earth." On the other hand, they, white Americans, would preserve their natural partiality to other white people by excluding nonwhites from membership in the universal republic. They would try hard to abolish slavery, with the understanding that abolishing slavery entailed excluding black ex-slaves from the body politic. Not every abolitionist thought this way, but the general trend was undeniably toward abolition coupled with, by whatever means, racial exclusion, which is to say white separatism.

The white separatism of the Revolution was distinctly American and deserves close examination. Most of the Revolution's luminaries opposed slavery, from John Adams, who flatly abhorred it, to George Washington, who might be described as uncomfortable with it. Revolutionary rhetoric concerning "enslavement" to Britain may, to a degree, be taken at face value. Jeremy Belknap, of Boston, later recalled how close the connection was between thinking about black slavery and thinking about American freedom: "The inconsistency of pleading for our own rights and liberties, whilst we encouraged the subjugation of others, was very apparent; and from that time, both slavery and the slave-trade were discountenanced." The committee that drew up the Declaration of the Causes and Necessities of Taking Up Arms, in July 1775, included Jefferson, Franklin, and John Jay. When they wrote that God and reason could not have "intended a part of the human race to hold an absolute power in, and an unbounded power over others"—that they "cannot endure the infamy and guilt of resigning succeeding generations to that wretchedness which inevitably awaits them, if we basely entail hereditary bondage upon them"—the committeemen meant what they said. And they were not blind to the fact that they used the most explicit antislavery language in arguing for the liberty of people who themselves owned others of the human race as slaves. (Eight years before, John Adams, under a pseudonym, had written of the British, "We won't be their negroes. Providence never designed us for negroes . . .") Most of the revolutionaries sincerely wished slavery in America to end. Had there been no opposition from South Carolina and Georgia—rich and populous states at the time and absolutely critical to the emerging nation—the white Revolutionary generation might well have abolished slavery. As it was, that generation did abolish it in many states and even agreed on a national policy to end (by 1808) the international slave trade.

However, abolishing slavery and welcoming black people into the body politic were two different matters. Very, very few white people advocated the latter. Abolition in New York—the major Northern slave state, along with New Jersey—was held up for fourteen years because enough white New Yorkers did not want freed blacks to be able to vote. Massachusetts's proposed constitution of 1778 barred "negroes, Indians and mulattoes" from voting. Although that constitution did not, for unrelated reasons, pass, when black freedom came Massachusetts voters forbade interracial marriages and sought to expel blacks who did not have citizenship in a state. (Some 240 faced deportation in 1800.) The new federal government, similarly, limited naturalization to foreign whites in 1790 and militia enrollment to whites two years later. To some extent, integration simply presented practical challenges so great as to seem insuperable. James Sullivan of Boston addressed those challenges in 1795: "As there is no way to eradicate the prejudice which education has fixed in the minds of the white against the black people, otherwise than by raising the blacks, by means of mental improvements, nearly to the same grade with the whites, the emancipation of the slaves in United America must be slow in its progress, and ages must be employed in the business. The time necessary to effect this purpose must be as extensive, at least, as that in which slavery has been endured here." By Sullivan's math, integration through education, under ideal conditions, would have been achieved by the 1960s.

More revealing was Sullivan's statement that the chief obstacle to black integration lay in the prejudiced minds of whites—their belief in their own special nature, superior to and distinguished from that of blacks. As we have seen, this idea about white people was exceedingly common in the Revolutionary era. It had support in science and philosophy. The Chain of Being, said to stretch from lowly beasts through blacks, then Asians, and on to its high end in white people, had steadily gathered white adherents since the 1740s. The Scottish philosopher David Hume's opinion, written in 1753, was influential but not entirely original: "I am apt to suspect the negroes, and in general all the other species of men (for there are four or five different kinds) to be naturally inferior to the whites. There never was a civilized nation of any other complexion than white, nor even any individual eminent either in action or speculation." This view would be echoed by other prominent Enlightenment figures such as Voltaire, Kant, and the authors of the *Encyclopédie*. It was the parlor version of white "prejudice" and appears to have become common opinion among whites by the time of the Revolution. Alexander Hamilton and John Laurens struggled with it when they sought to enlist black slaves as Revolutionary soldiers, in the process giving them freedom. Hamilton wrote in 1779, "I have not the least doubt, that the Negroes will make very excellent soldiers . . . I foresee that this project will have to combat much opposition from prejudice and self-interest. The contempt we have been taught to entertain for the blacks, makes us fancy things that are founded neither in reason nor experience; and an unwillingness to part with property of so valuable a kind, will furnish a thousand arguments to show the impracticability, or pernicious tendency, of a scheme which requires such sacrifices." Laurens plowed ahead with the project of convincing South Carolinians (of whom he was one) and Georgians to free slaves for the purpose of fighting the Revolution. But Hamilton had correctly anticipated the difficulties, and in 1781 Laurens wrote to him, "I was out-voted, having only reason on my side, and being opposed by a triple-headed monster, that shed the baneful influence of avarice, prejudice, and pusillanimity."

With regard to whiteness, the key factor here was white prejudice—the perception that whites were gripped by racial unreason. The Chain of Being (and similar theories) transformed this vague prejudice into a view of the world, an abstraction undisturbed by historical event. But it is worth remembering how *historical* white writers on white prejudice thought that prejudice to be. Hamilton understood white prejudice as learned behavior. So did James Sullivan, and James Madison, not to mention the many Quaker writers on the subject. Unfortunately, such a perception of white people was used to justify white separatism. As the colonizationist St. George Tucker wrote, "if prejudices have taken such deep roots in our minds, as to render it impossible to eradicate this opinion, ought not so general an error, if it be one, to be respected?" If white prejudice could not be overcome—and few believed it could, at least not with any speed—then blacks should be removed, leaving whites on their own. This was, of course, the position of Jefferson, Madison, Monroe, even, to a degree, Washington, a position later taken up by Henry Clay, Andrew Jackson, Stephen Douglas, and Abraham Lincoln, among so many others.

Yet the revolutionaries did not understand themselves as fighting to establish a white nation. Nor did they consider whiteness as intrinsic to the identity of the new republic. This may be explained, in part, by a reasonable reluctance to think of their national identity as based on racial prejudice. But it is also true that they didn't think it *was* based on prejudice. They believed their new American identity rooted itself in universal humanity. Both the newness and the inclusive universality of America were central to Revolutionary ideals. The newness had immediate racial implications. Given that almost no one wished to mount a racial defense of slavery, or to retain it indefinitely in the new country, the racial-slavery system had somehow to be placed outside the circle of American newness. One method was to blame it on England. Jefferson had done so in drafting the Declaration of Independence. James Monroe referred to slavery as "an existing evil which commenced under our Colonial System, with which we are not properly chargeable." Madison would later complain of English abolitionism on the ground that England had been "the quarter which obtruded the evil." The essence of these charges lay in the belief that new Americans were innocent of the past, specifically the white racial past with regard to blacks and Indians. Given that the new white Americans felt they had nothing else for which to apologize or feel guilty or even responsible, the newness of their country, in terms of moral responsibility (rather than political system), was precisely a repudiation of the white racial past. In this sense, the revolutionaries had rebelled against racial identity, while nonetheless retaining its vestiges in the form of white prejudice and racial slavery. And its vestiges in the physical form of black people and Indians.

The newness of America was threatened by these vestiges, not least in the prospect of a population of free blacks, who would one day perhaps, in the revealing words of St. George Tucker, attack "the innocent descendants of their former oppressors." These vestiges likewise threatened the inclusive universality of Revolutionary thought. In fact, the vestiges of pre-Revolutionary racial life—that is, the social results of whiteness and its institutions—were the *only* threats to Revolutionary newness, innocence, and universality. The republic faced many dangers to its physical existence, and its democratic institutions had many internal enemies. But the Revolutionary idea of a new man in itself foundered only on the belief in race, which included the question of slavery but was hardly limited to it. The belief in race, then, had an enormous pressure placed on it by Revolutionary thought. White Americans reacted to this pressure by denying the relevance of their racial past, placing the blame for it on others, excluding the nonwhite physical reminders of that past from society, regretting what had happened, despairing over the bad hand history had dealt them, feeling helpless, hoping that things would get better over the years—but above all by clinging tightly to the ideal of a humanity beyond race that was nonetheless, as far as anyone could tell, for the time being, restricted to white people. This was not so much hypocrisy as desperation. That generation knew white superiority was only a conjecture. Even Jefferson had advanced it "as a suspicion only." They knew that blacks and Indians were human. They had children with them. Yet they were stuck with an exclusive sense of closeness to other whites that they were unable to deny. In this predicament they could either sacrifice their humanity to whiteness or make their whiteness into humanity. Logically, these two options were identical (and, from a nonwhite viewpoint, practically indistinguishable). But emotionally and socially they were quite distinct. To become white was a degradation; to become human, of universal significance, was glorious. The Chain of Being helped a great deal. To be at the head of humanity's march was both to be white and to be beyond race—to be fully human.

The problem with this powerful conception was not only its inaccuracy, and its staggering cost in human lives and white souls, but its fragility. White racelessness had an inherent instability. One's whiteness only made sense in comparison to the characteristics of nonwhites; yet the goal of comparison was not to be white but to understand one's humanity. Therefore, one's humanity was always beyond reach, because part of the means for understanding it—the racial part—consisted in forever distinguishing oneself from other humans. Struggling toward one's humanity via race was, then, a doomed proposition. American racial thinking, as it had evolved by 1800, left white Americans with a nagging sense of incompleteness, because the goal they had for themselves could not be reached by the means they insisted on using.

It should be emphasized that this incompleteness would not have reached the level of ingrained social pathology—white "prejudice"—if the settler experience, and particularly the Revolutionary thought it formed, had not raised the human stakes so fantastically high. Most peoples elsewhere in the world were not risking their lives on a single bet having to do with the nature of humanity. They usually fought for social identities that already had a purchase on their minds, the types of identity that American colonists had once had themselves but slowly abandoned. American identity, by contrast, took its content from an idealized sum of the human past and the vision of its indefinite extension into the future. The American Revolution was nationalistic without having a nationality. It really had aimed at being universal, and so, when the Revolution ended and its highest hopes faded, white Americans had little in the way of nationality to fall back on, little to console them for their understandable failure to create a promised land of complete freedom. The new United States was radically incomplete, not least because it made a virtue out of its newness, its lack of a fixed past, indeed its break with the past.

The belief that the United States ought to be a laboratory for the creation of a new, better humanity—by definition, the place where people could be most truly human—had been wildly productive and would continue to be so. The democratic social institutions pioneered by American colonists were revolutionary almost beyond imagining. They created a social structure that was remarkably stable yet had change as its essence, particularly, though not only, the changing of individuals from place to place and from status to status. The new republic celebrated the changeability of individual fortune in a way unknown to human history. It celebrated the reality of not quite knowing who you were when you got up in the morning.

We may never know whether an individual or society can actually bear such an unhinging of the self. The price of Revolutionary faith in the universality of Americanness was that one could hardly know what, in particular, an American was. The wonderful and terrifying prospect of social fluidity made any national self-understanding seem almost a betrayal of principle. Complete freedom has no content. This may help us to grasp why race had been and would continue to be so central to white Americans. They had little else to cling to. Certainly, some might cling to Englishness or a mistier European essence, but this was a questionable urge given that the nation had just shot its way from under English rule and had emphatically rejected most aspects of European social structure. Some might cling to religion, and America was a somewhat Christian country, despite the fact that in 1790 only about one in ten white Americans was a member of a formal church. But religion-minded Americans had also shown, from the beginning, a spectacular talent for dividing into sects—usually in the name of freedom—a talent that would flower further in coming years and that Revolutionary leaders wisely sought to keep at a distance from the basically secular national institutions. The only aspect of the United States with national resonance and some rootedness in a collective, national past—the only aspect that was not, in principle, universal to humanity—was the racial thinking that divided people into white, Indian, and black, or into white and nonwhite. To the extent that Americans wanted a national identity as a people, rather than as human beings who happened to be in America, that identity almost had to be racial; given that white power, and the racial differences within which it developed and which it greatly extended, was already clear by the 1750s, if not earlier, "American" identity would be a white identity.

The white American obsession with racial purity makes more sense when viewed in this light. Just as white Americans had little other than race to cling to in their sense of themselves as a people, they had little else to defend. The defense of whiteness was simple. Once again, it defined itself in negative terms. Just as being free meant not being a slave, being white meant, above all, not being black. A little "black blood" could make you black, but it took a great deal of "white blood" to render a person white. Physical whiteness was not so much the presence of white ancestry as the absence of black ancestry. Thus the essentially negative quality of whiteness manifested itself in cultural imaginings about ancestry and sex.

At all levels, then, whiteness at the birth of the republic was a concept shaped by a set of absences. The sum of what you were not—Indian, black, slave—made you what you were, in that you were white. American whiteness appears as the mirror of American universalism. They shared an exclusive nature. American universalism excluded everything but the dictates of timeless reason. American whiteness simply excluded nonwhites. Neither could be sustained without the other. The nation could not build itself solely by consulting a recipe book of universal good ideas; nor could this nation, at least, build itself solely on white racial supremacy. Whiteness and universalism had become integral to American society over the course of a century and a half prior to the ratification of the Constitution. They flourished after 1795 as a hybrid of the universal and the particular, the raceless and the white.

"THE FREEST OF ALL HUMAN BEINGS"

WESTWARD EXPANSION AND THE PRICE OF LIBERTY

■

American whiteness at least carried the promise of its own extinction in American universalism. Practically speaking, however, the disappearance of whiteness was premised on the disappearance of nonwhites. That disappearance would mainly be achieved by a demographic and physical white expansion that would steadily reduce the nonwhite presence to something like unimportance. The Revolutionary generation, despite strong contrary tendencies in New England, had not doubted that the nation would expand, pursuing a destiny that Alexander Hamilton had called "imperial." John Quincy Adams, in an influential 1802 speech, urged, " 'Westward the star of empire takes its way.' Let us unite in ardent supplication to the Founder of Nations and the Builder of Worlds that what was then prophecy may continue unfolding into history . . . that the last shall prove the noblest empire of time." Adams played on the Christian underdog's theme of the last becoming the first, and the modern tragic thinker's pondering of the rise and fall of empires, only Adams had the tragedy removed. He also argued in this speech, not by coincidence, that early New Englanders had been kind to the Indians. Facing judgment after death, those pioneers would appear, he thought, in "the whiteness of innocence."

At the turn of the nineteenth century the connection between national growth and racial growth had begun to settle in the white mind. With regard to Indians this entailed an abandonment of (very uneven) assimilation and conversion, the Washington policy, in favor of war and expulsion. With regard to blacks the situation was more complicated. For white Northerners blacks were simply people one did not want around; the North then developed, officially and not, means of keeping blacks separate from whites, presaging the national system erected in the latter part of the century. For white Southerners who had the means, blacks were good to have around as slaves but bad as free neighbors. For white Southerners who could not afford slaves, blacks were unwelcome in every way. Finally, for white immigrants to America, free blacks stood in the way of their getting entry-level work, while enslaved blacks threatened to under-cut their labor in the new territories. The nature of early-nineteenth-century whiteness was, in broad terms, hammered out among these four white groups.

White workers and farmers did not want to compete with blacks, slave or free. Needless to say, no one in a market economy actually likes competition. In the circumstances, white capital did not face competition from black capital. White labor did compete with black labor. In the seaboard cities free blacks (and some slaves) had carved out niches for themselves, mainly after the Revolution. For the most part, they did jobs whites didn't want to do, either because they were unpleasant (such as dock work) or because they were tinged with servility (working as domestic servants and porters). In the first decades of the nineteenth century the labor market tightened as a result of immigration and natural population growth; the U.S. population nearly doubled between 1800 and 1820. White workers muscled their way into formerly black jobs, skilled and unskilled, backbreaking and servile. This was something of a formative experience for the small black seaboard communities and would intensify in the 1830s. It was also formative for the white urban working class—most importantly, for immigrants, who did not much hesitate to become white on our shores, to accept that the race card was about the only one they had to play and that their skin tone gave them entry into a collective that could secure work. They realized that, whatever else might happen, they at least were white. The relationship between this new status and black slavery was conjunctural at most. While slave labor did exist in the cities, it was hired out on an individual basis; one normally employed an enslaved worker, not a slave workforce. And the urban trend was toward more free blacks and fewer slaves. White urban workers competed not with slaves but with blacks. The social claim these white men and women made was purely racial. The power they had was a white power based on people asserting, not to say creating, their common interests by virtue of their skin color. This was the whiteness that immigrants discovered upon arrival and that they did their best to strengthen.

In racial terms, farming land differed little from caulking ships and ironing laundry. The sentimental approach to farm life—a mystical attachment to land, the magic of coaxing food from soil—tends not to be taken by actual farmers.

One farmed because one had no better choice. Working up a small farm was bitterly hard labor, not particularly healthful, and very difficult to do well. White laborers who couldn't get adequate work in the cities poured west. The competition for land was fierce, and farmers sought to reduce the competition as much as possible. Politically, the competitors they could exclude were Indians and blacks. These were excluded by law and by force (legal or not). Such exclusion gave westward expansion a racial character.

The initial expansion, into the Old Northwest (what would become Ohio, Indiana, Illinois, Michigan, Wisconsin, and a corner of Minnesota), was led by white Southerners. It was largely they who debated among themselves what form the new Western life would take. They tended to be middling or poor, part of that distinct population that had rolled westward for generations, moving on as Virginia's frontier moved, or up from South Carolina or Georgia, perhaps stopping awhile in North Carolina, Kentucky, or Tennessee—generations of transients, sons and daughters leaving their parents behind. They had learned, by the nineteenth century, that slavery did not necessarily benefit every white person. It tended to favor those who could make large investments in humans and land. White people outside that class repeatedly found themselves in the graceless position of being in a superior race without being very superior. Indeed, their whiteness was about the only superior quality they had—that, and their freedom, above all the freedom to move on and try again. In the nineteenth century, when they did move on their trying again often took the form of trying to build a new society without slavery. This is central to understanding the drama of white separatism in the early part of that century: in the Western theater, beginning just north of the Ohio River, white separatism was primarily shaped by white Southerners who had grown up with slavery and did not want to continue it.

It was a delicate business at the start. The Northwest Ordinance did not allow slavery in the territory. Slaveholders contrived to get around the prohibition, as under the odd "lifetime indenture" system in the Illinois and Indiana Territories, or a special law for the Shawneetown, Illinois, salt mines (renewed up through 1825). Slavery did not entirely disappear from Illinois until the 1840s. But too many people north of the Ohio preferred, as one group of Indiana petitioners put it, to live away from "People of Colour and Slaveholders." None of the Old Northwest lands, whether as territories or states, allowed full-blown slavery—though its Ohio advocates seem to have backed down only from fear that otherwise Congress might have rejected their statehood petition (in 1802), and a surge in pro-slavery feeling led to controversial referenda in the 1820s in Illinois and Indiana. The debates over slavery in the Old Northwest were murky, sometimes inconclusive, because they were not moral debates.

Most white people in the territories did not object to slavery in itself. They objected to living in a society where some labor (black slaves) could be used by some people to enrich themselves and gain a more or less permanent domination over their fellow whites. For the white majority the root of the problem was "People of Colour and Slaveholders" *together*. Some Indianans in 1809 appreciated the fact that "the lord of three or four hundred negroes does not easily forgive" those who oppose him. During the Illinois slavery referendum debates in the 1820s, an ex-Southerner sketched the scene of "haughtly slaveholders" sipping drinks in the shade while "the poor white" was out laboring with slaves on a public-works project; a former North Carolinian recalled "the servile drudgery of patroling through the neighborhood at night, in order to keep rich people's slaves at home." Such visions were rooted in the Southern experience and far from the dream of freedom in a new land.

Many whites in the Old Northwest, then, associated a slave society with their own unfreedom. It represented a humiliating relationship to power, one they sought to escape. Part of their escape consisted in escaping black people, slave or free—and many of the blacks in the region had been settled there by their former masters, a sloughing off of unwanted workers that struck hard at white self-estimation. As early as 1802 Ohioans prescribed in their constitution that blacks could not vote. Indiana joined in, a year later, with legislation forbidding blacks from testifying in court cases involving a white person. More laws quickly followed in the Old Northwest, requiring blacks to carry freedom papers, to post exorbitant bonds as guarantees of good behavior, not to marry whites. In 1813 Illinois's territorial legislature approved a bill requiring local lawmen to expel any arriving blacks or mulattoes; failure to leave brought thirty-nine lashes of the whip, repeated every fifteen days until departure. From 1802 into the Civil War no new state, from the Pennsylvania border to the Pacific Ocean, would allow blacks to vote. The same white population that settled the Old Northwest, though accompanied by more and more recent European immigrants, brought its worldview and experience to the plains and mountain territories and the West Coast. Like the momentum of their physical movement, the momentum of their laws increased with time.

The ultimate sanction of white separatism—total, official exclusion of blacks—took hold gradually. Missouri, applying for admission to the Union as a slave state in 1820, required in its proposed constitution that the state legislature pass laws "to prevent free negroes and mulattoes from coming to and settling in this state, under any pretext whatsoever." Pondering this clause, old James Madison wrote sadly to General Lafayette, "All these perplexities develop more and more the dreadful fruitfulness of the original sin of the African trade." Lengthy congressional argument resulted in a limp proviso intended to undercut the racial-exclusion provision, which it failed to do. Nonetheless, the grim debates in Washington had a chilling effect on would-be states until 1845, when Florida succeeded in gaining statehood with a constitution that expressly forbade free blacks from taking up residence. Free states and territories took the example to heart. Illinois adopted an exclusion provision in 1847, Ohio in 1850, Indiana in 1851. (The slave states had been likewise hardening their laws, from mandated "guardianship" statutes, applied to free blacks, to an 1850 Kentucky law that required five years in jail for any free black entering the state and any ex-slave remaining there upon emancipation.) Exclusion of free blacks became a common theme in Western conventions, whether at the strongly anti-slavery Topeka Convention of 1855 (where abolitionist Kansans voted for racial exclusion) or in New Mexico or Oregon (for exclusion in 1856 and 1858, respectively). There were local peculiarities. New Mexicans, for example, traded in Indian and Mexican slaves, within an elaborate debt-peonage system of quasi slavery. The Navajo and Ute tribes were particularly active in capturing and selling Indian slaves, and in the 1830s slave-raiding New Mexicans ranged as far as California. Utah, dominated by Mormons, also had its unique circumstances. Yet the general trend was clear, as enunciated in Walt Whitman's reflections on the separatist Oregon Constitution: "We shouldn't wonder if this sort of total prohibition of colored persons became quite a common thing in new Western, Northwestern, and even Southwestern States . . . Who believes that Whites and Blacks can ever amalgamate in America? Or who wishes it to happen? Nature has set an impassable seal against it. Besides, is not America for the Whites? And is it not better so?"

The debate over racial thinking in the California Constitutional Convention, in 1849, provides a useful summary of what was on white Western minds. It also has the advantage of conveying opinions among white men physically distant from Southern slavery, facing a minuscule black population—a somewhat abstract laboratory of white attitudes. They met in the Spanish coastal town of Monterey, in the autumn, forty-eight men who, on average, had lived in California for about two years. Most quickly agreed that slavery should not be allowed in California. The central question they faced was: Who can be a citizen of the new state? The *Californian* had published an item the previous year that declared, "We desire only a white population in California," and that may well have reflected the white consensus. It also begged the question of who was white. This question had special significance in a region with a large Hispanic (to use a later term) population. One man from that population, Noriega de la Guerra, suggested through his interpreter "that it should be perfectly understood in the first place what is the true significance of the word 'white.' Many citizens have received from nature a very dark skin; nonetheless, there are among them men who have heretofore [under Mexican government] been allowed to vote, and not only that, but to fill the highest public offices. It would be very unjust to deprive them of the privilege of citizens merely because nature had not made them white. But if, by the word 'white' it was intended to exclude the African race, then it was correct and satisfactory."

A Mr. Botts tried to clarify matters for Noriega. He said that color language was useful as it "indicated the inferior races . . . He would be perfectly willing to use any words which would exclude the African and Indian races. It was in this sense that the word white had been understood and used . . ." This remarkably straightforward definition of *white* as a term merely indicating a lack of non-whiteness, and a lack of the inferiority ascribed to nonwhites, ran up against several obstacles. Mexican law did not understand race in quite the same way. Mexico, as countless North American writers had been explaining for decades, was a "mongrel" nation. In law (though rarely in practice) it tended not to make racial distinctions in according citizenship rights such as voting. As elsewhere in Spain's New World, in Mexico the Spanish had frequently married Indians. Delegate O. M. Wozencraft pointed out, "Many of the most distinguished officers of the Mexican government are Indians by descent," that is, part Indian. However, the delegates knew that a part-Indian light-skinned person could be, and often was, functioning socially as white or, in Mexican terms, *español*. (Mexicans could acquire "higher" racial status by purchase.) The convention decided to admit to full citizenship "white male citizens of Mexico" resident in California, showing in legal terms the flexibility of whiteness that had already proved powerful back East. Noriega's concerns were then addressed by simply asserting that, in this nettlesome case, a person was white not "by nature" but by social agreement.

It was remarked that many California Indians had become "civilized," which mainly meant that they owned property. The delegates distinguished, in line with U.S. practice, between Indians as such and "Indians not taxed," that is, without property. (Historically, taxed Indians might become white, or they might become black.) In debating the fate of this population, the delegates were forced onto the comfortless ground of discussing Indian raceness rather than Indian individuals. They felt misgivings: "Mr. Dent observed that it might be a weakness in him, but he had always entertained a peculiar deference for the Indians. They were the original proprietors of the soil. From them we derived it, and from them we derived many of the blessings which we now enjoy . . . Why should we pursue them, and drag them down to the level of slaves? It appeared to him that the Indians should enjoy the right of suffrage, and that they should not be classed with Africans." Another delegate, Tefft, supported Dent: "It might be a prejudice which had grown with his growth, and strengthened with his strength; but from his earliest youth, he had felt something like a reverence for the Indians. He had ever admired their heroic deeds in defense of their ab-original homes, their stoicism, their wild eloquence and uncompromising pride . . . Were gentlemen aware, that, because a man is two-thirds Indian, he is not an Indian? . . . Has not injustice enough already been visited upon the Indian race? They have been driven back from the haunts of civilization into the wilderness, driven from one extremity of the land to the other; shall they now be driven into the waves of the Pacific? Shall we deprive them of the advan-tages of civilization? Shall we prevent them from becoming civilized? Surely the prejudice against color does not extend so far!"

But it did extend so far. Arguing over distinctions to be made among non-whites introduced confusion into a political process that needed clarity. Either a race was inferior, or it was not; either whiteness had meaning, or it had none. The delegates voted to eliminate their "not taxed" category and leave all Indians as Indians. As one delegate put it, "He did not believe the committee could adopt any better form than the words 'white male citizen.' " The economic dis-tinction between propertied and unpropertied gave way before the importance of white and nonwhite.

The possibility of racial mixing—rather, of becoming white—would have eased the doubts of those who regretted excluding Indians from voting. As Tefft reminded his colleagues, white was a fuzzy category in practice. This concep-tual weakness was also a strength, because it gave whiteness a certain malle-ability in responding to political pressure. In the California case whiteness succeeded in stretching to include many, probably most, Mexicans, including those of Indian descent, but failed (not by a unanimous vote) to encompass propertied Indians recognized as such by the white community. The debates show that *white* functioned as a flexible term to exclude some people from the body politic.

It did not—with, as we will see, one partial exception—function as a positive term. The delegates spoke of prejudice as a social or psychological force work-ing upon them. Importantly, they did not see prejudice as always negative. Tefft spoke of his prejudice *for* Indians. Racial prejudice seems to have named a float-ing interior force that these men felt unable to control in themselves. They were not masters of it; it mastered them. They sensed a helplessness before it, not knowing whence prejudice came or even what its purpose might be. Some sus-pected, as Alexander Hamilton and others had before them, that prejudice was instilled by habit and education, a legacy of the past, otherwise inscrutable, and not something for which one was profoundly responsible. Delegate Gilbert, urging that free blacks be admitted to the state, said, "Entertaining the feelings that I do upon this matter, and I grant that my prejudices against negroes are as strong as any man's can be, for my whole education has tended to make them repugnant to me, yet I am not willing to go this far, and say that a free negro, or any other freeman, shall not enter California." He pointed, as did many of his colleagues, to the Constitution and other founding documents, which they all understood as insisting that men are created free and equal. "Do not be partial in this matter," Gilbert warned. "You are treading upon the United States' Constitution itself."

Why did these Westerners feel so helpless before their own prejudices? And how is it that they were, at the same time, in the same debates, willing to codify those prejudices in the highest laws? We should recall that white Western men had a number of insecurities. They did not know, any better than their Eastern brothers, what an American was. They did not know who they were. Many of their fathers would not have been allowed to vote. The broad male franchise was rather new. Men such as these would-be Californians had taken the right to vote by force of numbers, as a result of great political pressure on the Eastern elites, whether in Boston or Charleston. Likewise, the aggressive settlement of the West, especially before Jackson, had not been done at the direction of Congress (though the national treasury profited from it through land sales), much less with the support of the state governments of the old thirteen colonies. New England, after all, repeatedly had thought to secede in order to avoid seeing its power diminished by the addition of new states; the Old South feared the same result for itself. The usual method for the creation of a new state was for a group of somewhat desperate men to push west, settle what they could hold on to, and present Congress with a political fact that it could not ignore. Some of these men would then stay on and become governors of Kansas or Arkansas. Others would sell up, their land having increased in value, and move westward to the next new frontier. It was a kind of rolling population of men with precious little in common. What they did share were a cloudy sense of whiteness, a sharp insecurity about their (or anyone else's) right to power, a wish for secure gains, a fear of each other, and a doubled fear of what they called "capitalists."

Whiteness—pathetic as it often seemed, even to them, obscure, unbidden, undefinable, a creature and creator of helplessness—enabled these white men to make some sense of what they were doing and who they were. It enabled them, in the context of U.S. history as they understood it, to command social respect as full humans. This respect or humanity did not come from oppressing Indians or blacks. There were few blacks in California or in any of the other new states and territories that went through similar dramas. There weren't many Indians ("full-blood," not taxed) either, in relative terms—not any longer. For these men the point of being white was not to command respect from nonwhites, nor to advance some notion of positive whiteness. The point was to command respect from other whites, and for oneself.

This becomes extremely clear when we look at the California debate on the admission of free blacks. The "free Negro," in the view of these white men, came in two forms: wolf and sheep. (Similar distinctions were made for Indians.) On one hand, free blacks were "idle in their habits, difficult to be governed by the laws, thriftless and uneducated." Wherever admitted to white society, they acted as "a foreign, poisonous substance, producing the same effect as in physical economy—derangement, disease, and, if not removed, *death*." Said the liberal Tefft, who had lived all his life in free states, "they are an idle, worthless, and depraved population . . . I have no prejudice against the Negro because of his color. I object to their introduction here because the experience of other states has proved that they are the worst possible class of beings we could have among us—the most idle, disorderly, and unprofitable." Hastings, of Sacramento, argued that "if they are introduced at all, I think they had better be introduced as slaves, for a free Negro is the freest human being in God's world. Let us not receive them at all; but if we do, let us receive them as slaves." To which Tefft replied, "As the gentleman has said, when negroes are free, they are the freest of all human beings; they are free in morals, free in all the vices of a brutish and depraved race."

On the other hand, according to delegate Wozencraft, "The African will always be subservient to the Caucasian. It is his nature to be so—he must be so." The delegate believed that "the instinctive feeling of the negro is obedience to the white man, and, in all instances, he obeys him, and is ruled by him." One colleague took this thought a step further, in favor of admitting free blacks: "They are required in every department of domestic life; they form a body that have become almost necessary for our domestic purposes . . . I do not want the people of California to be cut off from the services of any particular body of men. It matters not if they were baboons, or any other class of creatures."

When one group of people describes another group of people as having, in its essence, entirely opposite qualities, we must assume that the first group is having some trouble expressing its true thoughts about the second. (Wozencraft actually worked "foreign, poisonous substance" and "in all instances, he obeys" into the same long speech.) It is most likely that what worried these men was not the people seemingly under discussion but the qualities they were supposed to have. Most of the wolfish qualities—several delegates pointed this out—existed in non-Negro peoples, even in whites. The quality of submissiveness or obedience, however, they associated only with blacks (though it had been mentioned, feebly, with regard to Indians), and it troubled the delegates greatly. Black labor was mentioned most often as tending to "degradation" of whites: "It is a well established fact, and the history of every State in the Union clearly proves it, that Negro labor, whether slave or free, when opposed to white labor, degrades it." In all the many instances when delegates insisted on the degrading of white laborers through competition with blacks, they never explained what degradation meant or how it worked. By inference, however, degradation clearly referred to social submissiveness. The truism of white degradation appeared alongside vivid denunciations of "capitalists" and designing men who would use any means to establish a submissive labor force. Delegates spun visions of Southern slaveholders bringing their captive black workers into the very home of California wealth, the gold mine. But the convention had already agreed to forbid slavery, and the delegates' fears fastened not so much on real slavery as on effective social disfranchisement, on submission to the power of "capitalists." "Yes, Mr. President," one delegate said, "the capitalists will fill the land with these living laboring machines, with all their attendant evils. Their labor will go to enrich the few, and impoverish the many; it will drive the poor and honest laborer from the field, by degrading him to the level of the negro." Black labor frightened the Californians because blacks could be made to submit. If blacks were allowed into California, and if they submitted, as expected, to moneyed white power, then less powerful whites would have no choice but to submit to that power as well. They would lose their whiteness, in that their skin-color tie to power would be weakened, even broken. This would be their degradation.

Therefore, both the wolf and the sheep qualities that these white men saw in nonwhites they also saw in themselves. By excluding nonwhites, they thought to exclude qualities attributed to them. But because those qualities in fact existed among whites, we can see that the effort to exclude them by excluding nonwhites was bound to fail. The California debate suggests that the power of whiteness lay in the solidarity it created among competitive men; the strength it gave them when bargaining with a ruling class; and the fragile conviction, which it shored up, that whatever power other men might have over oneself, that power was temporary and had no basis in nature. The idea of a natural aristocracy—that society's rulers had some support in nature's scheme for their temporal power—was by no means dead in early-nineteenth-century America. It had formed a part of Federalist thinking, of recent memory; the concept still lived among Southern and Northern oligarchs. For a native-born man monarchy itself would have been a reality for his grandfather. For an immigrant, and there were many in the West, it would likely have been a reality of youth. To be a white American man meant to be free and independent *by nature*. A threat to one's whiteness was precisely a threat to that freedom and independence—and to little else.

Yet the limits of racial thinking were also apparent. First, it led nowhere; whiteness was an identity without a soul, an empty interior space created by negations and exclusion. It gave a faint sense of having been victimized by "prejudice" and a skulking racial past. Second, and relatedly, racial thinking was hard to sustain because it was hard to believe. This was true with regard not only to Indians, as in the remarks quoted earlier, but also to blacks. Delegate Dimmick opposed exclusion of blacks, describing them as "a class speaking our own language, born and brought up in the United States, acquainted with our customs, and calculated to make useful citizens . . . fully as intelligent as they [foreigners] are, possessed of as much physical energy, and better acquainted with our habits and customs." Dimmick then immediately assured his audience, "I have no partiality for the Negro race. I have the same personal antipathies which other gentlemen avow . . ." The delegates knew—at least, they could readily imagine—that nonwhites were not fundamentally different from them. If nothing else, the almost physical fear they expressed that the presence of blacks, controlled by powerful whites, would rapidly degrade many white men to the level of blackness logically implies that many white men felt that their hold on racial privilege was weak, that they could become black, that whiteness itself was a thin, wispy notion subject to revision, even elimination, by the powerful—by powerful whites. The whiteness of these Californians was provisional, which meant their freedom, independence, social stability, and dignity were provisional as well. Racial thinking could not help them overcome this radical insecurity. One might well argue that racial thinking prevented their overcoming it. To some degree, apparently, being white, rather than shoring up the self, actually kept it fragile. When these men knew themselves as white, they found it hard to bear.

The first governor of California, Peter Burnett, had previously served as a territorial legislator in Oregon. While in the future Beaver State, Burnett had introduced an act requiring that any free black person leave Oregon within a specified period. If this person failed to leave, he should be arrested, then whipped every six months until he had left. In California, Governor Burnett urged the new state to pass a black-exclusion law. Burnett's whiteness seems to have been hard for many of his fellow white Californians to stomach. His opponents denounced his idea as "unduly influenced by prejudice" and judged that the man himself, later to be chief justice of the state supreme court, had "many prejudices to overcome."

The Californians might have understood their whiteness more positively. Rather than viewing it as a mysterious prejudice, or an unthinking repugnance, they might have thought their whiteness an excellent characteristic, the key to their inner selves, and the personal quality that linked them to a glorious heritage. They had before them the example of Wozencraft, a physician out of Ohio who would go on, following the 1849 convention, to administer Indian policy here and there in California. During the constitutional debates Wozencraft provided an exhaustive résumé of positive whiteness. He alluded to Genesis and the blessing of God on "the family of Japheth." He spoke of "loving my kind," saying, "If you would wish that all mankind should be free, do not bring the two extremes in the scale of organization together; do not bring the lowest in contact with the highest, for be assured the one will rule and the other must serve." Wozencraft wanted a more level playing field for social advancement:

> The golden era is before us in all its glittering splendor; here civilization may attain its highest altitude; Art, Science, Literature will here find a fostering parent, and the Caucasian may attain his highest state of perfectibility. This is all before us. It is within our reach; but to attain it we must pursue the path of wisdom. We must throw aside all the weights and clogs that have fettered society elsewhere. We must inculcate moral and industrial habits. We must exclude the low, vicious, and depraved. Every member of society should be on a level with the mass—able to perform his appropriate duty. Having his equal rights, he should be capable of maintaining those rights, and aiding in their equal diffusion to others. There should be that equilibrium in society which pervades all nature, and that equilibrium can only be established by acting in conformity with the laws of nature. There should be no incongruities in the structure; it should be a harmonious whole, and there should be no discordant particles, if you would have a happy unity. That the negro race is out of his social sphere, and becomes a discordant element when among the Caucasian race, no one can doubt . . . Look at our once happy republic, now a contentious, antagonistical, discordant people. The Northern people see, and feel, and know, that the black population is an evil in the land . . .

In this unusually sophisticated rhapsody Wozencraft expressed a Northern and, especially, Western whiteness. While it still depended on nonwhites for its definitional sense, it proposed white superiority as something best developed in isolation, without nonwhites. Wozencraft's argument differed from that in the South, particularly the lower South. He did not explain how the republic could once have been happy with a large nonwhite population but could now be happy only without one. He was not alone, however, in believing that the republic *had* been happy, somehow, in the past but was now sliding toward misery because of the presence of nonwhites, who counted among the "weights and clogs" characteristic of every previous society. Wozencraft shifted whiteness away from prejudice with a nod to religion and a long embrace of nature. Nature had itself made whites superior to blacks; to ignore this was to deny not only Genesis but natural reality, which by 1849 had significantly displaced biblical interpretation as the key to universal understanding.

Among educated white people in the first half of the nineteenth century, the racial appeal to natural science had gained much ground. The rationalist spirit of the Enlightenment, as seen in the racial opinions of Hume, Voltaire, Kant, Jefferson, and others, had tended to array the evidence of white superiority in terms of civilizational accomplishment—literature, forms of government, art. Science-minded men raised on such thinking normally sought to translate it into scientific terms. Disputes raged as to whether the races had come from a single ancestor or had multiple, independent origins. Such arguments were significant initially in terms of an intellectual elite struggling with Christian doctrine. Voltaire had advocated the multiple-origins theory because he wanted to upset churchmen; it extended into the middle of the nineteenth century, when Josiah Nott and George Gliddon published their hugely popular *Types of Mankind* in Philadelphia. Arguing for multiple racial origins formed part of what Nott called "parson skinning." The differences between "monogenetic" and "polygenetic" approaches were not, however, very great. Both sides believed, on the whole, that blacks were inferior. The leading question concerned their "improvement"—whether they could reach the white, or civilized, state. Some scientists argued that blacks actually could turn white, usually over several generations, through exposure to cool weather or simply to civilized life. By the 1820s, however, a wide scientific consensus had developed, in Europe and America, that the races were inherently, or scientifically, different. The white race was all but universally thought, by white scientists, to be the best.

Scientific whiteness quickly ran into problems. Defining a race proved, despite vast expanses of research, practically impossible. Many fine minds expended themselves on this question, but the races, upon close examination, seemed always to merge into each other. And whiteness itself tended to fragment. The softer human sciences, particularly history, provided a place for tribal speculations intended to buttress national characters. The Revolutionary generation had occasionally dipped in such waters. Mercy Warren, in 1788, traced the right of trial by jury to "our Saxon ancestors," and the irrepressible

Jefferson had made a hobby of researching Anglo-Saxon, urging its study in American universities. English Anglo-Saxonism—the belief that the English had their racial essence in Germany—had been quite popular among the Puritans. In the time of Cromwell, Saxonism was associated with the mass of non-aristocratic Englishmen (the lords being thought Norman, that is, somewhat French). The central qualities of these supposed Saxons, the "true Englishmen," were independence and equality; their political nature was to resist tyranny. English concepts in the eighteenth century of freedom, the rights of Englishmen, and liberation from slavery and tyranny were often traced to the German forests. In his influential *History of England* (1762), David Hume attributed to northern Europeans, in particular Germans, "sentiments of liberty, honour, equity, and valour, superior to the rest of mankind." This tribal version of Englishness made its way to America; it blossomed in both countries in the 1840s. Even Harriet Beecher Stowe, in *Uncle Tom's Cabin* (1852), would refer to "the hard and dominant Anglo-Saxon race."

Nineteenth-century Anglo-Saxonism joined similar tribal phenomena in France, Germany, and indeed throughout Europe. Like Wozencraft in faraway California, European and Eastern American thinkers threw together a delirious medley of biblical genealogies (the usual off-key blend of Ham, Japheth, and Shem), racial science, and national-tribal specialness. The surge of tribal separatism in white countries did not necessarily weaken whiteness as an increasingly global idea. Each nation or tribe could, and most often did, see itself as first among white peoples. Frequently, each traced something of its essence to Germany, not least because German history, looked at in a certain way, offered two critical, complementary "racial characteristics": the will to conquer (against the Roman Empire, in France, in Britain) and the will to remain unconquerable. The logic of aggressive nationalism all but required these qualities to be placed at the heart of one's nation. In a milieu of nationalism combined with white superiority, Germanophilia or Teutonism provided a satisfyingly national-tribal essence that nonetheless could be accommodated within the grander scheme of imperial whiteness.

Studious white Americans frequently took their cues from learned Europeans, who in the post-Enlightenment period worked up an attractive set of racial dualisms: superior/inferior, masculine/feminine, active/passive, master/slave. All pointed to conquest as white racial destiny, even obligation. European race theories, in general, proposed an innovative form of human unity—a scientific or physiological reworking of biblical genealogy, marked by the transition from Japhetic to Caucasian and Aryan. The human races were united by their needs for each other. The master is not a master without a slave; there is no superior without an inferior, nor masculine without feminine. The influential social theorist Auguste Comte assigned white people intelligence, yellow people industry, and black people emotion, prophesying their eventual mixture because "the complete harmony of the Great Being requires the closest support of these three races, the speculative, the active and the affective." Comte's contemporary Count Gobineau, a famously melancholy white supremacist, wrote in 1856, "The black element is certainly indispensable for developing artistic genius in a race, for we have seen what outbursts of fire, flames, sparks, vivacity and spontaneity are intrinsic to its soul . . ." In the same period Gustav Klemm, whose standard *General History of Civilization* guided a generation of Germans, got at the heart of the new thinking. White people, led in this instance by Germans (and not including Slavs), needed the rest of the world: "I see in this fusion of active and of passive races which were originally separate, the realization of the purpose which is pursued by nature in all the domain of its organic creation . . . [A] people which is made up only of members of the active or members of the passive race remains imperfect and incomplete . . . It is only by mingling the two races, the active and the passive, by the marriage of peoples if I may put it thus, that humanity is completed . . ." For Klemm active white peoples were distinguished by "their love of freedom, their great courage, their awareness of their human dignity and of their human rights, by their sense of poetry and their love of power," and by their manly beauty.

And so by mid-century European racial theory, despite abundant internal contradictions and disagreements, had developed a concept of human racial unity that saw white people, in isolation, as "imperfect and incomplete." Whites needed other races in order to create a full humanity. Even those, such as Klemm, who reserved for whites the most magnificent human qualities still believed whites came up short somehow, that they could not develop alone beyond a certain limit. This was, in a way, the opposite of racial separatism. (European intellectuals did not, as yet, think that whites ought to exterminate nonwhites as nature's mistakes, though some did expect nonwhites to die off— or become white.) The new, rough European consensus on human racial unity in diversity did, logically, raise the question: Why had white people, in the millennia before 1850, been so slow to realize themselves? But the modern sensibility normally avoided this type of question, holding instead that the vast human past both had culminated only last week and was just now beginning its true adventure. In racial terms that adventure demanded white conquest, in the name of advancing human rights, human dignity, love of freedom, and love of power.

Such conclusions still had a speculative quality for Europeans at the time. They were sharper for Americans, who lived in a multiracial, or at minimum multiethnic, world, one created by an earlier, rather premodern drive for freedom and power. White destiny had a different character in practice than in theory. White Americans had experience of what white power meant on the ground, faced with real, living, nonwhite people. That experience took one beyond mild meditations about active races and human advancement. It could lead you to ponder the nature of Satan, for instance, particularly if you came from New England. New Englanders had a history of intense meditations on evil. "The New Englanders are a people of God settled in those, which were once the devil's territories," Cotton Mather briskly explained in 1693. Indians had been notable among the Devil's agents in combating God's people, as Cotton's father, Increase, had shown in his history of the most important war (1675–1676) against them and their leader, King Philip. "And we have reason to conclude," Increase wrote in 1676, "that *Salvation is begun,* and in a gracious measure carried on towards us. For since last *March* there are two or 3000 *Indians who have been either killed, or taken, or submitted themselves to the English.*" To Indians the New Englanders added other satanic enemies, such as Quakers, Baptists, miscellaneous freethinkers, and, in the Salem witchcraft trials of 1692, themselves.

This was a faraway world by the nineteenth century, yet one might, in imagination, reach back to it in trying to understand race and destiny. Two writers who did so were Washington Irving and Nathaniel Hawthorne. Irving, typically, wrote "The Devil and Tom Walker" (1824) as a haunted comedy. "About the year 1727" a "meagre, miserly fellow" named Tom Walker takes a shortcut while returning to his miserable home and a wife "as miserly as himself." (Cheapness may be the most lasting theme of New England humor.) Tom Walker wanders into a swamp, then finds higher ground, "one of the strongholds of the Indians during their wars with the first colonists." There he idly pokes in the earth with his walking stick "and lo! a cloven skull, with an Indian tomahawk buried deep in it . . . a dreary memento of the fierce struggle that had taken place in this last foothold of the Indian warriors."

> "Let that skull alone!" said a gruff voice. Tom lifted up his eyes, and beheld a great black man seated directly opposite him, on the stump of a tree. He was exceedingly surprised, having neither heard nor seen any one approach; and he was still more perplexed on observing, as well as the gathering gloom would permit, that the stranger was neither negro nor Indian.

The black man shows Tom the trees roundabout, on which he has carved the names of prominent men toward whom he bears ill will—notably Deacon Peabody, "an eminent man, who had waxed wealthy by driving shrewd bargains with the Indians." Having carved the names, the black man would chop the trees and bring death on the named men.

> "But what right have you," said Tom, "to cut down Deacon Peabody's timber?"
>
> "The right of a prior claim," said the other. "This woodland belonged to me long before one of your white-faced race put foot upon the soil."
>
> "And pray, who are you, if I may be so bold?" said Tom.
>
> "Oh, I go by various names. I am the wild huntsman in some countries; the black miner in others. In this neighborhood, I am known by the name of the black woodsman. I am he to whom the red men consecrated this spot, and in honor of whom they now and then roasted a white man, by way of sweet-smelling sacrifice. Since the red men have been exterminated by you white savages, I amuse myself by presiding at the persecutions of Quakers and Anabaptists; I am the great patron and prompter of slave-dealers, and the grand-master of the Salem witches."
>
> "The upshot of all which is, that, if I mistake not," said Tom, sturdily, "you are he commonly called Old Scratch."

He is indeed the Devil, which pleases Tom Walker, who sees in him a chance to make money. And what a Devil he is, a black spirit who hates white people for their cruelty and whose vengeance consists in turning them against each other and against blacks. One has to wonder what was on Irving's mind as he wrote this series of reversals, in which the Devil is Cotton Mather, or a slave dealer. Who did Irving think white people were? Who did he think he was? He seems to say that for the "white-faced race," the Devil appears as one of their own, leading them to torture each other and black people. The Devil does this in vengeance for what Irving had earlier described, in his immensely popular *Sketch Book*—the first American literary sensation—as "how the footsteps of civilization may be traced in the blood of the aborigines; how easily the colonists were moved to hostility by the lust of conquest; how merciless and exterminating was their warfare. The imagination shrinks at the idea . . ." Irving wrote that in an essay on King Philip. Interestingly, the Devil, spun into sleepless fury by the primal crime of white race war against Indians, continues his vengeance by prodding whites into the slave trade. (He tries with Tom, who refuses: "he was bad enough in all conscience; but the devil himself could not tempt him to turn slave-trader.") It is as if Irving, in narrative terms, needed that twist to keep the race drama going. His Devil is neither Negro nor Indian; his

Devil is, after a fashion, white. And because of what whites had done as a race, the Devil would always be with them.

Nathaniel Hawthorne, who was born in Salem, picked up the theme in his first collection of short stories, *Mosses from an Old Manse*, published in 1846. "Young Goodman Brown" also stages an encounter with Satan. Brown one evening leaves his pretty Faith, "as the wife was aptly named," for a rendezvous with the Devil. He walks down a "dreary road, darkened by all the gloomiest trees of the forest . . . It was all as lonely as could be." Soon he meets Satan, who looks much like the young man—"they might have been taken for father and son." They walk together, but Brown tells the Devil he has decided against selling his soul. "We are but a little way," the Devil replies, smiling, "in the forest yet."

> "Too far! too far!" exclaimed the goodman, unconsciously resuming his walk. "My father never went into the woods on such an errand, nor his father before him. We have been a race of honest men and good Christians since the days of the martyrs; and shall I be the first of the name of Brown that ever took this path and kept"—
>
> "Such company, thou wouldst say," observed the elder person, interpreting his pause. "Well said, Goodman Brown! I have been as well acquainted with your family as with ever a one among the Puritans; and that's no trifle to say. I helped your grandfather, the constable, when he lashed the Quaker woman so smartly through the streets of Salem; and it was I that brought your father a pitch-pine knot, kindled at my own hearth, to set fire to an Indian village, in King Philip's war."

The two debate awhile, the Devil's mockery rising as Brown urges the virtues of New Englanders. Various pious townspeople are revealed to be the Devil's disciples, until Brown sees a pink ribbon, the kind his wife had just been wearing, and he wonders whether Faith might herself be the Devil's own. Then he snaps, laughs, races into "the heart of the dark wilderness."

> The whole forest was peopled with frightful sounds—the creaking of the trees, the howling of wild beasts, and the yell of Indians; while sometimes the wind tolled like a distant church bell, and sometimes gave a broad roar around the traveller, as if all Nature were laughing him to scorn. But he was himself the chief horror of the scene, and shrank not from its other horrors.

"Ha! ha! ha!" roared Goodman Brown when the wind laughed at him. "Let us hear which will laugh loudest. Think not to frighten me with your deviltry. Come witch, come wizard, come Indian powwow, come devil himself, and here comes Goodman Brown. You may as well fear him as he fear you."

Having run as far as he can screaming into the wilderness that absorbs and expresses Goodman Brown's terror of himself the young man stops, facing a torchlit congregation of Salem's villagers. It turns out Cotton Mather had been right about witches; he and the hanging judge Samuel Sewall had merely stopped too soon. The whole village is there, and what remains of the local Indians, "[s]cattered . . . among their pale-faced enemies." The Indians, a Salem deacon has said earlier, "know almost as much deviltry as the best of us." At this point Hawthorne's description of Satan changes. The fallen angel no longer resembles Goodman Brown's father. Now he is "the dark figure," "the sable form," *sable* being a common adjective for Negroes at the time.

The Devil tells the people of Salem village to look upon each other, by firelight, in the forest clearing. Brown sees Faith, and she him. The Devil speaks:

"Lo, there ye stand, my children," said the figure, in a deep and solemn tone, almost sad with its despairing awfulness, as if his once angelic nature could yet mourn for our miserable race. "Depending upon one another's hearts, ye had still hoped that virtue were not all a dream. Now are ye undeceived. Evil is the nature of mankind. Evil must be your only happiness. Welcome again, my children, to the communion of your race."

"Welcome," repeated the fiend worshippers, in one cry of despair and triumph.

The active race, not in German forests but in those of the New World, encountered many difficulties planting its virtue in the stony ground. The difficulties lay within themselves, these harried so-called Saxons. What had God and His modern lieutenant nature done to them? Where now were the love of human rights, dignity, beauty, the love of freedom and of power? Hawthorne's New England nature screamed, laughed, annihilated. This world was no one's home; this world was a howling wilderness. The New England Protestant temperament had never allowed much doubt that men were sinners. They lived under the constraint of a failure before God that they merely inherited and to which they added their own little parcels of failure, such as the wretched war on King Philip, the persecution of Quakers, and finally, at Salem, the persecution of themselves. If anyone had doubted they were fallen, those doubts would have been cleared up by the early history of New England, which must explain why two of the modern North's greatest writers, the pioneers of the American short story—not to mention their colleague Fenimore Cooper—returned to that past with a palpable obsession. Could there really be any escape from it?

The white South, in considering racial destiny, faced a situation somewhat unlike that of the North. Southerners operated at a greater distance from an angry God, and their nature set different constraints. And obviously their thinking about whiteness occurred within a society variously between 25 and 60 percent black, with the great majority of these nonwhites in perpetual bondage to white owners. The belief of many Revolutionary Southerners—mainly, but not only, Virginians—that racial slavery might wither away had proved incorrect. With improvement in methods of raising and harvesting cotton in the South, and of manufacturing textiles from it in the North and Britain, plantation slavery had a renewed economic justification. Between 1807 and 1815 the number of cotton spindles in the country went from 8,000 to 130,000. Mississippi was admitted as a slave state in 1817, Alabama in 1819. Tobacco as a large-scale plantation crop had been in decline for some time, but rice (in the Southeast) and sugar (on the Gulf Coast) continued as profitable crops that gave their greatest returns to people who could afford slaves. Not more than a quarter of white Southerners were in slave-owning families, but slavery was still the overwhelming racial fact of life in the region. With white migration to the West, and the related drop in Southern political power at the national level, the slaveholding elite became both more important, in its slaveholding, to Southern society and more distinct, for the same characteristic, from whites outside the South. Elite whites' sense of their own whiteness as slaveholders consequently deserves close attention.

The distinctness of the South—that collection of beliefs and emotions that would, one day, be conveyed in the deceptively simple phrase "the Old South"—grew up in this period, say, from 1820 onward, as a form of defensive nostalgia. The growing, thrusting South, the cotton South, was entirely dependent on the North and on Europe. The Southern economy in its most developed aspect consisted in the transport of cotton, grown and harvested by black slaves, from the South to the Northern ports and on to Liverpool. All good roads led north; and back southward along those roads came Northern manufactures. The dependence ran both ways—the North needed the South, too, for its cotton and its consumers. But Northern money had a great many other things to do and places to go. It increased trade with Europe, with the expanding Great Lakes economies, and with the emerging breadbasket of the Middle West. Enjoying a complete flexibility in labor costs—being able to exchange one worker for another, as one would exchange a screwdriver for a hammer—Northern money could move about freely, always reaching for the main chance, in a physical environment steadily swelling with resources, a social environment swelling with cheap laborers and able artisans, an international market promising ever more partners and customers, and a technological scene blazing away with the laborsaving (or labor-intensifying), capital-rewarding innovations we associate with the machine age.

Although all this was not quite apparent in 1820, the basic trends were already surreptitiously winding their way through American society—except in the South. The fortunes made in cotton evolved, at best, into larger fortunes made in cotton. Slave-grown cotton rewarded investment for a greater number of investors than any other Southern product could. This was in part an accident of nature, in part a result of the innovative human accidents of the cotton gin and power loom. It was also a result of slavery as such. A decisive amount of that Southern money capable of transforming society was invested in the bodies of black people. In order for that money to increase in value, the work of enslaved blacks had to increase in value, and the critical means for this increase was in cotton plantations. Moneyed Southerners, the people with power, then faced a double dependency: on the North and on black people. The white Southern elite's relationship to its own whiteness has to be seen in the light of these twin dependencies.

Two additional factors should be kept in mind: the roiling character of Southern society during the expansionist, cotton-boom years, and the relationship between whites with much money and whites with little. The South was very far from stable in the early nineteenth century. Sizable parts of Georgia and Florida were still squeezing the mud between their toes when along came Alabama, Mississippi, then Arkansas, eventually to be joined by Texas and by Oklahoma, the last, curious theater for the process of frontier expansion begun in Jamestown. In its way the South was as much a frontier society as the Old Northwest and the West—especially the Deep South, well into the Jackson years. As Jackson himself had abandoned his ancestors' Southern graves, in his rough-and-ready style, so had many of his and later Southern generations. For every Virginian of high family who might have made his way to Mississippi in stately form, there were many more who hit their heads against some portion of the frontier until one or the other broke. Together, such people further developed the characteristic frontier love and terror of social violence; the tetchy individualism of men who nonetheless all behaved in about the same ways; the tight thrift and sudden extravagance of people accustomed to speculation and quick shifts in fortune; the camaraderie of fellow strivers in a tough environment, as well as their periodic cunning and need, as individuals, for deceit.

In the 1840s the hierarchical, big-planter-dominated, slavery-bound society known as the Old South at last came into its own. It had a great deal of new money in it, the subject of complaint among those few families whose fortunes had continually waxed since the days of William Byrd—but not much complaint, and no serious opposition, as money was money. And the Old South was uniquely situated to integrate, in the family sense, its parvenus. The region had a sparse population, compared with the North, and remarkably little white inmigration. White Southerners really were one big family, and imagination could readily traverse those gaps where fact refused to speak. In other words, the Alabama swindler who gulled enough hapless, hopeful ex-Virginians of their family money in land trades and made himself a prominent planter might rapidly come to understand himself, and be understood by others, as working out the destiny natural to a man with the blood of William the Conqueror and the Huguenot martyrs coursing in his veins. More importantly, perhaps, the man with twenty acres of hillside, not far from this newly prominent Alabaman's humming cotton plantation, might well have the same last name as the planter's maternal uncle, thereby establishing just enough of a common bond. And the truth was they could very well have been cousins.

Southern whites had this specific sense of blood ties, of family, that was foreign to the rest of the country and would become more so. It seems paradoxical that a society based on the repetitive turmoil of picking up and going west should, with a generation or two, appear one of timeless stability reaching back to Roanoke; that a society whose ruling class had had to revise its membership lists after each growing season should see itself as proudly organic and consistent; that a society of so many individual futures should abruptly stake its claim on yesterdays. Andrew Jackson was a terrified, torn-up, parentless boy uneasily apprenticed (through family) to the lawyer's trade, and Andrew Jackson was lord of the Hermitage, where slaves labored peaceably enough for him to afford the presidency. When we look at the South in this period, we find the eternal, self-made present typical of the country as a whole, but with an additional layering of pastness—of manners, ancestor worship, genealogical enthusiasm, and stable social relations based on some sort of warm logic.

One explanation for the apparent paradoxes of a roilingly stable, violently agreeable society may lie in the nature of this new Southern "heritage": the so-called Old South was not only new in fact, it was new in theory and very nearly so in content. To a timeless present it appended a timeless past, in other words, not a history but a wish: a wish for order; and a wish not to think one was missing the historical boat. A wish for order presumably springs from a fear of disorder. We need not search far to find the potential sources of disorder. They were, as so often, among the lower classes. Look at the Old South vision: planters, descended from the states' rights men who had forced the Magna Carta on King John, rightly at the top, preoccupied not with making money but with honor and "the chivalry"; and happy black slaves, deposited by Providence as children to the kind planter parent. What is missing? Poorer white people and unhappy slaves: together, the great majority of Southerners. Their absence from the Old South ideal must tell us something about what that vision sought to accomplish.

As to the absence of most whites from the dream of a white-supremacist society, we might note first that the point of white Southern institutions was not to make white people poor. "Among us," Chancellor Harper wrote in a defense of slavery, "we know there is no one, however humble his beginnings, who, with persevering industry, intelligence, and orderly and virtuous habits, may not attain to considerable opulence." However untrue this was, many people believed it and had a host of almost self-made men, including Jackson and Jefferson Davis, to whom they could point as evidence. The already wealthy certainly believed that their opulence and their virtue sprang from a single seed, some even speculating that there was a racial difference between successful whites and unsuccessful ones—raising the ever-present specter of a racial division within the white world. Besides, the plantation system didn't need non-planter white people, not much. Their labor was peripheral to the economy, and their only way up was to become like the planters above them, in every way, or to leave the cotton South. (This is, as we have seen, a central reason why so many ex-Southerners who had no moral qualms whatever about slavery nevertheless wanted their new states to be "free.") Finally, the lives of white small farmers were not necessarily miserable. At least one had one's land and the fruits of one's labors, and the distant-cousin planter nearby would help out if times got thin or an election close. And at least one was not black.

If planters depended on blacks economically, we might say that non-planter whites depended on them psychologically. Here was a white population (the majority) of little importance to the economy, of no importance to social ideals, and of military importance only as a barrier against racial enemies. Within the Old South as a planter-dominated whole, the only significant or valuable aspect of the white majority was its whiteness, which made its members free and full humans rather than slaves. It has sometimes been wondered at that the poorest Southern whites, who often had very little contact with blacks, exhibited such strong racial feeling. But the opposite would be more surprising, because skin color was all that pulled them over the line from insignificance to importance, from property to humanity, and from slavery to freedom. Crucially, that racial distinction was, at its heart, symbolic. It conveyed little real power, not even, in many instances, the right to vote, much less to receive any education. It did not have money attached, excepting perhaps some slight charity; as anyone knew, house slaves were warmer in winter and better fed than many a white man in the hills, a reality that lay behind President Johnson's shaking hurt when faced with Frederick Douglass. What Southern whiteness did give was a basement pride, a chance rescue from utter failure or degradation in one's own eyes and those of white society. It meant that at least one was a person and not a thing. One clung to it tightly for that reason.

Yet the prospect of being a failure and a thing, rather than a success and a person, was not limited to the white Southern dirt farmer. This prospect also lingered in the minds of the Southern elite. It was rather clear that cotton would not necessarily and always bring an adequate return. One could equally anticipate that the constant opening of land to cotton cultivation might increase production to the point where the price per unit would drop, a grim vision for old or somewhat old money resting on five hundred acres of Mississippi. Cotton cultivation was also not healthy for the land, and the example of land-destroying Virginia tobacco lay in the recent past for contemplation. Finally, the price of cotton was set at the North and in England, two places one therefore came rapidly to despise. (The Southern romantic attachment to Scottish ancestry, however genealogically dubious, had clear uses as a balm for English colonial subjection. The novels of Sir Walter Scott found especially eager readers in the South.) Elite Southerners knew they depended on the North and at least suspected that their leash would be getting shorter. "If we had less trade with and less dependence on the North," George Fitzhugh wrote in 1854, "all our [white] poor might be profitably and honorably employed in trades, professions, and manufactures. Then we should have a rich and denser population. Yet we but marshal her in the way that she was going. The South is already aware of the necessity of a new policy, and has begun to act on it. Every day more and more is being done for education, the mechanic arts, manufactures and internal improvements. We will soon be independent of the North." So Fitzhugh said, but the South was actually still going "in the way that she was going." This meant that Southerners might soon become no more than helplessly captive raw-material suppliers, subjects of selfish Northern caprice, even—here we see the eighteenth-century wheels turning again—something like slaves. Northern society was already much wealthier than Southern, its people rising in their own estimation and that of the world while Southerners were sinking. This had all the signs of humiliation. Better-off Southerners reacted in much the way the poor white farmer reacted: clinging to fancies of distinction that, in terms of solving the real difficulties at hand, did much more harm than good.

One of these fancies was the importance of light skin. However, elite ideas about the excellence of whiteness could not be identical with those of poor whites. For instance, a moment's observation revealed that the North was basically white, yet Northerners were not coming South. One might have thought that relocating to a place where one's skin color, rather than being of passing interest, conferred the psychic boon of unearned human fullness would have been attractive. That was not the case. Moreover, white (however defined) foreign immigrants were not coming South, either. And white Southerners were leaving—often banning slavery where they went. So it was a tricky business to portray the Old South as the most desirable site for whites as such to work out white destiny, simply because most whites, globally speaking, did not want to live there.

The elite could and did try a more negative racial appeal. Southern writers tirelessly pointed out that whites elsewhere did not want blacks living nearby, hoped to colonize them abroad, passed laws to exclude them, wouldn't let them vote, kept them in servile jobs, kicked and beat them. This argument was meant to unmask Northerners as hypocrites for opposing slavery and condescending to the South; or, more subtly, to encourage Northerners to recognize themselves as fellow white people not really that different from their Southern friends. However, Northerners could be antislavery and antiblack (and anti-Southern) with perfect consistency. Northern antiblack feeling did find expression in antislavery, and so appeals to that antiblack feeling were hardly a good way to gain allies in defense of slavery.

Thus the Southern racial system of white supremacy could not, beyond a certain point, defend itself to outsiders on the basis of whiteness. The planter did, successfully, make a racial appeal to his white social inferiors. That had become the basis of Southern Democratic politics, which had strikingly few other pursuits (such as road building or schools). But the evident disjuncture between Southern whiteness and whiteness elsewhere forced the elite back upon itself, such that race was only one element in the Old South mix. Instead of an overarching racial sense of mission, the South developed a local cultural patriotism. Within that patriotism the praise of whiteness played a small role. Prosperous white Southerners could at least find more to grasp, in rescuing themselves from insignificance and thingness, than could the poor farmer clinging to the human minimum of fair skin and a putative family tie to Master. The Old South's defense of itself focused rather on certain cultural distinctions and on analyzing the nature of black people.

The two were intimately related. As to the first, the notable Southern culture, it tended to fasten on such characteristics as personal honor, chivalry, generosity, cordiality, refinement, and good taste. What these had in common was a distance from moneymaking—more precisely, a belief that one's social world, and so oneself, was praiseworthy because it was based on cultural qualities higher than mere money power. This was the soul of pro-slavery or pro-Southern writing. One would expect such a view among people who feared their impotence as producer-puppets manipulable by pitiless Yankee financiers—by foreigners. But there was more to it than that. The abler Southern thinkers, for whom Chancellor Harper will serve as spokesman, believed their social system constituted a rebuke to modernity elsewhere—a soft capitalism better than the hard-eyed money madness of the North. Once again, the price of American freedom would be counted in American slavery. Harper paints an unattractive picture of modern life without slavery. The essential flaw of modern economies, he writes, is that they turn people into things: "The tendency of population is to become crowded, increasing the difficulty of obtaining subsistence. There will be some without any property except the capacity for labor. This they must sell to those who have the means of employing them, thereby swelling the amount of their capital, and increasing inequality . . . The remuneration of the laborer gradually becomes less and less; a larger and larger proportion of the product of his labor goes to swell the fortune of the capitalist; inequality becomes still greater and more invidious . . ." This process, which Harper saw as completed in England and on its way to completion in the North, was inevitable without slavery—and led to that social system which had played such a key role in American imaginations for two centuries, namely, whites enslaving whites: "This inequality, this vice, this misery, this *Slavery*, is the price of England's civilization."

Such was the root fear, inherited from the eighteenth century (if not the sixteenth) but altered by the experiences of industrialization and secularization: that a person's worth might be reckoned in money, that a person might be a thing, a piece of property, a slave. Southerners were hardly alone in this fear, and their turn to a local politics of cultural symbolism, a romantic mixture of sentimentality, genuine self-love, and rage against the inhumanity of the machine age, partook of a general modern trend toward cultural nationalism. But the white South was different in that its spokesmen railed against the figurative slavery of wageworkers in the North and England while defending the real slavery of workers at home. One might think this contradiction could have been resolved by simple reference to black inferiority—and Southern writers did discourse amply on the inherited flaws of black people, usually by disparaging reference to freedmen in the North. (Southerners took a sharp interest in Northern prison statistics.) Yet they could not stop there; they wandered forward instead into a blaze of contradictions about black people. They argued that slave labor was more expensive than free labor, because the master incurred cradle-to-grave costs; they also argued that slave labor alone provided an adequate return on investment, which could only mean that free labor was, at least on a broad view, more expensive than slave labor. They argued that blacks were grateful to be slaves, "so happy of mood, so jocund, and so generally healthy and cheerful," as W. Gilmore Simms put it. Slavery was an improvement on the barbarism of Africa, where, as everyone knew, blacks were already slaves in any case and often served up at banquets by their tyrannical black lords. Yet Southerners also argued that blacks could be stirred to open warfare against whites by the merest whisper of abolitionism, of the possibility of freedom and equality, for, as Governor James Henry Hammond of South Carolina wrote, "We have to rely more and more on the power of fear." They argued that slavery was a positive good for everybody involved; then they went out of their way to say that slavery had been thrust upon the South by necessity and by England, that they and their ancestors bore no direct responsibility for slavery's implementation, only the burden of making it function as well as possible. Finally, and most importantly, they argued that blacks as a race are naturally slaves of whites—and that, in the absence of black slaves, given the nature of modernity, the majority of whites would naturally, inevitably, become slaves themselves.

Is it too much, then, to say that slavery's advocates foundered in their arguments precisely on the realization that whites were not different from blacks? That, at least, they were not different enough from blacks in what mattered most—the capacity, right, or wish always to be fully human and not a thing? "We need never have white slaves in the South," George Fitzhugh wrote, "because we have black ones . . . We have introduced the subject of negro slavery to afford us a better opportunity to disclaim the purpose of reducing the white man anywhere to the condition of negro slaves here." The pro-slavery men, seeking, through logical argument and historical reflection, to posit the good of absolute racial separation, had ended by demonstrating the basic commonality of the races. And if they accepted this, without quite stating it, we may suspect that they felt that what they were doing was wrong. They blamed slavery on chance, England, necessity, historical circumstance. They desperately ransacked the Bible to find comfort for slaveholders. They admitted, unlike Northerners, that their social system as such sheltered evils, averring only that every human system did, and what man could take the place of God to determine which balance of goods and evils was best? They wrote, to take the words of Harper, that the tie between master and slave was "one of the most intimate relations of society"—that, as Fitzhugh urged, the white Southerner was "the negro's friend, his only friend."

If we put these varied thoughts together, the perception that blacks and whites were fundamentally alike, the recognition of evil's existence in society, the harried thumbings of the Bible, the ineffectiveness of economic rationalizing, and the stirring need to think of the interracial relationship as one of intimate friendship—if we join these as aspects of a unified view, we might penetrate a little further into the white mind as expressed in the 1850s, in the South. Professor Albert Bledsoe, of Thomas Jefferson's cherished University of Virginia, was possibly the least restrained and least clever of the pro-slavery writers, which makes him particularly valuable. In *Liberty and Slavery*, after a rambling condemnation of abolitionism as a form of radical socialism—a common Southern equation at the time, with socialism or communism often understood as the ultimate form of wage-slave capitalism—Bledsoe slopes into a discussion of human equality as sin:

> When Lucifer, the great bearer of light, himself was *free*, he sought equality with God, and thence became a hateful, hissing serpent in the dust. But he was not fully cursed, until "by devilish art" he reached "the organs of man's fancy," and with them forged the grand illusion that equality alone is freedom.
>
> For even sinless, happy Eve was made to feel herself oppressed, until, with keen desire of equality with gods, "forth reaching to the fruit, she plucked, she ate:"—
>
> > "Earth felt the wound, and Nature from her seat,
> > Sighing through all her works, gave signs of wo,
> > That all was lost."
>
> How much easier, then, to effect the ruin of poor, fallen man, by stirring up this fierce desire of equality with discontented thoughts and vain hopes of unattainable good! It is this dark desire, and not liberty, which, in its rage, becomes the "poisonous snake;" and, though decked in fine, allegoric, glowing garb, it is still the loathsome thing, the "false worm," that turned God's Paradise itself into a blighted world.

Here is a Southern cousin to Hawthorne's Goodman Brown. Poor, fallen man, thrashing about in a blighted world—not his home, but a howling wilderness. It was the wish to be like God that made us fall from grace and led nature to sigh at the loss. Bledsoe appears to believe that white people are these already fallen beings, and that the desire of blacks for equality with whites, if realized, would draw them into the miserable godlike white race—would destroy their innocence, make them as guilty as whites. Equality, then, would bring them into that last abyss, the abyss this pro-slavery professor associates with whiteness, where they might find for companionship one Bledsoe in his torment.

THE ETHIOPIAN OPERA

WHITE MASKS IN BLACKFACE MINSTRELSY

■

The sweating nights of Albert Bledsoe alternated with the warm and happy days of minstrelsy. The white association of black slaves with childlike innocence and, ultimately, with freedom reached its furthest development in minstrelsy. We may be surprised that slave society gave birth to a form of comedy. The terror of whites that they could become nonwhite had in it so many possibilities for tragedy. American racial history certainly possessed "all ills that there are names for," as Sophocles' messenger says in announcing Oedipus's blinding of himself. Aristotle believed that true tragedy pivoted on the making of a mistake, a "missing of the mark." The writer of tragedy moves his protagonist through a series of incidents, each building logically on its predecessor and consistent with the protagonist's dearest values, until a moment of reversal or recognition, when the protagonist realizes that he has fundamentally misapprehended his situation. Usually, he comes to understand that he has failed to identify someone in the story as a person he loves—most often a family member. By his actions he has caused that beloved person great pain. He has not done this because he is evil. The mere chronicling of evil could have no tragic profundity. Rather, the tragic protagonist is a normal, good man who has strayed unknowingly from his values and hurt the person he ought to have loved—hurting, of course, himself as well. Sometimes the protagonist's realization of his mistake comes too late, and the terrible damage is done.

In the finest tragedies, however, according to Aristotle, the protagonist recognizes what has happened. He has a chance to rethink the past—the linked series of events and humane values—before committing the final mistake, say the murder of a brother, mother, or child. This rethinking is not quite the same as replacing bad thoughts with good, or apologizing. The tragic protagonist in Greek drama always, for the most part, does good; he acts consistently with his values and has nothing to apologize for. It is the plot itself, rooted in the past and the fundamental misapprehension or mistake, that does the rethinking for him—enabling him to recognize a sister, for example, where previously he has seen an enemy. In tragedy this is a matter of actions, not words. Plot "is the principle," Aristotle wrote, "and, as it were, the soul of tragedy, while characters are second." It is with plot, what normal people actually do in the wending of a mistake, that "tragedy attracts the soul." And for the tragic protagonist to become a hero he must grow large with the past, not in recognition of his guilt but in recognition of reality of what happened, not what he thought. His heroism will likewise be manifest in action, not atonement, for atonement, in this tragic view, would be simply a repudiation of the past and so a mis-recognition of the real significance of events—possibly, just another mistake.

History as such is not tragedy, a point Aristotle emphasized. Yet there does seem to be a certain misapprehension in our American story so far, a mistake having to do with race. We might characterize this misapprehension as being the idea of racial incompatibility, or the idea that human inequality can be ordered in the categories of race. This misapprehension presides over a series of events in which protagonists act, more or less, according to their principles— mainly, in our case, principles of individual freedom that, owing to the mistake, constantly issue in racial separation. Incidents accumulate with a certain logic. Much harm is caused by the protagonists to people whom they might have recognized as family. But the moment of tragic recognition seems never to arrive. Guilt, certainly, and regret, and fears for the future, and pity for the dead, and self-pity. But how much true recognition? The tragic drama, in the classical sense, of racial separatism seems never to reach catharsis, that is, the casting out of collective fear through profound recognition.

There was no indigenous tragic theater of note in white American society in the first half of the nineteenth century. Whites chose comedy. In great numbers they chose minstrelsy, a comedy of the grotesque, of sentimental romance and social satire—comic solutions to a tragic dilemma. White people blacking their faces to enact racial dramas was itself hardly new. We have already observed the case of *Titus Andronicus* and the spectacle of a darkened Queen Anne, in 1605, bodying forth as a daughter of the river Niger. However, black dramatic characters presented "as blacks"—that is, being clearly distinguished from white characters by something other than skin color, land of origin, or historical circumstance—

was a later development. By the late eighteenth century two black racial stereotypes had established themselves on the English stage: the noble, suffering slave
(often speaking the King's English), and the ignorant, sympathetic fool-slave
(often using dialect). As early as 1768 Charles Dibdin's *The Padlock* had great
success in London: Dibdin himself was an impersonator of blacks. His play,
based on a Cervantes story, followed David Garrick as *Hamlet* on its premier
bill; it later had an American run. To a degree, these plays, and popular songs,
gained energy from British abolitionism. For example, "Yankee Doodle; or, The
Negroes Farewell to America":

> *Now farewell my Massa my Missey adieu*
> *More blows or more stripes will me e'er take from you*
> *Or will me come hither or thither me go*
> *No help make you rich by de sweat of my brow*
> *Yankee doodle Yankee doodle dandy I vow*
> *Yankee doodle Yankee doodle bow wow wow.*

More often, black characters in British theater and song were simply darkened
white servant characters, speaking what was thought to be West Indian slave
dialect—that is, a more interesting, because of its novelty, version of a white
stereotype.

American theater producers continued to import British plays and songs
after the Revolution, and with them the black characters they portrayed. The main
post-Revolutionary development in such works appears to have been the linguistic parody of pretension. Blackface characters, speaking in "dialect," increasingly imitated and mangled high-flown speech—a black or blackface comic
role that would last into the television era. But indigenous American minstrelsy,
while drawing heavily on British elements, had its origins more along the Western frontier and in the Northern cities, and not until the creative, nationalistic
period of the late 1820s. The British characters of suffering slave and (more
commonly) slave-fool were joined by the bragging frontiersman and the urban
dandy. These were, significantly, white stereotypes of white people. The wild
men of the frontier—Mike Fink, the fictionalized Davy Crockett, the unbound
braggarts of the Mississippi River waterfronts—provided the rudiments of Jim
Crow and Gumbo Chaff, the earliest developed minstrel roles. "I wip de lion ob
de west," sang Jim Crow, "I eat de allegator / I put more water in my mouf / Den
boil ten load ob tator." A man who could boil bushels of potatoes in his mouth
was someone to reckon with—the frontier hero, this magnificent, frightening,
childish fool. Where Davy Crockett claimed to be "half-horse, half-alligator,"
Jim Crow sang, "My mammy was a wolf / My daddy was a tiger." Early blackface dances—the famous breakdowns, the double-shuffle, chicken-flutter,

pigeon-wing, jig dancing—were also popular white frontier dances, while the tunes were nearly always "white" music, usually with antecedents in Britain.

As blackface entertainers in the 1830s found larger audiences in the growing cities of the Old Northwest and, especially, the Northeast, Jim Crow was joined by Zip Coon, the urban dandy. Zip Coon developed in tandem with the white Bowery Boy, a strutting citified frontiersman. Both boasted of having unchecked power over the ladies (as did Crockett and Jim Crow), but Zip Coon was different: he wore blue tails, sported a lorgnette, and drew meaningful distinctions between "nigga" gentlemen such as himself and "common niggas." With his specious claims to scholarship and silly use of big words, he was a more intensely self-deceived character than the rougher frontier types—and less important on the minstrel stage. Zip Coon was the closest of the minstrel roles to an actual figure of white apprehension, namely the free urban black. (An 1811 Zip Coon song was titled "The Free Nigger.") But, in terms of content, minstrelsy's energy came from white fantasies about black life, rather than black life as such, which may well explain why Zip Coon took a backseat to characters based on slaves (whom minstrel audiences rarely, if ever, saw) and half-alligator frontiersmen (who had never existed at all).

White fantasies about black life: it would be more accurate to say white fantasies about white life as portrayed by blackface actors, for minstrelsy was a conversation white culture had with itself. The actors were white, the audiences were white, much of the material was white, and even some of the originary stereotypes were white. Therefore, in examining minstrelsy, we may hope to learn something about how white people understood the meaning of race in their society. By the 1840s blackface minstrelsy had developed into the first distinctive white American theatrical form—and arguably, the last one—a form that commanded large white audiences from New York to San Francisco, from the White House to the slums.

The themes underlying minstrelsy are freedom from work and expressive freedom more generally. It would be later be argued that minstrelsy, by portraying black slaves as basically happy in their condition, was a popular dramatic version of the slaveholders' position that blacks were cheerful servants designed by nature for menial work and white domination. This argument falters on many grounds. To begin with, early minstrelsy was often antislavery. The popular song "Lucy Neal" concerned a happy slave couple torn apart when the husband is sold:

> Oh, dar's de wite man comin, To tear you from my side;
> Stand back you wite slave dealer, She is my betrothed bride.
> De poor nigger's fate is hard; De wite man's heart is stone.
> Dey part poor nigga from his wife, An brake dar happy home.

Minstrelsy's Northern and Western audiences had little, if any, fellow feeling for slaveholders; their legislators steadily resisted or abolished slavery. While slaveholders did maintain that slaves were happy, minstrelsy tended to portray slave happiness as a result of opportunities for laziness, which was quite the opposite of what slaveholders wanted in slaves. Minstrelsy also celebrated slaves' cunning, thievery, selfish trickiness, thirst for liquor, irresponsibility, and talent for making fun of, sometimes humiliating, their masters. Again, these were not the qualities a slave owner was likely to seek, or to brag about. Finally, if minstrelsy was meant to dramatize the rightness of slavery, we would have to ask: Where's the comedy in that? People rarely find anything deeply funny in the lives of those completely different from them—not night-after-night funny such that, as with minstrelsy, tens of thousands of white people would give up hard-earned money, over a span of decades, to attend theaters in every sizable town from Boston to Sacramento. Whatever one may say of pro-slavery arguments, they were not very funny, and could not have been the wellspring for a comic art. It is important to note that minstrels did not often, particularly as the form developed, use the words *slave* and *slavery*. This cannot have been due to minstrels' fear of giving offense. They specialized in giving offense. Coarseness was their calling. Yet they did not say, in blackface, "Dere's nuttin' bettuh fo' dis nigga den bein' owned fo' life." In minstrelsy slaves were not usually slaves. They were white men in blackface acting out roles for the entertainment of white people in, so to speak, whiteface.

What were those roles? They were, in fundamental respects, the opposite of actual slavery. Minstrels acted as characters with a great deal of leisure time, usually in a rural environment where the weather was always good and crops didn't fail. In the sentimental portions of the program they displayed strong family ties and ached with love for the man or woman of their choice. Their lives were remarkably stable and free from great worries. In the broader portions they deceived each other and their masters in the struggle for small advantages—that bottle of gin, that gal's company for the night. They did not hate their masters. Sometimes they loved them. More often, they simply tried to deceive them. Punishments were not severe. Black characters were treated like children, not slaves.

If this world was not slavery, then what was it? This was the world minstrel-show audiences had left behind, or thought they had left behind—a combination of happy farm life and childhood. They had left it in favor of towns and cities, places that were non-rural, unsentimental, and unstable, places built on abandonment of the past, where worries were great and one did not like one's masters at all. Punishments were severe. Or, out West, they had left the supposedly idyllic rural life—in many cases, the South—for hard farmwork in new lands, away from slavery. Minstrelsy, then, was a peculiar form of nostalgia. At its least restrained, minstrelsy communicated all the riotous joy of toddlerhood: the players were in constant fidgeting motion, interrupting each other, getting into harmless fights, scrapping over toys. They had the egotism of children, the delighted single-minded selfishness. They worried little because there was little to worry about. Massa and Missey were always there with light work and food. So one had the freedom to do what one liked, babble and cry and wheel about. In their dances the minstrels showed a new wildness of movement that played at chaos, a reeling ecstasy. In their songs and patter they introduced extended gibberish to the American stage, a cataract of absolute nonsense that harmonized with something deep in their white audiences.

Dan Emmett called it machine poetry. An Ohio man who, with three others, had formed the pathbreaking Virginia Minstrels, Emmett was among the giants of minstrelsy. Thin, angular, his blackened head planted atop him like a ball, Emmett would take a single tone from a simple melody and babble upon it, spewing barely connected words in a monotonous delirium. His biographer Hans Nathan describes Emmett's pose on an English song sheet, from about 1844, titled "History ob de World":

> Seated at his writing desk, he appears, with open eyes staring into the void and a long quill tensely held between his thick Negro lips, as the very image of inspiration. Around him are books with such facetious titles as *On Colour, The Dark Ages*, and *Blackstone*, and a jar labelled "Nigger Health"; in the background loom the busts of Byron, Shakespeare, and Scott. In view of the machine as the contemporaneous symbol of inventiveness and progress, "machine poet" might mean "poet and genius of the age." "Machine poetry" is his product . . .

It makes sense that a nostalgic art would parody progress, and that a democratic, popular theater would lampoon pretension. Minstrels produced many an "Ethiopian" opera, satirizing high culture to a fare-thee-well. They "Africanized" *Hamlet* and *Othello, William Tell*, the story of Damon and Pythias, and many another sacred text; Emmett once performed in "Old Uncle Ned or Effusions from Lord Byron." Minstrels were not slow to seize on, for example, Alexandre Dumas's *Camille*, with its sad portrayal of star-crossed lovers. In the new version Camille, as played by a white man with a black face, rues her fate—"Oh, Camille! You that was once the pride of the ball-room, and the envy of the envied; now pining away in a sick chamber for want of nourishment"— then explains her future to her beloved Armand, familiarly called Army: "Army, the jig is up—my mutton's cooked—I'm a gorner, Army—Army, I'm dying." Minstrels made fun of doctors and lawyers and any other professional or intel- lectual; they warned of the dangers of city life, such as con men, trolleys, and electricity. In the characteristic "stump speeches" and "larned" interjections they made a hash of high thought: "Transcendentalism is dat spiritual cognoscence ob psychological irrefragibilty, connected wid conscientient ademption ob incolumbient spirituality and etherialized connection—which is deribed from a profound contemplation ob de irregability ob dose incessimable divisions ob de more minute portions ob subdivided particles ob inwisible atoms . . ." But the thoughts, like Emmett's machine poetry, did not need to be high. They could simply be insane, "anapulated in de clarion tones of de clamorous roos- ter, de insignification of de—de—de—de hop-toad am a very big bird—du da—du da day—does it not prove dat where gold is up to a discount of two cups of coffee on de dollar, dat bolivers must fall back into de radience of de—de— anything else . . ."

A correspondent for *Putnam's Monthly*, writing in 1854, pointed out that while the "attempt to establish an Italian Opera here, though originating with the wealthiest and best educated classes, has resulted in bankruptcy, the Ethiopian Opera has flourished like a green bay tree." The writer described this flourishing in an intriguing fashion: "The only places of Amusement where the entertainments are indigenous are the African Opera Houses, where native American vocalists, with blackened faces, sing national songs, and utter none but native witticisms." Native and indigenous? Then why the blackened faces? Why did white American opera have to be African to be native American? One might assume that white American culture in isolation lacked the ability to entertain itself, even to understand itself.

Prewar minstrelsy, then, illustrates the impossibility of white American racial separatism at a deep imaginative level. The chief paradox of blackface minstrelsy is that it was acclaimed for bringing "black" people into precisely those parts of the country, the Free States, that didn't want black people. At the exact historical moment when "white America" was a rising notion, and calls for a white man's country came from the lips of any populist politician who wanted to fill a fairground—the period when states and territories with but a trembling handful of dark-skinned people still concocted laws to exclude them, even whipped them to the border—this was when white men with blackened faces thrived, to the entertainment of thousands. Having rid themselves, or so they hoped, of black people, whites couldn't wait to see them. From a much later perspective, we might think that minstrelsy appealed to these whites because it gave their self-love a boost. They could think, "I may be a wage- worker in the city, and a little thickheaded in my honest way, but at least I'm not like that, at least I'm not black." And minstrelsy did fulfill that simple psychological function. However, *I am not like that* could hardly be the sum of a native, indigenous, national art. We must look a bit further to find what made the minstrel heart beat.

The United States during minstrelsy's heyday was a nation expanding, consolidating, and defining itself—and falling apart. Minstrelsy grew up as the national art form that most thoroughly expressed these processes and attempted, in its way, to heal their contradictions. In minstrelsy white Americans found the freedom to imagine themselves. A Baltimore man, later a minstrel, recalled the night after his first boyhood show. "I found myself," he said, "dreaming of minstrels; I would awake with an imaginary tambourine in my hands, and rub my face with my hands to see if I was blacked up." The dream of minstrels was a dream of childhood, innocence, and racial wholeness. It seems that this dream could be artistically and satisfyingly realized only by white men pretending to be black, which meant, of course, that it could not be realized. Its dramatization was simply the best that white American culture could do for itself, under the circumstances.

Prewar minstrelsy was autistic, a flight from reality into hallucination, a theater not at all far from psychosis. Many thousands of people came to watch a blackened white man dance, dribble, and drool like an infant. These thousands were, to a degree, *like that*, when they found themselves dreaming of minstrels. In his biography of Emmett, Hans Nathan begins with an epigraph from John Bunyan: "Then read my fancies; they will stick like burs, / And may be, to the helpless, comforters." White Americans were helpless in many ways, not the least of which was that they fought tooth and nail to preserve their racial supremacy while knowing, somewhere, that their whiteness was itself an empty vessel—a culture without content, a social position that depended on nonwhites for its sense and therefore could never make sense in itself. Being white, in isolation, was senseless; the nonsense of minstrelsy proceeded from this psychological point, and the babbling infant was its child. The delirium of minstrelsy must indeed have given comfort to the helpless. But it is also true that the minstrel's fancies stuck like burrs.

The fundamental senselessness of being white, and the feeling of being helpless before it, only increased in the 1850s. White America was slouching toward John Brown's raid and the sound of guns before Fort Sumter, and minstrelsy, following its own strange logic and that of its raving, catcalling audiences, responded by growing more chaotic and more authentically black. It became more sentimental, and more violent. The antislavery elements dropped away; happiness and racial wholeness reigned on the minstrel plantation. Audiences demanded the complete illusion of real Africanness from their "Ethiopian delineators," and minstrels went south to research the thing in itself, returning with fresh material. The plotline of these years was propelling white Americans toward the completest misery, that of self-destruction and the murder of kin; their need to see racial happiness in the comic theater increased accordingly. The white need to believe that race was real, that it meant something, apparently intensified in these years just before the war. There had been identifiably black elements in minstrelsy from the beginning, particularly in the music— minstrels sang blue notes, favored the minor tonic, and noticeably preferred the offbeat. The improvisatory structures of minstrel music likewise do not seem to have any counterparts in British or white American music and so, presumably, were black. But in this later period Emmett's cakewalk, more or less directly African in origin, became a staple of minstrelsy, and minstrels boasted of lifting routines, sounds, lyrics, and dance moves directly from what they had observed in the South. White audiences, mainly outside the South, now needed to believe that the black race was a real and distinct category of being. They craved racial authenticity—for themselves. They craved racial innocence, but, like Albert Bledsoe, they realized that, because they were white, they could never be racially innocent. And so they hired white men in black faces to be the stand-ins for their missing innocence—to be racially happy for them. They wept, then, over the loss of this black past, the only form of racial happiness they could imagine.

It has been said that comedy reinforces social norms. Comedy points out folly so that folly can be avoided; it portrays deluded characters so that we may recognize our own delusions. The comic character proceeds from self-deception to self-understanding—or at least, we in the audience make this progress. In this respect, prewar minstrel comedy was a complete failure and a completely American one. It did not reinforce social norms so much as displace them. The whole premise of minstrel comedy was that you the white person were both the same as the minstrel character and completely different from him, given that his skin was black and yours white. The comedic conflict was yours—you identified with the minstrel then—but the resolution was not. Indeed, the resolution of the comedic conflict in minstrelsy was precisely that you were not black. This meant that minstrel comedy could not issue in self-understanding. On the contrary, it perpetuated the delusion that you could never be black, which is to say that your white color had meaning. This resulted in an intractable bafflement at reality. Minstrelsy couldn't resolve the conflicts that drove it, and neither could minstrelsy's audiences.

The contradictions involved here—the profound failure of minstrelsy—can be seen in the wanderings of that famous song "Dixie." Announced initially as "Dixie's Land" or "Way Down Souf in Dixie," it was a minstrel tune that Dan Emmett wrote for the New York City stage in 1859, a nostalgic song about a free black person in the North returning to the slave South. Minstrel songs advocating the return of black people to the South, as their natural home away from the perils of freedom, had become a standard feature by the mid-1850s. And in as pure a paradox as history is likely to offer, this black homeland of bondage was understood as the land of freedom. In the year before "Dixie" a blackface Emmett had sung of his decision to head south, "I'm bound for de land of freedom/oh, niggars! fare you well." The paradox was as pure as the trap white American culture had set for itself. As white minstrel audiences imagined individual freedom in a racially hierarchical society that reckoned a person's worth in money terms—and called their system the truest expression of human liberty—they constructed this figure of the fully racial person (the black man) choosing slavery as freedom. The nature of this man's freedom was that he could be happily, innocently racial, free to be himself, free from failure and the risks faced by white minstrels' white audiences, free from the exquisite modern pain of having to negotiate the price of his own life and carry it around in his pocket like a rosary without a string—so many beads for me. Minstrelsy had become a semiconscious parody, from a white point of view, of American liberty. The future hymn of white racial self-determination was sung in blackface dialect: "In Dixie Land I'll took my stand / To lib an die in Dixie," and "I wish I was in de lann ob cotton / Ole time darr am not forgotten." Emmett first sang it as part of his "walk 'round," probably the most African part of his shows.

"Dixie" caught on immediately. All the New York minstrels picked it up, adding their own lyrics as ambition and occasion demanded. In 1861, or a little before, a New York journalist wrote, " 'Dixie' has become an institution, an irrepressible institution in this section of the country." In May 1861, weeks after Beauregard emptied his guns on Fort Sumter, a Southerner reported that the song had "spread over the whole South. Considered as an intolerable nuisance when first the streets re-echoed it from the repertoire of wandering minstrels, it now bids fair to become the musical symbol of a new nationality." Union soldiers sang a version of Dixie into 1863. So did Confederate soldiers, with many new words and the dialect replaced by standard English. In this way white men marched singing to their deaths under the flag of racial comedy, and a blackface melody of impossible racial freedom became the nostalgic anthem of soldiers pitching into the unrestrained, monotonous gibberish of war.

One other important group of pre–Civil War white people remains to be considered: the abolitionists. Although there had been antislavery agitation from early times, and particularly around the Revolution, an organized mass of people with a national program did not appear until the late 1820s. Characteristically, the new abolitionism grew up in opposition to another program with which it had some things in common, and which it perceived as too weak and misguided; abolitionism was born in a fraternal split. It emerged from a disgust with the American Colonization Society among some of the society's supporters—Theodore Weld, James Birney, and, most importantly, William Lloyd Garrison. Garrison's break with black colonization, early in 1830, marked the beginning of abolitionism. In critiquing Henry Clay's recent pro-colonization address, he hit at the colonizationists' acceptance of racial inequality:

> The episode, at the commencement of the address, relative to the persecuted Indians, is replete with tenderness, truth, humanity, justice—spoken at an eventful crisis, and calculated to unite many discordant views. One cannot help remarking how much more freely Mr. Clay breathes in defending these poor red men, than in speaking of the Africans. Yet his notion about the *natural* physical and intellectual superiority of the whites over the Indians, is unphilosophical and absurd. I deny the postulate, that God has made, by an irreversible decree, or any inherent qualities, one portion of the human race superior to another.

This conviction led to Garrison's founding, in 1831, of the *Liberator*, which he edited from Boston, and the formation, in 1833, of the American Anti-Slavery Society. The clear, simple principles of racial equality, complete citizenship, and an end to slavery quickly foundered on the reluctance of Northern whites to accept them. (The abolitionists, unlike their Revolutionary predecessors, never made much headway in the South.) The jealous localism typical of Americans hardly helped; a northern Illinois chapter would not easily take suggestions from, say, a southern Illinois outfit, much less march to the dictates of high-handed Boston. On the ground abolitionist organizers often found themselves hedging. James Thome wrote to Theodore Weld of his February 1836 adventures before a Lyceum audience in Akron, Ohio:

> First I was particularly careful to *disclaim* certain things which are confounded with abolitionism; such as social intercourse, amalgamation, etc. I further stated that we did not claim for the slave the right of voting, immediately, or eligibility to office. Also that we did not wish them *turned loose*, having the possession of unlicensed liberty; nor even to be governed by the same *code* of Laws which are *adapted* to intelligent citizens. That on the contrary we believed that it would be necessary to form a *special code* of Laws restricting them in their freedom, upon the same general principles that apply to foreigners, minors, etc. By the time I had

got through with the *negative* part of the subject, my 20 [minutes] were up.

The abolitionists—many, such as Thome, were not long out of youth—clung to their own moral spotlessness. They thought like conspirators in a holy war. They therefore pictured their enemies, who were many, as conspirators, too. They often pictured their friends in the same way. Garrison was himself a cheerful extremist who issued denunciations with a free hand. His principled fierceness was his strength; it forced others to define themselves against him, to measure their own compromises against his refusal to compromise. It also left Garrison to define himself against others, and to define others as compromisers.

In 1837, just four years after the American Anti-Slavery Society's founding, the abolitionist movement was showing signs of factionalism. The serious splits began in 1840, essentially over the problem of political involvement. Some abolitionists wanted to enter party politics, even to field candidates. Garrison's position, however, was that the movement would only be corrupted by such means. Abolitionism, he had written in 1837, needed to limit itself to "the fire and hammer of God's word":

> As to the governments of this world, whatever their titles or forms, we shall endeavor to prove that, in their essential elements, and as at present administered, they are all Anti-Christ; that they can never, by human wisdom, be brought into conformity to the will of God . . . and that the followers of Jesus should instinctively shun their stations of honor, power, and emolument—at the same time "submitting to every ordinance of man, for the Lord's sake," and offering no *physical* resistance to any of their mandates, however unjust or tyrannical. The language of Jesus is, "My kingdom is not of this world, else would my servants fight."

Garrison urged that all Christians were "obligated to come out NOW, and be separate from 'the kingdoms of this world,' which are all based upon THE PRINCIPLE OF VIOLENCE."

The logic of come-outism and separation from worldly power led radical abolitionists to advocate Northern secession from the United States. Garrison and his followers held to this position from the early 1840s until the Civil War. Garrison never could adequately explain why secession by the Free States would not also be an abandonment of slaves to their fate. The come-outers did believe that an orphaned South would not be able to sustain itself or the slave system; the economic interests of the border states would pull them northward, undermining slavery. The Southern system would then collapse. What form that collapse might take, no one could say, and the Northern secessionists preferred not to dwell on the possibilities.

A further paradox of Northern secession was that it would have created, in effect, a white country—in the name of antislavery. That was not the abolitionists' intention, though even among the Massachusetts radicals one could find signs of antiblack feeling. Nevertheless, there was a certain resemblance between Free-Soil white supremacism and the radical abolitionist call "No Union with Slaveholders." The same practical result could be arrived at by following opposite principles. Free-Soilers also believed slavery would die a natural death in an isolated South. And there was some congruence between the fears of radical abolitionists and those of white-rights Free-Soil men. Both feared the possibility of slavery for themselves. But the Free-Soilers, to a great extent, rejected slavery for themselves on the ground of whiteness. The abolitionists, by contrast, rejected whiteness as a human irrelevance, a nonidentity.

This abolitionist rejection of whiteness, premised mainly on biblical doctrine of common humanity, had two signal difficulties. It led some abolitionists to emphasize that white people, being in essence no different from black people, could also be slaves. This was not a wise strategy for converting undecided whites to the doctrine of equality; their fears of becoming black, or unfree, tended to drive them away from a belief in common humanity, not toward it. The second difficulty of abolitionist anti-whiteness was that it entailed antiblackness. If white skin was irrelevant, then black skin was as well, and white abolitionists, somewhat gingerly, urged black abolitionists not to form black groups or hold colored conventions. Some black leaders, mainly in Philadelphia, also advocated this approach; others responded that when their color seemed unimportant in society, then they might consider making it unimportant to themselves. Until that time prudence, the voices of one's ancestors, and the realities of racial slavery and white contempt demanded that one remain black.

The radical white abolitionists basically maintained that if they were not acting white, then others should not act black. This raised the questions of what it meant to act white and of who could determine when somebody was acting white. As to the first, white abolitionists seem to have thought that acting white meant acting against blacks. As to the second, they evidently felt they could determine for themselves whether they were acting white or not. It was an altogether neat psychological business, very much resembling religious conversion, though it lacked reference to a second party (such as God) or to any strict code of verifiable conduct, acting as proof of conversion, such as one finds in religions. One could simply decide not to have a race, and so to be fully human; one could cleanse oneself of racial thinking before a jury of one or a few.

It could hardly escape the attention of nonwhites that this racial self-cleansing was something of a privilege. A white person might tell himself he had no race, and the world around him, if only by its silence, would probably do nothing to threaten his personal decision. A person not white, making the same decision, would face disbelief at best. This difference simply reflected the different positions of white and nonwhite with regard to determining the meaning of skin color or race. Whites had vastly more power than nonwhites to establish and enforce the meanings of race. More to the point, whites had the power to say race had no meaning at all; and nonwhites did not have that power.

The pain of this situation was especially acute in the context of slavery. Blacks, slave or free, had a sharp historical experience of the meanings of race, most of which had operated against them. That experience had led them as a group, and to an extent as individuals, to their present condition. To be told by a white person that one's racial experience had no great importance as such, and ought to be shed in the name of God and universal humanity, might reasonably have been regarded as a dismissal of one's life. In an abolitionist context it would have amounted to an acceptance that whites and blacks faced slavery on equal terms. The beyond-race principle lacked a historical element. Perhaps that is in the nature of a principle. But in the case of race in America it could have strange consequences, because race, being itself historical, resists ahistorical explanation. Indeed, a purely principled approach to race has impossibilities all its own, which in principled minds may create a pressure that could be relieved by making one's principle so large as to crowd out historical reality. For example, one might believe in racial equality enough to decide that it actually existed. Or one might take the principle of racelessness so far as to imagine that centuries of racial experience were actually centuries of consistently unfortunate coincidence.

Something like this occurred in radical white abolitionist circles. It may have been inevitable. Radical abolitionists came from a milieu keenly interested in human perfectibility, starting with themselves, and such a faith does tend to export fault for reasons of principle. One might say that only New Englanders would have thought of morally purifying the nation by withdrawing from it, or of "abolishing" slavery by casting it without the walls of the city of God. Besides, by 1850 it had become the white Southern habit to argue from history—to honor local ways of life and regional peculiarities, to meditate on the burdens of the past, as well as its glories—and the Yankee enemy, in battle, would naturally take the opposite tack, away from history and so into perfection. There was a tradition of that in the North; these were the terms by which many abolitionists could motivate themselves. However, it was all very well to hurl thunderbolts in a southerly direction—what about oneself? Certainly, abolitionists recognized the existence of white racial arrogance in their own communities. Yet the examples of it always seemed to lie outside the abolitionist camp. After all, racial prejudice was against their principles. Race itself was against their principles. And so it did not exist. Whatever content there was to race should and would pass away with the institution that had created it. Here lay the seeds of the most traumatic split within abolitionism: the break between Garrison and Frederick Douglass.

Almost from the beginning of his great crusade, Garrison had played on the theme of racial interchangeability. In his pivotal speech at Boston's Park Street Church, in 1829—he was twenty-four years old—Garrison asked the (white, by racial custom) congregation, What if "the slaves should suddenly become white"? The following year, penned up in a Baltimore jail, he wrote, "It is my shame that I have done so little for the people of color. A few white victims must be sacrificed to open the eyes of this nation, and to show the tyranny of our laws. I am willing to be persecuted, imprisoned and bound for advocating African rights, and I should deserve to be a slave myself, if I shrunk from that duty or danger." Garrison was a spectacularly brave man of principle. He was as strong in his principles, including the principle that race did not matter, as anyone in the abolitionist movement. Yet it does jar a little to hear him talk of being enslaved. He was never going to be enslaved. That was much of the point of being white, and Garrison was white—except in principle.

The condition of being subject to enslavement was not a condition of principle, or a natural condition, but a historical one, and the Garrisonians sometimes lost sight of this. They wanted to start over, make the past disappear into insignificance—the American racial past as a whole, the black past, and the white past—but one had to wonder which aspect of this disappearance was most important to white abolitionists. The lurid ferocity of the radicals' attacks on Southern whites, and the abolitionist advocacy of Northern secession, at least suggest a type of purification ritual in which the white North would be absolved. An abolitionist "Moral Map" from 1855 shows the South covered in black and the North all white. Logically speaking, shouldn't it have been the other way around? After all, the evils of slavery in the United States were, to an overwhelming degree, caused by white people acting as white people. True, the color black had conventional associations with evil. But if any white group should have been able to see the dangers of that association, wasn't it the abolitionists?

The beyond-race principle indeed provided a subtle way to continue an association of blackness with wrong. If one accepted that all good people (good Christians) had no race, then to "act black" was to step away from the desired purity. And for the Garrisonians acting black, in its threatening form, meant acting as if one's blackness, as a historical experience, gave one greater moral authority on racial questions than a white person of otherwise similar qualities could ever have. This was simply a confusion of matters from the radical white point of view, a failure to recognize the levelness of the playing field. It dragged historical experience, in the body of a black person, back into a realm of moral principle which had sought to exclude that very experience.

For abolitionists, and Garrisonians in particular, Frederick Douglass was the preeminent black body. "I was generally introduced," Douglass recalled in 1855, describing his early days as an antislavery speaker, "as a '*chattel*'—a '*thing*'—a piece of southern '*property*'—the chairman assuring the audience that *it* could speak." After his first great speech in Nantucket, Douglass wrote, "Mr. Garrison followed me, taking me as his text." Douglass was asked, he wrote, to imitate a certain type of black person, with something of the plantation and not too much philosophy—a type that abolitionists hoped to make extinct over time. He was, in a sense, expected to conspire in his own disappearance, to represent a historical figure, the heightened yet typical black slave, who would be gone when slavery was gone, and the blackness of both would be gone, too. Douglass, then, was expected to be *temporarily* black. Given that his white abolitionist friends were, in their opinion, no longer white—they had gone beyond that—Douglass's temporary blackness made him, as a matter of logic and principle, inferior. The projected end of his inferiority was to be the end of his history as a black man.

When Douglass broke with Garrison it was over the policy of disunionism. At the annual meeting of the American Anti-Slavery Society in May 1851, Douglass surprised his colleagues by announcing that he no longer believed Northern secession was a solution. His announcement had been prefaced by some jousting with the prominent white abolitionist Edmund Quincy. Quincy had characterized the South as "impudent." The word shook Douglass, particularly coming from a man who had once tagged him and another black abolitionist as "unconscionable niggers." Douglass toyed awhile with "impudent," saying he and his people knew about impudence and that he might take a different view of such judgments than would Quincy, because Quincy "was white, whilst he was black." This marked Douglass's departure from Garrisonian thought. Douglass was not going to move beyond race just yet, and didn't believe his white friends had either. They were still white. It was, ultimately, a question not of prejudices or bad thoughts but of reality and history, what people do rather than what they think. It makes sense that the issue at hand was disunionism. Northern secession was, so to speak, a thought in place of an action. Fighting slavery within the Union was an action. Secession aimed at ending racial history, while fighting slavery sought to transform it.

From this point Douglass began explicitly to defend black slave culture as legitimate and to defend blackness as an element in the full humanity of a person, in this case Frederick Douglass. When the conflict with Garrison finally boiled over, in 1853, these were precisely the terms of its expression. When

Garrison attacked Douglass as an "unscrupulous schismatic" who ought to behave better toward those "to whom he is eternally indebted for his emerging from obscurity," Douglass replied that Garrison ought not to expose "a fugitive slave to open shame." The implication that a slave might have a special moral claim enraged Garrison, who suggested that such "sufferers" might have suffered so much that they could not perceive clearly what the abolitionist cause required. Douglass responded by saying that Garrison's idea sounded like the "natural inferiority" argument in a different guise. In this way Douglass let the greatest white abolitionist in our history know that the racial past had a claim even on him. Principle alone could not solve the difficulties between them, or between North and South.

The radical abolitionists were exceptional white people. They keenly felt their minority status, and sometimes gloried in it. "Every principle we have laid down," Wendell Phillips noted in an 1853 speech, "has been denied by overwhelming majorities against us." This remained true down to the war. Looking at the nation as a whole, we can see that the attachment of white people, in all regions, to their own whiteness only intensified in the prewar decade, as did their desire to impart social significance to the darkness of others' skins. In this sense, white America was growing closer, in racial terms, prior to the war. The trend in the South was toward a tightening of racial distinctions and slave bonds. The border states and upper South talked of re-enslavement—or black colonization, possibly backed by the threat of re-enslavement. The condition of free blacks in these regions visibly deteriorated through the 1850s. In 1859 Arkansas passed a law requiring all free blacks either to leave the state or to be sold, with benefits from sales going to the state's schools. Missouri and Florida approved similar bills in their last sessions before the war; most other Southern and near Southern states were considering them. While these efforts had little practical effect—popular white opinion seems to have found them barbaric, particularly re-enslavement—they did reflect the rising pressure on racial thinking. Meanwhile, the North and West continued policies of racial exclusion, furthering the association of freedom with whiteness. The abolitionist doctrine of equality did gain adherents, but in a somewhat quiet way and against a backdrop of factionalism. Antislavery sentiment certainly grew, but it took anti-Southern and, relatedly, antiblack forms. And so as tensions rose, so did the fortunes of an antislavery political party that was also committed to white supremacy, that is, the Republican Party of Abraham Lincoln.

Frederick Douglass had succinctly described the Republicans in an 1855 speech. "The next recognized anti-slavery body," he told a Rochester audience, "is the Free Soil party, *alias*—the Free Democratic party, *alias*—the Republican party. It aims to limit and denationalize slavery, and to relieve the Federal Government from all responsibility for slavery. Its motto is, '*Slavery Local—Liberty National.*' The objection to this movement is the same as that against the American Anti-Slavery Society. It leaves the slaves in his [*sic*] fetters—in the undisturbed possession of his master, and does not grapple with the question of emancipation in the States." The Republican distancing from emancipation grew along with the party's power. In 1860 Abraham Lincoln's key ally William Seward could characterize the Negro as a "foreign and feeble element, like the Indian . . . a pitiful exotic"; an Iowa Republican slogan that year ran, "We are for land for the landless, not niggers for the niggerless."

The Republicans' opponents nonetheless argued that the party would bring about racial equality. Stephen Douglas of Illinois, in his senatorial campaign debates with Lincoln in 1858, had played hard on this theme. He styled Lincoln and the Republicans as abolitionists to the core, indeed as "black Republicans" whose whiteness was only skin-deep. (Republican activists responded in kind, with the epithets "Mulatto Democracy" and "Black Democracy.") Lincoln, Douglas said, believed that "the negro was endowed by the Almighty with the inalienable right of equality with white men":

> Now, I say to you, my fellow citizens, that in my opinion the signers of the Declaration had no reference to the negro whatever when they declared all men to be created equal. They desired to express by that phrase white men, men of European birth and European descent, and had no reference either to the negro, the savage Indians, the Fejee, the Malay, or any other inferior and degraded race, when they spoke of the equality of men. One great evidence that such was their understanding is to be found in the fact that at that time every one of the thirteen colonies was a slaveholding colony, every signer of the Declaration represented a slaveholding constituency, and we know that not one of them emancipated his slaves, much less offered citizenship to them, when they signed the Declaration . . . Instead of doing so, with uplifted eyes to heaven they implored the divine blessing upon them, during the seven years' bloody war they had to fight to maintain that Declaration, never dreaming that they were violating divine law by still holding the negroes in bondage and depriving them of equality.
>
> My friends, I am in favor of preserving this government as our fathers made it.

Douglas was the voice of moderation. He believed the Union would be split by war unless each state were left to decide racial questions on its own; and he wanted to preserve the Union. Douglas continually forced the racial-equality issue on Lincoln, sometimes on the high level of statesmanship, sometimes on the low one of sexual innuendo. When Lincoln finally took the bait, he did so on both levels:

> I will say then that I am not, nor ever have been in favor of bringing about in any way the social and political equality of the white and black races, [applause] — that I am not nor ever have been in favor of making voters or jurors of negroes, nor of qualifying them to hold office, nor to intermarry with white people; and I will say in addition to this that there is a physical difference between the white and black races which I believe will for ever forbid the two races living together on terms of social and political equality. And inasmuch as they cannot so live, while they do remain together there must be the position of superior and inferior, and I as much as any other man must be in favor of having the superior position assigned to the white race. I say upon this occasion I do not perceive that because the white man is to have the superior position the negro should be denied everything. I do not understand that because I do not want a negro woman for a slave I must necessarily want her for a wife. [Cheers and laughter.] My understanding is that I can just let her alone. I am now in my fiftieth year, and I certainly never have had a black woman for either a slave or a wife. So it seems quite possible for us to get along without making either slaves or wives of negroes. I will add to this that I have never seen to my knowledge a man, woman or child who was in favor of producing a perfect equality, social and political, between negroes and white men . . . I will also add to the remarks I have made, (for I am not going to enter at large upon this subject,) that I have never had the least apprehension that I or my friends would marry negroes if there was no law to keep them from it, [laughter] but as Judge Douglas and his friends seem to be in great apprehension that they [Douglas and his friends] might, if there were no law to keep them from it, [roars of laughter] I give him the most solemn pledge that I will to the very last stand by the law of this State, which forbids the marrying of white people with negroes. [Continued laughter and applause.]

Lincoln, like Douglas, believed racial decisions should be left to the states. He differed in portraying the slave states as expansionist. He drew a picture of slavery extending itself north and west, impoverishing free white people in the process and undermining their liberty as citizens and men. Unlike his opponent, he emphasized a firm policy of containment and argued that slavery would die a natural, if perhaps prolonged, death as a result of its failure in competition with white labor in free states and territories. As for ex-slaves, whose numbers in this scenario certainly would increase, they could evidently be kept in an inferior status by state laws and excluded piecemeal. And, of course, Lincoln had hopes for voluntary colonization in Africa, Central America, Haiti, anywhere but here. He lost the Senate race to Douglas but defeated him two years later in the contest for president. Some Southern states took this as the moment to secede, and soon the war began.

General Robert E. Lee surrendered his Virginian army to the Union on April 9, 1865, effectively ending a war that took the lives of more than 600,000 soldiers and wounded another half million, most of whom would have considered themselves white people and would have been considered white by others. The following morning President Lincoln, who would be dead in less than a week, was serenaded by a crowd before the White House. He greeted his well-wishers with some brief remarks, then added, "I propose now closing up by requesting you to play a certain piece of music or a tune. I thought 'Dixie' one of the best tunes I ever heard . . . I had heard that our adversaries over the way had attempted to appropriate it. I insisted yesterday that we had fairly recaptured it . . . I ask the Band to give us a good turn upon it."

What an intriguing choice, so obvious yet so psychically intricate: a tune written and sung by a white man imitating a black man, a nostalgic song about an imaginary racial freedom and innocence. A song that stroked white racial happiness by portraying black racial happiness, thereby demonstrating the impossibility of either, and the dependence of each on the other. Lincoln was toying with the song as a prize of battle. But wasn't "Dixie" also toying with him? After all, what really had been the point, in racial terms, of the Civil War? Given that the white consensus in all sections, going into the war, had favored white supremacy, how had the war altered that consensus? It is strange indeed to imagine the North's victorious president, the morning after Lee's surrender at Appomattox, whistling "Dixie." When, in wartime, Frederick Douglass met with Lincoln to discuss postwar civil rights, Lincoln had made it clear he didn't want anyone to be able to say that the war had been fought by white people on behalf of the Negro—as indeed it wasn't. In 1876, at a dedication of a Lincoln memorial, Douglass said of the late president, "In his interests, in his associations, in his habits of thought, and in his prejudices, he was a white man." What did that whiteness mean after this mysterious war?

The most obvious new element after 1865 was the absence of slavery. White people everywhere had associated blackness with slavery and whiteness with freedom. Now it was becoming clear, somewhat haltingly, that blacks would no longer be slaves. This raised, at least subliminally, the question of what, if any, distinction came with the possession of white skin. Whiteness had lost its anchor in a clear social status—racial freedom—which raised again the specter of racial sameness, even of human equality beyond race. In principle, this might have led to a wholesale abandonment of race ideas and the discovery of a previously unguessed egalitarianism waiting patiently in some recess of the American heart. This did not happen. There was, of course, no strong tradition on which to build. Moreover, the white South faced a tremendous labor problem—how to make the ex-slaves keep working—a problem that white Southerners spontaneously understood in racial terms as the challenge of keeping blacks working for them. And, finally, the radical Republicans in power at the North adopted racial terms for articulating their own desire to punish the Confederacy. Both sides—both white sides—chose the fate of Southern blacks as the key issue of political battle. One might say that the Civil War was a relatively nonracial preliminary to the race fight of Reconstruction.

Race provided the social form in which North-South political struggle made sense to those involved. Three formerly Confederate states had black majorities, while two others, under radical Reconstruction rules disfranchising ex-secessionists, had effective black majorities. Because Tennessee had already been readmitted, this meant that, in 1867, half the recalcitrant old Confederacy had black-majority voting populations. The Northern radicals in Congress believed that the white South would never extend full citizenship, or even something close to it, to black people unless forced to do so. They were probably correct in this assumption. Certainly, the white South had rounded on the freed-slave population even before the war had ended and soon passed Black Codes intended to keep all blacks, including those free prior to the war, in a subordinate position. The Ku Klux Klan and Knights of the White Camelia, the White Leagues and Red Shirts were the terrorist companions of such legislative initiatives, enforcing white power with rifle and firebrand. Southern blacks themselves had withdrawn very rapidly from white society after emancipation, forming racially separate institutions and preferring to work poor land in freedom than rich plantation land under the rule of a white landlord. The average ex-slave tried to get away from whites as well and quickly as he could. Radical Reconstruction did little to slow this rush toward separatism. In a way, Reconstruction exacerbated it, because the radicals were, to some degree, using Southern blacks to punish the white South—and, along the way, ensuring white Northern domination of the country as a whole. Reconstruction did have a racial divide-and-conquer aspect.

At the same time, some Northerners genuinely wanted to help the four million former slaves get a chance for themselves—acquire property, learn to read and write, be free from the fear of arbitrary murder, rape, or mutilation because of their skin color. Reconstruction had some success in this regard. Within a few years after the war, black per capita income relative to that of whites nearly doubled. A massive public-education effort benefited both whites and blacks: in 1876 more than 50 percent of white children and around 40 percent of black children were being educated in (nearly always segregated) schools. However, the Southern economy as a whole was stagnant or shrinking, which meant that the elevation of a group that had had nothing—former slaves—came at the expense of the group that had had everything, namely Southern whites. Over the course of Reconstruction the percentage of blacks who owned land increased from nearly nothing to 20, while white landownership dropped by 13 percent. Such redistribution of lands and income did not occur *because* people happened to be black or white. Land redistribution on a racial basis was derisory; the former slaves never did receive their promised forty acres and a mule. State-directed income redistribution was nonexistent. Nor was blacks' advancement a result of their working harder than whites. They worked less as free laborers than they had as slaves; their work hours were rapidly slipping down to white levels. In short, the racial redistribution of land and income did not come about for racial reasons as such. It came about because most blacks had not been paid for their work prior to 1865, and now that had changed. Redistribution resulted from blacks' change in class status—and slave owners' change in class status.

But if the alteration in Southern economic relations was not, strictly speaking, a racial event, it definitely could be understood that way. This white Southerners chose to do, particularly those who had the most to lose—and everything to gain by racializing class relations. The Southern elite needed other Southerners to work hard enough to generate a surplus that could support the elite. Before the war slave labor was all but entirely the source of that surplus. The postwar South offered a more complicated picture. Initial efforts at practical re-enslavement ran up against Reconstruction governments, federal occupation armies, and the manifest unwillingness of blacks, even in the face of the Klan and all it symbolized, to submit. The reassertion of the Southern white elite then proceeded on several fronts: control of political power, money power, and brute force. The Southern elite, whether the old plantation master or the local grocer/lender, once again addressed a labor problem with a racial solution. One-party rule, by Democrats, spread across the region. Force, persuasion, and law conspired to keep blacks from voting. Whites with money lent it along racial lines. The dispersal of former slaves onto lands of modest fertility enabled local whites, even those with very slight capital, to tighten the reins of credit (in goods as well as money) with remarkable speed. For most small farmers of whatever skin color, all it took was one bad year, if that, to put oneself in a debt to the local potentate that could never be repaid. Judicial and police power, shading effortlessly into quasi-public terrorism, was kept by whites and for whites: they were ferocious on this point. The Scottish romances of Sir Walter Scott had at last become socioeconomic textbooks as the South adopted a thorough feudalism.

Relations among Southern whites likewise underwent some innovation after the war. If white lower-class fears of becoming a thing, rather than a human being, had driven racial feeling in slave days, those fears could only have grown in a new world where the slave-person distinction no longer held. Light skin was a slender enough charter for full humanity back when blacks were slaves. Now blacks were neighbors and competitors, with powerful Yankee friends. Moreover, it was soon obvious that one's white social superiors were mobilizing to secure their own social dominance through the use of blacks. (In some localities the bosses encouraged black voting to block lower-class whites from dominating the party.) Southern blacks were shaping up as a client class under the old masters, and under an increasing population of new white masters pushing their way up—in the classic pattern, by buying a chunk of someone else's former plantation. At the same time, the previous restraints on white terrorism— mainly the desire of individual owners to protect their personal human property—had disappeared, and with them whatever brakes had existed to prevent the wholesale identification of whites with other whites, across class lines. In this context the bonds of war (and collective defeat) tightened the racial bonds of colonel and captain with their foot soldiers. Bested in war, the white South became more military in peace, and racially more militant. When industrialization did arrive, mainly in textile manufacture though also in metallurgy and raw-material extraction, it took over this military quality. The term *captain of industry* had a pure meaning. And the new industrial jobs were overwhelmingly, sometimes bloodily, reserved for whites. The redistribution of wealth from white to black lasted a decade at most, then stopped with a thunderous finality.

In the South, then, the postwar decade brought a strengthening of the racial bond among white people (and among blacks). Tied to blacks by circumstance and need, they tried in most every way to become a separate race, pouring the residuum of prewar economic status into a racial mold. No lever of power was too small for whites to grasp. However, in line with American racial tradition up to their time, Southern whites, even *in extremis*, remained unable to attribute much content to whiteness in itself. Theirs was an interestingly minimal whiteness, as may be seen in the mania for protecting white Southern women from rape by black Southern men, a mania that would wax with the century. Whatever else may be said of this complex, "no raping" is surely not the slogan of a confident culture full of purpose. Of all the things a culture might insist on preserving as central to itself, the freedom of its female half from sexual violence by outsiders is only a few steps advanced from insisting that outsiders not be allowed to slaughter innocent children at will. That it should be insisted on at all indicates the poverty of the culture in question, in this case that of white Southerners. So even as whiteness was being refined into a social category of towering importance, it amounted, in itself, to very little. Once white supremacy had been reinvigorated and the white Southern ship righted on its sea of black labor, the white South could turn its attention elsewhere.

Much the same thing occurred in the North. The interest of Northern and Western whites in their own nature as white people diminished with arresting speed after the war. As long as there was some subjugation of Southern whites to be done—as long as some important disagreement existed within the white world—then the racial question retained a certain power. The only other activity that made white people concerned with their own whiteness was a threat to it from outside the race, but such threats were small in the North, and in the racially exclusive West they came more from Indians and, mainly along the coast, Chinese, rather than from blacks. So as the war receded and the white South refined its power over blacks, the North paid less and less attention to racial matters.

We can see this in the development of minstrelsy. Minstrels had got measurably whiter by the 1870s, their performances less distinguishable from the variety troupes and Barnum extravaganzas touring the nation. Faced with the rising threat of girlie shows, minstrels responded by ceasing to imitate blacks and learning to imitate women. Minstrels had always been men-only, for the most part; that is, men played the female roles. But after the war female impersonators as such became major drawing cards in the minstrel theater. White Northerners no longer wanted to see blackened Jim Crow dance a jig; they wanted to see the famed Leon, also billed as "the Only Leon," batting his eyelashes and displaying the latest Parisian fashion. The raging Indian wars of the 1870s also produced Indian minstrelsy, a more bloodthirsty form than the prewar Ethiopian shows: the Indian farces often ended in massacres, perhaps the first appearance of ritualized murder in popular American comic entertainment. (Indians had been nobler folk in prewar minstrelsy.) Minstrelsy also adapted to its audiences' interests in urban immigrant communities. A catalogue list of "Ethiopian" plays from 1870 included "The Dutchman's Ghost"— "Jacob Schrochorn, the jolly shoemaker and his frau, are rare ones for raising a hearty laugh"—and another in which "[t]wo of the parts can be played in either white or black, and one in Dutch. Costumes Yankee and modern." Minstrelsy could batten on any ethnicity remotely known to its audiences, as shown by the brief career of "The Flying Black Japs" soon after Appomattox. Irish roles were common, Chinese somewhat less so. In 1877 Bret Harte and Mark Twain wrote a play about "the Chinaman," who Twain thought was "going to be a great political problem." But he proved not to be as big a draw as the Irishman or the German, much less the Only Leon.

Ethiopian acts continued to appear, but they had become one novelty among many. Northern blackface minstrels, sensitive as ever to their white audiences, found themselves dramatizing a double nostalgia: for happy prewar plantation days down South, and for the old-style blackface minstrel shows. Blackface minstrelsy had itself become a focus of nostalgic yearnings, an extreme example of American culture's apparently intractable need to think of life as coming after the Fall—not just the fall from grace in the Garden of Eden, long ago, but the fall from a better past whose distance from the present could be measured in months. Old Dan Emmett was periodically brought back for blackface revivals, but in a reduced capacity. The babbling, innovative intensity of prewar blackface, based on deep, nearly uncontainable audience desires, was replaced by a rather lifeless plantation ideal, innocently isolated from the present. The old comic rage now reclined beneath the magnolia and the weeping willow. Race no longer mattered as much. It was safely away in the South. Southern whites had succeeded, by the late 1870s, in reducing the millions of Southern blacks to immobility. They were not coming North. The white North and white South had made their bargain by 1877. White Northern race activists, such as Charles Sumner, had decided to leave well enough alone. The abolitionists had long since, with unseemly haste, folded their tents. That well over four million American citizens were effectively abandoned to serfdom and subject to random terror because of their skin tone meant remarkably little to their white co-citizens at the North, or even their Yankee helpers at the South— not to mention growing numbers of investors with old homes in New England and money in Georgia. In light of these developments, it seems less strange that Lincoln chose "Dixie." Whites North and South would be reconciled. The burdens of white racial consciousness would be, to an extent, pushed south, contained there—a victory of sorts for Free-Soil and Northern purity on the Moral Map. "Dixie" would be localized, a white Southern song of militant nostalgia;

indeed, the South would become known as Dixie. Many a black or pseudo-black artifact of prewar minstrelsy would reappear as a cherished item in the white American repertory—the songs of Stephen Foster, for example. The Northern white talent for forgetting, and the Southern white gift for combining forgetfulness with fantasy, would reach full speed by the 1880s. The early minstrels had actually had something to tell white people about themselves, at a time when they were prepared to listen. In 1873 Dan Emmett got back up on the stage in New York to deliver a "Negro sermon" on the theme of how people who expect nothing from life are blessed, because they won't be getting anything. Emmett ran through a series of oppositions between black and white, emphasizing the derivative nature of whites, both as people and as economic actors. "De niggar hoes all de corn an gits all de lickins, an he massa sells de corn an keep all de proffits": an echo of a slave song, "We Raise de Wheat," that Frederick Douglass included in his 1855 memoir. After explaining that Adam and Eve, Cain and Abel, were black, the darkened has-been minstrel identified the Devil: "dat dar white man settin in de corner laffin!" But the time for even such introspection as this had passed. The questions someone like Dan Emmett raised were no longer of interest to his old audience. The widespread need of everyday whites to imagine themselves as black had disappeared.

"OLD RACIAL CRIES,

OLD RACIAL TIES"

■

And yet the presence of nonwhites continued in American life and in some ways increased. Whites pursued various strategies of elimination, containment, and assimilation. From the Indian hunts of California to the battles and massacres of the Northwest, Great Plains, and Southwest, white (and, sometimes, black) Americans reduced the native populations to fragments that could be corralled onto reservations. The children of racially mixed unions—it's impossible to say how many there were—might merge into one or another population. People of Spanish-imperial ancestry went any number of ways, from perilous lives in Texas to prominence in New Mexico to disappearance (strictly speaking, whiteness) in California—and every combination of these. Chinese immigration was encouraged by some whites (employers) and hated by others (workers who had to compete with Chinese labor). This being a democracy, the majority eventually won; Chinese exclusion was made law by a series of congressional acts between 1882 and 1892. Blacks remained more or less cordoned in the South, with the exception of the Kansas Exodusters and the hopeful settlers of the Oklahoma and Indian Territories. Black life continued in the Northern and Midwestern cities but was increasingly marginal as European immigration swelled the urban population. Whites wrestled with whether the Irish, Germans, and others were actually white; the dominant opinion held that they were, if somewhat differently so.

Overall, the last quarter of the nineteenth century saw what we might call a consolidation of racial role-playing, its elevation into spheres of social science, art, law, and historical understanding. Nonwhite racial roles gradually slipped their moorings in social caste—slavery by 1865, Indian tribal freedom in the two anguished decades after the war—such that racial thinking came, more and more, to depend only on its own circular logic for validation. The nineteenth-century social sciences provide a fascinating spectacle of an elite class attempting to extract from circumstance a genealogical destiny. The basically white-supremacist terms of this attempt had already been set before the war and were undisturbed by the revelations of Charles Darwin. His *Origin of Species* did destroy the theory that races had separate origins, but that raised few obstacles to a belief in racial hierarchy. One could simply switch from a "polygenic" conviction that races were fundamentally different to an "evolutionary" view that some were more evolved than others. Darwin himself recognized differences among races but resisted giving them significance in his great work. His influential cousin Francis Galton, by contrast, coolly argued in 1869 that, for example, "The average intellectual standard of the negro race is some two grades below our own." Galton believed instances of "the inferiority of the white man" were few indeed. He coined the word *eugenics* to describe the breeding of higher stocks of human beings, as well as the phrase "nature and nurture." He was also a pioneer of mental testing.

Such a belief in biology as destiny seems to have filled a void within the American elite. The English philosopher Herbert Spencer's application of Darwinism to human societies provided the impetus for the founding of American sociology. Spencer divided racial intelligence into "complexity" and "mass," the latter being something like forcefulness of mind: the "dominant races overrun the inferior races mainly in virtue of the greater quantity of energy in which this greater mental mass shows itself." Such ideas had tremendous power and were adopted, in one form or another, by the pioneers of American social science. In some cases, as that of our first great political scientist, Francis Lieber, the Americans had a jump on Spencer. Lieber wrote in 1859, "We belong to that race whose obvious task it is, among other proud and sacred tasks, to rear and spread civil liberty over vast regions in every part of the earth, on continent and isle. We belong to that tribe alone which has the word Self-Government." The difficult truth is that few American scholars dissented from these views—they were part of the foundation of modern social thought among white people.

The Civil War did nothing to undermine white faith in white destiny. The opposite seems to have been the case: as the nation coalesced between 1870 and 1900, regional differences gradually yielded to a general whiteness. A belief in racial, often "Anglo-Saxon," destiny permeated the educated white classes and seems to have received passive assent among those with little or no education. In its strongest form, from Francis Lieber (who later recanted) through the Social Gospel prophet Josiah Strong and on to Theodore Roosevelt, militant Anglo-Saxonism tended to blend cause and effect: whites dominated because it was their nature to dominate. What would a belief in this require? First, there could be no debate, because one could not disprove a racial idea in its own terms. If whites failed to dominate, it was because they had failed to be sufficiently white. Thus the intense worry about racial mixture. The answers to racial questions (such as explaining white failure) had to be racial answers, otherwise racial thinking as a whole ceased to function. Second, there could be no free will. If an individual's racial destiny or responsibility was to embody his or her raceness, then self-realization became the same as self-obliteration, and oneself a mere instance of the race, individually faceless and helpless. Finally, being in a naturally dominant race raises the question: What is the purpose of other races? Are they to be dominated forever? Or is the final goal of racial struggle the complete mastery of oneself as a white person—that is, ceasing to need the other races to define oneself; that is, in the case of a naturally dominant race, eliminating all others?

The purpose of the United States has frequently been understood to be the creation of the purest human liberty. So we should pause to consider that a very popular belief of the American majority in the latter part of the nineteenth century—that white people were destined to dominate other races—held within it the demise of human liberty in the name of the white race's freedom to be itself. This dismal and somewhat contradictory philosophy is not necessarily rescued by the usual list of Anglo-Saxon virtues: the "liberal institutions and common law full of manly rights and instinct with the principle of an expansive life," as Lieber put it. If these were specifically racial virtues, then their transference to other races became problematic if not impossible. White domination or expansive separatism then became identical with the growth of human freedom and liberal institutions—for whites. White domination had incorporated this idea previously, but it included the forms of religious conversion and assimilation to a "higher" civilization. Such forms of uplifting integration were what went missing after the war.

Lieber's choice of *manly* to describe rights is important here. Militant Anglo-Saxonism took as its moral impulse a hatred of "sentimentality," a sense of unpleasant duty in humble obedience to the higher race cause, itself the cause of humanity, racially understood. One needed, as the cliché went, "the strength of the strong" to carry out the white task in "the struggle for existence" that led to "survival of the fittest" (two of Herbert Spencer's phrases). By 1871 Darwin had decided that the "wonderful progress of the United States, as well as the character of the people, are the results of natural selection," and he endorsed the remarks of one Reverend Foster Zincke: "All other series of events—as that which resulted in the culture of mind in Greece, and that which resulted in the empire of Rome—only appear to have purpose and value when viewed in connection with, or rather as subsidiary to . . . the great stream of Anglo-Saxon emigration to the west." Similar thoughts had often occurred to the Revolutionary generation. Now, however, they were explicitly racial. Their tie to an Enlightenment universal humanity and Christian doctrine had snapped. One might say universal humanity and whiteness had fused; whiteness was no longer a stage along the way but the thing itself.

Yet there remained those sentimental whites who thought otherwise. What was the nature of white racial sentimentality? It had two leading aspects. The first was a cultural or racial relativism. Ethnologists such as Lewis Morgan, Henry Schoolcraft, and John Wesley Powell found something worthy of preservation in Indian cultures, for example. This was sentimental in that it kept the Indians in a state beneath that of whites (the perfect human state of liberty and rights). It therefore did them a disservice, an act that could only be blamed on misplaced sympathy. It was also sentimental in that it preserved an economically inefficient society, which is, obviously, a weak and irrational thing to do. The second aspect of white sentimentality had to do with shrinking from the required hardness of mind. Some uncountable number of white Americans apparently thought that running about crushing other races was simply not appropriate. However, if they accepted the doctrines of secular, material progress, human perfectibility, and white supremacy, as most whites did, then it was difficult to say why, exactly, white violence against others was wrong.

Nevertheless, recourse to a rhetoric of strength did imply some dim racial misgiving. If white domination really was natural, inevitable, decent, and just, then presumably whites would not need to set their jaws and steady their hands when firing the fatal shot. Lynching and massacring ought to have required no more girding of the soul than did weeding the garden. Yet clearly the strong needed their peculiar strength. For whites, white supremacy could be demanding, a burden as well as a blessing. Did it sometimes hurt to kill, or to be associated with killers by the happenstance of birth? Did one sometimes look at one's pale hands in fresh wonder? Perhaps the surrender of one's personal liberty implicit in acting white required a type of strength—the strength to submerge oneself among the strong, trading one liberty for another.

Certainly one can see the attraction of everyday separatism as a social tool for avoiding what, ideologically, appeared a racial fight to the death. The institutionalization of informal racial segregation—leaving aside the long-standing segregation of Indian tribes—had begun well before the Civil War. Massachusetts had a segregated train by 1841, and its Supreme Judicial Court validated racially separate public schools in 1850. The pace of segregation picked up in the 1860s. Two hundred forty-two California blacks petitioned Congress in 1862 to colonize them "in some country in which their color will not be a badge of degradation": "It seems to be the settled policy of the nation . . . to discountenance in every manner the increase of persons of color in their midst." In 1863 and 1864 California officially segregated its public schools. (Legal segregation of Chinese and Japanese in the Golden State system would continue to 1929; blacks and Indians were integrated many years earlier.) Pennsylvania's supreme court approved segregation of trains in 1867; Ohio's supreme court upheld school segregation in 1871, Indiana's in 1874. The federal Civil Rights Act of 1875 outlawed racial segregation of public spaces, though not of public schools. (A clause against school segregation, kept by the Senate, was struck by the House.) The U.S. Supreme Court, however, ruled in 1883 that the act was unconstitutional. The majority opinion in *Civil Rights Cases* worried that enforcing integration would itself be racially discriminatory, but against whites, in that it would make blacks "the special favorite of the laws." Judicial argument on schools generally held, and would continue to hold, that it was legal to discriminate *between* or *among* races but illegal to discriminate *against* one or more races—racial separation without racial prejudice. As to private institutions such as railroads, hotels, and restaurants, it was argued that the state had no right to interfere with the power of property owners to determine who could use their property or how they could use it. In short, sophisticated pro-segregation (or anti-desegregation) arguments rested on conceptions of freedom, including the freedom to discriminate. In a situation such as ours, where the governing and property-owning classes were overwhelmingly of one race, whatever distinctions were made were likely to favor that race. Such had been the pattern, and formalized segregation reinforced it.

Segregation was in some ways spurred by a sense of racial competition, in particular competition in towns. Racial life in village and countryside proceeded somewhat informally; both cruelty and social peace occurred on a first-name basis. In older cities with large black populations, such as Charleston and New Orleans, established patterns of racial coexistence prevailed. But in Northern and Western cities, most with relatively small nonwhite populations, whites experienced the terms of racial engagement as unclear. Even a tiny number of blacks (and, on the West Coast, Chinese), pushing their way upward from the servile class, could threaten the racial order—suggesting, one more time, the fragility of whiteness. And white workers were, as ever, sensitive to the use of nonwhites as a semi-client population available to employers hoping to keep wages down, which is to say, most employers. With some exceptions formal segregation advanced southward as towns grew in such newer, formerly rural states as Mississippi, Florida, Texas, and Alabama. The older Southern societies in Virginia, the Carolinas, and Maryland were the last to develop thorough segregation. (Virginia waited until 1900.) In very broad terms, institutionalized segregation spread from the North and West to the South and was the creature of new, anxious white middle classes rather than of racial traditionalists. It was a symptom of social insecurity, not the seizing of some racial opportunity the white elite had failed to notice in the past.

One could see it as a form of self-determination: the races would be free to develop themselves fully in their own spheres. In order to preserve their privileges, whites had to make their race more manifest, to become "more white" as they went about their daily activities of riding streetcars, drinking at water fountains, and using the toilet. Whiteness had never before had such a twenty-four-hour public quality to it. And it does appear that this visible separatism, with its almost miniaturist logic, failed to ease the psychological pressures of being white at that time. Perhaps it worsened them. Formal segregation not only focused one's daily attention on race in general, it specifically brought attention to the racial body. In a sense, it heightened racial intimacy, one's awareness of the tactile bodies of others, and of one's own. The newer segregation laws concerned physically intimate spaces and things: beds, forks, cups, water fountains, toilet seats, telephone mouthpieces. Segregation, in its baroque period, so often had to do with things you put in your mouth and places where you were naked or physically exposed. From the heights of electoral office holding and public education it dove with neurotic energy into our most private functions as animals. White people were reducing themselves to racial beasts. They were doing this to others, but we should never forget that they were also doing it to themselves.

It would seem that segregation in the 1880s and 1890s was a symptom of some white racial failure. After all, nobody outside the white race was prodding whites into segregation. It is true that blacks in the same period increased their pace of self-segregation into racial institutions, but this was an effect of white segregation and discrimination, not a cause. One factor was the rise of a black middle class—the growing prosperity of some urban blacks—but the scale of that growth, relative to white wealth, remained so small that it is hard to imagine it as the basic motive for a wide-ranging social transformation. Besides, racial segregation had benefits for black businesspeople. It protected them, to a degree, from competition with whites, who otherwise had all the business advantages. Fear of a black middle class makes even less sense than the Reconstruction fear of Negro rule; to the extent that it animated white minds, it did so for racial rather than class reasons. The lack of extra-white explanations for segregation becomes even clearer when we consider the rise in lynching and the justification for it. The number of reported lynchings of black Americans steadily increased after 1884, from 51 in that year to 113 in 1891, with a slight dip in 1890. The number stayed over 100 for seven of the next nine years. The leading justifications for lynching highlighted black criminality and in particular a black male drive to rape white women and girls. No one has yet demonstrated that either of these racial propensities existed, much less why they would have increased after 1890. Indeed, given the nature and ferocity of white retribution, one would have to have been insane to rape a white woman. The raping by a black man of a white woman, then, was at once the most common justification for lynching and, in all probability, the one least likely to be true. Given segregation, it should have become still more unlikely. Like segregation, lynching was something whites did for reasons largely, if not entirely, in their own minds. They did not segregate because of what blacks did, and they did not lynch because of what blacks did. They did these things for themselves.

The similar, and similarly unlikely, natures of lynching and segregation suggest that whiteness lacked the power to convince whites of its validity, and so demanded ever more pathological demonstrations. Clearly whites were having difficulty understanding what made them different—what their skin meant—as they turned to more desperate means of enforcing that difference. The hopelessness of their task is illustrated by the fact that their strategies kept creating sameness. Both lynching and segregation had at their hearts a perverse mirroring. In segregation the white world doubled itself; it created a mirror. Seeking to establish a racial difference, whites ended up demonstrating sameness. With lynching they railed against black bestiality and proclaimed their racial triumph over it. Yet at the exact time when lynching became a public white spectacle— a broadly collective racial affair—whites engaged in the most bestial acts imaginable, and did so *as whites*. Put differently, they gave meaning to their whiteness by committing ultimate acts of animal transgression, which was exactly the behavior they attributed to their victims, rather, to their victims' blackness. They fought each other at the stake to cut off some part of the body of the lynched man (or, less commonly, woman). A white man or woman or child would take this fragment of a black body home as a trophy—keep it there, possibly display it. If the body had been burned, he or she would take home ashes.

In this system of difference as sameness—a white world created by white people in which they did nearly everything black people did, or which they *thought* blacks did—the major real difference was power. Perhaps this is the explanation for segregation and lynching: whites had power and would do anything to keep it. The problem with this explanation is that what white people did was so wildly out of proportion to any actual threat. Lynchings had occurred for many decades, not just in the South. But only after 1890 did people travel to them in specially hired train cars, follow them in the newspapers, buy souvenir photos and read souvenir pamphlets and mount trophies of the black dead. Unless we assume that a sizable portion of white Americans had simply lost its hold on sanity, we must look elsewhere for explanation than to an exaggerated defense of racial privilege.

The clue must lie in the nature of white racial power itself and the historical conditions in which it found expression. As we have seen, white fears of non-white sexual, political, and economic competition had been part of the white imagination for many decades and had normally found expression in imaginings of rampant sex between black men and white women, of slave revolts, Negro rule, blacks' exceeding whites in their natural ability to work, and employers' preference for black labor. From the Jacksonian period onward, white politicians had used all of these as valued political currency, up to and through the Civil War. However, in white minds, white power as such, after the war and emancipation, came to depend upon whiteness of a purity unknown prior to the conflict. Religious mission, Enlightenment civilizing, the sheer propulsion of land-grabbing in the drive to the Pacific—these had lost either their mental purchase or their purpose by the 1890s. The loss of a physical frontier threw white Americans back upon themselves. It made their whiteness problematic in a way it had not previously been. And whites reacted by refining their racial activities into the most implausible and unrealistic forms. That whites should have become most white, so to speak—most attached, judging from their actions, to the importance of their skin color—at the moment when their racial victory was most complete, that is, the 1890s, seems perverse in the extreme. Yet that is what happened, and it suggests that racial "victory" harbored within itself a type of impossibility. Like a religion that gets its energy from anticipation of the Last Days, whiteness was doomed to disappointment on its own terms.

The white racial mission as expressed among the elite was a mission of mastery—mastery of other races and, relatedly, mastery of oneself as a white man, an almost mystical self-ownership or self-determination, an ultimate form of liberty. It is telling, in this regard, that so many white commentators of the 1880s and 1890s perceived a *decline* of self-mastery. Here stirs the unquiet ghost of John Locke and his insistence that full human selfhood consists of complete ownership of oneself as a type of property. In 1887 E. L. Godkin, himself an immigrant, wrote of white men before the Civil War, "An American citizen who wrought with his hands in any calling was looked on, like other American citizens, as a man who had his fortunes in his own keeping, and whose judgment alone decided in what manner they could be improved." Now, however, there "has appeared in great force, for the first time on American soil, the dependent, State-managed laborer of Europe, who declines to take care of himself in the old American fashion." A failure to "take care" of themselves was also a common criticism of blacks. "Instead of clamoring for aid and assistance from the white race," Frederick L. Hoffman wrote in an 1896 book sponsored by the American Economic Association, "the negro should sternly refuse every offer of direct interference in his own evolution . . . Most of all there must be a more general recognition of the institution of monogamic marriage and unqualified reprobation of those who violate the law of sexual morality." In the same year that Macmillan published Hoffman's study, General Francis A. Walker wrote that newer immigrants "have none of the ideas and aptitudes which fit them to take up readily and easily the problem of self-care and self-government, such as belong to those who are descended from the tribes that met under the oak-trees of old Germany to make laws and choose chieftains." Needless to say, blacks also had not met under the old oak trees. (Walker taught history at Yale, once supervised the U.S. Census, and at the time of the above remarks, in the *Atlantic Monthly*, was president of the Massachusetts Institute of Technology.)

One problem with understanding self-mastery as a racial quality was that it simply couldn't work in a multiracial society. Thus a person might turn to morbid racial thoughts. It also could not work in an industrial economy, which necessitated various forms of dependence. Neither had it truly functioned before the Civil War. Without underestimating the reality of democratic individualism, we know that there were governments prior to the war, and powerful institutions and social classes, all of which acted as brakes on individual liberty. More important for our purposes, ownership of the self in Godkin's sense had been a white and male privilege, the privilege of a minority. And we have seen how the dependence of self-mastery on the condition of whiteness embodied a contradiction: that your individual freedom was an unearned inheritance, indeed a coincidence in which you had no role except acquiescence, and so was not individual freedom at all nor self-mastery. It was, in fact, conformity. It did give one mastery over others, and so one naturally took this second, conformist racial mastery as a substitute for self-mastery or complete selfhood in the Lockean sense.

This could have the unfortunate effect of leading you, as a white male, to perceive any threat to your individual freedom as, at some level, a racial threat. Alternatively, threats to the white race could be perceived as threats to your individual freedom. Life, as it happens, is filled with dangers to one's individual freedom. Some kind of constraint is ubiquitous to life outside of dreams. And because whiteness consisted essentially of arbitrary power, it, too, faced constant threats. Now, if one were to accept in oneself this white worldview, the likely results would include social hysteria, paranoia, fury, a deep sense of incompleteness and failure, a longing for a world in which one's high status was natural, unforced, inherent in something unalterable and mysterious even to oneself (such as blood)—and, when one realized that this longing could not be fulfilled outside of dreams or fantasy, one might turn to thoughts of death.

These were among the leading elements in Mark Twain's short and painful comic novel of 1894, *Pudd'nhead Wilson*. It was the only one of his works that Twain labeled a "tragedy." The simple plot begins with Roxana, a slave, who appears to be white and has a baby boy who is even lighter, for the usual reason. Roxana's owner, Percy Driscoll, and his wife have likewise just produced a son. The wife soon dies, leaving young Driscoll in Roxana's care. The infants are indistinguishable. Roxana, realizing this, and in despair at the thought of her son being sold away, switches the babies. The white baby grows up to be a black slave of good character, while the black baby matures into a white man with no known virtues and less sense. Roxana eventually explains to her son what happened. He takes the news poorly. ("I am a nigger! Oh, I wish I was dead!") At the end everyone left alive is miserable. The former slave becomes white and is rejected by white society. Roxana's reward comes in seeing her no-longer-white son at last sold into slavery, down the river. Two Twain aphorisms, attributed to his character Pudd'nhead, convey the base of his humor: "Whoever has lived long enough to find out what life is, knows how deep a debt of gratitude we owe to Adam, the first great benefactor of our race. He brought death into the world"; and, some pages later, "All say, 'How hard it is that we have to die'—a strange complaint to come from the mouths of people who have had to live." Washington Irving and Nathaniel Hawthorne at least had the Devil to turn to. Twain had only the America of the 1890s.

Twain was immensely popular with white American readers, who evidently possessed the mental tools necessary to appreciate the tragic comedy of *Pudd'nhead Wilson*. White skin had no meaning: that was the joke. And it was quite a joke in those days of spectacular lynchings, increased segregation, and operatic Anglo-Saxonism, a deadly joke twisting like a vine around the white heart, for whiteness did indeed have social meaning, plenty of it, but white skin did not. The physical marker that distinguished white people from other people was empty, insubstantial; it was literally nonsense. We cannot hope to understand what white Americans thought and did in this period without grasping, as did the popular white writer Twain, the senselessness of their identity. We might say of the 1890s that it contained two powerful impulses—to reject race, and to embrace it—and that these impulses functioned as perverse, battling twins. For example, between 1890 and 1892 the Populist movement worked to unite the white and black poor, end segregation, and generally eliminate race as a social category in favor of class. Yet a short time later the white Populist leadership flipped the movement toward white supremacy and race baiting of the most extreme type. It is a remarkable culture that could perform such an about-face within a four-year period. The Populist turnaround suggests a society in which racial roles had become so dependent on ritual performance, so baselessly imitative, that life begins to seem more dream than reality, a foreground without a background. As we might expect, such a society developed an unappeasable rage for authenticity.

Consider the one-drop rule, which came into its own during these years. The rule held that one drop of black blood made a person black. At first glance, this might seem to fix racial matters in a final shape and settle the problem of determining who's who. Yet it did just the opposite, as Twain demonstrated in his creation of Roxana, her pale son, and her master and mistress's baby. Seeking to pin down the essence of race, the one-drop rule actually made that essence unknowable, indeed invisible. It jettisoned the perceptible reality of skin tone for the dream of racial essence; it made the physical metaphysical. It was simply not possible to know whether you had one drop of black blood — to know whether you were a real white person or an imitation. There was no way to find out, no way to be sure. The one-drop rule made whiteness imaginary, pushed one's whiteness back into an indefinitely receding past of unknown ancestors. It took a crucial social fact of your life and made it a legacy bequeathed by ghosts — all in the form of a fine legal distinction meant to clarify a permanent system of racial separatism.

Here we have the structure of American racial thinking at its barest. We see its failure to give absolute form to the relatively formless, meaning to the meaningless, or sense to chance. The racial paradoxes of the 1890s — the one-drop rule, Twain's changelings, Populism's flip-flop, the mirror world of segregation and its nether cousin, the lynching spectacle — suggest that the failure at that time was of unprecedented scope.

In *Pudd'nhead Wilson*, Twain tried to show how the dream of race, in its misapprehension of the reality of kinship, led to misery and a certain gratitude for the release of death. His friend and colleague Joel Chandler Harris took a bloodier and more nuanced approach to the racial misery of his era. The white writer Harris, who created black Uncle Remus, was born in 1848. Abandoned by his father, he grew up with his mother in a small Georgia town. He published his first Remus tale, "A Story of the War," in 1877 in the *Atlanta Constitution*, where he would serve as editor for many years. The *Constitution* stories found an eager audience; in 1881 a collection, *Uncle Remus: His Songs and Sayings*, appeared.

This first volume sets down the basic structure of the Remus idea. In the book version of "A Story of the War" we learn that, during the conflict, Uncle Remus shot a white Union soldier who was about to fire on Remus's owner, Mars Jeems. The Union man, John, loses an arm as a result but is nursed back to health. He then marries Jeems's sister, Sally. They move to postwar Atlanta, taking along Remus as an employee. Remus's main work is telling stories to John and Sally's son, known to us as the "little boy."

In this way white North and white South, represented by John and Sally, are reconciled, a basic premise of the romantic plantation fiction so popular in both regions. More importantly, a white man could transform himself into a little white boy, then lose himself in the fictions, and the arms, of a black father figure. This racial positioning evidently acted as an elixir upon the minds of many thousands of whites, and some blacks, North and South. Harris and Twain occupied the summit of literary success, at least in sales terms, and their works share an obsession with race based on structures of imitation and doubling. Harris, as editor of the most important newspaper in Georgia, supported black education and voting rights and opposed lynching. He also, like Twain, trafficked in demeaning stereotypes of black characters. The most striking aspect of Harris's negative stereotypes is that they concerned blacks who were acting in what Harris considered white ways—"Dey er gittin'," Remus says of blacks in the city, "so dey b'leeve dat dey ain't no better dan w'ite folks." The black world as Harris imagined it was in many respects better than white folks' world. And Harris imagined it by listening to black people talk, and recording their stories.

Harris put on the mask of Remus in order to tell these black stories. It was a form of minstrelsy, and paralleled developments in the minstrel theater itself. Minstrelsy had become a theater of black people playing blacks. Black minstrels had been around since the 1850s, and the most renowned prewar minstrel dancer was black: William Henry Lane, the great "Juba." But black minstrelsy on a large scale began only after the war, just as white minstrelsy declined—a decline encouraged by black minstrel competitors. Black minstrel troupes emphasized their authenticity, constantly underlining that they were not white imitations of blacks. Their performances were advertised as more truthful to blackness. Black troupes also often claimed to be composed of genuine ex-slaves, and so especially able as "delineators of genuine darky life in the South," in the words of a New York journalist. Black minstrels soon ceased blacking up their faces, except for some comic roles, which furthered their claim to realism. On occasion a light-skinned black minstrel would blacken up in order to preserve the overall image of racial authenticity. Otherwise, audiences might have mistaken a light-skinned black man for a dark-skinned white man. Being both at once, needless to say, would have run contrary to the spirit of the theater.

Black minstrels enjoyed immense popularity with black audiences. Sometimes black minstrels played blacks-only theaters. But they also performed in white theaters, including on several European tours, and in integrated theaters—rather, in theaters that held blacks and whites in segregated sections. Blacks turned out in numbers at such theaters, occasionally leading the owners to expand black seating at the expense of white seating. Black minstrelsy was the incubator for the black theater that came into prominence after 1900. "All the best talent of that generation came down the same drain," as W. C. Handy, himself a black minstrel in the 1890s, put it. "The composers, the singers, the musicians, the speakers, the stage performers—the minstrel show got them all." Where white minstrelsy had produced Dan Emmett and his "Dixie," black minstrelsy gave the equally prolific and influential James Bland, a middle-class Northerner, and his classic "Carry Me Back to Old Virginny."

Black minstrelsy dealt in the same stereotypes of plantation life as had white minstrelsy. One difference between the two was that black minstrelsy preserved and elaborated slave spirituals. As we might expect, the relationship between spirituals and minstrelsy was complex. The Fisk University Jubilee Singers had created a sensation in 1871 with their performances of slave songs. They were black college students and naturally presented themselves in the costumes of the middle class. The serious collection of slave spirituals had begun just after the war, but received a substantial boost from the Fisk singers' success. They set in train several developments that, as always in the popular-entertainment business, came very rapidly. Some black groups sprang up with the idea of performing spirituals in, from a certain point of view, a more genuine way—they dressed as slaves, sometimes claimed to have been slaves, and emphasized that they had not needed any training to sing the old songs in the old way. Some of these groups added to their programs minstrel standards, including songs by white composers such as Stephen Foster. (Frederick Douglass, back in 1855, had mentioned the black music of Foster and other whites as part of the "national music.") Soon enough, white minstrels took up the singing of black spirituals, sometimes in parody of the black university students. And the white Ham-Town Students (after the starchy black Hampton Institute singers) were paralleled by the black Hamtown Quartette.

Slavery music became central to black minstrelsy, preserving for a wide audience some of the most beautiful music of prewar black life. The windings of authenticity and imitation did not end there. Black minstrels, wanting to emphasize their originality as individual artists, frequently claimed authorship of old songs that had no authors. At the same time, black minstrel spiritual performances were probably truer to the originals than those of their right-minded university colleagues. The Hampton and Fisk singers often used written scores, with all the regularity that entails; they formalized the songs to European standards, making it possible for anyone to imitate black sacred music as part of the act of preservation. Black minstrels, not least because they faced black audiences whose memories reached beyond 1860, performed more in the oral tradition from which the spirituals had come. The black minstrels, one might say, claimed more originality than they had, where for the college singers the opposite was true.

Both had large white audiences in a largely white society, and the desires of whites controlled the broad trends of racial performance. These trends ran toward a greater racial authenticity. The use of spirituals fed the sense, long present in white and black minstrelsy alike, that one could view life on a slave plantation as it really was or had been. That sense increased as slave reality receded in time and racial separation solidified as a national principle. Black minstrels turned out to have made something of a Faustian bargain. Having once billed themselves as real Negroes fresh from the plantation, they felt pressure, among white audiences and perhaps among black ones, to make the imitation ever more "realistic." Black minstrelsy entered its anthropological period of complete imitation, in parallel with the thoroughgoing imitativeness of high segregation.

Just as minstrelsy—mainly black, but also white—preserved much of prewar black song and dance, the Uncle Remus stories played a critical role in preserving black storytelling. The same is true of African elements within those songs, dances, and stories. It is not too much to say that racial imitation provided the forms through which a very great deal of African and African American culture was able to survive its passage through time down to us. We might even conclude that racial imitation, by people of varied physical appearance, gave us not only the content but the means to express it.

Harris's Uncle Remus provided the little white boy—the character who occupies the place of us as readers—with a racial past. As in minstrelsy, that past was a black past. But Harris's blackness was far richer than that of Dan Emmett. Using the African and African American stories he had collected as "editor and compiler," Harris created a racial dream time that reached explicitly back to Africa. "Dey wuz a time w'en all de w'ite folks 'uz black," Remus tells the little white boy. "Niggers is niggers now," he continues, "but de time wuz w'en we 'uz all niggers tergedder." Harris, through Remus, alludes to the old belief in the African origins of humanity. Remus explains that one day some people reached a pond and washed their color off, becoming white. Others arrived and became "merlatters," Indians, and Chinese. The last to arrive found enough water only to lighten the palms of their hands and the soles of their feet and therefore remained more or less black.

Harris followed this tale, which appeared in the 1881 Remus volume, with one in which Brer Rabbit overcomes his enemy, Brer Fox. Rabbit is an African trickster figure, funny, cunning, and merciless. Through trickery, he arranges for Brer Fox to be killed by Mister Man. Rabbit proceeds to dish up Fox's head to Fox's wife and son. Remus finishes by suggesting Rabbit may have married the widow Fox. Having completed this story of murder, revenge, cannibalism, and interspecies marriage, Remus suggests that he carry the little boy home to bed. He recalls that he used to carry the boy's Uncle Jeems around in the old days, the Jeems who would grow up to own Remus and whose life Remus would save by shooting the little boy's father.

Such were some of the tales that established the national reputation of Harris and his literary mask, Uncle Remus. We should notice their brutality. Many, many Remus stories were similarly bloody, so that the happy racial romance of plantation days, which Harris also portrayed, begins to seem distinctly strange, and we are invited to wonder which of Harris's dream times was more real. The white reader presumably identified with the white characters, but these were commonly passive and peripheral to the main action. Any reader must also have identified with Brer Rabbit—whose primary activity is subversion, not only of Fox but of Mister Man. Harris himself identified with Uncle Remus, sometimes signing his letters with the name of his black creation. Obituarists would write about Harris as if he actually had been the storytelling ex-slave. Mark Twain recalled hearing, as a boy, tales from Uncle Dan'l, a slave, "the immortal tales which Uncle Remus Harris was to gather into his books and charm the world with, by and by." "I understand that my relations toward Uncle Remus," Harris wrote to Twain in 1881, "are similar to those that exist between an almanac-maker and the calendar."

Why did Harris need this black Father Time? Importantly, the Remus calendar was for years past. Here we may see the one-drop irony working its way through fiction: the mystical, unknowable nature of race under a one-drop rule produced a mystical fiction of the racial past. As whites wrestled with the unknowability of their most important quality, their whiteness, Harris offered a national genealogy within the mythic frame of blackness—in fact, of Africa, and ultimately of a time when whites were black. During an era of the most rigid separatism, white Americans needed nonwhites more than ever, to give them a sense of themselves, to tell them who they were. On their own, white Americans were fundamentally parentless and pastless. That is why they could be deeply concerned about genealogical purity, to the point of committing ritual human sacrifices and something very close to cannibalism, while simultaneously crying out for black mammies (a movement sprang up to build mammy monuments) and turning to their Uncle Remus as the repository of national history. Evi-

dently, this was the only broadly convincing way to make sense of a white identity whose only real content, as Twain knew and Harris certainly suspected, was
arbitrary power. One needed the dominated race in order oneself to be whole.
And one needed the dominated race to be part of one's family, even to the point
of imagining a time "w'en we 'uz all niggers tergedder."

We can readily see the despair in this, for the recuperation of the past along
Remus lines required that the present be a failed replica. All of the races were
dying, fallen from grace together. The leading black writer at century's end,
Charles Chesnutt, wrote that African spiritual beliefs in America were "a pale
reflection of their former selves." In the story concerning African origins, "Why
the Negro Is Black," Harris has Uncle Remus remark that he has been in the
New World so long "dat I bin sorter bleach out." The anthropological trend in
black minstrelsy and the collecting of African American songs and stories grew
largely from a fear that black people were becoming less black or, if you like,
more white—in any case, a race in decline. The plantation romances portrayed
slavery days as a racial wonderland far better than the present, a time when
blacks were blacks and whites were whites and the two could meet in timeless,
doomed harmony. Genealogy was all the rage among postwar white Americans—everyone hoped to find a patent for power in his or her blood—to the
point that Twain, of course, satirized it. ("Yet this ancestor had good and noble
instincts, and it is with pride that we call to mind the fact that he was the first
white person who ever interested himself in the work of elevating and civilizing
our Indians. He built a commodious jail and put up a gallows . . ." Soon enough,
this ancestor becomes "the first white man ever hanged in America"—on his
own gallows.) White intellectuals, notably in New England, worried that their
race was becoming extinct through mixture with (white) immigrants and a
decline in vital energy since the stirring days of the Pilgrims. The New South
aristocracy likewise mourned the passing of the Old South aristocracy—the one
it had pushed aside—along with the old formal refinement, gracious manners,
and code of honor, fine qualities sadly fallen into disuse.

These were all dialogues with the racial dead, premised on a sense of inferiority to the ancestors. When faced with immigrants white in appearance, white
Americans spoke with the dead in tribal languages, Anglo-Saxonism, Teutonism, and Aryanism, Old New England and Old South; faced with nonwhites,
they addressed the white dead as a race. There were few consolations to be
found in either of these one-way conversations, as neither whiteness nor tribalism had much to give. Tribal genealogies held some slight promise in that one
might trace a cherished institution or two (individual liberty, self-government)
back to the German forest or at least a Rhode Island town meeting, though this
was rather thin and formal material with which to fashion the destiny of a peo-

ple. Whiteness, the more important ancestral quality, offered even less. It was an empty mansion built with borrowed labor. And so, seeking that which was absent from their racial selves, white Americans filled the mansion with a cast of racial characters whose main quality was their ability to get along in a white-dominated system. They had Uncle Remus to carry them there through the night in his strong arms.

The question remains: What was this really a nostalgia for? It cannot have been a nostalgia for whiteness as such, much less for some pulsing Anglo-Saxonism, because there was evidently so little there; one could not yearn for an old emptiness, except perhaps in that one yearned for the death so bitterly invoked by Twain. It cannot have been a nostalgia for slavery, either, that is, a nostalgia for the exercise of racial power. First, whites still had power; second, a very great deal of plantation nostalgia thrived among Northerners who had not known slavery; third, the slave system for which whites experienced nostalgia was a system in which one did not *exercise* power, one simply *embodied* it; finally, the longed-for old slave days were often not white at all, particularly in the more popular forms of black minstrelsy and the Remus tales, and it would be a curious thing to feel nostalgia for a past in which one was nearly absent.

Given all this, we may conclude, in broad terms, that white Americans in the 1890s pined for a lost world where their own dominance, by the accident of skin color, made sense to themselves and others. It was a nostalgia not for whiteness or power but for the legitimacy of white power. And whites would not have felt a nostalgia for such legitimacy if they had not also felt its lack in the present.

In 1893 a great many people visited Chicago to attend the World's Columbian Exposition, which marked the four hundredth anniversary of Christopher Columbus's first voyage. Twain even wrote an amusing piece about failing to get there. Henry Adams wrote that the fair "was the first expression of American thought as a unity," which makes one wonder why such an expression had taken so long to arrive. Frederick Douglass was there, representing Haiti and, by extension, "our common race," as the Haitians' commission letter put it. He was hosted by Fannie Williams, a black woman who often passed for white by insisting she was French. At the Haitian pavilion, Douglass set aside a desk for Ida B. Wells, who labored to bring some black content into the fair—she wrote a pamphlet describing the accomplishments of black Americans and exposing white injustices, notably lynching. Wells had begun her crusade against lynching early in 1892, when three of her close friends were shot to death north of Memphis. Her advocacy had led to the destruction of her newspaper office and type in Memphis; she relocated to New York. In Chicago she and the elderly

Douglass pressed their pamphlet on everyone who came by the Haitian site. In the pamphlet they described the fair's main attraction as a "whited sepulchre."

The 1893 Chicago fair represented one way out of the racial prison for white people. Historically, when whiteness functioned well for white people, it tended to have one or more supplements, supplements that made being white a route toward something beyond race, some version of fully realized humanity— Christianity, civilization, Enlightenment, natural superiority. These supplements had been in short supply since the Civil War, and white people had wandered into a world of mirrorings and animal savagery and desperate imitation and fantasy. They had become trapped by the terms of their own racial imaginations. What they found in Chicago was an appealing, if relatively meager, image of escape into the racial supplement of material progress, of technology. The centerpiece of the fair was the White City at the head of the Midway, a road that, as an observer wrote, depicted a "sliding scale of humanity. The Teutonic and Celtic races were placed nearest to the White City; farther away was the Islamic world, East and West Africa; at the farthest end were the savage races, the African Dahomey and the American Indian."

This was triumphalist anthropology run amok. Segregation had been applied to the entire world and to the sweep of human history. And this had been done in celebration of the marvelous diversity of human cultures, each one making its contribution, however rude, to the general advancement toward the White City. Part of the way along sat old Douglass and young Ida B. Wells with their pamphlet. Douglass had withstood much criticism for opposing the trend among blacks toward self-segregation—including black immigration, generally to Africa, which had become popular again in some black and white circles after 1880. (Even President Grant had advocated a black homeland in Santo Domingo, where Columbus had first brought racial thinking to the New World—a perfect closing of the racial circle, it would seem. James Garfield, president in 1881, merely hoped black Americans could be "colonized, sent to heaven or got rid of in any decent way.") Douglass wanted an America in which race did not matter. The Chicago exposition presented a world in which race did not matter if you were white. In the end, black Americans did get some handicrafts into the White City, though as examples of one among "the three modern types of savagery." And there was to be a Colored People's Day, complete with watermelons. Activists circulated "No Watermelon" leaflets in protest. That afternoon Douglass spoke at Festival Hall. As he read a paper, "The Race Problem in America," whites on the periphery began to jeer. Douglass put down his speech, and his glasses, and let loose a fighting voice that overwhelmed the catcalls. "Men talk of the Negro problem," he said. "There is no Negro problem. The problem is whether the American people have loyalty enough, honor enough, patriotism enough, to live up to their own Constitution . . . We Negroes love our country." He spoke for an hour.

Douglass was himself an exhibit: honorable old man with an honorable old idea. His speech and presence were no more than stones on the Midway. The path led out and upward, away from race, away from the pastness arrayed along the Midway so as to suggest that the darker you were the more you lived in the past—the dark child to the colorless adult. This was the other side of Joel Chandler Harris and the racial past he represented; this was Progress, the direction in which Harris's little white boy could go when he left his Uncle Remus. Progress hinged on the question of mobility. The plantation romance of racial immobility was, for all its cheeriness, a romance of despair. A fully realized race cannot, by definition, go anywhere, and the deathly nature of white nostalgia indicates some recognition of this fact. Whites needed an alternative vision, and they made one in Chicago: a future without nonwhites. Nonwhites from Dahomey through Persia (and Alabama) would remain fixed in time, immobile. The despair of whiteness could find relief in a cult of change. The chance to change and grow was the chief asset of membership in the dominant race.

The deepest tragedy of *Pudd'nhead Wilson* was that it could not have been written about two identical black babies. If Roxana had switched two dark babies, nothing, socially, would have happened. There would be no drama. Two black babies would just have been changelessly black; two white babies could have been white, or they could not have been. In the one-drop world of the 1890s, you could mistake someone for white, but you could not mistake someone for black. In the end, blackness was nature, whiteness was nurture. The intangibility and unknowability of whiteness under these circumstances created, as we have seen, vast anxieties. Yet that unknowability also preserved, for whites, some little maneuvering room in their relationship to their own skin color. At the period of greatest racial rigidity, it preserved for whiteness a flexibility of definition. Racial unknowability held out the possibility of further assimilation, for example, of new white people. More fundamentally, the upward mobility of white people away from whiteness—away from racial immobility— might be ensured in white minds. Whites alone would not be limited by their race. Paradoxically, their racial dominance could be secured because their race alone had the power to go beyond race. They could walk up and into the White City of the future with a light step. The whites Ida Wells knew, the many whites Douglass had known in his long life, were expected to be, like Douglass himself, part of the past.

From a national white point of view, the no-exit quality of high segregation had marked one terminus of racial thought and practice. Brighter prospects presented themselves in imperialism and assimilation—the work performed behind the scenes of the White City. The brief (about five months), popular war with Spain in 1898 seemed to herald a national career in foreign adventure. Here could be a new field for mastery. Spain was an ideal enemy; not just very weak, but very old. Catholic, monarchical, decrepit, it appeared to be the antonym of a progressive America. In short order, the United States acquired from Spain Cuba, Puerto Rico, and, nearly by accident, the Philippines. For a provincial nation, insecure and covertly admiring of the European powers then carving up Africa, China, Southeast Asia, South Asia, the Middle East, and the Levant as if at a vast human banquet, the 1898 war was a boon to self-esteem.

Yet there were problems with imperialism. After the first enthusiasm had dwindled, imperialism's cruelty did not go unnoticed. The Filipinos, guided by the able Emilio Aguinaldo, resisted the Americans after 1898 just as they had resisted Spain before 1898. It took American troops, 200,000 of them, more than three years of merciless fighting, and the capture of Aguinaldo, to subdue the Filipino forces. Although the anti-imperialist press was in the minority, reports did reach American readers of how savage their sons could be. There was, for example, the matter of prisoners. Unlike the experienced Filipinos, the Americans seem not to have held many prisoners of war; they killed them instead. Even official reports reflected this fact. Similarly, Filipino soldiers were not often wounded. They weren't given enough time to be wounded.

The news from the Philippines dampened American eagerness for war making overseas. It was also obscure to many what benefits our nation would receive from ruling a resentful people on the other side of the globe. Merchants hoping for a beachhead in the China trade squared off against domestic sugar producers who feared new competition—and labor leaders who also did not want cheaper competition. Finally, adventures abroad raised troubling racial questions, in a number of ways. The prospect of American colonies led to the prospect of new Americans. These prospective Americans were not, by the standards of the day, white. Imperialists and anti-imperialists alike took that into account. Imperialists argued that white people generally, white Americans in particular, inherited a racial obligation to expand their power indefinitely—Anglo-Saxonism had yet another popular surge around 1900. This did not, however, mean that newly subject nonwhite populations were to become Americans. Rather, they were to be ruled until they were fit for self-government. This conception of imperialism as educational outreach, or secular missionary work, had a jewel-like perfection in that it made serving oneself and serving others identical. And because, as the conquering party, one set the standard for self-government, the only way other people could prove themselves capable of self-government was to govern themselves in exactly the way one told them to. This could endlessly delay their self-government.

Put another way, to self-govern in the American sense meant to become American, which in turn meant, for many white Americans at the time, to become white. Again, we can foresee a long delay, particularly in the case of an imperialism that perceived itself as racially destined. Imperialists such as Albert Beveridge, Whitelaw Reid, Reverend Josiah Strong, Franklin Giddings, and Harry Powers accepted that whites or Anglo-Saxons were powerless, because of their race, to do anything but conquer. White Americans, Powers summed up, "want the earth not consciously as a formulated program, but instinctively." To become an American in this sense would mean to become a conqueror. Whatever else imperialists aimed at, it was not to create a world entirely populated by conquerors. The imperialists intended to keep the colonized as subjects, outside the nation. To the anti-imperialists' argument that this would be contrary to the values of a democratic republic, the imperialists deftly answered: it had already been done, with Indians. "The Declaration of Independence applies only to peoples capable of self-government," Beveridge said in 1899. "Otherwise, how dared we administer the affairs of the Indians? How dare we continue to govern them to-day?" The imperialist Henry Cabot Lodge noted that "this Republic . . . has held subjects from the beginning"; the United States "denied to the Indian tribes even the right to choose their allegiance, or to become citizens."

White opponents of imperialism used racial arguments as well. This was true of Southern anti-imperialists, who brought the principle of racial separatism to imperial debate. Speaking of the Philippines, Senator Benjamin "Pitchfork Ben" Tillman saw no reason why Americans should "mark their roads with our dead in a futile effort to call them from their 'loved Egyptian night' "—a reference to Rudyard Kipling's melancholy poem of conquest, "The White Man's Burden," which had raced from novelty to cliché across the popular press of 1899. Senator John Daniel of Virginia told Congress, "You may change the leopard's spots, but you will never change the different qualities of the races which God has created in order that they may fulfill separate and distinct missions in the cultivation and civilization of the world." Another anti-imperialist simply wondered why the United States would want to acquire "fresh millions of foreign negroes."

Both sides in the imperialism debate danced around the question of racial assimilation. President McKinley, to his party's regret, had mouthed the phrase "benevolent assimilation," which efficiently touched several sore points at once. Assimilation of foreigners was a political issue of vast import after the turn of the century. At the peak, foreign-born people would make up a fifth of the labor force and nearly half the urban population. This greatly concerned native-born Americans, who responded with various forms of legal coercion (laws against speaking foreign languages, for instance), extralegal coercion (a reborn Klan), and, most importantly, ideas of Americanism and programs of Americanization.

In general, the Americanizers advocated a racial nationalism that was anti-racial and anti-nationalist. The jurist Louis Brandeis, in a 1915 speech, wrestled with the nature of Americanism. He listed the basic liberties of the American system, then acknowledged, in the American universalist tradition, that democracy and free speech, while imperfectly present across the globe, were nonetheless highly developed beyond our shores and likely to become more so. Then what was unique to Americans, if not their ideals? The United States, Brandeis decided, uniquely "recognizes racial equality as an essential of full human liberty and brotherhood, and that it is the complement of democracy." Denis McCarthy's poem "The Song of the Foreign-Born" reflected this belief:

> O land of all lands first and best, —
> Come peace or conflict dread,
> Thy sons will bravely bear the test,
> Wherever born or bred.
> Old racial cries, old racial ties,
> For them will cease to be,
> And, over all, the thought will rise
> Of thee and only thee!

McCarthy's poem was meant to ease the considerable anxieties of wartime. The European powers in World War I were widely seen as in the grip of a race or nationalist madness, race being understood as similar to nationality. Native-born Americans feared that European immigrants would import this way of thinking as a social toxin, poisoning American unity. "No reverberating effect of the great war," Randolph Bourne wrote in the *Atlantic Monthly* in 1916, "has caused the American public more solicitude than the failure of the 'melting-pot.' The discovery of diverse nationalistic feelings among our great alien population has come to most people as an intense shock." There was the question of loyalty, then, and behind it the question of what, specifically, Americans were meant to be loyal to.

Loyalty was not too difficult to prove in wartime. You proved it by risking your life, or at least not saying or doing anything against the national cause. One faced a greater challenge in proving one's Americanness. Americanization programs provided some help, showing newcomers how to dress, speak English, cook properly, ventilate their tiny apartments, bake bread rather than buy it from the store. (Homemaking lessons were a prominent part of Americanist education.) Carol Aronovici, who chaired Minnesota's State Committee on Americanization, wrote in her 1919 pamphlet *Americanization*: "A new conscience has been evolved during the war relative to the assimilation of the for-eigner. It is almost the fashion now to talk, write or organize in the interest of Americanization work. Every existing organization has an Americanization committee, every city and every state is feverishly organizing for the organiza-tion of Americanization service, and folks who used to be just human beings are being classified into American and unAmerican, according to their willingness to agree or disagree with the Americanizers as to what their social, economic and political ideals should be."

It was not, however, simply a matter of willingness to agree with American-izers on social, economic, and political ideals. Americanizers had few enough of these with which to agree. Beyond standards of dress, housekeeping, and English-speaking ability, Americanism consisted more in forbidding certain things than in advocating them. Anarchism and communism were not allowed, but trade unionism and forms of anticapitalism were. Selling your vote, or vot-ing at the command of local ethnic captains, was strongly discouraged. So were many forms of group identity—except that a strong current ran within Ameri-canism of seeking to preserve Old Country ways in order to refresh the Ameri-can mainstream. Many Americanizers felt that incorporating newcomers and their ways formed part of the American tradition; it contributed to American vitality and further distinguished America from the racially and nationalistically stagnant societies common, so it was believed, everywhere but here. Some Americanizers even thought that foreign immigrants had a clearer idea of Americanism than did Americans. Speaking to an audience of new Americans, President Woodrow Wilson struck a plaintive, almost mystified note: "A man does not hope for the thing that he does not believe in, and if some of us have forgotten what America believed in, you, at any rate, imported in your own hearts a renewal of the belief . . . If I have in any degree forgotten what America was intended for, I will thank God if you will remind me."

We can only wish to know what those immigrants thought, sitting there in Philadelphia, when the president of the United States attributed to them the secret knowledge of what it meant to be an American—and hoped they might share it with him. But his was a truly American gesture, and generous in its way, and typical of introspective Americanizers. Many Americans, and not only Americans, believed that their liberal democratic system was the human ideal and so would be found everywhere people reached an ideal state of existence. The desire for it therefore inhered in all people. This could further mean that Americanism lived most purely as an ideal aspiration, indeed an abstraction, such that actual Americans, inevitably bearing the weight of having fallen short of American ideals, were less American than the new arrivals, who hadn't yet had the chance to fall short. One Americanizer argued in 1916 that " 'Americanism' is much more a matter of the future than of the past." Such a belief could have a warlike face, as in the 1919 remarks of Interior Secretary Franklin Lane, who believed "Americanism is entirely an attitude of mind"—one he was unable to specify. Lane linked Plymouth Rock, Jamestown, Valley Forge, Gettysburg, Santiago Bay (Cuba), and the Philippines in a delirium of mental attitude and American spirit, concluding, "We are to conquer this land in that spirit, and in our spirit we are to conquer other lands because our spirit is one that, like a living flame, goes abroad." The domestic field had a calmer aspect. Carol Aronovici looked hopefully to a Carnegie study she expected to show "the ways in which the various foreign cultures manifest themselves in our midst and to what extent an intelligent Americanization movement would assist in making these cultures a part of our heritage out of which will be realized a new world."

There is something very suggestive in Aronovici's scheme: a national culture making entirely new things into part of its *heritage*, then using that heritage to make a national culture that would be entirely new. The new provides the content of the old, which then leads to yet more newness—a heritage or history of fresh starts. In a way, each new immigrant could be conceived of as a pioneer. His or her "America" was a frontier to be conquered in the mind. While old Americans could no longer be pioneers, the immigrant could, and so he or she was most American. With immigration the frontier remained open as a state of mind. And this internal frontier had a close relationship to that external frontier represented by the physical reality of the non-American world. As Americans went abroad to make the world safe for democracy, Americanizers sought to make America safe for democracy. The language used was the same: Americans struggled against racial identity and nationalism, literally the genealogy of power, in the name of a universal human status and system. They sought to make the Old World new and to make the Old World peoples who came to America into new people.

Frontier settlement had been, on the whole, white settlement, and immigrants, settling their interior frontier, were expected to do so as whites. Legally, only "white" immigrants were eligible for citizenship. When Brandeis said that the United States alone "recognizes racial equality as an essential of full human liberty," he immediately followed with, "It has, therefore, given like welcome to all the peoples of Europe." President Wilson insisted to immigrant audiences that American identity was an individual identity, that "America does not consist of groups"; yet Wilson also segregated the federal government into two groups (white and colored) to a degree previously unknown. Theodore Roosevelt had spoken of Americans as "a new and mixed race—a race drawing its blood from many different sources." He also believed blacks to be "altogether inferior."

Americanizers did not, however, advocate a white America. Neither did Brandeis, Roosevelt, or Wilson. Apart from the dwindling Anglo-Saxonists and the Klansmen, the Americanizers were against racial identity, almost obsessively so. Races were what European immigrants had and would go beyond; that was much of the process of Americanization. To be American was to be raceless. It did not quite mean giving up one's past. Imaginatively, Americanists divided the immigrant's past into two categories: race, which is to say a past beyond individual will; and culture, a past that could be changed, improved upon, or discarded according to one's individual desires. The first, racial past had to be eliminated as un-American and contrary to Brandeis's spirit of racial equality. The second, cultural past could be retained, subject to some modifications. The person with a race could not be self-owned. He would be owned by his racial kingpin of the moment, the ward heeler or the kaiser; he would, in essence, be owned by his race. The person with a culture owned that culture himself and had the power to change it.

"An inherited past that controls you" was, in practical Americanizing terms, the definition of race. Understanding such a definition of race helps us see why Aronovici, in her thoughtful and closely argued pamphlet, shot through with racial language, rarely speaks of blacks or Indians. In Ellwood Griscom, Jr.'s compilation *Americanization: A School Reader and Speaker*, from 1920, blacks and Indians are similarly missing. The book contains several Lincoln tributes, including one from Emerson, who characterized Lincoln as "a quite native, aboriginal man." None of the Lincoln tributes mentions slavery or black emancipation, nor do the succeeding tributes to Robert E. Lee, Ulysses S. Grant, and the Confederate Stonewall Jackson. This may seem odd, but it makes sense in terms of the Americanizers' idealistic views on race and American racelessness. Becoming American meant giving up your race, defined as the hold of the past on your self, the inherited condition of unfreedom. People in America who had races were not, fundamentally, real Americans. They were what Theodore Roosevelt and others called "hyphenated" Americans (as in Italian-American). Rhetorically, their very raceness was the name for that part of themselves that had the power to keep them from assimilating as Americans and from reaching the human ideal. As Roosevelt put it shortly before his death, if the immigrant "tries to keep segregated with men of his origin and separated from the rest of America, then he isn't doing his part as an American."

The people who, by general consensus, had races, and were in fact segregated, were nonwhites, particularly blacks and Indians. In a curious fashion, Americanization was about distinguishing immigrants from blacks and Indians. The links among these groups were certainly there to be made. In discussing immigrants, Americanizers went on and on about race and spoke against "segregation," one might say just as if they were discussing blacks and Indians, who were, after all, the initial subjects of this way of speaking. (The Americanist terminology was uncannily familiar. "Americanization," the prominent Americanizer Frances Kellor wrote in the *Yale Review* in 1919, "is the science of racial relations in America, dealing with the assimilation and amalgamation of diverse races in equity into an integral part of its national life.") The influential Americanizer Edward Ross, a Wisconsin sociologist, wrote of "the simple-minded foreigner or negro" and "cities with many naturalized foreigners or enfranchised negroes." Yet Americanizers generally kept the two apart and kept immigrants separate from Indians—segregated them in the mind.

The ways in which they did so are revealing. Winthrop Talbot's lengthy 1917 compendium *Americanization: Principles of Americanism, Essentials of Americanization, Technic of Race-Assimilation*, revised and expanded in 1920, may serve as a guide. It included three selections on black Americans, all by black authors: W. E. B. Du Bois, Booker T. Washington, and R. R. Moton. Each of these proposed that blacks were nearing a more developed race conception of themselves. "Self-realization," Du Bois wrote, "is thus coming slowly but surely to another of the world's great races." Moton believed blacks increasingly accepted "the advice and leadership of their own race for racial betterment." What stands out about these contributions is that they are the only ones in the book that see heightened raceness as desirable. All other groups are supposed to be losing their separate raceness, while blacks are expected to gain theirs.

The case of Indians is somewhat different. Americanizers often noted that Indians were the exception to the rule that all Americans are immigrants or descended from immigrants. They then commonly proceeded to ignore them. However, Talbot's book does contain some reflections on Indians and their relation to Americanism. We hear from two men, the sociologist Fayette McKenzie and the editor Albert Shaw. McKenzie writes: "The Indian race is fast reducing the purity of its blood, but the Indian blood predominates and holds the succeeding generation out of the national thought and out of Caucasian social control. No one is free until he shares in the thought which controls his social life. The mixed blood in custom and tradition is Indian, or raceless, which is worse . . . The Indians are *not* assimilated. The assimilation of one race into another and surrounding race means bringing them into a full share in the life and thought of the latter." Shaw takes a more optimistic view of assimilation: "Certain Indian traits and qualities—those of physical courage and endurance, of silence and stoicism under conditions of danger and difficulty, of a certain unassailable personal dignity—have for a hundred years unquestionably so affected the American mind as to have entered very deeply

into the quality of what we may call American personality." For Shaw the Indianization of Americans in terms of character is paralleled by the whitening of
Indians in terms of blood: "All these red men of the Indian Territory will enter
into full American citizenship, and the process of absorption into the white
race will go on through intermarriage without hindrance or difficulty . . . We
shall always owe some traits and qualities of national character to our contact
with the North American Indians, but we shall assimilate them as a race with
results scarcely perceptible."

It would appear that the determining difference between immigrants, on
one hand, and blacks and Indians, on the other, is that immigrants are not
defined by race, while blacks and Indians are. Immigrants can and should give
up their race, while Indians and blacks cannot and possibly should not. As
McKenzie stated, the "raceless" Indian was the worst of all. White Americans
may acquire Indian traits through "contact," but Indians acquire white traits (or
enter "the national thought") only through the blood, through physical absorption rather than contact and acquisition. Similarly, blacks become more themselves, and perhaps more valuable to America, by becoming more black, which
is ultimately a condition of blood—while immigrants, as we have seen, become
more themselves, more American, and more part of the national thought by
becoming raceless and free of blood qualities.

But what, truly, was the quality of this racial blood? Why was it determining
for blacks and Indians and not for immigrants? The explanation must lie partly
in the Americanizers' desire that immigrants give up that aspect of their past
which might have control over them, so they might become fully American and
new—give up the historical aspect of selfhood that went under the name *race*.
Beyond this, one can't help but think that some of the Americanizers hoped
that their own past, the American heritage, would not have control over them.
They hoped for themselves not to have a race, thus to be free masters of themselves, unburdened by any past other than a list of place-names from Jamestown
to Manila or an ethereal genealogy of nearly indistinguishable men from Washington to Grover Cleveland. In this light, President Wilson's remark that foreigners, people with no American past, might remind him what it is to be
American seems slightly less bizarre. So does the ubiquitous combining, in
Americanist literature, of race with history—specifically, with the kind of history or past that affects what you do without your quite knowing it, thereby
undermining your independence, self-reliance, and individual liberty, in short,
all the ideals that are meant to go into making an American. Only a new American could be an ideal American. Wilson seemed to sense that.

Put differently, only a new American could not have an American racial
past. The Americanizers were demanding that foreign immigrants give up their
races partly because American society as it existed could not escape its own. We

should remember that immigrants did not have races. They had national loyalties, customs, languages, modes of dress, cuisines, but they did not have races. Their acquisition of racial identities, and subsequent transcending of those identities in favor of becoming American, occurred entirely in the minds of Americanizers. Native white Americans did have a race. The point is that they did not want one, not the one they had—the blood that formed you in spite of yourself and gave you a history that, to some degree, controlled you. Immigrants held the possibility of moving white society from one drop of blood to no blood; they seemingly had the potential to go beyond race in a way that white Americans could not. Their segregationist president would thank God if the newcomers could show him how to get there.

America had changed almost beyond recognition in the few decades after 1890. The country was becoming steadily more urban, with a vast population of people who had no links to the nation's history. Rail networks, radio broadcasting, the telephone, and the automobile shrank the country in countless ways, from private tourism to the creation of a truly national market for consumer products, including news and entertainment. American business and American political power had become steadily more international. Public education, and the access to nonlocal information an education provided, expanded spectacularly after 1890: in the fifty-year period to 1940 the proportion of children from five to seventeen years of age attending school went from 44 percent to 74 percent, expenditure per child increased sixfold, and the average number of attendance days more than doubled. Taking all these developments into account, we can see why formal American white separatism might have come to seem provincial, peculiar, and out-of-date. Racial segregation, the most visible form of separatism, had been the wave of the future in 1890. By the 1920s it had clearly become a legacy of the past. The Supreme Court had upheld a black disfranchisement law in 1903; it struck one down in 1915 and by 1917 was moving, however delicately, against segregation. President Wilson's creation of race-specific toilets in federal buildings turned out to be something of a turning point. So was his private screening of D. W. Griffith's film *The Birth of a Nation*, based on Thomas Dixon's novel *The Clansman*. The movie portrayed the righteous reassertion of social order by the Klan after a black beast attacked Southern womanhood. Wilson liked *The Birth of a Nation* and recommended it. More significantly, he received a great deal of abuse for his endorsement and was soon backpedaling to limit the political damage. He suggested the film be selectively banned. By 1922 an antilynching bill had actually passed the House, though it was filibustered to death in the Senate.

In one sense, white separatism became more localized—a Southern problem, with the understanding that the South was exceptional (and more "historical"). Senator Thomas Heflin of Alabama could, in 1930, introduce to the *Congressional Record* his thoughts on "the all-important question of preserving the integrity of our race": "The time has come for all true Americans of the Caucasian race to wake up to the dangers that threaten us." But he did so in defense of "what we used to call the land of Anglo-Saxon rule and white supremacy." Clearly the Southern man's confidence had been sapped—by white people. It is true that the revived Klan of the 1920s had its greatest strength in Indiana and extensive support in California, Oregon, Ohio, and Oklahoma, and these were not quite Southern states. However, the new Klan focused much of its energy against Catholics and Jews, that is, against immigrants. It reflected a national reality in which whiteness was failing to cohere in the post–Civil War fashion.

By the interwar period white American separatism had acquired a curiously ambivalent appearance. At once invisible and obvious, even to whites, whiteness was a tactical identity, a defensive resource useful on some occasions. Those occasions were becoming fewer in number, while the utility of racelessness was growing. The definition of race as a controlling past, and racelessness as freedom from such control, gave white culture an assimilative power it had previously lacked. To put it crudely, whites no longer had to put on blackface to assimilate nonwhite culture. When the raceness of whites was invisible to themselves—when they were universal humans, in the Americanist sense, rather than whites—the American majority acquired an ease of cultural borrowing that had been unavailable to earlier generations. It was not that the difference between white and nonwhite had disappeared. Rather, whites perceived their own whiteness as less thoroughly significant. Having gone so far into race in the 1890s, they were pulling away from it into a broader conception of Americanness. Segregation culture had sought to define what was white, which made segregation sexually paranoid, melancholic, sometimes desperately expansionist, and unoriginal. The new nationalism, after the transition of imperial Progressivism, sought a raceless America and was future-oriented, optimistic, and powerfully original.

Anything could feed such a nationalism. As Aronovici noted, the new America had the capacity to make new traditions part of its own past—a new past. An early example appears in the history of the cakewalk. This somewhat African combination of music and dance had, of course, reached a wide white audience through white minstrelsy, later through black minstrelsy. By the 1890s it had become popular among whites nationally and soon traveled to Europe. (Claude Debussy wrote a cakewalk.) However original turn-of-the-century white cakewalks were in fact, in imagination they remained imitative of black style—at least until the two-step promenade was taken up by John Philip Sousa and others as ideal for use with the brass bands they favored. The cakewalk split into a plantation variety (the "black" cakewalk), on one hand, and, on the other, a simple brass-band form that became central to numberless county fairs and small-town occasions. (There was also a more high-society cakewalk, here and in Europe. Cakewalk style had a profound impact on ragtime, too.) Whether the white sons of proud small-town burghers, puffing away at their tubas and high-stepping into the twilight one Fourth of July, were performing a "white cakewalk" or a "secretly black cakewalk" is a fine question. Probably they thought it was just a Sousa tune done in the traditional manner. This rather resembles the "Dixie" conundrum. The difference, particularly after World War I, was that white Americans were thinking not so much of making things white as of making a culture that was racelessly American. In the broadly Americanizing view, any cultural material that could be successfully integrated into American life was, by definition, either not racial at all or ceased to be racial by becoming American.

The interwar years brought "racial mixture" of an unprecedented type and intensity. Sousa's cakewalk is perhaps the least spectacular example. American music in those years could not have existed without blacks, Jews, and to a degree Italians. American popular dance was inconceivable without black and Latin forms, the latter being themselves partly African in inspiration. The quintessentially American wit of the time was an Indian, the "cowboy philosopher" Will Rogers. Western dramas on radio and in film would not have amounted to much without Indians. The Harlem vogue may have been a passing romance of the white elite, but jazz and swing were not. The limits of this integration or assimilation, in racial terms, were not cultural but personal. Ideally, a white person could do just about anything—sing a blues, build a tepee in the back yard—and not lose his or her authenticity, much less social power. One might say that, by imitating anything, white American culture had found the means always to be itself while always changing. The problem of white American lack of originality, which had haunted this settler society from the beginning, appeared to be resolved through something like minstrelsy without minstrels, or an assimilating imitativeness so thorough that it became authentic. However, only whites had the power to be authentic in this way—*whites* being understood to include most new immigrants. Blacks and Indians (and, in parts of the country, Chinese, Japanese, and people with Spanish surnames) could be authentic, in large part, only insofar as they behaved racially and appeared, physically, to be outside the expansive confines of whiteness.

In *Americanization*, Aronovici had written, "The foreigner who changes his whole mode of life with the ease and carelessness with which he takes off his coat is erroneously considered a good prospective American." She considered this "not assimilation but simulation." Yet the refusal of Americanists to attach much unique content to Americanism rendered the line between assimilation and simulation impossible to see. The perfect imitation American and the perfect American were practically identical—and, judging from Americanist writing, theoretically identical as well. Given the professed universality of American values, being American really was a matter of appearances. To a remarkable degree, the same held for being un-American, that is, having a race.

Florence Mills confronted the mysteries of assimilation and simulation during her brief reign as queen of the black musical theater in the 1920s. A small woman with a big voice, she perceived herself as a universal artist, not bound by racial conventions, outside the traditions of impersonation. Writing in 1927, George Jean Nathan, the preeminent white critic of the day, understood that Mills was doing something new:

> In her way she is an unusual creature. Our music show theater has never within the present memory known one like her.
>
> We have had any number of colored women performers since the day of Black Patti, who was little more than a portly mezzotint Homerically endeavoring to prove to all comers that black was white. Like Black Patti, all the colored women who have appeared before us, in terms of either larynx or foot or both, have simply striven to be as near white as possible and have succeeded as a consequence in being neither white nor black. Even Ada Overton Walker aped the manner and method of her white musical comedy sisters as the Black Patti before her aped the concert platform palefaces.
>
> But La Mills goes in for no such monkeyshines. She is a colored woman and her performances not only announce the fact but insist upon it. The song, the dance and the eyerolling and the abandon and the speech and the gesture of all Ethiopia are in that body of hers. She uses every last ounce of nervous power to merchant them nightly to her customers.
>
> Never for an instant does she try to do anything that is more natural to a white woman; never for a second is she in any department of her work other than the colored woman she is . . .
>
> When Florence Mills sings, the voice of her Negro people is in that singing, even when the lyrics of that song [are] out of the Yiddo-American Broadway music publisher's shop.

Nathan gives much to ponder. It appears that a black performer doing anything that was not intensely black was doomed to artistic failure because of her skin color. Against this inauthentic style Nathan, through Mills, proffers an authentic form of imitation, namely acting black. That, too, is clearly imitative, given that "any number of colored women performers" before Mills had, perversely, failed to act black, and given that Mills is able to be entirely Ethiopian even when performing material written by, in this case, Jewish Americans. Blackness, then, was a matter not of content but of behavior and appearance.

At the same time, however, Nathan finds that when Mills is acting black she is always, proudly, nothing "other than the colored woman she is"—which would mean that her black performance springs not from calculation but directly from her racial self, and is therefore not so much acting as simple honest existence. Strangely enough, a theater critic is praising an actress both for brilliant acting and for not acting at all. Perhaps more to the point, Nathan praises Mills for never doing "anything that is more natural to a white woman." We might well wonder, What is natural to a white woman? Nathan did not praise white actresses for acting white (or being white). He did not seek out intensely white performances or censure white actresses for not being white enough. On the contrary, what was natural to whites at this time was precisely acting as if they had no race. This would become so natural to whites that they wouldn't think of it as acting. It was simply normal behavior, springing untutored from their raceless selves. When white Americans did explicitly act white, as in the South, it seemed a little odd and un-American—given that the actors were white, and so had the social power to be the American norm, not limited by race. White Americans were not supposed to act white. Acting out racial roles was an activity one left to others.

At the national level the business of white separatism consisted in removing raceless people from the presence of those who had races. This soon became "natural" to white Americans—including immigrants, for whom the simulation of white Americanness was a novelty. As soon as black Americans began migrating into Northern cities and towns, just then nonblack Americans began leaving them. Dark skin had this magical ability to empty real estate. It was not only a matter of economic class. There were prosperous black neighborhoods, too, in the North and in parts of the South. They were still black neighborhoods. And, in the North, they were almost always formerly white or white-immigrant neighborhoods. We should note that black neighborhoods were sometimes nice places to live, and convenient, for residents of any appearance. Whites did not necessarily leave them because they did not like living there. They did leave if their homes were "turning black" in some way. When enough whites had left, the remaining whites began to see the values of their homes decline. The values did not decline because poor people were buying the houses. The values had to decline first, or poor people could not purchase the houses. The prime cause of the decline was racial, not economic.

The voluntary removal of white people, new or old, from certain parts of the country would constitute, in sheer numbers, possibly the largest race-based internal migration in the nation's history, comparable only to black out-migration from the South. Looked at over the decades from 1910 onward, it has the character of a bizarre game of "chase." Blacks leave white people in the South, and whites leave black people in the North. The motives of blacks are obvious, the motives of whites less so. It does not seem to have been a question of culture. Black American culture was not all that unusual or obscure. Besides, white removal occurred over the same period when white American culture demonstrated its amazing ability to assimilate cultural artifacts, behaviors, and styles of nearly every kind. What made black people different from Armenians, say, or Jews or Italians was primarily their color. But that's not enough; the mere fact of color explains nothing. There was, certainly, an economic explanation in the sense that an influx of black people, regardless of income, would predictably lead to a decline in property values (and in services from government and land-lords), which is to say an economic loss. But this loss occurred—would occur—independently of anything new black residents did. At this level, what white homeowners and renters feared was not black neighbors as such. They feared what their fellow whites would do, namely move away and, through the social consensus they controlled as a group but concerning which they felt helpless as individuals, cause the neighborhood to "go downhill," as if American racial cul-ture had a muddy river of the mind toward which it constantly threatened to slide. Economically, whites feared what the presence of blacks would make other whites do. Thus an entire community could relocate on a racial basis without any one person in that community feeling responsible.

White separatism of this type soon had little to do with immigrants. Ill feel-ing toward "foreign-born whites," to use the legal term, would diminish through the 1920s. This rapprochement was greatly aided by the 1921 immigration act, which established quotas: annual immigration from a given country could not exceed 3 percent of the number of persons from that country present in the United States in 1910. The National Origins Act of 1924 furthered the earlier act's goals by banning any East Asian immigration (Chinese immigration was already illegal). It also reduced the European quota to 2 percent of the number of nationals present in the country, not in 1910, but in 1890. This and succeed-ing legislation shrank the annual number of immigrants—approximately, from 800,000 in 1920 to 75,000 by the early 1930s—and carefully restricted most immigration to lighter-skinned non-Slavic Europeans. The melting pot then became white, without it being expressed in quite that way; and the racial language of the Americanists could return to its previous use as a way of thinking about whites and nonwhites. Reference to Italian or Greek "races" would soon be antiquated, if not mystifying.

Immigration laws and white removal were part of a larger process of separatism without strict segregation. The New Deal agencies, for example, formed to fight the Depression, discriminated against nonwhites, most explicitly against blacks. The Federal Housing Administration would not give mortgages to blacks who wanted to live in white neighborhoods. The Civilian Conservation Corps put blacks and whites in separate camps. When the federal Tennessee Valley Authority set up a model town, it would not allow blacks to live there.

That was a prophetic gesture. White removal to the suburbs was itself the creation of a model town, indeed a model America. Suburbanization exploded after World War II, at the very time of the largest migration of blacks to cities in American history—more than two million people over the course of the 1940s. Blacks were kept out of the suburbs by means formal and informal. The most famous incident occurred in Cicero, Illinois, an all-white town. More than three thousand whites rioted to prevent a black family from moving in. But in general postwar white separatism was preserved by quieter means: a simple refusal to sell to blacks, or, when blacks did succeed in finding a home, a simple removal from their midst to some whiter place.

The sheer oddness of white flight is striking. It showed a remarkable lack of attachment to place and tradition; it was fundamentally nomadic. The term *white flight* itself marks a departure without revealing any expectation of arrival, unlike the *white settlement* of an earlier era. One did not move to a suburb so much as to the suburbs, a generic non-place defined by its opposition to the city. We might also note the lack of coherence or group purpose. Although the suburbs were determinedly white, the people in them did not form white organizations as such or elaborate an explicitly white culture. The whiteness of the suburbs was a matter of exclusion rather than of racial identity in any positive sense. The suburbs were a place for escape, and a place to be new. They were themselves new, freshly built on exurban farms or wastelands. The things in them were often new, the consumer innovations of a booming middle-class economy: refrigerators, expansive cars, electric appliances such as the can opener, toaster, and mixer, lawn mowers, television sets. Suburban life was optimistic and forward-looking. Incomes were rising, and each passing year would bring some new thing to make life a little easier.

In this new world whiteness could be a thing of the past. The physical condition for the disappearance of whiteness was the exclusion of nonwhites. When everyone looked white, no one did. The white past could also be eliminated. "History offered a feeble and delusive smile at the sound of the word *race*,"

Henry Adams wrote in 1918; "evolutionists and ethnologists disputed its very existence; no one knew what to make of it; yet, without the clue, history was a fairy tale." Even in 1918 "fairy tale" was an unexpected choice of words. In the 1940s, after the Depression, two world wars, and many seasons of racial violence — 1943 had been the worst year since the rioting summer of 1917 — mainstream American thinking recognized mainly the present, a hideous recent past, and a pre-1914 world of more or less antiquarian interest. Cold War patterns of understanding, on any side, referred but dimly to the past; cold warriors competed over the present and the future, and in terms of human nature rather than historical circumstance or tradition. The contest was between two systems, not two peoples, much less two races. The world wars were themselves associated with race, with blood and nationalism and tribal genealogies that had clearly, by 1945, led to nothing one would want to respect — nothing but millions of the early dead, heaped on an Old World pyre. Nationalist, racial imperialism had likewise lost its honor and its appeal. And as such race movements constituted much of recent history, as well as Americans' main collective experience of the outside world, we can hardly wonder at the powerful wish to bury the past in oblivion. It offered little to celebrate other than the heroic sacrifices made to correct the mistakes of others.

There was no more reason to recall the mistakes Americans may have made. The success of Americanist assimilation of millions of people with no American past was taken to demonstrate the fundamental unimportance not only of immigrants' previous lives but of the American racial past in general. If immigrants could assimilate to the norm, after a period of transition, then anyone could. The timelessness of American values and democratic forms became mirrored by the timelessness of Americans. The affectless, democratic uniformity of suburban ideals, the belief that an entire nation could be in a "middle" class, the uneven but determined abandonment of regional and local identities, all pointed hopefully toward a stable future of perpetual newness and a culture based on repetition.

The makers of television programs and comic strips seized this vision as their own. Nonwhite characters and types persisted from the prewar years — Popeye's nemesis, Bluto; Amos and Andy; Jack Benny's servant, Rochester; the indestructible Buckwheat; Krazy Kat — but most gradually lightened or disappeared altogether. An imaginary world was created where only white people lived, the world of the situation comedy, newspaper comic, and weekly television dramas. These were all serial forms, repetitive by nature and crucially different in that respect from films, plays, and non-genre books. With the partial exception of comics they also differed from their serial predecessors — principally juvenile- and mystery-book series, and radio shows — in being visual. As repetitive visual media, they created a constant, stable imaginative life in which the leading characters did not die—indeed, did not age—and acted in highly predictable ways from episode to episode over years and even decades. This created a passive type of cultural consumption much like addiction and a rule-bound dramatic sense closer to that of sport than of art. In the lighter forms, from *Peanuts* to *Father Knows Best* and *Leave It to Beaver*, stories were commonly set in motion by children or by adults acting like children. One might say that the comic role once played by blacks and blackened whites in minstrelsy, up through *Amos n' Andy*, could now be handled by white children and childlike white adults. That is, the comedy of white American life no longer needed a nonwhite element. (Even the leading comedy of urban life, *The Honeymooners*, performed the counterfactual miracle of being all white, and non-"ethnic" white at that.) Popular American drama also had few roles for nonwhites. Even historical dramas, rather severely limited to Westerns, were overwhelmingly white. Indians appeared either as a peripheral threat or, as in the case of Jay Silverheels's Tonto in *The Lone Ranger*, as helpful assistants. Somehow Brer Rabbit had turned into Lassie.

Considering this postwar popular culture as a whole, in a historical light, we can see how profoundly radical it was. American popular culture, comic and dramatic, had included a sizable nonwhite element since at least the 1820s. And, given low literacy, few communications media, and a dispersed populace, one could argue that there was no American popular culture prior to the 1820s. Why did popular white American culture no longer need nonwhites? In part, cultural separatism reflected economic trends. With the regional exception of Mexican farm labor, the national economy—the white economy—did not need nonwhites in the ways it had. White immigrant labor, once it was white, and that didn't take long, filled the needs of manufacturers. Unemployment was low for whites in the long postwar expansion, so low that many white mothers could stay home and do domestic work that had been done by blacks. Many of the new appliances, particularly machines for washing laundry and sewing, reduced the demand for domestic services. Other technological innovations further shrank the need for black labor. A person traveling by car didn't need a railroad porter, and a man shaving at home with a safety or electric razor didn't need a barber as often. The middle-class ethos itself led away from direct employment of others in servile tasks: a man could shine his own shoes, or have his wife shine them. The ideal home, aided by technology and the electrification it depended on, was self-sufficient. That was part of its appeal, a source of stability and contentment. The privatization of public entertainment through television only furthered this splendid isolation.

But economic changes do not explain so much as mirror white separatism. Nonwhites were as qualified as whites to fill factory jobs. The difference was that they were not allowed to fill them. Asa Philip Randolph had forced

Franklin Roosevelt to permit black labor in wartime industries, but after the war, white labor, unionized and not, forced black labor back out. White-collar work was likewise kept white by custom—and when businesses relocated from cities to suburban towns, the labor force remained white because only white people lived nearby. Racial discrimination worked just well enough to keep the white economy white. That was all it was meant to do.

So why did whites create, for the first time in our history, a racially exclusive, secular popular culture of such extent? The clue may lie in the flat, repetitive, and timeless nature of that culture. *Flight* is the key idea—the wish to escape. What most distinguished white suburban culture was its escape from the past, its headlong pursuit of happiness as freedom from the past—an ultimate form of liberty. This particular conception of happiness and liberty had, as we know, long distinguished American culture, not only among whites. The circumstances of postwar America simply made it possible for whites to come closer than they ever had to fulfilling this dream. In fulfilling it, they preferred a popular culture that did not recognize the existence of the American past, just as they preferred cars, architectural and interior-design styles, gardens, place-names, and so on that steadfastly turned their backs on whatever had happened before 1945. Perhaps the crowning achievement of this vast effort was the conviction that such a life was normal, when it was not only unprecedented but about as artificial as one can imagine.

The fragility of the postwar white ideal can be seen in the fact that one black person riding down the street in the company of a real-estate agent could be perceived as a threat. A world so easily threatened cannot be considered rock-solid. Such fearfulness suggests the opposite. And we have to wonder why a dark skin could have this power to disturb. It seems likely that the dark person endangered the suburb's premise that it had no past—more precisely, the white person's freedom from a racial past as exemplified by the racelessness and timelessness, the special normality, of the suburban present. The dark person threatened the white person's claim to understand himself, particularly to understand himself as normal. Because the essence of whiteness, more than ever, was normality, nonwhiteness in itself, simple skin color, could endanger one's normality. Nonwhiteness could make you white, which meant giving you a racial past you did not want, a past that promised to diminish you. The peculiar nature of white suburbia, with its physical and psychological separation from that which was not white and not new, suggests that race and American history had become so deeply intertwined that white flight was specifically an attempt to escape them both.

————

The postwar civil-rights movement directly attacked white separatism in the name of personal freedom. The movement's language, particularly as crafted by Martin Luther King, Jr., avoided racial separatism and racial equality, two concepts that had moved in tandem through the nation's racial thinking for many decades, most famously in the "separate but equal" phrasing of the Supreme Court's 1896 decision in *Plessy v. Ferguson*. The movement reached instead toward a third point, usually a Christian one, that could take Americans away from racial consciousness in the present and away from the past that formed that consciousness. Integration meant the integration of black Americans into American life, not into white life.

It remained a question whether there was, in fact, a nonracial American life in which to integrate oneself. That question might be deferred by concentrating on white Americans who were confessedly, determinedly white, including to themselves. One could, as the movement did, divide the country into North and South and concentrate on Southern Jim Crow. The idea was to make the nature of the conflict clearer and to pick out the worst possible enemy—a role that police chief Bull Connor of Birmingham, Alabama, for example, was seemingly born to play. The civil-rights movement sought out and found the ultimate white people, so to speak. We can see how microscopically intransigent they could be in a meeting between five prominent white citizens of Birmingham and President John F. Kennedy in the autumn of 1963. The movement's Birmingham campaign had begun in April and had led to a shaky compromise with the city's white leaders. The five men were meeting with Kennedy to urge a cooling of federal activity in Birmingham. Kennedy had his own agenda—three concrete steps, at least one of which he hoped the leaders would agree to carry out. The steps were: hire some black salesclerks in white stores; open formal negotiations with local black leaders; hire one black police officer. The Birmingham group felt each of these demands was asking too much. They knew that Kennedy was pressing legislation to make the segregation of public accommodations illegal. The men felt that was going too far as well. "Oh, public accommodations is nothing!" Kennedy replied. "Nobody here is naive about it, or doesn't understand it, or doesn't see what's happening in Washington, where you've got fifty-four percent Negro and eighty-five percent in the schools, the whites just *running* out of Washington. Nobody wants that."

Although Washington, D.C., was more South than North, it was not Birmingham. What Kennedy feared was that his fellow white Americans throughout the nation would accept integration only up to a point, and that point would probably be in schools and the workplace, where racial policy might threaten class status rather than some other aspect of white life. The implications of

Northern-style voluntary white separatism were not lost on Kennedy, or on other observers. The term *white backlash* to describe national, not Southern, sentiment came into common journalistic use in 1964, the same year that Congress passed civil-rights legislation. The bill survived a Senate filibuster in June capped by Robert Byrd's record-breaking speech of fourteen hours and thirteen minutes. Byrd, famed for his eloquence, objected that the bill's passage would imply that most eminent American religious thinkers before 1964 had "failed to preach the truth." He also argued that Christ's command to love your neighbor did not mean "that we may not *choose* our neighbor . . . It does not admonish that we shall not build a wall betwixt us and our neighbor." Similarly, California voters came out for Lyndon Johnson in the presidential election, but they also passed, by a greater margin, a proposition that forbade the state from interfering with property owners' right to sell to whomever they wished. The proposition was meant to overturn a fair-housing act from the preceding year. It did so, importantly, in the name of personal freedom.

What Kennedy feared, Byrd argued, and the voters of California showed was that white Americans would experience the civil-rights movement as a threat to their own freedom. They would react to this threat by removing themselves to a white place where their freedom would be preserved. As Theodore White wrote in 1964, "the gross fact is that the great cities of America are becoming Negro cities." White believed that "these trends, if unchanged, will give America a civilization in which seven of her ten largest cities . . . will have Negro majorities; and the civilization in this country will be one of metropolitan clusters with Negroes congested in turmoil in the central cities and whites defending their ramparts in the suburbs." Rioting in urban black neighborhoods that year lent much support to White's prediction. Beginning in New York City—after an off-duty policeman shot a black teenager—rioting would occur in Rochester, New York, several places in New Jersey, and Oregon. This was something well worth fleeing, and riots in black neighborhoods would recur with terrible regularity until the end of the decade. However, riots did not take place because people were black. They took place because people were miserable and were being abandoned by white Americans in a way that seemed to indicate an indefinite future of decline and isolation. The pain of this can hardly be overestimated, because its primary cause was a separatism based on skin color, itself an accident of birth. Yet it seemed so evident that numbers of black people in town would lead to crime and violence that white Americans chose to run away, taking their money and political power with them, like nomads.

This was not what the civil-rights movement had had in mind—chasing white folks away, watching them stride toward freedom beyond the city limits. But most white Americans did not see themselves as Bull Connor, or see the

Bull Connor in themselves, and so the performance aspect of black people confronting a Bull Connor failed as a teaching tool. More importantly, most white Americans did not see black suffering as their own. The displays of black suffering did not propel whites to a realization of that common humanity which King held out to them as their own highest ideal and truest identity—which is perhaps why (mostly) black SNCC decided to use white bodies in Freedom Summer, 1964. A poll of New Yorkers that year showed a majority both supporting the Civil Rights Act and feeling the movement was going "too far." This occurred at a time before the Voting Rights Act when peaceful and proper black people were being jailed and beaten for nonviolent protests and killed for trying to register voters. Where was "too far"? White support for the movement had never been strong and already, in 1964, showed signs of receding. The abandonment of Negro cities and the abandonment of Southern blacks to Southern white mercies now appeared as two aspects of a single problem, namely the nature of white Americans. At this point the movement began to construe blacks and whites as separate races.

Perhaps the ultimate abandonment, or the ultimate pain, lay in the realization that white Americans did not care very much. If one were shot at, kept from casting a ballot, killed, left to fend for oneself in a torn-up and seemingly doomed city—what did it matter to them? One's life simply was not worth as much as one of theirs, and the determinant of that worthlessness was darkness of skin. The movement had played for stakes such as these, the highest stakes, and was abandoned by the American majority in the most profound fashion, an abandonment King understood as a refusal to love. The still-young preacher then began to thrash about in the wilderness that opened up all around his mountaintop, until a bullet ended his love and his misery in Memphis.

Yet what were white people to do? The civil-rights movement was unique in that it was the first and last broad, powerful movement in our history to accuse, however artfully, the American majority of being flawed human beings. The main reaction to this was a change in laws—to remove racial power from official hands and make segregation illegal. Such legislation did have the effect of transferring the flaw from people to laws, then correcting the laws. Nevertheless, even at the time a broad recognition existed that this might not be enough, since laws are just one form of social power, and it was hardly news to anyone that other forms had lives and consequences of their own. To alter such forms—most importantly, private decisions by whites only to hire and live near other whites—required a recognition of race as a social category. Thus a desire to eliminate race was almost immediately followed by a desire to recognize it. This desire was by no means widely shared in white America. Policies of affirmative action were not, and never would be, supported by a majority of white Americans. (The concept had been around since before the Civil War. Martin Delany used to attack white abolitionists by identifying their reluctance to hire blacks, and urged a change in the practice. In the 1860s Frederick Douglass's call for a black vice president was briskly met by the objection that such a post should be allocated on the basis of merit, not skin color.) Affirmative action did proceed, but surreptitiously, by executive orders, obscure regulatory maneuverings, and court decisions. Various arms of the state advanced the causes of minorities, with little reference to democratic debate. This backroom racial politics did not come about because of antidemocratic perversity among policy makers. Rather, those who pushed through programs aimed at helping minorities did so surreptitiously because they believed a more democratic process would not achieve the result they sought. And, given poll results from 1964 onward, the resistance of roughly one-third of Congress even to the Civil Rights Act, and the ongoing, spontaneous removal of whites to whites-only parts of the country, it is very difficult to maintain that apprehensions about the democratic process were misplaced. The white majority quickly came to perceive minorities as wards of the state benefiting from taxes paid by white people, a perception that dated back to Reconstruction—in some ways, back to early communities of freed slaves, as Samuel Sewall suggested in 1700—and had flitted through white politics ever since. The retention of local control over the funding, from local taxes, of police and schools marked the point at which state promotion of minority interests ceased and majority democratic politics took over. And that was, not coincidentally, the institutional place where white separatism survived the 1960s and survives down to our own time.

This was the main democratic white answer to efforts by the state, and by minorities whom the state was seen as representing, to tell one what to do and what to think, in racial terms. Affirmative action in whatever form, from school busing to quotas to the mild consideration of race as one factor in hiring and school admissions, implied two things about light-skinned people: that whites existed as a group; and that white Americans, left to themselves, would discriminate against nonwhites, even if they did not consciously intend to, in other words, that their race controlled them. Both were unattractive propositions, particularly the latter. While neither, except in specific legal cases, was directed at one as an individual, one could still feel as a white person in this period that one was on permanent probation from a charge of bad faith, a charge that could never be dismissed within the racial terms that made it comprehensible. Historically, this was a little like conceiving of white America as the South writ large. The civil-rights period had indeed been called a second Reconstruction, and many experienced the subsequent conservative drift of the nation—that part of it that voted—as resembling a second Restoration, one that began either with the Republican nomination of Barry Goldwater in 1964 or the election of Richard Nixon as president in 1968, and culminated with the presidency of Ronald Reagan in 1980. (Reagan had opposed the Civil Rights Act, headed Californians for Goldwater, supported the freedom of racial choice in housing expressed in 1964's Proposition 14, and opposed the Voting Rights Act of 1965.) Successful politicians now regularly ran *against* the state and *for* remarkably little, a paradoxical politics given that politicians don't have a function other than to run the state. But racially, there was little for white politicians to do except protect the white middle-class economy and reduce as much as they could, without causing riots or weakening American power overseas, government spending on anything else, such as civil rights.

However, the moral accusation of the 1960s—that white people were flawed as a race—did take hold in many white minds, and this had telling results for the history of white separatism. Within the academy and elite media, new histories began to be written and read, the histories of Indians and blacks, above all, but also of Jews and Chinese and Mexicans and others as these people had lived in the American past. Such histories gradually shrank the white share of the past, particularly as previously white groups—Irish, Italians, Jews, some Indians and Hispanics—became what might be called minorities of the historical imagination. This is hardly surprising, as the associations of whiteness as a historical identity were overwhelmingly negative. It was, collectively, a therapeutic use of the past, and its shrinkage of the specifically white claim to historical importance was part of the therapy, not only for nonwhites but for whites. One could almost imagine a certain vanishing point at which any white individual might claim a genealogical minority status, if only by loose adoption or membership in something other than the ruling class, so that the American past could appear a collection of minority contributions without any majority to which they might refer—a new, positive version of one-drop thinking, such that a little bit of something not utterly white could remove you from whiteness. The proliferation of ethnic, religious, and racial identities spread into popular culture and school curricula, and pointed to a future in which the many types of American would have everything in common and nothing in common at the same time. American individualism might become so elaborated that each person would have a unique past, and race, in Henry Adams's sense, would disappear. At the popular level, celebrations of diversity tended to posit, for each group, a distinct set of artifacts, cultural practices, and possibly worldviews that had a folkloric changelessness to them. This may be seen partly as a response to the enormous increase in nonwhite immigration following the 1965 immigration act. It was as if the Americanization thesis of the 1920s—that the European "races" would each contribute a heritage that could give America a new past as well as a richer future—had been expanded to include everything outside Europe. Thus racial separatism, except for whites, was legitimated as a questionless form of self-discovery and stripped of legitimacy as a form of social power.

The shrinkage of the white past as such enabled a new generation of whites to feel that the history of the white race had no claim on them. The longed-for white escape from racial identity—the freedom of racelessness that racial separatism had so often kept as its goal—seemed within reach. The widespread awareness that white people had once behaved very poorly encouraged whites to abandon that past altogether. One could hardly wish to live one's life in the constant honing of a sense of racial shame, and, of course, whiteness since the 1920s—in many ways, long before then—had steadfastly resisted attributions of positive content. At the same time, the acquisition of positive racial histories by nonwhites made them, from a white point of view, more racial, such that race itself might increasingly be seen as something other people had. And this, again, had been one white view of race for many years. White Americans after 1970 moved away from race, in the old sense, as others moved toward it. This explicitly occurred in terms of whites repudiating a racial past that controlled them—and nonwhites doing the opposite, embracing one that controlled them as a unique source of racial identity. Because whites no longer thought in terms of a positive white past, to be identified as white was in some sense to be victimized by the acts of one's ancestors. And that was just what white Americans had been seeking to escape, for so long, by constantly making themselves new.

The possibility of light skin having some social disadvantage awakened white Americans in a new way to the attractiveness of going beyond race. From the seventeenth century to the 1970s the desire of whites to go beyond race had customarily been expressed as a desire to separate from nonwhites. That separation continued in great stretches of the country that remained mostly white. But in some states, particularly California, the stability of a separate white life of raceless freedom was being threatened. In 1990 California was just over 57 percent white, and would soon be the third minority-white state (after Hawaii and New Mexico), with Hispanics understood as nonwhite. Californians then passed arguably the first civil-rights law in our history to favor whites, the California Civil Rights Initiative of 1996. It was a model of innocence, in a state that prided itself on not having a past. The initiative simply restated the language of 1964, that there shall be no discrimination on the basis of race or sex. In this way, California programs that favored nonwhites were made illegal because they discriminated against whites. This was the first time affirmative action had been subject to a popular vote, and the public voted against it. In a way, the California initiative indicated that white Americans were nearing a belief that white people no longer existed in a meaningful historical sense—specifically, that their racial past had been overcome, their notable tendency to favor each other had ended. Like the Garrisonians, they had become, in their own minds, color-blind. White history had ended. White people were free from it now. Whatever had happened since 1619, it had nothing to do with them.

The California initiative was still a dream when Timothy McVeigh parked his bomb by Oklahoma City's federal building. Those whites who cultivated, as McVeigh did, a positive, explicit white identity after the 1960s were few in number, even fewer than had been the case between 1945 and the civil-rights victories of the mid-1960s. Like their predecessors, they commonly reached toward something other than whiteness itself in their search for content. Where Southern segregationists had looked to regional custom and the blood sacrifices of the Confederacy—or, in the exotic case of the filibustering senator Robert Byrd, back to King John and the parable of the virgins—post-civil-rights race patriots sought hope in Aryanism, the example of Hitler, and above all in millenarian Protestant Christianity. Religious faith and a belief in racial destiny have certainly had a long, productive relationship. They fulfill so many similar functions, recognizing one's distinctiveness within the human mass yet also providing the guidance and nurture of membership in a group, and the liberation of anonymity. Both have been fairly well segregated, often self-segregated, in America since the early nineteenth century.

It may seem redundant to consider the members of a group believing in racial destiny to be self-segregated, but this type of separatism does have a substantial element of personal choice, if only in one's thoughts. Nature does not separate races. People do that for themselves. When people discover, as we say today, who they really are in racial terms, they are nonetheless creating, in part, the terms of their discovery. This creative aspect helps to explain why, looked at over a long period, races have been able to change shape. The American whitening of successive European groups, the creation of Hispanics and Asians, the elastic nature of Indianness, the variation in blood-quantum rules and community perceptions concerning who is black—all suggest that the boundaries of race are profoundly flexible.

For anyone who advocates positive racial identity, this vagueness may appear full of dangers. To the impossibility of racial separatism is added the difficulty of racial creation; they have accompanied each other. With respect to white people, the difficulty is compounded by the paradox of white separatism: that it has usually been in such determined flight from its own premise. And the desire of whites not to be white has probably never been stronger than at present; certainly, not since the Revolution. Those who advocate positive whiteness have never been so in the minority. They are in a wilderness, abandoned by the race they alone seek to advance in racial terms. No wonder, then, that their minds turn to the Last Days and visions of fire.

Yet even here there is room for surprise, and tangles of racial selfhood, and variations of the "tragic-comic attitude toward life" advocated by the Oklahoman Ralph Ellison. This was brought home to me in Oklahoma in the person of Anderson Clay Fields. I had noticed him in a Muskogee courtroom while I was observing the antiterrorism proceedings against Reverend Willie Ray Lampley. I asked Jay Willcoxen, Lampley's attorney, about the man I had seen on the fringes of the crowd. Willcoxen explained that he was Fields, Lampley's designated caretaker pastor of the Universal Church of God (Yahweh), who was to continue the ministry while Lampley was in prison. Willcoxen was himself a study: a big, young white man with a buzz cut and a modest practice, he had attended a black university on a minority scholarship. He told me that Fields was a farmer down in Vernon, a minuscule rural spot in the southeastern hinterland. Over ribs at a black restaurant, Willcoxen's favorite, the attorney diplomatically noted that Fields might have been, together with Lampley, as the story went, one of the two witnesses mentioned in Revelation as harbingers of apocalypse. Willcoxen was a Southern man and a discreet lawyer and so betrayed just the mildest hint of interest in the fact that Fields was black. Being new to the South but eager to learn, I was just quietly astonished. One does not expect to meet a black white separatist. Racial separatism is meant to be an exclusive creed. I arranged by phone to have dinner with Fields at his home.

It was the holiday season, and many Oklahomans had illuminated their private landscapes with reindeer, Santas, crèches, numberless lightbulbs in primary colors—even crosses, as if to say we should not forget the end of Christ's beginning. Driving at dusk to see Fields, I savored the fall of darkness and the rise of electrified Protestant ardor. Going west along Route 9 outside Eufaula, I passed a church with the sign IF YOU'RE GOING THE WRONG WAY, GOD PERMITS U-TURNS, then headed south on a dirt road (VERNON 4 MILES). My directions said to turn right at the first four-way intersection, and on up the hill to the end of the road, where I would find a black Comet, a brown-and-tan Chevy pickup, and a two-ton green Chevy. There I met Anderson Clay Fields and his wife, Elfrieda.

Elfrieda prepared dinner while Clay, as he is known, and I sat in the living room to talk. He met Lampley in 1990, and together they had traveled as far as Washington, D.C., to inform government officials that the nation was not in conformity with God's law and could expect to be invaded and destroyed, sooner rather than later, as a result. "So we worked together to make known to the people what we believe Yahweh would have them to do," Fields said in a voice unusually deep for a slight man. He spoke in the complete and weighty sentences of a preacher who expects attention. "And we visited certain government officials, and we went to several state capitals and talked to government officials and expressed to them the need to comply with Yahweh's law. Of course that was to no avail. But we nevertheless experienced being obedient to Yahweh when he commanded us to do a certain thing. So from that standpoint it was a success, even if they didn't hear us, or respond to the message."

Their quixotic journeyings created a closeness between the two men. "I considered him my friend," Fields said of Lampley, "and I still do." Fields believed that God, in wreaking destruction upon those who have strayed from his path, might use people such as Lampley and even himself. In Scripture, God had used people against sinners, "to place them in bondage and even to slay them." Fields gave Gideon as an example: "He was known for going and destroying all the false places of worship. And of course one of the places his father was involved in, and he destroyed it. And it would be the same, I would compare today, as a person blowing up a federal building. The federal building in no way represents Yahweh, and the federal government in no way complies with Yahweh's laws. Therefore it can be recognized as the same entity as, you know, Baalism during Gideon's time."

"So you feel there is a logic, a holy logic, to what happened in Oklahoma City?"

"There is. If people would be honest with themselves."

Fields's militant approach nevertheless had a distance to it. Unlike Lampley, he was far from certain that America would be invaded that Christmas. Nor did he look forward to the terror of apocalypse; he actually seemed to dread it. He had lost many family and friends, he said, to the drug trade—which he blamed on the government—and knew violent strife firsthand. Although he acknowledged that "it's a really kind of far-fetched-sounding scenario," he simply felt that American life had declined so far that divine retribution had to occur.

"Even among my people," Fields said, "the NAACP has ran its course." I was glad he brought up the subject of his people. I asked after his thoughts on the question of racial separatism. "That's one of the real touchy subjects that you can get on, and you can offend people rather quickly," Fields said. We both looked idly away into the distance for a moment, as Elfrieda clattered in the kitchen, then Fields continued: "I feel that there are some people who confuse the race issue, and feel like Yahweh chose one group of people over another group of people because of who the people were, or what color they were, and really that don't have anything to do with why he chose people. Because he chose people based on their response to him. If you read in the Scriptures, every tribe, all the twelve tribes of Israel, come from different ethnic backgrounds. Their parents were of one ethnicity and their mother was of another. And most of the women who married the Israelites, if you trace their background, they were of African descent.

"So when a white man claims to be a direct descendant of Israel, he don't know that I can in turn claim that same inheritance. I feel that there's proof that I can go to in the Scriptures, that I can prove that there were interracial marriages in those times. There's always been race mixing. Now, me personally, I feel like Yahweh made me who I am, and I feel that, personally, I should just kind of stick to that. That's just a personal belief, I'm not saying that's his law. I feel that he made everybody the way he intended to. And then he separated them. If you want to look at him as a separatist, then there's really no argument that I can say that he's not. Because in his divine plan he created mankind and gave them different shades of skin, and he set them in different places of the world. So I guess you could say he's the original separatist. But he didn't separate people because he felt that one group was better than the other. He intended all of us to have self worth and to have knowledge of our heritage. And I also believe that he believed for us to coexist peacefully with each other."

In the context of that evening this seemed to me surprisingly sane. He may be the only person to have done it, but Fields had combined Afrocentrism and white Israelitism into something like a multicultural racial chaos theory rooted in Scripture. Whether race had driven him to this, or religion, I could not say, but it was a remarkable synthesis. "We're fighting against something much greater than the color of our skin," he emphasized. "We're fighting for the will to control our minds."

And is race not something that controls our minds? Fields knew perfectly well that his friend Reverend Lampley believed himself, by virtue of his whiteness, to be identified with the Israelites. There was a joke there, too, however, because "you know, Mr. Lampley lives in this all-black community. So I guess you could call him a separatist in the true sense. Only he separated from his own people." We laughed about that for quite a while. In my polite cowardice I did not tell Fields what Lampley had told me earlier, that he believed blacks were designed by God to be a servant race.

Fields believed Vernon was the second all-black settlement in Oklahoma, after Boley. His own people had come up in a covered wagon from Waco, Texas, late in the nineteenth century, "as a way of getting their own land and getting away from some oppression during those times." The closest village, Hanna—a mile or two from the Fieldses—was a Creek settlement, with several stomp grounds nearby for the annual Green Corn dance. Presumably, the earliest blacks in this patch were former slaves of the Creeks or of the Seminoles, just to the west. The Seminoles had numerous slaves and free black tribal members, to such a degree that the African and Indian are practically impossible to separate. Coincidentally, *seminole* is from the Creek for "separatist," because the nucleus of the Seminoles separated itself from the Creeks and went to Florida. Then their respective descendants ended up here as neighbors north of the Canadian River. Oklahoma is a small world of human flight. Somehow black, white, and Indian separatism had come together within the tiny circumference of Vernon and Hanna, with a population that could be reckoned high in the dozens.

Fields had his own special view of white separatism. He noted, in particular, that the term made little sense because those called white separatists seemed always to be running away from white people in order to be white by themselves. "They labeled Randy Weaver [a militant besieged by federal agents] as a white supremacist, you know, as a white separatist rather," Fields said. "I mean, here's a man living off in the woods by himself. Who were his neighbors? If he was a white supremacist, it would seem more like him to move in a community where there was more, you know, white people. Where he was surrounded by those he felt he had something in common with. But he was just, like, out in the woods."

Elfrieda had prepared a lovely meal. We passed lightly among the somewhat related subjects of interracial love and Southern cooking and mourned that the homemade wine wasn't yet ready for drinking. After dinner Fields and I went outside and looked at the stars. There were so many. Fields said it was cloudy.

"This is cloudy?"

"Usually it's like a planetarium. Have you ever been to a planetarium?"

"Yes, I have."

"That's what it's usually like."

Fields said he looked forward to harvesting watermelons next summer, "if we're still here"—that is, if the apocalypse still hadn't come to make everything new and bring the reign of justice.

PART FOUR

A FAMILY IN TIME

History . . . is not merely something to be read. And it does not refer merely, or even principally, to the past. On the contrary, the great force of history comes from the fact that we carry it within us, are unconsciously controlled by it in many ways, and history is literally *present* in all that we do . . . And it is with great pain and terror that one begins to realize this. In great pain and terror one begins to assess the history which has placed one where one is and formed one's point of view. In great pain and terror because, therefore, one enters into battle with that historical creation, Oneself . . .

—James Baldwin

When we moved to Oakland, California, my parents bought a modest stucco house in the Fruitvale district and painted it an indescribable green. I was not yet seven years old. We were poised on a slope between the MacArthur and Warren freeways, closer to the former—between the Flatlands and the Hills, as they were called; also, though I did not understand this yet, between poverty and wealth, and between black and white. We had a tall pine in the back yard. I loved climbing trees and spent many contented hours with pitch on my hands and the pine smell so strong it clung to my shirt. I learned to imitate the questioning call of the mourning dove, and otherwise conversed with birds. I had an intense boyish love of animals, soil, wood, leaves, rocks, and water. I lived, as best I could, and remarkably enough for a city boy, in a state of nature. I carried a pocketknife and roved, alert and intrigued, about my private wilderness. My interest in human affairs was slight. We did see big animals at the Knowland Zoo, but there were no elk or bison foraging along Coolidge Avenue past our house, or anywhere else in Oakland. So I tracked mice in the back yard under the pine, as well as slugs and snails when it was damp. Nor was I above careful observation of insects, including ants, and even some little red bugs that were tinier than ants. At times a possum would visit, once in a while a raccoon. These I appreciated as proxies for the larger game among whom I assumed I would live when I was grown. Not that I condescended to the doves and possums I knew. A person capable of monitoring the progress of a snail or slug cannot be in a hurry. I was not in a hurry to grow up in those days.

From the swaying pine branches I looked out over our new home. Up the hill from us stood, most prominently, the Mormon temple. Windowless, its white stone walls crowned with gold steeples—one at each corner, a bigger, taller one in the middle—the Mormon temple looked very much like a space-ship from an alien civilization, one that had landed here for unknown reasons and therefore could be expected to leave at some point, probably at night, when it was illuminated and people like us visited to gawk and wonder at the expense. The Mormons also lit up their huge and repetitive, rigid garden: English ivy, cowering low in rectangles, cropped as if by a barber; trees one like the other; water in angular channels over a cement bed painted blue. All in all, a vision of nature subdued, not to say crushed, something I took rather personally, and altogether different from Joaquin Miller Park, farther up the hill. There I found a statue of the man for whom the park was named, a poet; some stone ruins he had left behind for me to climb on; a parking oval where families came in the day to take in the magnificent view, and lovers came at night; and rampant nature, redwoods, and madrones, which had smooth red bark that peeled, man-zanitas, flagrant rhododendrons, and acre upon acre of eucalyptus trees, rustling and clattering, with their gray frayed bark and their distinct scent, arid and sweet.

In the other direction, toward the water, the rooftops proceeded like a stair-case down to the freeway. A little rightward, as the land flattened, was China-town, then Lake Merritt, the city's aesthetic pride—one day I would scull on it—and then the skyline of downtown, distinguished by the curvy Kaiser build-ing and the green roof of the Oakland *Tribune* headquarters, then still owned by the Knowland family. Just down from there was Jack London Square, where the Alameda estuary met San Francisco Bay. A handful of restaurants, swank and therefore, to me, frightening, pressed in on a one-room cabin said to have been occupied by the writer Jack London. I was more interested in the estuary and what lived beneath its surface. I had a year of wanting to be a marine biologist; other years were devoted to chemist, geologist, astronaut, and through them all the dream of being a park ranger. And an Indian. I wanted to become an Indian. When *National Geographic* published a map of American Indian tribes, showing their (precolonial) lands, I taped it to the ceiling above my bed, the top bunk, and took myself to sleep memorizing names and territories, Chiricahua, Seminole, Nez Percé, Blackfoot, Cree. One of the surviving fragments of the language of the Ohlones, who lived in the Bay Area, is from a song. *Uxarat kai pire*, "dancing on the cliff of the world": that's what I was doing.

I did have some contact with living human society, through the Boy Scouts (after Cub Scouts), church, and school. My troop met at the one-room Boy Scout House in Dimond Park. The park lies in a steep crevice at the head of what early Oaklanders called Indian Gulch, because it had sheltered the main Ohlone village; the gulch drains into Lake Merritt. I did not know this, however, when my Scout troop met one evening each week. Dimond Park was damp and full of woodsy smells. We played brutal games of capture the flag. We clambered among the tree roots overhanging a muddy creek that ran through the park and searched for such things as worms and unusually shaped sticks. There were still some oaks around, and therefore acorns, which can be fun to play with if you apply yourself.

The Scout program sought to instill virtues by having us memorize lists of them from a book. These were mumbled in a low, rhythmic way at each meeting. We were likewise meant to develop an ethic of public service. We may have developed the ethic, but I don't believe we ever gave the service. The only official rituals that held any interest were when we had the chance to imitate Indians. There were no Indians in the troop. We labored at reciting long strange words, which in turn connected to a scheme having to do with unity of purpose and brotherhood. I can also remember color symbolism, animal totems, an emphasis on bird feathers, and the exchange of blood, through thumb pricks, with another boy. (My Indian blood brother was Jewish, a distinction I didn't recognize as important because he was my friend and neighbor and because I believed that Jews were much like us Baptists; my family reserved its doctrinal animus for Catholics, Mormons, Pentecostals, and the spineless Unitarians.) As Indians, we wore a length of fabric, the breechcloth, over our jockey shorts, and battled—because Indians are strong and laugh at pain—against the cold and discomfort of sitting on the ground cross-legged while listening to men tell incomprehensible, misty stories about our Indian ancestors. I adored these Indian times and felt them deeply. Today I can only recall one word, which sounds like wee-mock-ten-dink, and meant *brotherhood*, I think. It never did occur to me to wonder why the only ritual in all those years that had to do with ancestry, race, and blood was one connecting us to people who were not, as far as we knew, our ancestors. Nor did I stop to wonder why the only ritual tying us one to another as brothers, united in purpose and heritage, required us to be imitation Indians.

I thought little, if at all, about race in my first Oakland years. Oakland was a mixed-race town. Therefore, as a small child, one could not be greatly struck by physical differences, because there were too many and they were not yet fitting into a pattern; it would have been like wondering why all the trees weren't the same. My church was mostly white, but I did not yet think of those people as white except in the most cursory way (they looked white), any more than I dwelled on the blackness of my Sunday-school friends Mark and Curtis or the Chineseness of the Chin kids.

Race, however, was thinking about us, as when we Scouts unthinkingly became Indian blood brothers; in a manner of speaking, the past was waiting for our present to catch up. For example, when my family drove downtown from Fruitvale to the First Baptist Church, where my father was associate pastor, I saw to the left of the off-ramp FREE HUEY written on the side of a building. I saw it every Sunday morning. The words *Free Huey* told me we were about to reach the church. I am certain now that whoever wrote those words did not intend them as a reassuring memory aid for a pale red-headed boy going to church. Huey Newton and Bobby Seale had founded the Black Panther Party for Self-Defense in 1966 at an Oakland college; Huey went into prison in 1967 and became a symbol of the persecuted black man; "Free Huey" was the potent slogan of his supporters. But you never know how political speech may be interpreted. When I visited my father at his other job, working at the American Baptist Seminary of the West in Berkeley, I looked out his office window and saw a small park filled with tents and sleeping bags. Dad said this was People's Park. He probably explained why folks were camping there, but it went right past me. I already knew I supported them with all my fiber, because I loved camping.

In short, I had no idea what was happening around me. The central issues of American life—how much money you have and what color you are—had not quite gripped my consciousness. In elementary school I had black friends and white friends—yes, Jews and Gentiles!—Chinese and Japanese friends, and friends with Spanish surnames, Italian surnames, one with an Armenian name. And by Oakland standards my school, Sequoia, was not very integrated, whatever that meant. We made many distinctions among ourselves, some of which were racial in the sense that we could identify physical variation. We weren't blind. But, in truth, the important thing about Patty was not that she was black but that she was fat. The critical features of a boy named Severini were that he wore baggy pants and his name almost rhymed with Seven Weanies. My own first name, sad to say, rhymed with Snot. So much for the heroic Caledonian ancestry my parents had thought to evoke. Darryl was noted for his gentle manner (not his blackness), Laura for her athleticism and regal posture (not her blackness), William for his cruelty and Esther for her sweetness (not their Spanish names), Jeff for his speed and smile (not for being Chinese). Dino was the name of a Greek boy; more importantly, Dino was the name of Fred and Wilma Flintstone's yapping pet dinosaur. So the curiosities of race took a backseat to the curiosities of Seven Weanies and the magnificent nose of a girl named Susan, who explained that her mother was French, which made her jetty-like nose an icon of foreign beauty rather than a disfigurement. She was a smart little girl, Susan.

Yet, as I say, the past was waiting for us, to make us into Americans, give us our histories, and tell us the meanings of our names.

A PRESENT FROM JOHN SUTTER

■

My neighborhood, Fruitvale, was where the first non-Indians set themselves up on this side of the bay. They were of Spanish descent, as was the name California, which seems to have originated in Iberian romantic literature—that distinct synthesis of gallantry, racial and religious mixture, and dreamy power grabbing. Sometime in the late thirteenth or fourteenth century, the episodic saga *Amadís of Gaul* captured Portuguese and Spanish imaginations. A published version came in 1508, under the "authorship" of Garci Ordoñez (or Rodríguez) de Montalvo. To his version of *Amadís*, Montalvo added a sequel about Amadís's son, Esplandian. In the course of a battle with the sultan, Esplandian suddenly faces a second enemy—Californians.

> Know that to the right hand of the Indies was an island called California, very near to the region of the Terrestrial Paradise, which was populated by black women, without there being any men among them, that almost like the Amazons was their style of living . . . [T]heir arms were all of gold, and also the harnesses of the wild beasts, on which, after having tamed them, they rode; that in all the island there was no other metal whatsoever. They dwelt in caves very well hewn; they had many ships in which they went out to other parts to make their forays, and the men they seized they took with them, giving them their deaths . . .

This is the first known reference to a place called California, although the earlier *Song of Roland* has a mystifying line about "the Men of Africa and those of Califerne." Probably the name derives from Arabic *caliph*. Romance-addled Spanish Christians looking for California had dark-skinned Muslims and Muslim sympathizers very much on their minds and may have expected to find some north of Mexico. Historians have debated whether the name was lifted from fiction to fact with satirical intentions or as a sign of hope—that is, whether the Spaniards were making fun of themselves. But Spanish imperial culture was quite capable of being ironic and deluded at the same time. As it turned out, there were no black Amazons or Moors in California, and there was plenty of gold, and the Spaniards never found it.

Spain expanded slowly northward, in part because of persistently ambitious Jesuits. (The founder of their order, Ignatius of Loyola, had himself been fired in his expansionism by a fevered reading of *Amadís of Gaul.*) The great push came when Juan Bautista de Anza breached the San Jacinto Mountains in 1774, led by a Franciscan. The Order of Saint Francis would go on to build a string of missions up the coast as far as San Francisco, which Anza's lieutenant José Moraga settled in 1776. Along with Anza and Moraga on that colonizing expedition— the final effort in Spain's northerly growth—were Gabriel Peralta; his wife, Francisca Valenzuela; three sons and a daughter. Gabriel Peralta was born in 1718 in Córdoba, Spain, the old Moorish capital (until 1078); according to a distant relative, interviewed by a reporter around the turn of the twentieth century, the Peraltas were "descended from the union of a chivalrous Spanish knight and a beautiful daughter of the Moors, who were wedded despite the fierce war of the races. This was a blend of the best Andalusian and Moorish blood . . ." So although there had been no Moors previously in California, it appears that the Spanish brought some with them, a little trace of Africa.

"Word of the discovery of the New World," another Peralta descendant wrote, "is the biggest piece of news Man has ever had . . . Instantly, hopes were revived; life in the New World was to be worthwhile. To gather up the virtues and gleanings of Knowledge, to transplant them to this fertile new land—that was the thing to do." The writer is Ruperto Peralta-Galindo, in his unpublished "An American History (in 500 words)." Ruperto, Gabriel's great-great-grandson, wrote terrible short stories at the turn of the twentieth century and worked in the San Francisco Bay Area theater, including a stint as manager for, he reports, "MCIVOR-TYNDALL, the world's renowned mind reader." Ruperto writes that Gabriel's son Luis, in 1820, received from the king of Spain a vast ranch upon which "the cities of Oakland, Alameda and Berkeley, now stand." Luis's son Antonio "was the first white person to settle in what is now Alameda Co., that is outside of Mission San José. In 1820, he was sent by his father, to take possession of the 'Rancho', which he, his father, had just been granted. Young Antonio, was but eighteen years of age, and he was accompanied by an old retainer an Indian called Ramón; they arrived, and built a 'crow's nest', in a tree in which they slept at night, in order to warrant their safety, against bears, of which there were many . . . This place was in what is now called FRUIT VALE . . ."

Ruperto might also have said that Antonio Peralta was the first Moor to settle in what is now Alameda County (and the first Moor to live in a tree in Fruitvale). Spanish Northern California between 1776 and 1840 jutted into modern North America like a pier of late feudalism; it was to be the very last stage for that tragicomic Iberian opera that began with the Genoese captain-for-hire Christopher Columbus. Antonio and his "retainer" Ramón seem to have ridden in from *Amadís of Gaul,* or at least its satiric successor, Miguel de Cervantes's *Don Quijote.* Cervantes would have recognized immediately the comic perfection of the young nobleman and his dark servant hiding in a tree from bears. But who was Ramón? Ruperto relates that Antonio and his three brothers "lived a life of uninterrupted Joy, and pastoral pleasures, for years, with no one to trouble them, save their retainers." Similarly, Pearl Randolph Fibel, in her brief 1971 history of the Peraltas, writes of that first moment in the future Oakland: "What was here? Everything, it would seem, to make for man an earthly paradise: a mild Mediterranean climate, fertile earth, bountiful water, fish (including salmon) and shell-fish in the bay, ducks and small birds and game everywhere . . . and an indigenous labor force to be had for the training."

My little homeland turns out to have been yet another American paradise poised for its fall. California probably had the densest Indian population of any area comparable in size in North America. It possessed such an abundance of natural resources that people did not have to work very hard or develop sophisticated technologies to live adequately. They were therefore among the least pretentious Americans, and the most easily destroyed. Disease alone reduced them to people who had to sell their labor for survival. The Spanish priests and ranchers simply drafted those who survived into service. One prominent rancher recalled in 1844 that Indian men "tilled our soil, pastured our cattle, sheared our sheep, cut our lumber, built our houses, paddled our boats, made tile for our homes, ground our grain, slaughtered our cattle, dressed our hides for market, and made our burnt bricks; while the Indian women made excellent servants, took good care of our children, made every one of our meals." This left the ranchers and their wives the time for gracious living. An 1842 visitor described this same rancher's Indian workers: "Though not so recognized by law, yet they are thralls [slaves] in all but the name, borne to the earth by the toils of civilization superadded to the privations of savage life, they vegetate rather than live." There were perhaps 300,000 Indians living in California in 1792 and less than half that number sixty years later.

Northern California presents a chronologically intensified version of our North American history. About every broad social and economic trend from Columbus to the Civil War occurred there in the three generations between 1776 and 1866—from new frontier to cities, from imagined black Moors to slave society and the hierarchies of race and the wrinkled remembrance of honor-bound, happier times. The main missing elements were export-led plantation agriculture—California ranchers sold hides and tallow, not tobacco or cotton—and white Protestant salvationism, which would never get much purchase in a place of such abundance.

By the 1840s black and white Americans had begun to arrive from the East; the first wagon train set out from Missouri in 1841. Perhaps the most important of the whites, in retrospect, was Captain John Sutter. Born in the German-speaking mountain village of Kandern, just north of Basel, Switzerland, in 1803, Sutter (Johann Suter) spent his early adulthood going bankrupt, reaching California in 1839. Within two years he had built a would-be fort on the American River, headquarters for his projected New Switzerland. Sutter was among the few non-Spaniards (or non-Mexicans) to own considerable land prior to statehood. His "fort" became a base for the relentless Georgia-born explorer John Frémont, who in 1846 took it for the United States during the wishful quasi revolution against Mexico known as the Bear Flag Revolt. A visitor to Sutter's land in that year described his Indian workforce: Sutter "keeps 600 to 800 Indians in a complete state of Slavery and I had the mortification of seeing them dine I may give a short description 10 to 15 Troughs 3 to 4 feet long ware brought out of the cook room and seated in the Boiling sun all the labourers grate and small ran to the trough like so many pigs and feed themselves with their hands as long as the troughs contained even a moisture."

Sutter's neighbor on the American River William Leidesdorff was, in a sense, the first prominent black Californian. Born in the Virgin Islands to a Danish planter and his African wife, Leidesdorff arrived in San Francisco in 1841. He ran a schooner between that town and Honolulu, owned the bay's first steamboat, opened a hotel, served as San Francisco City Council treasurer, and generally made himself rich and respected. Leidesdorff became a Mexican citizen in 1844, receiving thirty-five thousand acres near Sutter's New Switzerland. Like Sutter, he involved himself in pro-U.S. politics, entertaining Frémont at his home. In 1845 President Polk made Leidesdorff American vice-consul. This may or may not be counted as a major racial event, because it appears that Polk did not know Leidesdorff was black. I do wonder what blackness meant to Leidesdorff. In 1846 his neighbor Sutter liquidated a third of his sizable debt to

Leidesdorff by giving him Indian slaves, including two "Girls, of which you will take which you like the best." Because the girl was intended for what was sometimes called "personal use," Sutter added that he would "make you a present with the girl."

Along with the trade in humans, the redwood business attracted Sutter and Leidesdorff, as it did lesser men. A vast forest of these huge trees covered the Oakland hills, so near to the growing town of San Francisco. Those trees belonged to the Peraltas, who were unable to prevent men from cutting them down by hand and dragging them to the shoreline. Sutter began building a mill in 1847, and, coincidentally, one of his carpenters (from New Jersey) happened to find some gold late in January 1848. That was quite a year for California. A week after Sutter's carpenter found gold, Mexico ceded California to the United States. In April, Leidesdorff died, his assets valued at over a million dollars. He was only forty-one and probably would have made a great deal more money, because Sutter and his carpenter failed to keep the gold news a secret. By the end of the year California's non-Indian population had doubled. In the next year San Francisco's population would grow by 1,000 percent; and in 1850 California became a state.

That meant an end to the Peralta life of uninterrupted joy. The boomtown of San Francisco burned down three times in a year and a half, and the lumber to rebuild it came principally from the Oakland hills. Within less than a decade all the redwoods would be gone and the hills covered with stumps; then the stumps were taken. The thefts and racial murders and creation of racial hierarchies that had been such conspicuous features of our national history since Jamestown occurred at a breathtaking pace in Northern California. Thousands upon thousands of men gripped by gold fever—mostly white, but also black (including some slaves) and Chinese and other sorts of folk as well—were not calm people. They were the most intense embodiment of lunatic American expansionism ever assembled, and if they had any principles other than self-advancement, they left little record of them. Non-Indian women were scarce, and many of those who did live in Northern California during these years found their sex to be their most lucrative possession. Indian women were taken, forcefully and not, as wives by whites—the so-called squaw men—or sold as sexual slaves. The market in Indians became brisk for a while as new Californians took up the practices of the Mexican ranchers. Writing of the Ohlones in 1850, an Indian agent reported: "Of the numerous tribes which but a few years ago inhabited the country bordering on the bay of San Francisco, scarcely an individual is left. The pale-faces have taken possession of their country and trample upon the graves of their forefathers."

The first governor of California had vowed "a war of extermination," and that is what took place, though often in an informal way. State funds went to volunteer militias. Their work is illustrated by the events of 1850 at Clear Lake, later a popular recreation spot for us Oaklanders. A newspaper account from the time described the militia coming upon two to three hundred Indians by the lake: "They immediately surrounded them and as the Indians raised a shout of defiance and attempted to escape, poured in a destructive fire indiscriminately upon men, women, and children . . . Little or no resistance was encountered, and the work of butchering was of short duration. The shrieks of the slaughtered victims died away, the roar of muskets ceased, and stretched lifeless upon the sod of their native valley were the bleeding bodies of these Indians—nor sex, nor age was spared; it was the order of *extermination* fearfully obeyed. The troops returned to their stations, and quiet is for the present restored." Within a decade of the discovery of gold two-thirds of California's Indians were dead. Their population stood at about thirty-five thousand in 1860. Twenty years later it would be sixteen thousand.

The non-Indian settlement of Oakland proceeded under the leadership of two groups of recent immigrants, one honest, one not. The second group, which ignored the Peraltas' title, prevailed. As one nineteenth-century historian wrote, "Sometimes, as in the notorious and infamous case of the first foundation of the now so fine and progressive city of Oakland, a great tract of land would be lost to its owners by the deeds of some crowd of deliberate and unprincipled trespassers . . ." Andrew Moon, Edson Adams, and Horace Carpentier came from Binghamton, New York, Fairfield, Connecticut, and Galway, New York, respectively. They were squatters, but Carpentier was a squatter with a law degree, and that made all the difference. He retired a wealthy man, living out his long life in New York City, on East Thirty-seventh Street. (He was notable for his philanthropy, giving generously to minority interests—Chinese, plus thirty thousand dollars to the Tuskegee Institute for a Booker T. Washington memorial—and to his alma mater, Columbia, which received a million dollars.) The Peraltas, meanwhile, saw their fortunes decline. Today you can visit their graves in Saint Mary's cemetery on a hill overlooking Oakland. Vicente died early and has a large vault at the top of the hill. It is a ruin now, but at least it was impressive when he died. Near it is a granite monument to his brother Ygnacio. The longer-lived Antonio—the first white person in the future Oakland, he of the bear-proof tree house—lies in an unmarked grave at the bottom of the hill.

Antonio and Ramón had sat in their tree a mile from our home. Later the Peraltas' Indian workers built an adobe house on the site, then a wood home that still stands, relocated next to a bitty park. This home was later divided into apartments and rented for quite a while. The last time I saw it, the place was empty and shut up, with a NO SMOKING sign by the door. There must have been some problems with people loitering on the porch. A few adobe blocks from the original house found their way into the Boy Scout House in Dimond Park. I remember carving into them with my pocketknife.

The new Oaklanders, like other Americans with a chance to start afresh, had a forgetful relationship with the past. The disappointed irony of the 1850s—two books from that decade were *The Land of Gold: Reality versus Fiction* and *Golden Dreams and Leaden Realities*—yielded to the go-ahead pioneer work of creating the best of all possible worlds. The coming of the railroad helped. The transcontinental line ran from New York to Oakland; service started in 1869. Commerce grew accordingly, magnificent hotels (the Tubbs, the Grand Central) sheltered travelers, the wealthy built mansions on Lake Merritt and private schools for their children. Oaklanders loudly urged the virtues of their town, in part because of a nagging awareness that another town, San Francisco, lay nearby and appeared to be growing as well. In 1875 the businessman D. L. Emerson harangued his audience: "When I first came to Oakland our population numbered less than 1000; and at that time this whole region of country above Seventh street was the most attractive cow pasture you ever beheld . . . At that time, also, we had a whole army, both *in* Oakland and *out of it* who seemed sworn to injure our city all they could. No *frog-pond* in the United States ever sent up, during the month of April, so infernal a din to the delicate ears of any nervous invalid as this army of human frogs poured into the ears of citizens and strangers in depreciation of our unrivaled city . . . If a people ever had occasion to curse Pharaoh and pity the Israelites, we were that people." But Emerson felt he had seen the end of that "old *habit*, once chronic and popular across the Bay, but not so any longer, of sneering at Oakland." In the mid-1870s it was the second-largest city on the Pacific coast—after San Francisco.

Industries expanded rapidly: lumbermills and carriage makers, German breweries, then canneries and, on a large scale, textile mills. In 1888 the *Oakland Tribune* could offer a special edition exulting in Oakland's prosperity and the bright future it promised. At the California Hosiery Company, "From 140 to 150 hands are employed in the factory, while 125 more are given employment at their homes on piecework—all white men, women, girls, and boys." The California Jute Company had even more workers: "At present about 225 white hands are employed and 100 Chinese. White applicants, with a genuine desire to learn and become useful operatives, are given the preference in every case . . . In securing and teaching so large a proportion of white labor, the management has conferred a benefit upon the community."

The labors of such people generated enough wealth that a good public-school system arose alongside the private one. Oakland began to bill itself as "the Athens of the Pacific." The University of California had its start in Oakland—the sort of fact known exclusively by Oaklanders—and the town was indeed peculiarly cultured. The writer Gertrude Stein spent her girlhood there, including a year at the Tubbs Hotel. She seems not to have looked back on it with warm affection, however: "What was the use of my having come from Oakland it was not natural to have come from there yes write about it if I like but not there, *there is no there there.*" Stein has been considered a traitorous liar ever since. There has never been a park named for her, and I expect there never will be.

Dearer to the memory of Oaklanders is the poet Joaquin Miller. Where Stein turned a cold shoulder to both punctuation and the Athens of the Pacific, Miller saved his scorn for spelling, and embraced his adopted city. He moved there in 1886, to what is now Joaquin Miller Park. He named his home The Hights. When I was a child, we did not read Joaquin Miller's work, nor did we know anything about him except that he had been a poet, with poetically long hair, but one did feel proud that a literary man had settled here and honored our city by association.

Miller was a strange man, from Indiana via Oregon and other parts. He dressed somewhat like a frontiersman. His real name was Cincinnatus Hiner Miller, known as Heiney. Joaquin sounded better, although the man was in no known sense of Spanish descent. One historian has described him as a "kind of literary cross between Walt Whitman and Buffalo Bill." He was almost certainly the versifying equal of Buffalo Bill, as can be seen in his poem "Oakland," written at The Hights:

> *Thou Rose-land! Oakland! Thou mine own!*
> *Thou Sun-land! Leaf-land! Land of seas*
> *Wide-crescented in walls of stone!*
> *Thy lion's mane is to the breeze!*

> . . .

> *Here men of God in holy guise*
> *Invoke the peace of Paradise.*
> *Be this my home till some fair star*
> *Stoops earthward and shall beckon me;*
> *For surely God-land lies not far*
> *From these Greek heights and this great sea.*
> *My friend, my love, trend this way;*
> *Not far along lies Arcady.*

Miller promoted himself as the Poet of the Sierras and strove to embody all things Western, which is to say he lied ceaselessly. He was a self-made poet, in that he didn't read books he hadn't written. He applied a similar discipline to drinking: "no whiskey before noon" became known as Joaquin's Law. According to Miller's biographer M. M. Marberry, young Jack London was a frequent guest at Hights bouts, along with local light George Sterling ("the hard-drinking sonnet writer") and Herman Whitaker, "then known for his novels and two-fisted drinking." Miller had his mane to the breeze.

He liked to tell, as one of what his friend Mark Twain called Miller's "muddy torrent" of stories, about how he had founded an Indian utopia around Mount Shasta, a snowcapped lonely volcano to the north. According to Marberry, "The plan, Joaquin said, was to rescue the noble Red Man from the corroding impact of white civilization. Mount Shasta was made sacred to the Indians, and all others were barred, excepting Joaquin. The tribes lived happily in their sanctuary in a communistic sort of way, with Joaquin officiating as the Great White Father." This was fantasy, but people occasionally believed it, as they believed Miller when he said he had fought on the Indian side during a famous battle-massacre at Pit River. "This is indeed a curious misrepresentation of the facts," the amiable Marberry wrote in 1953. "Actually, he fought against the Indians, and with the whites after the Pit River massacre, as Army records show. Joaquin's distortion of this episode is hard to understand and can only be explained in terms of the personal guilt he felt toward the Indians. While later in life he posed as their protector, there was an interlude here that he was none too proud of, when . . . he sired an Indian daughter and deserted her. Perhaps he preferred to appear as a traitor to his own race rather than to his own child, who must have been on his conscience—for Joaquin Miller did have a conscience."

I wish we had learned some of this during my school days. The Poet of the Sierras had been a squaw man. "This is indeed a lovely day," he wrote in his journal around 1856, "my squaw is out digging roots my dog is lying at my feet my riffle is by my side my pipe is in my mouth." The boundaries between white and Indian were fluid at that time, as were the moral considerations one might have brought to bear on them. Miller both lived with Indians and killed them, and more or less at the same time. A journal entry from 1857 reads, "Took 5 squaws and one buck hung the buck and freed the squaws." Miller's own "squaw" later married one Jim Brock. She died in 1908, in San Francisco, as Mrs. Amanda Brock, "greatly honored and respected," according to the San Francisco *Call*.

The racial boundaries were at times so fluid that one can only marvel at their persistence. For example, Miller took the name Joaquin from the Mexican bandit Joaquín Murieta. The legend of this man's career came largely from the pen of John Rollin Ridge (Yellow Bird)—eldest son of the Cherokee John Ridge and Sarah Bird Northrup, the mixed-race couple who had been ejected from Cornwall, Connecticut. Rollin Ridge had been a boy when he saw his father assassinated as a traitor to the tribe. It was, he recalled, "a scene of agony . . . which might make one regret that the human race had ever been created. It has darkened my mind with an eternal shadow." Sarah took the children out of Cherokee country. Ridge left for California in 1850 with his brother Aeneas and his slave Wacooli. Ridge tried mining and, like everyone else, hated it. "I have worked harder," he wrote back to his relative Stand Watie, "than any slave I ever owned or my father either." Ridge went into writing—journalism, the Murieta book, poetry—and became almost certainly the first Indian to earn his living as a writer. He defended the California Indians as best he could and had high hopes for an Indian state. He wrote the biography of Murieta essentially as revenge against his father's killers. Ridge put himself into Murieta, then had Murieta go along killing his many enemies one by one. This became the Murieta legend. And so the former squaw man Heiney Miller took on the name of a Mexican bandit whose legend was formed as an act of vengeance against a Cherokee assassination team by a part-white, part-Cherokee slave-owning poet. This is a true story of American authenticity. Miller enjoyed a great success in London—he met Tennyson and Trollope, held up the Langham hotel bar with Wilkie Collins and the peripatetic Twain—because literary people there knew that Miller embodied Americanness with a purity hard to surpass. And perhaps Miller knew it, too, when his conscience stirred with the noon whiskey on the Hights above Oakland.

My own literary idol was the Oaklander Jack London. He wrote about dogs, and I liked dogs. He enjoyed camping and the outdoor life, as did I. Jack London Square had been named for him, so he was clearly a person of importance, someone for a boy to emulate.

Born in San Francisco in 1876, London was the product of a one-year common-law marriage between Flora Wellman and a footloose no-account astrologer, William Chaney. When Chaney learned of Wellman's pregnancy, he left her. The man who would become the most successful fiction writer of his day was John Chaney for eight months, until Wellman married John London. Jack grew up in San Francisco, Oakland, and nearby farms, and in some ways I think of him as the quintessential white Oaklander in that era. "I have been alone with my many selves to consult and contemplate my many selves," he wrote in his last major work before dying, possibly a suicide, at age forty, in 1916. "I have gone through the hells of all existences to bring you news."

At fifteen London tapped the woman who had nursed him when his mother could not, the former slave Virginia Prentiss, for three hundred dollars—"my Mammy Jennie, my old nurse at whose black breast I had suckled," as he later wrote in his alcoholic's memoir, *John Barleycorn*. "She was more prosperous than my folks. She was nursing sick people at a good weekly wage. Would she lend her 'white child' the money?" She would. Young Jack bought the *Razzle Dazzle* for use in stealing oysters from the beds in the bay. "I wanted to be where the winds of adventure blew," he wrote, which first meant the scrappy tumbling life of the Oakland docks, the doubled universe of sober hard work and inebriated fancy, "life raw and naked, wild and free . . . And more than that. It carried a promise. It was the beginning. From the sandpit the way led out through the Golden Gate to the vastness of adventure of all the world . . ."

So it did. By the age of nineteen London had sailed the Pacific to Japan, an able seaman aboard the sealer *Sophia Sutherland*. He had tramped across the United States, with Coxey's Industrial Army of the Unemployed as far as Twain's town of Hannibal, Missouri, then on his own through Chicago (with a visit to the White City) and on to Buffalo, New York, where he was imprisoned for vagrancy and served thirty days. London then returned west across Canada on a coal car, south from Vancouver as a stoker; he sailed to Juneau for the Klondike gold rush, wintered on Split-Up Island, eighty miles from Dawson City, then rafted down the Yukon and, with just five dollars of gold dust, sailed home. Back in Oakland, in 1898, he found that his stepfather had died and he had a family to support.

London was no stranger to hard labor. He had already been in the cannery and the jute mill, the healthful industries that were meant to raise a prosperous white working class. He knew that a decade or so of such work would break any-one, even him—reduce him to an animal. "I would be a laborer," he wrote in an 1898 letter, "and by that I mean I would be fitted for nothing else but labor"; and "if I knew that my life would be such, that I was destined to live in Oakland, labor in Oakland at some steady occupation, and die in Oakland—then to-morrow I would cut my throat and call quits with this whole cursed business."

What saved London from suicidal despair, at that time, were ambition and socialism. He became a socialist after noticing, on his travels east, that healthy, decent people were destroyed by wage work. Prior to this teenage insight, "I could see myself only raging through life without end like one of Nietzsche's *blond beasts*, lustfully roving and conquering by sheer superiority and strength." Then he discovered that men "as good as myself and just as *blond-beastly*" could be "wrenched and distorted and twisted out of shape by toil and hardship and accident, and cast adrift by their masters like so many old horses." Not wanting this fate for himself or for others, London became the "boy socialist" of Oakland, and later ran for mayor as a socialist candidate in 1901 and 1905.

(Nearby Berkeley actually elected a socialist mayor in 1911.) London's radicalism had his characteristic intensity:

> I saw the picture of the Social Pit as vividly as though it were a concrete thing, and at the bottom of the Pit I saw them, myself above them, not far, and hanging on to the slippery wall by main strength and sweat ... [N]o economic argument, no lucid demonstration of the logic and inevitableness of Socialism affects me as profoundly and convincingly as I was affected on the day when I first saw the walls of the Social Pit rise around me and felt myself slipping down, down, into the shambles at the bottom.

London wrote, "my rampant individualism was pretty effectively hammered out of me," but he was wrong about that. He would remain a person at war with his individualism. As he had said, his "conversion" to socialism had come about from a terror of remaining in the working class; he genuinely wished to be of that class and above it and to work toward its demise. He did this out of fear for himself and as a hedge against despair at the human condition. When he began seriously considering suicide, "What really saved me was the one remaining illusion—the PEOPLE . . . I was born a fighter. The things I had fought for had proved not worth the fight. Remained the PEOPLE . . . Love, socialism, the PEOPLE—healthful figments of man's mind—were the things that cured and saved me."

Naturally they did not save him. London was a person devoted to identifying truth and whatever might seem elemental about life. It was not in his character to be saved by what he considered illusions and healthful figments. The great bulk of his work pointed in the opposite direction, toward the choices one reaches, alone, at the limits of endurance. This was what made him so popular with American readers, this ultimate lonely drama. London created his own unique landscape, a combination of Yukon and open seas, a last place for pioneers, utterly American yet utterly bizarre: at once American and bizarre because the emphatic Jack London landscape, with its heartbreaking solitude, its violence, its momentous choices made according to terribly simple codes, its Darwinism, greed, and belief in racial destiny, was evidently recognizable to white Americans, and yet hardly any of them had or ever would mush their dogs into Dawson or sail the high seas. Many, like young Jack, worked in jute mills or laundries, living the life he said he would rather die than perpetuate. He took them away from modernity to their frontier, a landscape that seemed not only made for them but made by them, where who they were and what they believed would become clear to them and to him.

It seems logical that his heroes were sometimes dogs. London had an attachment to the animalistic as an ultimate truth—that people were animals, biologically determined. One characteristically American means for translating this belief into human society was race. A faith in racial destiny allowed one to recognize the brutal, selfish, animal side of life while channeling it into some pattern that held meaning, beyond the murderous scrabbling of the Social Pit. London often felt pride in his race. In an essay on Kipling, from 1901, he wrote, "The Anglo-Saxon is a pirate, a land robber, and a sea robber . . . The Anglo-Saxon is strong of arm and heavy of hand, and he possesses a primitive brutality all his own . . . He loves freedom, but is dictatorial to others, is self-willed, has boundless energy, and does things for himself." The self-willed London hated half-breeds. As a correspondent, he blamed the Mexican-American war on that portion of Mexico's population he found to be of mixed racial parentage. "Like the Eurasians," he wrote, "they possess all the vices of their various commingled bloods and none of the virtues." His 1916 letters to a Greek ex-friend, Spiro Orfans, show London in full cry: "You . . . who are too heterogeneous through your bastard mixture of uncountable breeds, get up on your little dunghill and announce that all life is mongrel . . . Your logic is as rotten as your 2000-years degenerate race."

He accompanied his hatred of the mongrel with a liking for racial purity and purpose. London's most famous racial set pieces came in his coverage of the black boxer Jack Johnson's heavyweight title bouts: against Tommy Burns in Australia in 1908, then against James J. Jeffries, the Great White Hope, at Reno in 1910. "Personally, I was with Burns all the way. He is a white man, and so am I. Naturally I wanted to see the white man win." What could be clearer? Many things: Jack Johnson won both fights, and London was delirious in his praise. He went on and on about Johnson's coolness, intelligence, and grace, his "pure fun, gentle wit," this "amazing Negro from Texas, this black man with the unfailing smile, this king of fighters." Johnson was a lightning rod for white ill feeling at the time, not least because he had white lovers and because no white man could beat him. And after Jeffries's defeat, London the fighting Anglo-Saxon wrote, "Once again has Johnson sent down to defeat the chosen representative of the white race, and this time the greatest of them all. And as of old, it was play for Johnson." London admired Johnson as a fighter; he doubly admired him because he was black. "And he played and fought a white man in a white man's country, before a white man's crowd."

That London experienced such pleasure in a black man's victory over a white man suggests that the comfort he took from his own racial destiny was a cold one. He published "The Inevitable White Man" in the year Johnson beat Burns. A typical men-sitting-around-chatting yarn, it presents several white men in a New Hebrides bar debating white racial identity, specifically the white man's mission "to farm the world." One character explains: "Tip it off to him that there's diamonds on the white-hot ramparts of hell, and Mr. White Man will storm the ramparts and set old Satan himself to pick-and-shovel work." All the characters recognize this as in some way stupid. Most of the story is devoted to Saxtorph, "the one inevitable white man," as Captain Woodward describes him to his boon companions: "He was certainly the most stupid man I ever saw, but he was as inevitable as death." Saxtorph has the brain of a gnat, but he's an excellent shot. The story's central drama concerns a black slave revolt. Saxtorph kills the slaves, one by one, in an excruciating slaughter. This murderous imbecile London presents as the one truly inevitable white man. He has no good side, and there is no point or glory in what he does.

An earlier story, "The God of His Fathers," offers a less sadistic view of whiteness. "On every hand," it begins, "stretched the forest primeval,—the home of noisy comedy and silent tragedy. Here the struggle for survival continued to wage with all its ancient brutality." And here we are in pure London-land, the nearly empty place of elemental American humanity. London keeps us guessing whether his story is comic or tragic. He sets up the "sparse aborigines" still inhabiting this place and the arrival of their inevitable conquerors, "fair-faced, blue-eyed, indomitable men, incarnations of the unrest of their race . . . So many an unsung wanderer fought his last and died under the cold fire of the aurora, as did his brothers in burning sand and reeking jungles, and as they shall continue to do till in the fulness of time the destiny of their race be achieved." London describes two campsites, one Indian, one white. The Indian camp is governed by a part-white man named Baptiste, the other camp by the all-white Hay Stockard, who has an Indian common-law wife and, by her, a son. A white pastor has appeared, unwelcome, in Stockard's camp. Baptiste hates pastors even more than he hates whites. He demands that Stockard give the pastor up.

Stockard refuses: "He's worried me, Baptiste, in the past and now, and caused me all manner of troubles; but can't you see, he's my own breed—white—and—and—why, I couldn't buy my life with his, not if he was a nigger." This puzzling argument—that a white man must defend a fellow white even if the fellow is black—somewhat undermines the story's advocacy of "the love of race tradition," as does Stockard's insistence, once it's clear that the two camps will go to war, on having the pastor consecrate Stockard's marriage to his Indian wife. You do have to wonder what "destiny of their race" lies off in the fullness of time for the indomitable blue-eyes. When the battle comes, the white pastor has a vision of the half-breed Baptiste, "indifferent, indomitable, superb," as Christ—and, in the clinch, the pastor repudiates God before Baptiste. "Hay Stockard swept the blood from his eyes," London writes, "and laughed." Then Stockard lets his love of race tradition carry him away. Baptiste insists that Stockard, too, repudiate Christianity, and Stockard reiterates his belief in "the God of my fathers." Baptiste orders one of his Indian men to throw the spear. The ex-pastor watches Stockard's death. He "saw the ivory head stand out beyond his back, saw the man sway, laughing, and snap the shaft short as he fell upon it."

So "The God of His Fathers" is a tragedy about the comic things race can make you do, and a comedy about the tragic things. What a tremendous joke this manly whiteness played—a useless death, on openly laughable principle. It may seem strange that a racial impulse valuing indomitable individualism should end so often in death, except that a collective, involuntary, inherited individualism, in our case a racial individualism, does not make any sense. Neither does a self-mastery premised on the questionless inheritance of racial mission. And so someone believing in this individual-racial paradox would trend naturally toward suicide, as shown with outstanding verve by Jack London, the paradox's greatest American literary expositor.

London's fantasy world of rugged individualism, the American land Americans never see, the fighting and the majesty and the strength—I loved all of it when I was a child, perhaps because a good American boy always thinks he will win. I could not perceive the failure and the loneliness and the death. They were there; I just couldn't see them. London saw them clearly and tried to master them through heroic socialism and race. Neither did the trick.

In his last decade London turned increasingly to science fiction and fantasy. Here his conundrums assume rare and telling form. He allows himself to travel through time and space. He fragments himself, tears himself up—he all but destroys the individual, social class, and race—and the joy he feels in this process is palpable. At last he frees himself from the collective; rather, he scatters the individual self over time, creating an imaginary collective of selves unhindered by geography, liberating himself for adventures of identity that neither class nor racial solidarity could ever allow.

In his books the process began with *Before Adam*, in 1907, an obscure work today though widely read at the time. He told an editor that "it is the most primitive story ever written . . . It goes back before the cave-man . . . to a time when man was in the process of Becoming." In the novel the first-person narrator reveals his special ability to dream himself into an earlier existence. "Some of us have stronger and completer race memories than others . . . I am a freak of heredity, an atavistic nightmare." *Before Adam* is a weak, nearly lifeless novel, but a few passages stand out: the long description of the narrator's simian father, whom he sees in infancy and never again; and the scenes involving Red-Eye, the youthful narrator's unconquerable nemesis, who takes a wife as it pleases him, beats her, kills her, then finds another. He is truly a self-willed man. All that lives in the book's pages are the body of the absent father and the inevitable Red-Eye—"Red-Eye, the atavism," the book's last words.

In *Before Adam*, London found the dream device, and he returned to it shortly before his death in his last completed novel—*The Star Rover*. "All my life I had an awareness of other times and places," it begins. London's narrator posits an idea of childhood: "You were plastic, a soul in flux." Children, we learn, can dream their previous existences. While still an unformed soul, a child will yet scream in fear—but the fear is not the child's fear, it is the fear of the child's "shadowy hosts of progenitors," whose voices scream through the child's voice. The unknown ancestors' experiences are the child's reality: "The stuff of our sheerest dreams is the stuff of our experiences," that is, the experiences from the past that form us.

And at last the harsh realist London found the imaginary landscape he had been traveling toward, a vast semi-historical non-place in which his individualism and his collectivism could play at will. In *The Star Rover* he shatters his character into pieces and casts him over thousands of years. Where does the proud man choose to wander now that he is free, now that the only collective is memory? He changes form at will. He is a Roman slave, a medieval European aristocrat. He is a beggar in Korea, and a king, and a frontier boy. He falls in love with nonwhite women, fervently in love, and displays a tenacious loyalty to his lovers. He learns languages easily and merges with other cultures. *The Star Rover* is the only London novel in which the narrator has much fun. He manages, sometimes implausibly, to remain blue-eyed, male, smart, and physically fit. Yet he is as beyond race as London would ever get. The indomitable race mixers Baptiste and Stockard come to mind, as do the nonwhite children standing with ten-year-old Jack in a school picture back in Oakland—as does the ex-slave Virginia Prentiss, who nursed him when his soul was in flux and lent him the money to begin a life of adventure, and whom he supported when she and her husband hit hard times.

And yet: *The Star Rover*'s free, wandering narrator—Darrell Standing, a former professor—is a prisoner on death row. "They are going to take me out and hang me pretty soon. In the meantime I say my say, and write in these pages of the other times and places." He has learned the technique of time travel from a fellow prisoner. Standing travels under special conditions: when the warden has laced him into a straitjacket. The warden is torturing him to get information Standing does not have. Unable to move, unable to answer his jailer's questions, and soon to be dead, London's hero tells us: "I am life. I have lived ten thousand generations. I have lived millions of years. I have possessed many bodies . . . Cut out the heart, or better, fling the flesh-remnant into a machine of a thousand blades and make mince meat of it—and I, I, don't you understand, all the spirit and the mystery and the vital fire and life of me, am off and away. I have not perished. Only the body has perished, and the body is not I." Apparently, London, late in his brief life, found a country and a collective big enough that he could roam without feeling bound, without hating or fearing his companions and surroundings. The country was everything he could remember about history; the collective was all the people he could imagine and all the people he could imagine being. That London was only able to reach this free country through a tortured prisoner straitjacketed on a cell floor, anticipating death, is a paradox as close to truth as he could find.

The family that would dominate Oakland in the twentieth century was the Knowlands, which is why the zoo is named the Knowland Zoo and the extensive, lovely park around it Knowland Park. The Knowlands' rise to power overlapped the life of Jack London, and their slow downward arc somewhat resembled his own. Joseph Knowland was born on Long Island in 1833 and came to California via the Isthmus of Panama in 1857. Arriving in San Francisco, he pushed on to Yankee Jim's, a mining camp in Placer County, then back to San Francisco for some general laboring and clerking. By 1862 he had made it into the lumber business and prospered enough to marry Hannah Russell of Maine the following year.

Their first child, Sadie, took an interest in the arts. She completed a "Melodrama of Hiawatha" but died, still in her thirties, before finishing her big project, described by a relative as "nothing less ambitious than an opera. The plot was to be based upon the present relations between the American Indian and our Caucasian civilization; the music was to be in part a development of Indian material . . . [T]he hero was to be a young Indian for whom a life-tragedy was to grow out of an inner conflict between the two stages of culture which he should experience within himself." I wonder whether John Rollin Ridge wasn't somewhere in the back of Sadie Knowland's mind as she worked on her opera. He was well known in his day, and there had been so few local Indians able to leave a mark in Northern California.

The Knowlands' son Joseph, born in 1873 and destined to rule Oakland for decades, rose from his father's shadow into politics greatly on the strength of a self-serving investigation into a "Chinese slavery" ring. Joseph went from the state senate to the U.S. Congress, where he served from late 1904 to 1915. His feelings about Chinese people may be guessed from an anecdote he told late in life, in the early 1960s. He is being interviewed by a Mr. Fry about the Oregon forests that had made his father wealthy:

FRY: Did you spend much time in Oregon with the lumber mills?

KNOWLAND: Oh, I was up there several times. I brought home a bear with me once.

FRY: A bear?

KNOWLAND: A live bear. I kept it for a while, after I got home with it, then one day a Chinaman went by the house and said, "Say, that's a nice looking bear."

I said, "Do you want it?"

"Yes."

And so I said, "It's yours."

FRY: I wonder what he did with it.

KNOWLAND: I don't know. He may have eaten it. Some Chinamen were somewhat underfed then.

They were indeed. Many people were, as Knowland's short-lived contemporary Jack London could attest, but the Knowlands themselves were not close to the Social Pit, and Joseph Knowland could focus his main strength and sweat on acquiring power. As a strongly pro-business congressman, he found a welcome on corporate boards, although by his own account he had no management experience. Coming from a wealthy family helped.

Knowland believed in the self-made man. The prosperity of Oakland, however, received its greatest boost from an accident—the 1906 earthquake, which leveled much of San Francisco, thereby aiding the big city's rival across the bay. Thousands of refugees came to Oakland and stayed, causing a vigorous round of home building; Oakland's population more than doubled between 1900 and 1910. Self-making was also, as ever, easier for some than for others. Promoters of one new housing development, advertising around 1911, typically emphasized, "It is probably unnecessary even to mention that no one of African or Mongolian descent will ever be allowed to own a lot in Rockridge or even rent any house that may be built there." The city council and mayor publicly supported one such ordinance, enacting it on the same day the mayor saw off the first contingent of local black soldiers leaving to fight World War I. But in many areas it really was unnecessary to mention that only whites could live there.

Oakland blacks tended to respond in kind. San Francisco was not a particularly good place to have dark skin; many blacks migrated to Oakland after 1900, with a surge after the 1906 earthquake. The Pullman company's policy of employing black sleeping-car porters had led to a small but influential black middle class living in the Victorian houses of West Oakland, convenient to the transcontinental rail terminus. Oakland had a considerable number of black-owned businesses, along with the exclusive clubs and associations that seem to accompany a merchant class. In 1909 one of several local black papers, the *Sunshine*—founded by an ex-slave and longtime city-hall janitor—was advocating a separate destiny: "What the Sunshine would like to see, a colony of our people in every county in the State with the community under Negro rule." The *Sunshine* would rail against light-skinned fair-weather Negroes ("Just please stay on one side and don't keep flopping back and forth. We Simon pures don't need you. Keep passing.") and the flexible loyalties of wealthier blacks who acted black, so to speak, only when it suited their personal advancement.

The biggest push for black racial mobilization in the second decade of the twentieth century came in the form of a protest against certain ways of acting black. Aspiring black actors in those years lined up along Central Avenue, Los Angeles, hoping to be hired for the day to portray servants, Africans (for jungle pictures), and similar roles. A welcome increase in acting opportunities came with the filming of D. W. Griffith's *Birth of a Nation*. One might even get to play a soldier. The release of the pro-Klan picture, in turn, prompted protests, led by the young NAACP. The first major effort by the new Bay Area NAACP branch, based in Oakland, urged banning, or at least censoring, Griffith's film. Mayor Mott showed little sympathy to the protesters, but San Francisco's mayor pleaded with the San Francisco Moving Picture Censor Board to consider the film carefully. The board decided to cut those parts that showed physical contact between black men and white women, "to make the picture less offensive to all sides." The political principle of racial evenhandedness was thereby defended, and the NAACP's anger eased, by enforcing racial separatism—in a movie. *The Birth of a Nation* showed on local screens until 1921.

Joseph Knowland had lost his bid for the Senate in 1914 and turned to politics by other means. At the end of 1915 he bought a half interest in the Oakland *Tribune* from Herminia Peralta Dargie, the last of the prominent Peraltas. Knowland's *Tribune* supported the NAACP's *Birth of a Nation* effort on grounds of guarding the social peace. For those who had wealth and power, *peace* meant an absence of threat to their (well-deserved, as it was thought) social position. From their perspective, social conflict occurred only as a result of illegitimate demands by people acting as groups.

The main source of social conflict in this sense had, for some time, been the laboring class. Charter reforms in 1911 went far toward eliminating the Socialist Party threat. This was not enough, however, for the *Tribune* and the business class. By degrees, Knowland and his allies succeeded in reducing or eliminating the power of their rivals, first the Socialists and then the Democrats. After 1941 local elections became subject to the Knowland machine's direct control. The method was profoundly simple: council members resigned midterm, leaving the council to appoint a replacement. The replacement then had all the advantages of running for reelection rather than election—including a *Tribune* endorsement.

Oakland was a white city until the 1940s. This was considered normal, as were the restrictive housing policies and hiring practices that kept its small population of nonwhites physically isolated and, for the most part, unable to advance economically beyond a certain point. Many hotels and restaurants, theaters, swimming pools, and civil-service jobs (fire, postal, police) were, by custom, partly or wholly reserved for whites, without any need for whites-only signs. In 1926 the Oakland Chamber of Commerce boasted in a pamphlet that "Oakland skilled labor is almost 100 percent white, preponderantly native citizens with families and homes . . . Homeloving people are least susceptible to radical agitation, and Oakland is noted today for the absence of labor unrest and contention."

In 1929, just before the Depression, the county board of supervisors released *Oakland, Alameda County, California: The Highlighted Story of One of the Nation's Richest, Greatest Communities:*

> Lavishly, Nature set the stage. And now, in keeping with the bounteousness of natural resources, Man is acting a majestic part . . . speeding a destiny which international economists describe as certain, unlimited, glorious . . .
>
> Though the home cost $2500 or $250,000, here it can be and usually is distinctive, expressive of personality.
>
> So it is that residential districts stretch out instead of up. That tenements do not exist, that factory worker and professional man alike may trek nightly to the quiet, peaceful atmosphere of cozy suburban homes.
>
> Lauded to the world's end are Alameda County's super-facilities for education.

This was the idyll over which Joseph Knowland presided and in which his favorite son, William, was raised. Joseph nurtured the hope that Bill would become president. If ever a boy lived who could reasonably long to grow up to be president of the United States, that boy was William Knowland. He campaigned for the Harding-Coolidge ticket when he was twelve. His sixth-grade yearbook described him: "Appearance—politics. Besetting sin—politics." An average student, he concentrated his energies on Republican activism and wisely befriended his father's young ally Earl Warren, who one day as governor would appoint Bill to the U.S. Senate. Knowland graduated from the University of California at Berkeley in 1929 with a B-minus average, but he had also run the Oakland Young Republicans, and so earned praise at his commencement from both the president of the university and the governor of California.

Appointed to the California State Republican Central Committee in 1930, Knowland worked toward gaining an assembly seat. He won the election in 1932, when he was twenty-four years old. Two years later he made it, narrowly, into the state senate. The 1934 election was a strange one because the Democrats' gubernatorial candidate was a socialist writer, Upton Sinclair. The state's triumvirate of Republican newspapers—the *Tribune*, the San Francisco *Chronicle*, and the Los Angeles *Times*—were more than alarmed at the prospect of a socialist governor. The *Tribune* printed what it could from Sinclair's writings to make him look like Lenin. The Republicans, with Earl Warren running the campaign, portrayed Sinclair as a tool of Red revolution. Sinclair lost.

Anticommunism, while not new in California, reached a new level in the 1930s. Left-wing politics upended the chamber of commerce's worldview. Where the chamber saw freedom, the left saw bondage. Power and property were not the rewards of virtue but the fruits of oppression. Social conflict was part of the capitalist system, not an exception. There were no self-made men. Individuals did not make their own decisions. Their class interests made decisions for them—determined, in the end, what people thought and felt. This way of looking at things could make you paranoid if you were a communist, as some people were. More importantly, it reflected and teased out a fearful self-doubt within the chamber-of-commerce faithful, a self-doubt foreign to their character and to their happiness. Could it be that each man did not stand strong and independent in the world, and did not deserve what he had? Could it be that he was not in control, and a stranger to himself?

Anticommunism, in turn, saw leftists as controlled by others, foreign, strange, weak, dependent on powers outside themselves, not humans so much as tools and agents of social bondage—at best, unknowing evildoers. In later years Bill Knowland would say, "In the Communist world, nothing happens by accident," which is a terrifying way of looking at a large human society, and lacks humor, and is itself a very communist mode of thinking.

In 1945 Governor Warren appointed Knowland to fill a vacant U.S. Senate seat. Knowland successfully defended his seat the next year against Will Rogers, Jr., son of the Cherokee humorist. Knowland's campaign file included a press release claiming, "Junior Will Rogers over a period of years has commanded the sympathic interest of the Communistic press." Meanwhile, the elder Knowland, back in Oakland, was also facing some left-wing problems. The war, and in particular Henry Kaiser's fantastically successful shipbuilding operations, had brought tens of thousands of workers to Oakland, Richmond, Alameda, and other East Bay towns. For the chamber of commerce, the good side of this was that it brought in a lot of new money. The bad side was a lot of new people, most of them young workers and many of them black. Between 1940 and 1950 Alameda would grow by 77.7 percent, Oakland by 27.3 percent, and once-sleepy Richmond by 321.1 percent. Wages and working conditions were good enough to attract these tens of thousands of people, primarily from central states and, more so, from the old Southwest (Louisiana, Arkansas, Oklahoma, and Texas).

Wages and conditions were not, however, so good that workers saw no need for unions. And this revived the specter of communism, with all the world-upside-down dangers it held. Labor groups fielded a left-leaning slate in local elections in 1945. The *Tribune* ceaselessly baited the candidates as being communist. None of the candidates won. A vast general strike in 1946 did nothing to ease the Knowland machine's fears; organized labor shut the city down for two and a half days. A pro-labor council slate in the 1947 elections did surprisingly well in the primary (OAKLAND PRIMARY HAILED AS COMMUNIST VICTORY, the *Tribune* headlined) and got four of nine seats in the election.

The democratic demands of wageworkers were directed very specifically against the Knowlands and the *Tribune* and had a pronounced racial aspect. The most spectacular symbol of the 1946 strike was a parade float showing a black fist and a white fist together smashing the *Tribune* building, with the slogan "Take the Power out of the Tower." Joseph Knowland had hoped the *Tribune* tower would symbolize forward-looking prosperity; to wartime workers it represented undemocratic oppression. The white fist opposing management was not radically new to Oakland, but the black fist was. The black share of Oakland's population went from 2.8 percent in 1940 to 12.4 percent in 1950; the black population grew by 157.3 percent between 1940 and 1944.

White people responded to this increased black presence through racial separation. Suburbs, restricted by covenant to whites (mainly war workers) and often funded by the Federal Housing Administration, grew up in the undeveloped hinterlands. New housing tracts within the East Bay towns were also segregated. When blacks strayed into areas whites considered their own, they were sometimes forcibly expelled. The police swept through black neighborhoods, arresting men by the dozens. (Black leaders called for the hiring of black officers.) Everywhere, the solution to white racial tension—usually called just "racial tension"—was to isolate and harass blacks. When a riot connected with a Cab Calloway concert broke out in 1944, the chosen solution was to have black night at the Oakland Auditorium; other entertainment spots adopted similar policies. As elsewhere in West Coast war-boom cities, WHITE TRADE ONLY signs appeared in store windows. In the East Bay bowling alleys segregated; so did a cemetery. This was, to a degree, simply an extension and formalization of prewar practice. But the scale had increased and so had the cruelty. Segregation was not necessarily a conservative activity. Tolerance committees, too, advocated enabling a separate black life to reduce racial friction.

The *Oakland Observer* pushed segregation hard, wondering, in 1943, "who or what group will have the initiative and guts to make a stand for the segregation of the colored people." Following the 1944 riot, the *Observer* editors pondered the evolution of race relations:

> That riot on Twelfth Street the other day may be the forerunner of more and larger riots because we now have (a) a semi-mining camp civilization and (b) a new race problem, brought about by the influx of what might be called socially liberated or uninhibited Negroes who are not bound by the old and peaceful understanding between the Negro and the white in Oakland, which has lasted for so many decades, but who insist upon barging into the white man and becoming an integral part of the white man's society.
>
> Thus we see, in Oakland, white women taxicab drivers serving Negro passengers, and white women waitresses serving Negroes in white men's restaurants. If that is not a potential source of trouble, we do not know what is.
>
> There is no intention here to blame the Negro. That riot may have been entirely the doings of white men. We do not know. We do know, however, that the influx of the exuberant Negro has brought up the problem, and it is certain that the white man is not going to be pushed around in a civilization that is predominantly white.
>
> There is no doubt that a Negro can get just as hungry and thirsty as a white man. The Negro's money is as good as a white man's, coined by the same Government. The Negro needs transportation as much as the white man, and he is just as entitled to work as the white man. He is entitled to every right that our forefathers fought for, and which many honorable members of his race are also fighting for today.
>
> But the trouble is that the Negro newcomer does not concede that the white man has the right to be alone with his kind. If the white man does not want the Negro sitting alongside him in the white man's restaurants, or does not want the association of the Negro anywhere else, this may be attributed to racial prejudice. Yet, in final analysis, the white man has the right of race preju-

dice if he so desires. If he does not care to associate with anyone, he is not compelled to do so.

Right there is where the Negro is making his big mistake. He is butting into the white civilization instead of keeping in the perfectly orderly and convenient Negro civilization of Oakland, and he is getting himself thoroughly disliked.

For the *Observer* editors the only racial issue at hand in 1944 was the white person's right to live a white life. The racial desire to live apart apparently had no moral quality, one way or the other. The editors saw it rather as a natural reality of the white mind and a basic social fact. This fact gained legitimacy from "the right to be alone with his kind." Jack London would have recognized this combining of togetherness with aloneness. I don't think he would have seen it as a right, however; it was more like a lurching curse, to him.

But the editors did understand racial separatism as a right—a collective racial right to privacy. The idea of a group right to privacy is a little odd, at least in America, since our system usually conceives of privacy as an individual possession. The tension between the racial individual and the racial group may be seen in the editors' reference to "the white man," as in "the white man's restaurants" and "the white man's society." This individual, the white man, is evidently capable of having not just a restaurant but an entire society all to himself. Thus his individual right to privacy, to unencumbered enjoyment of white companionship, expands to include nearly everything. That is an extremely specific type of individualism.

Impressively, the editors did not consider this expansive right of the white man to be alone with his kind as interfering in any way with all the rights for which our forefathers died, and for which black men were dying at the moment of this editorial. On the contrary, they saw the right of racial separatism and the "right of race prejudice" as American norms—rights that were not local and existed without reference to the past or any tradition beyond the coincidence of a white majority. This was the almost unique genius of California conservatism, here in its hour of birth. It was a conservatism without a past. What it "conserved" was a language of individual rights and a reality of group power, with the shadowy figure of the white man shuttling between the two, expanding and contracting as required by circumstance. California was the last frontier in which this ghostly white pioneer would act out his drama, a new state with a fresh start on Americanism. The "past" that California conservatism preserved was simply a past without opposition or conflict, a pure freedom purely imaginary. The present of this past was, of course, always a bit disappointed, stiffly principled, easily hurt, condescendingly baffled (and sometimes intrigued) by its history-burdened predecessors on the other side of Nevada, and nostalgic for all its yesterdays when jute mills were peopled by cheerful yeomen and race was not an issue. In California, history was commemorated not in museums, re-enactments, books, or even one's Californian thoughts but in voiceless parks, to which Joseph Knowland devoted the bulk of decades of public service. He even helped fund a memorial plaque to the harried Cherokee poet John Rollin Ridge, whose grave lay near a little town not far from Oakland.

The result of such a conservatism for Oakland blacks was a ghetto. West Oakland, sun-drenched and built up with lovely Victorian houses, went from 16.2 percent black in 1940 to 61.5 percent black ten years later. The incidence of overcrowded homes (more than one person per room) doubled from 15 to 30 percent of the total over the same decade. Homeless black families begging for a place to sleep quickly became common. The postwar deterioration and destruction of public housing, combined with a thorough restriction of new private housing (in cities and suburbs) to whites, made the ghettos worse still. They took on a kind of permanence. This was as orderly and convenient a life as white Oakland was willing to allow for blacks. In this respect, Oakland was not at all unusual among West Coast cities.

And the blame for such misery was attributed to "the black man" himself—specifically (and by some black old-timers, too), to the black man up from the South with his mistaken expectation of a fresh start, a new freedom to integrate, in California. Everything that went wrong in California in those years was attributed to outsiders. Oakland's chief dogcatcher told the *Tribune*, "Most of the biting dogs in quarantine are from out of town." The dogcatcher's insight occurred in grander fashion to the city's police, politicians, newspapers, and pretty much everybody else. Whatever disturbed the social scene had to be foreign to it, because the basis of California conservatism was its own lost purity. And because this conservatism had no real past at all, nothing to conserve but the imaginary day before itself, history as other people knew it was merely another source of foreign trouble. Given the noticeable darkening of skin tones in California's war-boom cities, racial history promised to become an especially potent source of trouble.

The morality of an ahistorical conservatism is fairness without a past, and fairness was the stock-in-trade of William Knowland as he rose to become the second most powerful conservative politician of his time, after President Eisenhower. As Senate majority leader, then minority leader after Democrats took the Senate, Knowland stood out for his strictness, particularly when compared with his Democratic counterpart, Lyndon Johnson. Yet Knowland did have a swinging side. He liked to dance. He pursued a number of women other than his wife—in particular, the wife of a friend—and had a hearty appetite for both food and drink. He also had a reputation for not being the brightest of men. Eisenhower had noted this, and so had one of Knowland's closest aides.

A lack of mental agility was not necessarily a handicap in Washington, or even in campaigns; one pretty much knew what William Knowland was thinking. Besides, his milieu protected him from paying for flaws and vices. Senators of that era looked after each other. Their weaknesses were a principal source of amusement among themselves.

The way in which this class operated may be seen in their handling of Republican senator Joseph McCarthy. Knowland put in his files a copy of a typescript of a McCarthy Senate speech from 1950:

> We know that at Yalta we were betrayed. We know that since Yalta the leaders of this government by design and ignorance have continued to betray us. The depth and foulness of that betrayal no man can as yet outline for those of us who are its victims. We also know that the same men who betrayed America are still leading America. The traitors must no longer lead the betrayed. The international criminals must no longer splatter the pages of history with American blood.

McCarthy was just getting started in 1950. Over the next few years he behaved more and more like a nightmarish barfly. He raged, he lied, and he ruined people's lives. But what truly bothered his colleagues, as a group, was McCarthy's strong implication that they were not in control of their own power, that *they* were being manipulated by communists. Only when the senator crossed that line did Knowland, as majority leader, rebuke him.

What strikes me most about McCarthy was that he could say the United States was governed by traitors, and this charge could then be considered something about which reasonable men might disagree. But if McCarthy was correct, how could you possibly oppose him? By defending the rights of traitors? Knowland, who supported McCarthy, later criticized his colleague's refusal to bend: "I belonged to the school that, when the fight is over you shake hands and you're generous in offering your congratulations to the victor, and tried to have a humility when you were the victor. You work and live and fight with people and it's almost like a family." Such comradely moderation makes no sense when dealing with treason. The truth was that no one in power really believed McCarthy, not even Knowland, who acknowledged the senator "was loose with his figures." The Republicans lost control of the Senate in 1954; McCarthy then lost his committee chairmanship, and the Senate voted to censure him for poor conduct, effectively ending his career. The nation had not been governed by traitors after all.

Knowland's collegial world could handle a friend who thought the country

was run by communists because Knowland and the political class were in control of their power. McCarthy's looseness with figures did not matter much
because his class of men did not fear communist individuals so much as communism—not visible enemies, but an invisible one. In America this invisibility
was the essence of communism as understood by anti-communists. Obviously,
no genuine, free American could want to be a communist. American communism, therefore, had to be either a foreign plot or a psychological disease. Knowland did keep a file labeled "Mental Hygiene," which was one term for what
anticommunists hoped to foster.

The anticommunist worldview held enormous implications for race in
America, just at the point when civil rights reemerged as a significant subject for
the American majority. The old idea that individual self-determination, or freedom, was analogous to ownership of oneself as a type of property—personal,
human freedom as an aspect of social economy—had foundered for centuries
on the reality of people owning other people, and most vividly on the reality of
white people owning black people. And perhaps because most white people
down the years have known, sooner or later, that black people are as human as
anyone else, the association of blackness with a lack of self-ownership seems to
have stolen back upon the white majority's confidence in its own self-ownership
or freedom. This may well explain why black people as such have so often been
perceived, mainly among nonblacks, as threats to property—literally, in the
case of slave revolts, but also in the fear of losing social capital (in the form of
education) and the fear of declining property values, fears that were already
remaking how Americans lived. The endangered property is like an external
proxy for the endangered self. Modern race took shape as a property relation,
and although race has certainly gone on from there, it has never lost that original quality. Modern communism, of course, was specifically about property,
and in particular the property of one's labor, the property inherent in human
existence. And like race, communism threatened not only private property as
such but, more profoundly, one's ownership of oneself—one's liberty. There
was a real logic to the association of civil-rights activism, indeed of racial politics, with communism. Each seemed to propose that one's social status (or ownership of property) was an accident, at best, and that the leaders of the American
majority were not masters of their fates—not individuals in the American
sense—but subjects of forces (capitalism, white supremacy) over which their
personal control was incomplete, if it existed at all. In short, communism and
racial activism could be seen as ascribing a collective consciousness to people,
such as William Knowland, who believed in individualism. And unless the left-
ist and racial critiques of the American status quo were grounded in a strong historical sense of continuity and change—they usually were not—the conflict

would come down, sooner or later, to mental hygiene. The political duel would be between different conceptions of psychological disease. This type of politics was, of course, as old as racial thinking itself. Postwar anticommunism owed a great deal to American racial history.

Knowland faced the growing dangers of left-wing and racial opposition with individualism. He labored tirelessly for right-to-work laws, which prevented unions from determining who could be employed in a union shop. He likewise helped apply antimonopoly laws to unions. The theory was that social legislation should apply equally to people with great power (such as factory owners) and people with less power (union leaders) and people with next to none (nonunion workers), because, in Knowland's view, all these people were individuals and group power should not exist. Similarly, his most notable stand on civil rights came in antilynching bills. When he first held office as a state assemblyman, Knowland had joined a black colleague in sponsoring a law against lynching. (California had a high number of lynchings for a non-Southern state.) In 1946 Senator Knowland spoke out bravely against his Southern colleagues—Democrats, to be sure—in urging the FBI to investigate the lynchings of four black men in Walton City, Georgia, one of whom, like Knowland, was a veteran. Lynching was a distinctive civil-rights violation in that it involved people acting as a group against individuals. A white Southerner might see it as a tradition, but a mid-century California conservative would not. Californians were not traditionalists. On other civil-rights matters, however, Knowland tended to drag his heels. He did so out of deference to states' rights, an institutional form of individualism; out of reflexive Republican hesitancy in changing the social order; and because civil-rights laws so often implied that American society was divided into (racial) groups, and the point of Americanism was to honor the individual and eliminate the group. Knowland, like Eisenhower, had opposed his old friend Earl Warren's 1954 decision in *Brown v. Board of Education*, which was based on history and reality rather than timeless principle. Knowland hesitated at Eisenhower's own civil-rights bill, until party loyalty and self-preservation overwhelmed his misgivings.

Knowland's combining of stiff-necked individualist principle with political conformity typified his class of men. Bill had followed his father, Joseph, into the habit of somewhat smug self-effacement—the coolness of power. John Kennedy would raise this manly cool into a performing art. But an archconservative like Knowland could dance the dance, too, giving the exercise of rule a jauntiness that must have had its appeal and must have given Knowland some consolations when his career started sliding. He unwisely chose to run against Pat Brown for the California governorship in 1958. His campaign materials contained some questioning of Brown's patriotism, and Knowland stuck by his position on the right to work. He lost. This was something new for him. He threw himself into running the *Tribune* and the chamber of commerce, working connections at the Masons and the right clubs. Knowland had lost, but it was important to him that the class he symbolized, and whose values he cherished, not be lost as well.

The chief obstacle to Knowland's efforts lay in the voluntary abandonment by whites of the city. White status-quo urban politics was uniquely ill suited to handle this particular form of betrayal, which was at once individual or individualist and racially collective, at once blameless and horrifying in what it revealed about one's fellow white people and probably about oneself. This root treason, in the event, migrated into other, more imaginary and more customary specters of betrayal. What white people were doing to their country became, in the white imagination, what blacks and communists were doing. Late in 1961 Mayor Houlihan designated a special week for the coming year, "Anti-Communism Week in our City to coincide with the dates of the San Francisco Bay Region School of Anti-Communism," urging "that it be set aside as a week during which our citizens will join with others in this region to enlighten themselves on the insidious works of an international conspiracy that is dedicated to the destruction of our fundamental constitutional rights as free men." The *Tribune* eagerly promoted the event. On the last day of anticommunism week *Time* published an article on Oakland, and Knowland clipped it for his personal files:

> If ever a city seemed to be headed toward Skid Row, it was Oakland, California . . . [T]he city developed all the classic symptoms of metropolitan blight: the downtown area declined, citizens who could afford to fled to the suburbs, slums spread and schools disintegrated . . . The swelling Negro segment aggravated Oakland's fever chart. The schools got worse, crime and juvenile delinquency rose, slums spread.

Not all the schools had got worse. The city had redistricted the system in 1961 to create a white high school, Skyline, perched in the hills and complete with fraternities and sororities, in contrast to the other city high schools. The hill neighborhoods had their own elementary and junior high schools, too. The many private schools were also not disintegrating. The Knowlands themselves lived in Piedmont, a tiny, wealthy village with excellent schools (public and private) that was physically surrounded by Oakland but not part of it. But all this could be seen as peripheral to the Negro segment, with its mysterious, seemingly organic ability to cause social collapse. It was almost as mysterious as communism, if not quite as foreign to the white mainstream.

White Oaklanders continued to own most of the city. They continued to employ black people at a ratio far below the black share of the population, and black unemployment stayed at more than twice the rate of white unemployment. The police force, almost entirely white, had a well-earned reputation for brutality—some officers had sunk to the level of mugging black people for money. The white elite continued to eat at the waterfront restaurants in Jack London Square, and I suppose this life might have gone on indefinitely except that the money was leaking away and the younger black citizens of Oakland, particularly, were getting angrier. This was the environment in which racial activism grew large enough to confront William Knowland and destroy the coolness of rule.

Did it begin at a department store? The Oakland and Berkeley chapters of the Congress of Racial Equality (CORE) had been attracting students, inspired by the Southern civil-rights movement, since 1961. By 1963 CORE had documented the underrepresentation of blacks in the workforce at Oakland's Montgomery Ward store—25 percent of the population, 2 percent of the store staff. They picketed Montgomery Ward and after two weeks gained a commitment from the company to track minority hiring and recruit minorities according to specific goals. Success led to more volunteers, and Berkeley students started their own CORE chapter, which settled on Mel's Drive-In, later a location for the film *American Graffiti*. Two large demonstrations and many arrests later, Mel's agreed to hire blacks in positions visible to the general public. The distinctive feature of these protests, within the context of the times, was that they focused exclusively on hiring practices. The protesters insisted that business owners hire people partly according to their skin color, on the grounds that this was what business owners did anyway, only to the advantage of white job seekers. Racial preference was being confronted with racial preference, the goal being racial parity. This obviously meant that everyone would now have a race—a publicly acknowledged racial identity based on skin tone—in the important business of getting a job. Race was not to be eliminated as a personal and social characteristic, but intensified.

It was William Knowland's fate to become the local symbol of white supremacy. After the Mel's protest a black high-school senior from Berkeley joined white and black allies to form the Ad Hoc Committee to End Discrimination. The committee began picketing the *Tribune*, not with anything very specific in mind but as a general symbolic gesture. It made the *Tribune*, and Knowland in particular, symbolic of whiteness. He was not an individual but an effect of his race, a manifestation of it, and so no longer a free American.

In a 1964 editorial Knowland's paper gave its response to this conception of race: "That scraggly, unkempt group of young racists and bigots calling themselves the Ad Hoc Committee to End Racial [*sic*] Discrimination again pick-eted the Tribune this Saturday." The psychic cogs of what would later be called reverse discrimination, or reverse racism, had immediately clicked into place. Wasn't this mentally hygienic?

Mental hygiene would be preserved by repression. Knowland's reaction to the symbolic picketing of the *Tribune* tower was to attack the symbol of subversion, namely a group of tables set up by left-wing and racial-activist groups on a strip of sidewalk at the edge of the Berkeley campus. The subversive speech there had to be stopped, said this newspaperman, because it threatened freedom. What unforeseeable consequences one's actions can have. Feeling pressure from Knowland, the university moved against the radicals on that strip of sidewalk, the radicals resisted—and the Free Speech Movement was born. This was possibly the most significant political result of Knowland's lifelong engagement in politics, and it was the opposite of what he had intended. Within one eventful year Knowland had become a symbol of white power and, to some, a symbol of horrible political timing.

Even the archconservative could sense he had got out of step. He responded with attempts to rein in the world, through oratory ("It is not being an alarmist but a realist to state that this year [1967] we have come to the brink of armed insurrection") and through such activities as chairing the Statewide Respect for Law and Order Conference down at Goodman's in Jack London Square. He also, touchingly, closed his paper's suburban operations, hunkered down in the city concept—let the weak flee!—and "metropolitanized" the *Tribune*. Again, the man's timing was poor, because while his own commitment to the city might help it survive, the central fact remained the steady crawl of white money up the Oakland hills, cresting above Joaquin Miller Park, then downhill to Moraga, Orinda, and Lafayette, and on to where the ground levels a bit, the temperatures are warmer and the air drier and fruit trees grew until people came and built houses over the orchards because people wanted to get out of Oakland. When white people and their money did not head over the hills they went south along the Bay to San Jose. There they laid the basis for what would one day be Silicon Valley and a new era in American prosperity.

As Knowland lost control of the city he lost control of himself. He struggled with his weight, he struggled with cigarettes. Maybe a martini will get this day up on its legs? He struggled with money. His metropolitanized paper soon started losing money, the very money that was passing away south and over the hills. His mind seems to have been deeply reluctant to recognize the terrible logic of white flight. Perhaps he thought money and people and power were leaving him by some inexplicable mischance; in any case, he turned himself to games of chance, usually craps. Knowland was privately changing into the opposite of his public self. Rigid, humorless self-control gave way to nicotine and cocktails; the Republican virtues of hard work and proportionate reward yielded to tumbling dice. For the coolness of rule he substituted the ring-a-ding-ding cool of luck, and from believing in the inevitability of his success he left to woo inevitable failure.

In this condition he met the lovely Ann Dickson of Tulsa, Oklahoma, in Las Vegas. She was sitting at a bar one day in 1970 at the Tropicana. Knowland's biographers Gayle B. Montgomery and James W. Johnson describe the meeting:

> He sat at the bar beside her and began a casual conversation. Despite his stilted manner of small talk, when he introduced himself and offered a drink, Ann accepted readily.
>
> Although he usually had difficulty talking one on one, even with people he knew well, Ann was different. She made conversation easy, letting him know she knew who he was, how important he was, and that she remembered his background. He was flattered. Sometimes even in Oakland, where he should have been recognized, the senator felt he was ignored. With Ann, he felt important, and they got along from the start.

A little more than a year later Knowland's wife filed for divorce; within two years he and Ann were married, and not many months after that he began trying to find his way to a second divorce. In his personal files he started to keep notes of when his stocks did badly, and he started clipping horoscopes. The first one, from February 1972, read: "Domestic routine could be disrupted. Some relationships are reaching conclusion. Don't feel you must hang on to past. The world is out there in front, not back—step forward toward a new, vibrant life." The old Republican began sporting a mustache, and might be spotted smiling.

Knowland even bent a little on racial issues. The Black Panthers spent much of the latter part of 1971 trying to force black businessmen to contribute cash to Panther programs—education, food, and health care. The Panthers did not keep account books of a normal kind. Some were involved in crime. They turned to intimidation more often than not, at this stage, and the black businessmen would not be intimidated. The Panthers concentrated on picketing the liquor store of a prominent black leader, and Knowland was among the few to cross that line. He hated the Panthers, particularly Huey Newton. But when the boycott was settled, and the Panthers planned to turn their energies against white businesses, Knowland met with black leaders to form the New Oakland Committee. It had three caucuses—business, labor, and minority—which was somewhat comical since whites were nearly a minority, too. (In 1973 the public schools were just 21.1 percent white.) But the committee was, as they say, a step.

In the meantime Knowland was running through his money. What he didn't lose in Vegas he lost on Ann, who liked to spend, especially on clothes. The former senator's personal clipping file ends in January 1974, with an item from the Vegas Sun's "Social Whirl": "MRS KNOWLAND looked stunning in a smashing gown of iridescent sequins in shimmering shades of turquoise blue and soft greens. Knockout!" That last file also has some clips on the murder of Marcus Foster, Oakland's black superintendent of schools. Foster had been gunned down by the Symbionese Liberation Army (SLA), easily the strangest revolutionary group in those strange years. Knowland kept his backstage pass to the memorial service. He feared the SLA might want to kill him, too. He feared the Panthers. The abduction of Atlanta Constitution publisher Reg Murphy unnerved him, as did the SLA's kidnapping of Patricia Hearst, the daughter of the newspaper publisher.

On February 21, William and Ann Knowland attended various celebrations marking the hundredth anniversary of the Tribune. Both Knowlands were shaky and disoriented. That evening in Jack London Square, Governor Ronald Reagan gave a warm speech in praise of the Knowland family and their newspaper. Two days later, a Saturday, Knowland left home in his Cadillac. He filled it with five gallons of gas and drove north to his family's cabin on the Russian River. He parked in the garage, leaving the keys in the ignition. At the house he pulled a .32 pistol from his bedroom closet and walked down to the riverside. He was an orderly and careful conservative man. He fired once into the river to check the mechanism, then once into his head.

SEIZE THE TIME

■

The collapse of Knowland's world in Oakland coincided with the building up of my own. All these names around me—Knowland, Peralta, Huey, Joaquin Miller, Jack London, Ohlone—began to expand in significance, crowding out the possums and raccoons, snails and doves. The histories behind those names, the actions that formed them and formed the history of my hometown, began to push into my little mental sky and become my histories, whether I understood them or not and whether I liked them or not. I had few enough tools with which to enter this process, but that was true for everyone else in my generation as we went through it together.

I did have a prejudice, if that's the right word: a suspicion of white people. It was a suspicion only, a feeling that the people around me who looked white would begin acting white in some unknown way that might endanger my little personality. I was just a boy. It was just a suspicion, and I don't know where it came from.

My parents must have played some role. I don't recall them talking about race, but then I don't remember much of anything that they said before my adolescence. Theirs was not a generation of parents that sought opportunities for meaningful conversation with an eight-year-old. My moral education was in the hands of the church, my secular education in the hands of my schoolteachers. When my parents taught us children at all—I had an elder sister and a younger brother—it was through discipline and example. Ours was a loving household, and chatty at times, but in a way very oriented to the day at hand and the day to come. Our habits were extremely regular. They concerned meals, school, work, church, television programs, keeping the yard up, and going on vacation once a year.

Nonetheless, I must have absorbed something from my parents to have developed this suspicion of white people. Decades later I asked them to recall for me some of the basics of their thinking on racial matters. My father's childhood had been itinerant—a series of small towns in which, as he remembered, there were so few nonwhite people that racial questions did not often come up. However, his father, a Baptist minister from the near South, preached against racial prejudice on biblical grounds, and his mother at least went along with the idea. As a young adult in the early 1950s, my father grew fond of jazz, and he knew that most of the great jazz was made by black Americans—more evidence that white supremacy was incorrect. Having black roommates in college also made it difficult, for him, to entertain the idea of black inferiority.

The related opinion that white men, such as my father, were the social norm presented a more subtle challenge. He recalled this norm as being unshakable at the time. In 1963 a white friend, with some effort, convinced him to attend the March on Washington. My father was thirty-one years old. In Washington he heard the luminaries of the civil-rights movement, above all Martin Luther King, Jr. Like King, Dad was a well-educated Baptist preacher; he, too, had sifted through the works of twentieth-century theologians and wondered where faith might go in a turbulent era. He recognized King's rhythms that warm day on the Mall, the overstatement and the understatement, the incantations that pushed forward, then retreated a step, then pushed even further ahead, retreated, until you had the means to join the speaker at his destination. He knew a poor metaphor when he heard one ("America has given the Negro people a bad check"), and he knew a perfect one: "With this faith we will be able to hew out of the mountain of despair a stone of hope."

He knew which words were directed at him: "The marvelous new militancy which has engulfed the Negro community must not lead us to a distrust of all white people, for many of our white brothers, as evidenced by their presence here today, have come to realize that their destiny is tied up with our destiny and their freedom is inextricably bound to our freedom. We cannot walk alone." My father heard King's speech again on the radio on the train home.

We were then living in an old Connecticut village. (Until we reached Oakland, my parents would move every few years.) Dad carried a fresh stone of hope to Connecticut and wondered what he might do there. He talked with other white people, particularly in church circles, and they started a civil-rights group. There was not all that much to do except exhort one another, for nonwhite peo-

ple were thin on the ground in that part of Connecticut—sixty miles east of
Cornwall, where Elias Boudinot and his white bride had been burned in effigy,
thirty miles north by northwest of where John Mason had led the pivotal massacre of the Pequots in 1637, and about twenty-six miles northeast of the old
slave-trading river port of Middletown. The lack of nonwhites left little with
which to draw out the enemy. But one knew the enemy existed. There was
housing discrimination in the nearest sizable town, which had a small black
population. The group slowly evolved past black-white dialogues in the living
room—"that was kind of what you did in the early '60s." My father volunteered
for another group, which did find a focus: a black preacher, his family, a lake, a
beach, reluctant white neighbors, and a pall over the summertime pleasures of
swimming, boating, and fishing. After a struggle the landowners' association
allowed the black family beach access.

In 1963 we moved to Kansas City, Kansas, where my parents were active in
church civil-rights circles and in fair-housing efforts, that is, residential integration. They concentrated on the "good-neighbor pledge": the plan was to get
white people to sign a form saying they would be willing to live next to black
people; then their names would be published in the newspaper. My father was
more the instigator, my mother the soldier. She has told me that her earliest significant racial memory had to do with a black high-school classmate—the only
one, because, although my mother's hometown of Seattle was a liberal city, it
still had informally segregated schools in the 1940s. So her classmate Joyce
needed a ride to go to a party. My mother's best friend said her father would not
give a black person a ride in his car. My mother's parents were willing, however,
and everyone got to the party. My mother's father was, she said, "kind of a red-
neck," in a thoughtless way; but my mother's mother steered the family boat on
ideological questions, and she was under the influence of her pastor. He had
been an open pacifist during the war, and a regular visitor to Japanese internment camps, and encouraged fresh thinking among his congregation. When
my mother was still a young woman in Seattle, she had taken an imprudent (for
a white woman) liking to a Chinese American man, and later to a black man.
She remembers going on a bar crawl one day in New York City, 1953, with two
black male friends. A couple of white boys followed them, saying, "What's a
white gal like you doing with two black guys?" Her friends told her not to react,
so "we just quietly kept walking, and they gave up."

My mother has a long memory for being crossed on what she considers
moral matters. In Kansas a decade later she knocked on doors and asked white
people to sign the good-neighbor pledge. On the whole, she received "not very
good reactions": "I wouldn't say any of them were very positive." ("We had nuns
going around, too," my father added, "and people really had trouble throwing

them out. But they'd still do it.") This was the mid-1960s, which marked the high tide of white support for the civil-rights movement.

Whether, as a small child, I was aware of these heroics, I have no idea. Did my mother tell stories over dinner about her afternoon of being shunned by our own people? I imagine we did not think of them as our people. When faced with what was called racial prejudice, we were Christian rationalists—a happy marriage of contending doctrines—and expected society to advance through the gradual replacement of the wrong with the correct. This was being "liberal": to improve rather than conserve, to be open rather than closed, to become more than to be, and to explore rather than react. To have racial prejudice was to be conservative, closed, static, and reactive or "reactionary." The twenty years from the end of the war to 1965 were economically expansive, and one oriented one's thoughts toward problem solving. The middle class was expected to grow to include each American (maybe even the rich). An ever-increasing percentage of the population would complete college. Those few who might fail would do so as individuals, not as members of failure-prone groups.

Liberalism of this kind had a connection to social class, and so did the liberal understanding of racial prejudice. The theory was that the educated middle class lived in the process of becoming. By virtue of education and, perhaps, some economic comfort, members of the middle class had the ability to form themselves. They had an intellectual mobility that corresponded to their mobility of place and employment (liberalism being nomadic). They could change homes, jobs, and thoughts, because they had a certain distanced power over each of these. The lower class lacked that distance, the power to move. Without it, they could not control their own lives or, in the end, their own thoughts. Their selves were formed by their social position, independently of individual will; they were victims of history, not its makers, and questionlessly carried through time history's pluses and minuses. Among them racial prejudice thrived, not because they wanted it—that would have made them inhuman— but because they couldn't help themselves. This liberal middle-class view of how racial prejudice functioned was factually shaky but strong in principle. It promised a practical solution, through economic uplift and education of the white lower class, to the vestigial problem of racial prejudice (all problems being vestigial). It also placed the burden of racial history on a social class expected to disappear happily, and preserved the sense of the liberal white middle class that the past did not have a hold on them. They could choose not to have a race.

The attribution of whiteness, historical and moral, to other white people did not make it easy to identify. Someone might be acting normally for ages then suddenly act white, and just as suddenly become normal again. It was as if they, these other white people, had a double consciousness—two selves, one human, one white, in a single body. These two selves did not necessarily struggle one with the other. The white self could serve as a loam in which the preferred human self took root and grew; it could nurture and protect the freedom not to notice its existence, not to have a race. Far from being a choice, this was a psychic operation taking place in secret even from oneself; it showed a shortage of "racial awareness." Civil-rights activists, such as my parents, thought they knew how prejudiced people thought better than prejudiced people did. They would expose the white self to the light of faith and reason: by naming it, they could destroy it at last. When my mother knocked on doors in Kansas and asked people to sign the good-neighbor pledge, she was identifying those prospective good neighbors as white. That was the reason for her interest particularly in them. There was no point in asking black people whether they were willing to have black neighbors. So she was marking out these neighbors as white people; asking them to sign a declaration that publicly (and almost certainly for the first time) had them acknowledge their identity as white people; and further asking them to affirm as white people their power and desire to create a society in which their whiteness would become insignificant.

It was a lot to ask, one white stranger to another. She wanted them to recognize before society their whiteness and its power, then repudiate both. This would leave them with saying in public that they had a power they shouldn't have had, which was frighteningly close to acknowledging one had been deceiving oneself as to the nature of one's social position—that one had been living upside down in some way, and what one had considered normal was exceptional. In fact, you were accepting that you weren't normal and your abnormal part—your white self—was a mistake you needed to overcome. Why would anyone want to do this? Better to shut the door, as so many did, and hope my mother would go away.

The practical activism of the 1950s and early 1960s thus carried within itself what might be called psychoanalytic activism. The elimination of formal separatism implied, as a next step—if there was to be a next step—a self-examination by white people of what made them white, in order to identify and monitor their progress toward racelessness. (A psychologically healthy whiteness had no role in liberal thinking.) This logical movement *into* race in the subconscious sense, propelled by the hope of moving *away from* race—to break its power over oneself—also, of course, characterized the shift in black ideology at the time, as radicals sought to "eliminate white thoughts from our minds." The difference was that white liberals wanted to eliminate white thoughts from their own minds, too, without replacing them with black thoughts or racial thoughts of any kind. The past would not hold them. Allowing the past to hold you was what white conservatives did.

The political shift from practical, liberal integrationism to indefinite racial self-examination paralleled our own move from the relatively predictable racial world of Kansas City to the quite unpredictable world of Oakland. As white people, we had been in the surpassing majority in rural Connecticut and still in the dominant group in Kansas. In Oakland blacks were coming close to equaling whites, and there were substantial populations of Asians (mainly Chinese American) and Hispanics (mainly of Mexican descent). There was probably no place in the country further into race than Oakland in the late 1960s. And that made whiteness a distinctly problematic business. Racelessness was not really an available option, which may have made Oakland exceptional, but it also, I think, made the town, in its extremity, extremely typical.

So I had this suspicion of whites or whiteness, which my parents may have bequeathed to me, and I carried it into adolescence in the pivotal years 1972 1973. This was when I would begin to learn, through a type of social intuition formed by events, what those prominent names Huey and Knowland and Jack London might have meant. The process started, arbitrarily enough, with a spelling bee. I was a tremendous speller. Why I spelled so well, I can't say. My spelling talent existed at the level of primitive fact. You might guess that I was vain about my spelling, and you would guess right. I must have had several other vanities, too, because back in the misty time of the second grade my teacher had mentioned, in a note on my report card, the need for "bursting" my "ego balloon." That stung, not just because it was true. (I quickly decided that because I knew what "ego balloon" meant I deserved a big one.) It stung because I longed after my teacher, whom I found very pretty and who rode a motorcycle. From that day forward I lusted after the sort of woman who might ride a motorcycle and seek to burst my ego balloon. I note this simply to illustrate that careful planning in childhood may be less formative than coincidence.

Yes, I was quite a speller. We had awards assemblies each year, and my entire memory of them consists of me standing humbly at the back, hearing my name called, walking down an aisle lined by my cheering fellow children, and accepting yet another award for spelling. A temperamentally scornful and pinched person might say that spelling triumphs in the Oakland public-school system were, by nature, small triumphs. But isn't it something to excel in tough circumstances and raise one's orchard in a harsh land? By the end of elementary school I had been designated a "Master Speller." At some point in that term of 1972–1973 I went on to the citywide spelling bee.

There were, I think, twenty or twenty-four of us in a windowless room. We sat at tables flanking a dais. I advanced steadily, for a while. Then I missed a word—and another. Each of us was allowed to miss three. Soon only two people remained ahead of me, a white boy from the hills and an Asian girl. The word was *pear*—or maybe *pair*. Or *pare*. Probably it was *pare*. I had not been listening very closely to the definition given. That proved to be an error. I picked the wrong *pear*, and my glittering career as a speller came to a shameful end. I hadn't even misspelled the word, I had misunderstood it. I can't recall who won, pitched as I was into a murk of self-hatred and embarrassment.

The torment worsened. When whoever the victor was rose to accept his or her award, the presenter was the superintendent of schools himself, Marcus Foster. He was big and kindly, self-assured, filled with pride (so it seemed to me) at the excellent spelling of us twenty or twenty-four products of the Oakland public schools. What I knew about him was: he had come from Philadelphia, a major city in the dated section of America, to our little town; and he was the first black superintendent of the Oakland public schools, the first one from the beginning of human time to 1970. He had the most prominent position of any black person in Oakland over the same period. And I worshipped him because he was going to deliver us, not from bad schools—I thought the schools were fine—but somehow from the racial whatever-it-was that I suspected was hanging over our young lives. He would deliver us because he was capable and because he was black.

Why was it important that Foster be black? To me, at that time, the answer was simple. By the age of ten or eleven I had sensed the day approaching when we would all be told to start behaving as if we were racial beings. This command would run contrary to the known facts of life. The blackness of Marcus Foster was important, I thought, not because we were all such racial children, and blackness was somehow the ultimate raceness, and therefore to run the schools properly one had to be black. The opposite was the case. We were not racial children, but we did have that potential, and it seemed to me likely that the command to become racial would arrive from the white side of the adult tracks. And it seemed to me that a black person was the least likely to give that command.

Why did I, at such a young age, think the command to be racial would arrive at all? Why should it come from whites? My parents' antiwhite prejudices must have played some role, as well as little things I observed, such as the way families got whiter as I walked uphill and blacker as I walked downhill. Money worked the same way, as did the comforts it buys. So there was this pattern, this line of division. Even I could see it now. I did not know which had come first, the money or the skin color. But I did know that adults struggled with each other over money and that one racial side had more money. One side was winning. It appeared obvious to me that the winners must be controlling this game, one way or another. I just couldn't imagine that the losers were making themselves poor.

I did not care about the money. I was too young to care about money. My immediate needs were met, and immediate needs were the only needs I had. What I did care about was the skin-color aspect of this dividing line. I saw the money part and the skin part as distinct. Clearly, you could have more or less money. You could not have more or less race. That was nonsensical. Physical appearance was not a quantity. So you could not struggle over race. Therefore, the force behind this otherwise inexplicable division had to be the money. The white people had the money. So the people making this dividing line had to be white people.

And, by chance, I felt that the dividing line might run right through me and my little world. Because this line was being drawn by whites, I had to oppose them. Because he was black, I thought, Marcus Foster would not behave in a white way. You see, I was already caught up in racial thinking, almost instantaneously, trying to find my way through it. All I wanted was a delay. Marcus Foster would understand how race worked among adults, to whom the concept evidently belonged and whom we would be joining in the course of the years. He might give us children more time to judge ourselves by the bagginess of our pants and not the colors of our skins. But I suppose I was already lost, too, because I did not trust a white person to do the same.

So I thought a black superintendent might give me the chance not to become white, lose friends—lose my childhood freedom. I also had a glimmer of what might lie ahead, if white adults had their way, in the person of my sixth-grade teacher. I was in the gifted class. How we became gifted, I don't know. I do know that gifted classes were part of a scheme to keep white children in the public schools, and indeed there were no black students in my class. Our teacher was white, in her fifties. She drove her Cadillac down from the hills in the morning and back up in the afternoon. Between times, she encouraged us to think of ourselves as better than other children we knew. Therefore, we deserved better—we deserved her. She encouraged us to compete for her esteem. She encouraged us to give her presents and to flatter her. Valuable skills, certainly, and quickly acquired by a certain type of child. But I despised her. I despised what she was doing to us. I doubly despised her because she was not as intelligent as my other teachers had been. Her idea of smartness did have an academic connection, but her real interest was in deportment—posture, cleanliness, manners, deference to authority. All of these seemed to be folded back into what was called being smart—and being gifted. I found this insulting, and insidious. She was trying to draw us away from others for our own good. She did not make any racial judgments that I can recall. But the fact remained that there were no black kids in this special class. That could make an impression on a young mind. I still saw my black playmates at recess, yet a separation had begun. Black kids formed the *only* group that fell away. So you might say this was their introduction to being a group, and it was my first experience of racial separatism among my peers.

I have one other relevant memory from that period, when I suspected the advent of racial separation, a particularly vivid and painful memory. My family took my father's parents for a picnic. We went to a park somewhere, a great flat expanse of green lawn, on a sunny day. We were having a pleasant time when Grandma looked around and said, "There are a lot of colored people here." Her observation struck me with tremendous force. I had not noticed how many colored people there were. I was an observant child, yet I had not noticed. I adored my grandmother. What she said hit me like a blow to the stomach. I felt dizzy. I must have been expecting something like this to happen, someday, otherwise it would not have hit so hard, if at all. It would have been like saying, "Might rain tonight." But on that day Grandma's remark, "There are a lot of colored people here," suddenly made all those colored people seem so far away, indistinct, as if Laura and Patty and Lamont and Darryl and Denise were snatched away from me into the mass of colored people, and there we were in the sunlight on the grass with our picnic, transformed from people into white people. Maybe I just hadn't expected this to come from family.

It may sound silly, but I had thought that our talented and charming and black superintendent of schools might give us a chance to be free a little longer. I had that hope, almost without knowing it. If I had won the spelling bee, then I would have got to shake his hand.

I did get to shake Bobby Seale's hand. He came by our church that same spring when he was running for mayor against the white incumbent, John Reading— a Knowland man who had first gained the mayoralty by appointment. I supported Bobby Seale because my parents said he had frightened the minority-rule white conservative establishment. In retrospect, I can see that Foster's superintendency and Seale's mayoralty run marked the high points of my optimism, as far as race went. They coincided with a thickening horizon of pessimism. To think that I was just getting started on this race business, and already things were going so poorly. Eleven can be a pivotal age. I was leaving elementary school for junior high, where there would be more kids, kids I didn't know, and more work. I had begun to read adults' books—I was laboring through Rachel Carson's *Silent Spring*, worried about pesticides—and newspapers (the *Tribune*, which I also delivered) and magazines, *Time* and *National Geographic*. I felt I was at the point of moving from the corral of childhood into the open fields of pre-adulthood. Yet I also suspected, and this was a racial matter, however vague in my mind, that I might be moving from the open fields of childhood to a corral. Bobby fought Reading to a runoff, then lost by a mile.

The year 1973 was full of events. Bobby Seale ran for mayor, and my mother nearly died. I mention this because it encouraged in me a keen sense of life's fragility. She fell and hit her head; she went into a coma; the doctor came by Dad and me sitting on curvy plastic chairs in a hospital hallway and said she was likely to die. Maybe he said "not come back." Fortunately, I was somewhat prepared for such an outcome. My mother was diabetic, which meant to me that on occasion I would arrive home from school and find her unconscious. Because my parents were plain speakers by habit and on principle, I knew that her unconsciousness was a first step toward death. My job consisted in prying open her mouth, forcing food (bread or sugar cubes) into it. If she didn't respond, I held her head in one hand, her jaw in the other, and worked the jaw up and down until she had to swallow (assuming she was alive). Sometimes, she would wake a little and claim she was fine. Well, that wasn't entirely for her to say, was it? Then my diplomatic skills—whatever diplomacy a boy might know at the age of, say, seven—came into use. Cajoling, arguing, commanding. A few times I slapped her, as gently as I could, on the cheek, to keep her conscious. I couldn't fail.

Unfortunately, I could not bring her out of a coma. But as luck would have it—we attributed it to her stubbornness—Mom came out of the coma after eight days or so, during which time we watched the young man next to her die. She didn't really recognize us. Dad dressed up in an old suit that hardly fit him anymore, the suit he wore when we had a studio portrait taken of the family back in Kansas, and impersonated himself with the hope she would know who he was. She seemed to, a little. He asked her who she was (no idea), what day it was (same result), and who was president. That was a dangerous line of inquiry, at such a delicate moment. Nixon was still president, and she hated Nixon. I think she picked Roosevelt (meaning Franklin, no doubt) or maybe Kennedy. We would just have to fill in the rest. And that is what we did, Dad and I, for the summer. We taught her to use a spoon, a fork, a knife. We taught her who she was, who we were, and who was still president.

I cannot say with completeness what effects all this had on me because I don't know. I did develop an even temper in moments of crisis, and the reflex of responsibility—a useful sort of egotism. I decided that adults learned how to behave as they did; even a child could teach them. I gained a bottomless respect for, and fear of, the power of chance to determine one's path in life. My expectations of predictability and normality became quite loose. I grew reluctant to blame people for their individual circumstances, as the power of the arbitrary loomed so large. And, of course, I saw the precariousness of life.

Whatever doubts I may have had about this last lesson disappeared in the first few months of junior high school, at the end of 1973. As we began this new stage in our progress toward adulthood, Z—the only person I knew of Balkan ancestry—took me aside after I asked where J was. J had been a wiry, bouncy girl with an Irish name, small in stature, who had grown her hair long by sixth grade. Her hair had many different colors in it. She had a gap in her front teeth, which I saw often because she smiled often and generally had the cheeriest disposition of anyone in our class. Z described J taking a bath that past summer at home when her parents were out. According to Z, a man broke into the house, raped J, then stabbed her until blood flowed in the tub and she died. That was the end of J. The story circulated briefly, faded away. I can't say whether it was true. But we never did see J again or hear any news about her.

Then early one evening in November, on Election Day, Marcus Foster and his right-hand man, Robert Blackburn, left their offices and headed for Blackburn's car, a Chevy Vega, to go vote. When they entered the parking lot, Blackburn noticed two people leaning against a building to his right. He and Foster walked past them. As the two men neared the Vega, Blackburn hurried ahead to open the passenger door for his old friend and boss. He heard guns firing. Eight bullets from two pistols entered the hero of my childhood, killing him quickly. A shotgun blast staggered Blackburn; a second blast grazed him; he lurched ahead, making it about sixty feet to a doorway. He found the right key, unlocked the door, entered the building, and collapsed. One of the shooters, meanwhile, had giggled. The shooters packed their guns and ran off toward Lake Merritt.

Such was my boyhood introduction to political extremism. The murder of Marcus Foster—Blackburn survived—quickly proved a strategic mistake for the Symbionese Liberation Army (as well as its first "action"). Too many of the People had liked Foster; he became our own King or Malcolm or something like that, a dead black hope. Many thousands mourned publicly, at black churches and the Oakland Auditorium. Promise yielded to despair, the opposite of what Foster would have wanted. Nonetheless, the SLA represented a culmination of many 1960s trends, including trends that had led to the hiring of Marcus Foster. More than any other revolutionary group, the SLA strove to unite the varied ideologies of the period into a single, flexible political theory and practice. It had just ten members, and that surely helped.

Who were these killers? The most distinctive feature of the SLA was how it sought to go beyond race (in a revolutionary way). The four founders—Nancy Perry, William Wolfe, Patricia Soltysik, and Donald DeFreeze—were white, white, white, and black, respectively. Their initial innovation was to propose, within Bay Area radical circles, multiracial rebel units. The idea got a lukewarm response, even some hostility. Yet they pressed ahead, seeking also to integrate radical feminism and Marxism-Leninism. One member recalled, "the people who made up the SLA were influenced by the interplay between Marxism, revolutionary nationalism and revolutionary feminism." Their second innovation was the idea of federation. The vanguardist and central-command structures of other groups seemed too much like the authoritarianism and bureaucracy that many revolutionaries were pledged to end in their rush toward freedom. Russell Little, SLA member and Oakland native, describes the concept:

> [T]he federation took into account the antagonisms and distrust that exist among progressive people in this country, and allowed each group to retain its autonomy and self-reliance while still being able to coordinate activities with other groups around common needs and objectives. It leaves space for revolutionary nationalists to retain a separate stance but still work with other units. The same would apply for revolutionary women separatists and also for groups with different political philosophies—as long as there was a basic belief in the necessity to use armed force to destroy U.S. corporate fascism.

The SLA hoped to create a revolutionary federation of separatisms. Rebel energy increasingly ran in separatist channels, and the army of ten took this as a political given.

According to a report by the U.S. House Committee on Internal Security, written at a tense moment (the SLA had just kidnapped Patricia Hearst) and so probably overstating its case, the SLA had ties with: Venceremos (Maoist); Vietnam Veterans Against the War (one SLA man, who worked with VVAW, had served two volunteer hitches with the 101st Airborne in Vietnam); the Black Guerrilla Family and Black Liberation Army (influenced by Eldridge Cleaver after his break with Huey Newton and the Panthers); Nuestra Familia, a Mexican inmate group (rivals to the Mexican Mafia); and, not to be forgotten, the Polar Bears. The Polar Bear Party, according to the committee's investigators, "started out as a predominantly white group which followed the racist philosophy of the Aryan Brotherhood . . . It recently [1972–1973] joined in an alliance with the Venceremos organization and has established contact with the Venceremos members both inside and outside the prisons. As a result, the Polar Bear Party had begun to espouse the Maoist revolutionary line of the Venceremos."

According to Russell Little, the SLA "put great emphasis on respecting the freedom, self-determination and culture of all peoples." The new word *symbionese* indicated the central purpose of uniting diverse elements in working toward a common goal, as in symbiosis. The SLA's symbol was a seven-headed cobra, which may have derived from the album-cover art for Jimi Hendrix's

1967 record *Axis: Bold as Love* but which the SLA explained as among "the first symbols used by people to signify God and life." The SLA traced their cobra to "Egyptian temples and their seven pillars, to the seven candles of the pre-Zionist North African religions, to the Buddhist and Hindu religions and to North and South American Indian religions." Each head of the snake was assigned a Swahili word, in the manner of Kwanza images. Nor did the SLA neglect American traditions. The communiqué claiming credit for murdering Foster and wounding Blackburn arrived with a Revolutionary War Bicentennial commemorative stamp bearing the slogan "Rise the Spirit of Independence." The communiqué said, "we know that the enemy fears our understanding of the fact that nothing is more precious than freedom."

If one can generalize about ten people, the SLA at its height had a special attraction for whites. "The SLA actions presented white revolutionaries, especially women, in a positive role," recalled Little, who was white. "The 3 original white members of the SLA and the 5 who joined later were in part motivated by what we felt was a need for whites to intensify their participation in the underground struggle. We felt it was necessary to go beyond symbolic bombings to other guerrilla tactics that had formerly been the exclusive domain of non-whites in this country." It reveals much about the SLA synthesis that a white member could say, against all evidence, that guerrilla tactics had been "the exclusive domain of non-whites." He wanted to move in on that domain as a white person. I suppose he may have wanted the freedom of it, a freedom that enabled another white SLA man to refer to Foster as a "jive ass nigger." The mostly white SLA had so much confidence in its multiracial self-awareness that it felt entitled to murder a black man. The SLA formula for describing its constituency was "Black, Chicano, Asian and conscious White." The nature of conscious, as opposed to unconscious, whiteness was never explained. However, it seems clear that blacks, Chicanos, and Asians were inherently conscious whereas whites had to become conscious. Then you would have a perfect joint separatism; and then even a conscious white could join in the powerful separatist ritual of naming a person as not black enough, a "jive ass nigger," perhaps also voicing his opinion on who was not white enough, not Chicano enough, not Asian or feminist enough. Because these groups did not have much content or history to guide them (the goal being to go beyond history and start over) — because they moved rather as motiveless herds across the plains of late-1960s cultural thought — one man's opinion was worth as much as another's.

Or perhaps a conscious white man's opinion was worth a little more, because he had earned his consciousness through some unspecified effort rather than getting it for free at birth? This was certainly one white American tradition, and the SLA did run with the American grain. Its radical goal of everyone being equal but separate could hardly have been more traditional. I would say the same about its failure, its easy violence, its stupidity in shooting Marcus Foster to death there in the parking lot downtown, and its unshakable, one-man-one-universe self-absorption, as illustrated in the remarks of the four SLA survivors, the other six having been killed by the Los Angeles police: "Although we love and support each other totally, the four of us do not presently have the high degree of theoretical unity necessary to put together a comprehensive political perspective that truly represents each of our politics as they have evolved up to this point."

And I would say the same about the little boost I imagine some SLA members got from being consciously white rather than unconsciously black. Theoretically, the conscious white radical male of the period had this in common with the unconscious white ultraconservative male, such as William Knowland: he was a self-made man. Neither man could allow much room for chance or history in determining his social position. Just as Knowland believed nothing in the communist world happened by accident, the SLA believed most anything—for example, the school identification card and police-community programs for which they killed Foster—was an emanation of "the fascist government of Amerika." The radical white man reasoned his way to conscious power and freedom, while the conservative white man, more passive, simply asserted his freedom from unreason, that is, from a controlling past. Both kept their power and stayed white in their respective ways; and both thought their path to power was a path that led beyond race.

The beyond-raceness of the SLA had a mirror in the beyond-raceness of the Black Panther Party for Self-Defense. The Panthers had begun in opposition to black cultural nationalism. The general idea, as explained by Bobby Seale in his 1970 memoir *Seize the Time*, was that racism was a game whites couldn't lose. As he said in urging black kids not to gamble, "The house always wins." Black nationalism had to be ineffective and served mainly as a psychic balm for better-off blacks. Powerful whites, Seale wrote, "use blacks, especially the blacks who come out of the colleges and the elite class system, because these blacks have a tendency to flock toward a black racism which is parallel to the racism the Ku Klux Klan or white citizens groups practice . . . The ruling class and their running dogs, their lackeys, their bootlickers, their Toms and their black racists, their cultural nationalists—they're all the running dogs of the ruling class." Seale had been attracted to Huey Newton, when they were students at Merritt College, in part because Huey would readily argue with black nationalists (and anyone else). Seale believed the campus intellectuals saw Huey and him as "field niggers."

Bobby certainly did. He and Huey were proud products of the Oakland streets. Their parents had come up from the South to do war work. Every one of the tools white East Bay residents used to protect themselves from what they understood as blackness—segregated housing, criminal police, daily discrimination—went into forming Bobby and Huey. The time-honored romance of black-male criminality again came to the fore; the purer the oppression, the purer the person. As Seale wrote of the beginning:

> Huey wanted brothers off the block—brothers who had been out there robbing banks, brothers who had been pimping, brothers who had been peddling dope, brothers who ain't gonna take no shit, brothers who had been fighting pigs—because he knew that once they got themselves together in the area of political education (and it doesn't take much because the political education is the ten-point platform and program), Huey P. Newton knew that once you organize the brothers he ran with, he fought with, he fought against, who he fought harder than they fought him, once you organize those brothers, you get niggers, you get black men, you get revolutionaries who are too much.

Bobby and Huey had a belief in "cleansing" violence, which they combined with the conviction that "if you didn't organize the lumpen proletariat . . . if you didn't relate to these cats, the power structure would organize these cats against you."

The Panther founders had a strong practical sense. They felt that black nationalists were impractical, indeed anti-practical. The Panthers went in the opposite direction. They followed the police around to make sure officers obeyed the law. They forced the city of Oakland to put up a streetlight at a dangerous intersection. They helped educate white officers in the subtleties of constitutional law:

> Huey had said, "Go for your gun and you're a dead pig. Don't you know by the Fourteenth Amendment of the U.S. Constitution that you can't remove a person's property from them without due process of law." Huey was mad, loud, and articulate.
>
> The pig began to walk and he kind of did a half-moon, walking around and away from Huey, trying to walk back to his car . . . Black people began to come out of their houses, wanting to know what was going on. Huey said, "Come on out, black people. Come on out and get to know about these racist dog swine who been controlling our community and occupying our community like a foreign troop."

That was the Panthers all over: bold, practical, and so plain goofy, so disciplined and demented and dementedly disciplined that you had to pay attention. Bobby had, indeed, once been a comedian. Discussing the Constitution with a cop who might well like to kill you—it was at once so serious and so hilarious. When the California legislature, in reaction to the Panther police patrols, came up with a bill (its author lived in Piedmont) to restrict gun ownership, the Panthers drove to Sacramento and walked, fully armed, into the assembly chamber. (Governor Reagan had seen them coming, as he addressed a youth delegation outside, and absented himself from the scene.) So the Panthers asserted their right under the Constitution to bear arms, while Reagan and social conservatives passed a bill that amounted to gun control.

The Panthers resembled William Knowland in many ways, including their practical bent. They distrusted intellectuals. They prized physical bravery. They believed in the importance of political ideas, especially simple ones, and feared heresy. They honored every American tradition that served their purposes. They combined immense self-control with quick tempers. They believed firmly in law and order (their own). They urged a rigid public morality, far more rigid than what they followed in private. They looked hopefully to the power of government and business to correct social abuses. And from the start they showed an instinctive political-moral need to understand social disruption as foreign, to define it as such, the police "occupying our community like a foreign troop," the foreignness of money power in the form of (white, or treasonous black) property owners living "outside the community." Blacks were in an "internal colony," which the Panthers sought to make an *imperium in imperio*. They would police "their own" community.

And this is where the Panthers lapsed into a nationalism of racial separation, something they explicitly repudiated. It began as early as the first point of the first Panther document, the "Black Panther Party Platform and Program" of October 1966. "We want freedom" was the opening sentence, followed by "We want power to determine the destiny of our Black Community." It was as if freedom and racial separatism were inseparable twins, in America. The party platform cited the Second and Fourteenth Amendments to the Constitution. It ended with a call for "a United Nations–supervised plebiscite to be held throughout the black colony in which only black colonial subjects will be allowed to participate, for the purpose of determining the will of black people as to their national identity." The platform then quoted the opening of Thomas Jefferson's Declaration of Independence:

> When, in the course of human events, it becomes necessary for
> one people to dissolve the political bands which have connected
> them with another, and to assume, among the powers of the

earth, the separate and equal station to which the laws of nature and nature's God entitle them, a decent respect to the opinions of mankind requires that they should declare the causes which impel them to the separation.

Jefferson's document seems oddly suited to express both universal human longings and their American declension into racial separatism. It worked that way, in effect, for Jefferson and his white generation. The concept of "separate and equal" (as of "the black colony") certainly has proved a lasting one. Racial thinking, unbidden yet unstoppable, has tended to drain into those words as into tidal pools. The declaration functioned for the Panthers much as it had functioned for Jefferson. (A few years later it would reappear in an SLA communiqué.) The declaration summoned the ocean of human ideals, then somehow allowed the waters to recede into pools of race, which is roughly what the Panthers, the SLA, and their enemy William Knowland all did, after their particular fashions. Knowland wrote in his *Tribune* in 1968, "We should be talking American Power rather than Black Power or White Power." Yet the Panthers and the SLA *were* talking American power. They wanted American power. All of these people, including Knowland, wanted American power, but so much of the power they could actually get, actively or passively, was racial power. It was the most accessible form of American power. Jefferson would have understood that.

Knowland killed himself, whereas the suicides of the Panthers and the SLA were more complicated and involved many hands. The SLA never recovered from the fact that it had entered the world as a mostly white organization that killed a black man; and soon enough its warriors were either dead or in jail. The antiracial Panthers managed to ally themselves with the SNCC pioneers of Black Power. The SNCC people thought the Panthers were mistaken in accepting white comrades, and the SNCC-Panther alliance, oddly enough, in a roundabout way, ended up destroying SNCC and disabling the Panthers. The Panthers also had their deadly run-ins with the black-nationalist organization of Ron Karenga, who invented the race holiday of Kwanza. It went on like that, all these groups breaking and collapsing on the paradoxes of separatism and American universalism, with the police and FBI helping them along to explore every dimly lighted terror.

I would never forget that one of Foster's murderers—probably Patricia Soltysik, who took the name Mizmoon and wrote period verse—had been heard giggling from her hiding place. I had this image of killer comedians; it turned me serious for a while. As children, we were meant to come out from unnameable terrors, what were called "childish fears," and have our world steadily brighten as we approached maturity. It didn't quite work out like that. Rather, we were torn, and we tore, ourselves away from each other, and acquired racial fears in our progress away from childhood.

The process of racial separation that began with "tracking" continued with the practice of dropping out of school. At about twelve or thirteen years of age precocious boys started to drop away, mentored by older boys in their neighborhoods. They drifted into crime or just hanging out, being tough and fast, both too hard for the classroom and too soft. I watched my friend Lamont go this way, a round-cheeked, sweet, and energetic black boy. He had been over to the house for birthday parties until I was ten. We climbed the pine tree out back together. By my eleventh birthday we were already on separate tracks. I saw him very infrequently and by chance, on the street. He was bulking up early, the fat becoming muscle. His cheeks thinned and his face grew hard—not when he recognized me, but I could see it when he was at a distance, hanging with his set or staring coolly through the Cyclone fence at our poor little treeless, indeed bushless, junior-high-school playground baking in the California sun. I stayed in school, he didn't. We had less and less to talk about, and then nothing. In my child's mind he was a bit like J—an inexplicable loss, this time a gradual one. I wonder what happened to him. I know what was most likely. There were gangs, it was a violent time, and it got more violent as we aged.

Our school was named for Bret Harte, Twain's co-author on "The Heathen Chinee" and the sworn enemy of Joaquin Miller. Although the school had proportionately more black students than had been the case at my elementary school, I no longer had black friends, not close ones. That became a hole in the world. I'll put it this way: the black friends I had had were friends rather than black; now they were shifting to being black rather than friends. This happened to everyone. Dark-skinned kids became black, light kids became white, Pedro and Esther became Hispanic or Chicano, Jeff and Teri and Darrell became Chinese (whereas Darryl became black), Z became white and so, in a most reluctant way, did I. There were relatively more of all these groups at Bret Harte except whites. The whites began to drop out, a few to the streets, very few. Most went uphill, to whiter public schools or to private schools or to other towns entirely—white towns. Their separatism took the most decisive form of absence. This departure was in my view a defining move in their becoming white. Each person in each group was acquiring a racial consciousness and a racial identity.

How those words make me laugh now. How I wish we had known enough to laugh at them then. So we hung together in racial groups, patrolling the imaginary boundaries among us until they seemed as real as anything else. You could hear it in our slang. See that white dude over there? So this black dude says to me, that guy's a banana. Yellow on the outside, white on the inside. Or an Oreo . . . Poor Lisa had a white parent and a Filipino parent; when it came down to it, she was a Flip. (A few girls and boys did have a certain mobility, though, if they were supremely attractive—and not too dark.) We *identified* each other by race. The Chinese kids would say *hock* for black and *bock* for white, rough adaptations of their parents' Cantonese for "black devil" and "white devil."

Why did we do this? It was not a result of education. We had a standard education for the time—reading, writing, math, art, French or Spanish, physical education, shop class, typing. History, in any large sense, would not come until high school. If only our childish race fixation *had* been due to textbooks. You can always change textbooks. But there was nothing Afrocentric or Eurocentric or Confucian or Hispanophile about our education, and what do you know, we divided up into races anyway. I honestly don't understand why. It isn't as if we had always already had racial identities and they were just now coming up on nature's schedule, like the hair under our arms, the pimples on our faces, the growing breasts and hardening muscles. Maybe we just sought the protections of group identity for our twelve-to-fourteen-year-old selves, and here was where the possibilities lay; perhaps, as for our elders, race was the form power took in becoming accessible or articulate. This ran contrary to what we had known, but we did it anyway.

It seemed very unnatural to me and was not undertaken in any positive spirit. How could it have been? We were not discovering our true identities. Race had little or no positive content; one's new racial identity simply folded back in on itself. We were not discovering our roots, we were ripping them out—whatever shallow roots we had put down by the age of twelve. It may well be that the society of adults, which we were preparing to enter, had these racial identities waiting for us, and in our eagerness to mature we reached for them. But it was not a question of discovering who we were, it was a question of discovering who we had to be to fit in—a very different activity, in fact the opposite activity when looked at from a child's perspective. Only later, after much effort and many trials, could one possibly grasp this tearing and ripping and the baffled glances at ex-friends and these apparently senseless separations from other human beings as a method of becoming who you were—as if selfhood was a process of elimination and creative solitary confinement.

Personally, the racialization of life in junior high presented me with a quandary. I saw racial identity to some degree as a choice, and the racial path obviously open to me thanks to the accident of birth—becoming white—was not a path I was willing to take. I may have been more sensitive to the chosenness of race than were some of my peers. I was a pensive child. It could be that my chance acquaintance in the year 1973 with sudden death and racial terrorism had bled away my normal share of faith in inevitability and instilled a reluctance to accept what came my way. Further, there was an evidently dwindling number of white people with whom to identify—even had I been able to overcome my prejudices, which were in no way pro-white. And, of course, I did not feel white except in the eyes of others. But in that I was no different from anyone.

My solution, such as it was, became to identify with my Chinese American friends. I had a Chinese friend from up the street, Jeff. We began walking to school together every morning. The (now white) girl I had pursued in the first grade, he dated in the eighth. He developed a group of Chinese or quasi-Chinese friends who became my friends. We knew a complementary group of Asian girls—for the sexes had separated, too. Another old elementary-school playmate, Anthony, adhered to my group as well. He had been Italian in childhood but was now white like me. We were the two white boys who hung with the Chinese boys, and would remain so for years.

It was sometimes an awkward fit, but it was the best I could do under the circumstances. True, I could not understand their grandparents, sometimes their parents—though they didn't always understand their elders' Cantonese, either. Their bodies developed earlier, they were light, quick, and strong while their white friends kept inching upward, weak and ungainly. We had a uniform: black or navy Derby jackets, sky-blue cords or jeans (black or blue), collared long-sleeve shirts with the sleeves rolled up, Adidas or Tiger running shoes. I was usually just a little off the beat, in a brown Derby, in tennis rather than running shoes. But the exception proved the rule.

What did we do that was racial? At first, very little. We referred to others as *hock* and *bock*, to Asians as bananas or f.o.b. (fresh off the boat) or a.b.c. (American-born Chinese) or Jap or Flip. We said *ai-ya* in a wide variety of social situations. I probably don't need to mention that not one of us knew as much about Asian culture or the Asian heritage as a focused adult could glean from a day's reading in the library. We were, after all, Americans. My friends' parents were Americans, mostly second-generation, and did not talk about pre-America (not in English, anyway). Similarly, my own parents did not speak of pre-Oakland, much less of our heritage, whatever that might be. Soon Bruce Lee became of towering importance. We imitated everything about him that we could take from his movies except his bad haircuts: the walk, the moves, the stare, the cool stoicism. We practiced "martial arts." Non-Chinese practiced them, too, from the same sacred films and in the same way. Their efforts, however, like mine, lacked conviction, for the obvious reason that they were not

Chinese—rather, that they did not look anything like Bruce Lee. That was the difference, the only difference, one of appearance.

This made a truly perverse sense because at that time my friends' Chinese-ness, not to mention mine, really was a matter of appearance. And the essence of that appearance was a martial or warlike art, a defensive posture in the literal sense. But, *ai-ya*, defense against what? Some of my friends had well-off parents, by Oakland public-school standards, and some did not. All of us did fine in class, both through cheating, which we undertook together, and through study-ing, which we did separately. By and large, the wealthier would go on to col-lege, and the less wealthy would not, but that was all far away and did not affect our thinking yet, or our unity. What we were interested in was the appearance or imitation of power, which in the event was the appearance of racial solidarity and the imitation of race. It was something to do; it was kind of a joke, really, and a game, and then it wasn't.

My memories of our little race war are shaky now. I *think* it began with a stabbing. Either a Chinese boy stabbed a black boy or the other way around. There was a corner entrance to the schoolyard that had a long staircase and a high chain-link gate. The toughest kids hung around there, making a display of their nonattendance as far as classes went. Teachers avoided this area. Even the vice principal charged with enforcing discipline avoided it, and understandably so. An enraged fourteen-year-old is a confusing opponent. For an adult, she or he, especially he, incites pity and fear, condescension and terror all at once in a dismaying jumble of strong emotions. I'll never forget the day one black class-mate felt he had been disrespected by our math teacher, a white man with a temper, one of those rare, unfortunate souls who thought he could intimidate us with his touchy adulthood. My classmate got up and chased him out of the classroom and down the hall. That made quite an impression. The boy did not become a hero, and neither did the teacher. Each was humiliated in the same way. The boy was not going to come back and take over the class, although he had a talent for math. (I know, because I later tutored him.) The teacher was not going to recover what he had mistakenly built up for himself as his dignity. The boy and the man had backed themselves up against their respective honors. I pitied both of them, and I don't believe I was alone in that feeling.

Whether or not there was any stabbing, a situation soon developed in which the black kids and the Chinese kids squared off against each other. For a few days we carried more than the usual complement of weapons—in our phonetic renderings, *nunchaku* (two batons connected by a short length of rope or chain), *sherakins*, or "stars" (made of sharpened metal, for throwing), metal knuckles, and throwing knives. Guns were still rare at our school. We gathered at recess, grumbled, sought allies, strengthened our resolve, and traded rumors about the other side. We did everything armies do except fight. (Of course, most armies spend most of their time not fighting.) There were small skirmishes at the stairwell, but the school administration had wisely closed that entrance, so the few lead combatants met on opposite sides of the fence and threatened each other. It was very much like the many less-than-exciting parts of the Trojan War as recounted by Homer. When I finally read the *Iliad*, it seemed familiar.

I was torn by this conflict. I did not like conflict as such. I resented my classmates' insufficient (to me) appreciation of the fragility of life. I identified—on principle, and through what remained of my contacts with black classmates— with both sides. And I thought the basic premise of the clash, that one's race was worth fighting for, had too little a hold in reality. I don't remember being afraid of a just war. This simply did not seem to be that war. It was as if we, all of us, had been imitating something in all innocence, so to speak—imitating races— and now, all of a sudden and for no reason other than habit and the habit of imaginary honor, our racial imitations would become real in the sense of leading to stabbings, concussions, and final breaks between boys who had, in some cases, been friends before they became race beings. Because one day I did see Lamont there on the other side of the closed gate at the top of the stairs.

By some means I ended up in the principal's office to help "mediate" the "conflict." I put these words in quotation marks because the conflict was not about anything. The two groups, Chinese and black, had no competing group interests. They were not fighting "over" anything; they were just fighting. Therefore, "mediating" could only mean convincing all the parties that there was no "conflict" and nothing to mediate. In practice, as I remember, this meant gathering many small bits of information and cycling them through enough "meetings" such that everyone got tired and began to question their own memories. Fortunately, no one really wanted a race war. That had just been the available form into which a clash might fit. The forms had not yet acquired enough content so that a race war would have "made sense," in the way that the Panthers, the SLA, and the Oakland Republican Party made sense. Thank heaven we were still children and didn't know any better than to stop fighting.

At around this time I faced another, more subtle racial conflict. The truth was that my school tended toward violence, if not quite the gunplay of a succeeding generation. The city itself was violent; we beat out Detroit one year in per capita murders. Violence does interfere with one's education. Besides, I was not too challenged by the available courses. My parents quietly asked if I would like to attend a private school near our home. I knew the school. I had learned to swim and play tennis there in summers. (Of course, our elementary and junior high schools had no pools and no tennis courts. I don't remember their having summer programs at all.) This private school was another world. The students wore uniforms. I didn't know any of them, but I had observed them on occasion when classes were in session, from the other side of the high fence that surrounded their school. They looked cheerful and confident and heedless in a way I already associated with money. They also looked, most of them, white.

My parents were reluctant. They did not push me one way or the other. I considered the matter very carefully; it represented a turning point in my still-new career as a white boy. In my mind I related it to an earlier turning point, a moment of racial agitation and resolve that had occurred as I was sitting alone one day after school, on a hillside overlooking the city. I don't know why, but I was thinking about how racial trends seemed to be going in my narrow life and decided they were not going well. As I've said, I was a pensive child; I would have been about twelve. What I decided was that Martin Luther King believed race should not matter—I suspect I got that from Dad—and therefore I, Scott Malcomson, would no longer recognize its importance. Then I came down from the mountaintop back to junior high school and quickly determined that this was not up to me. The not-mattering of race seemed indisputable in principle. But in reality race clearly did matter, and even I could see that I and everyone I knew lived in reality rather than principle or fantasy. Although our juvenile races lacked much content, they already had effects—I was preoccupied, for example, with clear feelings of scholastic inferiority among my black classmates, feelings that seemed dangerous and illogical to me. The principle of no-race would in practice have been a denial; in a sense, it would have been a lie, in that it would have led to lies about the real world. At the same time, multiculturalism did not exist. There was no positive race principle with which to engage our race facts—a lack of racial principle doubtlessly related to our signal lack of racial heritages.

I did, of course, have one delusional choice available, namely to isolate myself from race so thoroughly as to believe it did not matter. I say "delusional" because, in practical terms, this choice could only mean going so far into my accidental race that it would become a seeming irrelevancy or a rule to which others were exceptions. In short, I would have had to choose white racial separatism in its physical and psychological forms, a choice that would express itself by my going to a white school.

I could not choose that as my future. To go to the white school would have been to give in to unreality. It would have made the life I had lived to that point a lesser form of life, or a mistaken one. It would have put me among people who had more money at their disposal than I had and whose sense of their own value as individuals was partly determined (so I thought) by their access to money, one might say their value in money. I found that idea offensive on its face, and more so because my limited exposure to such people suggested that they thought their pampered life was normal and unobjectionable in every way, which meant many of the lives I knew, including my own, were subnormal, a judgment I could not help resisting.

To have gone to the white school would have meant giving in to fear—running away from many things I feared. That was impossible. That would have meant taking a course opposite to the one I had been following since the eventful summer and fall of 1973, if not before, which had been to manage fear in my thoughts and actions, to get as close to it as I could in my weakness, to know those fears and live with them. I feared sudden death, women's vulnerability, and racial identity. Each of these seemed a threat to my existence or to the legitimacy of my short life as I understood it. Racial identity appeared to me as both a refuge and a threat, a relief and a personal disaster, a fact of life and an illusion of life. I was not going to run away from it, but I was not going to run toward it, either. I suspect I chose so-called Chineseness in hopes of keeping my denial and acceptance of race in suspension, or at a distance—to manage the reality of race and manage its unreality, to evade being mastered by race. The strained nature of this management was made apparent every day by the glaring fact that I was not Chinese. Physically, I could not pass for Chinese any more than I could be mistaken for a tree or a bird. I suppose I played with racial facts in this way because, ultimately, I did not believe they were facts. They were poised somewhere between facts and fantasies, and so was I.

To have entered the white school would have meant becoming white, a crucial aspect of which was becoming not nonwhite—which meant for me destroying parts of my life, large parts, that weren't white. This would have amounted to self-denial, and self-betrayal, in concrete terms: betraying friends, betraying the past. To have entered the white school would have meant entering what I imagined as a limitless arid present, a present of limitless cruelty because it was premised on withdrawal and abandonment; on a belief in the innocence of children such as myself, a belief that struck me, given my experience, as ridiculous; and on a related belief in the innocence of white people, which seemed to me equally absurd and even less defensible in the living world I knew. And it would have meant a betrayal of Marcus Foster. So I did not go to the white school.

The Chineseness of my group of friends did not deepen as time passed. Our shared culture did. It became more black. Whereas we had once listened to the ethnic medley that was Elton John, we now moved into Earth, Wind & Fire, the Stylistics, and the Ohio Players. "That's the Way of the World" and "Reasons" usually tied for favorite song, though we also liked "You Make Me Feel Brand New"—all romantic ballads. I read a great deal out of school, mostly morbid intellectual novels, such as Gide's *The Immoralist* and Camus's *The*

Plague, and philosophy (Plato's dialogues, *Zen and the Art of Motorcycle Maintenance*), and books about my favorite, appropriately fear-drenched sport, mountain climbing. But my friends did not read apart from class requirements, not even the papers, so the written word played a minimal role in our culture. Black music provided a sense of rhythm and improvisation and the words for imagining romance—a private lushness behind our habitual stoicism.

This was not exactly pro-black; it was more antiwhite. When we moved on to high school, we became exposed to a type of white person rather new to us. Our high school, Skyline, was the very high school created back in 1961 by the concerned white citizens of Oakland for the benefit of their children. This decisive bit of white affirmative action had lost some of its coherence in the intervening fifteen years. There were no more fraternities and sororities, the "senior lawn" was no longer reserved for seniors, and the student body was not all white. In relative Oakland terms Skyline was still a white school, though in suburban terms it was not. There we encountered white people from the upper middle class, kids whose parents gave them cars. The vague set of antiwhite prejudices we had harbored for some time—that whites were cowardly, clueless, physically unimpressive and sexually challenged (I'm speaking of the boys), and generally a lowish form of life—grew stronger. These kids had come from the white junior high, before that from the white elementary schools. They had led an entirely white life, as far as we knew, and looked as if they would contentedly go on living one. We were extraneous to it. Our experience had no interest or importance, particularly our racial experience, which had seemed so central. Therefore we removed still further, marking ourselves off. I think the turn to black music was part of this exacerbated "Chinese" separation. There was no Chinese music. The white kids listened to white rock and roll, which seemed like preciously self-involved noise designed for people with slow wits.

We did well in class, using the time-tested methods of cheating and study. Our dislike of white people, particularly white boys, did not result in academic failure, not at all. Whenever competition was involved, we simply assumed that we Asians could always win through hard work and mutual assistance. This was a clannish belief in racial superiority. It had almost no content beyond belief in itself. It scorned failure, and we were no more generous to others than we were to ourselves. We were what a teacher of that era would have called achievers. This successful "assimilation" to general norms on the basis of racial solidarity was quite a feat. Much of our Asianness, or Chineseness, had come to consist in beating whites at their own games by their own rules—with one critical departure from those rules, namely the suppression of individualism in favor of the collective. You might well wonder who was assimilating whom. Were we a model minority? Ours was a conception of race that could defeat almost any challenge because, in its competitiveness, it was so flexible. Its essential content was victory, which should not be confused with a racial heritage. It was just a strategy in a racial world. And because we felt free to take whatever we wanted, we were in that respect beyond race. Our race had little history of which we were aware, almost no unique content, and few constraints. To a great extent, raceness in the sense of history, content, and constraints was something we attributed to blacks and whites. They were stuck with race, and weakened by it, because they had the misfortune not to be Chinese. They lacked the assimilating confidence and power of Chineseness.

Whether this Chineseness had any connection to China—some inherited disposition coursing through my friends despite themselves—I do not know. But I doubt there was a connection. I think it is more likely that our Chineseness, at heart, worked as a third race whose shape, like its content, was formed primarily by blacks and whites and their relationships to each other. It created and filled a space between them and therefore was determined by them—however much we may not have desired that and felt we were beyond and above it. America has a long history of such third groups, from Ben Franklin's Germans through the numberless varieties of mulatto, through Irish Catholics, shtetl Jews, Hispanics and Armenians and Arabs, each with its own histories but each, also, waxing and waning as black and white wax and wane, and about as successful in separating from black and white as black and white have been in separating from each other.

So day after day through high school we stood by the same length of chain between two pillars in front of the same building at Skyline, wearing Derbys and tight jeans. We played mumblety-peg, throwing knives at each other's feet, the idea being not to flinch when the knife got close. We practiced Bruce Lee's "death punch." We were a gang without there being other gangs, a pure gang all dressed up with nowhere to go, training for challenges we knew would never arrive, jealous of a turf no one else wanted. That was just as well, and accounts for our perfect survival rate. We did engage in some small, interesting violence. This happened after one of us acquired a pellet gun. As a weapon, our gun was unimpressive, a toy. You could have done more damage with a rock than with that gun. But our toy gun did have the special quality common to all firearms: it substituted for physical bravery. A gun in hand can bring out the coward in anyone. And characteristically, I think, for a racial gang, we used our gun in a cowardly way against our fear of cowardice within our race and against the enemy race we could not reach. We went by V's house several times, a bungalow on a quiet street near Dimond Park. V was an uncool Chinese boy we had known since grade school. He was physically slack and had a silly name (silly by Chinese American standards). He submitted to his parents' will by wearing the traditional Chinese-boy buzz cut. We did not help him in school; his grades were average. Naturally, we strong boys confronted his weakness by substituting for it our own. We parked outside at night and fired into his family's front window. We laughed as we watched them scurry about their living room in fear, the glass broken. I would never lose the shame I felt at what we did, what I did, in particular that I had laughed when we fired. Sometimes you get to see things in yourself that are hard to bear.

Our other target was in the hills. The rich white people up there had their own shopping district, called Montclair. On its streets our murky hatred of whites and their money smugness, their impression of indifferent superiority that we did so much to imitate or assimilate, briefly found a focus. We cruised along at night and shot at their bank. I don't really know how it happened or whose idea it was. I believe we were simply pulled along by a logic that existed around us, a logic that led to the conclusion: shoot their bank. So we shot at the bank, and we felt pretty good about it, too.

I did not want to stay in Oakland. I had it in mind that there was a raceless world outside Oakland where people lived as part of some general, shared civilizational plan, with a common history of advances and setbacks that, however great the difficulties involved, had a shape and direction. That was my fantasy of the adult world, and I did not cling to my fantasy less tightly just because my Oakland experience contradicted it. One factor in my faith in a larger, sensible world was my study of Latin. The dead language of Rome had no apparent connection whatsoever to life in Oakland; thus, there must have been a non-Oakland where Latin had significance. Latin class survived at Skyline as a vestige of the school's white-separatist mission. Among the richer ironies of my Latin class was its popularity. Plenty of people took Latin, because Skyline was the best school in the system and the only one with Latin, which meant that if you were zoned for another, poorer high school and manifested a keen desire to learn the language of Cicero you could transfer to Skyline. In this way, studying Latin became a rather improbable method for escaping poverty and for integration on a tiny scale. You might not think a classical education could be so useful, but that's the way it was. So Latin class had many students, and attendance was strong.

After the first year we embarked on reading Virgil's Aeneid. It seems funny now that we would have studied the same book Elias Boudinot and John Ridge studied in Cornwall, Connecticut, a book that evidently made a strong impression on Ridge: the brother who accompanied Ridge's eldest son and his slave Wacooli to California had, after all, been named Aeneas. The Aeneid tells the story of a wandering tribe, led by Aeneas, that leaves Troy and eventually founds the Roman Empire. But that was not the part of the story that struck me in Oakland. What really captured me was the story of Aeneas and Queen Dido of

Carthage. Dido falls in love with Aeneas, a love that Virgil portrays as doomed madness. Of their love he writes, "The inward fire eats the soft marrow away, / And the internal wound bleeds on in silence." Aeneas cannot remain in love with Dido because he has to fulfill his destiny of founding Rome, while Dido is merely a queen in Africa. How different all our histories might be if Aeneas had stayed in Africa. In the poem Venus asks, concerning the will of Jupiter, "Does he approve / A union and mingling of these races?" The answer is no.

Why? That was the part I could not understand. Even the Trojan women had wanted to stay in Carthage. Why leave? Aeneas loved Dido, she loved him. Carthage was a perfectly nice city on the African coast, overlooking the Mediterranean and complete with its own empire. But no, Aeneas had to leave. Dido set herself on fire then, so you see Dido in flames, enraged, helpless, looking out at the departing ships of her lover. I couldn't crack the meaning of this story. I loved and hated and kept gnawing away at it. I think what bothered me most was that I wanted to save vulnerable Dido from her sudden and wrongful death, regardless of what Jupiter said about "races," yet I had to admit that something always took me away with Aeneas. When I left Oakland, I did feel that I was abandoning the city. Aeneas at least seemed to know where he was going, whereas I did not.

After the killings of the early 1970s there followed, in black Oakland, what might very cautiously be called a little hope. White rage showed signs of having spent itself. In 1977 Oaklanders elected a black man, Lionel Wilson, as mayor. A poll from the middle of the decade revealed a slight shift in black-elite thinking. Whereas 29 percent of those polled in the "traditional" black elite agreed that "the ultimate destiny of the Afro-American is likely to be extermination," the percentage dropped to 23 among "new urban elites." So not even a quarter of the presumably most optimistic segment of the Oakland black population believed that their race's final moment in American history would be a complete massacre. That is why I say "cautiously" and "a little" hope. Follow-up interviews traced the new hopefulness to a feeling that whites had lost interest in, or the political possibilities for, eliminating blacks from America.

Elimination of blacks was hardly necessary when abandonment of them was going so well and achieving some of the same results. A significant and growing portion of the American black population was no longer worth exploiting—the only fate, in a market system, worse than being exploited. Blacks got the husks of the cities, moving into the emptied palaces white nomads had left behind. What an extraordinary thing to do: *here, here are the clubs where you weren't welcome, the movie theaters and buses, here's city hall, here are the swimming pools and the post-office jobs and the boathouse and the newspaper, take them, we don't want them anymore.* In Oakland and other new-made black towns a particular emptiness settled in, that bowl-a-ball-down-Broadway feeling. Without a clear white establishment, anger at this condition had two obvious places to turn: against oneself and against one's neighbors. No one embodied that change better than Huey Newton. Huey had always been a bit of a thug, and soon enough a drug user. As time went by, that's all he was.

When Bobby Seale had a son, he told his wife and Huey that the boy's name would be Malik (after Malcolm X's Muslim name) Nkrumah (after the African revolutionary) Stagolee Seale. The *Stagolee* went way back. Stagolee was the mythical black outlaw, preying on everyone, bad to the bone. "Nkrumah," Seale wrote, "was a bad motherfucker and Malcolm X was a bad nigger. Huey P. Newton showed me the nigger on the block was ten motherfuckers when politically educated, and if you got him organized. I said, 'Stagolee, put Stagolee on his name,' because Stagolee was an unorganized nigger, to me, like a brother on the block. I related to Huey P. Newton because Huey was fighting niggers on the block. Huey was a nigger that came along and he incorporated Malcolm X, he incorporated Stagolee, he incorporated Nkrumah, all of them."

So Stagolee was going to be a freedom fighter but Stagolee's freedom was not of a shared kind, Stagolee had a killer freedom, he had the death addict's freedom. Huey Newton may once have incorporated all three men, Malcolm, Nkrumah, and Stagolee. For most of his last fifteen years or so he was only Stagolee, an addict raging through the streets of West Oakland in the small hours screaming "I am Huey P. Newton!" He ran those streets, beneath the overpasses white folks had built to commute from white place A to white place B, he ran around begging to be killed, writing a very long suicide note over the name Stagolee. And finally, quite early on a summer morning in 1989, at the corner of Ninth and Center Streets among the West Oakland Victorians, Huey got his three bullets in the head from two other nighttime ragers.

"We want freedom," he and Bobby had written in 1966 as point number one. Huey's funeral took place at Allen Temple Baptist Church in East Oakland. Thousands of mourners had already been to view his body in a beautiful casket at the mortuary. Thousands had been at Allen Temple for prayers the night before the funeral, and thousands came for the main event, filling the church, adjacent streets, and a nearby hall. Overnight, spray-painted silhouettes of Newton holding a gun had gone up along the Oakland streets, the shadow of a gunslinger. "Free Huey!" Reverend J. Alfred Smith cried out to the mourners, who took up the chant. "Free Huey!" Then Reverend Smith alluded to another dead man when he said of Huey, "He's free. He's free at last."

HAVE MERCY

■

Several years after Huey Newton died, I went back to Oakland and visited with Reverend Smith. He was a bantam man with the prominent hairstyle of an earlier era and the proper black suit of a still earlier one; he looked like a Black Power W. E. B. Du Bois. When he settled on the sofa in his spacious office overlooking the church parking lot Reverend Smith almost showed his sixty-five years, but then he would bounce up, and pace, and talk. When he spoke, his voice had a good bit of the South in it, along with the hard, enduring bass notes and jagged cuts that I believe came up here from the Delta and Texas only to be transformed into the distinct "Oakland blues"; he did work his voice as an instrument. "Bill Malcomson's *son*. Yes, yes, yes, *yesss*. Lord have mercy." I felt like the ghost of white folks past. I knew that Reverend Smith was a kind and generous and fun man by nature, and I knew that, because I was white as new snow, he was being kind and generous to me thanks only to his old friendship with my father. They had worked together in the early 1970s with the goal of integrating American Baptist church life in Northern California—that is, to join Baptists of all colors in the fellowship of worshipping Christ. They had labored hard and had some successes, but on the whole their efforts met with nearly complete failure. Yes, they had tried, he told me, "But today it looks like I didn't do anything. It looks like all the efforts that your daddy did were in vain."

So Reverend Smith gave up on white people around twenty years ago. "I see my commitment as trying to build a strong institution in this city, that's going to feed the community in the twenty-first century after I'm dead. That it's a waste of time for me to try to be a missionary to white America. Did I ever think that I was called to be a missionary? Yes. And did I ever think that I was going to be successful in converting white Americans? Yes." And, no, it did not work out. In retrospect, Reverend Smith sees what he was doing as a type of wishful imitation, a performance of hope. But "I'm too old to play-act now." He exploded into laughter; the explosion ended as suddenly as it began. "I'm too old to wear the mask, like African Americans have done, you know. You have one mask for the white man, and another mask for the black man. Well, I'm too old. And what they think is what they gonna get, and what they gonna get is not what they want. So . . . let's have *peace*. So I give them peace by staying away. You understand? Ha ha ha ha!"

"Is that a relief," I asked, my voice pitched down, "or disappointment?"

"It's a relief," Reverend Smith said, starting low to wind himself up. "I've gotten over the disappointment"—he began clapping slowly—"and I'm *happy*. I mean, I'm over the disappointment, and I'm *celebrating* being in my brier patch! Ha ha ha ha!"

Some white folks do worship at Allen Temple, say a dozen or two out of several thousand. Reverend Smith did not go looking for them: "What has happened is that the Lord has sent some white people who are Christians." He said they had left white churches to come to his. He mentioned in particular a woman who helps train young black ministers. "And these people," he said, "help me to remain Christian."

"In terms," I asked, "of your attitude to white people?"

"Yes. And people like your daddy. Ha ha ha! I have to put him in there. Yes, people like your daddy! Because, if it were not for your daddy I would not talk to you."

I wonder what mask my father was wearing back in the day and which one Reverend Smith wore for him. Brer Rabbit and Brer Fox, as well as Mister Man, and Master and John, not forgetting Stagolee and old Railroad Bill—the first mythical black cop killer, based on a real person from late in the nineteenth century—all these have been in the brier patch of Allen Temple Baptist Church over the years. Reverend Smith published a history of the church in 1973, *Thus Far by Faith*, prior to his giving up on white people and the white mask and choosing the "mask for the black man." Reverend James Allen, Smith wrote, "was among the earliest and possibly the first black Baptist pioneer in Northern California," up from Texas in 1893. By 1899 Allen had become pastor of Beth Eden in Oakland, the first black Baptist church in the county. That same year Allen helped organize a separate black Baptist association for north-

ern and central California, taking Beth Eden out of the white association—
what was henceforth the white association. Beth Eden, Reverend Smith wrote,
"chose voluntary separation . . . in order to help build black unity and solidarity
among those blacks who were migrating to California from the South." That
was one common mask at the time.

Reverend Allen soon faced a problem that beset many black pastors in the
North and West: he wasn't a shouter. He would not whoop. Blacks up from the
South, most at least nominal Baptists, needed and expected preachers who
could talk and sing at the same time and fall out and cry for them—they needed
shouters—but your Northern preacher often disliked shouting, which seemed
the activity of a desperate person and likely to undermine levelheaded faith,
social decorum, personal dignity, and middle-class progress in general. The
shouting pastor shouted in from the past and upset the delicate Northern negotiation between past and present. Reverend Allen and the other pioneers found
themselves unable to serve the majority of black migrants.

Yet Allen persevered, starting in 1919 what would become Allen Temple out
in the mostly white (Portuguese) wilderness of East Oakland. He kept on for five
years. His successor, Reed Thomas, took the church in a new direction, toward
political activism, including support of Marcus Garvey. (Oakland was home to
Division 188 of Garvey's African Army.) By 1930, however, Allen Temple had
come under the leadership of G. J. Wildy. "Much of the financial undergirding
which came to Allen Temple resulted from the excellent personal relationships
that Mr. Wildy established with generous Caucasian friends," Reverend Smith
wrote; and "Pastor Wildy saw to it that the membership would participate in
non-segregated and non-black Baptist activities." However, prosperity and integration failed to attract new black members—or many white members. Pastor
and Mrs. Wildy's "approach to worship was patterned more after a typical white
middle class Protestant church than after a typical black Protestant church. Pastor Wildy did not like emotional outbursts or 'shouting' in worship . . . Black
Baptist churches of mass appeal had as their pastors men who were known as
great 'whoopers.' " At the turn of the 1960s Allen Temple led the way among
black Oakland churches in joining with white churches. This was the effort in
which Reverend Smith proudly participated, along with my father, until his disappointment with white Baptists became too great.

When he was still talking with my father he was also talking with Huey and
Bobby and Bill Knowland. These were all connected. Reverend Smith worked
with my dad because Smith had hopes for white people. He worked with Bobby
and Huey and Elaine Brown because they were shaking up the go-along minds
of black Oakland—"the so-called nice people"—and getting the attention of white
folks like Bill Knowland. Smith worked with Knowland, was *able* to work with

Knowland in the basic activity of deciding who gets what money, because Huey and Bobby had got Knowland's attention. "It was better for me during the '60s," Reverend Smith said, "when we had a Black Panther Party, and when there was head-on confrontation. I could get jobs for African American youth. I could get all the summer jobs that they needed. The white community wanted to talk to me because I was *attractive,* I was a much more attractive choice than Huey Newton."

He was not under any great illusions about the Panthers. "There is the shady side of the Black Panthers. Huey Newton . . . Huey was buried out of this building, and I preached the funeral. Huey *was* somewhat of a crook. The people who placed the needs of the community first were people like Elaine Brown, JoNina Abroun, and Bobby Seale." A number of black Oakland preachers formed an advisory group to the Panthers "for the express purpose of trying to sensitize them to keep the needs of the community first. Don't get so caught up in revolutionary rhetoric that you forget about the needs of the people, and especially the children."

Reverend Smith missed the Panthers, and he missed Bill Knowland. He missed the power that came to people like him when there was a space created by people like Knowland and Huey Newton. They made the brier patch so big it wasn't a brier patch. "I miss the radical element to the left of myself. We need it. Because, who wants to talk to me now? Who wants to negotiate with me now? Who wants to be in—you see, after twenty-six years in this place, and after building such as we have built . . . You know, Scott, we have—all of the banks have left East Oakland, but the Allen Temple Credit Union is here. And we have assets of six million and we are giving people home loans, first-time buyers. And the Allen Temple Church is not only erecting housing for the seniors, but also housing for people who are HIV positive. We have a number of initiatives designed to strengthen life in the community. We are relating well to Hispanics, we are relating well to Koreans. You would think that business fathers would *want* to have me sitting in on some of their strategy sessions, where they are in a think tank plotting out the future of this city. But I have less dialogue now than I did when Bill Knowland was around."

Reverend Smith had even come to feel mercy for Knowland, because, in the end, and probably against his own wishes, but still and all Knowland may have believed, in the small window of time before he shot himself, that what black people thought about him mattered: "The man had pain that some of us did not understand. And I feel that he was having a very difficult time trying to live down the early, negative years, or the early years when the African American community had total unity in feeling negatively toward him. I really feel that in his later years, that may have haunted him." And the reverend reminded me— "maybe I'm thinking too much like a preacher"—that we will all be judged, all of us, including William Knowland and J. Alfred Smith.

I think Reverend Smith missed Bill Knowland in part because a new type of white person and white power was beginning to appear around him, a type that did not care, on principle, what black people as black people thought. Reverend Smith had been through all the postwar changes, civil rights and integration and Black Power and black power—he and the Panthers had used Allen Temple to register voters and get out the black vote that elected a black mayor—and he had lived through the long left-holding-the-bag period of a black city government with nothing but black money and all that white money just over the way, felling orchards, building malls, even building Silicon Valley and reshaping the economy of the entire world not an hour's drive from Allen Temple's East Oakland, which has been and still is a ghetto. (The Portuguese left and turned white decades ago.) He had lived through multiculturalism, the poor people's multiculturalism of reaching out and getting along and kind of ignoring or trying not to think too much about old what's his name who somehow got up over the hill to the suburb and has a Malcolm poster in his study and white peers and Duke Ellington CDs and a *kente* hat for Kwanza and a good safe public school for his children and wasn't this a little triumph for the race? He had been through that—maybe he was still in it a little—and on the horizon, dimly, he saw a somewhat new type of white person who liked jazz too and did not think in terms of race; rather, who thought that other people should not think in terms of race, whether about him or about themselves, and therefore when these other people did think that way, they were simply shouting up from a repudiated and irrelevant past and should not be listened to. J. Alfred Smith should not be listened to. "I think," he told me, "that the white community is mapping and rapping and strategizing to get the city back. I think they feel that we don't know how to run the city, that we have not done a good job in running the city, and that things were better when they were running it, and they want it back and they're going to get it back. And if they can promote a divide-and-conquer mentality, they will do that." So Reverend Smith will build an institution that will last after he is dead and has been judged, and it will be a black institution.

I needed to get out of that office and breathe some air. I felt I had brought a dark cloud in over Reverend Smith's happy clapping brier patch by stirring up ghosts, and I should not have done that. We rose from the sofa. I promised I would come to church. We talked a bit about my father—warmest greetings, hope everybody's well. He reached out and we embraced. He said, "I can't give up on white people." His eyes were damp and so were mine, glistening. God help me, I wanted to say, *Go on, please, give up on them, they are not worth the trouble, pretend that they are not there,* but of course I could not say that, because they are there, and there's no use lying about it. So I made it out to the car and drove off along East Fourteenth Street through what is still a ghetto, where it takes a church to make a bank in what Reverend Smith told me is "the most integrated city in the nation," the same ghetto where, twenty years before, I drove slowly along one afternoon and a few black boys came running after the car throwing rocks and shouting, *White boy, white boy, get out of here,* which made me afraid and silent at the time but today made me afraid and explode with laughter.

For a few days I felt happy to be back in Oakland. To the degree that I have ever had a home, this was home. I loved to catch the fragrance of eucalyptus again, taste the scented air. I liked to drive the roundabout "faster" routes that natives know, and look out at the bay, and walk up and down and around the old neighborhoods. I went by Sequoia and tried to see the principal. She was not receiving visitors, it seemed, not even an old alum. The Oakland schools were again taking a beating, this time over "ebonics," so maybe she was wary. The controversy over black English had a serious side, but, personally, it made me laugh, because I could remember the different Englishes we spoke at different ages and in different situations, including varieties of white English. One had to be multilingual within one language; besides, it was fun and kept us playing with words. The school appeared unchanged after twenty-five years. Wandering across the playground, I must have looked odd to the black children playing basketball. I heard a little voice speculating about the "white boy"—that would be me—so I guessed I had aged well. A girl came over to inquire after my purpose and managed two questions until a boy called out, happy and sarcastic, "Don't talk to strangers!"

I had been told that the neighborhood had become "more black" in the intervening decades. I suppose it had. I found it hard to tell, because my own memories tended to focus on the nonwhite and there is probably much of whiteness that I just can't recall. The school system had been just over 20 percent white in 1973. Now it was about 7 percent white—stay in there, you 7 per-centers!—not because the black population had risen but because whites had gone on leaving the system and the Asian population had soared. Interestingly enough, the white share of Oakland's population had remained pretty constant at about 40 percent. Whites had simply refined their ability to live in Oakland without living in Oakland. Housing was cheaper there. They could earn their money elsewhere, and it did look as if they were spending it elsewhere, because downtown still had a slightly after-the-war feel. And yet there were signs of revival—Asian money spreading out from Chinatown and considerable investment in Jack London Square.

I had worked for minimum wage in Jack London Square in the late 1970s, at a doomed cappuccino-and-sandwiches place thrown up by two hysterical, sleepless young white entrepreneurs, their eyes always wide and their hair lank. The restaurant appealed to my sense of humor. It was a start-up-failure-rate statistic from its inception. We of the staff helped matters along by eating all the food and drinking all the beer during our many customerless hours. We were actually able to save money on the minimum wage, emerging bloated and chipper at the end of each day. You might think that our profit-destroying work habits were an expression of urban pathology, but we treated our few clients very well, memorizing their names and preferences, and kept close track, I don't know why, of how much we were stealing, as though there were some accounting in life greater than knowing you had stolen what you could.

I worked with Sheldon, a black friend from early school days. We had drifted apart only to be reunited by chance selling sandwiches. Sheldon was tall and thin with big laughing eyes and an unshakable jheri-curl habit. He continually struck poses; he wanted to be a model. In those days modeling was about as unlikely a career as a black man could choose. This gave his ceaseless posing a brazen and forlorn charm. As for me, I wanted to be a globe-trotting writer and thinker of large thoughts, and struck my own poses accordingly. Sheldon and I had the minimum wage and maximal delusions in common. At the end of our "work" day we would boost a six-pack and slide over to the Sea Wolf. Named after Jack London's nautical novel, the Sea Wolf had been a flashy place in our childhood, a place where neither Sheldon's family nor mine would go—the hangout of Knowland-level people who wouldn't think twice about paying a valet to park their cars. There had been a clutch of such places around the square, and they had fallen from grace one by one, owing to the aforementioned departure of white money, until reaching the nadir of emptiness, unwanted, at which point Sheldon and I could slip in past the garbage cans, through a door we had jimmied, and take our places on the floor of the carpeted main dining room, overlooking the water. Rich white folks had built themselves a nice restaurant. It was very pleasant to sit on the red carpet with our backs against the wall, smoke a joint and sip our warming beers, watch the carpet fade and the water glisten as the sun climbed down. Those were great full-of-promise days.

The cappuccino place faced the old Goodman's, where the Law and Order conference occurred and where Ronald Reagan had praised Knowland just before the latter's suicide. A few steps farther along stood the cabin in which Jack London had wintered during the Klondike rush. I thought it an even lonelier home in Oakland than it must have been in Alaska—one wooden room, relocated here in the 1960s, set in an empty expanse of concrete. The windows and door were barred to keep people from sleeping in it; trash gathered instead.

Twenty years after Sheldon and I had drunk our last beer at the Sea Wolf,

London's house was still there, staggering distance from the incredibly long-lived saloon Heinhold's First and Last Chance. (London, as a boy, knew Heinhold.) But so much had grown up around it: a vast Barnes & Noble bookstore, busy restaurants, a functioning hotel or two, and, most difficult to believe, a farmer's market. Where once we human tumbleweeds had rested against the leeward side of London's cabin, now sated families promenaded with tummies full of quesadilla, and shoppers picked at chard. This had happened under two black mayors with black city-council members and (for a while) a black-run *Tribune*. The sauced Continental cuisine of the 1960s had yielded to the riotous freshness-worshipping pluralism of late-century Californian appetites. Jack London Square may have been the only part of Oakland undergoing a full-blown Renaissance, but you have to start somewhere.

Oakland is now an officially multicultural city. When it celebrates, it celebrates diversity. An advertisement for the Oakland Community Organizations sought to attract contributions with its annual fund-raising calendar, "Positive Images of Oakland." There were no white people in the six images used, I assume because you cannot really have a positive image of a white person as such, a white person just going through life "being white." Sheldon would be able now to get a modeling job, and that is something to celebrate.

One Sunday I drove downtown to Oakland First Baptist, the church in which I had been raised. The FREE HUEY graffito was gone, but I found the church anyway. One of the oldest churches in Oakland, First Baptist's cathedral is a vast redwood octagon vaulting upward, with little waterfalls of stained glass and an imposing pipe organ rising in tiers above the baptistery. The main corner spire lost its top in the 1906 earthquake, but otherwise the architect Julia Morgan's original building remains whole. Many, many years ago the size of the building must have been justified by the size of its congregation. I once came across some old church papers, the cradle rolls and nursery rolls, and was surprised by the numbers of children listed there. Oakland had been a busy and fecund white community in the second and third decades of the twentieth century. I could wistfully imagine all these white children playing in the wondrous crannies of the great cathedral—I know each one of those crannies—but when we arrived in 1968, there were maybe twenty children around. A decade later there may have been ten, and ours was, effectively, the last generation raised in that church. It was a source of much discomfort for my parents and some others at First Baptist that they were attending an almost all-white church in an almost all-black neighborhood, namely West Oakland. What made it worse, really, was that keeping this white church alive did constitute "trying to do something" about white flight—about racial abandonment. There was a sizable irony in that.

Dad, in particular, got some relief from this irony through his work with people like J. Alfred Smith. He also guest-preached on occasion at black churches. We went along sometimes, and it was a sight to watch him preach. He appeared, quite simply, larger than his usual size, fuller of humor and spirit. He showed signs of growing out of himself without having measured the route in advance. I can recall him showing a genuine nervousness (rather than preacherly humility) that had no fear in it, a public vulnerability peculiar to the refuge of a church. I cannot remember him showing quite that same vulnerability in white churches, though I imagine he would have over the years. We did visit a number of suburban white churches. We would park on new streets, walk along new sidewalks past new lawns and into new churches with new people, at which point my memories entirely end. Dad would have preached on these trips. I just can't remember anything, except backing toward the car away from a vista of white people on a perfect green lawn in the sun. Of course, our own church was a white church, but at least it had the dignity of a past and the enchanting honor of being a failure.

I went back to First Baptist on a Sunday and was pleased to see the old faces. I caught up on deaths. There hadn't been any births in the church, as far as I could tell. Of about seventy congregants huddled front and center in Julia Morgan's redwood cavern, maybe two were under fifty. This leaves out staff and the children from the Samaritan Neighborhood Center, which the church supported. What remained of First Baptist's congregation, prompted by a young white associate pastor, had abandoned the fruitless organic approach to integration of my youth for something more active. The result was an elderly white congregation (except for a few people) with about fifteen black children sitting in the front pew. The children's service and programs were now for other people's children; the parents, if they attended church, did so elsewhere. This struck me as intensely odd. Odder still was the fact—gleaned from conversations with several white people I had known since childhood and toward whom I felt great affection—that few of the church's members knew these children's names, although they saw them every Sunday. Their own children were long gone, like me. Everyone remembered my name.

The children's service involved a story from William Bennett's *Children's Book of Virtues* about a frog child and a snake child. It was said to be an African story. The snake child and the frog child play together. The snake teaches the frog to crawl, and the frog teaches the snake to hop. Then other snakes tell the snake child that snakes and frogs do not mix. On the contrary, snakes eat frogs. The snake child plans to eat his playmate but cannot do it. In conclusion, sometimes the snake and the frog just sit around together and remember how they used to play.

What point the children took from this pitilessly depressing story I can't say. They filed out when it was done, and part of me must have wandered off with them as the rest of the service is a blank. Afterward we gathered for "coffee hour" in a lounge off the sanctuary. The black children were not there. Coffee hour is the crucial community-reinforcing moment of the service. I knew just about everyone. I tried to buff my adult accomplishments to reflect well on the friends around me, to suggest that the interest and care they had shown years before had been to good effect. Most of the early jobs I had, unskilled manual jobs that enabled me to start college, had come from church connections. I mentioned that I was writing a book on racial separatism and asked who might have the longest and fullest memories of how separatism had evolved in Oakland. In the end it was determined that I should speak with Norm and Gladys.

Norm and Gladys lived in a well-appointed retirement home near downtown and received me in their apartment with a somewhat prickly graciousness. Norm and I sat in comfortable chairs by the window; Gladys took a straight-backed chair near the kitchen. I asked about their first experience with white flight. Norm said it occurred after the war, when black workers were losing their jobs in huge numbers and Norm and Gladys lived on Calmar Avenue: "Kaiser brought them in for the shipyards. In 1948 they moved up on Calmar Avenue—it was a white neighborhood, essentially. In 1955 the IQ in Crocker Highlands, where our daughter was going to school, had dropped—considerably." Their daughter was in elementary school. "We knew the principal—she was a member of our church—so we knew that IQ had been going down, property values were going down a bit, because the blacks were moving in. And we didn't like that, and we didn't want to be surrounded by blacks. And, personally, I had finished getting my CPA certificate, and so we bought a lot in Alamo." Alamo was a new white suburb outside the city.

They sold their house to a black family. "There were enough blacks in the neighborhood," Gladys explained, "that the whites weren't willing to buy. There was no market."

"When we sold our homes, we didn't take a racial line," Norm added. "We didn't think that was a Christian thing to do."

I asked, "Do you recall at all how your neighbors felt, how your white neighbors felt, at the time when you moved out?"

"Yes," Norm said. "The neighbor next door felt very badly about it, but we were not close friends or anything, so . . ."

Gladys had been on the First Baptist cradle roll in 1910. Norm had started delivering newspapers in West Oakland by 1918 and as a teenager joined the church in 1925. They remembered West Oakland as entirely white in 1910, mostly so in 1925. Norm said his high school, Oakland Tech, had been a white school, with a few exceptions. But even then the trend, he said, had been for "people" to move out of West Oakland. He attended college in Berkeley, then quit to work in an insurance company.

The migration of blacks for war work did not immediately spark white dislike, as Norm remembered it, because "at that time when they were brought in, they were needed. I think any real resentment came later." The resentment came when blacks were no longer "needed": "Because there was a tidal wave of them during the war years. It was just part of a natural attitude change, I think."

I mentioned that I had been down to Jack London Square and found it much improved from the 1970s. It seemed to me that Oakland was better-off than it had been in my youth. Did they think it had got better?

"I don't think so, Scott," Norm said in a pensive voice. "Because, well, we have a black mayor, we have a black council, we have a majority black in the city. I don't think it's gotten that much better."

And the relatively stable white community Norm and Gladys had known and liked was gone. All that remained was the church. That was going, too. "We're not replenishing ourselves," as Norm said. The last earthquake had damaged the old building enough that it faced being condemned unless substantial repairs were made, and many in the congregation felt the repairs were not worth paying for. First Baptist had begun meeting with the vestigial congregations of three other downtown white churches, thinking to unite into one white church that might have a chance at survival. Norm and Gladys asked after another white church I knew, in another city, and I said it was doing well, partly because there were enough young families nearby to keep the church going. There were, of course, also young families near First Baptist. However, "ours are not necessarily black all around us, but they're foreign. They're not church members."

"You see," Norm added softly, "we have outlived our generation there. Growing up, our close friends were church friends. We don't have the same close friends today, because we have just lived too long."

"Or they moved away," Gladys said.

"Yes. And of course we moved in and out of Oakland, but we still kept going to the church. Except that our group didn't grow. And we didn't continue making friends."

Norm paused, then said with mock irritation, "Now you're asking me to think, Scott!"

We all laughed heartily, I apologized, and their living-room clock rudely picked that moment to chime and mark in bright tones the passage of another hour. "You just go along," Norm said, "from week to week and month to month and day to day and you just don't think about—you just accept it. What can we do?"

The next time I attended services at First Baptist the judgments of Norm and Gladys weighed on me. The church was the only real institution I had known as a boy, and I had thought, in the way a child does, that it would continue forever. On the cover of the worship program was First Baptist's current slogan, "A Multi-cultural Church Serving the People of the City." "Today," the program announced, "we are giving special emphasis to the contributions of our African American Cultural heritage and the celebration of Black history month and Brotherhood/Sisterhood week." The white pastor and his associate wore *kente* scarves over their robes. The children were to attend the whole service. It was the one time in the year when the worship service was focused on them, and it happened that it was focused on them because they had dark skin. The young black program director of the Samaritan center had told me that some of the kids were still too young to think of themselves as black or of the church members as white—they thought the congregants were just "old people"—but, of course, through grown-up eyes, or at least for the purposes of a service celebrating "the contributions of our African American Cultural heritage," the kids were all already black. They had prepared a "rap" called "J-E-S-U-S" and were to read poems and sing "We Are Climbing Jacob's Ladder." But first we did a brief call and response—"Bear one another's burdens, and share each other's joys, / Love one another, and bring each other home"—and the pastor gave a Bible reading and some reflections on it. He chose Genesis 9:8–17, in which God promises the world to Noah and his sons. The pastor stopped just before the regrettable incident with the wine, the nakedness, and "Cursed be Canaan; lowest of slaves shall he be to his brothers."

The pastor took from his Genesis passage the thought that "God wants everyone to live together in peace and reconciliation with one another and with him, and will always be working with love to help us live together as one caring family." I realized that his message was directed at the black children in the front pew. The pastor had simplified his language in hopes of reaching them. His central points were that the black children should understand that we are all one family; violence is wrong; and it was somehow up to them to take this message of family unity into the world. Do we, the pastor asked rhetorically, look at everyone we meet as family? For example, do you, when seeing a stranger on the street, regardless of his or her physical difference from you, say, "Hey, cuz?"

A little girl in the front pew mistakenly thought the pastor wanted an answer, so she said, "No." He phrased the question a bit differently, the girl again said, "No," then he quit asking.

———

When, as a teenager, I left Oakland, I also left the church. Being a preacher's child, you see perhaps too much of the little deceptions and omissions that go into keeping the faithful together. (The pastor's child knows that the pastor dispenses hope he doesn't have.) Besides, I could not choose to be in a white church. That would have been like choosing a white school (or a white town). But even more than schools or towns, churches replenish themselves the way families do—thus, in part, the churchly obsession with children. A church reaches into the past and extends into the future in much the way a family does, and in the way a race does. My feelings about this were ambivalent in the extreme. I cherished the community, the tradition, the respect for death and the dead, the music and the prayer and the literature and the preacherly performance, and, above all, the sense that one could aspire to something higher than self-advancement. However, church life also had many hypocrisies, thoughtless formalities, false intimacies, dubious received wisdoms, unacknowledged conformities. And I could not embrace the role of race continuer that seemed, in a quiet way, also part of the church mission.

One possibility would have been to attend a black church. The music is undeniably better, there's more to eat at socials, and grief is not treated as a life stage or a character flaw. Where the white church is a lake, the black church is an ocean. But the black church does sustain and continue the race, a task for which nature unfitted me. It isn't my family or my home. Nevertheless, I wanted to try Allen Temple and had promised J. Alfred Smith I would attend services. I stopped by his office to pay my respects early one Sunday morning. There was a guest preacher that day, Dr. Charles E. Booth, a tall, slender man of notable gravity wearing a perfectly cut dark suit. Reverend Smith introduced us, and together we held hands in a circle in his office and prayed.

I took my place in the sanctuary with two thousand other people. It was still February, still Black History Month, so more people than usual wore at least one element of African clothing. We stood and clapped and marked the beat, swaying, shifting from foot to foot, as the choir danced in from the back, singing. Then came more songs, and more songs, and perorations, for most of which we stood. The only point of sitting down was to lend emphasis to your next standing up. I began to think the pews had been a waste of church funds. I was getting winded, and Dr. Booth's sermon, during which I expected to rest, was still distant on the horizon. Then a young boy got up in the choir for a solo. We the two thousand sat respectfully. The song had to do with Jesus being the boy's light. The singer had a high piping voice that was not far from breaking. He couldn't remember the words. He would get partway through then go blank, gazing out at the thousands with a look of endless shock. At first, people smiled understandingly. The music minister walked over to help the child, the musicians went back a few bars and started again, the boy would begin, then hit the wall once more. At one point, when all seemed lost, the boy just burst into it a cappella, and that pretty much put all of our hearts right up in our throats, we were standing now and sending two thousand longings for success into that child. We were not going to let him fail. Two thousand standing people fervently wishing, in total silence, for this one little thing to go right. The music again, the piping voice, the faltering steps—he got through it, more or less, and we broke down into clapping, laughter, tears, as if the sea had just been parted and we were going to make it out of Egypt after all.

Dr. Booth began his sermon in a dull, deep monotone. He said his text would be Psalm 137. "By the rivers of Babylon," he read, "there we sat down, yea, we wept, when we remembered Zion. We hanged our harps upon the willows in the midst thereof. For there, they that carried us away captive required of us a song, and they that wasted us required of us mirth, saying, 'Sing us one of the songs of Zion.' How shall we sing the Lord's song in a strange land?" Dr. Booth stopped there, leaving out the rest of the chapter, which ends on a vengeful note with regard to the Babylonian slavers: "Happy shall he be, that taketh and dasheth thy little ones against the stones."

"I want to preach," Dr. Booth said, "upon the theme 'Once upon a time when we were colored.'" This was the title of a recent memoir by Clifton Taulbert, who came from "a tiny hamlet of Mississippi" and went on to business success in Tulsa, Oklahoma. Dr. Booth mentioned his own homecoming trips to his grandmother's little town in Virginia. Taulbert's story "is the story of all of us who are of African American descent, for all of us come from little places, places that are not necessarily marked by those of the dominant culture. But there are places in your life and mine that will be riveted always in memory as sacred and enchanted land. And as I looked earlier at these beautiful young children, and at the young man, though nervous, *singing his song*, I could not help but think of my own life, and how so many wonderful figures, some living and some yet passed beneath the veil, have had a tremendous impact and an influence on who it is and what it is that I have become."

Dr. Booth identified those black Americans who had risen into the middle class or higher as breakers of a covenant between black people and God. They have forgotten they are in Babylon: "Now there are those of us who feel very much at home in America. But I've come by, for these moments this morning, to remind all of us that still this is a strange land. You may have your undergraduate and graduate degrees, 'doctor' may even grace your name by way of title. You may live in two-car-garage homes and have a Louis Vuitton bag under one arm and a Gucci bag under the other. But I am here to *remind* you that in many instances America is still not the land of the free. Nor is it the home of the brave." People began to clap now, a few people. "This is a strange land"—*yes*— "and God is calling upon us to sing *his* song"—*yes, yes*—"not the song of our middle-class accomplishments, not the song of our bourgeois attainments, but *his song.*"

He paused to let the clapping die away. "We've lost something. I know you don't want to hear it—get in your cars and drive away to the places that represent your abode—but we *have lost* something. And I claim today that we need to reach back and find that which has been lost. Once upon a time when we were colored people we had a sense of *community.*" Dr. Booth pointed out that the verse read *we* sat down when *we* wept and *we* remembered Zion, that the Israelites, "even under the oppressive stroke of slavery, when they were commanded to make bricks out of straw, still they had a sense of community . . . There was a time when we had a sense of community, and we honestly believed in all for one and one for all. But it seems to me that we have come to a new day, and we have adopted a new slogan: 'I've got mine, and you've got yours to get.' Come on, don't get quiet on me. Many of us feel that because we are where we have always dreamed of being, that we no longer have an obligation to those behind. Well that's *not* how we acted when we were colored people."

Dr. Booth said he had grown up in a Baltimore ghetto, and back then "whenever mama would run out of flour, run out of sugar, she would say, 'Take a cup up the street to Miss Frances, and ask Miss Frances to give me a cup of sugar till my paycheck comes.' We helped each other. Somebody died, we rallied around one another. When somebody got sick, we learned how to support one another. We were a family then." Now we were not a family. Now even African dreams could divide the people, with some thinking themselves better because they were more with Africa while the low-down folks were stuck with America: "We have all this African pride, *dress up* in all this African garb. Yet we won't speak to each other. Won't say amen. Some of us have gotten so sophisticated we don't *shout* anymore. You sittin' up there with all your bourgeois arrogance with your arms folded and your legs crossed acting as if you are somebody but let me *tell* you something, when we were *colored* people you didn't have to *wait* for an amen, you didn't have to wait for somebody to *shout*, when you just thought about how good God has been and when you remembered how far that God has brought you you *Made Some Noise!!*"

When that very noise had wound down, Dr. Booth went quiet again; he talked about Herodotus and how the Israelites, like the Egyptians, had been dark-skinned. The ancient people of God in Egypt and the Africans sold into slavery were practically the same people, and the identification of black with Jew naturally led to a healthy collective pride when one remembered Zion. "I can stand up," Dr. Booth said, his voice rising, and each one of us standing when the moment seemed right, "with my knotty-head self, my black face, my thick lips, my broad nose, and declare honey that I know I am somebody! 'Cause I've been made in the image of almighty God and I've been created after his likeness! I am just as fine as I wanna be and I'm not gonna let anybody in the dominant culture or anybody else define who I am because I *remember . . . my . . . Zion!!*" Dr. Booth was screaming. We cheered, and said *yes yes*. He said, "Can I get an amen in here? Anybody in here know what I'm talkin' about? Anybody in here can say, 'I'm black and I'm proud'? " Two thousand people minus six or so shouted, "I'm black and I'm proud!" Or maybe my fellow white folks did say they were black and proud and I was the only one who went quiet for that moment. I could not say I was black. It would have been disrespectful, as well as untrue. That was a song I could not sing and so I left my harp hanging upon the willow without a clue as to how to remember Zion and, yes, even wondering whether I shouldn't dasheth the heads of my little ones against the stones.

"Hold on now I ain't ready to go yet. Come on, we gonna go on a few minutes. Can you give me about five more minutes. Come on don't fool me I know you gotta go but can you give me about five more minutes. Once upon a time, when we were colored, we had community, we had a glorious past that we not only knew but we articulated." That may well be but it was beside the point because we were now going to do some shouting, we were going to do some *inarticulate* speech, and everyone knew it. Soon we were up and running. You could barely hear Dr. Booth, who was singing and screaming about how his faith was built on the rock of Christ—you could barely hear him because we were screaming too, since what did it matter, everyone knew what the language was—and Dr. Booth began to strip off his tie, his shoes, his beautiful coat, even a sock went out into the roiling congregation as he whooped.

> *In the high and stormy gale*
> *my anchor holds within the veil*
> *not the money in my pocket*
> *on Christ!*
> *not the tie around my neck*
> *on Christ!*
> *not the clothes on my back*
> *on Christ!*
> *not the shoes on my feet*
> *but on Christ*
> *the solid rock I stand*
> *the lily of the valley*
> *the rose of Sharon*

> *the bright and morning star*
> *on Christ*
> *that wheel in the middle of a wheel*
> *on Christ*
> *my way out of no way*
> *my doctor who never lost a patient*
> *my lawyer who never lost a case*
> *on Christ on Christ on Christ*

In the heat of it I'm sure I was not the only person who thought of throwing off his own tie and coat and shoes and even socks, particularly when the woman up in the front rows started screaming above the screaming in a perfect wail, but I did not take off my own tie and neither did anyone else.

Dr. Booth had asked whether anyone in the congregation was in pain. As a general proposition, this question is not asked in this way in white churches, at least not in the North. White people have troubles, black people have pain, the difference being that troubles can go away. Being in a family can ease one's pain, up to a point. Being in a race eases one's pain, too, in a similar way, and also up to a certain point and not any further than that, for any of us. Once upon a time we were white, once upon a time we were colored, and the two depended on each other and still do. As you leave one, you enter the other. America is such a religious Christian country that it is a curiosity we have no Zion all of us can remember or even imagine. Well, we were supposed to *be* Zion, weren't we? Maybe that is why we can't remember it? It is a strange land, our Babylon. "This was a few days after I had been drafted into the military service," an old man told me, "and I had a question with regard to my service record. And I went back to get an answer, and it just happened that when the enlisted person who was handling it for me, when he pulled my service record out, there was a circle in blue with a big W in the middle of it. And so after he had taken care of my problem, I said, 'By the way, what does that W mean?' He said, 'Oh, you don't have to worry about that, it doesn't mean anything. It just means you're white.' And I said, 'Well, somebody's made a mistake.' So he was embarrassed, and he reached down under the counter—he crossed out that W and pulled out another stamp that had a C—colored."

"Was he white himself?"

"Yes, he was white."

"Do you think a black person would have made that same mistake?"

"No." He began smiling, then laughing. "No."

Judge Lionel Wilson related this story as we sat in his office downtown. The building, one of the pretty West Oakland Victorians, apparently belonged to his brother, who had a law practice. I briefly met the brother, who proved Judge Wilson's remark that he was himself dark for that family. The place had been well restored and had a glow and airiness, though Judge Wilson's office was just a small room with a desk and a phone. He was entering his last months. J. Alfred Smith had wished I could have met Wilson in his athletic prime. I wish I could have, too, but by this time he had grown frail and small, with a weak voice, and the vitality left in him concentrated in his amused eyes. Wilson had been both a talented ballplayer and an excellent student. He had been the first black this and the first black that almost since college days at Berkeley. Sports desegregated slowly in California as elsewhere. Wilson remembered all of the stages, for basketball, baseball, football, because he had lived them. His great natural abilities and fair skin had made racial segregation particularly sharp, as the distinctions segregation made were in his case particularly whimsical. Once upon a time when we were white and colored, Wilson and a brother applied to the post office. Lionel scored much higher on the employment test, but on this occasion his brother passed for white, while Lionel did not. So one brother got a job while the other did without. Their father had worked at the post office before them, as a white man.

Judge Wilson's father and brother were never the first black anything. Judge Wilson became the first black mayor of Oakland. The reality of "the black vote" had, of course, been growing steadily if unevenly since the 1920s (not to say since emancipation, but its growth was interrupted after 1875). In Oakland, Marcus Foster had been the first big victory. Black activists had insisted on a "physically and psychologically black" schools superintendent—the phrase is that of Paul Cobb, a young leader at the time—and they got Foster. The candidates' blackness was to be determined by black leaders, rather in the spirit of Wilson's punch line to the army anecdote: a white person might not be able to tell, but a black person would. Then in the year Foster was murdered, Bobby Seale ran for mayor, putting a scare into the old Knowland machine. Few whites or blacks doubted Bobby's blackness. In 1977 Seale and what was left of the Panthers under Elaine Brown worked to register black voters and elect Judge Lionel Wilson as the first more or less physically and psychologically black mayor of Oakland. Like J. Alfred Smith, Judge Wilson would miss the Panthers in later years. "Without a doubt, the fear of the Panthers enabled some of us to do some of the things, in a positive way, that were good for the city," Wilson told me that day in his office. "It's sad to say, but, as you know, fear can play a major role in almost any situation, and frequently does."

Fear of Panther blackness helped to make Wilson the first black mayor and to destroy what remained of the Knowland–John Reading machine. Wilson ran the city's government for thirteen years, through two recessions that hit Oakland as hard as you would expect. (His successor was black, too.) Oakland had at last become "a black town." Wilson was always at pains to say he governed for everybody—that he was not just mayor for blacks. He explained to me that, in a city with a black plurality, it seemed to him redundant to insist on his blackness as mayor. Further, his ability to work with what he called "the good white people" was crucial to his success.

There were disappointments. Many black mayors gained office in those years, yet the millennium did not arrive. Oakland did not rocket to prosperity when released from white dominance at the polling booth, any more than Philadelphia and Chicago did. Marcus Foster had warned that "superblacks" like him would only gain power over what whites no longer wanted or could no longer control. They got places like Oakland, which were not entirely unlike Indian reservations. In these places blacks might, as Andrew Jackson had hoped for the Indians he was expelling westward, raise up "an interesting commonwealth, destined to perpetuate the race." Yet black Oaklanders were no more free from white America than the Cherokees had been. White abandonment was not a kindly act; people had been left a wasteland and told to cultivate their own gardens there. They did what they could, and that turned out to be quite a lot, but a city cannot be independent of its surroundings and thrive. Oakland seems destined to live in extremity. Geographically, it lies at about the center of the greatest wealth-creating region of the late twentieth century—a boom still in the future when I was a child—and for all that, it has got a good bookstore and some fine restaurants down at Jack London Square and some investment around Chinatown.

You can see why white folks might have thought that with a white mayor and a white city council Oakland would have participated more in the high-technology boom, if only for the very practical reason that the money behind that boom was white money, the same money that had left Oakland because Oakland had too many black people who were no longer, so to speak, "needed." This analysis is accurate as far as it goes. The problem with it is that black people are human beings with the same gifts and shortcomings as anyone else and just as needed. Their exclusion from Silicon Valley prosperity (for example) is a result, in the end, of white action. White people created black poverty in Oakland job by job, house by house, classroom by classroom, over many years. What makes this so remarkable is not that it illustrates the vastness of the gulf between black and white. Rather, it shows how much time and effort are necessary to make that gulf, which in turn suggests how comically small the differences are. No one, perhaps, could understand this quite so well as Lionel

Wilson, whom ambition and fate made into the first black mayor of Oakland and therefore a symbol of the city's blackness, that raceness which, because of what whites did, created poverty. He would know the limits of family and of race in easing one's pain, because Wilson, of course, did not have to be black, at least not all the time. He did not have to tell the enlisted man that someone had "made a mistake." If he had insisted on his whiteness, who is to say he would have failed? A black person would not have been likely to give him up; black Americans have been consistent on this point over the decades, not least because letting others pass supports the dignity of not passing. Lionel Wilson let just about his entire family pass. "I was the oldest of eight children," he told me, "and most of my family went the other way." He had two sisters and five brothers, "and most of them have gone the other way. And so we've had very little family life as a result of this. Well, because they pass as white. They live as white. It's important enough to them. And they're raising their children as white."

"Do you have nieces and nephews who don't know you?"

"Yes."

So you don't need a once-upon-a-time. Those two families within a family have existed and will continue to exist. You might say that Judge Wilson was physically white and psychologically black. It was hot in that room, and the mayor was noticeably fading, so I decided to leave. I wanted to say something to him—I wanted desperately to say something—but I could not figure out what it was. "It's an endlessly complicated subject," he said in his soft dying voice, "yes it is." I thrashed in my mind trying to find what I wanted to say and came up with an anecdote that may or may not have been appropriate. I told him about the sermon the other day at Allen Temple and how afterward I went back to see Reverend Smith in his office. "He started pulling me along by the arm," I said in a rush, feeling like a child, to Judge Wilson, "introduced me to a few people and stuff, I mean, you know how he is. He's jumping around and everything. And he said, 'We have such—you can see there's such *richness*, there's such *richness* in the black church! White people just don't *care* about it, and I don't care about them anymore, and I'm not sure there's even any *hope* for them anymore.' And he's going on in this vein. We're all sort of laughing in fairly high spirits. Then eventually he turned to me and said, 'Don't you think so, Scott, don't you think so? Just give up on them?' And I said, 'Well, I don't really disagree, but when you're white it's hard to give up on white people entirely.' "

The old man laughed, "yes, yes" he said, and chuckled away.

I have to say that when I went back to Oakland I felt both happily at home and utterly adrift. I liked the caressing warmth and smells of the air, the relative lack of white people, and the persistence of Oaklanders in believing that their home was a special site for the working out of human destiny. It really is a place blessed by nature in every way except for the historical American circumstance of race, which is why Oakland seems to me the most American place I have ever been, and I feel lucky to have grown up there. Oakland abundantly demonstrates that American racial separatism moves money and power around according to no logic other than the baffling logic of racial separatism itself. Oakland, to me, also demonstrates that racial separation is impossible and tears one apart. I felt adrift there because the pre-racial materials of my childhood at its best were just as gone now as they had been when we first split into races around 1973. Adult life had not become any less racial in Oakland in the intervening years—with multiculturalism, it may have become more so. I made only faint efforts to find my childhood peers. I think I was afraid they would have become fully race beings, and seeing them might have destroyed whatever pre-racial ideal I had left

I did try to find Lamont, and failed. I mentioned him to Captain Reginald Lyles, a former Panther and Oaklander who is now a police officer in a white suburban "community," if that is the right word—"community policing" had been the party principle that most attracted Lyles to the Panthers. He suggested checking the prisons, saying that the California prison population had gone from 30,000 in 1985 to 150,000 a decade later. Yes, of course, the prisons. Is it because we are a nomadic nation that we exceed all other democracies in immobilizing our citizens? Lyles called the incarceration boom "the new slavery," but, in contrast to slaves, prisoners don't produce much. The national rise in imprisonment simply removed part of several American generations from daily life—black generations, many thousands of young men, not "needed." Thirteen percent of illegal-drug users in America are black, and 74 percent of the people imprisoned for possession of illegal drugs are black. Most white drug users could not get into jail on a bet. I did not look for my boyhood friend in prison, because I thought I might find him, there, enacting one of the most bitter race roles of our period.

I felt adrift because, while the white share of Oakland's population had stayed at around 40 percent, the ratio of white students in the public schools had dropped to 7 percent, two-thirds less than when I was a child. Given such a trend, the pre-racial years I had enjoyed as a child would become impossible. And this trend had occurred at the same time that white Oaklanders, and not only Oaklanders, had abjured racial hatred, the systematic oppression that had been such a marked feature of our society in the centuries prior to 1973 or so. They had abjured every form of this hatred except one: a belief that the racial past had no hold on them, that they were free. This was not a form of hatred, really. It was just a mistaken self-love and selfish ignorance.

Coincidentally, while I was in Oakland two obscure California academics were cooking along with their California Civil Rights Initiative, which would eventually be passed by California voters. There is always something new out of white California. One of the professors explained to a journalist, "Affirmative action has been losing steam with the general public, and we think we've hit upon the sure way to finally reverse it and restore true color-blind fairness in the United States." I could not help wondering when there had been a color-blind fairness in America that might now be restored. But you hardly need to refer to a past that never existed in order to breathe new life into one past that certainly did, a past in which raceness was something black people did, for inscrutable reasons known only to them, while white people did not have a race. White people were beyond race. Just as radical white abolitionists knew that race no longer existed after emancipation, just as Louis Brandeis knew in 1915 that the distinguishing characteristic of American society was "racial equality," just as the historian Oscar Handlin knew that Americans had "ceased to believe in race" after the 1930s, so today many white Americans appear to believe that race does not matter. More specifically, they appear to believe that their race does not matter, and therefore nobody else's should either, and if somebody else's race does seem to matter, then that is his cross to bear.

So the California Civil Rights Initiative passes. So a federal judge in Boston decides, in opposing desegregation policies that resulted in a white person being unable to attend a particular school, that a public high school's using race as a "determining factor in the admission of a subset of each year's incoming classes, offends the Constitution's guarantee of equal protection." Thus the equal-protection clause of the Fourteenth Amendment, which was intended to prevent the state from marking blacks with the badge of inferiority, is now used to prevent whites' being marked with the badge of superiority. Once upon a time when we were white and colored, a federal judge wrote, "Courts will not say in one breath that public school systems may not practice segregation, and in the next that they may do nothing to eliminate it." But that was the 1960s. Today it appears that our jurisprudence is moving more in the direction of Justice Henry Billings Brown, writing in 1896: "If the two races are to meet upon terms of social equality, it must be the result of natural affinities, a mutual appreciation of each other's merits and a voluntary consent of individuals." Justice Brown's opinion, of course, cleared the way for legal segregation throughout our country.

So the struggle against affirmative action began with universities and moved on to high schools and now is proceeding to elementary schools. The fault for racial disparities in achievement always seems to lie with the next level down: the universities should not be held responsible for the high schools' failures, the high schools should hardly have to make up for the deficiencies of middle schools, middle schools cannot be expected to correct the elementary schools' shortcomings, and the elementary schools . . . it is hardly the kindergarten teacher's fault that certain parents, so often black, did not read enough to their toddlers. In this way, racial disparities in educational achievement actually have nothing to do with the educational system. They were already present at the teething stage, if not in the womb—if not in the genes. In any case, American society cannot solve this riddle. Probably blacks should just get their own house in order—as if their house stood somewhere outside American society, as if ours is a two-house town, as if racial separation is the solution we turn to not only at our worst (say, the 1880s) but at our best (today, of course, always today).

In any case, white children should not be hindered from getting whatever they can get under any circumstances, just as their white parents should not be hindered from getting jobs, government contracts, low-income housing, or, indeed, anything at all. And there is nothing wrong with this, because whatever white people may get in the world, they do not get it because they are white, since, as everyone knows, we have gone beyond race. If there might be some aspects of American life that remain racial, the good ones are *cultural heritages*, and the bad ones are *vestiges* of past discrimination, *vestiges* of history, it being understood that unpleasant continuities in America consist entirely of vestiges. It is in the nature of vestiges to die. We seem constantly as Americans to stand in confident expectation of the death of our past. We white Americans, in particular, seem to relish this trampling of graves. Unlike the dead, we can always start over in the morning, can't we, in complete freedom?

Judge Wilson believed "the Asians" were likely to run Oakland next. The Indian village that became a white town and then a black town would become an Asian town—another racial fresh start. Reverend Smith thought whites would take it over, a new generation of whites, on the grounds that blacks had had their chance and proved themselves not ready, not quite yet, for self-government. Bill Knowland's biographer Gayle Montgomery, a former *Tribune* political editor now settled into retirement in a mostly white suburb, also thought a white takeover likely. I met Montgomery for happy hour in a tavern near his home. He had the forthrightness of an old-school reporter on a bar stool, and he described white people as being rather like Huns are said to have been long ago. They had left the city in ruins. "We whites always do that. Destroy." But soon the wheel would turn, and "we'll move in, kill off the wounded, and take it back. Let the blacks go elsewhere."

I spent several pleasant hours in Oakland with Paul Cobb. My parents had had him over to the house back in 1971, when he was running for office. (He lost.) Cobb had spent his lifetime in black activism. From street corners he was exhorting passersby as early as 1962 with such slogans as "Honor Grades Make

You Feel Good Like a Black Man Should." Cobb had a fanciful turn of mind. He told me how he had got a draft deferment, in Vietnam days, by threatening to sue the draft board for conflict of interest—because there were two morticians on the board. When we met for dinner at a nice little restaurant he had suggested downtown, Cobb brought along a white longtime political ally, one of many; after dinner he bearded the white owner of the restaurant, and praised his entrepreneurship, and urged him to stick with it and help build this great city. Yet Cobb was a race man of long standing. He still lived in a West Oakland Victorian, a gracious home packed with African art, a home well within the "community." When I visited him there late one afternoon, he told me that his brother and Eldridge Cleaver were sitting in jail together once and decided Paul should be the Panthers' minister of information. He demurred, instead setting up the Black Caucus. Cobb said he had known Bobby and Huey from school days. Cobb led discussions for the Afro-American Association, and Bobby and Huey "were the study group."

Sitting in a Victorian home stuffed with African art and talking with a lifelong black activist, I was reminded of an exchange between Bobby Seale and his mother, which Seale put in his book:

> She said, "Oh, yes, Bobby, I'm with y'all, I'll always be with you, because I know you're doin' right. Way back yonder, in the days when my mama was just mauled over, and our peoples was owned like animals, I remember my mother tellin' me that we shouldn't have to be over here in this country treated like we was, and that somehow or other we should be back over in Africa."
>
> "Mama," I said, "you know we ain't ever going back to Africa. We can't."
>
> "Sure, I know that," she said. "I'm just telling you what my mother felt."

Cobb had inherited his racial politics from his father and grandfather, who were Garveyites back in Oklahoma. (Paul was conceived in Muskogee, so he claims Oklahoma roots. In his black West Coast generation one needed a Southern link for credibility and social networking.) What Cobb took from this tradition was an Africanism of the mind, and possibly of the heart, and a mimicry of the social body. The Afro-American Association organized book clubs, for example, that read Ayn Rand and Thorstein Veblen's *Theory of the Leisure Class*, "talking about why blacks need to *mimic* the economic activity of the Asian community in forming restaurants and businesses, and following certain aspects of the Jewish community in pooling resources, and so forth." Cobb said he used to quote

The Federalist Papers to white people in advocating the black cause, as the Panthers had quoted the Declaration of Independence: "You literally can take their own words and sell that message. And it's shocking, because it's all the things they believe in." When Cobb and his allies faced down Bill Knowland and his, they patiently explained that all they wanted was what white people had. They wanted it for the same reasons and in the same way, except that they hoped to get what white people had in a legal manner and soon, rather than in a vicious manner and over the long term, as whites had. Cobb recalled telling Knowland and the chamber of commerce, " 'You should have a vested interest in our economic advancement, because it creates more commerce for everybody.' I mean, how do they say no to that in public? Because that's different from saying, 'We're gonna shoot you, you know, were gonna break your door down because you've treated us bad.' " The black message to powerful whites, in short, was "what they'd say, if they were black."

We both knew this message had been repeated by black activists since the 1790s and with greater plausibility since 1865. We both knew that black Americans, day by day, over the long term, probably have been the most conservative, self-help-oriented group of people in our history, as well as the most generous, under the circumstances, in interpreting the American dream. Cobb is an optimist. I had to respect him for that, as we stood in front of his house in the waning light on a cliff at the edge of the world and at the center of the world, where the Ohlones cleansed themselves in their sweat houses, where Jack London consulted and contemplated his many selves, where the Pullman porters organized their union, where Huey had lived and Stagolee had died, where by now several generations of men had been flown away to prison, or been killed by their brothers, or killed them, such that the streets were a bit empty. Cobb is an optimist. He said he'd been noticing white people moving into the neighborhood, fixing up Victorians. They could buy them cheap. Transportation was good. These were young people, a new white generation that did not have the old phobias about black people and were content to live among them—even pleased, because they appreciated diversity. Cobb liked these young white people. The only thing that worried him was that they seemed to believe that there was, in their case, no history. They seemed to believe that, in racial terms, they were free from it. They then felt free enough to move into West Oakland.

We said good night, and I walked off onto the quiet street. I thought about this new generation. It is my white generation and the generations younger than mine. And I felt I could see what might happen with us, because I had seen it elsewhere, in other cities. We would arrive in all our freshness, with the money and confidence we believed to be our natural race-free attributes. In a book called *Babylone*, René Crevel wrote, "Memory is the tattooing by which the weak, the betrayed, the exiled, believe they have armed themselves." I would say lack of memory is the tattooing by which my white generation and younger ones, who are not weak, betrayed, or exiled, believe they have armed themselves. So it will be said that *people are moving back into the city* and *more people are looking at that area.* Purchase prices will rise, rents will rise. The schools will develop gifted programs, and every white couple that moves in will be certain, against every law of averages, that their children will be gifted. They will raise them from birth in the serene knowledge that they are gifted; and so they will be, enough of them. (The stubbornly giftless will go to private schools.) The police will respond to crimes against these new people, because these are the people bringing the neighborhood up, and they think of the police as the police think of them, as friends and allies. Poorer people will find the area harder to afford; and they will move away, because they have to.

Now, the people who are moving back to the area will never have been there before, so technically they are not moving "back." Technically, indeed, there will already have been *people* there. But those people will have been black, in one way or another, and the new people will be white, in one way or another, which is to say the new people will be full people rather than partial people. The new people will be free from whatever it was that had kept the neighborhood from coming up in the world; whatever it was, it had nothing to do with them. The new people will not be stuck in the immobility of being, they will be free nomads in the state of becoming, ever improving, as all Americans should be. The neighborhood they improve, however old and previously peopled, will be new, in the same way that America was new and empty when the English arrived and when John Locke saw that a land ruled by an Indian king was not really his land because he had not "Reason to guide him," and so had not fully used the land, and so should be displaced by more gifted people.

Yet I think that all these people will still be close enough to each other, as they have been since Locke, that the displacement by whites of nonwhites will not be altogether successful. A lack of memory is not unique to my white generation, nor is the belief in a fresh start which makes that lack of memory look like a virtue rather than a mistake. There will not be a fresh start now any more than there has been one in our past. A lack of memory is not armor; it is just something written on the skin. White and nonwhite will still be members of one divided family, their ancestors will not sleep, and if they do not attend to the graves with love, then they will again go to racially separate graves in the mistaken belief that that is freedom.

DOWN TO THE RIVER

■

When the subject came up, which was not often, Grandma said we came from France. This was an excellent place to come from, as it meant so little. Grandma demonstrated that we came from France by turning her head in profile and offering her nose. Grandma's nose, with its careful molding and frank boniness, clearly spoke the name France, and so, she thought, did mine. Because our French heritage consisted of a body part, we did not dwell on our Frenchness. What possible heritage could attach to a physical characteristic, even a visible one, inherited, as all such things are inherited, by accident? Our Frenchness was just something Grandma and I noted affectionately, as evidence of our blood tie; and maybe there was a suggestion of "French sophistication," which I understood to be the signal quality of French people.

This thimble-deep French heritage perfectly suited our Christian rationalist liberalism. We had come from somewhere, of course, possibly France. My father's kin were, in the male line, said to be from Scotland, my mother's from England, and the ancestors had thoughtlessly drifted and hopped from East to West over the generations until we collectively hit our heads against the wall of the Pacific. But none of that was important, because as hand luggage we had our rational minds, our Christian faith, and our basic goodness with us wherever we went. The moral instruction of the past consisted mainly in providing the opportunity to imagine how much better one would have done, because one entered the past as oneself, and by definition one always possessed a clearer mind, and more information, than had the dead in their time.

When I was an adolescent or a teenager—when I was in my period of asking what I thought were pointed questions—Grandma gave me a supplement to our nasal history. She had been born in Oklahoma, in 1903, "when it was still Indian Territory." She was just a small girl when her (English) mother died, leaving her French father with a large number of children from this marriage and his previous one. Here was Grandma's burning memory: a motherless child, without shoes, in a dust storm, unable to see anything, dizzy and afraid. She said her father was a great man, though a little weak, especially in choosing his first and third wives. She felt absolutely certain that he had loved her. However, he lacked means. So she and a sister were packed off to a childless aunt in Vevay, Indiana, on the Ohio River. This aunt, Lutetia, had married money, and Grandma grew up in a splendid house looking across the river to Kentucky. Another sister was sent up from Indian Territory to her grandmother's in Prairie Home, Missouri. These, then, were the places where the family had some roots. Lutetia is, of course, a French name—the Romans' name for Paris. My great-grandfather's name was George Granville Lacy. Grandma told me he had said they came from France, he and his siblings with their father and mother. Possibly they hailed from Alsace, or from a town Grandma thought was named Granville-by-the-Sea.

Many years later, as Grandma was closing in on death, I drove to Missouri from the West Coast. I drove a small old car that had grown asthmatic and tired of life. We did all right across the expanse of eastern Washington, with its baking orchards and the Indian reservations off to the north, and across a bit of Idaho and a lot of Montana, fashionable destinations for the white separatist. I stopped by Yellowstone, which had changed since my childhood car-camping visit: the idea now was to let the animals live and nature do her work, so that one had to elbow one's way through the grazing mob of elk and buffalo. Down across the treeless steppes of the Wind River reservation antelope ran. Stubbornness alone got that car over the Rockies. We descended with relief into the grim eastern Colorado desert. I had a strong sense of proceeding backward, since all those wagon trains had worked so hard to go the other way. Was this a rudeness to the past? Near the Kansas border a storm came up. The man on the radio said some tornadoes were traveling northeasterly from Oklahoma. You have probably heard tests of the Emergency Broadcasting System. They always end with "This is only a test." It was disorienting to realize I actually was listening, after all those years of tests, to the Emergency Broadcasting System itself. Although hours remained before dusk, someone had tarred over the sky. All I could see were distant crashings of light, the highway, sudden swipes of rain, and the cargo trucks on every side. Our fellow passenger cars seemed to have left the scene. Although the repeated instructions over the radio on how to pull over and lie down in a ditch—it wasn't too complicated—rattled me, I felt confident that the truck drivers, experienced men and women of the road, knew what they were doing in continuing down the highway. The radio announced the position, path, and speed of each tornado or storm. Looking at the map and watching the speedometer, I soon realized that my brothers and sisters on the highway were timing the tornadoes, threading between them. What a harried life people can lead, racing across the plains in pursuit of money to the point of risking their lives. Self-preservation is not the highest instinct of man.

I got off the road to find a motel that was not labeled AMERICAN OWNED AND OPERATED. These signs began appearing a few years ago across the country, after a South Asian (or Indian) clan, the Patels, worked its way into owning a large number of motels. If you go to a motel trade meeting today, about half the people you meet will be named Patel. In motel land there are essentially two races: Patels and non-Patels. Some among the race of non-Patels advertise themselves as "Americans" or "Natives." (The NATIVE OWNED signs led to some real confusion when I was looking for a place to rest in Indian country.) Soon I found a motel that was not American owned. There are plenty of them these days, and they're easy to find.

Another day of driving brought me near to Prairie Home. Is there a more American-owned name than Prairie Home? Does it not bespeak tranquillity, semiskilled physical work, and the best of Protestantism? I left the interstate at Boonville and went southeasterly on Route 87, one of those wondrous old two-lane highways that roll like the most pleasant of dreams. There were red-winged blackbirds fluttering from the verge and red-tailed hawks coasting high above them, hunting, and sometimes the shy gabbling bustle of a wild turkey, and it was too early for the dogwoods to bloom but the redbuds had. Route 87 would have brought out the Edenic hillock-and-glen poetry of Thomas Morton, that satyr who had tormented the Puritans with his maypole and verse. Car and road and sky and grassy rises hummed a restful meandering lullaby. The sign at Prairie Home announced a population of 215. The village center had a small shop, a church, and a Masonic lodge. The residential neighborhood to the north could not have been more than a quarter-mile square; most of its homes came from the nineteenth century. You could safely say that Prairie Home was a quiet place. There were farms within an easy walk from the center, not that anyone was out walking.

Here I met my cousins Dub and Jeanne Lacy, who were well on in years. They lived in a graceful handmade home on a soundless road near the limits of the village; the other side of the street was farmland. In the spacious, formal front room Dub and Jeanne had hung pictures of the ancestors. The shades were down, so we turned on the lights to look at the portraits. There were enough of them that they soon blurred together in my mind—now, was that Grandpa Johnston or Grandpa Lacy? Dub and Jeanne spent their time in the TV room, or family room, which had the kitchen on one side, big comfortable chairs, and a door on the other side that gave onto the gravel driveway. Jeanne was the younger, more energetic, and more talkative of the two, sitting forward on her chair by the kitchen. She had taught English in the public schools for decades and was still active in teachers' and church groups. Dub had farmed all his long life and was quiet like a man who knew that nothing in the world ever happened until the time was right—though he did have mischief in his eyes. His wife's words kept the room occupied and purposeful. Because he was small Dub disappeared somewhat in his chair. He wasn't farming anymore. I have noticed with farmers that when they are through farming the strength leaves them in a hurry, as if it needs to get on to the next generation before sunup.

Dub and Jeanne were well informed about family history. George Granville Lacy, my great-grandfather, had been born here rather than in France. The Lacys had come up from Virginia, via North Carolina, in 1836. Cousin Dub's great-grandfather Dr. Archibald Lacy was my great-great-grandfather. He had been born in Stokes County, North Carolina, just over the Virginia line, and came to Missouri with his parents, Dr. William and Agnes (Johnston) Lacy. They took their place among the pioneer families of central Missouri—as late as 1820, this was the western edge of American settlement, or the eastern edge of Indian settlement. They married in with Millses, Joneses, more Johnstons, Hunts, Burruses, and Gales, to whom Dub, in marrying Jeanne, had added the Poindexters. These were said to be English families.

Dub took me out in the pickup to look at graves. We stopped first at the feed cooperative, because I had asked what people do socially in Prairie Home and, apart from church, this was what they did. The co-op had been born early in the twentieth century, in that period when agriculture was consolidating and the small family farm becoming unviable. The co-op enabled farmers as a collective to boost themselves up a notch, capitalism-wise. It was effective for a while. We went inside, where men, most of them elderly, sat along one wall, and we said hello. We bought a pop. "Sometimes you'll have some interesting discussions there," Dub had told me earlier, his eyes twinkling, "and the rest of the time you don't." I could see what he meant. He said his generation had outlived their day, as had many of the farms they worked, and there were fewer and fewer men at the co-op as time went by. In various ways the small farms were returning to what they had been when they began. You might survive on them. In principle, because the land had not been depleted, a family could push into this territory and live almost exactly as our pioneer ancestors had lived. However, the likelihood of anyone wanting to live as our ancestors had was quite small. So the biggest farms might be bought and combined with others to make an enterprise large enough to be profitable, a scale of activity basically beyond the reach of the men at the co-op. Smaller farms might be kept for hay or other feed crops, but this was somewhere between a business and a hobby. The smallest farms would return to forest, scrub, or prairie and had been doing so for some time.

The other possibility was country life, that is, vacation properties or rural homes for people who didn't mind driving a long way to work or could work at home (via computers and phone lines, for example). Dub and I drove over to his grandparents' farm. We met the young man who lives there. He had been fixing up the place, bit by bit; he worked in a city, I can't remember which one. He had not fixed up—why would he?—the patch by a tree that holds the remains of William and Nannie Lacy and their son Archibald, who died young of TB in 1912. (In the nineteenth century and into the twentieth somewhat more than half of my relations made it to adulthood. Childbirth took several of the women early, such as my great-grandmother Mills. TB killed quite a few, men and women equally.) Dub and I tried to put back together some of the broken gravestones that indicated who was there and when he or she had lived. I think Dub felt badly about letting the graves get to this state. He said that the wild turkey and deer were multiplying at a fantastic rate, even the squirrels might be coming back, threatening the primal chaos (for a farmer) of leaving the crops unprotected. But since practically no one needed these crops anymore—in that sense, no one much needed central Missouri—folks would not bother to go out and kill the deer, turkeys, and squirrels. So it was hard to get one's motivation up for such projects as tending graves or anything else, except maybe the highway.

Out the other end of town on Route 87 we visited a proper cemetery, which was fenced against deer and other animals and where Dub said my great-grandfather was buried. Not only was George Granville Lacy not born in France, he did not die in Oklahoma. After my great-grandmother died, and my grandmother was sent to her Indiana relations, George married again, to a woman much younger than he named Hattie. They had four children, three of whom lived to adulthood. George seems to have gone from failure to failure throughout his life, as far as money was concerned, and Dub remembered seeing him in his last years. One of our relations had taken in George, who was penniless, abandoned by his wife and, evidently, by his numerous children. This relation cleared a closet in the house and fashioned it into a bedroom, where my great-grandfather George, who had the force of life in him if not much else, lived until his death in 1932. Dub was certain George had been buried in this cemetery. I looked at each stone in the place—there were two or three hundred—and Dub kept searching, his small body bent over to peer, but we couldn't find George's grave. Soon it was getting dark. Dub pronounced himself stymied. Well, we weren't going to find George in the dark. Somehow this seemed appropriate to me, because George, the old liar, was beginning to take on the qualities of a ghost. It surprised me not at all that the family had kept him in a closet. Dub and I tried again later and never did find the man's grave.

I had noticed, in going around Prairie Home, that everyone appeared to be white. You might think this unremarkable in a tiny Midwestern village, but I remarked it. Back in the TV room Jeanne said that there had once been many black residents of Prairie Home. Grandpa Johnston, for example, had owned a man named Clarkson, who raised a family in Prairie Home after the Civil War. Jeanne could remember one Albert Clarkson calling often at her grandmother's. Dub said that *his* Grandma Johnston had never said anything about any slaves. She had said that she was constantly frightened during the war, and on one occasion a rider came to the house saying slaves were on their way up the main road from Jamestown, nine miles away—"she said they were just pillaging and doing anything they could"—so she, her sister, and their mother fled to Pisgah, as they would several times during the conflict, although the pillaging-slaves alarm turned out to be false. I had some trouble keeping the Johnstons straight, perhaps because I was adjusting to the news that my people had been slave owners.

In 1876 Henry Levens and Nathaniel Drake published A *History of Cooper County, Missouri, from the first visit by White Men, in February, 1804, to the 5th day of July, 1876.* Prairie Home lies within Cooper County, so I took an interest in the book. The authors' description of the settlers begins as one might expect: they were "industrious, hardy and honest; a better class of people never emigrated to any country." However, Levens and Drake further note, "At that time, people cared very little about accumulating wealth." Much of the work was done collectively. Settlers enjoyed frequent games, and the young respected the old: "The maxim at that time was, 'Old men for counsel, and young men for war.'" William Foreman Johnson, in his 1919 *History of Cooper County, Missouri,* wrote, "When the first settlers came to what is now Cooper County, wild game of all kinds was very abundant, and was so tame as not to be easily frightened at the approach of the white man. This game furnished the settlers with all their meat, and, in fact, with all the provisions that they used for most of the time they had little else than meat ... The settlers spent most of their time hunting and fishing, as it was a needless waste to plant crops to be destroyed by the wild game . . . Thus were the early settlers and their families abundantly provided with meat and food by nature . . . The grasses were so good during the whole year that the stock lived without being fed by their owners . . . The only use for corn, of which the settlers planted very little, was to make bread."

I particularly like the idea of expecting deer to grasp the significance of white skin. I can see why the poor animals might have been slow on the uptake, since these so-called whites were not farming, were enjoying their leisure, and did not care about accumulating wealth. They were not yet acting white. I suppose they must not have wanted to. Like most pioneers—like most people—they did not seek out a new life with hopes of working themselves into early graves. They wished to start easier lives. Understandably, the local Sauk and Fox Indians treated them as they would treat Indian invaders. They traded with them and tried to keep them from taking over the land. Cooper County would be named for the Indians' most prominent early victim, Captain Sarshall Cooper. Johnson writes:

> The night of April 14, 1814, was dark and stormy, and the watchful sentinel could not see an object six feet in front of the stockade. Captain Cooper lived in one of the angles of the fort, and one day while sitting at his fireside with his family, his youngest child on his lap, and the others playing around the room, his wife sitting by his side sewing, the storm raging without, a single warrior crawled up to the fort, and made a hole just large enough for the muzzle of his gun through the clay between the logs. The noise of his work was drowned by the howling storm; he discharged the gun with effect fatal to Cooper, and Sarshall Cooper fell from his chair to the floor, a lifeless corpse, amidst his horror-stricken family.

Beginning in the winter of 1816, large numbers of white people—the dreaded "newcomers," with their settle-down ways—arrived in central Missouri, pushing at the Indian border. The Sauk and Fox were driven away; later they would be packed into Indian Territory.

With white people came black people. "The slaves," Levens and Drake wrote in 1876, "were universally well treated, being considered almost as one of the owner's family, the only difference being, that they ate their meals from the kitchen and lived apart from the family. They were allowed to have their own parties and gatherings the same as the whites, and in all things enjoyed life about as much as their owners." *Almost* family and enjoying life *about as much.* The recorded testimonies of former Missouri slaves indicate that they were not treated any better than slaves elsewhere in the nation. If they had been, it would then certainly be true that "a better class of [white] people never emigrated to any country."

According to census records, my great-great-great-grandfather Dr. William Lacy in 1840 owned thirteen people, men and women, from children to a man of middle age. Another ancestor of that generation, Dr. Robert Gale, in 1850 owned a twenty-three-year-old man and a forty-five-year-old woman. The census records give the names of owners but not of the owned. The Millses owned slaves (my great-grandmother was a Prairie Home Mills), as did the Hunts and the Poindexters and so many other of the old white families. I do wonder how white these slaves were. In 1850 about a fifth of the slaves in Cooper County were recorded as "mulattoes."

Dr. Lacy's slaves disappear from the census slave schedules after 1840. It may just be an error, or perhaps he sold them. The prices for enslaved humans in Missouri held up well, until the war. The war was also when these darker-skinned (on the whole, one assumes) people began acquiring family names. The recruitment of slave soldiers by the United States started early in Missouri, because Missouri was a slave state yet stayed in the Union. They were not emancipated, exactly. My great-great-great-grandfather Gale still had a man and a boy in his estate in 1863. (Appraisers considered the man "worthless." The boy, seven years old, was priced at one hundred dollars, about the same as a mule.) But white men from slave-owning families tended to go south and fight on the Confederate side, or remain in Missouri as irregulars; in either case, they were not in a good position to keep slaves down on the farm. And the Union army in Missouri was not in a position to turn down volunteers. There are black Lacys listed as fighting in black Union regiments from Missouri.

After the war Missouri required ex-slave couples to register their marriages, and so we get more names: Philis Lacy to Rial McFaden, George Mills to Nancy Poindexter, Jack Mills to D. A. Johnston, Sampson Mills to Matilda Poindexter, Add Lacy to Dany Douglass, A. Johnston to C. Johnston, George Gale to Harriet Thompson. Not all slaves took the names of their former owners, but many did, and it is strange to see all these names together, these names that are identical to the names of the white people of Prairie Home. These names went on to the children, for example, W. A. Johnston and William and Mary and James Lacy. All one really has, today, for non-prominent people of these generations—and there was no one from Prairie Home with name recognition much farther afield than Boonville—is names, just these names with a C or B or W or M next to them. Sometimes census takers distinguished among children of the same parents, marking one as mulatto and another as black, because what mattered, in terms of race, was not parentage as such, not literal genealogy, but the appearance of membership in a racial "family." By the 1880s the black families had mostly left Prairie Home, though a number of mulatto families remained, including the Clarksons whom Jeanne had mentioned as descended from a slave of Grandpa Johnston.

The county histories of 1876, 1883, and 1919 do not mention black or mulatto people by name. They are rarely mentioned even as a group, although Cooper County's nonwhite population would have reached somewhere near 20 percent of the total, prewar. Their names do appear in the sense that their names are the same as those of the white people about whom the histories are written. So you will find a biographical sketch of the white W. A. Johnston, whose picture hangs in Dub and Jeanne's front room, and one of the white William Lacy, whose name my father bears, and these sketches may note, as in Johnston's case, that the subject was "strongly southern in sympathies." But you will not find it said that they purchased people nor that the work of those people greatly aided the white Johnstons and Lacys (and Millses and Gales) in reaching the position of meriting biographical sketches in county histories—that, if you will, the black pioneers of Cooper County lent the luster of their lives to the white people who bore their names. There is a compelling logic to the practice of former slaves adopting their old masters' names. Because it was, after all, to a great extent a man's slaves who made his prosperity and therefore *made his name*. And it would make perfect sense, in freedom, to take that name, not because it was his but because it was yours. As a slave, you had earned it, free and clear and then some. It was the master who did not deserve his name, who was in effect hiding behind it because he could not share it. It was not really his name at all, any more than America was the name of a white country.

These old county histories are fascinating documents. There was a vogue for them between the end of Reconstruction and the turn of the century. I have read many county books, from the South, near South, Midwest, and West, and I would guess few American counties lack a narrative history from that thirty-year period after 1875. The approach of their authors was the opposite of that taken by the former slave. The county historians built up the white names through elimination: elimination of Indians, of blacks (free and slave), of white women, of the black children of white men and women, and of the many, many failures in the families of the white names. And in the process of this heroic separatism they created the names of founding fathers, county by county, of impossible and incomparable virtue, from whom later generations descended in a ragged line. In this way, by writing celebratory history, by creating a genealogy of positive history, they placed a rather oblique curse on the present. Levens and Drake, for example, writing in 1876, believed that young white Americans had departed disastrously from the simplicity of the ancestors. Now "they must commence with a fine, costly house, elegantly furnished, with a fine piano and other finery in proportion; but they shortly find themselves at the foot of the ladder, too proud to beg and too lazy to work. What then is the result? Some resort to stealing, robbery, arson or murder, and are sent to the penitentiary or the gallows. While others, in desperation, seek refuge in death, and commit suicide rather than reform." What is it about Americans that has led them so often to create recent pasts from which to measure their own declines, pasts so pure in good names that one could never love them? Why seek to be haunted by ghosts of unreal virtue? I wonder whether it wasn't this, partly, that drove my great-grandfather out to Indian Territory, trying to be free, free, free by taking about the only Indian land left and starting over, again. Maybe it was these virtuous names that he thought he could trick by telling his children they were from France.

The unreal pasts of the postwar county histories eventually birthed their desperate soothsayer, an unreal future in which everything would get better. Writing in 1919, William Foreman Johnson described how in Cooper County the schools—he would have meant the segregated, white schools—"have multiplied and towns have been built upon the broad expanse of her territory; the old trails have given way to well-kept highways; steam locomotives haul palatial trains where once the slow moving ox-teams transported merchandise to and from the Missouri. Even the buggy and carriage, once the evidence of prosperity, have been superseded by the more elegant, more comfortable and speedier means of travel, the automobile. The telegraph, the telephone and the wireless have bound together distant communities. Distance has been eliminated and time conserved." But lurking behind Johnson's rhapsody was the knowledge that the black and white people that had made all this possible were also being abandoned. Distant communities were not being bound together; most of them, slowly, were dying, and the labors of the ancestors, the places they built at such cost, were being left on the vine, and those speedy automobiles were whistling right past the family graves. The distance between Americans and their past was being increased. Places like Prairie Home were easier to reach but farther from the mind. Time was not being conserved so much as crushed. Soon no one would need Cooper County and many other counties like it, and you might wonder what all the fuss had been about, or why the ancestors had bothered.

"It's hard for me to understand the settlers," Wilbur Schilb told me in Prairie Home. I had met him down at the co-op. "Why people, with what they had to put up with, would keep pushing west. But I guess they thought it was better.

We've made trips out west, and some of that rugged terrain, I don't know why—they really wanted something awful bad to travel through this kind of country in a covered wagon. I don't know how they did it. Or even why they did it, really. But it's a good thing they did, I guess, settle the country. I guess."

One side of his family all went out to Oklahoma for the 1891 land run. He had visited them—years after 1891, of course, Schilb is old but he isn't that old. "I don't know what in the world they wanted with that land out there. One of my second or third cousins come back here one time, she said that too, 'Why would anybody leave this country, go out there for that flat dry land out there?' 'Course she's went on to Oregon. I don't know, it was free land. I guess they had a rough time making a living here, probably, and whatever." Some of his family stayed on in the new land, some returned partway, to Kansas, others pressed ahead to California and Oregon.

Schilb's people came from Germany; there was a mid-nineteenth-century surge of immigrants from Prussia, Bavaria, Coburg, Bohemia, and Hesse. "They were antiwar," he said, " 'cause they came over here to get out of the draft in Germany, a lot of 'em did. I don't know if all of them did. My folks did. Germans, well, they were a warring nation through those years, and they put everybody in the army." In addition to being unwarlike, these German immigrants were "antislave, I guess." The Civil War cut quite neatly through the village of Prairie Home: one side of the road through town was Union, the other was Confederate. The Germans had not been eager to integrate with the people they called "the English" or "the Americans." People in Prairie Home still talk about families being either English or German, although some English families are not too English, and Germany was not a unified nation in 1845, and some of the Germans were Swiss. Many of the Germans, so-called, were Catholic or Lutheran, new faiths in central Missouri. They spoke dialects of German at home and often in church. Schilb said many of the German families kept their language until World War I, anti-German hysteria, and Americanization.

The Germans, then, resident here for fifteen or twenty years, fought to preserve the Union. My people, the English, went south. General Sterling Price camped his army out front of our family farm on Route 87 in 1861. Many of the men joined up. Dr. Archibald Lacy served as a surgeon in Shelby's Brigade. Price and Joseph Shelby spent much of the war ranging in and out of Missouri from camps in Arkansas. Dr. William Lacy served in a Confederate cavalry unit. The white W. A. Johnston went with Price, then was captured and paroled. Dub suspected Grandpa Johnston had been a "bushwhacker," an impolite term—the polite one was "guerrilla"—for someone who rode with the pro-Southern gangs that aided Price and Shelby when they were around and committed less formal violence when they weren't. The loyal Home Guards, many of them German, were not necessarily much better, nor were the federal troops. This part of Missouri, and parts west and north on either side of the Missouri River, had no law during the war. Neither party could triumph for long, so the land was given over to terrorism. By 1862 Union general John Schofield had issued an order: "The time is passed when insurrection and rebellion in Missouri can cloak itself under the guise of honorable warfare. The utmost vigilance and energy are enjoined upon all the troops of the State in hunting down and destroying these robbers and assassins. When caught in arms, engaged in their unlawful warfare, they will be shot down upon the spot." Later that year Schofield noted that among his uniformed hunters "there has been perpetrated pillage and marauding of the most unsoldierlike and disreputable character." Even scorched-earth policies, mass arrests, and confinement of suspected Southern-sympathizer families to their homes could not prevent the breakdown. In November 1862 Union general Loan wrote about the Central District, which included Cooper County: "It is much easier to catch a rat with your hands in a warehouse filled with a thousand flour barrels than it is to catch a band of guerrillas where every, or almost every, man, woman, and child are their spies, pickets, or couriers. There are some 200 here held as prisoners on the general charge of disloyalty. They are generally actively disloyal. The remainder of the disloyal inhabitants I propose to have brought in as rapidly as possible." The total-war methods used in the Civil War were particularly thorough in Missouri, particularly prolonged, and fruitless.

After the war the white survivors came home and the black survivors left home. They did not go very far, at first. "There were at one time," Schilb said, "a lot of colored people around through this part of the country. When I started carrying mail—I was a rural letter carrier down north here, around Gooch's Mill—and I went through that part of the country, and there were old cabins sitting around on pretty near every hill down there. That's where the Negroes used to live. 'Course, they were all vacant by that time. So there had to be quite a number of Negroes down there. And they had a church down there, a graveyard down there, too. It used to be quite a thriving community. There's nothing there now." Schilb said there were no black people left in the area, "as far as I know," but that "when I was young, there was not many, but there was a few black people around in this community yet. They just gradually, well, either died or went to the city." The land they had farmed after the war has gone to waste. "The dirt itself I think is not that bad," Schilb said, and as he had farmed all his life he was in a position to know. "Not very rocky, but it's pretty hilly."

Schilb did say that black people appeared around here in great numbers once or twice a year: "It is amazing. We've got an old black church right around the corner down the hill, down there, and it's just amazing—the first of May, and otherwise the first of October—and people will come. And they don't have services there at all anymore. And there's terrific crowds come down there. They've even had a bus from Kansas City come in one year. That's Splice Creek. Well, I'm sure it's Baptist. Most of the coloreds were Baptist. That's Splice Creek church, colored church."

I asked eighty-six-year-old Lela May, who was raised a Patterson, about these May meetings. Although she lived in Boonville, she knew the Prairie Home black community well. She had spent part of her childhood there in the village's last black family—keeping in mind, of course, that, as she said, "my grandfather, he had brothers that had different names than his, you know. Those slave women, seem like they had, I don't know, they had white children, and black children." The Prairie Home black community now was an imaginary community. The descendants of the families who came out of slavery returned each year to claim their home churches. As to Splice Creek, "that just closed down last year. They just got three members now, that I can think of. You know, nobody's been living down there for years. You know, wasn't no country people down there. But they went there every month and had church. In May and October they'd have homecoming, and call it a basket-dinner day. Everybody that ever lived there, they would come back and bring dinner. Everybody was glad to see everybody. They were worshipping also. And that's what they called a basket-dinner day."

Of the four original black churches, Splice Creek and Clark's Fork were able to sustain homecomings all through the twentieth century. Splice Creek may yet keep it going, as they do at Clark's Fork—"Oh, they just feel *good* out there," Lela May said. The Clark's Fork church even had electricity put in. She said she had thought of bringing people from the old churches to her church in town, and people did come, but not at the price of abandoning their old churches forever. "I wouldn't even ask them. That would hurt their feelings, that would make them feel real bad." Her sister grew up in Prairie Home and was a member of Clark's Fork, "and that would hurt her feelings if anybody would say, 'Why do you all keep on going back to that old church?' " Giving up on the old churches, she said, "I think that's just about like giving up your mother, or your dad, or somebody close to you."

I went by those churches late one afternoon. Splice Creek was small and falling down. At its cemetery, which was a struggle to get to up a hazardous slope, I saw some of the old family names, and there they were again at Clark's Fork, which had a large white wooden church with a center steeple and a green roof that was in trouble. Clark's Fork had once been headquarters for the bushwhacker Bloody Bill Anderson, but all was tranquil now. The small, newer building next to the church would be where they had the electricity that kept the coffee urn going at May meetings. A young white woman drove up in a late-model car with children in it, then got out and walked over. Her family lived across the road. They weren't really farmers, but they liked the country life. She said she and her husband maintained the large cemetery—"we just try to keep it up"—a bit of news that made me inexplicably happy. I walked on a ways and around a bend down toward the creek where Gooch's Mill had been. There were trees all around on the steep slopes rising from the creek and not too much brush, so you could see here and there on the heights what remained of the homes where some of the Millses, Lacys, Joneses, Hunts, and Johnstons had first established themselves in freedom. It was so still and quiet there, a place to hang your harp on the redbuds, sing a song.

Genealogy is a strange pursuit. After Alex Haley's book *Roots* was published, the writer Ishmael Reed wisely wondered what the story would have been if Haley had traced his white ancestors back to Ireland, rather than following his black ancestors to Africa. Haley grew up black, was considered black by the people around him, and so was black. Yet the African story was not his whole past; it was only the past that he was permitted to have by the accident of skin color, the people around him, the many influences that had worked on those people, and perhaps by his own imagination. These attitudes and accidents—apart from his imagination—set the limits of what he could inherit that would seem believable, and therefore meaningful, to the public, and maybe to him. So the racial present determined what of the past Alex Haley could plausibly inherit. Considering how wide the genealogical field was, as a factual matter—and most of us Americans have very wide genealogical nets to cast over the waters—Haley's African inheritance was comparatively small.

The pursuit of genealogy can lead to strange places. My great-grandfather George Granville Lacy, for example, who went to start over on Indian land, married an Indian. One of his daughters, my grandmother's sister Georgia, also married an Indian, a Cherokee, indeed a distant cousin of John Ridge, the slave-holding student of Virgil and unloved martyr. A granddaughter of this marriage, Danna, out in Oklahoma, told me once in the most delightful rueful way that she was qualified to join both the Daughters of the American Revolution and the Cherokee Nation. She could also, for that matter, qualify for the Daughters of the Confederacy, and no doubt she had some Union ancestors, too.

Against the backdrop of such a potential inheritance, I think it is clear that we Americans, on the whole, inherit very little. We live in such silence. Most of us do not discuss matters at length with our grandparents; more to the point, our grandparents did not discuss matters at length with their grandparents, and so on back to the Founding Fathers, who made it clear, especially Jefferson, that they were inheriting as little as possible. (Who cared even then what George Washington's father had to say? Who of us even remembers his name?) America is the only well-established nation in the world that still insists on having Founding Fathers, as if we had but two generations, a tiny founding one and a vast and disappointing second one. All we are *meant* to inherit are the principles of the Founding Fathers. Doesn't that create something of a void after 1792? It is a void we have filled, principally, with race, time out of mind. We took the idea of freedom and made it a racial idea, which meant it had to appear as racial separatism, in one form or another, which means that we have been chasing our freedom like a dog chasing its tail.

I think we have inherited far less than our ancestors had, and may still have, to give. If only I could have inherited the knowledge from the white Johnston and the black Johnston of what it was like to be them in their time. That inheritance would be more precious than pearls. But we are Andrew Jackson's grave tramplers, and what we really have inherited is so small, a few thoughts and thoughtless reactions that we tend to repeat. Among these often repetitive small inheritances is the conviction, particularly strong among white Americans, that we do not repeat ourselves. In despair we inherit a belief that the past does not matter—we can start over, we can go beyond the racial thinking that, deep down, nearly every American has known is not a wise way of thinking—the funny and often tragic part being that this antihistorical belief itself is an inheritance from our past. And each person who comes here becomes an heir to that doomed freedom from the past that the American past gives us. And when each person who comes here acquires a race, in the American sense, as each person has and does, that person will pour freedom into a racial mold, where it will cool and harden. May I put it another way: this cup of timeless, unreal freedom we keep inheriting in each generation is a poisoned cup; the wine we drink from it makes us do foolish things.

We have inherited some few small thoughts and thoughtless reactions. I asked my father to query his mother as to whether there had been black Americans in Vevay, Indiana, when she was growing up. There had been some. The one she remembered well was Alice Andrews—Aunt Alice Andrews—the woman who raised her. Grandma was about ninety-three years old when she mentioned Alice Andrews. I had never heard before of Alice Andrews, and neither had my father, her only child, which would make for just under sixty years of silence about Alice Andrews. Grandma told Dad that Alice Andrews had raised her, that when she needed comfort she went to Alice Andrews, that when she cried out at night the name she cried was Aunt Alice, that, in short, Alice Andrews was the most important adult of her childhood, she just had not thought to mention her before. I would guess she did not mention Alice Andrews to her child and grandchildren because she didn't think it was important to, or even very interesting. Grandma was not interested in race. I never once heard her say an unkind thing about nonwhite people or a nonwhite person. She did not think race mattered particularly, and as long as everyone around her was white, which was most of her life, it in fact seemed not to matter. She hardly gave it a thought. But race was thinking about her—this is why Americans are a paranoid people—it was thinking about her, because her freedom from race was a racial freedom. Alice Andrews was not worth recalling because she wasn't family. The odd thing is that Grandma's family, the one she did remember for us, was itself just barely family. Grandma was in effect a white orphan raised by a black woman.

The only inheritance all of us, including orphans, receive from our parents is appearance. Coincidentally, race as such is a matter of appearance. In a racial society even orphans have family. Grandma was raised by a black woman, yet her family was white because her race was white, her inheritance was white. This occurred not because she adored the color of her own skin, or despised the color of Alice Andrews. It occurred because she was American, poor motherless child whirling in the dust, and we can trample graves all we want, and risk our lives racing across the plains in search of money, and forget everything and start over again and again in freedom and we still have these families called races we cannot shake, because they really are our only families, not in fact but in the more powerful realm of imagination. What did Grandma mean that sunny day in the park when she said, "There are a lot of colored people here"? Perhaps she was simply observing a fact. But that fact is not a fact; it is a dream, it's magic, and that dream fact was Grandma's chief inheritance, proving conclusively that we were not from anywhere but America.

The racial inheritance would have been working through her even if we had been in another park somewhere in the suburbs and she had failed to notice that everyone was white. When white Americans are among themselves and do not see that there are people missing from the family, do not see that this whites-only situation is partial, incomplete, then they are failing fully to understand what it means to be an American. That common failure is itself an inheritance, with its origins in the greater failure to recognize nonwhites as fellow human beings, as brothers and sisters—the mis-recognitions of slavery and conquest. I have read that some difficulties experienced by black Americans are a legacy of slavery, and no doubt, in some ways, that is true. There is, however, a much larger legacy of slavery, and that legacy is white people. When you encounter a group of white Americans, you are encountering the legacy of slavery. Similarly, Indian Americans have had problems linked to the conquest of America. But the most sizable legacy of the conquest of America is white people. Conquest and slavery formed white people every bit as much as they formed black and Indian Americans, and form them still. As a nomadic people, we Americans carry these inheritances with us when we travel through space and time.

We all share them, we all inherit them, not through our families in the strict sense but through the imagined families of race. That is the American norm. The norm cannot exist in a single person, which is one of the beauties of our nation. An individual alone cannot be an American; an American truly alone, as Jack London knew, is a suicide. An American race in isolation is likewise not fully American and is likewise a suicide. No American race can, in isolation, put its house in order, because we are all in the same house. To be an American is necessarily collective, an identity no one of us can fully have.

This structure of identity is determined by our past and by now has become as permanent and real as an identity can be. As an individual American, one has simply to accept its incompleteness. An American race, in its American-ness, must also accept this incompleteness. In the particular case of white Americans—and they are a particular case—this acceptance has been greatly complicated by the delusion that their race can absorb or supersede all others, can go beyond race either by becoming the only race or by being the only race that is fully human and therefore not really a race. What white Americans have done, when in the hold of this delusion, is not a pretty matter for investigation. They have committed horrible acts of a size and frequency disproportionate to their numbers. We might then assume that they are a wicked race—and many of us have reached for this answer, including many white people, in various ways. But to assign a race wickedness gives away the power of wickedness, which is a great power; it likewise gives power to the idea of race as such; and it gives the non-wicked a powerlessness that has no more use than powerlessness ever has.

America is not a crime scene. If we were to envision America as a crime scene, then apologies would be due from white people. But the apologizer retains the power of apology, the power to create his own innocence, and the racial power to create white innocence has been used so many times in America, to so little good effect, that we should, I think, look elsewhere than to contriving apologies. I doubt that the past can be apologized for in any case, because it is beyond the reach of forgiveness. The past can only be understood and integrated into the present—its effects on the present recognized and incorporated into a daily practice of repair that cannot have an ending any more than the past has an ending. This is not apology but a moral life in a tragic world. One person telling another, after a misunderstanding, that he is sorry is how comedies end, not tragedies.

If America were a crime scene, then we could punish the guilty, but the American body, if you will, has, to put it crudely, three heads, black, white, and Indian. In his short story "Those Extraordinary Twins"—it was the genesis of *Pudd'nhead Wilson*—Mark Twain wrote about a community faced with a crime. The accused man was one of a pair of Siamese twins (you could tell which was which because one had lighter skin). The court decided to hang the guilty twin, accepting the inevitable death of his brother as a by-product, however regrettable, of serving justice. Similarly, if we were to eliminate one American race, the others would, if only symbolically, also die.

Some have said that, because their own family was not here in 1619, 1792, 1862, or 1964, they had no part in the racial drama, as Americans. But races in America have functioned so much as families do, and once you are in the family you receive your part of the inheritance, and the American past becomes your past. America is not a crime scene; it is a place for the performance of a tragic drama. Aristotle wrote that in tragedy "the solutions of plots ought to happen as a result of the plots themselves, and not from a contrivance." The tragic figure is "the sort of man who . . . changes to misfortune, not because of badness or wickedness, but because of some mistake . . ." The tragic mistake is his failure to realize that he is harming someone he loves. This mistake is caused not by his evil but by his misapprehension of reality. And the resolution of the tragic plot comes about not through his recognition of the wrong itself—that was never the problem—but through his recognition of the wronged as a person or as persons he loves. He may then also recognize the wronged as part of himself. Sometimes classical tragedies end when the moment of recognition takes place too late, when the wronged is not recognized in time. The tragic figure has already killed his loved one, and so kills himself. Aristotle considered such dramas unsuccessful tragedies because they failed fully to evoke the fear and pity the tragic audience needed.

The American tragedy need not be unsuccessful. We should not look for angels in our past. We should not, I think, make rough angels of children or look for innocent victims or innocent victors. We should look for ghosts and try to recognize them in time as loved ones.

"Genealogical trees do not flourish among slaves," Frederick Douglass once wrote. Nor do they flourish among the conquered. But isn't it also true that genealogical trees do not flourish among the grave tramplers, the slave owning and the conquerors? When such trees do flourish, they normally have required heavy pruning. The first Lacy to reach America, James, came to Roanoke Island in 1587. Like everyone else in that colony, he was gone the next time a ship arrived from England. He either died or became an Indian. In general, Lacys came from Ireland, not England. It is largely an Irish name, and Lacy genealogists have traced it to distinguished Irish forebears and, beyond them, to the Norman invasion, which could mean that, in an extremely faraway sense—the first Norman Lacy reached England in about 1071—we really were French, except that the Normans were Vikings. And the name Lacy itself, as Latius, was a bequest of the masters from Rome.

These distant genealogical tracings are of limited credibility. American genealogists commonly face a gap at the water's edge, or succeed in tracking a male line as far as the first person to leave the Old World. They may have a town or county name to hold on to in Ireland, France, Germany. Then the leap begins to aristocracy—a leap to the Norman invasion, the Scottish clans, the *limpieza de sangre* (clean blood) of Old Castile, an Ashanti prince. I have seen the Lacys confidently descended from Charlemagne, a linkage by no means unique to that family's genealogists. This is a secular version of Christian Identity, tying one through blood to the greatest of the great. It is not merely a product of narcissism, for the names we follow through time were, for the most part, the names of our masters. In Europe and in Africa most people labored for someone else, as slave, serf, or tenant. For people of European descent, particularly, the names we own as ours would have been, more often than not, the names of people who owned our ancestors—at any rate, owned our ancestors' labor. These were, so to speak, serf names, and not altogether different in character from slave names. They were the names average people built up for others and took with them as one fruit of their labors.

And when our ancestors brought those names to America, they must have thought they would now own them completely; from being identified by their masters, they would become identified by their mastery (under assumed names), their self-mastery, their power of freedom from the unfree past that gave them their names. Yet as some became masters, they found it necessary to master others—not least, to master other ex-Europeans—and the language of freedom grew dependent on the language of slavery, just as mastery of oneself depended on mastery of others. This intolerable, chaotic conflict among freedom-seeking people soon eased into the categories of race, the great names we gave ourselves to identify with, the great parentless families. In this way the especial failure of former Europeans, now white Americans, to be free and independent masters of themselves could be partially erased from their minds. If the race device failed, as it so often did, and one felt oneself developing a sense of bondage, one left to start over out West.

The first of my line of Lacys to reach America appears to have been a William, who came to Virginia in 1652 under indenture to Captain John West.

After gaining his freedom, William settled in New Kent County, twenty miles northwest of Jamestown. New Kent did not have the best of land. It marked the border of substantial English settlement in the mid–seventeenth century and attracted men who had no better choice than to live near Indians and carve out a very rough living. The early white revolts against Virginia's white leadership, notably Bacon's Rebellion, received disproportionate support in New Kent County. The white freemen there hated their masters, who clearly wished to keep them in the servitude they had come here to escape. It was the genius of Bacon and men like him to turn that hatred into racial hatred of Indians—to shape the bitterness of white men and women who felt oppressed by their white betters into a racial mission and make massacre and enslavement of racial enemies into a social good. Wealthier white Virginians could buy people of one race to do the work that made mastery possible. Poorer free whites had to kill one race in order to get the land and amass the wealth necessary to buy people of a second race and ascend to mastery. All this occurred among a small number of people in a small corner of the world over a brief period of time. In New Kent County, it seems, my ancestors first purchased a person: a man named Anthony. The land there is thickly forested now by slender trees; its general flatness breaks at times into shallow undulations of fields long ago plowed into regularity. This fought-over land is of little importance to anyone today, and you can just smell the sea nearby when the breeze is right.

The Lacys tumbled westward into North Carolina and Georgia, up into Tennessee and Kentucky, pushing against whatever Indians were over the next hill and particularly against the populous Cherokees. At least three Lacys served in the units that removed the Cherokees to Oklahoma; other Lacys married into the tribe and even went west with it. A few Cherokees did hold out in the North Carolina mountains, pressed against the Tennessee border. Their descendants live there today, and do a lively business in imitating the Cherokees of yesteryear for tourists, mainly white tourists.

The westering Lacys married into families similar to their own, such as the Craigs. The Craigs made their long trek out of Virginia leading the Traveling Church, a faith-crazed Baptist band of unwanted white believers who managed to cover many miles in prayerful caravan, their slaves traveling with them (and organized into a separate church). God love them, the Craig brothers Lewis and Benjamin brought the Baptist faith, black and white, to Kentucky. They had more than worn out their welcome in Episcopal Virginia. Lewis Craig, for instance, had been, according to one biographer, "a valiant champion of the cause in Virginia":

> He was several times imprisoned in that state for preaching the
> gospel. The first time, he was arrested in company with several

other ministers. The prosecuting attorney represented them to be
a great annoyance to the county by their zeal as preachers. "May
it please your worships," said he, "they cannot meet a man on the
road but they must ram a text of scripture down his throat." As
they passed on to prison, through the streets of Fredericksburg,
they united in singing the lines,

"*Broad is the road that leads
to death,*" &c.

The biographer went on to note: "As an expositor of scripture," Lewis Craig
"was not very skillful, but dealt closely with the heart." Brother Benjamin dealt
closely with baser materials, and suffered frequent expulsion from the church
for drinking and dancing, prior to his drowning in the Ohio River.

The Craigs settled on both sides of that river, below Cincinnati. They laid
out towns and built plantations and farms. They intermarried with Irish or
"Scotch-Irish" families (such as the Malcomsons) and the Swiss families who,
on the Indiana side, had settled after 1815, at the limit of Indian territory, with
high hopes of making it big in the wine business. (Sadly, there are good reasons
why you have not heard of Indiana wines. The vintners did not prosper, though
one took a few cases to Thomas Jefferson, and it is said that the aging president
appreciated them.) They named their main town Vevay, projected capital of
New Switzerland. Here is where my grandmother was raised by Alice Andrews
and where I went to meet my cousin Roger, a tobacco farmer and one of the few
remnants of the founding families in Switzerland County.

At eighty-two, Roger was slowing down in his work farming in the hills
above the Ohio. He raised enough hay to feed his cattle, and a small tobacco
crop. His wife, who served up a lovely cold lunch for us in their neat, small
farmhouse, had part of one lung gone, while his sister was dying of lung cancer
in a convalescent home down by the river. Cousin Roger took me to his barn
and showed how he cured the tobacco leaves. He asked whether I had raised
tobacco out in Oakland. I said I had raised tomatoes, beans, and radishes in our
back yard, but no tobacco, and so far as I knew no one farmed tobacco in Oakland, California, all of which information Roger took in with the friendly, light
grace that characterized him. He reminded me of my grandfather Malcomson,
who had grown up here on these hills and whose death I was still mourning. My
grandfather, however, had gone to college, and traveled, while Roger was a
local man. His language spoke up from the past in such words as *ye, chimbley,
holler* (for *hollow*) and *feller, reckon, no 'count, yonder.* Also *nigger,* that amaz-
ingly long-lived word. We looked out, through a horizontal slot in the side of the
barn, across a field and a holler to a clear crest with a couple of trees and no

brush. On that clearing Roger sometimes put meat, then waited back in the barn for coyotes to come, his rifle resting in this slot. I gathered he rarely missed. He was expecting wolves now, too, because the state had decided to reintroduce the old game, including predators, since this region, at least the hill country, was no longer economically needed. Roger was not needed, nor were the younger people round about. Unlike Roger and his generation, they turned, as unwanted youth will in their distress, to the glories of crime and inebriation, and angry fancies. (Amphetamines were the drug of choice.) The community was falling apart, and the fact that the state was scheming to give the land back to the wolves and the deer struck the rural holdouts with great force. Their absentee masters were replacing them with animals.

Looking from the shooting slot in the barn, you saw the land drop to the right of the clearing, then rise steeply as a cleared slope to a small ridge Roger called Nigger Ridge. He called it Nigger Ridge because, in slave days, a man had escaped from slaveholding Kentucky across the Ohio and fled into these hills. Vevay was full of slave catchers. One of them tracked this man and saw him running up the slope. The escaped man had a brass pistol. The slave catcher, Roger said, shouted at the man, "Surrender." The man didn't know the meaning of that word, and so was shot to death on the spot, and buried on the ridge. Roger had heard that the body had later been moved, but he knew that was not the case, because he had himself witched Nigger Ridge with wires. The wire witching revealed that the body was still there along with the brass pistol. So cousin Roger was something of a witch as well as a farmer. He did not have the power, he said, of the late Shenandoah or of the so-called Amish pastor, who had a tomahawk that spun, something that happens when a tomahawk's owner was killed violently or in a premature and sudden manner, such that the man's energy is trapped in the hatchet and cannot dissipate, much as his soul does not have enough time to escape his body. Roger was just a minor witch.

Roger took me across the road from his house to one of the old Malcomson farms. No one was at home. The owners were a professional couple, British, I think, living in Cincinnati. They had fixed the place up as a vacation home. They tore down the outhouse and the carriage house and filled in the well. The orchard was gone, and the chestnut tree with the fence to keep the horses from eating the nuts. They did not cultivate the land, which caused Roger pain, because he knew how hard it had been to make the land productive. They had added a solarium, which looked odd, though not as odd as the peacock. This was the hope of the country, to attract people of such wealth that they could maintain a farmhouse which they would visit a few weeks in the year to enjoy rural quiet and a peacock. Although just across the road, we had gone far from Roger's world. People, he said, did not know each other's names anymore or recognize their faces. They did not wave from cars. They posted their land and watched television. They did not go to church. It had become a lonely life here, even with television.

Roger led me down from the hills, nearer to the river, and we visited the old Thiebaud house. Roger and I had the same Thiebaud ancestors—perhaps the source of my French nose. The Thiebauds had been among the first Swiss families, they of the ill-fated vineyards that had returned to wasteland on the hill above us. Across the driveway from the house stood a stone building with eight-inch vertical slits, flared outward. The early families had used this as a defense post against Indians. Many Indians had been killed in this area as part of the settlement process. Some were in unmarked graves below this house. Others had been hanged in the trees hereabouts, Roger said, after a fierce encounter. "They hung a number of them in the trees up the hill there," he said, "and just left them there. There was a taboo." Roger said that the county line west of here had been set by the Treaty of Greenville, in 1795, as the Indian boundary. The Indians tore it down, the whites put it back up, and this went on for some years. "Eventually, they got it to keep up," Roger said. This was the punch line, and we laughed.

It was not the only punch line, however, for Roger was himself part Indian. He found this out, first, when his father saw him walking up one day barefoot and said, "That's the Blackfoot in you." "He let that slip," Roger told me. Years later someone said to Roger, "You're more Indian than white. Ask your dad." His dad did not want to discuss it, but Roger queried a distant relation who was passing through and discovered that he had a Choctaw grandmother and a Blackfoot grandfather. This at last made sense of a strange feature of his boyhood. His grandmother's half brother had often followed Roger around. The half brother didn't say much. He went shirtless and barefoot and trailed Roger and his boyhood friends when, for instance, they went swimming. Roger would watch his great-uncle over his shoulder, and he was always there, his black hair reaching to his waist. Sometimes he plaited it, and he always held up his pants "with an ordinary vine."

Below the Thiebaud house, on Ohio River bottomland, we passed a plowed field, smooth as a table except for a mound of earth in the middle that had a few trees. This hump was one of several that lined the Ohio, remnants of an ancient culture known, not too imaginatively, as the Mound Builders. I asked Roger why it had not been plowed under. He said that plowing under Indian mounds was illegal, but of course it was not illegal in 1820, and this was prime land. Roger suggested that the settlers might not have had the necessary equipment. We both knew that to be untrue, so Roger tried again: Could it have been a shade spot for cows? No, it could not have been. You would not pasture cows in a tilled field. Roger said, hopefully, "There was always a good breeze there. It was pleasant and cool to sit up there." Roger smiled, and I let him go. Witches like keeping secrets, although it was plain as day that the mound was haunted, and generations of white people who had not hesitated to kill any living thing in their path had nonetheless been unable to plow under the mound. They knew it was sacred. Roger tended many graves in this part of the county, and I suppose that, in his way, he tended the Indian mound too, just as he had witched for the dead man on Nigger Ridge.

There were, apparently, no Indians any longer in Vevay—except in the sense that Roger was an Indian—nor did there seem to be any black people. Vevay was a white small town that strained to attract city dwellers seeking a rest from the stress of urban life. The visitors were no darker in appearance than the residents of Vevay, and I doubt that this restful homogeneity was accidental. There had been a black population here, once, including a separate black school. The Kentucky farms, across the river, had been worked by slaves, including the substantial Craig plantations along the shore. Indiana did not allow slavery, despite the frequently expressed wishes of some white Hoosiers, mainly because Congress would not permit it. However, an 1807 territorial law allowed the import of "negroes and mulattoes" for use as indentured servants. Such people were normally slaves whose masters brought them to Indiana under contract. If the newly indentured person lived out the contract, he or she would be free. Slave owners also brought slaves into free Indiana for temporary work, then took them back to a slave state. These arrangements would not have been difficult, because the old river families usually had relations over the water in Kentucky. For most of the year the Ohio was easily crossed. There were regular ferries. In a cold winter you could walk across it; in a dry summer you could swim it. Not surprisingly, many black slaves escaped across the Ohio. If they were lucky, they crossed Switzerland County and reached the shelter of small black towns strung in a belt north of the hills where my family farmed—towns that are gone now—or the Quaker safe houses northwest of Cincinnati. From there they might press on to Michigan and Canada.

After the war, of course, free blacks were not wanted in Indiana, any more than they were wanted elsewhere. Roger said that a small black population had lived in Vevay until about 1900, when a white man named Hines was murdered. Local whites believed that a black person, or "the blacks" generally, was responsible. Vevay's black population tried to flee. Some succeeded; others were hunted down and killed. Roger's mother saw a family coming up the hill with all their things wrapped in cotton ticking. They were terrified. She helped them on their way. Another man, Roger said, hid himself near town in the shallows, among the logs, with water and mud up to his shoulders and his rifle on a log by his head. A white man saw him and walked over to shoot him, but another man nearby shot him first, and "he just dropped down into the dark water and never came back up." Roger believed there had not really been blacks in Vevay since then. Alice Andrews would have had to stay close to the home where she raised my grandmother or else live on the Kentucky side at night and work in Indiana by day.

When the Klan revived in the 1920s, its most spectacular growth and power came in Indiana. Switzerland County had a klavern, which met weekly above the Vevay post office. Roger remembered fondly the big outdoor meetings, the coal-oil-soaked rags burning, wrapped around crosses, the speeches and pageantry and excitement. Americans were big joiners in those days. Roger's dad joined the Klan. So did many others in the county, including Thomas Banta (a friend of our family), who was Night Hawk, in charge of investigations; Edwin Ferguson, Klexter, who ran a drugstore; Leland Courtney, Kligrapp, another family friend; Reverend Schmuck, Klokard, whom my granddad did not like; and Reverend Frank Hammel, Exalted Cyclops, that is, chief of the klavern, who used to take Grandma on church trips. Fortunately, because there were, in effect, no likely race enemies left in the county, the Klan there seems to have done very little.

I had expressed an interest in the Underground Railroad, so Roger took me to a stone house next to the Ohio. There, three white people of modest means, a woman and two men, were gathered around a picnic table. They seemed to have some informal arrangement to occupy the old house. The woman went inside to bring fresh Bud Lights against the afternoon heat. One of the men was short and had an impressive beer belly; the other was very big and carried a holstered pistol on his hip. A discussion ensued as to why their house was haunted and in what way. Some maintained that the house had been built by whites over from Carrollton, straight across the river—a town founded by the Traveling Church Craigs—and that the Indians would tear it down, the whites would return, and so on; others believed the Indians had built it to defend against marauding whites crossing the river. (The first stage of white American expansion across the Ohio had consisted entirely of quick strikes aimed at burning crops and homes.) Everyone agreed about the culmination, which was that the whites had massacred the Indians. It was these Indians who had been hanged from the trees on the hill until they rotted.

The stone house later served as a hideaway for escaped slaves, Roger said. A tunnel from the creek led to a cellar. "Lotsa niggers lived there," Roger told us as we stood by the river. It had been owned by a Baxter. The woman who brought the beers said they had put a microcassette recorder in the cellar and captured the sounds of ghosts. The machine, she said, recorded a little girl crying for her mama, music, a crackling fire, and someone walking up more steps than there were from the cellar. Roger volunteered that a former resident had slept with a 30.06 rifle under his pillow. "Hell," the short man with the big belly said, "that ain't gonna do no good against a ghost!" We all laughed, except for Roger, who, being a witch, just smiled his faint smile and told another story. There had been an old woman ghost in a house nearby. She scared the family so badly that they moved out in an instant, leaving all their furniture behind. Roger had asked his father, Was that really a ghost? His dad said, "Don't you pay that no mind. Dead ghosts ain't dangerous. It's the living ghosts that are dangerous."

We left the threesome to drink by the river and drove off. I was still curious about these escaped slaves. Why did people help them? Why, given that there were rewards for escapees, given that there were bounty hunters, known to everyone, in Vevay? Why, given that this was a place that had posted a NIGGER DON'T LET THE SUN GO DOWN ON YOU IN THIS TOWN sign at the town line up until the Truman administration, if not later? Roger's answer was quick: "I think they kinda felt sorry for them. You know, down South, sometimes they were mistreated."

And he told me the story of a pair of lovers across the river. Around the turn of the twentieth century, there lived a black man who would come down the river at night to the home of a young white woman from a prosperous family. He would stay the night with her, then slip out before light and return to his home. Someone happened to observe this, and one day a group of people went to the woman's house at night and captured the lovers. These people tied the pair together, and built a raft. After dawn, they stripped the couple naked, then covered them with hot tar. "They would have been hot," Roger said in his practical way, "all covered in that hot tar, out in the hot sun." The captors covered the sticky tar with feathers. The lovers "were screaming and hollering." The villagers put this couple on the raft, "and put them out in the river. They floated on down the river. And nobody ever saw them again. Never heard tell of 'em."

So they were together. My family, my family, thank you for telling me in time. This world is a howling wilderness, yes it is, and this world is our home. For all I know, those lovers were my cousins, too, and I would like to recognize them. So at night I went, fearful, down to the river that runs through our little Babylon, our small, intimate America, and hanged my clothes on the trees waving over the dark water. Where did the lovers go together? I walked into the water, swam out until the current pulled, and floated away to find them.

NOTES

ACKNOWLEDGMENTS

INDEX

■

NOTES

THIS BUSINESS OF ANGELS

3 Epigraph: Translated by John Felstiner in his *Paul Celan: Poet, Survivor, Jew* (New Haven, Conn.: Yale University Press, 1995), p. 278. The original is in Celan's *Gesammelte Werke*, eds. Beda Allemann and Stefan Reichert, with Rolf Bucher (Frankfurt, 1983), vol. 1, p. 227.

6 Oklahoma is an extreme: Russell Thornton, citing U.S. Department of the Interior and U.S. Bureau of the Census records, has the Cherokee population in Indian Territory around 1902 at 35,000, while the resident population in Cherokee territory alone in 1900 was 101,754; "the difference, of course, was primarily composed of nontribal whites and blacks." Russell Thornton, *The Cherokees: A Population History* (Lincoln: University of Nebraska Press, 1990), pp. 116–17.

7 The name Oklahoma: *Okla* for "people," *homma* or *humma* for "red." It was first applied to Indian Territory by the Choctaw chief Allen Wright in negotiating an 1866 Reconstruction treaty with the Chickasaws; Wright was at the time working toward an Indian state. Muriel H. Wright, *A Guide to the Indian Tribes of Oklahoma* (Norman: University of Oklahoma Press, 1986), p. 4; H. Wayne Morgan and Anne Hodges Morgan, *Oklahoma: A History* (New York: Norton, 1984), p. 35.

AN INDIAN COUNTRY

15 Dawes Commission: The initial allotment legislation was the Dawes Severalty Act of 1887. The Cherokees did not agree to allotment until 1899; even then, the process stalled, and only after a special election in 1902 did a majority of Cherokees agree to enroll with the U.S. gov-

ernment individually as Cherokees and accept allotment. See Wilma Mankiller and Michael Wallis, *Mankiller: A Chief and Her People* (New York: St. Martin's, 1993), pp. 133–38; Grace Steele Woodward, *The Cherokees* (Norman: University of Oklahoma Press, 1963), pp. 319–23 (which notes that "enrolling centers were jammed with white applicants"); Thornton, *Cherokees*, pp. 116–23.

15 "The head chief": Dawes was addressing the third Lake Mohonk Conference, an annual gathering of reformers at the upstate New York resort of Albert K. Smiley, a member of the Board of Indian Commissioners. The conference attendees were usually affiliated with the Indian Rights Association, a non-Indian group formed in 1882. Quoted in Janey B. Hendrix, "Redbird Smith and the Nighthawk Keetoowahs," *Journal of Cherokee Studies* 8, no. 1 (Spring 1983), p. 32.

18 Redbird Smith: The best single source on Redbird Smith and the Nighthawks is Hendrix, "Redbird Smith and the Nighthawk Keetoowahs," published consecutively in *Journal of Cherokee Studies* in the spring and fall of 1983. I have drawn on it extensively here.

"ALL THINGS IN ABOUNDANCE": COLONIAL AMERICA AS EDEN

21 Native tribes generally: Edmund S. Morgan, *American Slavery, American Freedom: The Ordeal of Colonial Virginia* (New York: Norton, 1975), pp. 54–55, citing several primary sources. Thomas Morton, *The New English Canaan* (about 1634), in Peter Force, ed., *Tracts and Other Papers, Relating Principally to the Origin, Settlement, and Progress of the Colonies in North America, from the Discovery of the Country to the Year 1776*, vol. 2 (Washington, D.C.: Peter Force, 1838), p. 37, wrote: "this custome of firing the Country is the meanes to make it passable, and by that meanes the trees growe here, and there as in our parks; and makes the country very beautifull, and commodious."

21–22 "Upon the banks": Abbott quoted in Katherine McKinstry Duncan and Larry Joe Smith, *The History of Marshall County, Alabama*, vol. 1: Prehistory to 1939 (Albertville, Ala.: Thompson, 1969), pp. 23–24.

22 The several million: Morgan, *American Slavery*, p. 7, citing Sherburne F. Cook and Woodrow Borah, *Essays in Population History: Mexico and the Caribbean*, vol. 1 (Berkeley: University of California Press, 1971), pp. 376–410.

22 The Spaniards and Portuguese: This was true from the beginning. Peter Martyr was an Italian at the Spanish court and commenced writing his account of New World exploration in 1493. His *Decades* (groups of ten letters), "published in at least nineteen editions and eight languages between 1504 and 1563, offered Europeans a well-informed running account of the discovery and other events of the New World," according to Benjamin Keen in the introduction to his translation of *The Life of the Admiral Christopher Columbus by His Son Ferdinand* (New Brunswick, N.J.: Rutgers University Press, 1992 [1959]), p. xxiii. In the first *Decade*, Martyr described Columbus and the Hispaniola colonists as already engaged in a race to the bottom by 1498. Writing to the king, unhappy colonists characterized Columbus and his brother as "unjust men, cruel enemies and shedders of the Spanish blood, declaring that upon every light occasion they would rack them, hang them, and head them, and that they took pleasure in this." Columbus replied that his accusers "were naughty fellows, abominable knaves and villains, thieves and bawds, ruffians adulterers and ravishers of women, false perjured vagabonds, and such as had been either convicts in prisons, or fled for fear of judgment . . . and so given to idleness and sleep, that whereas they were brought thither for miners, laborers, and scullions,

they would not now go one furlong from their houses except they were bore on men's backs . . . For, to this office, they put the miserable island men, whom they handled most cruelly. For lest their [the colonists'] hands should discontinue their shedding of blood, and the better to try their strength and manhood, they vied now and then for their pastime to strive among themselves and prove who could most cleanly with his sword at one stroke strike the head of an innocent." I have adapted the translation of Richard Eden in his compilation *The First Three English Books on America* (1555), the Kraus reprint (New York, 1971) of an 1885 Birmingham edition edited by Edward Arber, p. 91.

22 "The most disturbing": Robin Blackburn, *The Making of New World Slavery: From the Baroque to the Modern, 1492–1800* (London: Verso, 1997), pp. 12–13.

23 "reputation and honor": Pedro de Castañeda, *The Narrative of the Expedition of Coronado* (c. 1562), excerpted in Giles Gunn, ed., *Early American Writing* (New York: Penguin, 1994), pp. 48–49.

23–24 "This sentiment roused" and "Conferring": Álvar Núñez Cabeza de Vaca, *Cabeza de Vaca's Adventures in the Unknown Interior of America*, trans. Cyclone Covey (New York: Collier, 1961), p. 128; "And to think" and "to the last": Cabeza de Vaca, *Adventures*, p. 127.

24–25 "One of the marvellous": Adapted from Eden, *First Three English Books on America*. López de Gómara seems nearly addled by the human possibilities, as when he notes of Caribbean natives that they "are altogether in general either purple, or tawny like unto sodde quinces, or of the color of chestnuts or olives, which color is to them natural and not by their going naked as many have thought, albeit their nakedness has somewhat helped them thereunto." The editor of this 1885 edition of Eden, Edward Arber, unfortunately substituted his own judgment for that of López de Gómara: "The future of Mankind lies with the Anglo-Saxon race: and of all English books relating to the American portion of that race, the three reprinted in this volume are the very *first*" (p. vi).

25–26 The earliest multiracial: My account of Drake and the Cimarrons is largely based on that of Morgan, *American Slavery*, chs. 1 and 2. Morgan relies on Irene A. Wright's collection of Spanish archival sources, *Documents concerning English Voyages to the Spanish Main, 1569–1580* (London: Hakluyt Society, 1932); David B. Quinn, *The Roanoke Voyages, 1584–1590* (London: Hakluyt Society, 1955); and E. G. R. Taylor, ed., *The Original Writings and Correspondence of the Two Richard Hakluyts* (London: Hakluyt Society, 1935). See also Kenneth Andrews, *Trade, Plunder, and Settlement: Maritime Enterprise and the Genesis of the British Empire* (Cambridge, U.K.: Cambridge University Press, 1984), pp. 131–52.

26 "This league": Andrews, *Trade, Plunder, and Settlement*, p. 132.

26 One English sailor: He was Miles Phillips. People of African descent were common in New Spain. In 1570 blacks and mulattoes were about equal in number to Europeans, criollos, and mestizos combined. The first blacks to reach California's San Francisco Bay came with Drake in 1579. In 1636 over half the population of Lima, Peru, the Spanish viceroyal capital, was of African descent to some degree. See Quintard Taylor, *In Search of the Racial Frontier: African Americans in the American West, 1528–1990* (New York: Norton, 1998), pp. 27–37 and 320 n. 11. On Lima, see Blackburn, *Making of New World Slavery*, p. 143.

27–28 Upon Drake's arrival: Lane's previous relevant experience had been in Ireland. There is a substantial literature on the importance of the conquest of Ireland in shaping English racial attitudes and policies. Theodore Allen has explored this literature in great, revealing detail in *The Invention of the White Race*, vol. 1: *Racial Oppression and Social Control* (London: Verso, 1993).

29 "so as it was" and "drawne away": William Bradford, *History of Plymouth Plantation* (Boston:

Massachusetts Historical Society, 1856 [1630–1651]), ed. Charles Deane, pp. 23, 24–25. I
have modified, here and elsewhere, the more potentially misleading spellings.

29 "the Lord": John Winthrop, *A Modell of Christian Charity* (1630), in *Winthrop Papers* (Boston:
Massachusetts Historical Society, 1931), pp. 294–95.

29–30 "may carrie a greater spite" and "ye salvage people": Bradford, *History of Plymouth Plantation*, pp. 385, 25.

30 "this Morton": Bradford, *History of Plymouth Plantation*, pp. 236–37. On Morton, Indian
images, Puritan fears, and much else, see Karen Ordahl Kupperman's extraordinary work *Settling with the Indians: The Meeting of English and Indian Cultures in America, 1580–1640*
(Totowa, N.J.: Rowman and Littlefield, 1980).

31 "drinking": Bradford, *History of Plymouth Plantation*, pp. 236–37. Bradford dwells on how
Morton's crew were "quaffing and drinking both wine and strong waters in great excess" (p.
237). He also, more importantly, notes that Morton had begun teaching the Indians all about
guns. Bradford regarded this as a very serious danger and implied that other Europeans were
likewise instructing Indians (p. 238). The control of firearms, and of knowledge concerning their
use and repair, was of course critical to the early organized colonists' competitive advantage.

31 "The more I looked," "lusty trees," and "dainty fine round rising hillucks": Morton, *New English Canaan*, pp. 41–42; "make a great show" and "For in a place": Morton, pp. 97, 18. Morton
asserts his loyalties early in the book: "In the yeare since the incarnation of Christ, 1622, it was
my chance to be landed in the parts of New England, where I found two sorts of people, the
one Christians, the other Infidels, these I found most full of humanity, and more friendly than
the other" (p. 15).

31 "Wotowequenage": Morton, *New English Canaan*, p. 76; see Alfred A. Cave, *The Pequot War*
(Amherst: University of Massachusetts Press, 1996), pp. 46–48.

32 "The setting up" and "A conclusion was made": Morton, *New English Canaan*, pp. 90, 97.

32–33 European arrival vastly expanded: Francis Jennings's *The Invasion of America: Indians,
Colonialism, and the Cant of Conquest* (New York: Norton, 1976) handsomely lays out the
reciprocal quality of Indian-European trade and development, while never losing sight of
power imbalances. On the fur and textile trades, see ch. 6; on agriculture and hunting, see pp.
61–72; on infrastructure, see esp. pp. 173–74; on medicine, see p. 52, based on Virgil J. Vogel,
American Indian Medicine (Norman: University of Oklahoma Press, 1970); on guns and gun
repair, see p. 40. The South Carolina deerskin export figures are from William G. McLoughlin, *Cherokee Renascence in the New Republic* (Princeton, N.J.: Princeton University Press,
1986), p. 5. McLoughlin discusses changes to the Cherokee diet on p. 6.

36 "The ends of": Jennings, *Invasion of America*, p. 76.

36 The Ottoman conquest: Captain John Smith of Jamestown had fought the Ottomans before he
came to Virginia.

36–37 "There is scarce": The three quotations concerning the uses of Indians are in Morgan,
American Slavery, pp. 99–100; Purchas is quoted in Jennings, *Invasion of America*, p. 78.

37 Some English: See James Axtell, "The White Indians of Colonial America," *William and
Mary Quarterly*, 3rd ser., no. 32 (1975), pp. 55–88.

37–38 "also my Indians": Winthrop's will is mentioned in Alison Wheeler Lauber, *Indian Slavery
in Colonial Times within the Present Limits of the United States* (Williamstown, Mass.: Corner
House, 1979), p. 216. Lauber also notes on that page "a bill of sale of an Indian man, given by
Governor John Winthrop of Massachusetts to John Mainford of Barbadoes," citing *Massachusetts Historical Society Collections*, ser. 3, vol. 1, p. 27. On Indians selling other Indians, and
the Cherokee chiefs' complaint, see Woodward, *Cherokees*, pp. 58–59, and McLoughlin,
Cherokee Renascence, p. 16. On slavery in Cherokee society before European arrival and in

early-colonial times, see Theda Perdue, *Slavery and the Evolution of Cherokee Society, 1540–1866* (Knoxville: University of Tennessee Press, 1979), pp. 11–33.

38 Carolina slavery-regulation act: On judicial and legislative moves to define Indians as black, and the extreme muddiness of these and other racial terms in the early English colonies, see Jack D. Forbes's brilliant study *Africans and Native Americans: The Language of Race and the Evolution of Red-Black Peoples*, 2nd ed. (Urbana: University of Illinois Press, 1993), pp. 190–264. Forbes's book is filled with such revealing phrases as that of a 1719 South Carolina act: "all such slaves as are not entirely Indian shall be accounted as negroe" (p. 223). The 1712 Carolina phrase is mentioned, among many similar colonial usages, some even earlier, in Forbes, pp. 211–18.

"A NEW KIND OF DISORDER": A CHEROKEE UTOPIA AND
THE RISE OF RACIAL SEPARATISM

39 A sober spiritual cousin: My account of Priber draws mainly on Rennard Strickland, "Christian Gotelieb Priber: Utopian Precursor of the Cherokee Government," *Chronicles of Oklahoma* 48, no. 3 (1970), pp. 264–79; Verner Crane, "A Lost Utopia of the First American Frontier," *Sewanee Review Quarterly* 27 (1919), pp. 48–61; James Adair, *Adair's History of the American Indians*, ed. Samuel Cole Williams (Johnson City, Tenn.: Watauga Press, 1930) in the National Society of the Colonial Dames of America, in Tennessee, reprint of 1953, pp. 252–57; Ludovic Grant, "Historical Relation by Indian Trader Ludovic Grant," *South Carolina Historical and Genealogical Magazine* 10, no. 1 (1909), pp. 54–65.

39 "About Seven": "Colonel Chicken's Journal," in Newton B. Mereness, ed., *Travels in the North American Colonies* (New York: Macmillan, 1916), p. 141.

40 Sir Alexander Cuming: The Cuming information is in a note to Grant, "Historical Relation," pp. 54–55. Grant emphasized, "I was there present the whole time and am positive that there was not the least word spoke about surrendering any lands" (p. 57).

40 "This was a Day": Cuming's journal is quoted in Woodward, *Cherokees*, pp. 63–65; the remark about "our own pleasure" was made by Attakullaculla, the Little Carpenter, in an interview with the governor of South Carolina appended to Grant, "Historical Relation," pp. 65–68. Attakullaculla emphasized that the agreement with King George concerned military alliance (it also covered trade relations) and in no way ceded Cherokee land to Britain — "nor had we power to agree to any such proposal."

40 "We look upon": Woodward, *Cherokees*, pp. 66–67.

41–43 Antoine Bonnefoy: Bonnefoy's story is from "Journal of Antoine Bonnefoy, 1741–1742," in Mereness, ed., *Travels in the North American Colonies*, pp. 239–55.

42 Jean-Jacques Rousseau: Crane, "Lost Utopia," pp. 53–54.

43 French America: The relative strengths and weaknesses of the English and French are lucidly discussed in a 1754 letter from Edmond Atkin to the lords commissioners for trade and plantations, reprinted in Wilbur R. Jacobs, ed., *Indians of the Southern Colonial Frontier: The Edmond Atkin Report and Plan of 1755* (Columbia: University of South Carolina Press, 1954). The report is on pp. 3–74. Interestingly, Atkin believed that in "all ruptures of consequence between the Indians and the white people . . . the latter were first the aggressors; the Indians were driven thereto [i.e., to violence] under oppressions and abuses, and to vindicate their natural rights." He then gave several examples, beginning with the burning of an Indian town in Virginia in 1585. Atkin's letter reached London in the course of the French and Indian War. "The importance of Indians is now generally known and understood," Atkin wrote. "[A] doubt

remains not, that the prosperity of our colonies on the continent, will stand or fall with our interest and favor among them." This opinion was shared by a young George Washington, who was, of course, still English at the time. See Woodward, *Cherokees*, pp. 69–70.

44 "man of ill principles": Letter from Colonel William Bull, dated October 5, 1739. "Cherokee Documents in Foreign Archives," Museum of the Cherokee Indian Archives, Cherokee, N.C., microfilm no. 165.

46 "whatsoever English": Cited in Blackburn, *Making of New World Slavery*, pp. 264–65.

46 regulating *whites*: The creation of the not-white is a fundamental concern of Morgan in *American Slavery* and Forbes in *Africans and Native Americans*, as well as of Lerone Bennett, Jr., in *Before the* Mayflower: *A History of Black America* (New York: Penguin, 1988 [1961]). For the American colonial period, in terms of secondary sources, I have relied mainly on Morgan; Winthrop Jordan, *White over Black: American Attitudes toward the Negro, 1550–1812* (Chapel Hill: University of North Carolina Press, 1968); and Jennings, *Invasion of America*.

46 Fernão Mendes Pinto: "I had the misfortune to be purchased by a Greek renegade, whom I shall curse as long as I live," wrote Mendes Pinto. "He used me so badly that during the three months I was his slave there were at least six or seven times when I nearly took my life with poison . . . At the end of three months, thanks be to God, some of his neighbors warned him that he was running the risk of losing all the money he had invested in me, a possibility that frightened him into trading me for about twelve thousand *reis* worth of dates to a Jew by the name of Abraham Mussa . . ." Fernão Mendes Pinto, *The Travels of Fernão Mendes Pinto*, trans. and ed. Rebecca D. Catz (Chicago: University of Chicago Press, 1989), p. 11.

47 "the right of birth": John Milton, *The Tenure of Kings and Magistrates* (1649), in Merritt Y. Hughes, ed., *John Milton: Prose Selections* (New York: Odyssey, 1947), p. 319. Milton uses similar imagery in *The Ready and Easy Way to Establish a Free Commonwealth* (1660), in the same prose collection, pp. 364 and 369. In *Tenure*, published within weeks of the execution of King Charles I, Milton wrote "that to say, as is usual, the king hath as good right to his crown and dignity as any man to his inheritance, is to make the subject no better than the king's slave, his chattel, or his possession that may be bought and sold" (p. 281). I want to emphasize that English Puritan thought placed slavery within debates on the relation of the subject, through Parliament, to the king, as well as of the landless to the propertied. This helps us understand why a refusal of slavery was such a feature of colonizers' struggles with colonial masters, and later of the American colonists' revolt against their king. These English Puritan arguments preceded large-scale racial slavery in the colonies and had very little relation to it. See A. S. P. Woodhouse, *Puritanism and Liberty: Being the Army Debates (1647–9) from the Clarke Manuscripts with Supplementary Documents* (Chicago: University of Chicago Press, 1951). These fascinating debates present non-theologically inclined Puritans arguing with each other about Puritanism. They show that, for these men, *liberty* could be defined as "social power or standing" and was sometimes used as a synonym for *property*. That is, property represented not only land and/or wealth but also the social personhood these conveyed to an individual—so much so that the debaters sometimes used *property* to express that power later Englishmen would express as the right to vote. When Puritans (and others) tried to articulate the opposite of property or personhood, the word they often used was *slavery*. The language was not entirely adequate to its tasks. For example, within it, to acquire "liberty" might well mean to take someone else's "property." As one debater said, "Sir, I see that it is impossible to have liberty but all property must be taken away . . . But I would fain know what the [Puritan] soldier hath fought for all this while? He hath fought to enslave himself, to give power to men of riches, men of estates, to make him a perpetual slave" (p. 71).

47 Alexander Whitaker: In Gunn, ed., *Early American Writing*, p. 105.

48 "Every freeman": Locke was persuaded to be secretary to the lords proprietors of Carolina by

his friend Anthony Ashley Cooper (later Lord Shaftesbury) in 1668; the constitution was drafted in 1669. Locke was not its sole author, but he did influence its design. See Maurice Cranston, *John Locke: A Biography* (London: Longmans, Green, 1957), pp. 119–20. In 1671 Locke was made a "landgrave" in the proposed aristocracy of Carolina—a hereditary title—and given four thousand "baronia" of land. The constitution never took effect, and neither did the aristocracy. Locke appears to have earned no money from "his" American land. Cranston, *John Locke*, p. 120. However, he had, for example, four hundred pounds sterling in the Royal African Company in 1674, two hundred more the next year. One hundred pounds in the Bahama Adventurers in 1675 brought twenty-seven pounds ten shillings profit in 1676. Cranston, *John Locke*, p. 115. The figure of 372 meetings and the quote from the Carolina Constitution are in Blackburn, *Making of New World Slavery*, pp. 264, 275. The Council of Trade and Plantations was an information-gathering body, and its secretary the most important member. The council promoted in particular the Southern and Caribbean slaveholding colonies, because, unlike New England, they did not, and were strongly encouraged not to, compete with English raw goods and manufactures. At the Board of Commissioners for Trade, Locke took a strong interest in Virginia. He helped prepare a lengthy report on that colony and, among other activities, engineered the appointment of Francis Nicholson to replace Edmund Andros as governor there. Locke counted several American governors among his circle. Cranston, *John Locke*, pp. 153–55 (on the council), 420–27 (on the board).

48 "Lives, liberties": John Locke, *Two Treatises on Government* (1690), in the version edited by Peter Laslett (Cambridge, U.K.: Cambridge University Press, 1960), p. 123. In summarizing Locke's thought, I am indebted to Michael P. Zuckert's subtle and measured analysis in *Natural Rights and the New Republicanism* (Princeton, N.J.: Princeton University Press, 1994), especially chs. 8 and 9.

48 healthy English beggars: Cranston, *John Locke*, pp. 424–25. Additionally, writes Cranston, "Methods were suggested for 'taking away the pretence' that there was no work for the idle to do. First, guardians should have power to put the idle to work with private employers for less than the usual rate of pay . . . Secondly, pauper schools should be set up in every parish to enable both mothers and children to work productively. As an economical diet for the pauper children, Locke suggested that they should have their 'bellyful of bread daily . . . and to this may also be added, without any trouble, in cold weather, if it be thought needful, a little warm-water gruel; for the same fire that warms the room may be made use of to boil a pot of it' " (p. 425).

49 "a king": Locke, *Two Treatises*, pp. 41–42. Locke's ideas on property, in the context of Indian–non-Indian relations, appear in an American text as early as 1724. Zuckert, *Natural Rights*, p. 21.

49 "the state of war": Locke, *Two Treatises*, p. 24.

49 "Whenever he finds": Locke, *Two Treatises*, p. 23. Zuckert (among others) sees Locke's discussion of slavery as central to his philosophy, in particular his movement from God as owner of the human self to "self-ownership." There was a tradition at work here, parallel to that of English Puritanism (and of the broader world of Calvinist Puritanism) but more secular in spirit, which wrestled with slavery. Hugo Grotius, who laid the basis for modern international law in *De Jure Belli ac Pacis* (1625), wrote: "To every man it is permitted to enslave himself to any one he pleases for private ownership, as is evident from both the Hebraic and the Roman law. Why, then, would it not be permitted to a people having legal competence to submit itself to some one person, or to several persons, in such a way as plainly to transfer to him the rights to govern, retaining no vestige of that right for itself?" The idea of people deciding to be slaves remained current enough later in the century for Gilbert Burnet to write, in his "Enquiry into the Measures of Submission to the Supream Authority" (1689): "As a private person can bind himself to

another man's service . . . or by a total giving himself up to another, as in the case of slavery . . . so likewise bodies of men can give themselves upon different degrees to the conduct of others," such as kings. See Zuckert, *Natural Rights*, pp. 110–11. In short, slavery as a social status was among the richest, and most common, concepts in seventeenth-century political debate, both in more and less secular circles. The extent to which such writings influenced Americans has been much debated. To my mind, Zuckert's argument for significant influence is fair and convincing (*Natural Rights*, pp. 18–25, 297–305). For a nuanced, brief summary of the continuity of slavery language into the Revolutionary years—and a powerful argument that the secular and religious could not really be separated, at least among Americans considering slavery—see Barry Alan Shain, *The Myth of American Individualism: The Protestant Origins of American Political Thought* (Princeton, N.J.: Princeton University Press, 1994), ch. 8.

50 "many threw themselves": McLoughlin, *Cherokee Renascence*, pp. 17–31.

50–51 "No nation was ever infested" and "an Ishmaelitish period": Woodward, *Cherokees*, pp. 83–85; "we have now the pleasure": Alvin M. Josephy, Jr., *500 Nations: An Illustrated History of North American Indians* (New York: Knopf, 1994), p. 249. Lieutenant Francis Marion wrote of a 1761 action, "We proceeded, by Colonel Grant's orders, to burn the Indian cabins. Some of the men seemed to enjoy this cruel work, laughing heartily at the curling flames, but to me it appeared a shocking sight. Poor creatures, thought I, we surely need not grudge you such miserable habitations . . . Thus, for cursed mammon's sake, the followers of Christ have sowed the selfish tares of hate in the bosoms of even Pagan children." John P. Brown, *Old Frontiers* (Kingsport, Tenn.: Southern Publishers, 1938), p. 111.

51–53 "It is a little": Corn Tassel (or Old Tassel), "Cherokee Reply to the Commissioners of North Carolina and Virginia, 1777," *Journal of Cherokee Studies* 1, no. 2 (Fall 1976), pp. 128–29, reprinting from *Tennessee Historical Magazine* 7, no. 2 (July 1921). The speech was translated and written down by William Tatum. Corn Tassel was murdered by whites in 1788.

53 Skiagunsta: McLoughlin, *Cherokee Renascence*, p. 6.

54 "a devout and zealous": The missionary was David Brainerd. Gregory Evans Dowd, *A Spirited Resistance: The North American Indian Struggle for Unity, 1745–1815* (Baltimore: Johns Hopkins University Press, 1992), p. 29. I have relied mainly on Dowd's account of emerging Indian racial identity in what follows.

56–57 a seer arose: The description of Tenskwatawa is from R. David Edmunds, *Tecumseh and the Quest for Indian Leadership* (Boston: Little, Brown, 1984), pp. 74–85; Josephy, *500 Nations*, 304–14.

57 By the middle of 1806: The Harrison story and quotes from Tecumseh are in Josephy, *500 Nations*, pp. 307–13. The secretary of war's 1805 memo is in McLoughlin, *Cherokee Renascence* (p. 97), which also has the Cherokee visions, pp. 168, 176–85, to be supplemented by Dowd, *Spirited Resistance*, pp. 174–79.

58–59 Tecumseh turned to war: On the Creek War, see McLoughlin, *Cherokee Renascence*, pp. 186–205; on population figures, the disintegration of Pan-Indianism, and the uses of Tecumseh, see Dowd, *Spirited Resistance*, pp. xiv–xv, 181–90, 190–201; Josephy, *500 Nations*, pp. 314–17 (the sculpture, by Ferdinand Pettrich, is shown on p. 316). For a general account of Tecumseh and the Prophet, see John Sugden, *Tecumseh: A Life* (New York: Henry Holt, 1997). Sugden discusses the metamorphoses of Tecumseh in historical memory on pp. 388–401.

60 Linguistic borrowing: For Indian words, see Charles L. Cutler, *O Brave New Words!: Native American Loanwords in Current English* (Norman: University of Oklahoma Press, 1994). The rate of borrowings is charted on p. 2

60 "notwithstanding the obloquy": Washington Irving, "Traits of Indian Character," *The Sketch Book of Geoffrey Crayon, Gent.* (New York: Signet Classics, 1981 [1819–1820]), pp. 280, 282.

61 "is either an European": J. Hector St. John de Crèvecoeur, *Letters from an American Farmer* (1782), in Gunn, ed., *Early American Writing*, pp. 476, 479.

61–62 The notion: William Byrd, *Histories of the Dividing Line betwixt Virginia and North Carolina*, excerpted in *The Annals of America*, vol. 1: *1493–1754, Discovering a New World* (Chicago: Encyclopedia Britannica, 1968), p. 383; "you will mix" (Jefferson) and Washington's Indian policy: McLoughlin, *Cherokee Renascence*, pp. 34–37; "They would have mixed": Jefferson quoted in Jordan, *White over Black*, p. 480.

62–63 *Hobomok*: This is the argument of Priscilla Wald in her "Terms of Assimilation: Legislating Subjectivity in the Emerging Nation," in Amy Kaplan and Donald E. Pease, eds., *Cultures of United States Imperialism* (Durham, N.C.: Duke University Press, 1993), pp. 68–70.

63–64 *The Pioneers*: The denouement of the story, from Chingachgook's death through the hero's being revealed as Indian only by adoption ("I have no other Indian blood or breeding") and the graveside meditation, are on pp. 381–436, *The Pioneers; or, The Sources of the Susquehanna; A Descriptive Tale* (New York: New American Library, 1980 [1823]). The legal question of land tenure is central to the plot and remarkably specific, as in this exchange between the hero and a Mr. Jones (p. 226): "Said he nothing of the Indian rights, sir? The Leatherstocking is much given to impeach the justice of the tenure by which the whites hold the country."

"I remember that he spoke of them, but I did not clearly comprehend him and may have forgotten what he said; for the Indian title was extinguished . . . and no court in the country can affect my title."

As he prepares to die, Chingachgook argues (against a white woman) that the land was taken unjustly. He also rejects Christian deliverance, despite her urgings. When Leatherstocking arrives, Chingachgook can already glimpse heaven: "I look—but I see no white skins" (p. 401). I have in most respects followed here the argument of Eric Cheyfitz on *The Pioneers* in "Savage Law: The Plot against American Indians in *Johnson and Graham's Lessee v. M'Intosh* and *The Pioneers*," Kaplan and Pease, eds., *Cultures of United States Imperialism*, pp. 118–26. The extent to which Cooper was taken seriously as a scientist of white-Indian relations may be questioned. Writing in the *North American Review* of July 1895, Mark Twain expressed his doubts: "Cooper's gift in the way of invention was not a rich endowment; but such as it was he liked to work it . . . In his little box of stage properties he kept six or eight cunning devices, tricks, artifices for his savages and woodsmen to deceive and circumvent each other with, and he was never so happy as when he was working these innocent things and seeing them go. A favorite one was to make a moccasined person tread in the tracks of his moccasined enemy, and thus hide his own trail. Cooper wore out barrels and barrels of moccasins in working that trick." "Fenimore Cooper's Literary Offences," in Mark Twain, *Tales, Speeches, Essays, and Sketches*, ed. Tom Quirk (New York: Penguin, 1994), pp. 379–80.

64 "The new and old members": *Johnson and Graham's Lessee v. M'Intosh*, 8 Wheat 543, 572–92 (1823), in H. L. Pohlman, ed., *Political Thought and the American Judiciary* (Amherst: University of Massachusetts Press, 1993), pp. 16–20.

64–65 "ambition and lust" and succeeding quotes: Joseph Story, "History and Influence of the Puritans" (1828), in Pohlman, ed., *Political Thought*, pp. 20–24.

"WELCOME, NEGRO, WELCOME": THE INDIAN AS SLAVE AND SLAVEHOLDER

66 Elias Boudinot: My main sources for the Boudinot story are McLoughlin, *Cherokee Renascence*, pp. 366–451; Theda Perdue, ed., *Cherokee Editor: The Writings of Elias Boudinot* (Athens: University of Georgia Press, 1983 [1966]); John Ehle, *Trail of Tears: The Rise and Fall*

of the Cherokee Nation (New York: Anchor Books/Doubleday, 1989); Edward Everett Dale and Gaston Litton, eds., *Cherokee Cavaliers: Forty Years of Cherokee History as Told in the Correspondence of the Ridge-Watie-Boudinot Family* (Norman: University of Oklahoma Press, 1995 [1939]); Ralph H. Gabriel, *Elias Boudinot, Cherokee, and His America* (Norman: University of Oklahoma Press, 1941); Thurman Wilkins, *Cherokee Tragedy: The Story of the Ridge Family and the Decimation of a People* (New York: Macmillan, 1970). Gabriel and Wilkins are the best sources for Boudinot's early years, though they should be supplemented by Andrew Wiget, "Elias Boudinot, Elisha Bates, and *Poor Sarah*: Frontier Protestantism and the Emergence of the First Native American Fiction," *Journal of Cherokee Studies* 8, no. 1 (Spring 1983), pp. 4–21, which makes excellent use of Moravian sources. For Boudinot's later years, after he became editor of the *Cherokee Phoenix*, Perdue provides clear introductory texts and careful notes.

67 19,000 head of cattle: Cherokee material advances are concisely presented in William G. McLoughlin, "Who Civilized the Cherokees?" *Journal of Cherokee Studies* 13 (1988), pp. 55–81. For demographic changes, see Thornton, *Cherokees*, ch. 3.

67–68 "the adult real Indian": Quoted in McLoughlin, *Cherokee Renascence*, pp. 70–71, 213; Meigs's (and the U.S. government's) about-face is in the same source, ch. 6.

68–69 "in agriculture & domestic": Ehle, *Trail of Tears*, pp. 83–84; "deturmed to move": McLoughlin, *Cherokee Renascence*, p. 149.

70–71 an evening in New Jersey: Biographical information for the white Boudinot is from *Dictionary of American Biography* (New York: Scribners, 1964), vol. 2, pp. 477–78; Elias Boudinot, *A Star in the West; or, A Humble Attempt to Discover the Long Lost Ten Tribes of Israel, Preparatory to Their Return to Their Beloved City, Jerusalem* (Freeport, N.Y.: Books for Libraries Press, 1970 [1816]), pp. i–v. James Adair, among others, also toyed with the Israel-Cherokee connection.

72 "becoming like the white people": Calhoun was then secretary of war. Ehle, *Trail of Tears*, p. 156.

72–73 a short story: I am citing the version of "Poor Sarah" printed with Legh Richmond, *The Officer's Servant: An Authentic Narrative* (Philadelphia: Perkinpine & Higgins, 1864[?]); the publication history for "Poor Sarah" and some important biographical details for Boudinot are in Wiget, "Elias Boudinot."

72 "Oh, what a lesson" and "Then I kneel down": Richmond, *Officer's Servant*, pp. 13, 46.

75 "the smoke of their torment": Harriet Gold may have borrowed this image from Revelation 9:2.

76 material prosperity: The material and demographic changes are in McLoughlin, "Who Civilized the Cherokees?" p. 61; the evolution of Cherokee racial laws may be traced in Perdue, *Slavery and the Evolution of Cherokee Society*; Tennessee governor Joseph McMinn's remark of 1816 and Georgia governor George Troup's similar assertion from 1824 about Indians being "of color" are in McLoughlin, *Cherokee Renascence*, pp. 212, 273. On the categorization of Indians as free people of color, see Forbes, *Africans and Native Americans*, pp. 250–64. On the vogue for re-enslavement, see Ira Berlin, *Slaves without Masters: The Free Negro in the Antebellum South* (New York: New Press, 1992 [1974]), ch. 11, and Kenneth M. Stampp, *The Peculiar Institution: Slavery in the Ante-Bellum South* (New York: Vintage, 1989 [1956]), pp. 215–17. At the same time, in Southern courts Indian blood was generally understood as closer to white blood than was Negro blood. See Ariela J. Gross's article "Litigating Whiteness: Trials of Racial Determination in the Nineteenth-Century South," *Yale Law Journal* 108, no. 1 (1998), pp. 109–88, esp. pp. 141–42. (Gross's footnotes are a remarkable resource in themselves for twentieth-century race literature.) The 1840s and 1850s saw enormous pressure placed on the concept of free person of color. The number of such people was increasing in both slavery and freedom. "During the decade of the 1850s slavery was becoming whiter, visi-

bly so and with amazing rapidity. White people were enslaving themselves, as it were, in the form of their children and their children's children. While black slavery increased in numbers only 19.8 percent in the decade, mulatto slavery rose by an astounding 66.9 percent." Joel Williamson, *New People: Miscegenation and Mulattoes in the United States* (Baton Rouge: Louisiana State University Press, 1995), p. 63. Meanwhile, about a fifth of Petersburg, Virginia, free blacks owned slaves as early as 1830; Frederick Law Olmsted, traveling in 1853–1854, noted of Richmond free blacks, "About one quarter seemed to me to have lost all distinguishing African peculiarity of feature, and to have acquired, in place of it, a good deal of that voluptuousness of expression which characterized many of the women of the South of Europe." Writers' Program of the Works Progress Administration in the State of Virginia, *The Negro in Virginia* (Winston-Salem, N.C.: John F. Blair, 1994 [1940]), pp. 136 and 132, respectively. The WPA volume includes the lively story (pp. 185–86) of a light slave with a dark master who sold his master. The hardening of racial distinctions in these decades has to be understood in the context of the visible breakdown of those same distinctions.

76–77 integration into U.S. society: For courts and the federal government a crucial distinction was made between Indians not taxed and other Indians. Essentially, untaxed Indians were those who retained a tribal or national identity, which was almost always tied to such groups' control of land. When Indians (as individuals or groups) lost land, they entered the general American racial system of classification, becoming white, Negro, free colored, or, least often, Indian. To lose land, then, meant in most cases to become second-class citizens. For Indians in this period "becoming Negro" was not a threat so much as a likely destiny if tribal independence, based on sovereignty over land, were lost. Indian defenses of land title were not, by any means, only defenses of title; nor were they, as we will see, only, or even necessarily, defenses of Indianness.

77–78 "An Address to the Whites": All quotations of Boudinot are from Perdue, ed., *Cherokee Editor.*

79 voter suffrage: On the expansion of the electorate, see Alan Brinkley, *The Unfinished Nation: A Concise History of the American People*, 2nd ed. (New York: Knopf, 1997), pp. 236–37; on the composition of Jackson's Democratic base, see Alexander Saxton, *The Rise and Fall of the White Republic: Class Politics and Mass Culture in Nineteenth-Century America* (London: Verso, 1990), ch. 6; on Benton, see Reginald Horsman, *Race and Manifest Destiny: The Origins of American Racial Anglo-Saxonism* (Cambridge, Mass.: Harvard University Press, 1981), pp. 89–92, and Thomas Hart Benton, *Thirty Years' View* (New York: D. Appleton, 1858).

80 "have retained their savage": Andrew Jackson, "First Annual Address to Congress," in James D. Richardson, comp., *Messages and Papers of the Presidents*, vol. 3 (New York: Bureau of National Literature, 1897), pp. 1020–21.

81 "To follow to the tomb": Jackson, "Second Annual Address to Congress," in Richardson, comp., *Messages and Papers*, vol. 3, pp. 1083–84.

82 Andrew Jackson was born: The biographical facts for Jackson are in the introductions and chronology provided in the first five volumes of *The Papers of Andrew Jackson*, an ongoing project under various editors (Knoxville: University of Tennessee Press, 1980–). This is also the source for the sale of Nancy (vol. 1, p. 432, app. 3), the remark on Indians and treaties (vol. 1, p. 40, letter to John McKee, 1793), fear being better than love (vol. 2, p. 305, letter to Willie Blount, 1812), and the desirability of frequently whipping Betty (vol. 5, p. 66, letter to James Craine Brunaugh, 1821).

83 "To better their condition": Jackson, "Second Annual Address to Congress," pp. 1083–84.

84 Jackson greatly feared: On the secession issue, see Ronald N. Satz, *American Indian Policy in*

the Jacksonian Era (Lincoln: University of Nebraska Press, 1975), pp. 1–12, 47–53; also Edwin A. Miles, "After John Marshall's Decision: *Worcester v. Georgia* and the Nullification Crisis," *Journal of Southern History* 39 (1973), pp. 519–44.

86 Ross negotiated: The elite desire to assimilate has, in hindsight, often been attributed to Boudinot, the Ridges, and their allies, with the Ross side standing more for cultural autonomy. However, on this question the elite was not particularly divided; the later factional split was much more political than ideological. For example, John Ross, Major Ridge, and two other chiefs wrote to President James Monroe in 1824: "The ignorant and wretched condition of your red children makes them in some degree inferior to their white brethren, but as a Parent, you have not despised them on account of their unfortunate situation . . . The liberal encouragement given by the nation for general improvement, cannot fail to accomplish their complete civilization. True, there are many who have been raised under the native habits of their ancestors, who cannot be expected to abandon wholly the favorite customs which have been imbibed in their youth, their partiality and prejudices in favor of their Fathers are naturally strong, but under the present aspect of improvement, they will not fail to encourage their children to adopt the prevailing habits of industry and civilizations; therefore as the old stubbles disappear, the new sprouts will flourish under cultivation." Gary E. Moulton, ed., *The Papers of Chief John Ross* (Norman: University of Oklahoma Press, 1985), vol. 1 (1807–1839), p. 59. The letter to Adams is in the same source, pp. 104–5. The Mexico proposal is in *Papers*, vol. 1, p. 330 (letter to Friedrich Ludwig von Roenne) and pp. 334–36 (letter to Joaquín María de Castillo y Lanzas, the Mexican chargé d'affaires). In the latter Ross wrote, "it does appear to me, that the Cherokees will be compelled by the force of circumstances to remove from *the land of their Fathers* and to seek a home elsewhere . . . [T]he Cherokee people never can reconcile it to their own feelings ever to reestablish themselves in any country where they would be exposed to a similar treatment in future, consequently they would at once remove out of the limits of the United States . . . [S]uch tribes of Indians who may find an asylum within the bosom of your Govt. would no doubt prove themselves to be worthy of your confidence and protection by their peaceful demeanor, as well as patriotic loyalty to the interest & welfare of the Mexican Govt." The negotiations with Washington over removal are in, for example, *Papers*, vol. 1, pp. 331–32 (letter to Lewis Cass, March 6, 1835). Also see Gary E. Moulton, *John Ross, Cherokee Chief* (Athens: University of Georgia Press, 1973), pp. 60–63.

88 committee of assassins: See Grant Foreman, "The Murder of Elias Boudinot," *Chronicles of Oklahoma* 12 (March 1934), pp. 19–24.

88 "Several persons" and "I think there": Dale and Litton, eds., *Cherokee Cavaliers*, pp. 30, 32–33.

88–89 "The traveler": The Lewis Ross figures and the remarks of the trader (Josiah Gregg) are in Perdue, *Slavery and the Evolution of Cherokee Society*, p. 72. The following discussion of the role of slavery after removal, and of the evolution of Cherokee racial laws, is based on Perdue's fifth chapter, "Post-Removal Chaos," pp. 70–95.

90 "They was always": Morris Sheppard, interviewed in T. Lindsay Baker and Julie P. Baker, eds., *The WPA Oklahoma Slave Narratives* (Norman: University of Oklahoma Press, 1996), p. 377. Sheppard's owner had been the Cherokee Joe Sheppard.

91 African colonization: The Wills Valley Benevolent Society hoped to raise enough to send one person to Liberia, "but never realized their goal although the slaves did make remittances to the national [American Colonization Society] treasurer in 1830 and 1831 of twelve and eight dollars, respectively." Perdue, *Slavery and the Evolution of Cherokee Society*, p. 93.

91 "between the North and South": Perdue, *Slavery and the Evolution of Cherokee Society*, p. 119.

91–92 "The National Idea": Seward quoted in Laurence M. Hauptmann, *Between Two Fires: American Indians in the Civil War* (New York: Free Press, 1995), p. 11.

92 Evan Jones: Perdue, *Slavery and the Evolution of Cherokee Society*, p. 123.

92 "Slavery has existed": John Ross, "Annual Message" (1860), *Papers*, vol. 2 (1840–1866), pp. 449–50; "Annual Message" (1861), *Papers*, vol. 2, pp. 492–95. Ross's ownership of fifty slaves in 1860 is in Daniel F. Littlefield, Jr., *The Cherokee Freedmen: From Emancipation to American Citizenship* (Westport, Conn.: Greenwood Press, 1978), p. 13 n. 12.

92–93 The Confederacy: On the progress of the war in Cherokee territory generally, see Woodward, *Cherokees*, ch. 13, and Hauptmann, *Between Two Fires*, ch. 3. The murder of the black soldiers—the men, from the First Kansas Colored Infantry, were attacked as they were cutting hay near Fort Gibson—is in Hauptmann, p. 55. Watie was then sharing command with General Richard Gano, who was white, as were most of his troops; Watie's force included Creeks and Seminoles as well as Cherokees.

93 "Tues. 15th": Linda Finley, "Notes from the Diary of Susan E. Foreman," *Chronicles of Oklahoma* 47, no. 4 (1969–1970), pp. 396–97.

94 The emancipation: On the Washington emancipation, Samuel Pomeroy, and the Central American and Haitian ideas, see Benjamin Quarles, *Lincoln and the Negro* (New York: Da Capo, 1991 [1962]), pp. 109–23; the similarities between Lincoln's thinking on blacks and on Indians are outlined in David A. Nichols, *Lincoln and the Indians: Civil War Policy and Politics* (Columbia: University of Missouri Press, 1978), pp. 186–91. Nichols quotes Pomeroy on removal into "one distinctive Indian country" on p. 191.

94 "We pale-faced": Lincoln quoted in Nichols, *Lincoln and the Indians*, pp. 187–88.

95–97 all three races: The following description of the Battle of the Crater is based on Hauptmann, *Between Two Fires*, pp. 150–60; see also James M. McPherson, *Battle Cry of Freedom: The Civil War Era* (New York: Oxford University Press, 1988), pp. 756–60, and Henry Pleasants, Jr., *The Tragedy of the Crater* (Boston: Christopher Publishing House, 1938).

"GRAND AND GREAT—THE FUTURE STATE": SOME TWENTIETH-CENTURY SOLUTIONS TO THE INDIAN PROBLEM

98 "started back": Interview with Patsy Perryman in Baker and Baker, eds., *WPA Oklahoma Slave Narratives*, pp. 314–16. Of the many efforts to collect the WPA interviews with ex-slaves, the Bakers' strikes me as the best. It is well-sourced, includes many interviews not sent on to Washington (as well as lines struck by the federal editors, which were often sentences that were strongly antiwhite or had to do with sex), and explains the nature of the interviewing, which was done with a set list of questions. It is interesting to contemplate the degree to which the interview questions have shaped our understanding of slavery. For example, voodoo and black magic are thought to have permeated slave life, and the WPA interviews support that belief; however, it is equally true that all the WPA interviewers were required to ask about voodoo. Along similar lines, interviewers normally attempted to write in "dialect," a language that seems to have been codified at least as much in the (usually white) interviewers' minds as in the voices of their subjects. The interpretive problems raised by WPA methods really become apparent only when you look at the original typescripts, which are available on microform in larger public libraries. The comic possibilities of the interview situations likewise come across much more clearly when reading the originals.

99 Some slaves of Indians: Thornton, *Cherokees*, pp. 101–2; Littlefield, *Cherokee Freedmen*, ch. 2; Taylor, *In Search of the Racial Frontier*, pp. 114–21.

100 Cherokee Outlet: Wright, *Guide to the Indian Tribes*, pp. 14–19; Woodward, *Cherokees*, pp. 303–15 (Ross quoted p. 307).

101 "adventurous spirit": Woodward, *Cherokees*, pp. 315–16; also Amos Maxwell, "The Sequoyah Convention," *Chronicles of Oklahoma* 28, no. 2 (Summer 1950), pp. 161–65.

101 "gradual blending": Woodward, *Cherokees*, pp. 316–19; Annie H. Abel, "Proposals for an Indian State, 1778–1878," *Annual Report of the American Historical Association, 1907*, vol. 1 (Washington, D.C.: Government Printing Office, 1908), pp. 100–2.

102 Cherokee Outlet: Morgan and Morgan, *Oklahoma*, pp. 49–55.

102 Cherokee opposition: This account of the Keetoowahs is based on Hendrix's two-part article "Redbird Smith and the Nighthawk Keetoowahs."

103 thousands of interviews: Thornton, *Cherokees*, pp. 98–109, 116–23. Thornton quotes a U.S. Census report from 1894: "A serious difficulty was met in the answer to 'Are you an Indian?' Under the laws of the Five Tribes or nations of the Indian Territory a person, white in color and features, is frequently an Indian, being so by remote degree of blood or by adoption. There are many whites now resident claiming to be Indians whose claims have not as yet been acted upon by the nations. Negroes are frequently met who speak nothing but Indian languages, and are Indians by tribal law and custom, and others are met who call themselves Indians, who have not yet been so acknowledged by the tribes. These circumstances necessarily produced some confusion as to the number of Indians separately designated" (pp. 107–8).

103 "Plenary authority": *Lone Wolf, Principal Chief of the Kiowas, et al., v. Ethan A. Hitchcock, Secretary of the Interior, et al.*, 187 U.S. 553, pp. 565–66.

104 On August 21, 1905: Maxwell, "Sequoyah Convention," p. 180. The following discussion of the Sequoyah Convention is based on Maxwell's two-part article, *Chronicles of Oklahoma*, 28, nos. 2 and 3 (Summer and Autumn 1950).

106 At the official: The description of the statehood ceremonies is in Woodward, *Cherokees*, pp. 323–24. Remarkably, Woodward does not mention the Sequoyah Convention.

106 "a white man's state": Morgan and Morgan, *Oklahoma*, p. 139. On statehood, early segregation, and Indians as whites, see Morgan and Morgan, pp. 84–91, and Jimmie Lewis Franklin, *Journey toward Hope: A History of Blacks in Oklahoma* (Norman: University of Oklahoma Press, 1982), pp. 34–50.

107 "After statehood": Woodward, *Cherokees*, p. 325.

107 "Our pride": Hendrix, "Redbird Smith and the Nighthawk Keetoowahs," pt. 2, pp. 82–84.

108 allotment: Mankiller and Wallis, *Mankiller*, p. 135; Wright, *Guide to the Indian Tribes*, p. 21.

108 "the Indian population": Wright, *Guide to the Indian Tribes*, p. 3; Thornton, *Cherokees*, p. 141.

109 Bill of Rights: Mankiller and Wallis, *Mankiller*, pp. 62–69, 172–76, 273–75.

110 "all persons": Thornton, *Cherokees*, p. 124. The following discussion of census tactics and results is based on Thornton, pp. 123–203.

111 "We are products": The Youth Conference is quoted in Mankiller and Wallis, *Mankiller*, pp. 178–81; the conference's "Declaration of Purpose" is in Alvin Josephy, Jr., Joane Nagel, and Troy Johnson, eds., *Red Power: The American Indians' Fight for Freedom*, 2nd ed. (Lincoln: University of Nebraska Press, 1999), pp. 13ff.

111–12 in November 1969: Mankiller and Wallis, *Mankiller*, p. 188. This account of Alcatraz is based on Adam Fortunate Eagle, *Alcatraz! Alcatraz!: The Indian Occupation of 1969–1971* (Berkeley, Calif.: Heyday Books, 1992), which includes a long version of the occupiers' proclamation on pp. 44–48; Steve Talbot, "Indian Students and Reminiscences of Alcatraz," in Troy Johnson, Joane Nagel, and Duane Champagne, eds., *American Indian Activism: Alcatraz to the Longest Walk* (Urbana: University of Illinois Press, 1997), pp. 104–12; and Mankiller and Wallis, pp. 188–93. Wilma Mankiller, who became principal chief of the

Cherokees in 1985, was among the occupiers of Alcatraz. Adam Fortunate Eagle was a leader of the effort.

112 A certain Indian: On these films and others of the time, see Peter C. Rollins and John E. O'Connor, eds., *Hollywood's Indian: The Portrayal of the Native American in Film* (Lexington: University Press of Kentucky, 1998).

113 American Indian Movement: On AIM, see Peter Matthiessen, *In the Spirit of Crazy Horse* (New York: Viking, 1983).

HOMELANDS

115 The word *powwow*: According to Cutler, *O Brave New Words!*, p. 15, *powwow* first appeared in English in James Rosier's *A True Relation of the Most Prosperous Voyage Made This Present Yeere 1605 by Captain George Waymouth*. Rosier rendered it as *Baugh Waugh*.

116 "promoting tribal": 25 U.S.C. sec. 2702 (1) (Declaration of Policy).

116 "[T]here were about": Captain John Underhill, quoted in Jennings, *Invasion of America*, p. 223. A few pages later in his *Newes from America*, Underhill noted, "Our [allied Narragansett, Niantic, and Mohegan] Indians came to us, and much rejoiced at our victories, and greatly admired the manner of Englishmen's fight, but cried Mach it, mach it; that is, It is naught, it is naught, because it is too furious, and slays too many men" (Jennings, p. 223). In *History of Plymouth Plantation*, Governor William Bradford wrote, "It was a fearful sight to see them [the Pequots] thus frying in the fire and the streams of blood quenching the same, and horrible was the stink and scent thereof; but the victory seemed a sweet sacrifice, and they [the English] gave praise to God, who had wrought so wonderfully for them, as to enclose their enemy in their hands and give them so speedy a victory over so proud and insulting an enemy." Cave, *Pequot War*, p. 152.

Prior to the Pequot War, the Mohegans had been part of the Pequot Confederacy; undermining the confederacy was the colonists' chief goal. Indeed, Uncas's brother-in-law was the principal Pequot chief Sassacus. For careful analysis of the alliances of that time, see Eric S. Johnson, "Uncas and the Politics of Contact," and Kevin A. McBride, "The Legacy of Robin Cassacinamon," both in Robert S. Grumet, ed., *Northeastern Indian Lives, 1632–1816* (Amherst: University of Massachusetts Press, 1996), pp. 29–47, 74–92.

117 a tiny church: According to Melissa Jayne Fawcett, the church was built in order to demonstrate, for the federal government, Mohegan acceptance of Christianity: "Mohegans resisted Federal relocation by claiming to be already 'civilized' and 'christianized.' To support that claim, they founded a Christian church and school on their reservation in 1831." The church and tribal cemetery were all that remained of Mohegan territory by 1872. Fawcett, *The Lasting of the Mohegans, Part 1* (Uncasville, Conn.: Mohegan Tribe, 1995), pp. 21–22, 47–48. On the fund-raising for tribal recognition and casino construction, see Mohegan Sun, "Chronology," October 1996; Lyn Bixby, "A New Player at the Table," *Hartford Courant*, October 5, 1996, p. A1; and Bruce Orwall, "The Federal Regulator of Indian Gambling Is Also Part Advocate," *Wall Street Journal*, July 22, 1996, p. A1.

117 At this point: On Sol Kerzner in South Africa and Connecticut, see Roger Gros, "Here Comes the Sun," *Casino Journal* 9, no. 12 (December 1996); Lyn Bixby, "Casino Backer Faces No Charges in Old Case," *Hartford Courant*, December 9, 1995, p. A3; Howard Rudnitsky, "Big Chief Kerzner," *Forbes*, April 22, 1996, p. 176; Tom McEwen, "Entertainment Shines in Sun City," *Tampa Tribune*, July 2, 1995, Travel section, p. 1. Several articles in the

534 NOTES

Atlantic City *Press*—April 14, May 10, and June 16, 1983—concerned racism charges against Kerzner.

117 pony-hide banquettes: For an appreciative view, see Jerry Adler, "Knocking Their Eyeballs Out: David Rockwell's Casino Says 'Native American' with a Little Class," *Newsweek*, October 7, 1996.

118 "We must burn them!": This was the phrase of Captain John Mason; Cave, *Pequot War*, p. 150. For the history of tribal recognition, see Bixby, "New Player at the Table."

120 "freedman": According to Mankiller and Wallis, *Mankiller*, p. 218, the constitution of 1976 excluded freedmen.

THE REPUBLIC OF NEW AFRICA

125 one of twenty-nine: The number of black towns is from Quintard Taylor, *In Search of the Racial Frontier: African Americans in the American West, 1528–1990* (New York: Norton, 1998), p. 149. Taylor also names four black towns in California, one each in Colorado and Kansas (Dearfield and Nicodemus), three in New Mexico, and eleven in Texas. On early black settlement in Oklahoma generally, see Taylor, pp. 143–50; Jimmie Lewis Franklin, *Journey toward Hope: A History of Blacks in Oklahoma* (Norman: University of Oklahoma Press, 1982), pp. 9–23; and William Loren Katz, *The Black West: A Documentary and Pictorial History of the African American Role in the Westward Expansion of the United States* (New York: Touchstone, 1996), pp. 245–64. Katz reprints Booker T. Washington's article, from *Outlook*, January 4, 1908, as appendix 2, on pp. 327–31. The article about "complete freedom" I noted down from a copy shown to me in a Boley dry-goods store.

127 "Oh, 'tis a pretty country": Uncle Willie Jesse quoted in Thomas Knight, *Sunset on Utopian Dreams: An Experiment of Black Separatism on the American Frontier* (Washington, D.C.: University Press of America, 1977), p. 78.

128 as Ashley and other: There is, as you might expect, more than one version of the founding of Boley. "Boley was founded in the former Creek Nation in 1904 by two white entrepreneurs, William Boley, a railroad manager, and Lake Moore, a former federal officeholder. They hired Tom Haynes, an African American, to handle town promotion." Taylor, *In Search of the Racial Frontier*, pp. 149, 151.

128–29 black leaders organized: The leader of the black-state effort was Edwin P. McCabe. See Franklin, *Journey toward Hope*, pp. 12–16; William Loren Katz, *Black People Who Made the Old West* (Trenton, N.J.: Africa World Press, 1994), pp. 163–69; Taylor, *In Search of the Racial Frontier*, pp. 144–46. In 1891 a black correspondent to the American Colonization Society wrote, "[W]e as a people believe that Africa is the place but to get from under bondage we are thinking of Oklahoma as this is our nearest place of safety." Katz, *Black West*, p. 250. On the Klan in Tulsa, see Scott Ellsworth, *Death in a Promised Land: The Tulsa Race Riot of 1921* (Baton Rouge: Louisiana State University Press, 1982), pp. 20–22, 102–3.

"THE GRAND HAM": RACIAL IMAGINATION IN THE OLD WORLD

133 The geneticist: Luigi Luca Cavalli-Sforza and Francesco Cavalli-Sforza, *The Great Diasporas: The History of Human Diversity* (New York: Addison-Wesley, 1995), pp. 55, 66–69, 112–13; Louise Levathes, "A Geneticist Maps Ancient Migrations" (interview with Luigi Luca Cavalli-Sforza), *New York Times*, July 27, 1993, p. C1.

133 the art of Egypt: See Frank Snowden, *Before Color Prejudice: The Ancient View of Blacks* (Cambridge, Mass.: Harvard University Press, 1983), pp. 10–12. The literature on Egyptian art is more than vast. Snowden's book is accessible and reliable. See also the first two volumes of *The Image of the Black in Western Art* (New York: Morrow, 1976, 1979). For the Bible, I have usually used the King James, because I find its language the most beautiful. I have also relied on the New Revised Standard Version in *The HarperCollins Study Bible*, which has excellent notes (New York: HarperCollins, 1993), and *The Five Books of Moses: Genesis, Exodus, Leviticus, Numbers, Deuteronomy* (vol. 1 of the Schocken Bible), Everett Fox's extraordinary translation with notes of the Pentateuch (New York: Schocken, 1995).

134 The Greek historian: The interview with the king of the Ethiopians is in Herodotus, *The History*, 3:21; I am using David Grene's translation (Chicago: University of Chicago Press, 1988), pp. 219–20. Cambyses, according to Herodotus, went "insane" after hearing the Ethiopian boasts and sent an army to Ethiopia. However, Cambyses had not got his supply lines organized very well, and his army apparently went no farther than a desert where "some of the men did something dreadful. They cast lots and chose one out of every ten men among them and ate him. When Cambyses learned of this he was afraid—of the cannibalism—and abandoned the expedition against the Ethiopians . . . Herodotus 3:25. most beautiful men": Herodotus 3:20 (later, at 3:114, "tallest, handsomest, and longest-lived"). Herodotus made a connection between skin color and semen. Speaking of a group of subcontinental Indians, he wrote, "their skin is as black as that of the Ethiopians. The seed that they ejaculate into their women is not, like the rest of mankind, white but black, as their skin is. The seed of the Ethiopians is likewise black." Herodotus 3:101. On race concepts in classical literature generally, see Snowden, *Before Color Prejudice*, pp. 85–97; Frank Snowden, *Blacks in Antiquity: Ethiopians in the Greco-Roman Experience* (Cambridge, Mass.: Harvard University Press, 1970), chs. 3 and 6. James S. Romm, in *The Edges of the Earth in Ancient Thought* (Princeton, N.J.: Princeton University Press, 1992), points out that Greek commentary on distant peoples tended to waver between extreme praise and extreme criticism. In each case the point was to comment on Greekness by counterexample. Much Greek writing on non-Greeks could be understood, then, as anti-Greek, if you want to look at it that way. See Romm's second chapter and, on Ethiopians particularly, pp. 49–60. "It is because Cambyses . . . cannot accept any challenge to the worldview which places Persia at the all-important center of things," Romm writes, "that the whole episode ends as a disaster for him; while on the other hand the Ethiopian king, who freely acknowledges the areas in which his culture has been bested by others . . . remains unharmed and even triumphant" (p. 59).

134 Ethiopian community on Cyprus: Herodotus, *History* 7:90. Herodotus actually locates two populations of Ethiopians, one close to Egypt, one farther away (3:97), as well as the Cypriot colony. For the varied possibilities in locating Cush, Sheba, Ethiopia, and Zipporah, see the relevant entries in Charles E. Pfeiffer, Howard F. Vos, and John Rea, eds., *Wycliffe Bible Dictionary* (Peabody, Mass.: Hendrickson, 1999).

135 Ham, the son of Noah: Interestingly, the list of Noah's progeny sets up the story of Babel, which involved all the world's people: "Now they said: Come-now! Let us build ourselves a city and a tower, its top in the heavens, and let us make ourselves a name, lest we be scattered over the face of all the earth! But YHWH came down to look over the city and the tower that the humans were building. YHWH said: Here, (they are) one people with one language for them all, and this is merely the first of their doings—now there will be no barrier for them in all that they scheme to do! Come-now! Let us go down and there let us baffle their language, so that no man will understand the language of his neighbor. So YHWH scattered them from there over the face of all the earth, and they had to stop building the city. Therefore its name

was called Bavel/Babble, for there YHWH baffled the language of all the earth-folk, and from there, YHWH scattered them over the face of all the earth" (Fox's translation). The point seems to be that the human effort to make all people the same, and to glorify the species thereby, was experienced by God as an affront to his power. Metaphorically, the building of Babel resembles the building of an empire, in that both aim at a certain uniformity. Classical writers often struggled with the moral and spiritual implication of international trade and empire building. Such activities pointed toward an extension of one human model across the world and implied a discontent with one's life—again, possibly an insult to the gods and a taking of their power. Expansion might also lead merely to war. Seneca the Younger wrote, in *Natural Questions*, "What of the fact that the winds have allowed all peoples to traffic with one another and have mixed peoples from disparate locales [*gentes dissipitas locis miscuit*]? A great kindness on nature's part, if the madness of the human race did not turn it toward self-destruction. As things are, though, one could say of the winds what people said of Julius Caesar, according to Titus Livy: It's not certain which way the republic would be better off, if Caesar had been born or not . . . A great measure of peace would be granted to humans if the seas were closed" (5:18). Some Renaissance thinkers would take this passage to heart when pondering America. See Romm, *Edges of the Earth*, ch. 4. "It is not enough," Seneca concluded bitterly, "to be insane in our own part of the world." I have modified slightly the translation in Seneca, *Natural Questions*, trans. Thomas H. Corcoran (Cambridge, Mass.: Harvard University Press, 1972), vol. 2, pp. 115–21.

136 "Those who live": Aristotle, *Politics* 7:7, in the Oxford translation, Richard McKeon, ed., *The Basic Works of Aristotle* (New York: Random House, 1941), p. 1286. As to skin color, Aristotle was certainly aware of it (*On the Soul* 3:1, 3:5). Aristotle tended to see the sameness in difference and argued that one had (or a sense had) to be between extremes in order to perceive at all: "What is 'in the middle' is fitted to discern; relatively to either extreme it can put itself in the place of the other. As what is to perceive *both* black and white must, to begin with, be actually neither but potentially either" (*On the Soul* 2:2); and later, "even if you assert that what is white is not white you have included not-white in a synthesis . . . [T]here is not only the true or false assertion that Cleon is white but also the true or false assertion that he *was* or *will be* white" (*On the Soul* 3:6). Aristotle believed species of beings could not be defined by dichotomies such as black and white (*On the Soul* 1:3). Our own species is "not differentiated into subordinate groups" (*On the Soul* 1:5), but it does have shades of skin color, and these could be understood as arrayed from black to white. Aristotle perceived the range of possible effects and had an idea of what caused them and of their unpredictability: "Further, children are like their more remote ancestors from whom nothing has come [nothing physical, e.g., semen], for the resemblances recur at an interval of many generations, as in the case of the woman in Elis who had intercourse with the Aethiop; her daughter was not an Aethiop but the son of that daughter was" (*On the Generation of Animals* 1:18). Snowden has a wonderful passage on the frequent mixing of black and white peoples in Greek literature and legend (*Before Color Prejudice*, pp. 94–97).

The first Greek prose romance that may be considered a good novel, Heliodorus's *Ethiopian Story* (third or fourth century A.D.), pivots on an interesting case of interracial sex. The heroine, Chariclea, is the white child of two black parents, the king and queen of Ethiopia. When Chariclea enters the world, her mother abandons her for fear of being accused of adultery. Chariclea returns, after many adventures, to her parents. The king is understandably suspicious: "I still am not sure. For, apart from the other reasons, your complexion is of a bright fairness foreign to the Ethiopian colour." It turns out that, while the king and queen were making love, the queen gazed upon a picture of white Andromeda, and this caused her daughter to come out white. Everyone is relieved; the parents rejoice; the assembled populace cheers; and Chariclea, after some slight challenges, goes with her (white) beloved to a happy future in Ethiopia. There is no hint of discomfort or surprise about these minglings in Heliodorus (or in Aristotle). Indeed, among the Ethiopian king and queen's ancestors in the novel are the Sun, Dionysus, Perseus, Memnon—and Andromeda, which is why the white woman's picture was on the palace wall that afternoon. Heliodorus, *Ethiopian Story*, trans. Sir Walter Lamb (London: J. M. Dent & Sons, 1961), pp. 95, 254–59, 278. Lamb, in his introduction, finds Heliodorus's influence at work on Sir Philip Sidney, Lesage, Tasso (who describes the white daughter of a black mother in his 1575 masterpiece, *Jerusalem Delivered*), Guarini, Rabelais, Racine, Shakespeare, and Montaigne.

136–37 Origen argued: The quotations from the Church Fathers are in Snowden, *Before Color Prejudice*, pp. 99–104. Snowden argues that "the Christian writers developed an exegesis and a black-white imagery in which Ethiopians illustrated the meaning of the Scriptures for *all* men. In short, antiquity as a whole was able to overcome whatever potential for serious anti-black sentiment there may be in color symbolism" (p. 101). The more important point, it seems to me, is that the Ethiopians were required to illustrate something—anything—by means of their skin. Specifically, they illustrated a human extreme in terms of relationship to God. This may be a characteristic problem with universalist monotheisms. Fortunately, we had and still have more than one monotheism. The Isis cults, by contrast, were more on the polytheist side, had their heartland in the Ethiopian–Upper Egyptian zone, were much more popular than (early) Christianity in the Mediterranean and Levant—and did not conjure meanings out of skin color. On race in the Isiac cults, see Snowden, *Before Color Prejudice*, pp. 97–99; on the extent of Isiac worship in the eastern Roman Empire, see, for example, Maurice Sartre, *L'Orient roumain* (Paris: Seuil, 1991), pp. 472–77.

137–38 There are, however: On Ethiopian ties to early Muslims, see the entry for Ethiopia in Cyril Glassé, *Concise Encyclopedia of Islam* (San Francisco: Harper & Row, 1975); and entries for Rukayya and Bilal in *Encyclopedia of Islam*, 2nd ed. (Leiden: E. J. Brill, 1960).

138 "Though I am a slave": Bernard Lewis, *Race and Slavery in the Middle East: An Historical Enquiry* (New York: Oxford University Press, 1990), p. 28. The best source for English translations of original Arabic sources on Africa is N. Levtzion and J. F. P. Hopkins, eds., *Corpus of Early Arabic Sources for West African History* (Cambridge, U.K.: Cambridge University Press, 1981). The earliest source, if the attribution to Munabbih (around 732) is correct, is from Ibn Qutaybah, writing in 879–880, who mentions Noah's curse. (Ham "was a white man having a beautiful face and form," but God "changed his colour and the colour of his descendants because of his father's curse," p. 15). However, Al-Yaqubi, writing in 872–873, maintains that Noah cursed Canaan, not Ham (p. 20). And so it begins, with the sources indulging various theories over the next few centuries, some mentioning skin color, some not, some finding an explanation in the curse on Canaan or Ham, some not. The earliest reference to black kings selling their people as slaves is also in a source attributed to Al-Yaqubi. In the middle of the tenth century, Ibn Hawqal floats the theory that blacks who come north turn white, and whites going south turn black, in either case after seven generations (p. 51).

138 Malao and Opone: See Keith Bradley, *Slavery and Society at Rome* (Cambridge, U.K.: Cambridge University Press, 1994), pp. 32, 38.

139 "who are done to a turn": John Owen Hunwick, "West Africa and the Arab World: Historical and Contemporary Perspectives," *The J. B. Danquah Memorial Lectures*, ser. 23, February 1990 (Accra: Ghana Academy of Arts and Sciences, 1991), p. 5; Albertus Magnus, *De Natura*

locorum, quoted in Seymour Phillips, "The Outer World of the European Middle Ages," in Stuart B. Schwartz, ed., *Implicit Understandings: Observing, Reporting, and Reflecting on the Encounters between Europeans and Other Peoples in the Early Modern Era* (New York: Cambridge University Press, 1994), pp. 45–46.

139 You might think Europeans: Benjamin Braude, "The Sons of Noah and the Construction of Ethnic and Geographical Identities in the Medieval and Early Modern Periods," *William and Mary Quarterly*, 3rd ser., 54, no. 1 (January 1997), p. 109. Unless otherwise noted, the discussion of Ham below is from Braude, who seems now to be the principal authority on Ham and his brothers. The story of Ham's wanderings through Christian, Muslim, Jewish, and various African literatures is a fantastically complex world unto itself. To judge from recent uses of Ham and his brothers in Africa and among American whites of a racial-theological bent, the story is far from over. Ole Bjorn Rekdal summarizes some of the African Hamitic literature in "When Hypothesis Becomes Myth: The Iraqi Origin of the Iraqw," *Ethnology* 37, no. 1 (Winter 1998), pp. 17–38, with particular reference to the Iraqw of Tanzania. Essentially, European thinkers and administrators in the late nineteenth century and through the middle of the twentieth developed the idea that peoples favored (by Europeans) in Africa were descended from Ham, whether literally, as it were, or metaphorically. This had the effect of helping some Africans feel racially superior to others, putting a bargain-basement, yet positive, spin on status as a son of Ham. The Iraqw became one such superior people, the Tutsi another. This forms part of the background to the recent massacring of hundreds of thousands of human beings in east-central Africa. For Rwanda, see Gerard Prunier, *The Rwanda Crisis: History of a Genocide* (New York: Columbia University Press, 1995), pp. 5–9, 37–40. For the United States, see my passages below on Christian Identity.

One point I would like to emphasize is that Genesis does not describe people by skin color. This is not too surprising, since the book does state that all humans are descended from the three sons of Noah and his wife. Only one wife of Noah is mentioned. Presumably his three sons looked similar; no color distinctions are made among them. Nonetheless we find Lewis, for example, writing of "Canaan, who was white," and "Kush, who was black" (*Race and Slavery*, pp. 123–25 n. 9). As Lewis abundantly shows elsewhere, such distinctions were read back into the text and served later purposes foreign to those of Genesis. We might also remember, because it has proved so easy to forget, that Genesis is not, in all likelihood, describing real people or events.

For the Ham story in North America, see Thomas Virgil Peterson, *Ham and Japheth: The Mythic World of Whites in the Antebellum South* (Metuchen, N.J.: Scarecrow Press, 1978).

140–41 slavery's decline: I am, of course, greatly simplifying the multiple processes by which slavery died out in Europe. An interesting example comes from the Byzantine Empire under Manuel I Comnenus (ruled 1143–1180): "[In] the cities a great many sold their freedom in order to find protection in the service of some powerful lord, a practice by no means unusual in Byzantium. Manuel tried to stem this development by a law by which any freeborn man who had sold himself into slavery was allowed to get back his freedom, and the Emperor even seems to have provided the ransom from the state treasury, at least in the capital. But the whole trend of the times, with the growth of the great estates, and the overburdening and impoverishment of the lower classes, made it inevitable that ever wider strata of the population were bartering their freedom to become, if not slaves, then at least serfs. In the end, the triumphant advance of feudal processes weakened the authority of the state and undermined the Byzantine polity's power of resistance." George Ostrogorsky, *History of the Byzantine State*, trans. Joan Hussey (New Brunswick, N.J.: Rutgers University Press, 1969), rev. ed., pp. 394–95. The nature and extent of slavery were the subjects of long struggle among Europeans; and the difference between slavery and serfdom is not easy to measure. The essential themes were, first, pressure from below and, second, the contest between central authorities (such as the emperor Manuel) and more local lords for control of the laboring populace. A good basic source is Charles Verlinden, *L'Esclavage dans l'Europe médiévale* (vol. 1, Brugge: Tempel, 1955; vol. 2, Ghent: Rijkuniversiteit, 1977). By the sixteenth century in Europe this contest had resulted in something like modern nationhood. In particular, membership in a nation began to acquire the quality of a personal inheritance, a "natural" state. When English and Continental writers contemplated slavery in this context, they reached for natural metaphors such as "free soil" and "free air." The English, then, for example, were naturally free, or, as we would say, genetically free. This helps us understand why, in the early modern period, the bondage of the unfree was so often expressed in terms of a natural inheritance. For "free air" in England and elsewhere, see Helen Catterall, *Judicial Cases concerning American Slavery and the Negro* (Washington, D.C.: Carnegie Institution, 1926–1937), vol. 1, pp. 1–5; Robin Blackburn, *The Making of New World Slavery: From the Baroque to the Modern, 1492–1800* (London: Verso, 1997), pp. 60–63.

141 Rebel serfs: See Paul Freedman, "Sainteté et Sauvagerie: Deux images du paysan au moyen âge," *Annales* no. 3 (May–June 1992), pp. 539–60.

142 In the Mediterranean: The slave-color descriptions are from Jack D. Forbes, *Africans and Native Americans: The Language of Race and the Evolution of Red-Black Peoples*, 2nd ed. (Urbana: University of Illinois Press, 1993), pp. 26–27. Forbes gives similar descriptions from contemporary slave records in Provence and Italy. The trans-Saharan figures are from Ralph Austen, "The Trans-Saharan Slave Trade: A Tentative Census," in Henry A. Gemery and Jan S. Hogendorn, eds., *The Uncommon Market: Essays in the Economic History of the Slave Trade* (New York: Academic Press, 1979), p. 66. Austen notes that "females outnumbered males" among sub-Saharan slaves brought north to Muslim markets, and had children: "The fathers, in a very large number of cases, were not black, so that the children became genetically mulatto but socially 'white' " (p. 44).

142–43 "The people who": Moses Maimonides, *The Guide for the Perplexed*, trans. M. Friedlander (New York: Dover, 1956 [1904]), p. 384.

143 "close to those": Ibn Khaldun, *The Muqaddimah: An Introduction to History*, trans. Franz Rosenthal, ed. N. J. Dawood (Princeton, N.J.: Princeton University Press, 1989 [1958; rev. ed. 1967]), pp. 58–61. For Ibn Khaldun the temperate peoples, who monopolize human virtues, extend from Spain to China. Climate is not the only factor he recognizes. There is also, for example, overeating, which makes people pale and stupid, as with some Berbers; a frugal diet in the temperate zone can produce such as the Spaniards, who have "a sharpness of intellect, a nimbleness of body, and a receptivity for instruction such as no one else has" (p. 66). The temperate peoples include among their features a "temperate . . . colour" (p. 58).

Maimonides also does not mention the Ham myth. Ibn Khaldun notes it in order to refute it. He took a hard line against the Ham myth, which evidently had gained enough ground in some quarters that it appeared common sense. Genealogists, he wrote, "declared all the Negro inhabitants of the South to be descendants of Ham. They had misgivings about their color and therefore undertook to report the aforementioned silly story. They declared all or most of the inhabitants of the north to be the descendants of Japheth and they declared most of the temperate nations . . . who cultivate the sciences and crafts, and who possess religious groups and religious laws as well as political leadership and royal authority, to be the descendants of Shem. Even if the genealogical construction were correct, it would be the result of mere guesswork, not of cogent, logical argumentation" (p. 61).

143 "The inhabitants": See Ibn Khaldun, *Muqaddimah*, pp. 60–61.

144 dumb animals: The earlier northern Mediterranean Europeans reaching Africa were from Ibn Khaldun's temperate zone, though Norman freebooters were present very early as well; Normans raided along the Tunisian and Libyan coasts from 1087 into the next century. Ira M. Lapidus, *A History of Islamic Societies* (Cambridge, U.K.: Cambridge University Press, 1990), p. 370. The peninsular slave population, too, as we have seen, had a substantial element of Slavs and other "whites" who would qualify, in Khaldunian terms, as dumb animals. The later English, French, and Dutch were indisputably intemperate. The English, in particular, would carry the Ham myth into modernity.

144–45 Muslim slave traders: Austen, "Trans-Saharan Slave Trade," pp. 64–67; Lapidus, *History of Islamic Societies*, p. 368 (on Aghlabids); Marshall G. S. Hodgson, *The Venture of Islam: Conscience and History in a World Civilization*, vol. 2: *The Expansion of Islam in the Middle Periods* (Chicago: University of Chicago Press, 1977), p. 399 (on Fatimids); and the ʿAbd (slave) entry in *Encyclopedia of Islam*, 2nd ed.

145 "Reconquest": Felipe Fernández-Armesto, *Before Columbus: Exploration and Colonization from the Mediterranean to the Atlantic, 1229–1492* (Philadelphia: University of Pennsylvania Press, 1987), pp. 126–42.

146 "the kingdoms of Africa": Fernández-Armesto, *Before Columbus*, pp. 152–53, 169–77.

146–48 "It was the custom": This account of the initial conquest of the Canaries is based on Pierre Bontier and Jean Le Verrier, *The Canarian* (London: Hakluyt Society, 1872), trans. Richard Henry Major. The manuscript was written between 1402 and 1406. This edition includes the French text, and I have at times departed slightly from Major's translation. For example, Major sometimes translates *gens* and *peuple* as "race" rather than "people." He also, remarkably, translates "ceux qui estoient desce[n]dus de Sem l'aisne fils de Noe tendroient Asie; et ceux qui estoient descendus de Cam l'autre fils de Noe tendroient Afrique" as "Those which were descended from Shem, the eldest son of Noah, should have Asia. Those who were sprung from Ham, the second son of Noah, should have Africa; and the descendants of Japhet, the third son, should have Europe" (p. 83). Among several additions, Major has entirely imported Japheth and his claim to Europe, which is not in the original text. Along similar lines, Major describes some of the Canarians as having "very brown complexions" while others "were more or less fair, or even quite blonde" (p. xxxix). This does not come from *The Canarian*. Such color distinctions were very likely the result of uneven colonization of the Canary Islands, by European women as well as men and by Africans, including dark-skinned sub-Saharans brought in for labor. For the conquest generally and its place in the evolution of southern European politics and economy, see Fernández-Armesto, *Before Columbus*, esp. chs. 7–9, and Eduardo Aznar Vallejo, "The Conquests of the Canary Islands," in Schwartz, ed., *Implicit Understandings*, pp. 134–56.

148–49 alleged Spanish friar: The "source" of this story is presumably the "Libro del conscimiento" of 1360, by an anonymous friar. The "Libro" is reproduced in Youssouf Kamal, *Monumenta cartographica Africae et Aegypti* (privately printed, 1937), vol. 4, fascicle 2, pp. 1258–60. The friar notes the gold-digging ants and mentions black skin color several times—far more often than in the much longer work of Bontier and Le Verrier. He also writes, "estas gentes son negros pero son omes de buen seso e an saberes e ciencias e an tierra muy abondada de todos los bienes porque ay muchas aguas e buenas de las que salen del pollo. antarico do diz que es el paraiso terrenal." In short, the friar's Africans have everything one could want (knowledge, sciences, abundant food, good water), as well as proximity to the earthly paradise, *even though* they are "negros." If this was indeed Bontier and Le Verrier's source, they managed to ignore these racial shadings of meaning. The story is considered fictional, though that did not, of course, hinder its influence on factual adventurers.

149–50 when Portuguese captains: See John Thornton's invaluable book *Africa and Africans in the Making of the Atlantic World, 1400–1680* (Cambridge, U.K.: Cambridge University Press, 1992). This paragraph and the next are based on his first chapter.

150 "shouting out": Gomes Eanes de Azurara (Zurara), *The Chronicle of the Discovery and Conquest of Guinea*, trans. Charles Raymond Beazley and Edgar Prestage (London: Hakluyt Society, 1896), p. 66. Zurara describes a number of such encounters. The last one on the trip was abortive, "for the Moors had caught sight of the first party, and fled at once from that place; so that they only found one girl, who had stayed sleeping in the village; whom they took with them, and returning to the caravels, made sail for Portugal" (p. 78).

151 "great sorrow" and "a marvellous sight": Zurara, *Chronicle*, pp. 78, 81–82. The perception of the captives' sorrow Zurara attributes to Lancarote, the leader of the voyage.

151 "and then it was needful": Zurara, *Chronicle*, p. 82.

151–52 "good and true," "free servants," "set free," "And here you must," and "had no knowledge": Zurara, *Chronicle*, pp. 83, 84, 84, 54, 85. According to Braude ("Sons of Noah," p. 127), the Portuguese original has Caim, rather than Cain. Cain and Ham were frequently confused.

152 Zurara seems: Immediately before describing the division of the captives, Zurara asks of God, "I pray Thee that my tears may not wrong my conscience; for it is not their religion but their humanity that maketh mine to weep in pity for their sufferings." *Chronicle*, p. 81.

152 Most Portuguese: Verlinden writes of the separation scene in Zurara, "We should note in particular the surprise, mixed with indignation, of the Portuguese population. Slavery, certainly, was not something new for these people. But it was a misfortune that hit isolated individuals and which had become, it seems, relatively rare in a country cut off from direct contact with Islam. To see a compact mass of some hundreds of human beings delivered into servitude in a single moment was a new spectacle. And if some townspeople of Lagos or some peasants of the Algarve wept or cried out at this sight, it was because something new was being born, the horror of which far surpassed anything they had known: the modern trade, a mass phenomenon, an anonymous misfortune swooping down on backward colonial populations with the blind fatality of a force which overran them . . ." *L'Esclavage*, vol. 1, p. 620.

153–54 But the Atlantic slave trade: This discussion of the early Atlantic trade, and what follows on African slavery and the mixed communities along the coast and on the islands, is based on Thornton, *Africa and Africans*, ch. 2 ("The Development of Commerce between Europeans and Africans"), ch. 3 ("Slavery and African Social Structure"), and ch. 4 ("Enslavement and the Slave Trade"). Some coastal and riverine states did not export slaves, and some of these imported them, including from European suppliers. Some further details (such as African imports of tobacco) are in David Richardson, "West African Consumption Patterns and English Slave Trade," in Gemery and Hogendorn, eds., *Uncommon Market*, pp. 319–21; the reference to African smelting methods being used in Brazil is in Basil Davidson, *The Search for Africa: History, Culture, Politics* (New York: Random House, 1994), p. 58. Gemery and Hogendorn demonstrate that, apart from the human costs—above all, the vast numbers of humans who died in the Middle Passage and in their early years in the New World—the

Atlantic trade operated at an overall loss to West Africans, that is, the economic advancement of individual states and merchants worked against that of West Africa as a whole: "The fact that voluntary trade with Europeans occurred despite a negative economic impact on West African society as a whole suggests that, because decision making occurred within relatively narrow geographic bounds, calculations of cost and benefit were made on a level more consistent with private than social perceptions. At that level, capture costs were the only relevant private costs and social costs were perceived as nonexistent or were, at best, severely underestimated. Political fragmentation and the resulting dominance of a private cost-benefit calculus thus explains the continuance of trade despite the adverse bargain." "Economic Costs of West African Participation in the Atlantic Slave Trade," in Gemery and Hogendorn, eds., *Uncommon Market*, p. 161.

154 Seville and Lisbon: The population figures are in Blackburn, *Making of New World Slavery*, pp. 112–13.

154–55 "one thing leading": *The Life of the Admiral Christopher Columbus by His Son Ferdinand*, trans. Benjamin Keen (New Brunswick, N.J.: Rutgers University Press, 1992 [1959]), pp. 14–15.

155 "At daybreak": Ferdinand's *Life of the Admiral*, pp. 59–60. Bartolomé de Las Casas, in *Historia de las Indias*, ed. Agustín Millares Carlo (Mexico City: Fondo de Cultura Economica, 1951), has Columbus saying that the Indians did not have crinkly *(crespo)* hair and were not black *(negro)*, "except in that they were the color of Canarians" (vol. 1, p. 205).

156 "The Indians": Peter Hulme, "Tales of Distinction: European Ethnography and the Caribbean," in Schwartz, ed., *Implicit Understandings*, p. 161. The whiteness passage is in Las Casas, *Historia*, vol. 1, p. 202. Later, Las Casas states that all people have "natural law" in common, regardless of "sect, law, state, color, and condition" (p. 232).

156–57 "With what right": Montesinos quoted in Anthony Pagden's introduction to Bartolomé de Las Casas, *A Short Account of the Destruction of the Indies*, trans. Nigel Griffin (New York: Penguin, 1992), pp. xx–xxi. Las Casas suggested importing African slaves in his reform plans of 1516 and 1518. He continued to champion it in 1531 and pleaded for a license to import blacks in 1544. See Juan Friede, "Las Casas and Indigenism in the Sixteenth Century," and Marcel Bataillon, "The *Clérigo* Casas, Colonist and Colonial Reformer," in Juan Friede and Benjamin Keen, eds., *Bartolomé de Las Casas in History: Toward an Understanding of the Man and His Work* (De Kalb: Northern Illinois University Press, 1971), pp. 165–66 and 515–18, respectively, plus the relevant notes; and Las Casas, *Historia*, vol. 3, pp. 177–78.

157 "They all made fun": *Britannica* (1975) entry for Columbus; "I believe those from Guinea": Columbus quoted in Forbes, *Africans and Native Americans*, p. 23; Forbes gives sources for the importation of American slaves to Europe and the Afro-Atlantic islands on pp. 22–25. In his first communication to King Ferdinand and Queen Isabella after reaching the New World, Columbus promised them not only "as much gold as they want" but slaves, "as many as they shall order." Columbus, "Letter to Lord Raphael Sanchez, Treasurer to Ferdinand and Isabella," in Giles Gunn, ed., *Early American Writing* (New York: Penguin, 1994), pp. 30–31.

157–58 Pope Paul III: In the bull *Sublimis Deus*, quoted in Peter Hulme, "Tales of Distinction," p. 189. The pope was responding to a letter from the first bishop of Tlaxcala, who was worried about mistreatment by Spaniards of Indians and its justification by reference to Indians' subhumanity. See James Muldoon, *The Americas in the Spanish World Order: The Justification for Conquest in the Seventeenth Century* (Philadelphia: University of Pennsylvania Press, 1994), pp. 58–67.

158 A number of factors: Some argued that Africans could be enslaved as captives in a "just war," while Indians could not, the African "war" being against Muslims. This was a very long reach.

158 "may well bee lykened to": Eden, in Edward Arber, ed., *The First Three English Books on America* (New York: Kraus, 1971 [1885]), p. 57. The impression of early European arrivals to the New World that Indians were at once like them and unlike them led to an absolute carnival of shape-shifting in the contact literature. Las Casas, for example, compared the Spaniards in America to the Moors who had ruled Spain not so long before and threatened (through the Ottoman fleet and armies) to do so again. He referred to the Spanish conquest as "Mohammedan"—that is, Muslim, and Moorish—and wondered whether the (real) Moors might not be sent back by God to reconquer Spain as punishment for Spain's impious acts in America. (See Pagden's introduction to Las Casas, *Short Account*, pp. xxxviii–xxxix.) So Las Casas thought Spaniards might be punished by Moors for having turned into Moors. Similarly, though in different terms, Francisco de Victoria (Francis Vitoria) argued that New World infidels were just as human as Spanish Christians, and so attacking them was no different from attacking Seville. (Victoria's opinions were presented in lectures circa 1532. See Muldoon, *Americas in the Spanish World Order*, pp. 28–33, and Las Casas, *Short Account*, p. 41 n. 53.) Among English colonists, it was common to believe that Indians were "white," both in color and, so to speak, genealogically. See Karen Ordahl Kupperman, "Presentment of Civility: English Reading of American Self-Presentation in the Early Years of Colonization," *William and Mary Quarterly*, ser. 3, 54, no. 1 (January 1997), pp. 193–252. Yet another metaphor Europeans used to include (and exclude) Indians was that of "lost tribes of Israel," or simply "Jews." See Djelal Kadir, *Columbus and the Ends of the Earth: Europe's Prophetic Rhetoric as Conquering Ideology* (Berkeley: University of California Press, 1992), pp. 182–92, and Don Cameron Allen, *The Legend of Noah: Renaissance Rationalism in Art, Science, and Letters* (Urbana: University of Illinois Press, 1949), pp. 113–37. Black Africans did not receive anything like this chaotic intensity of identification from European Christians, nor had any other people, with the possible exception of Jews (real and imagined).

159 bitterly regretted: Friede, "Las Casas and Indigenism," p. 166.

"COAL BLACK IS BETTER THAN ANOTHER HUE": LOVE AND RACE IN SHAKESPEARE'S ENGLAND

160 Robert Gainsh: See Alden T. Vaughan and Virginia Mason Vaughan, "Before *Othello*: Elizabethan Representations of Sub-Saharan Africans," *William and Mary Quarterly*, 3rd ser., 54, no. 1 (January 1997), pp. 24–25.

160 "considering with himself": Peter Martyr in Arber, ed., *First Three English Books on America*, p. 88; Cunningham and Best in Vaughan and Vaughan, "Before *Othello*," pp. 24, 26–27.

161–63 "negars and Blackamoores": On Elizabeth's edicts and blacks in Elizabethan life, see Gretchen Gerzina, *Black London: Life before Emancipation* (New Brunswick, N.J.: Rutgers University Press, 1995), pp. 3–5; for Mandeville, see Vaughan and Vaughan, "Before *Othello*," pp. 22–23. I am using *The Riverside Shakespeare*, ed. G. Blakemore Evans (Boston: Houghton Mifflin, 1974), for *Titus Andronicus*, at pp. 1023–54.

163–66 "in form and colour": I am using Peter Whalley's edition of Jonson's complete works (London: Private printing for D. Midwinter et al., 1756), which includes Jonson's own introductory texts and footnotes. The two masques are in vol. 5.

165 the conquest of Ireland: The connection between Ireland, the other Atlantic islands, and the New World existed in literature long before it took the form of fact. This is why, for example, the name Brazil is linked to *Hy-Breasail*, "the island of the blessed," as learned of in the tenth-century *Navigatio Brendani*, which relates the island-hopping adventures of the Irish Saint

Brendan. Phillips, "Outer World," pp. 32–34. Phillips (pp. 44–45) notes a general European Christian drift toward the West from the fourth century onward, "the belief that civilization had gradually moved westward after its beginnings in the East, but that when it reached the uttermost limits of the West the human race would meet its doom and extinction." The intense westering apocalypticism of imperial Puritanism—at once chronological, geographic, and ethnological—makes more emotional sense when placed within this tradition.

167 "And there will I": Purchas's prayer is in Braude, "Sons of Noah," pp. 135–37.

168 The passage Purchas quoted: Purchas's change of tactic and the identification of Sandys as source are in Braude, "Sons of Noah," pp. 137–38. Sandys's account, from his own North African travels, appeared in 1615. It's worth noting that Sir Walter Raleigh, in his 1614 *History of the World*, argued at tiresome length that the Cushites were in Arabia and not black (bk. I, ch. 8, sec. 10), further that "the known great lords of the first ages were of the issue of Ham" (bk. I, ch. 2, sec. 2). Raleigh connected Ethiopians, "Negroes," and "blackamoors" to sons of Ham only by proximity.

168–70 He arrived there: My account of the Sandys brothers and their Virginia efforts is based on Edmund S. Morgan, *American Slavery, American Freedom: The Ordeal of Colonial Virginia* (New York: Norton, 1975), chs. 5 and 6; some biographical details (such as Pope's endorsement of George's poetry) are from the brothers' respective entries in *Encyclopaedia Britannica*, 15th ed. (1975).

170 "He maketh us": In Morgan, *American Slavery*, p. 121.

171 they cost too much: On slave-labor prices, transport costs, and British labor costs, see Richard N. Bean and Robert P. Thomas, "The Adoption of Slave Labor in British America," in Gemery and Hogendorn, eds., *Uncommon Market*, pp. 378–98. The black-slave-race concept itself was certainly available to British colonials from Virginia's earliest days. George Sandys had expressed it in his writings by 1615, as had Shakespeare before him. The idea did not impinge on Virginian reality, however, until the 1670s.

171 "more easily kept": Winthrop Jordan, *White over Black: American Attitudes toward the Negro, 1550–1812* (Chapel Hill: University of North Carolina Press, 1968), p. 64. For the various possibilities open to Virginia blacks at the time, see WPA Writers' Program, *The Negro in Virginia* (Winston-Salem, N.C.: John F. Blair, 1994 [1940]), pp. 3–17; Catterall, ed., *Judicial Cases*, vol. 1, pp. 53–61. Indians and blacks would be prohibited from "purchasing christian servants" in Virginia by 1670, "yet not debarred from buying any of their owne nation" (Catterall, p. 58).

172 an act specifically discriminating: For the 1639 law and the Casor decision, see WPA Writers' Program, *Negro in Virginia*, pp. 13–15; for the Puritans' Providence Island, see Jordan, *White over Black*, pp. 63–64, and Karen Ordahl Kupperman, *Providence Island, 1630–1641: The Other Puritan Colony* (Cambridge, U.K.: Cambridge University Press, 1993), esp. ch. 6 on the transition from servants to slaves; for the Virginia laws in general, see Catterall, *Judicial Cases*, vol. 1, pp. 57–60. The earliest reference to a somewhat black person (Manuel, a mulatto) being sold "for life" is from 1644; lifetime servitude was imposed as a punishment on a black man in 1640. The legal construction of black slavery did not really get under way until the early 1660s. See A. Leon Higginbotham, Jr., *In the Matter of Color: Race and the American Legal Process: The Colonial Period* (New York: Oxford University Press, 1978), pp. 28–37.

172–73 By the 1650s: On Bacon and the restive landless, see Morgan, *American Slavery*, pp. 215–70; the poem was Lucy Terry's "Bars Fight," in Deirdre Mullane, ed., *Crossing the Danger Water: Three Hundred Years of African-American Writing* (New York: Doubleday, 1993), p. 26; for legislation on enslaving Indians, see Catterall, *Judicial Cases*, vol. 1, pp. 61–65.

173 "Negro and Slave": Reverend Morgan Godwyn, *The Negro's and Indians Advocate*, quoted in

Jordan, *White over Black*, p. 97; on the waning of Christian as a legal identifier, see Jordan, pp. 92–97.

174 Of particular concern: On the sexual question in early race laws and decisions, see Higginbotham, *In the Matter of Color*, pp. 42–47, and Joel Williamson, *New People: Miscegenation and Mulattoes in the United States* (Baton Rouge: Louisiana State University Press, 1995), pp. 6–11.

175 racial code: Jordan, *White over Black*, pp. 109–10 (South Carolina law) and p. 111 (Governor Spotswood).

175 inclining to revolt: To some degree, lifetime slavery made social violence more likely. As early as 1669 Virginia legislators recognized that, because nonphysical punishments hardly existed when a master was dealing with a slave, physical violence was about all a master could use. In many cases, the act stated, "obstinacy" on the part of an enslaved person could not be "by other than violent meanes supprest." Higginbotham, *In the Matter of Color*, p. 36.

176 "which if granted" and "You have afforded us": James Oakes, "Slavery as an American Problem," in Larry J. Griffin and Don H. Doyle, eds., *The South as an American Problem* (Athens: University of Georgia Press, 1995), pp. 88–89.

176–77 "'Tis an ill-grounded opinion": Benjamin Franklin, "Observations concerning the Increase of Mankind," in *The Magazine of History with Notes and Queries* 16, extra no. 63 (Tarrytown, N.Y.: William Abbatt, 1918). Franklin's essay was originally published in Boston by S. Kneeland in 1755. By "red" Franklin meant the color white people show when, for example, they blush.

178 "have these Negroes": "Against the Traffic of Mens-body," *The Annals of America*, vol. 1: *1493–1754, Discovering a New World* (Chicago: Encyclopaedia Britannica, 1968), p. 275; "deprave the Mind": Jordan, *White over Black*, p. 274.

178 "The Colonists are" and "we must assert": Jordan, *White over Black*, p. 278 (James Otis), p. 292 (George Washington).

179 "rendered impossible": Jordan, *White over Black*, p. 552. Madison retained this view, writing of "existing and probably unalterable prejudices" in 1819. Matthew T. Mellon, *Early American Views on Negro Slavery: From the Letters and Papers of the Founders of the Republic* (New York: Bergman, 1969 [1934]), p. 133.

181 Jefferson refers: Jefferson summarizes the proposal in "Notes on the State of Virginia," in Adrienne Koch and William Peden, eds., *The Life and Selected Writings of Thomas Jefferson* (New York: Random House, 1993), pp. 236–37.

181–82 "It will probably be asked": Jefferson, in Koch and Peden, eds., *Life and Selected Writings*, pp. 238–39.

182 "It is for the happiness" and "stop the increase": Koch and Peden, eds., *Life and Selected Writings*, pp. 204–5.

183 "removed beyond": Jefferson, in Koch and Peden, eds., *Life and Selected Writings*, p. 243; "I am drawn along": WPA Writers' Program, *Negro in Virginia*, p. 41.

183 "Who is there" and "prejudices, sentiments": Jordan, *White over Black*, pp. 558, 554.

184 the states most likely: Laws against free blacks entering Ohio (in 1804), Maryland (1806), Delaware (1811), Kentucky (1799, 1808): Jordan, *White over Black*, p. 410.

"WE CAN BE AS SEPARATE AS THE FINGERS": SEGREGATION FROM THE AMERICAN REVOLUTION TO THE GILDED AGE

185 "We are willing": Wilson Jeremiah Moses, ed., *Classical Black Nationalism: From the American Revolution to Marcus Garvey* (New York: New York University Press), pp. 7–8. See also

St. Clair Drake, *The Redemption of Africa and Black Religion* (Chicago: Third World Press, 1970), pp. 23–24.

186 At St. George's: The Philadelphia church story is in Lerone Bennett, Jr., *Before the* Mayflower: A *History of Black America* (New York: Penguin, 1988 [1961]), pp. 80–81.

186 "African blacks": Prince Hall is quoted in Moses, ed., *Classical Black Nationalism*, pp. 8–9; see Bennett, *Before the* Mayflower, pp. 82–85.

187 "I have nothing": Bennett, *Before the* Mayflower, p. 126; "Liberty and equality": Jordan, *White over Black*, p. 396, and Drake, *Redemption*, p. 34.

187 Within one: On Massachusetts, see Jordan, *White over Black*, pp. 410–11; see also Leon F. Litwack, *North of Slavery: The Negro in the Free States, 1790–1860* (Chicago: University of Chicago Press, 1961), p. 16.

188 Around 1810: My discussion of colonization in this period is based on P. J. Staudenraus, *The African Colonization Movement, 1816–1865* (New York: Columbia University Press, 1961), and Early Lee Fox, *The American Colonization Society, 1817–1840* (Baltimore: Johns Hopkins University Press, 1919). See also Floyd Miller, *The Search for a Black Nationality: Black Colonization and Emigration, 1787–1863* (Urbana: University of Illinois Press, 1975), which is particularly good on Cuffe (ch. 2). Fox thought colonization of black Americans was a pretty good idea, and so he gets more deeply into what (white) colonization activists were thinking. "Unquestionably, the one supposed solution [to 'the great negro problem of that time,' 1815] to which the leaders of thought in every part of the Union, except possibly the extreme South, turned was that of colonization. The free negro would be transported to the land whence his fathers came; the danger from the alarming increase in the free negro population would vanish as ghosts vanish with the coming of the morning; slaveholders could then safely and gradually emancipate their slaves, and the negro problem would be solved" (pp. 44–45).

190 White American opinion: Apart from Staudenraus and Fox, see also, for this period, Eugene Berwanger, *The Frontier against Slavery: Western Anti-Negro Prejudice and the Slavery Extension Controversy* (Urbana: University of Illinois Press, 1967), p. 54; Litwack, *North of Slavery*, pp. 20ff.

191 "Indeed, the people of color": James Forten, "Letter to Paul Cuffe," in Moses, ed., *Classical Black Nationalism*, p. 51. Forten later turned against colonization.

193 "the ancient Egyptians" and "How are we astonished": Volney, *Travels through Syria and Egypt in the Years 1783, 1784, and 1785* (London: Robinson, 1787), pp. 81, 82–83; "A race of men" and "we have": Volney, *The Ruins: or, Meditations on the Revolutions of Empires; and the Law of Nature*, trans. Joel Barlow and the author (New York: Peter Eckler, 1890), pp. 17, 16. Volney's *Travels* was first translated into English in 1787, *The Ruins* in 1795. According to *Encyclopaedia Britannica* (1975), "Volney frequented the salon of Anne Catherine, widow of the philosopher Claude Helvetius in the company of the Encyclopedist Baron d'Holbach and Benjamin Franklin." Volney in America "was warmly welcomed by George Washington; returned home in 1798 denounced by John Adams as a secret agent to help France recover Louisiana." (Biographical note by the editor to Cheikh Anta Diop, *The African Origin of Civilization: Myth or Reality?* ed. and trans. Mercer Cook [Chicago: Lawrence Hill Books, 1974], p. 304.) Also see Théophile Obenga, *Cheikh Anta Diop, Volney et le Sphinx: Contribution de Cheikh Anta Diop à l'historiographie mondiale* (Paris: Présence Africaine/Khepera, 1996), pp. 53–70. In *Volney et l'Amérique, d'apres des documents inédits et sa correspondence avec Jefferson* (Baltimore: Johns Hopkins University Press, 1923), Gilbert Chinard demonstrates an affectionate relationship between Volney and Thomas Jefferson. (Volney let Jeffer-

son know by letter when Madame Helvetius died; Chinard reproduces the letter on p. 123.) Volney also knew Madison and Monroe. Chinard argues convincingly that Jefferson, rather than their common friend Barlow, translated the invocation and first twenty chapters of Volney's *Ruins* (pp. 109–18). This would mean that the man who made a case for African inferiority also—and at roughly the same time—translated a historically pivotal document which made the case that black Africans had been the earliest civilized peoples and the fount of Western civilization. In twenty-first-century terms this would make Jefferson both an influential "racist" and a pioneering (though secretive) handmaiden of American "Afrocentrism."

It is easy to forget how small the elite world was in 1790. The New York Public Library has, for example, a copy of *The Ruins* that Volney gave to Aaron Burr. Volney's last large work, on the climate and soil of the United States, was first translated into English by Brockden Brown. Judging from Brown's many notes, he was no fan of Volney. Brown pioneered the North American novel, most famously with *Wieland*. His novels are frightening tales in which people stand day and night in danger of losing their minds. He wrote four novels in a mental fever between 1798 and 1800, then gave up fiction. The Volney translation was one of his last significant literary jobs before his early death. Brown believed black people would turn white after a few generations in a northern climate, a view aired, though not endorsed, in Volney's America book.

193–94 "The natives of Africa": Henri Grégoire, *On the Cultural Achievements of Negroes* (Amherst: University of Massachusetts Press, 1996 [1808]), trans. Thomas Cassirer and Jean-François Brière, p. 74. Grégoire cites Volney most significantly on p. 10 and attacks Jefferson directly on pp. 20–21 and 64. Jefferson's letters to Grégoire and Barlow are on pp. xliv of Cassirer and Brière's excellent introduction. The classical sourcings appear in ch. 1, the gallery of distinguished blacks mainly in ch. 8. By the way, Grégoire explicitly connected the fate of blacks with those of Jews and the Irish. Blacks and Irish "have already been linked in a manner that is equally insulting to the inhabitants of Africa and Ireland, by being represented as hordes of brutes who are incapable of self-government and must be subjected for all time to the iron scepter that the British government has held over them for centuries . . . Irishmen, Jews, and Negroes, your virtues and talents are your own; your vices are the work of nations who call themselves Christian. The more you are maligned, the more these nations are indicted for their guilt" (p. 39). Grégoire grew up near a large, much oppressed Jewish community in Lorraine; the first English translation of *On the Cultural Achievements of Negroes* was by David Bailie Warden, who had been exiled from Britain for his part in the 1798 Irish rebellion (pp. x, xvi).

194 "Mankind generally allow": The *Freedom's Journal* article is in Moses, ed., *Classical Black Nationalism*, pp. 53–59. The editors, Samuel E. Cornish and John B. Russwurm, eventually split over emigration, as Moses discusses in his valuable introduction (p. 14). Cornish had left the paper by the fall of 1827. Russwurm carried on, taking the paper slowly in a procolonizationist direction. *Freedom's Journal* folded in 1829; not long afterward, Russwurm left for Liberia. Cornish, meanwhile, started *The Rights of All* and agitated against colonization, as in August 1829: "The ridiculous doctrine of a *separate people, separate interests, extraneous mass, dangerous evil,* &c., is fraught with 10,000 evil consequences . . ." See Miller, *Search for a Black Nationality*, pp. 82–90.

I regret that I have not had the opportunity to trace further Volney's and Grégoire's possible influence on Americans. Diop, in *African Origin of Civilization* (pp. 50–51 and 73), argues that Volney's view was rather orthodox in France at the time, only to be overturned by Jean-François Champollion and Gaston-Camille-Charles Maspero, two important figures in early- and mid-century archaeology. Diop quotes Champollion: "The opinion that the ancient population of Egypt belonged to the Negro African race, is an error long accepted as the truth . . . A serious authority declared himself in favor of this view and popularized the error. Such was the effect of what the celebrated Volney published on the various races of men that he had observed in Egypt."

194 *Ethiopian Manifesto:* In Moses, ed., *Classical Black Nationalism*, pp. 60–69.

194–95 "When I contemplate": Alexis de Tocqueville, *Democracy in America* (New York: Knopf, 1945), trans. Henry Reeve, vol. 1, pp. 378–79. Tocqueville saw blacks and whites, unlike Indians, as doomed to coexistence: "The Indians will perish," but blacks and whites are "two races . . . fastened to each other without intermingling; and they are alike unable to separate entirely or to combine" (vol. 1, p. 356). He felt they never would combine ("I do not believe that the white and black races will ever live in any country upon an equal footing" [vol. 1, p. 373]), and so the long-term possibilities were either everlasting racial oppression or exterminating war of some kind.

195–96 "I know that the blacks": I am using the version of Walker's *Appeal* excerpted in Moses, ed., *Classical Black Nationalism*, pp. 68–89.

196 a passage in Psalms: The tradition of "Ethiopianism" is treated at length in Drake, *Redemption*.

197 the Great Disappointment: On William Miller, Millerites, and the Great Disappointment, see Paul Boyer, *When Time Shall Be No More: Prophecy Belief in Modern American Culture* (Cambridge, Mass.: Harvard University Press, 1992), pp. 80–86; Ruth Alden Doan, *The Miller Heresy, Millennialism, and American Culture* (Philadelphia: Temple University Press, 1987), p. 52 (for Great Disappointment of October 22, 1844), pp. 202–6 (aftermath of the Disappointment). Doan sketches some interesting ties between Millerism and abolitionism on pp. 180–87.

197 "the children glide away": The European visitor was Basil Hall, quoted, as is Tocqueville, in Robert H. Wiebe, *Self-Rule: A Cultural History of American Democracy* (Chicago: University of Chicago Press, 1995), p. 48.

198 "merged in the habits": Martin R. Delany, *The Condition, Elevation, Emigration, and Destiny of the Colored People of the United States* (Baltimore: Black Classic Press, 1993 [1852]), p. 209; "although it may seem": "An Address to the Colored People of the United States, from the Colored National Convention of 1848," in Mullane, ed., *Crossing the Danger Water*, p. 111; "You had better all die": Henry Highland Garnet, "An Address to the Slaves of the United States of America," in Mullane, ed., p. 119; "the great law of progress" and "military tactics": "An Address . . . 1848," in Mullane, ed., pp. 108–9.

Delany wrote about merging in the habits of oppressors around 1836; the remark appears in an appendix (on African migration) to *Condition . . . of the Colored People*. Delany, like most black leaders, argued that blacks had internalized the judgments of whites as to the nature of blackness. Thus the need for a racial-psychological tonic of some kind and, to a degree, the need for avowedly black leaders. Delany rejected whites' negative judgments and any further merging with oppressors—including, on the whole, the belief that black skin had significance—except in that his solution was for blacks to separate racially. The point was that blacks should be separate and equal, rather than separate and inferior. Black leaders tended to arrange themselves along a line from nonracial, reformist integration to racial separation. Nonracial reformism was, by its nature, a less articulated and visible position. One group in Philadelphia, however, did advocate abandoning the use of *colored* and *African* altogether, preferring *oppressed Americans*. *Colored American* editor Samuel Cornish, in New York, replied, "Nonsense brethren!! You are COLORED AMERICANS. The indians are RED AMERICANS, and the white people are WHITE AMERICANS and *you are as good as they, and they are no better than you.*" Litwack, *North of Slavery*, pp. 238–39. See Sterling Stuckey, *Slave Culture: Nationalist Theory and the Foundations of Black America* (New York: Oxford University Press, 1987), ch. 3.

198–99 as did Delany: Delany discusses various proposals for moving abroad in *Condition . . . of the Colored People*, pp. 160–89, 209–15. For a broader treatment, see Miller, *Search for a Black Nationality*. Miller's second part (pp. 93–274) is dominated by Delany and his milieu. On the Haiti projects, also see Miller, pp. 232–49. On the West, see Berwanger, *Frontier against Slavery*, pp. 34–37, and Taylor, *In Search of the Racial Frontier*, ch. 3.

199 "the savage chiefs": Frederick Douglass, "African Civilization Society," in Moses, ed., *Classical Black Nationalism*, p. 139. The possibility of using cotton grown in Africa to undercut the economy of the slave South is mentioned in Delany (citing Robert Campbell), *Official Report of the Niger Valley Exploring Party* (1861), in Moses, ed., *Classical Black Nationalism*, pp. 158–59.

200 "No one idea": Douglass, "African Civilization Society," p. 137; "the ancient Egyptians" and "The poor bondman": Douglass, "Negro Claims Ethnologically Considered," in Philip S. Foner, ed., *The Life and Writings of Frederick Douglass* (New York: International Publishers, 1975), vol. 2, pp. 296, 308.

200–1 "Is it not apparent": Crummell's speech is reprinted in Moses, ed., *Classical Black Nationalism*, pp. 169–87. See also Moses's biography, *Alexander Crummell: A Study of Civilization and Discontent* (New York: Oxford University Press, 1989), pp. 130–40.

201–3 "I need not recount": Lincoln's remarks were taken down by an official recorder. They are reprinted in Moses, ed., *Classical Black Nationalism*, pp. 209–14. See also Benjamin Quarles, *Lincoln and the Negro* (New York: DaCapo, 1991 [1962]), pp. 115–23. Black reaction was generally negative. On blaming blacks for the Civil War, Douglass wrote, "A horse thief pleading the existence of the horse as the apology for his theft, or a highwayman contending that the money in the traveler's pocket is the sole first cause of his robbery are about as much entitled to respect as is the President's reasoning at this point." Lincoln's hope, expressed to the delegation, that blacks would enjoy themselves somewhere in Central America inspired one contemporary parodist: "The festive island of Nova Zembla has been in existence for some time, and is larger than any smaller place I know of. A trip on your part to Nova Zembla will benefit both races. I cannot promise you much bliss right away. You may starve at first, or die on the passage; but in the Revolutionary War George Washington lived exclusively on futures." Quarles, *Lincoln and the Negro*, pp. 118–19.

204 "apart from the antipathy" and "It is useless": *Report of the Select Committee on Emancipation and Colonization* (Washington, D.C.: Government Printing Office, 1862), pp. 11–13. The committee briefly examined history, finding that the Revolutionary generation "had been constantly exclaiming against the influx of this evil, and attributing it to the rapacity of British merchants, sustained by a partial government at home, at the expense of the colonists and to their great detriment"—though the committee also reached further afield, characterizing slavery as "this barbarous relic of Asiatic policy" (pp. 5–6). The committee emphasized the national character of slavery: "The fortunes which have in times past been accumulated by the purchase of negroes on the African coast and their sale to southern planters were mostly amassed by people residing in those States where slavery had long been abolished by law. Moreover, from the time when the northern States began to declare the children of slave mothers thereafter born should be free, the slaves in those States began to decline in their

market value, and many owners, actuated by self-interest, transported their slaves to the more southern States for better markets. Thus it will be observed that the responsibility for the evil of slavery in the southern States rests not alone upon the people of those States" (pp. 14–15). Finally, the House committee found that white dislike of blacks was greater in the North than in the South: "in proportion as the legal barriers established by slavery have been removed by emancipation, the prejudice of caste becomes stronger, and public opinion more intolerant to the negro race" (p. 15).

204 "Our republican institutions": James Mitchell, *Letter on the Relation of the White and African Races in the United States, Showing the Necessity of the Colonization of the Latter. Addressed to the President of the U.S.* (Washington, D.C.: Government Printing Office, 1862). Mitchell also blamed slavery on England (pp. 12–13) and, significantly, linked Western support for the Union to Western white dislike of blacks (p. 8).

205 "I cannot make it": Abraham Lincoln, "Annual Message to Congress," December 1, 1862, in *The Life and Works of Abraham Lincoln* (New York: Current Literature Publishing Company, 1907), vol. 5, pp. 530–37. Lincoln's mention of black people needing a suitable climate, which was typical of colonization writing, particularly white colonization writing, is interesting in view of the powerful and long-standing pro-slavery argument that blacks were needed as labor in the South because the climate *there* better suited blacks than whites. This climate theory was considered, at once, one of the most rational arguments for black slavery and against having blacks in North America.

205 One Lincoln cabinet member: Gideon Welles. Quarles, *Lincoln and the Negro*, pp. 132–33. On Redpath, see Staudenraus, *African Colonization Movement*, p. 344, and the advertisements placed by Redpath in *Douglass' Monthly*, November 1862. One advertisement above his name, dated November 30, 1860, is addressed, "To the Blacks, Men of Color, and Indians in the United States and British North American Provinces," and includes the offer of a "Guide Book for the use of those persons of African or Indian descent" interested in immigrating to Haiti.

205–6 "It is no less true": Lincoln, "Annual Address," 1862, pp. 531–32.

206–7 "This is the trouble": Douglass, "Spirit of Colonization," in Foner, ed., *Life and Writings*, vol. 3, p. 263; "he has gone about": *Douglass' Monthly*, August 1862.

207 "The establishment": Douglass, "The Douglass Institute," in Foner, ed., *Life and Writings*, vol. 4, pp. 178–79.

208 "will end in a contest": The interview with President Johnson is in Douglass, *Life and Writings*, ed. Foner, vol. 4, pp. 183–91.

209 "The last vestiture": Elliott's speech is quoted in Bennett, *Before the* Mayflower, pp. 242–43.

210 "Slavery is dead": Phillips quoted in Bennett, *Before the* Mayflower, p. 260.

211 "The white race": Harlan's dissent quoted in H. L. Pohlman, ed., *Political Thought and the American Judiciary* (Amherst: University of Massachusetts Press, 1993), p. 221.

211 "look into affairs": Committee member Henry Adams quoted in Cedric J. Robinson, *Black Movements in America* (New York: Routledge, 1997), p. 89. Robinson gives a concise summary of the Exodusters on pp. 89–92. The basic work on the exodus is Nell Irvin Painter, *Exodusters: Black Migration to Kansas after Reconstruction* (Lawrence: University Press of Kansas, 1986).

212 "the idea that colored people" and "Suffering and hardships": Douglass quoted in William S. McFeely, *Frederick Douglass* (New York: Norton, 1991), pp. 300, 303; "somewhere where we could live": Henry Adams quoted in Robinson, *Black Movements*, p. 91.

213 "perhaps the Negro's": Bennett, *Before the* Mayflower, p. 296.

213 "you have at no time": Bennett, *Before the* Mayflower, pp. 278–79.

213–14 "the most patient": Washington's speech is quoted in Bennett, *Before the* Mayflower, pp. 264–65.

214–15 "It is not a pleasing": Chesnutt quoted in Bennett, *Before the* Mayflower, p. 265; "Be the requirement": Griggs quoted in Wilson Jeremiah Moses, *The Wings of Ethiopia: Studies in African-American Life and Letters* (Ames: Iowa State University Press, 1990), pp. 229–30.

215 "professed abolitionists": Wilson quoted in Bernard W. Bell, *The Afro-American Novel and Its Tradition* (Amherst: University of Massachusetts Press, 1987), p. 49.

216 "the best blood": Harper quoted in Bell, *Afro-American Novel*, p. 58.

216–17 "we spend four years," "Float on," and "if we die": Sutton Griggs, *Imperium in Imperio* (New York: AMS Press, 1975 [1899]), pp. 200, 263, 221. Belton chooses his death by refusing to go along with the Imperium's bloody race-war plans. Bernard's graveside speech occurs just after he and the other Imperium leaders have executed Belton. Griggs basically brings Tocqueville's despairing vision of the 1830s up to the turn of the century. Griggs was still in his twenties when he wrote this stilted, deeply touching, hopeless novel.

218–19 "God has given": Ferris quoted in Moses, *Wings of Ethiopia*, p. 101, on Ferris and his circle, see Kevin K. Gaines, *Uplifting the Race: Black Leadership, Politics, and Culture in the Twentieth Century* (Chapel Hill: University of North Carolina Press, 1996), ch. 4.

219 "the future belongs": Barber quoted in Gaines, *Uplifting the Race*, p. 109.

THE NEW NEGRO: THE BEAUTIFUL DESPAIR OF THE HARLEM RENAISSANCE

220 "To promote" and "really unfit": Garvey quoted in Judith Stein, *The World of Marcus Garvey: Race and Class in Modern Society* (Baton Rouge: Louisiana State University Press, 1986), pp. 30–31. The following discussion of Garvey is based primarily on Stein's book.

221 "The black and white races": Marcus Garvey in Amy Jacques Garvey, comp., *The Philosophy and Opinions of Marcus Garvey, or, Africa for the Africans, Volumes I and II* (Dover, Mass.: Majority Press, 1986 [1923 and 1925]), p. 89.

222 "impractical": John Bruce quoted in Stein, *World of Marcus Garvey*, p. 64.

222–23 "will send a thrill": Ferris quoted in Stein, *World of Marcus Garvey*, p. 81; "by the principle" and "we also demand": Garvey, comp., *Philosophy and Opinions*, pp. 138, 140.

223 "the foremost pro-negro," "redeem Africa," and "I am writing": Stein, *World of Marcus Garvey*, pp. 84, 101.

223 "This is a white man's": Stein, *World of Marcus Garvey*, p. 154.

224 "I was speaking": Stein, *World of Marcus Garvey*, p. 159; "through an honest" and "Between the Ku Klux Klan": Garvey, comp., *Philosophy and Opinions*, p. 71.

224 "intense hatred": the letter is reproduced in Garvey, comp., *Philosophy and Opinions*, pp. 294–300; the hatred quote is on p. 295. The eight signers were a mix of newspaper editors, NAACP leaders, and businessmen.

225–26 "I'm going home" and Sina Banks's remarks: T. Lindsay Baker and Julie P. Baker, eds., *The WPA Oklahoma Slave Narratives* (Norman: University of Oklahoma Press, 1996), 34; "Ha! Ha! White folks" and "The Patteroll Song" are on pp. 434–35 and 96.

227 "The Negro could not ever": LeRoi Jones, *Blues People: Negro Music in White America* (New York: William Morrow, 1963), p. 80. Jones was, of course, sharply aware that the refinement of an American beauty within the confines of an American racial separation was just the beginning of irony—the first in an ironic series. Elsewhere he writes, "Ragtime was a Negro music,

resulting from the Negro's appropriation of white piano techniques used in show music. Popularized ragtime, which flooded the country with songsheets in the first decade of this century, was a dilution of the Negro style. And finally, the show and 'society' music the Negroes in the pre-blues North made was a kind of bouncy, essentially vapid appropriation of the popularized imitations of Negro imitations of white minstrel music, which, as I mentioned earlier, came from white parodies of Negro life and music. And then we can go back even further to the initial 'steal' American Negro music is based on, that is, those initial uses Euro-American music was put to by the Afro-Americans. The hopelessly interwoven fabric of American life where blacks and whites pass so quickly as to become only grays!" (pp. 110–11). See also Albert Murray, *Stomping the Blues* (New York: Da Capo, 1989).

229 "Melanophobia, or fear": Zangwill quoted in Moses, *Wings of Ethiopia*, p. 26.

229 The Atlanta riot: See Gaines, *Uplifting the Race*, ch. 2.

229–30 "Recall how suddenly": Alain Locke's essay has been widely anthologized. I am using the version in Mullane, ed., *Crossing the Danger Water*, pp. 481–90.

231 "One of the most promising": "The Negro Artist and the Racial Mountain" originally appeared in *The Nation*, June 23, 1926. I am using the reprint in Mullane, ed., *Crossing the Danger Water*, pp. 503–7.

232 "Just as soon": Du Bois, "Criteria of Negro Art," in David Levering Lewis, ed., *W. E. B. Du Bois: A Reader* (New York: Henry Holt, 1995), p. 515; originally published in *The Crisis*, October 1926.

233 "There are mountains": Arna Bontemps, "Golgotha Is a Mountain," in David Levering Lewis, ed., *The Portable Harlem Renaissance Reader* (New York: Penguin, 1994), p. 225.

233 African visual arts: The rediscovery of African art in the United States via Germany is discussed in Malgorzata Irek, "From Berlin to Harlem: Felix von Luschan, Alain Locke, and the New Negro," in Werner Sollors and Maria Diedrich, eds., *The Black Columbiad: Defining Moments in African American Literature and Culture* (Cambridge, Mass.: Harvard University Press, 1994), pp. 174–84.

233 "Dese spirituals": Eric J. Sundquist, *To Wake the Nations: Race in the Making of American Literature* (Cambridge, Mass.: Harvard University Press, 1993), pp. 472–73. The unnamed woman was first quoted in Jeanette Robinson Murphy, "The Survival of African Music in America," *Popular Science Monthly* 55 (1899).

234 "song of the end" and "The folk-spirit": Jean Toomer's unpublished autobiography, quoted in Mullane, ed., *Crossing the Danger Water*, p. 510; "Now just before an epoch's sun": from the section of *Cane* titled "Song of the Son," in Mullane, ed., *Crossing the Danger Water*, p. 511.

235 "I is got to see": Sterling Brown, "Long Gone," in Lewis, ed., *Portable Harlem Renaissance*, p. 235.

235 Sadness: A character in Dunbar's novel *The Sport of the Gods*.

235 "Gee, brown boy": Helene Johnson, "Poem," in Lewis, ed., *Portable Harlem Renaissance*, pp. 277–78.

236 "van vechtening": Gwendolyn Bennett quoted in Steven Watson, *The Harlem Renaissance: Hub of African-American Culture, 1920–1930* (New York: Pantheon, 1995); "Jazz, the blues": Van Vechten quoted in David Levering Lewis, *When Harlem Was in Vogue* (New York: Knopf, 1981), p. 98; "write about this": Van Vechten quoted in Watson, p. 101; "Savages! Savages": Van Vechten, *Nigger Heaven* (New York: Harper Colophon, 1971 [1926]), pp. 89–90.

236 "one damned orgy": Du Bois, "On Carl Van Vechten's *Nigger Heaven*," in Lewis, ed., *W. E. B. Du Bois*, p. 517; originally published in *The Crisis*, December 1926. On the same page Du Bois notes, "Van Vechten is not the great artist who with remorseless scalpel probes the awful depths of life. To him there are no depths. It is the surface mud he slops about in."

On the reception of Van Vechten's novel, see Watson, *Harlem Renaissance*, p. 113; Lewis, ed., *Portable Harlem Renaissance*, p. xxxiii, 108–9 (James Weldon Johnson), 169–70 (Claude McKay).

236 "the real stuff," "it is the finest thing," and "out-niggered": In Watson, *Harlem Renaissance*, pp. 82, 84; "*Nigger Heaven* in a larger and more violent": Bell, *Afro-American Novel*, p. 116. James Weldon Johnson, cited above, discusses the novels together.

237 "the Aframerican is merely": Schuyler, "The Negro-Art Hokum," in Lewis, ed., *Portable Harlem Renaissance*, pp. 96–99; originally published in *The Nation*, June 16, 1926.

237 "laughing all the time": Hughes, *Not without Laughter* (New York: Knopf, 1951), p. 313. At the very end Hughes's hero, Sandy, threatens to drift into the high life until he sees his aunt Harriett, a nightclub singer who urges his mother to keep him in school: "This boy's gotta get ahead—all of us niggers are too far back in this white man's country to let any brains go to waste!" (p. 323). Sandy and his mother then walk off through the Chicago streets. They pass a church, and from a hymn Hughes takes his last lines: "An' we'll understand it better by an' by" (p. 325).

238 "in practically every instance," "Everybody," and "And So On". Schuyler, *Black No More. Being an Account of the Strange and Wonderful Workings of Science in the Land of the Free*, A.D. *1933–1940* (Boston: Northeastern University Press, 1989 [1931]), pp. 218, 222. Schuyler had one child, Philippa. His wife was a white woman from Texas. Philippa had a gift for music. Her parents tended to do behavioral experiments on her, but she turned out charming. When she began to succeed as a pianist, she tried changing her name and saying she was various things (such as Spanish) to avoid the penalties of blackness. When George, who clearly loved his daughter and took pride in her, wrote a lengthy (and never published) manuscript history of notable blacks in America, he gave her a few pages. She insisted she be taken out of "The Negro in America." If you go to the Schomburg Center of the New York Public Library, in Harlem, you can find the manuscript. Leontyne Price is featured on p. 979. The bottom part of the page has paper pasted over the type. Pages 980 to 982 are missing, and the top of 983 is covered over. Then we learn about Hale Smith. See Kathryn Talalay, *Composition in Black and White: The Life of Philippa Schuyler* (New York: Oxford University Press, 1995).

238–39 "break the chains," "free himself," "Paul the debonair," and "Ironically enough": Wallace Thurman, *Infants of the Spring* (New York: AMS Press, 1975 [1932]), pp. 144–45, 147, 280, 283–84.

"THIS SPECIAL WAY OF LIFE"

240 "so he could get a son" and "free transportation": Elijah Muhammad quoted in Martha F. Lee, *The Nation of Islam: An American Millenarian Movement* (Syracuse, N.Y.: Syracuse University Press, 1996), pp. 22, 24. Concerning the Nation of Islam, I have relied on Lee's concise and careful account.

241 "the largest mechanical," "our former," and "observe the operations": Muhammad quoted in Lee, *Nation of Islam*, pp. 34, 32, 31; Malcolm X gives a vivid version of the Yakub story on pp. 190–94 of *The Autobiography of Malcolm X* (New York: Ballantine, 1992 [1964]), identifying the island as Patmos.

241–42 "revolutionary" and "archaic": I am using the version of Richard Wright's "Blueprint for Negro Writing" in Lewis, ed., *Portable Harlem Renaissance*, pp. 194–205.

243 "the most important": E. Franklin Frazier, *The Negro Church in America* (New York:

Schocken, 1974 [1964]), p. 75. This edition includes a companion text by C. Eric Lincoln, *The Black Church since Frazier*.

245 "debauched tenth": Du Bois was commenting on Claude McKay's *Home to Harlem*. After reading it, Du Bois claimed to feel "like needing a bath." Lewis, ed., *Portable Harlem Renaissance*, pp. xxxiv–xxxv.

246–48 In his moment of greatest doubt: I am using the version of King's "Letter from Birmingham City Jail" in Mullane, ed., *Crossing the Danger Water*, pp. 633–46. "When you ask a man": quoted in Richard H. King, *Civil Rights and the Idea of Freedom* (Athens: University of Georgia Press, 1996), p. 51; "traitors to the race" and "inflamed tensions": Taylor Branch, *Parting the Waters: America in the King Years, 1954–63* (New York: Simon and Schuster, 1988), pp. 727, 737. For the civil-rights era I have relied greatly on Branch's book and its successor, *Pillar of Fire: America in the King Years, 1963–65* (New York: Simon and Schuster, 1998).

247 "the one people": Malcolm X, *Autobiography*, p. 189.

248 "This is what you get": Carpenter quoted in Branch, *Parting the Waters*, p. 745. The Moore story is from the same source, pp. 747–50.

251 "racist movement": Moses quoted in King, *Civil Rights*, p. 166.

251 "will no longer speak": Moses quoted in Branch, *Pillar of Fire*, p. 590.

251 peaceful desegregation: I don't mean to underestimate white Southern resistance to desegregation, whether in the 1960s or later. For a summary of scholarship on this subject, see Hugh Davis Graham, "Since 1965: The South and Civil Rights," in Griffin and Doyle, eds., *The South as an American Problem*, pp. 145–63.

252 "It is absolutely necessary": King quoted in Lincoln, *Black Church since Frazier*, p. 126.

252–53 "The fundamental distortion": The 1966 statement appears as appendix A to Frazier, *Negro Church in America*.

255 "the problem is whether": Moses quoted in King, *Civil Rights*, p. 175.

255 "learning to think," "with Hatred," and "the white man": King, *Civil Rights*, pp. 153, 169, 160.

256 "the white Christian churches": The manifesto appears as appendix B to Frazier, *Negro Church in America*.

256 "We [Americans] are a people": Frazier, *Negro Church in America*, p. 193.

257 "There were tens of thousands": Letter is in Malcolm X, *Autobiography*, pp. 391–92.

257 "if he could accept": Cleaver told this story in *Soul on Ice* (1965); the passage appears in Mullane, ed., *Crossing the Danger Water*, p. 675.

WHITE FLIGHT

269–70 The theology: This summary description of Christian Identity is based on Michael Barkun, *Religion and the Racist Right: The Origins of the Christian Identity Movement* (Chapel Hill: University of North Carolina Press, 1994). "Communism can never be checked": William H. Murray, *Adam and Cain: Symposium of Old Bible History, Sumerian Empire, Importance of Blood of Race, Juggling Juggernaut of the Leaders of the Jews, the Gothic Civilization of Adam and the Ten Commandments of His Church*, 2nd ed. (Boston: Meador Press, 1952), p. 113. *The Protocols of the Elders of Zion* takes up ch. 5.

270 the Order and Aryan Nations: Concerning the white underground, I benefited greatly from Kevin Flynn and Gary Gerhardt, *The Silent Brotherhood: Inside America's Racist Under-*

ground (New York: Free Press, 1989). See also James Ridgeway, *Blood in the Face: The Ku Klux Klan, Aryan Nations, Nazi Skinheads, and the Rise of a New White Culture* (New York: Thunder's Mouth, 1995). Raphael Ezekiel's *The Racist Mind: Portraits of American Neo-Nazis and Klansmen* (New York: Viking, 1995) gives a more personal view. Lyman Tower Sargent, ed., *Extremism in America: A Reader* (New York: New York University Press, 1995), collects many useful post–World War II documents. Oklahoma-bombing conspiracy theories are generously covered in Jim Keith, *OK Bomb!: Conspiracy and Cover-Up* (Lilburn, Ga.: IllumiNet Press, 1996). On Waco, see Stuart A. Wright, ed., *Armageddon in Waco: Critical Perspectives on the Branch Davidian Conflict* (Chicago: University of Chicago Press, 1995).

"THE ESSENCE OF WHITENESS": SPAIN, ENGLAND, AND THE COLORS OF EMPIRE

277 light people cannot help: The persistence of "natural aversion" ideas to explain white dislike of nonwhites, and in particular blacks, is something to reckon with. For example, Winthrop Jordan, in his massive, classic work *White over Black: American Attitudes toward the Negro, 1550–1812* (Chapel Hill: University of North Carolina Press, 1968), offers the fantasy of Robert Pyle, a Pennsylvania Quaker. In the story, Pyle finds a black pot along the road. He carries the pot to a ladder, "up which I must go to heaven with the pott in my hand." But the ladder is too steep, and unsecured, "at which I steps down and laid the pot at the foot of the ladder, and said them that will take it might, for I found work enough for both hands to take hold of this ladder." Jordan writes, "When he awoke this good Quaker considered the matter and decided firmly, in an astonishing phrase, 'self must bee left behind, and to lett black negroes or pots alone.' " Jordan continues in a footnote, "If these materials have no particular psychological significance, a whole generation of American mothers has been hoodwinked by Dr. Benjamin Spock on the subject of toilet training. There is voluminous scholarly and clinical literature which does not of course support any single interpretation of the symbols and 'meaning' of these fantasies but which also does not permit us to pronounce them meaningless or unconnected with an important function of the body. There are many kinds of 'pots' (not all of them 'black') but only one which could have been associated with such 'motion' and with the obligation to leave part of the 'self,' i.e. selfishness, 'behind' " (p. 256). I find Jordan's interpretation considerably clearer in meaning than Pyle's dream. Jordan is struggling to suggest that some whites unconsciously associate blacks with excrement. He leaves it an open question whether whites will always feel this way: "although the fantasy of Robert Pyle in 1698 suggests that repulsion for blackness may in some individuals have derived from deep levels in the personality which were associated with or perhaps even dependent upon purely physiological processes, the fact remains that Pyle perceived blackness in a specific and derogatory social context. So the historian, rather like the modern student of race-awareness in very young children, must remain tentative and baffled as to whether white men originally responded adversely to the Negro's color because of strictly accidental prior color valuation *per se*, instinctual repulsion founded on physiological processes or perhaps fear of the night which may have had adaptive value in human evolution, the association of dirt and darkened complexion with the lower classes in Europe, or association of blackness with Negroes who were inferior in culture or status" (p. 257). This is, I think, a great insult to "the historian" and his or her capacity for understanding, though it does, inadvertently perhaps, mark an important continuity

in white thinking—to find a warrant in nature, that is, outside of social responsibility and will, for white racial feeling.

281–82 "English men": The Rhode Island law is in Jordan, *White over Black*, p. 70; the Virginia law of 1691 in A. Leon Higginbotham, Jr., *In the Matter of Color: Race and the American Legal Process: The Colonial Period* (New York: Oxford University Press, 1978), p. 44; the 1664 Maryland law, and its uses, in Joel Williamson, *New People: Miscegenation and Mulattoes in the United States* (Baton Rouge: Louisiana State University Press, 1995), p. 10; for a fuller text of the law and of its 1681 successor, see Lerone Bennett, Jr., *Before the* Mayflower: *A History of Black America* (New York: Penguin, 1988 [1961]), pp. 301–2; "though they are black": "Against the Traffic of Mens-body," in *The Annals of America*, vol. 1: *1493–1754, Discovering a New World* (Chicago: Encyclopaedia Britannica, 1968), p. 274.

282 Europeans, Hindus: François Bernier quoted in Leon Poliakov, *The Aryan Myth: A History of Racist and Nationalist Ideas in Europe*, trans. Edmund Howard (New York: Barnes & Noble Books, 1996 [1971]), p. 143.

283 "whereof white," "When I consider," "how certain soever," and "certainly knows": John Locke, *An Essay concerning Human Understanding* (Oxford: Clarendon Press, 1975), ed. Peter H. Nidditch, pp. 607, 319, 474, 62; see the discussion by Poliakov, who relates Locke's thinking to that of Leibniz: *Aryan Myth*, pp. 145–47 and 349 n. 52.

284 "all things considered": Samuel Sewall, *The Selling of Joseph: A Memorial*, in *Annals of America*, vol. 1, p. 317. Sewall also rejected the curse-of-Ham explanation as irrelevant. He published this antislavery memorial just a few years after publicly apologizing for killing witches (in his capacity as a judge).

284 "When *Self-love*": John Woolman, *Some Considerations on the Keeping of Negroes* (1754), in Giles Gunn, ed., *Early American Writing* (New York: Penguin, 1994), p. 393.

285 "In the formation": Noah Webster, "An Examination into the Leading Principles of the Federal Constitution," October 17, 1787, in Bernard Bailyn, ed., *The Debate on the Constitution: Federalist and Antifederalist Speeches, Articles, and Letters during the Struggle over Ratification*, vol. 1, p. 129; "By adopting this system": James Wilson, "Summation and Final Rebuttal," in Bailyn, ed., *Debate on the Constitution*, vol. 1, p. 868.

285–86 "The inconsistency": Jeremy Belknap quoted in Leon F. Litwack, *North of Slavery: The Negro in the Free States, 1790–1860* (Chicago: University of Chicago Press, 1961), p. 8; the Declaration of the Causes, etc., is quoted in Higginbotham, *In the Matter of Color*, pp. 374–75. Higginbotham also offers several examples of white revolutionaries decrying slavery for themselves, as does Litwack (pp. 8–11). John Adams, under the man-of-the-people pseudonym Humphrey Ploughjogger, is quoted in Alexander Saxton, *The Rise and Fall of the White Republic: Class Politics and Mass Culture in Nineteenth-Century America* (London: Verso, 1990), p. 30. Saxton notes that Adams's Ploughjogger letters "solicited artisan and yeoman support through excoriations of aristocracy and assertions of a white egalitarian ethic" (p. 30). That, it seems to me, is the central point, not only for whites but for blacks in that they had to deal with white people, which they obviously did.

A particularly vivid example of a white Revolutionary writer using slavery language in terms of intra-white relations is the text of "John Humble" originally published in the Philadelphia *Independent Gazetteer*, October 29, 1787, which begins: "The humble address of the *low born* of the United States of America, to their fellow slaves scattered throughout the world—greeting." Bailyn, ed., *Debate on the Constitution*, vol. 1, p. 224–26. See, in the same volume, Luther Martin's "The Genuine Information" (originally published 1787–1788 in Maryland), pp. 631–61, esp. pp. 642–43 and 645–47. Martin uses the language of slavery both for whites and blacks, and in similar ways, while recognizing that it is a more concrete issue for the latter.

The use by whites of slavery language was not just an intriguing hypocrisy, any more than was the keeping by free whites of nonwhites in slavery. Whites most commonly used slavery language in examining the relations between laboring and shopkeeping men, on one hand, and aristocrats (real or potential) and men of property, on the other. Both aristocracy and significant property holding were, of course, inheritable, and most often inherited, conditions, which is to say blood privileges, and so eminently comparable to racial status. In this sense, "slavery" for whites and blacks had much more in common than is usually supposed. If we fail to appreciate this, then our history of slavery and race will always end up being a history of (separate) races rather than a shared history of human beings—that is, we will have one history (of race) running parallel to another, larger history (of America). For example, Gordon Wood, in his invaluable 1969 history, *The Creation of the American Republic, 1776–1787* (New York: Norton, 1972), analyzes at length the political and social debates over aristocracy and property. This is the very arena in which white slavery language played such a significant role. Yet Wood does not discuss race in any way. I find this an important omission, even allowing for the necessary limits of his study. Either all the people in North America at that time were making American history together, or some (white) people were making real history and everyone else was making something exceptional and only of specialized interest, if of interest at all. I incline toward the former view. It seems to me truer to the past, and therefore to the past which has molded our present.

286 Abolition: The New York, Massachusetts, and federal government events are discussed in Litwack, *North of Slavery*, pp. 8, 16, 30–31; James Sullivan quoted in Jordan, *White over Black*, p. 557.

287 "I am apt to suspect": David Hume quoted in Jordan, *White over Black*, p. 253; the efforts of Alexander Hamilton and John Laurens are described in Matthew T. Mellon, *Early American Views on Negro Slavery: From the Letters and Papers of the Founders of the Republic* (New York: Bergman, 1969 [1934]), pp. 51–57.

287 "if prejudices have taken": Tucker quoted in Jordan, *White over Black*, p. 558.

288 "an existing evil": Monroe quoted in Jordan, *White over Black*, p. 563; "the quarter which obtruded": Madison quoted in Mellon, *Early American Views*, p. 140.

288 "the innocent descendants": St. George Tucker quoted in Jordan, *White over Black*, p. 559.

290 a new, better humanity: I do not mean to suggest that the Revolutionary experience was wholly new; rather, that the goal of radical newness had a critical place in people's minds, particularly as the war went on. For a brief treatment, see Edward Countryman, *Americans: A Collision of Histories* (New York: Hill and Wang, 1997), ch. 3.

"THE FREEST OF ALL HUMAN BEINGS": WESTWARD EXPANSION AND THE PRICE OF LIBERTY

292 " 'Westward the star' ": Adams's speech quoted in Saxton, *Rise and Fall*, pp. 34–35.

295 "People of Colour," "the lord of three or four hundred," and "haughtly slaveholders": Eugene Berwanger, *The Frontier against Slavery: Western Anti-Negro Prejudice and the Slavery Extension Controversy* (Urbana: University of Illinois Press, 1967), pp. 19, 18, 26. On the Indiana indenture system, see Berwanger, pp. 10–11. These Indiana Territory laws encompassed Illinois, which was initially part of the territory, and were carried over into Illinois law when it

became a separate territory in 1809. My discussion of the Old Northwest is based on Berwanger's essential work.

295–96 "All these perplexities": Madison quoted in Mellon, *Early American Views*, p. 153. On exclusion laws, see Berwanger, *Frontier against Slavery*, pp. 38–51; on guardianship statutes, see Ira Berlin, *Slaves without Masters: The Free Negro in the Antebellum South* (New York: New Press, 1992 [1974]), pp. 318, 357; on Kentucky laws, see Helen Catterall, *Judicial Cases concerning American Slavery and the Negro* (Washington, D.C.: Carnegie Institution, 1926–1937), vol. 1, p. 276, and Berwanger, p. 45; on slavery in New Mexico, see Quintard Taylor, *In Search of the Racial Frontier: African Americans in the American West, 1528–1990* (New York: Norton, 1998), pp. 74–76; "We shouldn't wonder": Whitman quoted in Saxton, *Rise and Fall*, p. 154 (originally published in the Brooklyn *Daily Eagle*, May 6, 1858).

296–302 "We desire only": *Californian* editorial of March 15, 1848, quoted in Tomás Almaguer, *Racial Fault Lines: The Historical Origins of White Supremacy in California* (Berkeley: University of California Press, 1994), p. 34; "that it should be perfectly understood": all quotations from the California constitutional debate are from Robert Fleming Heizer and Alan F. Almquist, *The Other Californians: Prejudice and Discrimination under Spain, Mexico, and the United States to 1920* (Berkeley: University of California Press, 1977), ch. 4.

302 The first governor: On Burnett, see Heizer and Almquist, *Other Californians*, pp. 123, 127, and Berwanger, *Frontier against Slavery*, pp. 70–73. The quotations from Burnett's opponents are in Berwanger, p. 71. Burnett's proposal was defeated in this first legislature, known as the "legislature of a thousand drinks." Despite the antislavery constitution, blacks were from time to time bought and sold in California until the eve of the Civil War.

304 "parson skinning": Nott quoted in Thomas F. Gossett, *Race: The History of an Idea in America*, new ed. (New York: Oxford University Press, 1997), p. 64.

304–5 "our Saxon ancestors": Mercy Otis Warren, "Observations on the Constitution," in Bailyn, ed., *Debate on the Constitution*, vol. 2, p. 291; "sentiments of liberty": David Hume, *The History of England from the Invasion of Julius Caesar to the Abdication of James the Second* (Boston: Aldine, n.d. [1762]), vol. 1, p. 152. Hume portrays the northerners as cherishing "a fierce and bold liberty," which the Germanic Saxons brought to bear as "founders of the English government" (p. 153). However, the Saxons did tend to take liberty too far, both in their distinctively exterminationist military policy (p. 152) and in an addiction to "intemperance, riot, and disorder," which led to the "want of humanity in all their history" (p. 177); "the hard and dominant": Stowe, preface to *Uncle Tom's Cabin*, quoted in Saxton, *Rise and Fall*, p. 237. The best single source on early-nineteenth-century Anglo-Saxonism in England and America is Reginald Horsman, *Race and Manifest Destiny: The Origins of American Racial Anglo-Saxonism* (Cambridge, Mass.: Harvard University Press, 1981).

306 "the complete harmony," "The black element," and "I see in this fusion": Comte, Gobineau, and Klemm quoted in Poliakov, *Aryan Myth*, pp. 224, 235, 252, respectively.

307 "The New Englanders": Cotton Mather, *The Wonders of the Invisible World* (Boston: Benjamin Harris for Samuel Phillips, 1693), unpaginated, section 2. Mather goes on at length about how "never were more *Satanical Devices* used for the Unsetling [sic] of any People under the Sun, than what have been Employ'd for the Extirpation of the *Vine* which God has here *Planted*" (section 2). This book is Mather's great witchcraft text, and provides case studies, with names, of various witches in his community. At the same time, he notes proudly in section 1, "Such great persons as *Budaeus*, and others, who mistook *Sir Thomas More's* UTOPIA, for a Country really Existent, and stirr'd up some Divines Charitably to undertake a Voyage thither, might now have certainly found a Truth in their Mistake; *New-England* was a true *Utopia*."

307 "And we have reason": Increase Mather quoted in S. T. Joshi, ed., *Documents of American Prejudice: An Anthology of Writings on Race from Thomas Jefferson to David Duke* (New York: Basic Books, 1999), p. 227.

307–8 "About the year 1727": I am using the version of "The Devil and Tom Walker" in Charles Neider, ed., *The Complete Tales of Washington Irving* (New York: Da Capo, 1998), pp. 437–48.

309–10 "as the wife": Hawthorne, "Young Goodman Brown," in Norman Holmes Pearson, ed., *The Complete Novels and Selected Tales of Nathaniel Hawthorne* (New York: Modern Library, 1965), pp. 1033–42.

314 "Among us": Chancellor Harper, "Harper's Memoir on Slavery," in *The Pro-Slavery Argument; as Maintained by the Most Distinguished Writers of the Southern States, Containing the Several Essays, on the Subject, of Chancellor Harper, Governor Hammond, Dr. Simms, and Professor Dew* (New York: Negro Universities Press, 1968 [1852]), p. 20.

315 "If we had": George Fitzhugh, *Sociology for the South; or, The Failure of a Free Society* (1854), excerpted in Joshi, ed., *Documents of American Prejudice*, p. 284. Like several other defenders of slavery, but more so, Fitzhugh staged a defense of slavery as an attack on industrial capitalism. He was influenced by Karl Marx, especially the *Communist Manifesto*. See C. Vann Woodward, *The Future of the Past* (New York: Oxford University Press, 1989), p. 284.

317 "The tendency" and "This inequality": Harper, "Memoir on Slavery," pp. 22–23, 24.

318 "so happy of mood": Simms in "The Morals of Slavery"; "We have to rely": Hammond in "Letter on Slavery," both in *Pro-Slavery Argument*, pp. 217 and 126, respectively.

318 "We need never": Fitzhugh, *Sociology for the South*, p. 284; "one of the most intimate": Harper, "Memoir on Slavery," p. 34; "the negro's friend": Fitzhugh, p. 285.

319 "When Lucifer": Bledsoe, *Liberty and Slavery*, in E. N. Elliott, ed., *Cotton Is King, and Pro-Slavery Arguments: Comprising the Writings of Hammond, Harper, Christy, Stringfellow, Hodge, Bledsoe, and Cartwright, on This Important Subject* (Augusta, Ga.: Pritchard, Abbott & Loomis, 1860), p. 408.

THE ETHIOPIAN OPERA: WHITE MASKS IN BLACKFACE MINSTRELSY

320–21 "missing of the mark": I am using Kenneth A. Telford's translation of Aristotle's *Poetics* (South Bend, Ind.: Gateway, 1961).

322 Dibdin himself: On Charles Dibdin and for the lyrics of "Yankee Doodle," see Hans Nathan, *Dan Emmett and the Rise of Early Negro Minstrelsy* (Norman: University of Oklahoma Press, 1962), pp. 20–21, 11.

322 "I wip de lion": Nathan, *Dan Emmett*, p. 56; "My mammy was a wolf": quoted in Saxton, *Rise and Fall*, p. 168.

323 Zip Coon and "The Free Nigger": See Nathan, *Dan Emmett*, pp. 57–59.

323 "Oh, dar's de wite man": "Lucy Neal" quoted in Robert C. Toll, *Blacking Up: The Minstrel Show in Nineteenth-Century America* (New York: Oxford University Press, 1974), p. 80.

325–26 "Seated at his writing desk": Nathan, *Dan Emmett*, p. 217; "Oh, Camille!": an undated version of a minstrel *Camille*, published by Happy Hours in New York, probably around 1865; "Transcendentalism" and "anapulated": Toll, *Blacking Up*, pp. 70, 55. A good, accessible selection of minstrel materials is Jack Haverly, *Negro Minstrels: A Complete Guide to Negro Minstrelsy, Containing Recitations, Jokes, Crossfires, Conundrums, Riddles, Stump Speeches, Ragtime and Sentimental Songs, etc., Including Hints on Organizing and Successfully Presenting a Performance* (Upper Saddle River, N.J.: Gregg Press, 1969 [1902]). Haverly was a very successful minstrel producer. An excellent collection of (mostly) recent essays is Annemarie Bean, James V. Hatch, and Brooks McNamara, eds., *Inside the Minstrel Mask: Readings in Nineteenth-Century Blackface Minstrelsy* (Hanover, N.H.: Wesleyan University Press, 1996).

326 "attempt to establish" and "The only places": Nathan, *Dan Emmett*, p. 218.

327 "I found myself": Toll, *Blacking Up*, p. 33.

329 "I'm bound": Nathan, *Dan Emmett*, p. 243; the "Dixie" lyrics and the story of the song's wanderings are from Nathan, ch. 4.

330–31 "The episode": Garrison's editorials on Clay, from *The Genius of Universal Emancipation*, quoted in John L. Thomas, ed., *Slavery Attacked: The Abolitionist Crusade* (Englewood Cliffs, N.J.: Prentice-Hall, 1965), pp. 6–10; "First I was": Thome to Weld, in Thomas, ed., p. 29.

331 "As to the governments": Garrison in *Liberator*, December 15, 1837, excerpted in Thomas, ed., *Slavery Attacked*, pp. 76–79.

332 Northern secession: For an example of an anti-Union abolitionist document, see the Massachusetts Anti-Slavery Society document of 1844 in Thomas, ed., *Slavery Attacked*, pp. 87–93.

334 "the slaves" and "It is my shame": Garrison quoted in Henry Mayer, *All on Fire: William Lloyd Garrison and the Abolition of Slavery* (New York: St. Martin's, 1998), pp. 66, 94. The Park Street Church was addressing slavery on Independence Day.

334 "Moral Map": In Mayer, *All on Fire*, with the illustrations following p. 232.

335 "I was generally": Douglass in *My Bondage and My Freedom* (1855), quoted in Eric J. Sundquist, *To Wake the Nations: Race in the Making of American Literature* (Cambridge, Mass.: Harvard University Press, 1993), p. 90. Parker Pillsbury thought Douglass should keep "a *little* of the plantation," while Garrison advised him not to sound too "learned": William S. McFeely, *Frederick Douglass* (New York: Norton, 1991), p. 94.

335 "impudent" and "unconscionable": Quincy quoted in McFeely, *Frederick Douglass*, pp. 168, 147; "was white": Douglass quoted in McFeely, p. 169.

335–36 This marked: This discussion of the break between Douglass and Garrison is based on McFeely, *Frederick Douglass*, pp. 168–82; Mayer, *All on Fire*, pp. 370–74, 428–34; and Litwack, *North of Slavery*, pp. 237–44.

336 "Every principle": Phillips's speech excerpted in Thomas, ed., *Slavery Attacked*, pp. 142–47. On re-enslavement and the Arkansas and other laws, see Berlin, *Slaves without Masters*, pp. 369–80.

336–37 "The next recognized": Douglass's speech on abolitionism is excerpted in Thomas, ed., *Slavery Attacked*, pp. 126–31; "foreign and feeble": Seward quoted in Berwanger, *Frontier against Slavery*, p. 123; "We are for": in Berwanger, p. 131.

337 The Republicans' opponents: On the racial rhetoric of Republicans and Democrats in the late 1850s, see Litwack, *North of Slavery*, pp. 268–77; Berwanger, *Frontier against Slavery*, pp. 128–32. Stephen Douglas used the image of Frederick Douglass sitting in a coach with a white woman to stir the crowd during one 1858 debate with Lincoln: McFeely, *Frederick Douglass*, p. 188.

337 "the negro was endowed": Douglas, in the third joint debate, at Jonesboro, in Arthur Brooks Lapsley, ed., *The Writings of Abraham Lincoln* (New York: G. P. Putnam's Sons, 1923), pp. 324–25.

338 "I will say": This was in the fourth debate with Douglas; excerpted in Joshi, ed., *Documents of American Prejudice*, pp. 287–90.

339 "I propose now": Lincoln quoted in Nathan, *Dan Emmett*, p. 275.

340 "In his interests": Douglass quoted in Sundquist, *To Wake the Nations*, p. 133.

343 We can see this: On the postwar changes in minstrelsy, see Toll, *Blacking Up*, pp. 138–55; Jacob Schrochorn appears in the catalogue for DeWitt's *Ethiopian Comic Drama*, c. 1870. The Flying Black Japs and other nonblack minstrel roles are discussed in Toll, pp. 164–67.

345 "De niggar hoes": Emmett's 1873 "sermon" is in Nathan, *Dan Emmett*, pp. 410–12.

"OLD RACIAL CRIES, OLD RACIAL TIES"

347 "The average": Galton, *Hereditary Genius*, quoted in Gossett, *Race*, p. 156.

347 "dominant races": Spencer quoted in Gossett, *Race*, p. 150; "We belong": Lieber quoted in Gossett, p. 94.

348–49 "wonderful progress" and "All other series": Darwin and Zincke cited in Gossett, *Race*, pp. 311–12.

350 "in some country": The 1862 California petition is in Litwack, *North of Slavery*, p. 262; for prewar Northern segregation generally, see Litwack, chs. 3–5. Gossett, *Race*, p. 274, cites several important cases. On California, see Taylor, *In Search of the Racial Frontier*, pp. 92–94, and Almaguer, *Racial Fault Lines*, pp. 38, 133, 163. "The special favorite" is from Justice Bradley's majority opinion in *Civil Rights Cases*, 109 U.S. 3 (1883), p. 25. The five cases variously concerned refusal of service to "persons of color" in hotels, theaters, and a railroad car. Bradley wrote: "When a man has emerged from slavery . . . there must be some stage in the progress of his elevation when he takes the rank of a mere citizen, and ceases to be the special favorite of the laws . . . There were thousands of free colored people in this country before the abolition of slavery, enjoying all the essential rights of life, liberty, and property the same as white citizens; yet no one, at that time, thought it was any invasion of their personal status as freemen because they were not admitted to all the privileges enjoyed by white citizens, or because they were subjected to discriminations . . ." Justice Harlan replied in dissent that it was "scarcely just to say that the colored race has been the special favorite of the laws. What the nation, through congress, has sought to accomplish in reference to that race is, what had already been done in every state in the Union for the white race, to secure and protect rights belonging to them as freemen and citizens; nothing more." 109 U.S. 3 (1883), p. 61. H. L. Pohlman, ed., *Political Thought and the American Judiciary* (Amherst: University of Massachusetts Press, 1993), excerpts some of the relevant decisions, such as *Strauder v. West Virginia*, pp. 203–13, 218–23. The back-and-forth between House and Senate on school segregation is in Bernard Schwartz, *A History of the Supreme Court* (New York: Oxford University Press, 1993), pp. 165–68.

350–51 With some exceptions: The basic work on the rise of formal segregation is C. Vann Woodward, *The Strange Career of Jim Crow*, rev. ed. (New York: Oxford University Press, 1974 [1955]), supplemented by his article "*Strange Career* Critics: Long May They Persevere," reprinted in Woodward, *Future of the Past*, ch. 17. My thinking on the South, segregation, and lynching has been greatly influenced by Grace Elizabeth Hale's *Making Whiteness: The Culture of Segregation in the South, 1890–1940* (New York: Pantheon, 1998), as well as by W. J. Cash's ageless 1941 work, *The Mind of the South*.

353–54 "An American citizen," "Instead of," and "have none": Godkin, Hoffman, and Walker are quoted in Gossett, *Race*, pp. 298, 281, and 303, respectively.

355 "I am a nigger!" "Whoever has lived," and "All say": Mark Twain, *The Tragedy of Pudd'nhead Wilson* (1893–1894), in *The Unabridged Mark Twain* (Philadelphia: Running Press, 1979), vol. 2, pp. 60, 29, 60.

357 "Dey er gittin' ": Harris quoted in Sundquist, *To Wake the Nations*, p. 338.
358 "All the best": Handy quoted in Toll, *Blacking Up*, p. 195. This discussion of black min-
    strelsy is based on Toll's seventh and eighth chapters.
358 "national music": Douglass is quoted on Stephen Foster in Sundquist, *To Wake the Nations*,
    p. 91. Foster was singing "Zip Coon" and "Jump Jim Crow" even as a child. John Tasker
    Howard, *Stephen Foster: America's Troubadour* (New York: Thomas Y. Crowell, 1953
    [1934]), pp. 121–25.
359 "Dey wuz a time," "Niggers is niggers," and "merlatters": Harris, "Why the Negro Is Black," in
    Richard Chase, comp., *The Complete Tales of Uncle Remus* (Boston: Houghton Mifflin,
    1955), vol. 1, p. 110; "The Sad Fate of Mr. Fox" is in the same volume, pp. 111–15. Strictly
    speaking, according to Harris's narrator, "The Injun and de Chinee got ter be 'counted 'long
    er de merlatter."
360 Harris himself: For Harris's use of Uncle Remus's name, the obituaries, and the letter to
    Twain, see Hale, *Making Whiteness*, pp. 310–11 n. 28.
361 "a pale reflection": Chesnutt quoted in Sundquist, *To Wake the Nations*, p. 297; "dat I bin":
    Harris, *Complete Tales*, p. 110; "Yet this ancestor": Twain, "A Burlesque Biography," in
    Unabridged Mark Twain, vol. 2, p. xiii.
362 "was the first expression": the quote from Adams and the description of Douglass and Wells at
    the Chicago fair are all in McFeely, *Frederick Douglass*, pp. 366–72.
363 "colonized, sent to heaven": Garfield quoted in Kenneth O'Reilly, *Nixon's Piano: Presidents
    and Racial Politics from Washington to Clinton* (New York: Free Press, 1995), p. 56; the
    Grant information is also in O'Reilly, pp. 52–53.
366 "want the earth" and "The Declaration": Powers and Beveridge quoted in Gossett, *Race*, pp.
    314 and 329, respectively; "this Republic": Lodge quoted in Alan Brinkley, *The Unfinished
    Nation: A Concise History of the American People*, 2nd ed. (New York: Knopf, 1997), p. 574.
366 "mark their roads" and "You may change": Tillman and Daniel quoted in Gossett, *Race*, p.
    337.
366 "benevolent assimilation": McKinley quoted in Gossett, *Race*, p. 338.
367 "recognizes racial equality": Brandeis's speech is in Philip Davis, ed., *Immigration and Amer-
    icanization* (Boston: Ginn and Company, 1920), pp. 639–44; "The Song of the Foreign-
    Born" is in Winthrop Talbot, ed., *Americanization: Principles of Americanism, Essentials of
    Americanization, Technic of Race-Assimilation, Annotated Bibliography* (New York: H. W.
    Wilson Company, 1920), p. 280; "No reverberating": Bourne's article, "Trans-National
    America," excerpted in Talbot, ed., *Americanization*, pp. 51–52.
367–68 "A new conscience": Carol Aronovici, *Americanization* (St. Paul, Minn.: Keller, 1919),
    pp. 46–47.
368 "A man does not hope": Wilson's speech in Talbot, ed., *Americanization*, pp. 78–81. Philip
    Davis included the same speech in his collection.
368–69 " 'Americanism' is much more": Grace Abbot (director, Immigrants' Protective League,
    Chicago) in Talbot, ed., *Americanization*, p. 53; "Americanism is entirely" and "We are to
    conquer": Lane in Davis, ed., *Immigration and Americanization*, pp. 617 and 619; "the ways
    in which": Aronovici, *Americanization*, p. 31.
369 "It has, therefore, given": Brandeis in Davis, ed., *Immigration and Americanization*, p. 643;
    "America does not": Wilson in Talbot, ed., *Americanization*, p. 79; "a new and mixed" and
    "altogether inferior": Roosevelt quoted in Gossett, *Race*, pp. 319, 268.
370 against racial identity: Aronovici ridicules current ideas of racial purity, especially of white or
    Anglo-Saxon purity, and briefly mentions blacks in that regard. She does not otherwise speak

of blacks or Indians. Minnesota, then as now, had a large Indian population. St. Paul in those days had a small, though long-established, black community.

370 "a quite native": Emerson in Ellwood Griscom, ed., *Americanization: A School Reader and Speaker* (New York: Macmillan, 1920), p. 86; Roosevelt discusses hyphenated Americans in a 1915 address to the Knights of Columbus, in Davis, ed., *Immigration and Americanization*, pp. 645–60; "tries to keep segregated": Roosevelt in Griscom, ed., *Americanization*, pp. 56–57.

371 "Americanization": Kellor in Davis, ed., *Immigration and Americanization*, p. 625; "the simple-minded": Ross in Talbot, ed., *Americanization*, p. 312.

371 "Self-realization": Du Bois reprinted in Talbot, ed., *Americanization*, pp. 119–27; "the advice": Moton in Talbot, ed., pp. 131–39.

371 "The Indian race": Fayette McKenzie's article is on pp. 142–45, Albert Shaw's on pp. 139–41, in Talbot, ed., *Americanization*.

373 President Wilson's: On President Wilson, segregation, and *The Clansman*, see O'Reilly, *Nixon's Piano*, pp. 82–94.

374 "the all-important": Heflin quoted in Joshi, ed., *Documents of American Prejudice*, pp. 331–33.

374–75 An early example: The history of the cakewalk is from Sundquist, *To Wake the Nations*, pp. 282–94.

375–76 "The foreigner": Aronovici, *Americanization*, p. 21.

376 "In her way": George Jean Nathan in the *New York Telegram*, April 16, 1927; copied in the Florence Mills file, Schomburg Center for Research in Black Culture, New York City.

379 White removal to the suburbs: On the suburbs generally, see Kenneth T. Jackson, *Crabgrass Frontier: The Suburbanization of the United States* (New York: Oxford University Press, 1985); also see Rosalyn Baxandall and Elizabeth Ewen, *Picture Windows: How the Suburbs Happened* (New York: Basic Books, 2000), esp. ch. 11 (on lifestyle) and ch. 13 (on segregation).

379–80 "History offered": Adams quoted in Gossett, *Race*, p. 414.

383 Kennedy had his own: In Taylor Branch, *Parting the Waters: America in the King Years, 1954–63* (New York: Simon and Schuster, 1988), pp. 896–97.

384 "failed to preach": Byrd's filibuster speech is quoted in Taylor Branch, *Pillar of Fire: America in the King Years, 1963–65* (New York: Simon and Schuster, 1988), pp. 334–36.

384 "the gross fact": White quoted in Branch, *Pillar of Fire*, p. 419.

386 The concept: Delany criticized abolitionists in his *The Condition, Elevation, Emigration, and Destiny of the Colored People of the United States* (Baltimore: Black Classic Press, 1993 [1852]), pp. 26–29; Douglass's call for a black vice president is in McFeely, *Frederick Douglass*, p. 317; the polls on affirmative action are in Robert H. Wiebe, *Self-Rule: A Cultural History of American Democracy* (Chicago: University of Chicago Press, 1995), p. 235.

A FAMILY IN TIME

400 Huey Newton: In researching the Panthers, I have not felt able to rely on any one source, or any two. Those interested in the Panthers tend to have strong, often overpowering feelings about them. Michael Newton's *Bitter Grain: Huey Newton and the Black Panther Party* (Los Angeles: Holloway House, 1991) and Hugh Pearson's *The Shadow of the Panther: Huey Newton and the Price of Black Power in America* (New York: Addison-Wesley, 1994) may usefully be read together. Pearson's is better researched, but he is so disappointed by the Panthers that

you finish the book mystified as to why anyone ever admired or followed them. Of the Panther memoirs, such as David Hilliard's *This Side of Glory* and Elaine Brown's *A Taste of Power*, I still am most struck by Bobby Seale's *Seize the Time: The Story of the Black Panther Party and Huey P. Newton* (Baltimore: Black Classic Press, 1991). Seale wrote his book in 1969 and 1970, at the height of events, and the story benefits from his lack of perspective; he makes you feel why events happened the way they did. I have also benefited greatly from conversations with people who knew those days, in particular Judge Lionel Wilson, Captain Reginald Lyles, Paul Cobb, and Reverend J. Alfred Smith.

A PRESENT FROM JOHN SUTTER

403 "Know that to the right": The *Amadís* story is from Dora Beale Polk, *The Island of California: A History of the Myth* (Lincoln: University of Nebraska Press, 1991), pp. 123–25.

404 The founder: On Loyola's reading habits, see Hernan Lara Zavala, "Amadís, Iñigo, Alonso," in Julio Ortega, ed., *La Cervantiada* (Rio Piedras, P.R.: Editorial de la Universidad de Puerto Rico, 1994), pp. 289–90; Peralta history is from David Weber, *Oakland: Hub of the West* (Tulsa, Okla.: Continental Heritage Press, 1981), pp. 38–40; Pearl Randolph Fibel, *The Peraltas: Spanish Pioneers and the First Family of the East Bay* (Oakland, Calif.: Peralta Hospital, 1971); Beth Bagwell, *Oakland: The Story of a City* (Oakland, Calif.: Oakland Heritage Alliance, 1996), pp. 8–16; Peter Thomas Conmy, *The Beginnings of Oakland, California, A.U.C.* (Oakland, Calif.: Oakland Public Library, 1961), pp. 3–6. For Oakland history in general, I have relied heavily on Bagwell, less so on Conmy. "Descended from the union": undated *San Francisco Examiner* article, "From the Throne of Spain," in the Peralta-Galindo Family Papers, Bancroft Library, University of California, Berkeley.

404 "Word of the discovery": typescript in Peralta-Galindo Family Papers, Bancroft Library.

405–6 "tilled our soil" and "Though not so recognized": The rancher was Salvador Vallejo. Quotes in Tomás Almaguer, *Racial Fault Lines: The Historical Origins of White Supremacy in California* (Berkeley: University of California Press, 1994), p. 50.

406 "keeps 600": trapper James Clyman quoted in Almaguer, *Racial Fault Lines*, pp. 50–51.

407 "Girls, of which you will take": Sutter quoted in Quintard Taylor, *In Search of the Racial Frontier: African Americans in the American West, 1528–1990* (New York: Norton, 1998), p. 47.

407 "Of the numerous": Almaguer, *Racial Fault Lines*, p. 119.

408 "They immediately surrounded": Almaguer, *Racial Fault Lines*, p. 122.

408 "Sometimes, as in": Josiah Royce quoted in Conmy, *Beginnings of Oakland*, p. 11.

409 two books: The disillusioned book titles are in Almaguer, *Racial Fault Lines*, p. 112; D. L. Emerson, "Speech by D. L. Emerson," is at the Bancroft Library.

409 "From 140" and "At present": Bagwell, *Oakland*, pp. 77, 88.

410 "What was the use": Stein, in *Everybody's Autobiography* (1937), quoted in Bagwell, *Oakland*, p. 214.

410 "Thou Rose-land!": Miller's poem is in Conmy, *Beginnings of Oakland*, pp. 17–18; the discussion of Miller, unless otherwise noted, relies on M. Marion Marberry, *Splendid Poseur: Joaquin Miller, American Poet* (New York: T. Y. Crowell, 1953).

412 "a scene of agony": Ridge quoted in John Ehle, *Trail of Tears: The Rise and Fall of the Cherokee Nation* (New York: Anchor Books/Doubleday, 1989), p. 376; "I have worked harder": Ridge's letter to Stand Watie in Edward Everett Dale and Gaston Litton, eds., *Cherokee Cav-*

aliers: Forty Years of Cherokee History as Told in the Correspondence of the Ridge-Watie-Boudinot Family (Norman: University of Oklahoma Press, 1995 [1939]), p. 76.

412 Born in San Francisco: This section on London is adapted from an article I wrote for the *Voice Literary Supplement* (February 1994). I will give here only the years of letters; I have used Earle Labor, Robert C. Leitz III, and I. Milo Shepard, eds., *The Letters of Jack London*, 3 vols. (Stanford, Calif.: Stanford University Press, 1988). I will likewise refer to stories by name; the source is Earle Labor, Robert C. Leitz III, and I. Milo Shepard, eds., *The Complete Short Stories of Jack London*, 3 vols. (Stanford, Calif.: Stanford University Press, 1993). References to novels and nonfiction are to Donald Pizer, ed., *Jack London*, 2 vols. (New York: Library of America, 1982), unless otherwise noted.

412 "I have been alone": London, *The Star Rover* (New York: Macmillan, 1920), p. 3.

413 "my Mammy Jennie" to "life raw and naked": London, *John Barleycorn* (1913).

414 "I saw the picture" to "What really saved me": London, "How I Became a Socialist."

415 Kipling, Mexican-American war, and Johnson: In King Hendricks and Irving Shepard, eds., *Jack London Reports: War Correspondence, Sports Articles, and Miscellaneous Writings* (Garden City, N.Y.: Doubleday, 1970).

417–18 "Some of us" and "Red-Eye": London, *Before Adam* (New York: Grosset and Dunlap, 1907), pp. 19–20, 242.

418 "All my life" to "The stuff of": London, *Star Rover*, p. 1.

418–19 "They are going" and "I am life": London, *Star Rover*, pp. 8, 123.

419 a "Melodrama": The description of Sadie Knowland's opera is in George Albert Coe, *Sadie Knowland Coe* (privately printed, 1906), at the Bancroft Library.

420 "Did you spend": Fry's interview with Joseph Knowland is in typescript with the Regional Oral History Office, Bancroft Library.

420 "It is probably": Bagwell, *Oakland*, p. 206.

421 one of several: The *Sunshine*'s founder was John A. Wilds: Weber, *Oakland*, p. 127. "What the Sunshine" and "Just please stay": In Will D. Tate, *The New Black Urban Elites* (San Francisco: R&E Research Associates, 1976), pp. 13–14.

421 A welcome increase: The *Birth of a Nation* story is in Taylor, *In Search of the Racial Frontier*, pp. 238–39.

421–22 Charter reforms: For the political changes and Knowland's role, see Edward C. Hayes, *Power Structure and Urban Policy: Who Rules in Oakland?* (New York: McGraw-Hill, 1972), pp. 12–17; also Gayle B. Montgomery and James W. Johnson, in collaboration with Paul G. Manolis, *One Step from the White House: The Rise and Fall of Senator William F. Knowland* (Berkeley: University of California Press, 1998), pp. 7–10, 13–18.

422 "Oakland skilled": Bagwell, *Oakland*, pp. 201–2.

422 "Lavishly, Nature": *Oakland, Alameda County, California: The Highlighted Story of One of the Nation's Richest, Greatest Communities* (Oakland, Calif.: Alameda County Board of Supervisors, 1929).

422 "Appearance": Montgomery and Johnson, *One Step from the White House*, p. 20. My discussion of Knowland is based greatly on Montgomery and Johnson's book; on reading through the extensive William Fife Knowland (WFK) Papers at the Bancroft Library; on interviews with people who knew him, in particular Judge Lionel Wilson, Reverend J. Alfred Smith, and Paul Cobb; and on the recollections of my family and our friends.

423 The 1934 election: See Greg Mitchell, *The Campaign of the Century: Upton Sinclair's Race for Governor and the Birth of Media Politics* (New York: Random House, 1992).

423–24 "In the Communist": Knowland editorial in *Tribune*, April 16, 1969, in WFK Papers;

"Junior Will": from campaign file for 1946, in WFK Papers. The population figures are from Marilynn S. Johnson, *The Second Gold Rush: Oakland and the East Bay in World War II* (Berkeley: University of California Press, 1993), p. 35.

424 OAKLAND PRIMARY: quoted in Johnson, *Second Gold Rush*, p. 204.

424–25 The democratic demands: This paragraph and the next are based on Johnson, *Second Gold Rush*, chs. 6 and 7.

425–26 "That riot": The *Observer* editorial is excerpted in Bagwell, *Oakland*, pp. 240–41.

427 William Knowland: See Montgomery and Johnson, *One Step from the White House*, pp. 142–43 (compared with Lyndon Johnson), ch. 23 (the swinging Knowland), p. 150 (Eisenhower's notes on Knowland's mind), p. 143 (the former aide was James Gleason).

428 "We know that": McCarthy Senate speech of December 6, 1950, copy of typescript, in WFK Papers.

428 "I belonged" and "was loose": Montgomery and Johnson, *One Step from the White House*, p. 157.

431 "Anti-Communism Week" and "If ever a city": The Anti-Communism Week proclamation and the *Time* article (from February 2, 1962) are in the WFK Papers.

432 The Oakland and Berkeley: This discussion of the civil-rights movement in the East Bay is based on Taylor, *In Search of the Racial Frontier*, pp. 289–92, 296–99; Pearson, *Shadow of the Panther*, ch. 3.

432–33 "That scraggly": Knowland's *Tribune* editorial in WFK Papers.

433 "It is not being": Knowland editorial of October 20, 1967, in WFK Papers.

434 "He sat": Montgomery and Johnson, *One Step from the White House*, p. 283.

434 "Domestic routine": The horoscopes appear in Knowland's personal clipping files, in WFK Papers.

SEIZE THE TIME

446 The murder of Marcus Foster: This history of the SLA is based largely on Vin McLellan and Paul Avery, *The Voices of Guns: The Definitive and Dramatic Story of the Twenty-one-Month Career of the Symbionese Liberation Army—One of the Most Bizarre Chapters in the History of the American Left* (New York: Putnam, 1977), supplemented by Les Payne and Tim Findley, *The Life and Death of the SLA* (New York: Ballantine, 1976).

446 Who were these killers?: The discussion of the SLA's uniqueness, and the quotations, are from *The Last SLA Testament: An Interview with Russ, Joe, Bill, & Emily* (Berkeley, Calif.: Bay Area Research Collective, 1976).

447 "started out": This information is from House Committee on Internal Security, *The Symbionese Liberation Army* (Washington, D.C.: U.S. Congress, 1974).

447–48 According to Russell Little: All SLA quotes in this paragraph and the next are from *Last SLA Testament*.

449 "The house," "use blacks," and "field niggers": Seale, *Seize the Time*, pp. 42, 72, 25.

450 "Huey wanted brothers": Seale, *Seize the Time*, p. 64.

450 "if you didn't": Seale, *Seize the Time*, p. 64.

450 "Huey had said": Seale, *Seize the Time*, pp. 95–96.

451–52 "We want freedom": The Black Panther Party platform is in Seale, *Seize the Time*, pp. 66–69.

458 I was preoccupied: This detail appears in a diary I briefly kept. All my other recollections are just memories.

463 "the ultimate destiny": The poll results are in Tate, *New Black Urban Elites*, p. 42.

464 "Nkrumah was a bad motherfucker": Seale, *Seize the Time*, p. 4.

464 For most of: See Pearson, *Shadow of the Panther*, for Huey Newton's last days (pp. 310–16) and the funeral (pp. 322–24).

HAVE MERCY

466 "was among the earliest": All quotes concerning Allen Temple history are from J. Alfred Smith, *Thus Far by Faith: A Study of the Historical Backgrounds and the First Fifty Years of the Allen Temple Baptist Church* (Oakland, Calif.: Allen Temple Baptist Church, 1973).

485 the California prison population: See, in general, David Cole, *No Equal Justice: Race and Class in the American Criminal Justice System* (New York: New Press, 1999).

486 "Affirmative action has been": Glynn Custred quoted in R. Drummond Ayres, Jr., "Conservatives Forge New Strategy to Challenge Affirmative Action," *New York Times*, February 16, 1995, p. A1.

486 So a federal judge: Judge Selya, in *Wessmann v. Gittens*, 160 F. 3d 790, p. 792. Despite its startling pomposity of tone, Selya's opinion is a good summary of current judicial opinion when read in combination with Judge Boudin's concurrence and Judge Lipez's dissent. See also Tamar Lewin, "Public Schools Confronting Issue of Racial Preferences," *New York Times*, November 29, 1998, p. A1.

486 "Courts will not say" and "If the two races": in H. L. Pohlman, ed., *Political Thought and the American Judiciary* (Amherst: University of Massachusetts Press, 1993), pp. 226, 221.

488 "She said, 'Oh, yes' ": Seale, *Seize the Time*, p. 259.

489–90 "Memory is": René Crevel quoted in Robert McAlmon and Kay Boyle, *Being Geniuses Together, 1920–1930* (San Francisco: North Point Press, 1984), p. 334.

DOWN TO THE RIVER

496–97 "industrious," "At that time," and "The maxim": Henry C. Levens and Nathaniel M. Drake, *A History of Cooper County, Missouri, from the first visit by White Men, in February, 1804, to the 5th day of July, 1876* (St. Louis, Mo.: Perrin and Smith, 1876), pp. 119–20; "When the first": William Foreman Johnson, *History of Cooper County, Missouri* (n.p.: VKM Publishing Company, 1978 [1919]), vol. 1, p. 64.

497 "The night": Johnson, *History of Cooper County*, vol. 1, p. 113.

497–98 "The slaves": Levens and Drake, *History of Cooper County*, p. 120. For slavery in Missouri, see Lorenzo J. Greene, *Missouri's Black Heritage*, rev. ed., revised and updated by Gary R. Kremer and Antonio F. Holland (Columbia: University of Missouri Press, 1993).

499–500 "they must commence": Levens and Drake, *History of Cooper County*, p. 123.

500 "have multiplied": Johnson, *History of Cooper County*, vol. 1, p. 53.

502 "The time," "there has been," and "It is much easier": Richard S. Brownlee, *Gray Ghosts of the Confederacy* (Baton Rouge: Louisiana State University Press, 1984), pp. 81, 85, 160.

508 "the solutions" and "the sort of man": Aristotle, *Poetics*, trans. Telford, pp. 28, 23.

508 "Genealogical trees": Douglass quoted in Eric J. Sundquist, *To Wake the Nations: Race in the Making of American Literature* (Cambridge, Mass.: Harvard University Press, 1993), p. 100; my sources for Lacy genealogy are too many and too obscure to be listed here. The best starting point for Lacy research is Steve Lacy's Web site, gengateway.com.

510–11 "He was several times imprisoned" and "As an expositor of scripture": these lines are quoted from notes and clippings in the files of William Davis, a Craig descendant in Ghent, Kentucky.

511 Sadly, there are: The pioneer Swiss emigrant, Jean-Jacques Dufour, brought in his small collection of books Count Volney's *Soil and Climate*. Perret Dufour, *The Swiss Settlement of Switzerland County, Indiana* (Bowie, Md.: Heritage, 1987 [1925]), p. 337. This has been my main source for Vevay history, along with *History of Switzerland County, Indiana* (Chicago: Weakley, Harraman, 1885).

515 a klavern: D. C. Stephenson, "List of Indiana Ku Klux Klan Officials, 1924–25," n.d.

ACKNOWLEDGMENTS

■

My first thanks must go to the people featured in the preceding pages, for giving me stories to tell. I would also like to thank the small group of colleagues, friends, and family who have steadfastly supported this work: Faith Childs, Bruce Robbins, Caryl Phillips, Mike Vazquez, Rebecca Saletan, William, Laurel, and Christi Malcomson, James and Janet Martin, Margaret Martin, and above all my wife, Rebecca Martin. Special thanks also to Billie Poole, Steve Molton, Steve Lacy, Bill Davis, and Ronan Bennett.

As to research sources, I should let the endnotes speak for themselves; without the work of William McLoughlin, Wilson Jeremiah Moses, Eric Sundquist, Quintard Taylor, Theda Perdue, and so many others, I would have been lost. There are, however, works that do not appear in the notes but to which I owe a great deal: Toni Morrison's *Playing in the Dark: Whiteness and the Literary Imagination*, for example, and especially the essays by James Baldwin collected in *The Price of the Ticket*. When I could not find my way forward, I would often turn to Baldwin, and he always helped. I hope that the many, many writers whom I have failed to acknowledge here or in the notes will at least know they're in excellent company.

Finally, I would like to recognize the libraries and archives where most of my research was done: the New York Public Library at Forty-second Street and Fifth Avenue, which became a second home; the affiliated Mid-Manhattan Library and Schomburg Center for Research in Black Culture; the New York

City and Philadelphia branches of the National Archives; the Cherokee National Museum Library, Cherokee, North Carolina; Library of Congress; Cherokee National Historical Society Library, Tahlequah, Oklahoma; Northeastern State University Library, Tahlequah, Oklahoma; Bancroft Library, University of California, Berkeley; and the main public libraries in Huntsville, Alabama; Vevay, Indiana; Boonville, Missouri; St. Joseph, Missouri; Carrollton, Kentucky; Oakland, California; and Philadelphia (the Free Library).

INDEX